Frommer's®

Montana & Wyoming

8th Edition

by Eric Peterson

Bancroft

WILEY

Wiley Publishing, Inc.

ABOUT THE AUTHOR

A Denver-based freelance writer, **Eric Peterson** has written and contributed to numerous Frommer's guidebooks covering the American West and *Ramble Colorado* (www.fulcrumbooks.com), as well as numerous travel features for in-flight magazines and newspapers. He's an avid camper and hiker, a lifelong Broncos fan, and rock star (at least in the eyes of his niece, Olivia, and nephews, Mitch and Sam).

Published by:

WILEY PUBLISHING, INC.

111 River St.
Hoboken, NJ 07030-5774

ISBN 978-0-470-59150-5

Editor: Billy Fox and Anuja Madar
Production Editor: Jana M. Stefanciosa
Cartographer: Andrew Murphy
Photo Editor: Richard Fox
Production by Wiley Indianapolis Composition Services

Front cover photo: Montana: Beargrass, Mt. Reynolds Glacier National Park ©David Muench / Muench Photography Inc.
Back cover photo: Bighorn Sheep Portrait ©Mark Karrass/Corbis

For information on our other products and services or to obtain technical support, please contact our Customer Care Department within the U.S. at 877/762-2974, outside the U.S. at 317/572-3993 or fax 317/572-4002.

Wiley also publishes its books in a variety of electronic formats. Some content that appears in print may not be available in electronic formats.

Manufactured in the United States of America

5 4 3 2 1

CONTENTS

4 SUGGESTED MONTANA & WYOMING ITINERARIES   46

5 THE ACTIVE VACATION PLANNER   54

6 GLACIER NATIONAL PARK   63

7 MISSOULA, THE FLATHEAD & THE NORTHWEST CORNER   90

8 HELENA & SOUTHWESTERN MONTANA   144

9 THE HI-LINE & NORTH- CENTRAL MISSOURI RIVER COUNTRY 183

10 BOZEMAN, SOUTH-CENTRAL MONTANA & THE MISSOURI HEADWATERS 207

11 BILLINGS & EASTERN MONTANA 239

12 YELLOWSTONE NATIONAL PARK 258

13 JACKSON HOLE & GRAND TETON NATIONAL PARK 306

14 CODY & NORTH-CENTRAL WYOMING 350

15 SHERIDAN & EASTERN WYOMING 372

16 SOUTHERN WYOMING 393

17 FAST FACTS 414

INDEX 421

LIST OF MAPS

HOW TO CONTACT US

In researching this book, we discovered many wonderful places—hotels, restaurants, shops, and more. We're sure you'll find others. Please tell us about them, so we can share the information with your fellow travelers in upcoming editions. If you were disappointed with a recommendation, we'd love to know that, too. Please write to:

Frommer's Montana & Wyoming, 8th Edition
Wiley Publishing, Inc. • 111 River St. • Hoboken, NJ 07030-5774

AN ADDITIONAL NOTE

Please be advised that travel information is subject to change at any time—and this is especially true of prices. We therefore suggest that you write or call ahead for confirmation when making your travel plans. The authors, editors, and publisher cannot be held responsible for the experiences of readers while traveling. Your safety is important to us, however, so we encourage you to stay alert and be aware of your surroundings. Keep a close eye on cameras, purses, and wallets, all favorite targets of thieves and pickpockets.

FROMMER'S STAR RATINGS, ICONS & ABBREVIATIONS

Every hotel, restaurant, and attraction listing in this guide has been ranked for quality, value, service, amenities, and special features using a **star-rating system.** In country, state, and regional guides, we also rate towns and regions to help you narrow down your choices and budget your time accordingly. Hotels and restaurants are rated on a scale of zero (recommended) to three stars (exceptional). Attractions, shopping, nightlife, towns, and regions are rated according to the following scale: zero stars (recommended), one star (highly recommended), two stars (very highly recommended), and three stars (must-see).

In addition to the star-rating system, we also use **seven feature icons** that point you to the great deals, in-the-know advice, and unique experiences that separate travelers from tourists. Throughout the book, look for:

(Finds)	Special finds—those places only insiders know about
(Fun Facts)	Fun facts—details that make travelers more informed and their trips more fun
(Kids)	Best bets for kids, and advice for the whole family
(Moments)	Special moments—those experiences that memories are made of
(Overrated)	Places or experiences not worth your time or money
(Tips)	Insider tips—great ways to save time and money
(Value)	Great values—where to get the best deals
(Warning!)	Warning—traveler's advisories are usually in effect

The following **abbreviations** are used for credit cards:

AE	American Express	DISC	Discover	V	Visa
DC	Diners Club	MC	MasterCard		

TRAVEL RESOURCES AT FROMMERS.COM

Frommer's travel resources don't end with this guide. **Frommers.com** has travel information on more than 4,000 destinations. We update features regularly, giving you access to the most current trip-planning information and the best airfare, lodging, and car-rental bargains. You can also listen to podcasts, connect with other Frommers.com members through our active-reader forums, share your travel photos, read blogs from guidebook editors and fellow travelers, and much more.

The Best of Montana & Wyoming

A mix of the rugged Wild West, the even more rugged Rocky Mountains, and a few almost-modern cities—or what some might call overgrown cow towns—make the states of Montana and Wyoming delightful vacation spots. This is especially true for people who savor outdoor adventures, but it's also the case for those looking to discover a part of the United States that many of us have seen only in the movies and on television (and that's a rather distorted view). Here you'll find some of the most breathtaking scenery in America; a vast array of wildlife that not only thinks it owns the place, but actually does; and even some first-class Western-style lodges, restaurants, and museums.

Following are what I consider some of the best experiences in Montana and Wyoming.

1 THE BEST VACATION EXPERIENCES

- **Glacier National Park** (MT): The best vacation spot in Montana is also the most obvious one. By the standard of other crowded national parks, this spectacular country is virtually undiscovered. See chapter 6.
- **Yellowstone National Park** (WY): It's the crown jewel of American parks, and it remains the prime attraction in the Rocky Mountains. This unique park offers visitors an extraordinary combination of wilderness, wildlife, and geothermal wonders. See chapter 12.
- **Grand Teton National Park** (WY): The Grand Tetons are an excellent short course in Rocky Mountain parks for travelers with less time: magnificent peaks rising from the Snake River plain, alpine lakes, wildflowers, and wildlife, all in a relatively small park that can be seen in a few days or combined with Jackson for a longer vacation. See "Grand Teton National Park" in chapter 13.

2 THE BEST OUTDOOR ADVENTURES

- **Exploring the Bob Marshall Wilderness** (MT): The 1.5-million-acre Bob Marshall Wilderness Complex in northwest Montana is one of America's most spectacular wild places. Lace up your hiking boots, tie on your bandanna, and take to the high country in Montana's northwest corner. See section 7, "The Bob Marshall Wilderness Complex," in chapter 7.
- **Enjoying the Yellowstone Backcountry** (WY): Outfitters from ranches around Yellowstone National Park will take you into the deep wilderness that surrounds the busy attractions at the park's center, and there you'll get a flavor of the wild as rich as the Rockies can offer. If you have experience, you can go on your own—paddling Yellowstone Lake, backpacking along Slough Creek, or Telemark skiing the powder around Shoshone Lake. See chapter 12.

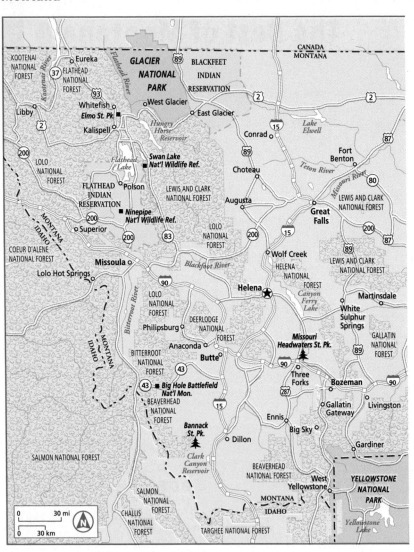

3 THE BEST WILDLIFE VIEWING

- **Glacier National Park** (MT): The experience of watching wildlife amid the imposing terrain of Glacier National Park is tough to beat. With a little energy, you can see mountain goats, moose, elk, and other native animals in their natural habitat. Keep a good distance, and be aware of all bear restrictions and

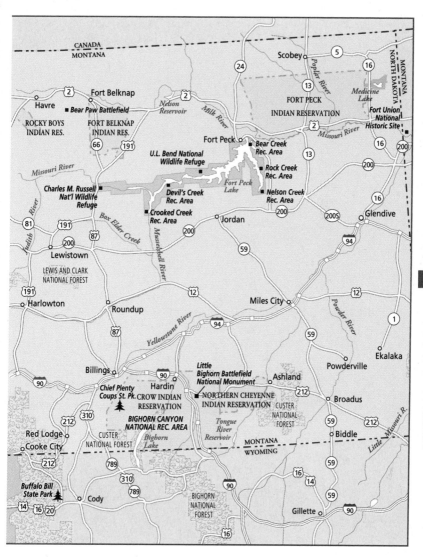

regulations—the grizzly is the park's unofficial mascot. See chapter 6.

- **The Bob Marshall Wilderness Complex** (MT): Just south of Glacier, in the Bob Marshall Wilderness Complex, roam a full complement of Rocky Mountain wildlife—although you have to wander into the backcountry to find it. See section 7, "The Bob Marshall Wilderness Complex," in chapter 7.

- **The Lamar Valley** (WY): You can see wildlife in many parts of Yellowstone,

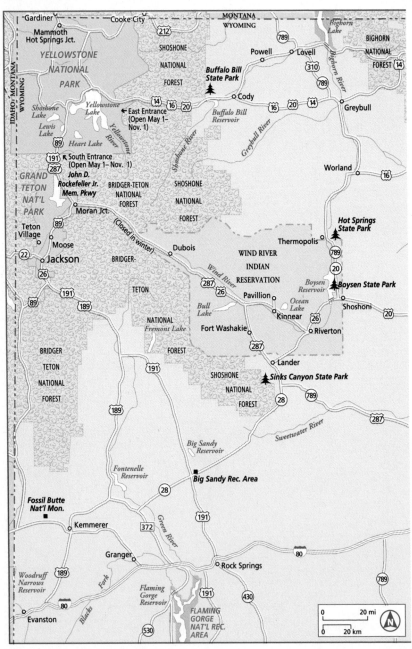

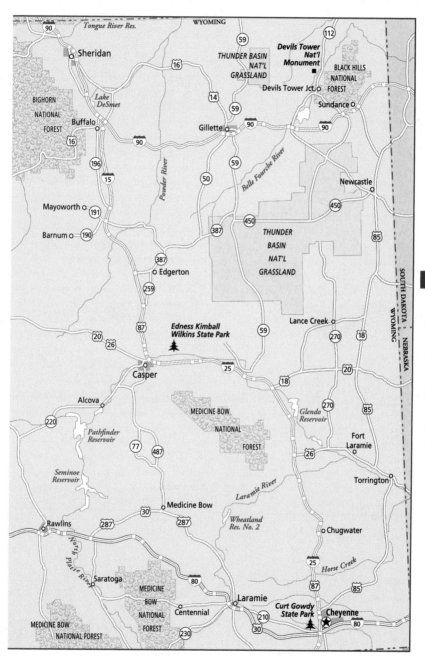

including the meadows across from the Old Faithful complex. But the richest trove of wildlife is in the park's northeast corner, in the valley nicknamed "The Serengeti of United States." See chapter 12.

4 THE BEST WINTER VACATIONS

- **Skiing at Whitefish Mountain Resort** (MT; ✆ **800/858-3930;** www.ski whitefish.com): With an annual snowfall of 300 inches, a vertical drop of 2,500 feet, a superpipe for the snowboarding crowd, and virtually no lines, Whitefish Mountain is one of the best ski areas in the northwestern United States. See p. 131.

- **Skiing at Big Sky and Moonlight Basin** (MT; Big Sky ✆ **800/548-4486,** www.bigskyresort.com; Moonlight Basin **877/822-0430,** www.moonlight basin.com): Big Sky and the much newer Moonlight Basin have connected their trail systems, making for a combined 5,300 acres of terrain—the largest ski area in the country, not to mention the one with the most vertical drop. See p. 225.

- **Wintering at Old Faithful** (WY): The chilly season in Yellowstone is increasingly popular, and it's bound to be even more so now that the **Old Faithful Snow Lodge** (✆ **866/439-7375;** www. travelyellowstone.com) has been transformed into a handsome, comfortable facility. You can take a snowcoach into the park, or cross-country ski or snowshoe to the Lonestar Geyser and other attractions. See p. 303.

- **Skiing at Jackson Hole Mountain Resort** (WY; ✆ **888/333-7766;** www. jacksonhole.com): Jackson Hole offers a vertical drop that will take your breath away. There are a variety of ways to get to the bottom, from double black diamonds to intermediate slopes. Skiers who like a challenge should come here and mix the visit with some ballooning, tours of the elk refuge, and other adventures. See p. 310.

5 THE BEST HOTELS & RESORTS

- **Many Glacier Hotel** (Glacier National Park, MT; ✆ **406/892-2525;** www. glacierparkinc.com): The best thing about Many Glacier, apart from its elegant mien, friendly service, and cozy rooms, is the setting; it sits along Swiftcurrent Lake and in the shadows of Mount Grinnell and Mount Wilbur. See p. 80.

- **The Pollard** (Red Lodge, MT; ✆ **800/765-5273;** www.thepollard. net): You can join Buffalo Bill on the guest register at the Pollard, a historic spot that proves that a hotel doesn't need to sprawl all over the place to set the highest standard of comfort and elegance. See p. 236.

- **Old Faithful Inn** (Yellowstone National Park, WY; ✆ **866/439-7375;** www. travelyellowstone.com): If you ever wonder whether there's really art in architecture, look at the way the rustic simplicity and monumental structure of this inn make a perfect fit just across the way from one of nature's most astonishing creations. A lattice of logs climbs to an 85-foot ceiling. You can find peace in the upper balconies, or join the convivial crowds around the big stone fireplace below. See p. 302.

- **Four Seasons Resort Jackson Hole** (Jackson, WY; ✆ 307/732-5000; www. fourseasons.com/jacksonhole): The most deluxe lodging option in Teton Village, the chic Four Seasons opened in December 2004 and immediately set a new standard for ski-in, ski-out luxury. See p. 320.

- **Jenny Lake Lodge** (Grand Teton National Park, WY; ✆ 800/628-9988; www.gtlc.com): My favorite property in any national park, this small cabin-resort offers seclusion, top-notch food, and individual attention. The property is a hybrid of mountain-lake resort and dude ranch, with many extras included in its prices. See p. 344.

- **The Chamberlin Inn** (Cody, WY; ✆ 888/587-0202; www.chamberlin inn.com): A block from the center of town, the new and improved Chamberlin Inn is Cody's best lodging option. It features charming historic rooms and apartment units. Consider asking for the Hemingway Suite, where "Papa" stayed in 1932. See p. 358.

- **The Occidental Hotel** (Buffalo, WY; ✆ 307/684-0451; www.occidental wyoming.com): Born as a tent in 1878, the Occidental has burned to the ground and been lost in a poker game in its storied history. The hotel has been beautifully restored for the new millennium. See p. 381.

---

6 THE BEST GUEST RANCHES

- **Triple Creek Ranch** (Darby, MT; ✆ 800/654-2943; www.triplecreek ranch.com): This place is wonderful. It's pretty much the perfect guest ranch, where guests are pampered like European royalty, and the prices reflect it. It has all the traditional dude ranch activities, as well as a pool and a fitness room. See p. 106.

- **Lone Mountain Ranch** (Big Sky, MT; ✆ 800/514-4644; www.lmranch.com): Lone Mountain Ranch is a winter and summer resort that has views into the Spanish Peaks Wilderness Area. In winter there are 45 miles of cross-country trails over terrain that will challenge every level of skier. In summer, you can ride, hike, fish, or simply relax and eat in the popular restaurant. There are bird walks with naturalists and forays into Yellowstone. See p. 227.

- **Lost Creek Ranch** (Moose, WY; ✆ 307/733-3435; www.lostcreek.com): Positioned next door to a national park and possessing a beautiful view of the Tetons on one side and the Gros Ventres on the other, Lost Creek layers on the comforts and activities. You can ride, hike, swim, fish, float, play tennis and billiards, shoot skeet, and eat gourmet food. Regulars return every year. There are only 10 cabins, but if you can get a reservation, it's worth it. See p. 322.

- **Eatons' Ranch** (Wolf, WY; ✆ 800/210-1049; www.eatonsranch.com): The oldest guest ranch in the country, the Eaton is also one of the best. The ranch got its start in North Dakota in 1882 before relocating in 1904 to isolated Wolf Creek Canyon, about 20 miles west of Sheridan. It's a gorgeous location for a dude ranch. See p. 378.

7 THE BEST BED & BREAKFASTS

- **The Garden Wall Inn** (Whitefish, MT; © 888/530-1700; www.gardenwall inn.com): This delightful B&B, built in the 1920s, is full of charm—all of the furnishings are period antiques, including claw-foot tubs and Art Deco dressers. Gourmet breakfasts include specialties such as wild huckleberry crepes. See p. 134.

- **The Sanders B&B** (Helena, MT; © 406/442-3309; www.sandersbb. com): Built in 1875, this historically important B&B has been beautifully restored. You'll relax on original furniture under the eyes of portraits hung by the original owner, U.S. Sen. Wilbur Fiske Sanders. See p. 154.

- **The Symmes-Wicks House** (Lewistown, MT; © 406/538-9068; www. symmeswickshouse.com): This lovingly restored 1909 Arts and Crafts home is in the heart of the Silk Stocking District. The stately home is distinguished by rich hardwood floors, Tiffany glass, and period antiques. See p. 198.

- **Lehrkind Mansion Bed & Breakfast** (Bozeman, MT; © 800/992-6932; www.bozemanbedandbreakfast.com): Located in the Historic Bozeman Brewery District, the Lehrkind Mansion looks like something out of a fairy tale. Everything is period, from the rare

1897 Regina music box in the parlor to the many original fixtures in the bathrooms. See p. 216.

- **Wildflower Inn** (Jackson, WY; © 307/733-4710; www.jacksonholewildflower. com): A B&B on 3 acres near Teton Village, the Wildflower Inn features luxurious rooms named after local wildflowers, with private decks, exposed logs, and exceptional privacy. See p. 319.

- **Spahn's Big Horn Mountain Bed and Breakfast** (Big Horn, WY; © 307/674-8150; www.bighorn-wyoming.com): With a 100-mile view from a secluded peak tucked amid the Bighorn Mountains, this rustic hideaway features a massive three-story living area and rooms decorated with country quilts and lodgepole furniture. See p. 378.

- **Nagle Warren Mansion Bed & Breakfast** (Cheyenne, WY; © 800/811-2610; www.naglewarrenmansion.com): Originally built in 1888 by famed architect Erasmus Nagle, the mansion was converted into a bed-and-breakfast in 1997. The grand three-story mansion is luxurious and filled with regional antique furniture. It boasts a stately spire that anchors the building's southeast corner. See p. 401.

8 THE BEST RESTAURANTS

- **Cafe Kandahar** (Whitefish, MT; © 406/862-6247; www.cafekandahar. com): The chef here is inspired by French and Creole traditions but also loves to experiment. Local produce and meat dominate the menu; favorite creations include seared elk roulade with forest mushroom, as well as creative seafood and pasta dishes. See p. 138.

- **Second Street Bistro** (Livingston, MT; © 406/222-9463; www.secondstreet bistro.com): In the lobby of the Murray Hotel, this stylish bistro serves a creative, French-inspired menu. All of the produce in summer comes from the chef's garden, and in winter much comes from a greenhouse. See p. 233.

- **Snake River Grill** (Jackson, WY; *C* **307/733-0557**; www.snakerivergrill. com): Locals, including celebs who spend time in the valley, love this place. It's won awards for both its wine list and its menu, which features fresh fish, crispy pork shank, and game meat like venison chops and Idaho trout. See p. 324.
- **Jenny Lake Lodge Dining Room** (Grand Teton National Park, WY;

C **307/733-4647**): The five-course dinners here (from prime rib of buffalo to smoked sturgeon ravioli) are so good you might be distracted from the spectacular scenery just outside the window. You may be roughing it in the park, but you'll need to dress properly at this establishment. See p. 346.

9 THE BEST FLY-FISHING

- **The Madison** (MT): Brown trout aren't native to this area, but no one's asking them to leave; on this popular river running from Yellowstone National Park into Montana, they're the big attraction. The Madison converges with its "holy trinity" counterparts, the Jefferson and Gallatin, near Three

Forks, but lots of anglers fish it around Yellowstone. See chapters 10 and 12.
- **The Snake** (WY): It seems somehow fitting that the menacing-sounding Snake River is home to a feisty strain of cutthroat trout, making it one of the most satisfying Western rivers to fish. See chapter 13.

10 THE BEST GOLF COURSES

- **Old Works** (Anaconda, MT): Jack Nicklaus has created a course that is as much fun to play as it is beautiful to look at. The course wonderfully integrates the rocky bluffs, the historic nature of the old copper-processing sites, and prairie grasses and sage. See p. 158.
- **Teton Pines** (Jackson, WY): You won't find a more beautiful view from any

golf course in the country—except maybe the neighboring Jackson Hole club—with the granite Grand Teton looming over every shot. See p. 312.
- **The Powder Horn** (Sheridan, WY): Under the majestic Bighorn Mountains, this gorgeous 27-hole course mixes Scottish-style golf, wide-open fairways, and some serious target practice. See p. 375.

11 THE BEST MUSEUMS

- **Lewis & Clark National Historic Trail Interpretive Center** (Great Falls, MT; *C* **406/727-8733**; www.fs.fed.us/ r1/lewisclark/lcic): This offers a great perspective on the Corps of Discovery, from its conception back East to its endpoint at the mouth of the Columbia

River at the Pacific Ocean. Films, lectures, and demonstrations are among the offerings. See p. 189.
- **Museum of the Rockies** (Bozeman, MT; *C* **406/994-3466**): The centerpiece of this first-rate museum is the fabulous dinosaur exhibit. The exhibit,

which just had a stellar makeover, has made the place one of the premier paleontological attractions in the world. See p. 215.

- **Buffalo Bill Historical Center** (Cody, WY; ✆ **307/587-4771;** www.bbhc. org): An art museum, a firearm gallery, the memorabilia of the West's great showman, and exhibits about the Plains Indians comprise the finest museum in the Rocky Mountains. See p. 356.

- **National Historic Trails Interpretive Center** (Casper, WY; ✆ **307/261-7700;** www.blm.gov/wy/st/en/NHTIC. html): State-of-the-art exhibits give modern travelers an idea of what life on the "road" was like for the emigrants who passed through here in the mid-1800s on the Oregon, Mormon, California, and Pony Express trails. See p. 389.

12 THE BEST PERFORMING ARTS & CULTURAL FESTIVALS

- **International Wildlife Film Festival** (Missoula, MT; ✆ **406/728-9380;** www.wildlifefilms.org): This film festival has become a required festival for international filmmakers who specialize in wildlife. It goes for a week, from early to mid-May, and includes panel discussions and workshops, as well as screenings of the world's best wildlife films. See p. 92.

- **Montana Cowboy Poetry Gathering** (Lewistown, MT; ✆ **866/912-3980**): Held each year in mid-August, this is a rhyming good time for the bowlegged and horse-drawn set. In addition to a healthy dose of range rhyme, there are booths full of leather and arts-and-crafts shows. See p. 196.

- **Grand Teton Music Festival** (Jackson, WY; ✆ **307/733-3050**): Talented musicians from well-known orchestras participate in this summer festival. Tickets can usually be obtained on short notice, especially for the terrific weeknight chamber music performances. See p. 327.

- **Cheyenne Frontier Days** (Cheyenne, WY; ✆ **800/227-6336**): The "Daddy of 'em All," Cheyenne Frontier Days is 10 days of parades, rodeo, dances, and concerts. This is the most vivid demonstration of Western hospitality you'll encounter in the modern world. See p. 398.

Montana & Wyoming in Depth

Spectacular scenery combines with a genuine frontier history to create what I consider the real American West. The land is mostly uncluttered—even the so-called cities are little more than overgrown cow towns—and the setting is one of rugged beauty: the remote wilderness of Yellowstone's Thorofare country, the Gallatin valleys where Sacajawea led Lewis and Clark, and the sandstone arroyos of famed outlaw Butch Cassidy's Hole-in-the-Wall country.

There's a little more pavement here than there was in years gone by, but the open horizon and hospitality—along with a pronounced independent spirit among the locals—still exist in Montana and Wyoming. Your first visit will likely be centered on the scenery, the outdoor recreation, and the region's Wild West history, but these two states have even more to offer.

1 MONTANA & WYOMING TODAY

Since the 1950s, the story of Montana has been an evolving one, with tourism and agriculture playing key economic roles. Primary crops include wheat, cherries, sunflowers, and sugar beets, as well as beef. Growth has emerged as a key, often divisive issue, as areas like Whitefish and Bozeman have attracted wealthy newcomers from out of state and the population has steadily ticked toward 1 million. But large chunks of Montana are far outside the fast track and have remained relatively unchanged for several generations.

Unfortunately, mining, logging, and housing developments have impacted the area known as the Greater Yellowstone Ecosystem that surrounds Yellowstone and Grand Teton national parks. The ecosystem is an interdependent system of watersheds, mountain ranges, wildlife habitat, and other components extending beyond the two parks into seven national forests, an Indian reservation, three national wildlife refuges, and nearly a million acres of private land. To put it into perspective, the ecosystem's 18 million acres span an area as big as Connecticut, Rhode Island, and Delaware combined. It is one of the largest intact temperate ecosystems on the planet.

Park officials have the dual—and often contradictory—missions of conserving the natural environment and providing recreational access to three million visitors a year, each with a different definition for the word "wilderness." The roads and facilities necessary to open the parks to the public are often at odds with the concept of conservation, and the human impact on the environment is no small thing.

Gray wolves, which were eliminated in the 1920s and reintroduced in 1990s, have been a crucible for conflict. Many ranchers whose lands border the parks have fought the reintroduction tooth and nail, despite the fact that they are compensated when they lose livestock to a wolf. Gray wolves now number about 1,500 in Idaho, Montana, and Wyoming; single animals have turned up in Utah and Colorado, but permanent populations have yet to be established. With Montana's first legal wolf-hunting season in 2009 taking the life of a prominent alpha female wolf, the controversy is not going away soon.

Snowmobiles in Yellowstone have also generated their fair share of controversy in the past decade. While the machines were to be banned under a plan put in place by the Clinton administration, the Bush administration implemented an alternative compromise of a quota system and best-available technology. The gateway towns of West Yellowstone, Jackson, and Gardiner remain popular jumping-off points for park tours, park officials are still studying the long-term environmental impact of the machines, and snowmobiles still share narrow trails with wildlife during months when the animals' energy levels are at their lowest.

Though the ranching community has dominated Wyoming politics for most of the past century, the modern economic hammer in the state is undoubtedly the energy industry. The state's fate has been closely tied to oil, gas, and coal, with the economy rising and falling in synch with world prices. But in recent years, the state has tallied billion-dollar surpluses thanks to the extraction industries. The boom and bust of the energy industry has prompted repeated calls for a more diversified economy, and in recent years Wyoming's tourism industry has begun to have an impact. Nonetheless, Wyoming remains a predominantly rural state—and by far the least populous in the union, with about 530,000 residents as of 2009.

2 LOOKING BACK AT MONTANA & WYOMING

MONTANA

IN THE BEGINNING The first people believed to have wondered at the land we now call Montana was Folsom Man, who arrived sometime after the end of the last Ice Age about 12,000 years ago, and lived here until superseded by the Yuma culture about 6,800 years ago.

Then, about 3,000 years ago, a more modern American-Indian culture began to emerge, eventually evolving into the

Kootenai, Kalispell, Flathead, Shoshone, Crow, Blackfeet, Chippewa, Cree, Cheyenne, Gros Ventres, and Assiniboine.

EUROPEAN EXPLORERS The first European known to enter Montana was Pierre Gaultier, de Varennes, sieur de La Vérendrye.

Vérendrye had heard of a river that flowed to the western sea and was looking for the Northwest Passage. He came in

MONTANA DATELINE

- **11,000 B.C.** Earliest evidence of humans in Montana.
- **A.D. 1620s** Arrival of the Plains Indians.
- **1803** The eastern part of Montana becomes a territory through the Louisiana Purchase.
- **1805–06** Explorers Lewis and Clark journey through

the northern Rockies to and from the Pacific coast.
- **1864** Montana becomes an official territory. Gold is discovered at Last Chance Gulch in Helena.
- **1876** Defeat of George A. Custer at the Battle of the Little Bighorn.
- **1877** Chief Joseph of the Nez Perce tribe surrenders to U.S. soldiers in the Bear Paw Mountains.

- **1880** The Utah and Northern Railroad enters Montana.
- **1883** The Northern Pacific Railroad crosses Montana.
- **1889** Montana, on November 8, becomes the 41st state in the Union.
- **1893** The University of Montana in Missoula and Montana State University in Bozeman are founded.
- **1910** Glacier National Park is established.

1738, but retreated. Two of his sons, Pierre and François, returned in 1743 and described the "shining mountains," generally believed to be the Bighorns of southern Montana and northern Wyoming. But threats of a looming Indian war discouraged the brothers and they returned to Montreal. No other white men are known to have come here for another 60 years.

When they finally did arrive, they were with the expedition of Lewis and Clark. The explorers reached the mouth of the Yellowstone River on April 26, 1805, and pushed upriver to the Shoshone, where they were warmly greeted, the result of having coincidentally brought Shoshone chief Cameahwait's long-lost sister, Sacajawea, with them as one of their guides.

SETTLEMENT The first industry in Montana, at least for non-Indians, was trapping. John Jacob Astor, Alexander Ross, and William Ashley brought in their hearty *voyageurs* to clear the country of beaver for the European hat market.

The discovery of gold opened Montana's Wild West era. The lure of easy money plus the fact that these towns were some 400 miles from official justice attracted outlaws, con artists, and ladies of the night from all over the West.

In 1864, just as gold was discovered in Last Chance Gulch in present-day Helena, the Montana Territory was formed and

Sidney Edgerton became the first territorial governor. The capital was moved to Virginia City and a constitutional convention was called as the first step toward statehood. A constitution was drafted and sent to St. Louis for printing, but was lost somewhere along the way.

In 1884, another constitution was drafted. This one didn't work either, for one reason or another, and in 1889, the now well-practiced delegates came up with a third one. Taking no chances, they prefaced it with the Magna Carta, the Declaration of Independence, the Articles of Confederation, and the U.S. Constitution. Montana finally became a state in November 1889.

TROUBLE BETWEEN THE INDIANS & THE SETTLERS Montana's Indian tribes were not at first invariably hostile to the whites, and signed a number of treaties signaling their peaceful intentions. But the influx of settlers and the confinement of tribes to reservations resulted in dissatisfaction among the original inhabitants, and escalating hostilities against the whites. In 1876, the War Department launched a campaign against the Sioux and Cheyenne. At the end of June that year, this culminated in the **Battle of the Little Bighorn** and the death of all of the command under Gen. George Armstrong Custer.

- **1917–19** Missoula native Jeannette Rankin, a Republican, becomes the first woman elected to U.S. Congress and votes against U.S. participation in World War I.
- **1940** Fort Peck Dam is completed.
- **1965** Construction of Yellowtail Dam is completed.
- **1973** Montana's third state constitution goes into effect.

- **1983** Anaconda Copper Mining Company shuts down.
- **1986** Montana spends $56 million on environmental protection programs.
- **1995** Wolves are reintroduced into Yellowstone National Park. Daytime speed limits are abolished (but later reestablished).
- **1996** Recluse Theodore Kaczynski, dubbed the Unabomber, is arrested at

his cabin near Lincoln and is later sentenced to life in prison for sending a series of mail bombs that killed three people.
- **1998** The $6-million Lewis & Clark National Historic Trail Interpretive Center opens in Great Falls.
- **2000–01** A series of forest fires—mostly wildfires but some caused by careless humans—drive thousands

continues

The Indian victory was only a temporary setback for the whites, however, and by 1880 all the Indians had been forced onto reservations. The last action of the Indian War period occurred in Montana with the heroic flight of Chief Joseph's Nez Perce from their northern Idaho reservation toward Canada in 1877.

INDUSTRIALIZATION When copper was first discovered in the silver mines in Butte, no one could have foretold its effects on Montana's future. When copper wiring became an integral part of several new electrical technologies, Butte copper became an important resource for America. One of the first men to profit was Marcus Daly, an Irish immigrant who arrived in Butte in his mid-30s and purchased his first mine, which yielded incredibly large amounts of the purest copper in the world.

William A. Clark, another copper-mine baron, was a Horatio Alger type. An average youth from Pennsylvania, he rooted around in mines until his efforts took him to Montana. He had a keen business acumen that prompted him to purchase mining operations, electric companies, water companies, and banks. He quickly amassed a great deal of wealth; then his inflated ego drove him to the political arena. His was the major voice in the territorial constitution proceedings in 1884,

and when Montana held its last territorial election, Clark was determined to get into public office as Montana's representative.

A war commenced between Daly and Clark, rooted in Clark's determination to hold political office and Daly's unwillingness to see him do it. Montana finally became a state in 1889, after 5 tough years of appeals to the U.S. Congress. The bellicose millionaires were so set on controlling the young state's political interests that they purchased or created newspapers to give themselves a printed voice. They stuffed money into the pockets of voters and agreed on nothing. In Montana's first congressional election, Clark fell three votes shy of his bid, and the legislature adjourned without selecting a second senator, leaving Montana with only half of its due representation in Washington.

The fight for capital status came along in 1894. Helena had been the capital, but the constitution held that the site must be determined by the voters. Daly wanted his newly created Anaconda to be the capital; Clark was happy with the status quo. The fact that Anaconda was ruled by the strong arm of the Anaconda Mining Company caused voters to turn to the diversified ways of Helena. For once in his life, William Clark was not only rich but also appreciated by the masses. Or so it seemed.

of people from their homes and do millions of dollars in damage.
- **2003** Wildfires burn 140,000 acres in Glacier National Park.
- **2005** The grizzly bear is removed from the endangered-species list.
- **2006** A powerful November rainstorm washes out a chunk of Going-to-the-Sun Road in Glacier National Park.
- **2007–08** Over 1500 Yellowstone bison are killed as they cross into Montana due to brucellosis fears.

With his thirst for public office revitalized, Clark did his best to buy his way into the U.S. Senate, and actually pulled it off. Daly, infuriated by the way his bitter enemy achieved his seat, demanded an investigation by the Senate. The investigation uncovered a wealth of improprieties on Clark's part, so he resigned. Down, but not out, Clark took a deep breath and plunged immediately back into the thick of things. Once when Robert Burns Smith, governor of Montana and hardly an ardent admirer of Clark's, was out of town, Clark arranged for his friend A. E. Spriggs, the lieutenant governor, to appoint Clark to the U.S. Senate. This lunatic act embarrassed the state of Montana, causing Smith to nullify the appointment upon his return. Meanwhile, Daly had sold his Anaconda Copper Company to Standard Oil to form the Amalgamated Copper Company, and Clark was now up against a nameless, faceless opponent.

He chose to link his fate with another, younger copper king, Augustus Heinze, hoping to form an alliance that Amalgamated couldn't match. At this time, Heinze was more influential than the older, less active Clark, and the team of Heinze and Clark soon had complete control of the mining world in Montana. It seemed as if Clark's last wish—to garner the Senate post he had been denied for so long—would be realized with Heinze's help. And

so it was—Clark served his state as a senator from 1901 to 1907.

THE 20TH CENTURY At the beginning of the 20th century, Montana experienced a boom of a different type. The Indian Wars had ended, and white settlers declared the land a safe and fertile haven for farming. The U.S. government helped things along in 1909 when it passed the Enlarged Homestead Act, giving 320 acres to anyone willing to stay on it for at least 5 months out of the year for a minimum of 3 years. Homesteaders arrived from all over the country to stake a piece of land.

Sentiment for the homesteaders was never good, and the generalization that homesteaders were stupid, dirty people became increasingly popular. The truth is that Montana's agricultural backbone was created by these extraordinary people who came west to establish farms. Wheat became—and still is—the major crop in such areas as the Judith Basin, in the center of the state, and Choteau County, north of Great Falls.

When the Great Depression hit Montana, farming was challenged by severe drought, and jobs were nowhere to be found. Roosevelt's New Deal was a lifesaver. Without the jobs created by the Civilian Conservation Corps and the Works Progress Administration, the state might have never recovered its economic

MONTANA & WYOMING IN DEPTH

2

LOOKING BACK

WYOMING DATELINE

- **18,000 B.C.** Earliest evidence of humans in Wyoming.
- **A.D. 1807** John Colter explores the Yellowstone area, coming as far south as Jackson Hole.
- **1812** Fur trader Robert Stuart discovers South Pass, the gentlest route across the northern Rockies.

- **1843** Pioneers begin traveling west on the Oregon Trail through Wyoming.
- **1848** The U.S. Army moves into Fort Laramie to protect Oregon Trail travelers from Indians.
- **1852** The first school in the state is founded at Fort Laramie.
- **1860** The Pony Express begins its run from Missouri to California, through Wyoming.

- **1867** The Union Pacific Railroad enters Wyoming.
- **1868** The Treaty of Fort Bridger creates the Shoshone Reservation in northwest Wyoming.
- **1868** The Territory of Wyoming is created by Congress.
- **1869** Wyoming Territorial Legislature grants women the right to vote and hold elective office.

balance. Of particular help was construction of the Fort Peck Dam in the mid-1930s, which employed more than 50,000 workers. The earth-filled dam, the largest of its kind in the world, took almost 5 years to complete.

WYOMING

IN THE BEGINNING   The earliest indications of man in what is now Wyoming date back some 20,000 years. No one knows the identity of these early inhabitants, nor can anyone say with certainty who created the Medicine Wheel in the Bighorn Mountains or the petroglyphs found in various parts of the state. The earliest identified settlers were the Crow, Sioux, Cheyenne, and Arapaho—tribes that came from the east—as well as the Shoshone and Bannock, who came from the Great Basin, more closely related to the peoples of Central America. The lifestyles of these tribes were greatly changed by the arrival of two European innovations—the horse and the gun. The first white men in Wyoming were fur trappers, and the first of them was John Colter, who left the Lewis and Clark expedition in 1806 to wander south through Yellowstone and possibly Jackson Hole.

SETTLEMENT   The Oregon Trail and other major pioneer routes west cut right through Wyoming and the territories of the Sioux, Shoshone, Arapaho, and other tribes. Without much regard for the people they were displacing, the non-Indians killed a great deal of the game the Indians depended on; Indian bands, in turn, harassed and sometimes attacked the travelers. Indian tribes were increasingly pushed west into tighter spaces, and there was warfare among tribes.

In a series of treaties, beginning with the Fort Laramie Treaty of 1851, the tribes gave up rights to some of their homelands in return for reservations and other considerations. The discovery of gold in areas like the Black Hills and South Pass, and the routes of settlers, led to numerous treaty violations and continued conflict. Tribes in the east were being evicted and shipped west. Treaties that might have protected Indian rights were modified and broken, and U.S. Army troops were sent in to keep the peace. Some tribal leaders, recognizing the inexorable advance of the whites, decided the only alternative was to fight the invaders.

TROUBLE BETWEEN THE INDIANS & THE SETTLERS   Sitting Bull and Crazy Horse of the Hunkpapa Sioux joined forces with members of the Cheyenne and Arapaho tribes along the Little Bighorn River. It was here in June 1876 that a huge gathering of Indians defeated George Custer and his men. Inevitably this led to

- **1870** Esther H. Morris becomes the nation's first female justice of the peace.
- **1872** Yellowstone National Park is established as the nation's first national park.
- **1884** First oil well is drilled in Wyoming.
- **1886–87** Great blizzard decimates ranches of eastern Wyoming, sending many cattle barons into bankruptcy.
- **1889** The state constitution is adopted.
- **1890** Wyoming becomes the nation's 44th state.
- **1892** The Johnson County War breaks out over a dispute about cattle rustling.
- **1897** The first Cheyenne Frontier Days rodeo is staged.
- **1906** Devils Tower is established by President Theodore Roosevelt as the country's first national monument.
- **1910** Buffalo Bill Dam is completed.
- **1925** Nellie Taylor Ross becomes the nation's first female governor.
- **1927** Man claiming to be Butch Cassidy visits Wyoming from Washington, suggesting that the outlaw was not killed in Bolivia as was generally believed.
- **1929** Grand Teton National Park is established, consisting of only the peaks.
- **1929** Oil thefts discovered on federal land at Teapot

a backlash, a series of attacks on Indian communities, culminating in the death of Sitting Bull and the massacre of Spotted Elk and his Sioux followers in 1890 at Wounded Knee, South Dakota. Chief Washakie of the Shoshone was one of the few great Indian leaders still alive, though his star was diminished by his decision to ally his tribe with the whites. That alliance got his people one of the finest reservations in the West, and the only one in Wyoming—Wind River. Then the U.S. Army moved the now threadbare Arapaho, traditional enemies of the Shoshone, to Wind River "temporarily," and the two tribes began an uncomfortable coexistence that continues to this day.

INDUSTRIALIZATION & THE 20TH CENTURY Big cattle operators moved into Wyoming in the 19th century, controlling the territory's economy and political scene through such organizations as the Cheyenne Social Club. A couple of severe winters in the 1880s and the influx of new settlers building fences raised tensions. When the cattle barons brought in hired guns to clear out the newcomers, the Johnson County War of 1892 erupted. The wealthy cattlemen claimed the newcomers were rustlers. But that show of muscle was futile in halting the longtime decline of the big livestock owners.

3 LAY OF THE LAND

In Montana and Wyoming, the earth seems to have turned itself inside out, its hot insides leaking into hot springs and geysers, its bony spine thrust right through the skin of the continent to form the Continental Divide, making it a geologist's dream. And to a biologist it's heaven, one of the last regions in the United States with enough open space for animals like elk and grizzly bears to roam free.

Plains, basin, and range alternate in this high-altitude environment that is in large part defined by its extremes of weather

and climate. These changing landscapes make Montana and Wyoming two of the best vacation spots in the country for travelers who like their scenery dynamic and dramatic.

The western side of both states is mountainous, dragging moisture from the clouds moving west to east and storing it in snowpack and alpine lakes. Because the ridge of the Rockies wrings moisture from the atmosphere, you find deeper, denser forest extending far to the west, while on the east side, the lodgepole pine, spruce,

Dome, a scandal that rocks the Harding Administration.

- **1950** National forest and private lands are added to form Grand Teton National Park as it is today.
- **1965** Minuteman missile sites are completed near Cheyenne.
- **1973** The Arab oil embargo sends oil prices skyrocketing, instigating a huge oil-drilling boom in Wyoming.

- **1988** Five fires break out around Yellowstone National Park, blackening approximately one-third of the park.
- **1996** The National Park Service institutes a voluntary ban on climbing Devils Tower during June to respect American Indian religious ceremonies.
- **1998** Gay University of Wyoming student Matthew Shepard murdered.

- **2002** The $10-million National Historic Trails Center opens in Casper.
- **2004** The state enjoys a nearly $1-billion surplus in its annual budget, thanks to increased drilling and mining activity.
- **2006** The famed tram at Jackson Hole Mountain Resort closes.
- **2008** The tram reopens in time for the ski season.

continues

and fir forests give way to the Great Plains, a vast, flat land characterized by sagebrush, native grasses, and cottonwood-lined river bottoms.

But a lot of the landscape dates back more than 100 million years to when the collision of tectonic plates buckled the earth's crust and thrust these mountains upward. Later, glaciers (of which some vestiges remain) carved the canyons. The tallest peaks in Wyoming are located within the Wind River Range, which rises from the high plains of South Pass and runs northwest to the Yellowstone Plateau. Nine of the peaks in the Winds have elevations over 13,000 feet; **Gannett Peak,** at 13,785 feet, is the highest in the state. Several other mountain ranges are found to the south of Yellowstone—including the Absarokas and the stunning Tetons—and from Yellowstone north into Montana run other dramatic ranges, including the Gallatin, Madison, Mission, Bitterroot, Cabinet, and Beartooth, where you'll find Montana's highest point, **Granite Peak,** at 12,799 feet.

The **Continental Divide** enters Montana from Canada and traces a snaking path through the two states. Both Montana and Wyoming have rivers flowing west to the Pacific and east to the Atlantic. Here you'll also find the headwaters of major river systems—the Flathead and Clark Fork heading west into the Columbia from Montana, along with the Snake from Wyoming; the Yellowstone, North Platte, and Madison joining the Missouri bound east; and the Green from Wyoming emptying into the Colorado heading south. These rivers are the lifeblood of the region, supplying irrigation, fisheries, and power from dams. Montana also boasts the country's largest freshwater body of water west of the Mississippi River: **Flathead Lake. Yellowstone** and **Jackson lakes** are Wyoming's two largest natural bodies of water.

Montana is the greener of these two states, with more abundant alpine wilderness

and bigger rivers. Wyoming, however, has been dealt a more interesting hand of natural wonders: waterfalls, geysers, and other geothermal oddities at Yellowstone; as well as the natural landmark of clustered rock columns that rise more than 1,280 feet above the surrounding plains at **Devils Tower National Monument,** near the state's Black Hills region of the northeast. At Wyoming's Red Desert, south of Lander, the Continental Divide splits to form an enclosed basin where no water can escape, and nearby you find **Fossil Butte National Monument,** an archaeological treasure chest of fossilized fish and ancient miniature horses.

The states are characterized by long, cold winters and short summers of hot days and chilly nights. Temperature ranges are dramatic, and are largely dependent on elevation. Except along the far western edge of Montana, precipitation here is less than 30 inches a year. It's considerably less as you journey east and south. But the snowpack in the high mountains—more than 300 inches accumulate in some areas—melts through the summer and keeps the rivers running.

Planning a trip to Montana and Wyoming can be done in several ways. Those interested in a particular activity, such as hiking, might choose two or three locations and divide their time among them. Conversely, one could first select a destination, such as one of the national parks or an Old West town, and then determine the activities to be pursued there.

This book is organized geographically. Because these states are so large, many visitors will limit their vacations to one or two regions.

MONTANA

GLACIER COUNTRY & THE NORTHWEST CORNER
This includes Glacier National Park, the Flathead Valley and northwest corner of the state, and Missoula, one of Montana's three largest cities. The national park draws millions of visitors annually

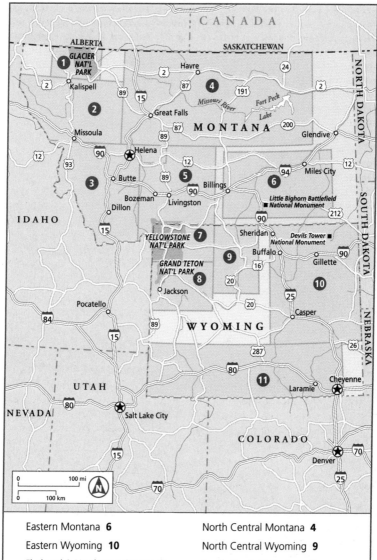

Eastern Montana **6**	North Central Montana **4**
Eastern Wyoming **10**	North Central Wyoming **9**
Flathead & Northwest Corner **2**	South Central Montana **5**
Glacier National Park **1**	Southern Wyoming **11**
Jackson Hole & Grand Teton National Park **8**	Southwestern Montana **3**
	Yellowstone National Park **7**

who come to see its soaring peaks, varied wildlife, and innumerable lakes and streams. The **Going-to-the-Sun Road,** a 50-mile scenic highway that cuts through the heart of the park from southwest to northeast, makes Glacier surprisingly accessible. Elsewhere in the region, the increasingly popular Big Mountain draws downhill skiers, and Flathead Lake is a magnet because of its excellent watersports and quality golf courses. One of the fastest-growing areas in the state, the **Flathead Valley** shelters an interesting mix of residents: Farmers and loggers share ski lifts and trout streams with transplanted urbanites and big-bucks entrepreneurs, all looking for their slice of paradise. On the southern edge of the region is **Missoula,** a vigorous college town with good restaurants, interesting shops, and bits of Montana history.

SOUTHWESTERN MONTANA This area is extremely diversified. **Helena,** a town centered on arts and politics (though not necessarily in that order), has a beautiful historic district filled with classic architecture and access to tremendous fishing on the Missouri River. **Butte,** on the other hand, is working hard to overcome the decay caused by the exploitation, then abandonment, of its mines. Other areas in this part of the state are full of lore. Vigilantes and corrupt sheriffs dominate the stories of the "ghost towns" of Virginia City and Nevada City, both of which are kept alive today by tourists seeking a realistic glimpse into America's past, and Bannack, an abandoned ghost town that's now a state park.

MISSOURI RIVER COUNTRY One of the least populated areas in the state, this region stretches from the mountains to the eastern border and is distinguished by prairies that roll along for hundreds of miles. **Great Falls,** the region's largest city, is a mecca for those interested in the story of famed explorers Lewis and Clark. U.S. 2, or the **Hi-Line**—that long stretch of

pavement that runs across the northern part of the state—cuts by a series of farms and ranches that perpetuate the homesteader life. New farming equipment and satellite dishes are just modern polish on an old tune.

SOUTH-CENTRAL MONTANA (YELLOWSTONE COUNTRY) Though this region is almost a twin of the northwest part of the state in many ways—a nearby national park, renowned ski resorts, a university, lots of tourists—it has a unique personality. The city of **Bozeman** is home to Montana State University and a vibrant downtown. Anglers come from all over the world to fish these blue-ribbon trout streams, but the main attraction in this part of the state is **Yellowstone National Park.** Still, even the valleys that lead to it—the Madison, Gallatin, and Paradise—are spectacular destinations themselves.

EASTERN MONTANA The geography in this part of Montana is similar to its neighboring region to the north, but there are more people and more things to do here. **Billings** is the supply center for eastern Montana and northern Wyoming. It's easily the largest city in Montana and has prospered, even without the helpful hand of tourism that the western side of the state has seen. The Bighorn Canyon and the Yellowtail Dam draw their share of visitors, especially hunters and anglers, but this region's main attraction is **Little Bighorn Battlefield,** where Gen. George Armstrong Custer led the 7th Cavalry to defeat at the hands of the Sioux and the Northern Cheyenne.

WYOMING

YELLOWSTONE PLATEAU Yellowstone sits atop a volcanic caldera that periodically blows its top—once every 600,000 years, give or take—but in the interim provides a largely intact ecosystem in this park of 2.2 million acres. Protected from major development by the National Park Service, Yellowstone provides habitat no longer found elsewhere in the Lower 48, and is home to herds of bison, elk, grizzly bears, trumpeter swans, Yellowstone cutthroat trout, and more subtle beauties such as wildflowers and hummingbirds. The geothermal area is greater than any other in the world, with mud pots, geysers, and hot springs of all colors, size, and performance, indicative of a complex natural plumbing system that pulls water down into the earth's crust and regurgitates it at high temperatures. More than three million visitors come here annually, not just to pay homage to Old Faithful, but also to fish, hike, camp, and boat.

THE TETONS & JACKSON HOLE The Tetons are a young range, abrupt and sharp edged as they knife up from the plain below. And while the photogenic peaks get top billing, it's the valley of Jackson Hole that provides the more varied environments and experiences. **Grand Teton National Park** offers some of the most stunning scenery most of us will ever see—shimmering lakes, thickly carpeted forests, and towering peaks that are blanketed with snow throughout most of the year. It's an easy-to-see park—you can catch its breathtaking beauty on a quick drive—but you'll find lakes and waterfalls and even better views and adventures if you leave your car and take to the trails and waterways. The Tetons are especially popular with mountain climbers, who scale its peaks year-round. Elsewhere in the valley you can float the lively Snake River, visit the National Elk Refuge in the winter, or play cowboy at one of the dude and guest ranches that dot the valley. Skiers and snowboarders have a blast at the resorts here, as well as Grand Targhee on the other side of Teton Pass. And the snug town of **Jackson,** with its antler-arched town square and its busy shops, offers everything from classy art galleries to noisy two-steppin' cowboy bars.

NORTH-CENTRAL WYOMING This is the sort of basin settlers were looking for

when they came this way in the 19th century—mountain ranges on all sides cradling wide, ranchable bottomlands, and some mineral wealth to pay for ranch kids' college educations. More and more, though, the oil and gas development, sheep herding and cattle driving, and beet and wheat growing are giving way to recreation and tourism. The beautiful mountains here—the Wind Rivers, the Owl Creeks, the Absarokas, the east side of the Bighorns—get less attention than the Tetons, but that only makes them more attractive. Historically, the area learned its lessons in tourism from the West's greatest showman, Buffalo Bill Cody, who helped build the fun-loving town that still bears his name. The rodeo and great museum of **Cody** are joined by other attractions, including the **Bighorn Canyon National Recreation Area,** the hot springs of **Thermopolis,** and the **Wind River Indian Reservation,** home to the Shoshone and Arapaho peoples.

EASTERN WYOMING The plains don't begin when you pass east over the Continental Divide; there's another mountain range to cross, and then another—first the Bighorns, then the Black Hills—before you're really out there on the howling flats. The **Bighorns** are a treasure of steep canyons, snow-crowned peaks, good fishing, and good hiking, and at their feet sit two of Wyoming's nicest communities, **Sheridan** and **Buffalo.** Some of the prize ranches in this valley have become some of the best dude ranches in the country. Farther east, across the plains beyond the energy boomtown of Gillette, stands the unmistakable geological landmark that is **Devils Tower,** and along Wyoming's eastern border rise the Black Hills. The region's other claim to fame lies in its history. This is the land of Butch Cassidy and his Hole-in-the-Wall Gang (also known as the Wild Bunch), of cattle rustlers, cowboys, and outlaws.

SOUTHERN WYOMING To the millions of drivers who cross Wyoming on

I-80, this is the empty quarter, consisting of mostly barren, wind-swept plains. But it also has its own mountainous corner—the craggy **Medicine Bow**—a lot of history, and mineral wealth of many varieties, from natural gas to trona. More discerning travelers will not see a wasteland: They'll follow the routes of Oregon Trail pioneers (you can still find the wagon-wheel ruts and graves), get off the freeway to visit historic sites such as Fort Laramie, and throw out a fishing line on the North Platte near Saratoga or in Flaming Gorge Reservoir south of Green River. In this country you'll find both old and new— from the historic getaway of **Saratoga** to the capital city of **Cheyenne,** where the city throws the biggest rodeo party in the West during July's Cheyenne Frontier Days.

4 MONTANA & WYOMING IN POPULAR CULTURE: BOOKS, FILM, TV & MUSIC

In addition to the books discussed below, those planning an extended trip to Yellowstone and/or Grand Teton national parks will find an abundance of information in *Frommer's Yellowstone & Grand Teton National Parks* (Wiley Publishing, Inc.).

FICTION A. B. Guthrie's *The Big Sky* (Houghton Mifflin, 1947) is now a Montana classic, as is Owen Wister's *The Virginian* (Macmillan, 1929), set in frontier Wyoming. Then move on to contemporary fiction, like the classic fly-fishing novella *A River Runs Through It* (University of Chicago Press, 1976), by Norman Maclean. *Fool's Crow* (Viking Penguin, 1986), by James Welch (a native Montanan), and *Heart Mountain* (Viking Penguin, 1989), by Gretel Ehrlich, are fictional stories that revolve around American-Indian and Asian characters. Annie Proulx's *Close Range: Wyoming Stories* (Scribner, 1999) and *Bad Dirt: Wyoming Stories 2* (Scribner, 2004) are recent additions by a fine writer who's spent considerable time around Sheridan. Poet James Glavin's beautifully written *The Meadow* (Henry Holt, 1992) is set in the Tie Siding area of southeast Wyoming.

Montana is fortunate to have the best of its literature compiled in one volume, *The Last Best Place* (University of Montana Press, 1988), the definitive anthology of Montana writings, from American-Indian myths to contemporary short stories.

NONFICTION Novelist Ivan Doig wrote a beautiful memoir about his youth in Montana, *This House of Sky* (Harcourt Brace Jovanovich, 1978). Gretel Ehrlich's *The Solace of Open Spaces* (Viking Penguin, 1986) is a beautifully written, evocative account of Wyoming ranch life. Paul Schullery's *Searching for Yellowstone* (Mariner Books, 1997) is a great look at the ecology of the world's first national park and mankind's impact on it. Eric Sorg's *Buffalo Bill: Myth and Reality* is an informative read about the man who truly defined the mythos of the West.

If your interests lean more toward geography, check out the *Roadside Geology of Montana* (Mountain Press, 1986), by David Alt and Donald W. Hyndman, and the similar *Roadside Geology of Wyoming* (Mountain Press, 1988), by David R. Largeson and Darwin R. Spearing.

HISTORY Perhaps the best, and easiest, read about the history and culture of Montana is found between the covers of *Montana, High, Wide and Handsome* (University of Nebraska Press, 1983), written by Joseph Howard and first published in 1944. Another interesting historical tome is Aubrey Haines's two-volume *The Yellowstone Story* (University Press of Colorado, 1977).

FILMS Hollywood adapted Norman Maclean's *A River Runs Through It* in 1992 with Brad Pitt; *Rancho Deluxe* (1975) is set in Livingston, Montana, and depicts a rapidly changing place through cattle rustlers played by Jeff Bridges and Sam Waterston; *Little Big Man* (1970) is a revisionist Western that covers Custer's Last Stand and much more. Wyoming films of note include the made-for-HBO *The Laramie Project* (2001), an adaptation of a stage play about the murder of gay college student Matthew Shepard; *Shane* (1953), the Western classic shot in Jackson Hole; *Heaven's Gate* (1980), the Michael Cimino film about the Johnson County War whose title became synonymous with bloated Hollywood budgets, and *Close Encounters of the Third Kind* (1977), Steven Spielberg's UFO epic that climaxes at Devils Tower National Monument. *Brokeback Mountain* (2005) took place in Montana and Wyoming, but most of the movie's Rocky Mountain exteriors were actually shot in Canada.

TV A number of 1950s and 1960s Western shows were set in Montana and Wyoming, including *Buckskin* (Montana) and *Laramie, The Lawman,* and *The Virginian* (Wyoming). However, the states have been ignored by most networks outside of PBS and Animal Planet in recent years.

MUSIC Late country singer-songwriter Chris LeDoux lived on a ranch in Kaycee, Wyoming. Blackfeet singer-storyteller Jack Gladstone has been called "Montana's troubadour." Grunge-rock pioneers Bruce Fairweather of Mudhoney and Pearl Jam's Jeff Ament both hail from Montana.

Planning Your Trip to Montana & Wyoming

Montana and Wyoming are both huge states, and there are countless vacations around the states. You can focus on the national parks, or the Wild West history, the ski resorts, or a little cabin in the woods that is truly away from it all—no Internet, no cellphones, and no city lights.

The places that get the most attention—Yellowstone, Jackson Hole, the Flathead and Gallatin valleys—also get the most visitors. If it is peace and quiet you're after, some of the roads less taken are where you'll want to steer your route. But modern conveniences can be hard to find in the most far-flung locales of these states; urban types will be more interested in Jackson, Missoula, and Bozeman, where a day trip to the great outdoors can be bookended with a night's sleep in a first-rate lodging and dinner at a terrific eatery.

Few things can ruin a much-anticipated vacation more than poor planning: for instance, arriving at a national park in mid-January, only to discover that it's almost totally closed by snow until early May, or discovering that you missed that dog-sled race you would have loved to see by 2 days. This chapter is designed to assist you in sorting out the details that could make the difference between a trip you'll never forget and one you'd rather not remember.

1 WHEN TO GO

Summer, autumn, and winter are the best times to visit the Northern Rockies. The days are sunny, the nights are clear, and humidity is low. A popular song once romanticized "Springtime in the Rockies," but that season—or what most people think of as springtime—lasts about 2 days in early June. The rest of the spring season is likely to be chilly with snow or rain; most of the annual moisture in these states falls during March and April.

Summer is the best season to visit for hiking, fishing, camping, and wildlife-watching. It will be warm during the day and cool at night. In **Montana,** average highs in July run from 79°F (25°C) in **West Yellowstone** to 89°F (32°C) in **Miles City;** lows at night range from 38°F (3°C) to 60°F (16°C). In **Wyoming,** the average high temperatures in July range from 80°F (27°C) to 90°F (32°C)—at high elevations, it almost never gets above 100°F (38°C), and it's dry. The plains tend to get hotter than the mountains.

Fall brings spectacularly clear days; cool, clear nights; and calm winds up until late October, when things get iffy again. Weather is changeable, however, and snow is possible—even likely—in the high country, so don't try an extended backpacking trip unless you are experienced and well prepared. Actually, this is a requirement year-round; you can get caught in mountain snowstorms in July and August.

Winter is a glorious season here, though it can be very cold. Lows in Havre, Butte, West Yellowstone, and Jackson average single digits Fahrenheit (about –15°C) in January.

And it can be very windy in some parts of these states, especially on the plains. But the air is crystalline, the snow is powdery, and the skiing is fantastic. If you drive around Montana and Wyoming in the winter, *always* carry sleeping bags, extra food, flashlights, and other safety gear. You need to be prepared to survive if your car breaks down or you get stuck in a blizzard or snow squall. Every resident has a horror story about being caught outside unprepared. Only the north entrance at Yellowstone National Park is open to automobiles in the winter. Lodging is available in the park only at Mammoth and Old Faithful. Ski resort towns, such as Jackson and Kalispell, stay lively all winter, but summer tourist towns, such as Cody, are quiet.

Montana's Average Monthly Temperatures (High/Low)

	Jan	Feb	Mar	Apr	May	June	July	Aug	Sept	Oct	Nov	Dec
Billings												
°F	32/14	38/19	45/25	57/34	67/44	77/52	86/58	85/57	72/47	61/37	45/26	36/18
°C	0/–10	3/–7	7/–3	13/1	19/6	25/11	30/14	29/13	22/8	16/2	7/–3	2/–7
Bozeman												
°F	28/2	34/9	39/15	54/28	65/37	72/44	83/48	82/47	71/39	59/30	43/19	34/10
°C	–2/–16	1/–12	3/–9	12/–2	18/2	22/5	28/8	27/8	21/3	15/–1	6/–7	1/–12
Butte												
°F	28/2	33/6	39/14	51/26	61/34	68/40	80/45	78/43	68/35	56/27	40/15	33/8
°C	–2/–16	0/–14	3/–10	10/–3	16/1	20/4	26/7	25/6	20/1	13/–2	4/–9	0/–13
Dillon												
°F	31/8	36/12	42/18	55/28	64/36	71/43	84/49	82/47	71/39	59/31	43/19	35/14
°C	0/–13	2/–11	5/–7	12/–2	17/2	21/6	28/9	27/8	21/3	15/0	6/–7	1/–10
Glasgow												
°F	20/0	27/7	39/18	56/31	68/43	77/51	85/57	84/55	71/44	59/33	40/19	26/7
°C	–6/–18	–2/–13	3/–7	13/0	20/6	25/10	29/13	28/12	21/6	15/0	4/–7	–3/–13
Great Falls												
°F	31/12	37/17	43/22	55/32	65/41	74/49	83/54	81/53	70/44	59/36	44/25	35/16
°C	–1/–11	3/–8	6/–6	13/0	18/5	23/9	28/12	27/11	21/7	15/2	7/–4	2/–9
Havre												
°F	24/3	32/10	43/20	57/31	68/41	77/49	84/54	84/52	71/42	60/31	41/18	29/7
°C	–4/–16	0/–12	6/–6	13/0	20/5	25/9	28/12	28/11	21/5	15/0	5/–7	–1/–13
Helena												
°F	29/9	36/15	44/22	56/31	65/40	74/47	83/52	82/51	70/41	58/31	42/21	32/12
°C	–1/–12	2/–9	6/–5	13/0	18/4	23/8	28/11	27/10	21/5	14/0	5/–6	0/–11
Kalispell												
°F	28/13	35/18	43/23	55/31	65/39	72/45	81/48	80/47	69/39	55/30	39/24	31/17
°C	–2/–10	1/–7	6/–5	12/0	18/3	22/7	27/8	26/8	20/3	12/–1	3/–4	0/–8
Lewistown												
°F	32/9	35/11	42/18	55/28	64/37	72/44	82/49	80/47	70/39	59/31	45/20	37/14
°C	0/–12	1/–11	5/–7	12/–2	17/2	22/6	27/9	26/8	21/3	15/0	7/–6	2/–10
Libby												
°F	32/16	39/19	48/25	57/30	68/38	75/45	83/48	85/47	71/38	57/30	41/25	32/18
°C	0/–8	3/–7	9/–4	14/–1	19/3	23/6	28/9	29/8	21/3	14/0	4/–4	0/–7
Miles City												
°F	25/5	33/11	43/21	58/33	69/44	79/53	89/60	87/58	73/46	61/35	43/21	31/11
°C	–3/–15	0/–11	6/–6	14/0	20/6	26/11	31/15	30/14	22/7	16/1	6/–6	0/–11

	Jan	Feb	Mar	Apr	May	June	July	Aug	Sept	Oct	Nov	Dec
Missoula												
°F	30/14	37/20	46/25	57/32	66/39	74/46	84/50	83/49	71/40	57/31	40/24	31/17
°C	-1/-10	2/-6	7/-3	13/0	18/3	23/7	28/10	28/9	21/4	13/0	4/-4	0/-8
Sidney												
°F	20/-3	29/5	35/13	56/29	68/41	76/49	83/53	83/52	71/41	59/30	42/18	30/8
°C	-6/-19	-1/-15	1/-10	13/-1	20/5	24/9	28/11	28/11	21/5	15/-1	5/-7	-1/-13
W. Yellowstone												
°F	25/-1	31/2	39/7	49/19	59/27	68/33	79/38	77/35	67/28	53/21	37/9	27/1
°C	-3/-18	0/-16	3/-13	9/-7	15/-2	20/0	26/3	25/1	19/-2	11/-6	2/-12	-2/-17

Wyoming's Average Monthly Temperatures (High/Low)

	Jan	Feb	Mar	Apr	May	June	July	Aug	Sept	Oct	Nov	Dec
Casper												
°F	33/12	38/16	45/22	56/30	67/39	78/48	87/54	86/53	74/43	61/33	44/22	35/15
°C	0/-11	3/-8	7/-5	13/-1	19/3	25/8	30/12	30/11	23/6	16/0	6/-5	1/-9
Cheyenne												
°F	38/15	41/18	44/21	55/30	64/40	75/48	83/54	81/53	72/44	60/34	47/23	40/17
°C	3/-9	5/-7	6/-6	12/-1	17/4	23/8	28/12	27/11	22/6	15/1	8/-5	4/-8
Cody												
°F	36/12	40/14	47/21	57/31	66/40	76/47	85/54	83/51	72/42	61/33	46/22	38/15
°C	2/-11	4/-10	8/-6	13/0	18/4	24/8	29/12	28/10	22/5	16/0	7/-5	3/-9
Devils Tower												
°F	33/7	40/13	47/19	57/28	68/39	77/48	86/53	86/51	75/41	64/31	45/20	37/12
°C	0/-14	4/-10	8/-7	13/-2	20/3	25/8	29/11	29/10	23/5	17/0	7/-6	2/-11
Dubois												
°F	33/10	37/12	41/16	50/24	60/31	70/38	79/42	78/41	67/34	56/26	42/18	35/12
°C	0/-12	2/-11	5/-8	9/-4	15/0	21/3	25/5	25/4	19/0	13/-3	5/-7	1/-11
Gillette												
°F	32/11	36/14	43/20	55/30	66/40	76/48	87/56	85/54	75/45	61/34	44/23	36/15
°C	0/-11	2/-10	6/-6	12/-1	18/4	24/8	30/13	29/12	23/7	16/1	6/-5	2/-9
Jackson												
°F	27/5	32/8	41/15	52/24	63/31	72/37	82/40	80/38	71/31	58/23	39/16	28/6
°C	-2/-15	0/-13	4/-9	11/-4	17/0	22/2	27/4	26/3	21/0	14/-4	4/-9	-2/-14
Kemmerer												
°F	29/5	33/7	40/14	54/25	65/33	74/38	82/44	80/42	71/34	59/26	41/16	34/10
°C	-1/-15	0/-15	4/-10	12/-3	18/0	22/3	27/6	26/5	21/1	15/-3	5/-8	1/-12
Lander												
°F	32/8	37/14	45/21	56/31	66/40	77/49	86/55	84/54	73/44	60/33	43/19	33/11
°C	0/-13	2/-10	7/-6	13/0	18/4	25/9	30/12	28/12	22/6	15/0	6/-7	0/-11
Rawlins												
°F	31/11	34/15	39/18	52/27	64/37	76/44	83/51	81/50	71/40	58/31	40/19	33/15
°C	0/-11	1/-9	3/-7	11/-2	17/2	24/6	28/10	27/10	21/4	14/0	4/-7	0/-9
Riverton												
°F	35/7	41/12	48/20	58/29	67/38	77/46	85/51	84/49	74/41	63/31	45/18	37/9
°C	1/-13	5/-10	9/-6	14/-1	19/3	24/7	29/10	28/9	23/4	17/0	7/-7	-2/-12

	Jan	Feb	Mar	Apr	May	June	July	Aug	Sept	Oct	Nov	Dec
Rock Springs												
°F	28/10	33/13	39/19	53/29	63/38	73/46	83/54	81/52	72/43	58/33	40/20	32/14
°C	–2/–12	0/–10	3/–7	11/–1	17/3	22/7	28/12	27/11	22/6	14/0	4/–6	–0/–10
Sheridan												
°F	33/9	38/14	46/21	57/31	67/40	76/48	86/54	86/52	73/42	62/32	45/20	36/12
°C	0/–12	3/–10	7/–6	13/0	19/4	24/8	30/12	29/11	22/5	16/0	7/–6	2/–11
Thermopolis												
°F	34/5	40/10	49/20	61/31	71/39	81/47	91/53	89/51	78/41	64/30	48/18	37/9
°C	1/–15	4/–12	9/–6	16/0	21/3	27/8	32/11	31/10	25/5	17/–1	8/–7	2/–12
Yellowstone												
°F	22/–2	28/–1	34/3	43/15	52/25	61/32	71/38	71/37	61/29	49/22	34/11	25/3
°C	–5/–19	–2/–18	1/–16	5/–9	11/–3	16/0	21/3	21/2	16/–1	9/–5	0/–11	–3/–16

MONTANA & WYOMING CALENDAR OF EVENTS

For an exhaustive list of events beyond those listed here, check **http://events.frommers.com**, where you'll find a searchable, up-to-the-minute roster of what's happening in cities all over the world.

JANUARY

Montana Pro Rodeo Circuit Finals. Montana's best cowboys compete in the final round of this regional competition in Great Falls. Call ✆ **406/727-8900** (www.montanaprorodeo.com) for information. Second or third weekend in January.

FEBRUARY

Winter Carnivals. In Whitefish, Montana, there are a parade, a hockey tournament, the "penguin plunge," fireworks, and a dance. Call ✆ **406/862-3548** (www.whitefishwintercarnival.com). First weekend in February.

Novelty ski races and rodeo events take center stage during a similar Jackson, Wyoming, event that includes cowboy poetry readings, Dutch-oven cook-offs, and a barn dance. Call ✆ **307/733-3025** (www.jacksonholewintercarnival.com) for information. First weekend in February.

Wyoming State Winter Fair. They hold this one indoors in Lander, except for the chariot races. There are booths galore, music, entertainment, a livestock competition, and a big dance.

Call ✆ **307/332-9321** for information. Late February or early March.

MARCH

C. M. Russell Auction of Original Art. This is the finest Western art auction in the country, with exhibitors and attendees from around the world. Great Falls, Montana. Call ✆ **800/803-3351** (www.cmrauction.com) for information. Mid-March.

St. Patrick's Day in Butte. This wild and woolly (and often booze-soaked) outdoor party pays homage to Butte, Montana's Irish heritage. Call ✆ **406/723-3177** for more information. March 17.

APRIL

Montana Storytelling Roundup. Thousands turn out for this annual celebration of storytelling in Cut Bank, Montana. Call ✆ **406/336-3253** for the schedule. Late April.

MAY

International Wildlife Film Festival. This unique, juried film competition in Missoula, Montana, has more than 100 entries from leading wildlife filmmakers.

Call ✆ **406/728-9380** (www.wildlife films.org). Early to mid-May.

Miles City Bucking Horse Sale. A "3-day cowboy Mardi Gras," this stock sale in Miles City, Montana, features street dances, parades, barbecues, and, of course, lots of bucking broncos. Call ✆ **406/234-2890** (www.buckinghorse sale.com) for information. Third weekend in May.

Elk Antler Auction. Nearly 10,000 pounds of bull-elk antlers are auctioned off in Jackson's town square. Call ✆ **307/733-3316** (www.jacksonhole chamber.com or www.elkfest.org) for information. Third Saturday in May.

JUNE

Plains Indian Powwow. Indian dancers from around the region compete in various dance categories, accompanied by traditional drum groups, on the Robbie Powwow Garden next to the Buffalo Bill Historical Center in Cody, Wyoming. Call ✆ **307/587-4771** (www.bbhc.org) for information. Mid- to late June.

Chugwater Chili Cook-Off. Thousands of hot-food pilgrims come to Chugwater, Wyoming, to taste the spicy contenders in this contest. Call ✆ **307/422-3345** (www.chugwaterchilicook off.com) for information. Mid- to late June.

Lewis & Clark Festival. Commemoration of Lewis and Clark's journey in and around Great Falls, Montana, with historical reenactments, buffalo roasts, and float trips. Call ✆ **406/452-5661** (www.lewisclarkia.com) for information. Late June.

Eastern Shoshone Indian Days Powwow. A celebration of American-Indian tradition and culture that's followed by one of Wyoming's largest powwows and all-Indian rodeos, in Fort Washakie, Wyoming. Call ✆ **800/645-6233** (www.easternshoshone.net) for information. Late June.

JULY

Cody Stampede. There are rodeo nights all summer in Cody, but this long weekend is the big one, and the rodeo ring excitement carries over to street dances, fireworks, and food. Call ✆ **800/207-0744** (www.codystampede rodeo.com) for details. July 1 to July 4.

Legend of Rawhide Reenactment. An overeager gold miner comes to an untimely end in this production of the popular Western legend in Lusk, Wyoming. Call ✆ **800/223-5875** (www. legendofrawhide.com) for information. Second weekend in July.

International Climbers Festival. Speakers, music, demonstrations, and climbing at the famed Wild Iris and other rock faces in Fremont County attract rock climbers from around the world to this gathering in Lander, Wyoming. Call ✆ **307/349-1561** (www. climbersfestival.org). Second weekend in July.

North American Indian Days. The Blackfeet Reservation hosts a weekend of native dancing, singing, and drumming, with crafts booths and games, in Browning, Montana. Call ✆ **406/338-2344** for information. Mid-July.

Grand Teton Music Festival. Fine musicians from around the world join this orchestra every summer. A varied classical repertoire includes numerous chamber concerts and some premières in Teton Village, Wyoming. Call ✆ **307/733-3050** (www.gtmf.org) for information. Mid-July to the end of August.

Cheyenne Frontier Days. One of the country's most popular rodeos, the "Daddy of 'em All" entertains huge crowds for a full week in Cheyenne, Wyoming. Call ✆ **800/227-6336**

(www.cfdrodeo.com) for information. Last week in July.

Evel Knievel Days. Butte, Montana honors its favorite son and one-time problem child, late daredevil Evel Knievel, with parades, stunt shows, and children's events. Call ☎ **406/723-3177** (www.knieveldays.com) for more information. Last week in July.

Happy Jack Music Festival. Bluegrass and fiddles prevail over this free festival of mountain music in Curt Gowdy State Park near Cheyenne, Wyoming. Call ☎ **307/433-9463** (www.hjmusic festival.com) for information. Late July or early August.

Sweet Pea Festival. This full-fledged arts festival in Bozeman, Montana, with fine art and musicians, has varied entertainment for all ages. Call ☎ **406/586-4003** (www.sweetpeafestival.org) for information. First full weekend in August.

Grand Targhee Bluegrass Festival. This 3-day celebration of music, arts, food, and entertainment is held at Grand Targhee Resort near Jackson, Wyoming. Call ☎ **800/827-4433** (www.grandtarghee.com) for information. Mid-August.

Crow Fair. This festival is by far one of the biggest and best American-Indian gatherings in the Northwest, with dancing, food, and crafts in Crow Agency, Montana. Call ☎ **406/638-3700** (http://crowfair.crowtribe.com) for information. Mid-August.

Montana Cowboy Poetry Gathering. This 3-day event features readings and entertainment from the real McCoys in Lewistown, Montana. Call ☎ **406/535-5436** for information. Mid-August.

Nordicfest. This Scandinavian celebration in Libby, Montana, features a parade, a juried craft show, headliner entertainment, and an international Fjord horse show. Call ☎ **800/785-6541** (www.libbynordicfest.com) for information. First weekend following Labor Day.

Western Design Conference. Western-style furniture and clothing fashions are displayed on the runway in Cody, Wyoming. Call ☎ **307/354-3466** (www. westerndesignconference.com) for more information. Early or mid-September.

Buffalo Bill Historical Center Art Show and Patrons Ball. With a big art sale to support the museum and a black-tie dinner and ball, this is one of the Rockies' premier (and only) formal social events, in Cody, Wyoming. For information, call ☎ **307/587-4471** (www.bbhc.org). Late September.

Hatch Fest. Unspooling over 6 days, this audiovisual arts festival in Bozeman includes film screenings, workshops, filmmaker Q & As, and live music after dark. For information, call ☎ **406/586-2635** (www.hatchfest.org). Early October.

Glacier Jazz Stampede. This 4-day event brings ragtime, swing, and blues musicians to multiple venues in Kalispell, Montana. Call ☎ **406/755-6088** (www.glacierjazzstampede.com) for more information. Early October.

Christmas Strolls and Parades. Statewide, Montana and Wyoming. Check with local chambers of commerce for specific dates and locations.

PASSPORTS

Virtually every air traveler entering the U.S. is required to show a passport. All persons, including U.S. citizens, traveling by air between the United States and Canada, Mexico, Central and South America, the Caribbean, and Bermuda are required to present a valid passport. U.S. and Canadian citizens entering the U. S. at land and sea ports of entry from within the Western Hemisphere will need to present government-issued proof of citizenship, such as a birth certificate, along with a government-issued photo ID, such as a driver's license. A passport is not required for U.S. or Canadian citizens entering by land or sea, but you are highly encouraged to carry one.

VISAS

For information on obtaining a visa, please see "Fast Facts," on p. 414.

The U.S. State Department has a **Visa Waiver Program (VWP)** allowing citizens of the following countries to enter the United States without a visa for stays of up to 90 days: Andorra, Australia, Austria, Belgium, Brunei, Czech Republic, Denmark, Estonia, Finland, France, Germany, Hungary, Iceland, Ireland, Italy, Japan, Latvia, Liechtenstein, Lithuania, Luxembourg, Malta, Monaco, the Netherlands, New Zealand, Norway, Portugal, San Marino, Singapore, Slovakia, Slovenia, South Korea, Spain, Sweden, Switzerland, and the United Kingdom. (*Note:* This list was accurate at press time; for the most up-to-date list of countries in the VWP, consult http://travel.state.gov.) Even though a visa isn't necessary, in an effort to help U.S. officials check travelers against terror watch lists before they arrive at U.S. borders, visitors from VWP countries must register online through the Electronic

System for Travel Authorization (ESTA) before boarding a plane or a boat to the U.S. Travelers will complete an electronic application providing basic personal and travel eligibility information. The Department of Homeland Security recommends filling out the form at least 3 days before traveling. Authorizations will be valid for up to 2 years or until the traveler's passport expires, whichever comes first. Currently, there is no fee for the online application. *Note:* Any passport issued on or after October 26, 2006, by a VWP country must be an **e-Passport** for VWP travelers to be eligible to enter the U.S. without a visa. Citizens of these nations also need to present a round-trip air or cruise ticket upon arrival. E-Passports contain computer chips capable of storing biometric information, such as the required digital photograph of the holder. If your passport doesn't have this feature, you can still travel without a visa if it is a valid passport issued before October 26, 2005, and includes a machine-readable zone, or between October 26, 2005, and October 25, 2006, and includes a digital photograph. For more information, go to **http://travel.state.gov**. Canadian citizens may enter the United States without visas; they will need to show passports (if traveling by air) and proof of residence, however.

Citizens of all other countries must have (1) a valid passport that expires at least 6 months later than the scheduled end of their visit to the U.S., and (2) a tourist visa.

CUSTOMS
What You Can Bring into the U.S.

Every visitor more than 21 years of age may bring in, free of duty, the following: (1) 1 liter of wine or hard liquor; (2) 200 cigarettes, 100 cigars (but not from Cuba), or 3 pounds of smoking tobacco; and (3) $100 worth of gifts. These exemptions are offered to travelers who spend at least 72 hours in the United States and who have not claimed them within the preceding 6 months. It is forbidden to bring into the country almost any meat products (including canned, fresh, and dried meat products such as bouillon, soup mixes, and so forth). Generally, condiments and appetizers including vinegars, oils, spices, coffee, tea, and some cheeses and baked goods are permitted. Avoid rice products, as rice can often harbor insects. Bringing fruit and vegetables is not advised, though not prohibited. Customs will allow produce depending on where you got it and where you're going after you arrive in the U.S. International visitors may carry in or out up to $10,000 in U.S. or foreign currency with no formalities; larger sums must be declared to U.S. Customs on entering or leaving, which includes filing form CM 4790. For details regarding U.S. Customs and Border Protection, consult your nearest U.S. embassy or consulate, or **U.S. Customs** (www.customs.gov).

What You Can Take Home from Montana & Wyoming

For information on what you're allowed to bring home, contact one of the following agencies:

Canadian Citizens: Canada Border Services Agency (© 800/461-9999 in Canada, or 204/983-3500; www.cbsa-asfc.gc.ca).

U.K. Citizens: HM Customs & Excise (© 0845/010-9000, or 020/8929-0152 from outside the U.K.; www.hmce.gov.uk).

Australian Citizens: Australian Customs Service (© 1300/363-263; www.customs.gov.au).

New Zealand Citizens: New Zealand Customs, the Customhouse, 17–21 Whitmore St., Box 2218, Wellington (© 04/473-6099 or 0800/428-786; www.customs.govt.nz).

MEDICAL REQUIREMENTS

Unless you're arriving from an area known to be suffering from an epidemic (particularly cholera or yellow fever), inoculations or vaccinations are not required for entry into the United States.

3 GETTING THERE & GETTING AROUND

BY PLANE

Travelers flying into Montana can choose to land in one of the state's six major airports: Billings, Bozeman, Great Falls, Helena, Kalispell, or Missoula. In Wyoming, Jackson, Casper, Cheyenne, Cody, Gillette, Laramie, Riverton, Rock Springs, and Sheridan have airports with commercial intrastate airline service. To find out which airlines travel to Montana and Wyoming, please see "Airline, Hotel & Car-Rental Websites," p. 418.

Montana and Wyoming's airports are dwarfed by **Denver International Airport** in Colorado and **Salt Lake City International Airport** in Utah. However, connecting flights are available from Denver and Salt Lake to almost all of the regional airports in Montana and Wyoming, and—if you have time—renting a car in one of these larger cities can make for a nice scenic drive to your final destination.

BY CAR

In Montana, **I-90** runs west to east from St. Regis to Wyola, near the Wyoming border southeast of Billings. **I-94** goes east from Billings to Glendive and the North Dakota border. **U.S. Hwy. 2,** called the "Hi-Line," is another east-west alternative, stretching across the northern reaches of

Montana from Bainville to Troy. The major interstate traversing the state from north to south is **I-15,** from Sweetgrass to Monida.

Wyoming is crossed through the southern part of the state by **I-80,** a huge trucker route from Pine Bluffs in the east to Evanston in the west. **I-90** begins in the north-central part of the state near Ranchester and comes out in the northeast near Beulah. Just outside Buffalo is I-90's junction with **I-25,** a north-south route that runs through Cheyenne. The western part of the state, north of Rock Springs, is dominated by U.S. highways and secondary state-maintained roads.

Renting a Car

You'll find rental-car outlets at the airports and in major cities in Montana and Wyoming, but there are great swaths of land in both states where you simply can't rent a car. National companies with outlets in Montana and Wyoming include **Alamo** (© 877/222-9075; www.alamo.com), **Avis** (© 800/230-4898; www.avis.com), **Budget** (© 800/527-0700; www.budget. com), **Dollar** (© 800/800-3665; www. dollar.com), **Enterprise** (© 800/261-7331; www.enterprise.com), **Hertz** (© 800/654-3131; www.hertz.com), **National** (© 800/227-7368; www.nationalcar. com), **Payless** (© 800/729-5377; www. paylesscarrental.com), and **Thrifty** (© 800/847-4389; www.thrifty.com).

Car-rental rates vary even more than airline fares. The price you pay depends on the size of the car, where and when you pick it up and drop it off, the length of the rental period, where and how far you drive it, whether you purchase insurance, and a host of other factors. A few key questions could save you hundreds of dollars.

- Are weekend rates lower than weekday rates? Ask if the rate is the same for pickup Friday morning, for instance, as it is for Thursday night.

- Is a weekly rate cheaper than the daily rate? Even if you need the car for only 4 days, it may be cheaper to keep it for 5.

- Does the agency assess a drop-off charge if you don't return the car to the same location where you picked it up? Is it cheaper to pick up the car at the airport than at a downtown location?

- Are special promotional rates available? If you see an advertised price in your local newspaper, be sure to ask for that specific rate; otherwise, you may be charged the standard cost. Terms change constantly, and reservations agents are notorious for not mentioning available discounts unless you ask.

- Are discounts available for members of AARP, AAA, frequent-flier programs, or trade unions? If you belong to any of these organizations, you may be entitled to discounts of up to 30%.

- How much tax will be added to the rental bill? Local tax? State use tax?

- What is the cost of adding an additional driver's name to the contract?

- How many free miles are included in the price? Free mileage is often negotiable, depending on the length of the rental.

- How much does the rental company charge to refill your gas tank if you return with the tank less than full? Though most rental companies claim these prices are "competitive," fuel is almost always cheaper in town. Try to allow enough time to refuel the car yourself before returning it.

Some companies offer "refueling packages," in which you pay for an entire tank of gas upfront. The price is usually fairly competitive with local gas prices, but you don't get credit for any gas remaining in the tank.

Many available packages include airfare, accommodations, and a rental car with unlimited mileage. Compare these prices with the cost of booking airline tickets and renting a car separately to see if such offers are good deals. Internet resources can make comparison-shopping easier.

Surfing for Rental Cars

For booking rental cars online, the best deals are usually found at rental-car company websites, although all the major online travel agencies also offer rental-car reservations services. **Priceline** (www.priceline.com) and **Hotwire** (www.hotwire.com) work well for rental cars; the only "mystery" is which major rental company you get, and for most travelers, the difference between Hertz, Avis, and Budget is negligible. Also check out **Breezenet.com**, which offers domestic car-rental discounts with some of the most competitive rates around.

Demystifying Renter's Insurance

Before you drive off in a rental car, be sure you're insured. Hasty assumptions about your personal auto insurance or a rental agency's additional coverage could end up costing you tens of thousands of dollars—even if you are involved in an accident that was clearly the fault of another driver.

If you already hold a **private auto insurance** policy in the United States, you are most likely covered for loss of or damage to a rental car, and liability in case of injury to any other party involved in an accident. Be sure to find out whether you are covered in the area you are visiting, whether your policy extends to all persons who will be driving the rental car, how much liability is covered in case an outside party is injured in an accident, and whether the type of vehicle you are renting is included under your contract. (Rental trucks, sport utility vehicles, and luxury vehicles may not be covered.)

Most **major credit cards** provide some degree of coverage as well—provided they were used to pay for the rental. Terms vary widely, however, so be sure to call your credit card company directly before you rent. If you don't have a private auto insurance policy, the credit card you use to rent a car may provide primary coverage if you decline the rental agency's insurance. This means that the credit card company will cover damage or theft of a rental car for the full cost of the vehicle. If you do have a private auto insurance policy, your credit card may provide secondary coverage—which basically covers your deductible. *Credit cards do not cover liability* or the cost of injury to an outside party and/or damage to an outside party's vehicle. If you do not hold an insurance policy, you may want to seriously consider purchasing additional liability insurance from your rental company. Be sure to check the terms, however: Some rental agencies cover liability only if the renter is not at fault; even then, the rental company's obligation varies from state to state. Bear in mind that each credit card company has its own peculiarities; call your own credit card company for details before relying on a card for coverage.

The basic insurance coverage offered by most car-rental companies, known as the **Loss/Damage Waiver (LDW)** or **Collision Damage Waiver (CDW),** can cost as much as $20 per day. The former should cover everything, including the loss of income to the rental agency, should you get in an accident (normally not covered by your own insurance policy). It usually covers the full value of the vehicle, with no deductible, if an outside party causes an accident or other damage to the rental car. You will probably be covered in case of theft as well. Liability coverage varies, but the minimum is usually at least $15,000. If you are at fault in an accident, you will be covered for the full replacement value of the car—but not for liability. Most rental companies require a police report in order to process any claims you file, but your private insurer will not be notified of the accident. Check your own policies and credit cards before you shell out money on this extra insurance because you may already be covered.

(Tips) Weather & Road Conditions

For up-to-date information on current weather, contact the National Weather Service at 📞 **406/449-5204** in Montana, 📞 **307/772-2468** in Wyoming, or online at www.wrh.noaa.gov. For statewide road conditions, contact the Montana Department of Transportation (📞 **800/226-7623,** or 511 in Montana; www.mdt.mt.gov) or the Wyoming Department of Transportation (📞 **888/996-7623,** or 511 in Wyoming; www.wyoroad.info).

BY TRAIN

Amtrak's *Empire Builder* (📞 **800/872-7245;** www.amtrak.com) provides daily rail service along the northern tier of Montana, traveling west from Chicago and east from Seattle. The train stops at Wolf Point, Glasgow, Malta, Havre, Shelby, Cut Bank, Browning, East Glacier, Essex, West Glacier, Whitefish, and Libby. There are presently no Amtrak stops in Wyoming.

GETTING AROUND
By Car

Most visitors to Montana and Wyoming travel the state in a car. In fact, in some areas, it's a necessity. Planes, trains, and buses do not cover many areas of these states.

Before you set out on a road trip, you might want to join the **American Automobile Association** (AAA; 📞 **800/222-4357;** www.aaa-montainwest.com), which has hundreds of offices nationwide. The Billings office is located at 3320 4th Ave. N. (📞 **406/248-7738**), and is open Monday through Friday from 8:30am to 5:30pm. AAA also has offices in Missoula (📞 **406/542-5008**), Bozeman (📞 **406/586-6156**), Helena (📞 **406/447-8100**), Great Falls (📞 **406/727-2900**), Cheyenne (📞 **307/634-8861**), and several other locations. Members receive excellent maps and emergency road service, and AAA will help you plan an exact itinerary.

If you're visiting from abroad and plan to rent a car in the United States, keep in mind that foreign driver's licenses are usually recognized in the U.S., but you may want to consider obtaining an international driver's license.

By Plane

There is regional air service between cities in Montana and Wyoming, but your options are limited, and you'll almost always need a rental car.

Some large airlines offer transatlantic or transpacific passengers special discount tickets under the name **Visit USA,** which allows mostly one-way travel from one U.S. destination to another at very low prices. Unavailable in the U.S., these discount tickets must be purchased abroad in conjunction with your international fare. This system is the easiest, fastest, cheapest way to see the country, but you'll likely still need a rental car after landing in Montana and Wyoming.

By Train

International visitors can buy a **USA Rail Pass,** good for 15, 30, or 45 days of unlimited travel on **Amtrak** (📞 **800/872-7245;** www.amtrak.com). The pass is available online or through many overseas travel agents. See Amtrak's website for the cost of travel within the western or northwestern United States. Reservations are generally required and should be made as early as possible. Regional rail passes are also available. *Note:* Keep in mind that Wyoming has no train service.

By Bus

Greyhound (© 800/231-2222; www.greyhound.com) is the sole nationwide bus line. International visitors can obtain information about the **Greyhound North American Discovery Pass.** The pass, which offers unlimited travel and stopovers in the U.S. and Canada, can be obtained from foreign travel agents or through www.discoverypass.com. **Rimrock Stages** (© 800/255-7655; www.rimrocktrailways.com) operates intrastate service in Montana.

4 MONEY & COSTS

The Value of the U.S. Dollar vs. Other Popular Currencies

US$	C$	UK£	Euro€	A$	NZ$
1.00	1.06	0.62	0.68	1.10	1.41

Frommer's lists exact prices in the local currency. The currency conversions quoted above were correct at press time. However, rates fluctuate, so before departing consult a currency exchange website such as **www.oanda.com/convert/classic** or **www.xe.com/ucc** to check up-to-the-minute rates.

As most parts of Montana and Wyoming are connected to the broadband backbone, you'll find credit cards are accepted at most lodgings and restaurants, and many attractions. ATMs are also fairly common in towns of all sizes, and even in the national parks. But these states also have numerous back roads that lead to out-of-the-way places with establishments that do not accept credit cards; I recommend you carry at least some cash on hand (about $200 is a good amount) while traveling in either state.

While the states are still relatively inexpensive in terms of the cost of hotel rooms and lodging, there are also many luxury establishments in places like Whitefish

What Things Cost in Montana & Wyoming

Night in moderately priced hotel room	$70.00–$160.00
3-course dinner for two without alcohol	$50.00–$100.00
Taxi from Billings Airport to Downtown	$5.00–$10.00
Bus fare	Free–$2.00
Entry into Yellowstone and Grand Teton	$25.00 for a week
Full-day bus tour in Yellowstone	$70.00 per person
Entry into Glacier	$25.00 for a week
Guided backcountry trip in Glacier	$150.00 per person per day
Tent campsite in a national park	$10.00–$23.00
RV campsite in a national park	$20.00–$54.00
Tent campsite in a national forest	Free–$15.00
RV site in a city or town	$25.00–$50.00
Full-day adult ski lift ticket at Jackson Hole	$55.00–$91.00
Full-day adult ski lift ticket at Bridger Bowl	$45.00
A cup of coffee	$1.00–$3.00
A domestic beer in Jackson, Wyoming	$3.00–$5.00
A domestic beer in Butte, Montana	$1.00–$3.00

and Jackson Hole. You'll find plenty of $50 double motel rooms, but lodgings in Yellowstone gateway towns and ski resorts average about $150 in peak season for a standard room. Nevertheless, there are vacations for almost any budget, from camping and cooking out in the national parks to the pricey rooms at Four Seasons Jackson Hole. Be sure to pay special attention to the "Where to Stay" and "Where to Dine" sections in each chapter, which break down your choices by cost.

5 HEALTH

STAYING HEALTHY

Montana and Wyoming's extremes—from burning desert to snow-covered mountains—can cause health problems for the ill-prepared. If you haven't been to the desert before, the heat, dryness, and intensity of the sun can be difficult to imagine. Bring a hat, strong sunblock, sunglasses with ultraviolet protection, and moisturizing lotion for dry skin. Hikers and others planning to be outdoors should carry water—at least a gallon per person, per day.

Another potential problem for short-term visitors is elevation. There's less oxygen and lower humidity in the mountains, which rise to over 13,000 feet. If you have heart or respiratory problems, consult your doctor before planning a trip to the mountains. Even if you're in generally good health, you may want to ease into high elevations by changing altitude gradually. Don't fly in from sea level in the morning and plan to hike in the high country of Yellowstone or Glacier that afternoon. Spend a day or two at a lower elevation to let your body adjust.

GENERAL AVAILABILITY OF HEALTHCARE

Hospitals with 24-hour emergency rooms can be found in most cities and large towns in Montana and Wyoming, as well as Yellowstone National Park, which has three clinics within its borders.

COMMON AILMENTS

ALTITUDE SICKNESS Because most of us live at or near sea level, the most common health hazard is discomfort as we adjust to Montana and Wyoming's high elevations. Acclimation to high elevation is a process that can take a day or more. Symptoms include headache, fatigue, nausea, loss of appetite, muscle pain, and lightheadedness. Doctors recommend that, until acclimated, travelers should avoid heavy exertion, consume light meals, and drink lots of liquids, avoiding those with caffeine or alcohol.

EXTREME WEATHER EXPOSURE The weather in the Northern Rockies is capricious—it can snow in July or give you serious sunburn in February. If your wilderness activity takes you to a body of water, have extra clothes available in case you get wet, preferably wool and fleece fabrics, which wick away moisture. Hypothermia occurs when the body can no longer warm itself, and you're especially susceptible if you're wearing wet wool or cotton clothing. Many Western streams, rivers, and lakes are glacier-fed and run high during spring; they can be difficult to negotiate and are extremely cold. Winter backcountry explorers should always be equipped with a shovel, a sectional probe, and an avalanche transceiver, since avalanches are common.

WATERBORNE ILLNESSES Two waterborne hazards are **giardia** and **campylobacter,** with symptoms that wreak havoc on the human digestive system. If you pick up these pesky bugs, they might accompany you on your trip home. Untreated water from lakes and streams should be boiled for at least 5 minutes before consumption or pumped through a fine-mesh water filter specifically designed to remove bacteria.

WILDLIFE CONCERNS Be especially cautious around wildlife, particularly with children. Bison are not big sheepdogs, and bears are not stuffed animals; they are wild animals that can turn on you suddenly if you get too close. Never—I repeat, never—get between a mother bear and her cub. If you're exploring during the summer, carry a can of pepper spray (bear mace), an effective deterrent to bears, available at local sporting goods stores. Also keep an eye out for rattlesnakes and ticks.

WHAT TO DO IF YOU GET SICK AWAY FROM HOME

Hospitals with emergency rooms tend to be in the major cities in each of the states, with satellite clinics in smaller communities. In the case of a medical emergency, call ℂ **911.**

If you suffer from a chronic illness, consult your doctor before your departure. Pack **prescription medications** in your carry-on luggage, and carry them in their original containers, with pharmacy labels—otherwise they won't make it through airport security. Visitors from outside the U.S. should carry generic names of prescription drugs. For U.S. travelers, most reliable healthcare plans provide coverage if you get sick away from home. Foreign visitors may have to pay all medical costs upfront and be reimbursed later.

---

6 SAFETY

While there are many reasons to visit Montana and Wyoming, the two cited most often are visiting historic sites and exploring the magnificent outdoors—especially the three national parks. However, visiting historic sites and participating in outdoor activities can lead to accidents.

When visiting such historic sites as ghost towns, gold mines, and railroads, remember that they were likely built more than 100 years ago, when safety standards were extremely lax, if they existed at all. Never enter abandoned buildings, mines, or rail cars on your own. When touring historic attractions, use common sense, and don't be afraid to ask questions.

Walkways in mines are often uneven, poorly lit, and sometimes slippery due to seeping groundwater that can stain your clothing with its high iron content. In old

buildings, be prepared for steep, narrow stairways, creaky floors, and low ceilings and doorways. Steam trains are wonderful as long as you remember that steam is very hot, oil and grease can ruin your clothing, and, at the very least, soot will make you very dirty.

As you head into the great outdoors, bear in mind that injuries often occur when people fail to follow instructions. Take heed when the experts tell you to stay on established ski trails, hike only in designated areas and carry rain gear, and wear a life jacket when rafting. Mountain weather can be fickle, and many beautiful spots are in remote areas. Be prepared for sudden changes in temperature at any time of year, and watch out for summer afternoon thunderstorms that can leave you drenched and shivering in minutes.

---

7 SPECIALIZED TRAVEL RESOURCES

In addition to the destination-specific resources listed below, please visit

Frommers.com for additional specialized travel resources.

PLANNING YOUR TRIP TO MONTANA & WYOMING

3

SPECIALIZED TRAVEL RESOURCES

GAY & LESBIAN TRAVELERS

Wyoming and Montana do not have the reputation of being the gay-friendliest states in the Union, especially in the wake of the Matthew Shepard murder in Laramie in 1998. But larger cities tend to have a gay scene of some kind, especially Missoula and Bozeman in Montana; and there is little for gay travelers to worry about. However, some of the more rural destinations are still rife with homophobia.

The **International Gay and Lesbian Travel Association (IGLTA; ⓒ 800/448-8550** or 954/776-2626; www.iglta.org) is the trade association for the gay and lesbian travel industry, and offers an online directory of gay- and lesbian-friendly travel businesses and tour operators.

Many agencies offer tours and travel itineraries specifically for gay and lesbian travelers. Based in Red Lodge, Montana, **OutWest Global Adventures (ⓒ 800/743-0458** or 406/446-1533; www.outwest adventures.com) offers gay and lesbian adventure travel packages, including ranching vacations in Montana and backpacking trips in Yellowstone.

TRAVELERS WITH DISABILITIES

Most disabilities shouldn't stop anyone from traveling. There are more options and resources out there than ever before. But that said, Wyoming and Montana are not necessarily ahead of the curve when it comes to accessible facilities: There are only a handful of accessible trails in the main attraction—the national parks.

The **America the Beautiful—National Park and Federal Recreational Lands Pass—Access Pass** (formerly the **Golden Access Passport**) gives visually impaired people and people with permanent disabilities (regardless of age) free lifetime entrance to federal recreation sites administered by the National Park Service, including the Fish and Wildlife Service, the Forest Service, the Bureau of Land Management, and the Bureau of Reclamation. This may include national parks, monuments, historic sites, recreation areas, and national wildlife refuges.

The America the Beautiful Access Pass can be obtained only in person at any NPS facility that charges an entrance fee. You need to show proof of medically determined disability. Besides free entry, the pass also offers a 50% discount on some federal-use fees charged for such facilities as camping, swimming, parking, boat launching, and tours. For more information, go to **www.nps.gov/fees_passes. htm**.

The **Montana Independent Living Project,** 1820 11th Ave., Helena, MT 59601 (ⓒ **800/735-6457** or 406/442-5755; www.milp.us), operates an information and referral service for travelers with disabilities, providing information relating to such topics as accessibility, recreation, and transportation.

Organizations that offer a vast range of resources and assistance to travelers with disabilities include **MossRehab** (ⓒ **800/** 225-5667; www.mossresourcenet.org); the **American Foundation for the Blind** (AFB; ⓒ **800/232-5463;** www.afb.org); and **SATH** (Society for Accessible Travel & Hospitality; ⓒ **212/447-7284;** www. sath.org). **AirAmbulanceCard.com** is now partnered with SATH and allows you to preselect top-notch hospitals in case of an emergency.

Access-Able Travel Source (ⓒ **303/ 232-2979;** www.access-able.com) offers a comprehensive database on travel agents from around the world with experience in accessible travel; destination-specific access information; and links to such resources as service animals, equipment rentals, and access guides.

Amtrak will, with advance notice, provide porter service, special seating, and a discount (ⓒ **800/872-7245;** www. amtrak.com) for travelers with disabilities.

If you're traveling with a companion, **Greyhound** will give your companion a 50% fare discount (📞 **800/231-2222** or 800/752-4841 for the Disabilities Travel Assistance Line; www.greyhound.com).

Many of the major car-rental companies now offer hand-controlled cars for drivers with disabilities, and can provide those vehicles with advance notice. **Wheelchair Getaways** (📞 **800/642-2042**; www. wheelchair-getaways.com) rents specialized vans with wheelchair lifts and other features for drivers and/or passengers with disabilities, with outlets in both states.

FAMILY TRAVEL

Montana and Wyoming are full of great family destinations, especially Yellowstone, Grand Teton, and Glacier national parks. Many properties in these areas have family cabins that include kitchens, and most motels have family rooms or suites tailored to the needs of parents traveling with their kids. To locate accommodations, restaurants, and attractions that are particularly kid-friendly, refer to the "Kids" icon throughout this guide.

Recommended family travel websites include **Family Travel Forum** (www. familytravelforum.com), a comprehensive site that offers customized trip planning; **Family Travel Network** (www.familytravelnetwork.com), an online magazine providing travel tips; and **TravelWithYour Kids.com** (www.travelwithyourkids.com), a comprehensive site written by parents for parents offering sound advice for long-distance and international travel with children.

Family groups should always ask about discounts for attractions and accommodations. If you plan to stay a week at a ski resort or dude ranch, you may find a better value by renting a condominium or lodge than multiple rooms. Ski areas often offer packages that include accommodations and lift tickets; check with a ski resort's reservation service for current prices. Before booking any type of room, event, or activity, inquire whether there are discounts for children or age restrictions.

The U.S. National Park Service offers an **America the Beautiful—National Park and Federal Recreational Lands Pass** for $80 for 1 year into all national parks and federal fee areas. For more information, go to **www.nps.gov/fees_passes. htm**.

Montana Kids (www.montanakids. com) is a website from Travel Montana that's for kids, with games and such, and their parents, with information about places to go and things to do with families. As for books, *Frommer's National Parks with Kids* (Wiley Publishing, Inc.) is an excellent resource.

SENIOR TRAVEL

Most lodging establishments and museums in Montana and Wyoming offer discounts to seniors. Mention the fact that you're a senior when you make your travel reservations. Although all of the major U.S. airlines except America West have canceled their senior discount and coupon-book programs, many hotels still offer discounts for seniors. In most cities, people 60 and over qualify for reduced admission to theaters, museums, and other attractions, as well as discounted fares on public transportation.

Members of **AARP,** 601 E St. NW, Washington, DC 20049 (📞 **888/687-2277;** www.aarp.org), get discounts on hotels, airfares, and car rentals. AARP offers members a wide range of benefits, including *AARP The Magazine* and a monthly newsletter. Anyone 50 or over can join.

The U.S. National Park Service offers an **America the Beautiful—National Park and Federal Recreational Lands Pass—Senior Pass** (formerly the **Golden Age Passport**), which gives seniors 62 years or older lifetime entrance to all properties administered by the National Park

Service—national parks, monuments, historic sites, recreation areas, and national wildlife refuges—for a one-time processing fee of $10. The pass must be purchased in person at any NPS facility that charges an entrance fee. Besides free entry, the America the Beautiful Senior Pass also offers a 50% discount on some federal-use fees charged for such facilities as camping, swimming, parking, boat launching, and tours. For more information, go to **www.nps.gov/fees_passes.htm**.

Many reliable agencies and organizations target the 50-plus market. **Elderhostel** (© **800/454-5768;** www.elderhostel.org) arranges worldwide study programs for those age 55 and over. **ElderTreks** (© **800/741-7956** or 416/588-5000 outside North America; www.eldertreks.com) offers small-group tours to off-the-beaten-path or adventure-travel locations, restricted to travelers 50 and older.

WOMEN TRAVELERS
Founded in 1982 and the first of its kind, **AdventureWomen** in Bozeman, Montana (© **800/804-8686,** or 406/587-3883 outside the U.S.; www.adventurewomen.com) offers customized trips to just about anywhere in the world for active and adventurous women, age 30 and older. In Montana, the company guides hiking trips as well as skiing and guest-ranch trips.

Check out the award-winning website **Journeywoman** (www.journeywoman.com),

a real-life women's travel-information network, where you can sign up for a free e-mail newsletter and get advice on everything from etiquette and dress to safety. The travel guide *Safety and Security for Women Who Travel,* by Sheila Swan and Peter Laufer (Travelers' Tales Guides), offers common-sense tips on safe travel.

TRAVELING WITH PETS
While Montana and Wyoming seem like natural destinations for bringing Fido along, the national parks are absolutely awful destinations for pets—they aren't allowed on the trails or many in-park hotels. If your itinerary is focused on national forests and dog-friendly cabin resorts, however, it can be workable to bring a dog on the trip.

Keep in mind that dogs must be leashed at all times on all federal and state lands. However, because many of the public lands in these states have bears and other wildlife, there are sometimes site-specific regulations regarding pets. Aside from regulations, be attentive to your pet's well-being. Just as people need extra water in this dry climate, so do pets. And keep in mind that trails are often rough, and jagged rocks can cut the pads on your dog's feet. Remember, too, that dogs that usually spend most of their time sleeping aren't used to 10-hour hikes up mountainsides.

8 SUSTAINABLE TOURISM/ECO-TOURISM

The perpetual debate continues throughout Montana and Wyoming: natural gas drilling and mineral extraction versus recreation and conservation. The Pinedale anticline south of Jackson Hole in Wyoming has been heavily drilled for gas in recent years, sometimes marring the once crystalline Teton views. The Berkeley Pit in Butte, Montana, is a stark reminder of the price to be paid, a mile-long gash in

the earth where a copper-rich mountain once stood.

Numerous lodgings in both states have initiated procedures to be greener, from recycling to water conservation programs. At Teton Village in Wyoming, **Hotel Terra** (© **800/631-6281;** www.hotelterra jacksonhole.com) is the first LEED-certified hotel in the state. The "localvore"

General Resources for Green Travel

Resources are above and below, and not plentiful. The following websites provide valuable wide-ranging information on sustainable travel. For a list of even more sustainable resources, as well as tips and explanations on how to travel greener, visit www.frommers.com/planning.

- Responsible Travel (www.responsibletravel.com) is a great source of sustainable travel ideas; the site is run by a spokesperson for ethical tourism in the travel industry. Sustainable Travel International (www.sustainabletravel international.org) promotes ethical tourism practices, and manages an extensive directory of sustainable properties and tour operators around the world.
- In the U.K., Tourism Concern (www.tourismconcern.org.uk) works to reduce social and environmental problems connected to tourism. The Association of Independent Tour Operators (AITO; www.aito.co.uk) is a group of specialist operators leading the field in making holidays sustainable.
- In Canada, www.greenlivingonline.com offers extensive content on how to travel sustainably, including a travel and transport section and profiles of the best green shops and services in Toronto, Vancouver, and Calgary.
- Carbonfund (www.carbonfund.org), TerraPass (www.terrapass.org), and Carbon Neutral (www.carbonneutral.org) provide info on "carbon offsetting," or offsetting the greenhouse gas emitted during flights.
- Greenhotels (www.greenhotels.com) recommends green-rated member hotels around the world that fulfill the company's stringent environmental requirements. Environmentally Friendly Hotels (www.environmentally friendlyhotels.com) offers more green accommodations ratings.
- Sustain Lane (www.sustainlane.com) lists sustainable eating and drinking choices around the U.S.; also visit www.eatwellguide.org for tips on eating sustainably in the U.S. and Canada.
- For information on animal-friendly issues throughout the world, visit Tread Lightly (www.treadlightly.org).
- Volunteer International (www.volunteerinternational.org) has a list of questions to help you determine the intentions and the nature of a volunteer program. For general info on volunteer travel, visit www.volunteerabroad.org and www.idealist.org.

movement is especially strong in Montana in the Whitefish, Missoula, and Bozeman.

In Yellowstone and Grand Teton national parks, heavy summer auto traffic and the annual impact of millions of human beings have raised questions about the sustainability of these national parks. But a visit to Yellowstone and Grand Teton national parks can be a relatively green vacation. In Yellowstone, concessionaire **Xanterra Parks & Resorts** (© **866/439-7375** or 307/344-7311; www.travelyellowstone.com), has implemented numerous environmental initiatives, including a recycling program, sourcing seafood from sustainable fisheries, and encouraging guests to reuse towels and conserve heat. Campgrounds have recycling bins near the entrance. In Grand Teton, the **Grand Teton Lodge Company** (© **800/628-9988** or 307/543-2811; www.gtlc.com) has also implemented very successful sustainability programs to lessen the human impact on the park. The company purchased wind credits to offset its energy use and diverted 50% of its waste into reusing and recycling everything from aluminum cans to horse manure to food waste. But perhaps the best way to look at sustainability is by connecting with the parks' wild soul by hiking the trails and camping in campgrounds. One of the best ways to lessen one's impact is to go off the grid on an overnight backpacking trip. **Leave No Trace** (www.lnt.org) is the backpacker's ethic to leave any campsite in the same condition—or better—than when one found it. Backpacking is a refreshing counterpoint to modern life that will give perspective on the issues of sustainability and personal energy dependence. For more on backpacking, see the sections on each park's backcountry in chapters 12 and 13.

9 SPECIAL-INTEREST TRIPS & ESCORTED GENERAL-INTEREST TOURS

Escorted tours are structured group tours, with a group leader. The price usually includes everything from airfare to hotels, meals, tours, admission costs, and local transportation.

Despite the fact that escorted tours require big deposits and predetermine hotels, restaurants, and itineraries, many people derive security and peace of mind from the structure they offer. Escorted tours—whether they're navigated by bus, motorcoach, train, or boat—let travelers sit back and enjoy the trip without having to drive or worry about details. They take you to the maximum number of sights in the minimum amount of time with the least amount of hassle. They're particularly convenient for people with limited mobility and they can be a great way to make new friends.

On the downside, you'll have little opportunity for serendipitous interactions with locals. The tours can be jampacked with activities, leaving little room for individual sightseeing, whim, or adventure—plus they often focus on the heavily touristed sites, so you miss out on many a lesser-known gem.

For more information on organized tours, see chapter 5.

10 STAYING CONNECTED

Most long-distance and international calls can be dialed directly from any phone. **For calls within the United States and to Canada,** dial 1 followed by the area code and the seven-digit number. **For other international calls,** dial 011 followed by the country code, city code, and the number you are calling.

To make a direct call to the U.S. from outside of North America, first dial 001, followed by the area code, and phone number.

Calls to area codes **800, 888, 877,** and **866** are toll-free. However, calls to area codes **700** and **900** (chat lines, bulletin boards, "dating" services, and so on) can be very expensive—usually a charge of 95¢ to $3 or more per minute, and they sometimes have minimum charges that can run as high as $15 or more.

Online Traveler's Toolbox

Veteran travelers usually carry some essential items to make their trips easier. Following is a selection of handy online tools to bookmark and use.

- Airplane Food (www.airlinemeals.net)
- Airplane Seating (www.seatguru.com; www.airlinequality.com)
- Foreign Languages for Travelers (www.travlang.com)
- Maps (www.mapquest.com)
- Time and Date (www.timeanddate.com)
- Travel Warnings (http://travel.state.gov, www.fco.gov.uk/travel, www.voyage. gc.ca, www.dfat.gov.au)
- Universal Currency Converter (www.xe.com/ucc)
- Visa ATM Locator (www.visa.com), MasterCard ATM Locator (www.master card.com)
- Weather (www.intellicast.com; www.weather.com)
- Other tourism websites: Montana (www.visitmt.com); Wyoming (www. wyomingtourism.org); National Park Service (www.nps.gov)

For **reversed-charge or collect calls,** and for person-to-person calls, dial the number 0 then the area code and number; an operator will come on the line, and you should specify whether you are calling collect, person-to-person, or both. If your operator-assisted call is international, ask for the overseas operator.

For **local directory assistance** ("information"), dial 411; for long-distance information, dial 1, then the appropriate area code and 555-1212.

CELLPHONES

Just because your cellphone works at home doesn't mean it'll work everywhere in the U.S., thanks to our nation's fragmented cellphone system. It's a good bet that your phone will work in major cities, but take a look at your wireless company's coverage map on its website before heading out; T-Mobile, Sprint, and Nextel are particularly weak in rural areas. If you need to stay in touch at a destination where you know your phone won't work, **rent** a phone that does from **InTouch USA** (© **800/872-7626;** www.intouchusa.com) or a rental car

location, but beware that you'll pay a premium for airtime.

If you're not from the U.S., you'll be appalled at the poor reach of our **GSM (Global System for Mobile Communications) wireless network,** which is used by much of the rest of the world. Your phone will probably work in most major U.S. cities; it definitely won't work in many rural areas. And you may or may not be able to send SMS (text messaging) home from some of these states' most secluded corners, either, including areas in the national parks.

INTERNET/E-MAIL
Without Your Own Computer

Easy Internet access is coming quickly to Montana and Wyoming, with major tourist areas such as Jackson and the ski resorts leading the way. You'll have more trouble in rural communities, although cybercafes are beginning to pop up even there, and most public libraries offer Internet access. Cybercafes can be found in the downtowns of most major cities.

Most major airports have **Internet kiosks** that provide basic Web access for a per-minute fee that's usually higher than cybercafe prices. Check out copy shops like **FedEx Office,** which offers computer stations with Internet access.

The national parks have limited connectivity; Yellowstone has almost none.

With Your Own Computer

Most hotels, resorts, airports, cafes, and retailers have installed Wi-Fi (wireless fidelity), becoming "hotspots" that offer free high-speed Wi-Fi access or charge a small fee for usage. Wi-Fi is even found in campgrounds, RV parks, and even entire towns. Almost all laptops sold today have built-in wireless capability.

11 TIPS ON ACCOMMODATIONS

Accommodations in Montana and Wyoming range from mom-and-pop motels to major chain hotels, bed-and-breakfasts to ski condos, and getaway cabins to dude ranches. See the individual chapters for recommendations.

SURFING FOR HOTELS

In addition to the online travel booking sites **Travelocity, Expedia, Orbitz, Priceline,** and **Hotwire,** you can book hotels through **Hotels.com, Quikbook** (www.quikbook.com), and **Travelaxe** (www.travelaxe.net).

HotelChatter.com is a daily webzine offering smart coverage and critiques of hotels worldwide. Go to **TripAdvisor.com** or **HotelShark.com** for helpful independent consumer reviews of hotels and resort properties.

It's a good idea to **get a confirmation number** and **make a printout** of any online booking transaction.

SAVING ON YOUR HOTEL ROOM

The **rack rate** is the maximum rate that a hotel charges for a room. Hardly anybody pays this price, however, except in high season or on holidays. To lower the cost of your room:

- **Ask about special rates or other discounts.** You may qualify for corporate, student, military, senior, frequent-flier, trade union, or other discounts.

- **Dial direct.** When booking a room in a chain hotel, you'll often get a better deal by calling the individual hotel's reservation desk rather than the chain's main number.
- **Book online.** Many hotels offer Internet-only discounts, or supply rooms to Priceline, Hotwire, or Expedia at rates much lower than the ones you can get through the hotel itself.
- **Remember the law of supply and demand.** Resort hotels are most crowded and therefore most expensive on weekends, so discounts are usually available for midweek stays. Business hotels in downtown locations are busiest during the week, so you can expect big discounts over the weekend.
- **Look into group or long-stay discounts.** If you come as part of a large group, you should be able to negotiate a bargain rate. Likewise, if you're planning a long stay (at least 5 days), you might qualify for a discount. As a general rule, expect 1 night free after a 7-night stay.
- **Sidestep excess surcharges and hidden costs.** Many hotels have the unpleasant practice of nickel-and-diming their guests with opaque surcharges. When you book a room, ask what is included in the room rate, and what is extra. Avoid dialing direct from hotel phones, which can have exorbitant rates. And don't be tempted by the

room's minibar offerings: Most hotels charge through the nose for water, soda, and snacks. Finally, ask about local taxes and service charges, which can increase the cost of a room by 15% or more.

LANDING THE BEST ROOM

Somebody has to get the best room in the house. It might as well be you. You can start by joining the hotel's frequent-guest program, which may make you eligible for upgrades. A hotel-branded credit card usually gives its owner "silver" or "gold" status in frequent-guest programs for free. Always ask about a corner room. They're often larger and quieter, with more windows and light, and they often cost the same as standard rooms. When you make your reservation, ask if the hotel is renovating; if it is, request a room away from the construction. If you're a light sleeper, request a quiet room away from vending or ice machines, elevators, restaurants, bars, and dance clubs. Ask for a room that has most recently been renovated or redecorated.

If you aren't happy with your room when you arrive, ask for another one. Most lodgings will be willing to accommodate you.

Suggested Montana & Wyoming Itineraries

Montana and Wyoming are two of the bigger states in the country, and all of that land and sky makes for something of a blank canvas when it comes to planning a trip to theses parts. Most visitors come here to see their natural wonders in general and Yellowstone, Grand Teton, and Glacier national parks in particular, but there is plenty to see beyond their boundaries: top-notch museums; fun college, resort, and authentic Western towns; crystal-clear lakes and rivers for paddling and fishing; and vast tracts of open space.

As far as a time commitment goes, 1 week is a bit short for a trip to Montana and Wyoming, but you can scratch the surface of one region in that time—say, Yellowstone or the Flathead Valley in Montana. Two weeks is much better, giving the opportunity to delve deeper into one region or travel between the Greater Yellowstone Ecosystem and Glacier National Park.

But with all of that real estate, it's important to not stretch yourself too thin: It's better to be out on the trails in the Rockies than behind the wheel of a car. Take time to explore places well off the beaten tourist track and breathe the fresh air, take in the views, and really, truly get away from it all.

1 MONTANA & WYOMING IN 1 WEEK

This route brings you to the northwest corner of Wyoming and south-central Montana: the 18-million-acre parcel known as the Greater Yellowstone Ecosystem.

Day ❶: Arrive in Jackson, Wyoming ★★

Start your Rocky Mountain getaway in the world-class resort town of Jackson. Serviced by more airlines than any other town in the state, Jackson is relatively easy to get to and a comfortable launching pad for a Montana/Wyoming vacation. Check out **Town Square,** with its famed antler arches, and the downtown area for window-shopping and lunch, before heading up to the **National Museum of Wildlife Art** (p. 315) for the afternoon. In the evening, drive to **Teton Village** or nearby **Wilson** for dinner, perhaps with a stop to fish on the **Snake River** en route, or if time permits, a ride up the tram at the **Jackson Hole Mountain Resort.** Take your pick of lodgings in and around Jackson. See chapter 13.

Day ❷: Grand Teton National Park ★★★

But of course you didn't come to Wyoming for the civilization. Get up early and head immediately for **Grand Teton National Park.** Stop at the visitor center in **Moose** before catching a boat across **Jenny Lake** to the trail leading up **Cascade Canyon;** take it at least to **Hidden Falls** and **Inspiration Point,** but you'll get away from most of the crowds if you continue up the canyon for another mile or two. Either bring lunch with you or come

WEEK 1

1 Jackson, WY

2 Grand Teton National Park

3-5 Yellowstone National Park

6 The Paradise Valley and Bozeman, MT

7 Bozeman, MT

WEEK 2

8 Butte, Helena, and Great Falls, MT

9-11 Glacier National Park

12-13 The Flathead Valley

14 Montana's Gold West Country

down to one of the numerous eateries in the park. Spend the afternoon ogling the majestic mountains from the numerous overlooks, and take a stroll around **Willow Flats** and look for moose or hike up **Signal Mountain** (you can drive to the summit as well) for a magnificent perspective. For hungry, budget-minded types, I love the nachos at **Deadman's Bar** in Signal Mountain Lodge (p. 347). Spend the night in one of the park's lodgings or campgrounds. See chapter 13.

Day 3: Arrive in Yellowstone National Park ★★★

You got a taste of the in-your-face grandeur of the Tetons, now it's time for the subtler, wilder confines of **Yellowstone National Park** and its amazing amalgam of wildlife, geysers, and hiking trails. You'll drive out of **Grand Teton National Park** through the **John D. Rockefeller, Jr. Memorial Parkway** before entering Yellowstone, and will soon arrive at the trail head to **Lewis River Channel** to Shoshone Lake, the largest backcountry lake in the Lower 48. Pack a lunch or plan for a late lunch at **Old Faithful,** where you'll spend the night after a stop at **West Thumb** en route. In the evening, watch the famed geyser erupt, and then stroll the boardwalks for a glimpse at some of the lesser-known thermal features here: Castle,

Grand, and Riverside geysers are all awe-inspiring sights to behold. Stay at one of the myriad lodging options at Old Faithful; eat here as well. See chapter 12.

Days ❹ & ❺: Yellowstone National Park ★★★

Now that you've whet your Yellowstone appetite, you've got 2 full days to get your fill of hiking, wildlife-watching, sightseeing, or whatever else might tickle your fancy. I recommend visitors spend the first half of Day 4 exploring the **Grand Canyon of the Yellowstone** area, gawking from the overlooks but also hiking one of the **rim trails,** visiting **Clear Lake** and **Lily Lake,** or walking down the metal staircase known as **Uncle Tom's Trail** for an unbeatable perspective of the base of **Lower Falls.** Drive up to Tower-Roosevelt in the afternoon to unwind on the porch at **Roosevelt Lodge** (p. 303), where you'll sleep in a dinky cabin after enjoying a cookout on the trail. The next day, you're in prime position for an early start of wildlife-watching in the **Lamar Valley**—"the Serengeti of North America." Have lunch in Cooke City and perhaps do a little fishing in Trout Lake or Soda Butte Creek before reversing course for **Mammoth Hot Springs.** After walking the boardwalk here, have dinner at **Pedalino's** (p. 268) in Gardiner, Montana, or have a quick bite at Mammoth before heading to **Boiling River** for a soak before the sun sets. Stay in either Mammoth or Gardiner. See chapter 12.

Day ❻: The Paradise Valley ★★ & Bozeman, Montana ★★

From Mammoth or Gardiner, drive north on U.S. 89 up the idyllic **Paradise Valley** to **Livingston, Montana.** Wander downtown Livingston, visiting one of the town's three museums, check out a gallery or two, and have a bite to eat. Next, drive west on I-90 to downtown **Bozeman, Montana,** for the evening. Spend the afternoon strolling **Main Street,** and settle on a restaurant downtown—there are plenty to choose from—and perhaps a watering hole for an after-dinner drink. As for accommodations close to downtown, I can't recommend the **Lehrkind Mansion** enough (p. 216).

Day ❼: Bozeman, Montana ★★

After breakfast at the Lehrkind or one of the noshing spots on Main, head south to the **Museum of the Rockies** (p. 215), on the campus of Montana State University. This top-flight museum offers a view into one of the best and brightest paleontology programs in the country and a look at the largest collection of American dinosaurs in the world. Either have lunch at the museum cafe or head back downtown before venturing south into the **Gallatin National Forest** for an afternoon hiking or fishing expedition. For dinner, try **Montana Ale Works** (p. 218) or the **Mint** (p. 217) in nearby Belgrade, a very Montana kind of place.

2 MONTANA & WYOMING IN 2 WEEKS

Start with the preceding 1-week itinerary, then from Bozeman, Montana, make your way northwest to Glacier Country, the Flathead Valley, and many more of the natural wonders that give the Treasure State its nickname.

Days ❶ to ❼: Montana & Wyoming in 1 Week

Follow the itinerary outlined above.

Day ❽: Butte, Helena ★ & Great Falls, Montana

This is a big driving day, covering about 80 miles on I-90 W. and another 150 miles on I-15 N. But it also puts you within a relatively short drive of **Glacier National Park** and gives you an opportunity to visit one or both of Great Falls's terrific museums: the **Lewis & Clark National Historic Trail Interpretive Center** (p. 189) and the **C. M. Russell Museum Complex** (p. 188). I'm also a sucker for the **Sip 'n Dip Lounge** (p. 191), the kitschiest watering hole in the West. En route from Bozeman, stop for a peek at the **Berkeley Pit** (p. 161) in Butte and lunch on **Last Chance Gulch** in Helena (p. 150).

Days ❾, ❿ & ⓫: Glacier National Park ★★★

Visit another museum in Great Falls or head directly to **Glacier National Park.** Before ascending **Logan Pass** on Going-to-the-Sun Road, stop at Sunrift Gorge for a hike up toward Siyeh Pass, where there's a nice view of a hanging glacier. Camp or stay at one of the many nice hostelries in the park; eat in the park as well. The next day, take your pick of activities: **rafting** out of West Glacier; **hiking** to Avalanche Lake or another trail; or **sightseeing** in Glacier's many nooks and crannies. Stay in the park again on night 10, or take your choice of one of the hostelries in the gateways of East Glacier, West Glacier, St. Mary, Essex, or Polebridge. Explore more of Glacier by car or foot on Day 11 before leaving the park for Whitefish. In Whitefish, stay at the **Garden Wall Inn** (p. 134) and walk downtown for dinner. See chapter 7.

Days ⓬ & ⓭: The Flathead Valley ★★

Use Whitefish as a base for exploring the Flathead Valley. After breakfast, take a scenic cruise or fishing charter on **Flathead Lake,** then spend the remainder of the day in **Bigfork,** shopping, strolling, and having dinner at one of the terrific eateries. Perhaps take in a play at the **Bigfork Summer Playhouse** (p. 114). Stay at one of the many lodgings in or around Bigfork for the evening. On the next day, drive south to **Missoula** for a peek at the **Rocky Mountain Elk Country Visitor Center** (p. 97) and the University of Montana campus before getting in one last hike in the **Rattlesnake Wilderness Area** just outside of town. In the evening, venture into downtown Missoula for dinner and drinks. See chapter 7.

Day ⓮: Explore Montana's Gold West Country

You might end your trip in Missoula and spend the final day enjoying a slow start and a good breakfast. But if your schedule allows, take the day for a **scenic drive** through the Bitterroot Valley, south of town via U.S. 93, and over Lost Trail Pass. From there, you'll have an opportunity to visit one of Montana's historic mining towns: **Virginia City, Nevada City,** or **Bannack.** (The latter is a ghost town that's now a state park.) From any of these, you're in a good position to get to Salt Lake City (if you arrived by air) and I-15 (if you're driving home). See chapter 8.

3 YELLOWSTONE & GRAND TETON NATIONAL PARKS FOR FAMILIES

Yellowstone and Grand Teton national parks can be challenging destinations for families. Many of the recreational activities (particularly hiking) can be taxing for little ones, who might also find too much time in the car a bit of a bore. The following itinerary offers a few tips for everybody to get the most out of a week in the parks.

Day ❶: Arrive in Cody, Wyoming ★

Cody is the ideal gateway for a family vacation in Yellowstone: Kids will surely enjoy the shootouts in front of the **Irma Hotel** (p. 359) downtown, and the nightly **Cody Nite Rodeo** (p. 357) has kiddie rides beforehand and a participatory "calf scramble" that allows youngsters to get in on the action and chase a bewildered calf around the arena in between the events. (The kids are trying to grab the coveted ribbon tied to the animal.) Older kids might even like the **Buffalo Bill Historical Center** (p. 356). As for food and lodging, try **Shiki** (p. 361) or **Cassie's** (p. 361) for the former and the **Buffalo Bill Village Resort** (p. 358) or the **Chamberlin Inn** (p. 358) for the latter.

Day ❷: Arrive in Yellowstone National Park ★★★

Head straight into **Yellowstone** on Day 2, stopping for a picnic along the shore of **Yellowstone Lake** once you've entered. **West Thumb** is an excellent primer for introducing tykes to the park's geothermal underpinnings. Spend the night at **Old Faithful,** where you can see more incredible displays produced by the heat, water, and geology below. See chapter 12.

Days ❸ & ❹: Explore Yellowstone ★★★

While many hikes in the first itinerary in this chapter may not be suitable for all children, there are two in particular for people of all ages: **Artist Paint Pot Trail** south of Norris, and the **Forces of the Northern Range Self-Guiding Trail** near Mammoth (neither trail is detailed in this book, so ask a ranger for more information). Both are short, level, and give a good glimpse at different phenomena that have shaped Yellowstone's ecosystem over the eons. On Day 3, tackle Artist Paint Pot Trail, then wander Norris's boardwalks before making your way to Mammoth for the evening. Get a room, cabin, or campsite here, and hit **Boiling River** (p. 284)

for a soak before exploring more thermal features at Mammoth via boardwalk. The next morning, you're in prime position for the Forces of Nature Self-Guiding Trail, which gives a look at the effects of a forest fire, before driving west for an afternoon exploring the Lamar Valley in search of wildlife—the **Yellowstone Association Institute** offers customizable expeditions that will allow mom and dad a break from the wheel. Spend the night at **Roosevelt Lodge** (p. 303)—a family favorite—after enjoying a signature chuck-wagon cookout on the trail. See chapter 12.

Days ❺ & ❻: Grand Teton National Park ★★★

It's a pretty good drive from Roosevelt to Grand Teton, so plan a stop at the **Grand Canyon of the Yellowstone,** and picnic in the southern reaches of the park en route. You'll probably get your first peek at the Tetons in the early afternoon. Pick a base in the park—your choices range from campgrounds to luxury cabins. **Colter Bay Village** (p. 345) is a particularly family-friendly spot, and gives you the opportunity to set out to moose-watch in Willow Flats or around Jackson Lake Lodge. The next day, take the boat across **Jenny Lake** and hike as far up Cascade Canyon as you see fit. In the afternoon, take a **scenic cruise** on Jackson Lake. See chapter 13.

Day ❼: Jackson, Wyoming ★★

Your last day will be well spent in Jackson. At **Town Square,** there are nightly shootouts and stagecoach rides. You might check out the alpine slide or miniature golf at **Snow King Resort** (p. 311), or the excellent **National Museum of Wildlife Art,** which has kid-oriented interpretation and activities. Grab dinner at **Billy's Giant Hamburgers** at the **Cadillac Grille** (p. 324) and stay at the **Virginian Lodge** (p. 317); it has a big grassy courtyard centered on a pool. Jackson has an airport and is an easy drive from I-15 at Idaho Falls. See chapter 13.

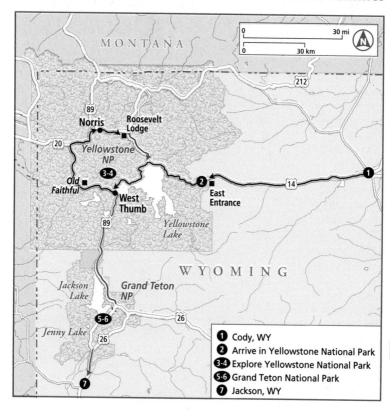

- **1** Cody, WY
- **2** Arrive in Yellowstone National Park
- **3-4** Explore Yellowstone National Park
- **5-6** Grand Teton National Park
- **7** Jackson, WY

4 EXPLORING THE WILD WEST PAST OF MONTANA & WYOMING

Many visitors come to the region for the sublime views and superb recreation, but many others come in search of the real West that's slowly but surely fading into the history books. There are pockets of fascinating history that shaped the nation's culture and textbooks, vestiges of the Old West amid the developments of the new in Wyoming and Montana.

Day **1**: Arrive in Cheyenne, Wyoming

Begin your day downtown at the beautifully restored Union Pacific Depot and the **Cheyenne Depot Museum** (p. 399) for a look at how the railroad shaped the history of this part of the West. Pick up their brochure *Tracking Trains in Cheyenne*, and dig a little deeper into this fascinating chapter. Another interesting (and intertwined) tale is told at the **Cheyenne Frontier Days Old West Museum** (p. 399).

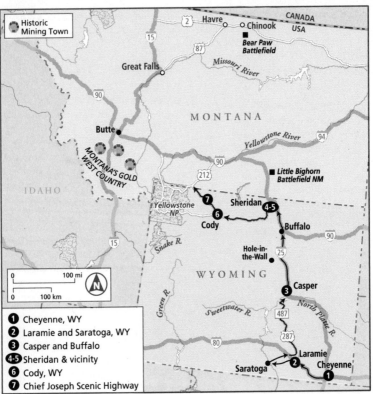

4

Stay at the historic **Nagle Warren Mansion Bed & Breakfast** (p. 401) downtown after a dinner at **Poor Richard's** (p. 402).

Day ❷: Laramie & Saratoga

On your second day, head west into Laramie for a visit to the **Wyoming Territorial Prison State Historic Site** (p. 405), and then continue into the Snowy Range Mountains to visit **Saratoga, Centennial,** and/or **Woods Landing,** and stay for the night. Saratoga's historic **Hotel Wolf** and **Woods Landing** (p. 408) are particularly interesting.

Day ❸: Casper & Buffalo ★

Return to Laramie, and drive north through the Shirley Basin on U.S. 287 and

Wyo. 487 to Casper and the excellent **National Historic Trails Interpretive Center** (p. 389). Perhaps lunch at the **Wonder Bar** (p. 391) before continuing north to **Hole-in-the-Wall** (p. 381), a hide-out favored by Butch Cassidy and the Sundance Kid. Stay in Buffalo at the **Occidental Hotel** (p. 381). Explore Buffalo's other historic attractions, Fort Phil Kearny and the Jim Gatchell Memorial Museum, while in town. See chapter 15.

Days ❹ & ❺: Sheridan & Vicinity ★

From Buffalo, continue north on I-25 to Sheridan for a look at its numerous **historic attractions** (p. 375). Use Sheridan as a base for exploring the rest of the area, especially **Little Bighorn Battlefield**

National Monument (p. 251), the site of Custer's infamous Last Stand. If you're looking for a knowledgeable guide, Ron Spahn of Spahn's Big Horn Mountain Bed and Breakfast offers daylong **historic and cultural tours** (p. 374) of the area, including spots well off the beaten track.

Day ❻: Cody ★

No Old West trip would be complete without a visit to the town founded by and bearing the name of William "Buffalo Bill" Cody. The **Buffalo Bill Historical Center** (p. 356) is a must-visit, with a great look into the life of Cody himself as well as many other aspects of the area's history. Stay at **Pahaska Tepee Resort** (p. 360), Buffalo Bill's old hunting lodge, or in town at the **Chamberlin Inn** (p. 358).

Day ❼: Chief Joseph Scenic Highway

From Cody, drive north out of town and get on the **Chief Joseph Scenic Highway** (p. 352), which connects to the Beartooth Scenic Byway, an awe-inspiring route into **Yellowstone National Park.** The road follows the route taken by the Nez Perce tribe, which fled the U.S. Army and its attempt to force relocation to Oklahoma. The flight of the Nez Perce in summer 1877 snaked through Yellowstone but ended in Hi-Line country at **Bear Paw Battlefield** (p. 200). From here, you could head in that direction and later hit Butte and Montana's Gold West Country for a look at the region's mining history, or into Yellowstone for an adapted version of the first itinerary in this chapter. The **Yellowstone Association Institute** (p. 296) also offers a number of history-oriented classes and expeditions.

5

The Active Vacation Planner

Montana and Wyoming are among the greatest the great outdoors has to offer, in the United States or anywhere in the world. There are literally millions of acres of public spaces where you can cast for native cutthroat trout or herd cattle, go rock climbing or four-wheeling, raft, or ski. These states collectively boast a trio of spectacular national parks, four national monuments, one national recreation area, two national historic sites, five national historic trails, 14 national forests, one national grassland, more than 20 million acres administered by the federal Bureau of Land Management (BLM), and 62 state parks. All things considered, there are many lifetimes of outdoor recreation to be experienced in these parts.

If you're a seasoned active traveler, you might want to skip section 1; it should be a good primer, though, for those who are new to this kind of travel. Section 2 provides some up-to-date information on visiting Montana and Wyoming's national parks. Following that are descriptions of activities you can pursue, from A to Z. I'll point you to the best places in the state to pursue your interests, and give you the information you'll need to get started. You'll find more details in the appropriate regional chapters.

1 PREPARING FOR YOUR ACTIVE VACATION

WHAT TO PACK & WHAT TO RENT

Planning for a trip into the great outdoors may conjure images of vacationers loaded down with golf clubs, skis, cameras, tents, canoes, and bikes. If a car or light truck is your mode of transportation, try to keep the heaviest items between the axles and as close to the floor of your vehicle as possible; this helps improve handling. If you have a bike rack on the rear bumper, make sure the bike tires are far from the exhaust pipe; one bike shop owner told me he does a good business replacing exhaust-cooked mountain-bike tires. Those with roof racks will want to measure the total height of their packed vehicles before leaving home. Underground parking garages often have less than 7 feet of clearance.

One alternative to carrying all that stuff is renting it. Many sporting-goods shops in Montana and Wyoming rent camping equipment; virtually all ski areas and popular mountain-bike areas offer rentals; and major boating centers such as Flathead Lake, Jackson Lake, and Lake Flaming Gorge rent boats. You'll find many rental sources listed throughout this book.

In packing for your trip, you'll want to be prepared for all your favorite activities, of course, but you'll also want to be prepared for an unforgiving climate and terrain. Those planning to hike or bike should take more drinking water than they think they'll need—experts recommend at least 1 gallon of water per person per day on the trail—as well as high-SPF sunscreen, hats and other protective clothing, and sunglasses with ultraviolet protection. Summer visitors should carry rain gear for the typical afternoon thunderstorms, plus jackets or sweaters for cool evenings. Winter visitors will need not only warm parkas and hats, but also lighter clothing—the bright sun at midday, even in the mountains, can make it feel like June.

STAYING SAFE & HEALTHY IN THE OUTDOORS

The wide-open spaces and rugged landscape that make these states such a beautiful place to explore can also be hazardous to your health, especially if you're not accustomed to the extremes here; see "Health" and "Safety," in chapter 3, for details on dealing with wildlife and high altitudes. The isolation of many of the areas that you'll seek out means there may be no one around to help in an emergency, so you must be prepared, like any good scout. See "What to Pack & What to Rent," above, for tips on what to bring. Also, be sure to carry a basic first-aid kit. Most important, check with park offices, park rangers, and other local outdoor specialists about current conditions before heading out.

OUTDOOR ETIQUETTE

Many of the wonderful outdoor areas you'll explore in Montana and Wyoming are quite isolated; although you're probably not the first human being to set foot here, you may feel like you are. Not too long ago, the rule of thumb was to "leave only footprints"; these days, we're trying to not even do that. Being a good outdoor citizen is relatively easy—it's mostly common sense. Pack out all trash, stay on established trails, be careful not to pollute water, and, in general, do your best to have as little impact on the environment as possible. The best among us go even further, carrying a small trash bag to pick up what others have left behind.

2 ADVENTURE TRAVEL

There are plenty of opportunities for adventure in Montana and Wyoming—and some terrific outfitters to help you plan and execute your trip. You can take part in a cattle drive; thrill to the excitement of white-water rafting on the Snake or Flathead rivers; scale a mountain in Grand Teton National Park; or head out into some of the most spectacular scenery in the country on foot or on bicycle, or in a four-wheel-drive vehicle. The variety of tours available seems almost endless, but the tour operators can help you find the one for you. In many cases, you can work with an operator to plan your own customized trip—all it takes is money.

Below are some of the most respected national companies operating in Montana and Wyoming. Most specialize in small groups and have trips geared to various levels of ability and physical condition. They also offer trips in a range of price categories, from basic to luxurious, and of varying length. Numerous local outfitters, guides, and adventure travel companies are discussed throughout this book. For a complete list of outfitters in Montana or Wyoming, as well as a lot of other useful information and Web links, contact **Visit Montana,** P.O. Box 200533, 301 S. Park St., Helena, MT 59620 (© **800/847-4868** or 406/841-2870; www.visitmt. com), or the **Wyoming Business Council Travel & Tourism Division,** 1520 Etchepare Circle, Cheyenne, WY 82007 (© **800/225-5996** or 307/777-7777; www.wyomingtourism.org).

- **AdventureBus,** 375 S. Main St., Ste. 240, Moab, UT 84532 (© **888/737-5263** or 909/633-7225; www. adventurebus.com), offers trips on its customized buses with an emphasis on outdoor adventures, including multisport and mountain-biking tours in the Yellowstone and Grand Teton national parks areas.

- **Austin-Lehman Adventures,** P.O. Box 81025, Billings, MT 59108 (© **800/ 575-1540** or 406/655-4591; www. austinlehman.com), offers guided multiday mountain biking, hiking, and combination tours in the Yellowstone and Grand Teton national parks areas.
- **Backroads,** 801 Cedar St., Berkeley, CA 94710-1800 (© **800/462-2848** or 510/527-1555; www.backroads.com), offers a variety of guided multiday road biking, mountain biking, and hiking tours in the Glacier, Yellowstone, and Grand Teton national parks areas.
- **Escape Adventures,** 8221 W. Charleston Ave., Ste. 101, Las Vegas, NV 89117 (© **800/596-2953** or 702/838-6968; www.escapeadventures.com), offers guided mountain biking and road cycling in Yellowstone National Park and Jackson Hole.
- **Ski the Rockies,** 4901 Main St., Downers Grove, IL 60515 (© **800/ 291-2588** or 630/969-5800; www. skitherockies.com), provides customized skiing and snowboarding packages at the major resorts in Montana and Wyoming.
- The **World Outdoors,** 2840 Wilderness Place, Ste. D, Boulder, CO 80301 (© **800/488-8483** or 303/413-0938; www.theworldoutdoors.com), offers a variety of trips, including multisport adventures that include hiking, mountain biking, rock climbing, and rafting in the Grand Teton and Yellowstone national parks areas.

3 VISITING MONTANA & WYOMING'S NATIONAL PARKS

For many people, including me, the best part of a vacation to Montana and Wyoming is exploring the state's three national parks: **Glacier, Yellowstone,** and **Grand Teton** (www.nps.gov). Unfortunately, these beautiful national treasures have become so popular that they're being overrun by visitors when the federal government is cutting budgets, making it difficult for the parks to cope with their own success.

To get the most out of your national park visit, try to go in the off season. The parks are busiest in summer, when most children are out of school, so try to visit at almost any other time. Fall is usually best. Spring is okay, but it can be windy and there may be snow at higher elevations. Winter can be delightful if you don't mind snow and cold. If you have to travel in summer, be patient. Allow extra time for traffic jams and lines, and try to hike some of the longer and lesser-used trails. Rangers will be able to tell you which trails are best for getting away from the crowds.

4 OUTDOOR ACTIVITIES A TO Z

Montana and Wyoming offer a surprisingly wide range of outdoor activities, from desert hiking and rafting to fly-fishing and skiing. Among the many online outdoor recreation information sources are the very informative and user-friendly Public Lands Information Center website, **www.publiclands.org**, and the **GORP** (Great Outdoor Recreation Page) website, at **www.gorp.com**.

Throughout this book, you'll find contact information for national and state parks, national forests, and the like. Here are some key statewide and regional resources. The **U.S. Forest Service** has information about national forests and

Passes Offer Free Admission on Most Federal Lands

Those who enjoy vacationing at national parks, national forests, and other federal lands have opportunities to save quite a bit of money by using the federal government's annual passes. The America the Beautiful—National Parks and Federal Recreational Lands Pass costs $80 for 1 year from the date of purchase for the general public. It provides free admission for the pass holder and those in his or her vehicle to recreation sites that charge vehicle entrance fees on lands administered by the National Park Service, U.S. Forest Service, U.S. Fish and Wildlife Service, Bureau of Land Management, and Bureau of Reclamation. At areas that charge per-person fees, the passes are good for the pass holder plus three additional adults. Children 15 and under are admitted free.

The passes are also available for U.S. citizens and permanent residents 62 and older for a lifetime fee of $10 (Senior Pass), and are free for U.S. residents and permanent residents with disabilities (Access Pass). The Senior and Access passes also provide 50% discounts on some fees, such as camping.

The Senior and Access passes must be obtained in person at national parks, U.S. Forest Service offices, and other federal recreation sites, but the general public version (the $80 one) can be purchased in person, by phone (© **888/275-8747,** ext. 1), or online at http://store.usgs.gov/pass, a website that also provides complete information about the passes.

wilderness areas in Montana, as well as **Bridger-Teton National Forest** in Wyoming, at the Northern Region Office, Federal Building, 200 E. Broadway, Box 7669, Missoula, MT 59807 (© **406/329-3511;** www.fs.fed.us/r1). The rest of Wyoming's forests, as well as **Thunder Basin National Grassland,** are covered by the Rocky Mountain Region Office, 740 Simms St., Golden, CO 80401 (© **303/275-5350;** www.fs.fed.us/r2).

The federal **Bureau of Land Management** also manages millions of acres of recreational lands and can be reached at its Wyoming state office, 5353 Yellowstone Rd., Cheyenne, WY 82009 (© **307/775-6256**), or its Montana state office, 5001 Southgate Dr., Billings, MT 59101 (© **406/896-5000**).

For information on Montana state parks, fishing, and hunting, get in touch with **Montana Fish, Wildlife, and Parks,** 1420 E. 6th Ave., P.O. Box 200701, Helena, MT 59620 (© **406/444-2535;** www.fwp.state.mt.us). In Wyoming, contact **Wyoming State Parks and Historic Sites,** 2301 Central Ave., Cheyenne, WY 82001 (© **307/777-6323;** http://wyoparks.state.wy.us). For hunting and fishing, contact **Wyoming Game and Fish,** 5400 Bishop Blvd., Cheyenne, WY 82003 (© **307/777-4600;** http://gf.state.wy.us).

You'll have no trouble finding detailed topographic maps—essential for wilderness trips—plus whatever equipment and supplies you need. And despite the well-publicized cuts in budgets and workforces in national parks, recreation areas, and forests, every single ranger I encountered was happy to take time to help visitors plan their backcountry trips. In addition, many sporting-goods shops are staffed by area residents who know local activities and areas well, and are happy to help the would-be adventurer. In almost all cases, if you ask, there will be someone willing and able to help you make the most of your trip.

BACKCOUNTRY SKIING There is nothing as thrilling as skiing deep, untracked powder in completely wild terrain. To enjoy this sport you need a good set of Telemark skis, good information about where to go, and expert knowledge of snow conditions and avalanche risks. One of the best places to pursue this sport is **Togwotee Pass** in Bridger-Teton National Forest in Wyoming (p. 329). Otherwise, check at local ski shops and ask at the headquarters of national forests and state parks. The **Jackson Hole Mountain Resort** (p. 310) decided in 1999 to allow skiers to ski beyond the boundaries of areas it grooms and patrols—as long as they sign waivers. Check with other ski resorts about out-of-bounds forest areas that might be accessible for backcountry adventures.

BIKING Mountain biking is a fast-growing sport. Some folks take it easy, pedaling their way to wild country on smooth, easy-grade paths; others are looking for a fast ride down on bumpy, steep trails. Bring your own bike or rent from a local bike shop that will likely assist you in finding the best spots to ride. Bicycling on roads is also popular, but there are limitations: While automobile traffic on many roads is light, there isn't much room, because most of the roads have skimpy shoulders—Yellowstone roads are among the worst. Nor are drivers in this region terribly respectful of bicyclists. So be watchful, research your routes so you can keep to the wider roads, and always wear that helmet.

BOATING & SAILING Serious sailors are not likely to live full time at this altitude; even weekend sailors would be wise to look elsewhere for their kind of fun. But if you insist on trying, you'll find a few sails spread on the bigger lakes of these

mountains. You can take a pretty big boat on pretty big **Flathead Lake** (p. 109), **Jackson Lake** (p. 335), or even **Yellowstone Lake** (p. 286) if you're careful about the weather. Smaller boats such as Hobie Cats, in some ways, better suit the sudden, swirling winds typical of these mountains.

Powerboating is another matter; if you've got a motor, pack a lunch and head for any of the many lakes that dot Montana and Wyoming's landscape. **Canyon Ferry** (p. 149) is a popular Montana water-skiing spot, and you'll see Wyoming powerboats cruising **Boysen Reservoir** (p. 363) or the many impoundments on the **North Platte** (see section 4 in chapter 16). Just make sure to check around locally regarding access if you're uncertain about it. All types of boats are available locally for rent.

CAMPING These states are ideal places to camp; in fact, at some destinations, such as Yellowstone National Park, it's practically mandatory. Most communities have at least one commercial campground, and campsites are available at all the national parks and national recreation areas, though these campsites are often crowded in summer. Those who can stand being without hot showers for a day or so can often find free or very reasonable campsites just outside the national parks, in national forests, and on Bureau of Land Management lands. Other good bets are found at state parks.

A growing number of state and federal campgrounds allow visitors to reserve sites, although more often than not only in the busy summer months. Throughout Montana and Wyoming there are more than 100 national forest campgrounds and numerous state parks that will also reserve sites. To check on campground reservation possibilities for many National Park Service, U.S. Forest Service, and other federal properties, contact the new **Recreation. gov,** which combines the old **ReserveUSA** and **National Park Reservation Service**

(Fun Facts)   **Are You a Dude or a Guest?**

A century ago, it was common courtesy in the West for ranches to feed and lodge travelers who stopped by on their treks across the great empty spaces. Gradually it became acceptable to accept a few dollars from guests, and by the 1920s, a ranch visit was a full-fledged vacation.

When you make your ranch reservations, it's wise to know the difference between a "dude ranch" and a "guest ranch." A dude ranch typically requires a 1-week minimum stay, and they give you the entire package: riding, fishing, trips to the rodeo, and family-style meals. Dude ranchers look down their noses at "guest" ranches, which will take guests staying just 1 night and charge extra for activities such as riding.

---

into one portal (📞 **800/444-6777** or 518/885-3639; www.recreation.gov). For information on Montana state parks, get in touch with **Montana Fish, Wildlife, and Parks,** 1420 E. 6th Ave., P.O. Box 200701, Helena, MT 59620 (📞 **406/444-2535;** www.fwp.state.mt.us). In Wyoming, contact **Wyoming State Parks and Historic Sites,** 2301 Central Ave., Cheyenne, WY 82001 (📞 **307/777-6323;** http://wyoparks.state.wy.us).

CROSS-COUNTRY SKIING If you don't plan to pound down the backcountry powder on Telemark skis but you want to get out in the snow, cross-country skiing can be practiced on any relatively flat, open meadow or plain where there's snow on the ground, or along old roads in the region's forests. Scores of guest ranches now groom trails for both track and skate skiing, and almost every ski resort in the region has a trail. If you don't want to pay to ski, **Forest Service logging roads** are typically used for cross-country trails. Many golf courses are also regularly groomed for track skiing; some are even lighted for night skiing. The best place to cross-country ski in Montana is **West Yellowstone** (p. 258), training ground of U.S. Nordic and Biathlon ski teams; in Wyoming, try the **Jackson Hole** area and **Grand Teton National Park** (see chapter 13).

DOWNHILL SKIING There are over 20 downhill ski areas in Montana and Wyoming, scattered amid the towering mountain ranges found predominantly in the western parts of both states. Breathtaking summit vistas are standard fare. Usually operating from late November to mid-April, and with comparatively shorter lift lines and less expensive lift tickets than most other ski areas in the country, Montana and Wyoming ski resorts are great values for the ski enthusiast. Don't fret if you're not skiing black-diamond runs; all ski resorts have acres of beginner and intermediate trails, and seasoned instructors provide lessons at extremely affordable prices. More and more often, you'll find Telemark skiers honing their skills on packed resort slopes. The best skiing in Montana can be found at **Big Sky Resort** (p. 225), near Bozeman, which is the biggest ski area in Montana, with runs for all abilities. West of Glacier National Park, **Whitefish Mountain Resort** (p. 131) prides itself on a family atmosphere. In Wyoming, the Jackson Hole area wins hands down, with the **Jackson Hole Mountain Resort, Snow King,** and **Grand Targhee** ski hills just a short drive apart (see chapter 13).

DUDE RANCHES The dude ranch is the fabled Western experience come to life: daily rides by horseback, cowboy coffee beneath an expansive blue sky, campfire sing-alongs, and homemade food served in rustic lodges. Accommodations are usually in a comfortable cabin or lodge. You need not have any riding experience before your visit; ranch hands are trained to assist even the greenest of greenhorns. For additional information on dude ranches in both Montana and Wyoming, as well as other Western states, contact the **Dude Ranchers' Association,** P.O. Box 2307, Cody, WY 82414 (✆ **866/399-2339;** www.duderanch.org). The best dude ranches can be found in the **Paradise and Gallatin valleys** in southwest Montana, and in the **Sheridan** area and the **Wapiti Valley** west of Cody in Wyoming.

FISHING   Montana and Wyoming have long been known for world-class fly-fishing, their streams and creeks teeming with native trout—rainbow, brook, brown, mackinaw, golden, and cutthroat—as well as kokanee salmon, yellow perch, largemouth bass, and northern pike. Warmwater species include sauger, channel catfish, and smallmouth bass. Best places to fish in Montana: on any one of the world-class, blue-ribbon streams in the southwest part of the state. In Wyoming, head for the waters of the **North Platte River** (p. 408) near Saratoga and the Miracle Mile, or the high lakes of the **Wind River Indian Reservation** (p. 370).

GOLF   Golfers may be pleasantly surprised at the number of exceptional courses found in both states, particularly in Bigfork and Anaconda, Montana. Summer's long days make this a perfect place to play a round, especially when you take into consideration that average daily temperatures and humidity are much lower here than at destinations in Florida. Reserve tee times well in advance. Best Montana courses: the **Old Works** (p. 158) in Anaconda and **Eagle Bend** (p. 112) in Whitefish. In Wyoming: the **Jackson Hole Golf and Tennis Club** (p. 312) and

Teton Pines (p. 312) in Jackson; and the **Powder Horn** (p. 375) in Sheridan.

HIKING   Hiking gives you the added bonus of moderate to strenuous cardiovascular exercise while you're seeing the sights. Remember, though, that these are the mountains, and the elevation you gain over the course of the hike is a much better indication of how difficult the hike will be than the actual distance traveled. Be sure to wear comfortable hiking shoes that have been broken in, and if you plan on hiking in prime grizzly country, be sure to carry bear mace and check with rangers for what to do in case you actually see a bear. Best place to take a hike in Montana: **Glacier National Park** (chapter 6). In Wyoming: the **Wind River Mountains** (section 5 of chapter 14) or **Bighorn Mountains** (section 1 of chapter 15).

MOUNTAINEERING: ROCK & ICE CLIMBING   The Northern Rockies provide superb opportunities for climbers to experience the year-round beauty of Montana and Wyoming's mountains, whether you seek a daylong rock climb during the height of summer in Montana's Beartooths or a technical climb up one of the faces of the Tetons. Ice climbing is becoming a hot ticket in the dead of winter, when many of the world's finest climbers congregate in Cody, Wyoming, for unforgettable winter mountaineering. Not for the faint of heart, the sport is highly technical and requires extreme fitness and stamina. Best place to climb in Montana: **Granite Peak,** the state's highest (chapter 10). In Wyoming: **Grand Teton National Park** (chapter 13) or **Wild Iris** south of Lander (p. 369).

SNOWBOARDING   Forget all those stereotypes you've heard about snowboarders: This sport is a simple combination of speed, air, and style. If you've never done it, realize that you may have a very sore butt during your first few days, although seasoned shredders swear that the learning

Fishing Licenses

Both Montana and Wyoming require fishing licenses, which are available from most sporting goods stores, outfitters, or tackle shops. Yellowstone National Park requires an additional fishing permit (see chapter 12), and American Indian tribes located in the two states have special regulations and may require permits for fishing in their waters.

In Montana, all nonresident anglers 15 and older are required to buy fishing licenses. Those 14 and under do not need a fishing license as long as they are with an adult who has a valid fishing license. A license for the period of March through the following February is $60. A consecutive 2-day license is $15. In addition to fishing licenses, however, nonresident anglers of all ages must also possess conservation licenses, which cost $10 each. For information, contact the **Montana Department of Fish, Wildlife, and Parks,** 1420 E. 6th Ave., Helena, MT 59620 (© **406/444-2535;** www.fwp.state.mt.us).

You'll also need a Wyoming state fishing license if you plan to fish that state's waters. An adult nonresident license costs $14 per day and $92 for the season. Youth fees (ages 14–18) are $3 per day and $15 for the season. A $13 Conservation Stamp is also required for all licenses except the 1-day variety. No license is required for kids 13 and under, as long as they are accompanied by an adult who has a valid fishing license. You'll also have to check creel limits, which vary from year to year and place to place. Information is available from the **Wyoming Game and Fish Department** (© **307/777-4600;** http://gf.state.wy.us).

curve is much shorter than that for skiing. Experienced snowboarders will find Montana and Wyoming ski areas to be snowboard-friendly. If you're really into riding, ask around at local ski shops for winter backcountry options or summer snowboarding—**Glacier Park's Logan Pass** (chapter 6) is a popular destination. Best place in Montana: **Whitefish Mountain Resort** (p. 131).

SNOWMOBILING With more than 3,000 miles of trails in Montana and 1,300 in Wyoming, snowmobilers have a vast winter playground to explore. Though rental shops are plentiful, machines are in high demand, so you're wise to make a reservation well in advance. Though snowmobiling doesn't require an extreme level of physical fitness, you have to be able to adequately handle the snowmobile and be

well versed in safety measures because avalanches are common in the areas some of these trails traverse. Best bets for snowmobiling in Montana: **West Yellowstone** (chapter 12) and the **Seeley Lake Valley** (p. 119). In Wyoming: **Yellowstone National Park** and the surrounding national forest lands, depending on whether a long-looming ban ever becomes law.

WATERSPORTS: CANOEING, KAYAKING & RAFTING Paddlers have a wealth of choices here. Montana is particularly rich in rivers worth floating: the Flathead, the Blackfoot, the Madison, the Clarks Fork near Missoula, the Dearborn, the Yellowstone, and even the big old Missouri. In Wyoming there is less variety, but you'll find some fine stretches of river on the Snake, the Platte, the Hoback, and

Clarks Fork through Sunlight Basin. If you choose white-water rafting, leave the driving to someone else (that is, sign up with an outfitter that will provide an experienced person to pilot your craft), though you may be asked to paddle. The smaller rivers have no dams to regulate flows, which means kayakers seeking fast, scary runs should come during runoff in June, while canoeists wanting to relax and bird-watch can easily handle the upper Snake or Flathead late in the summer. For thrills, try the **Yellowstone River** at Gardiner, Montana (p. 267), and the **Snake River** in Wyoming (p. 313).

Glacier National Park

Majestic and wild, this vast preserve overwhelms visitors, beckoning with stunning mountain peaks (many covered year-round with glaciers), verdant mountain trails that cry out for hikers, and the sheer diversity of its plant and animal life. The unofficial mascot in these parts is the grizzly, a refugee from the high plains.

Named to describe the slow-moving glaciers that carved awe-inspiring valleys throughout this expanse of over 1 million acres, Glacier National Park exists because of the efforts of George Bird Grinnell, a 19th-century magazine publisher and cofounder of the Audubon Society. Following a pattern established with Yellowstone and Grand Teton, Grinnell lobbied for a national park to be set aside in the St. Mary region of Montana, and in May 1910 his efforts were rewarded. Just over 20 years later, it became, with its northern neighbor Waterton Lakes National Park in Canada, Glacier-Waterton International Peace Park—a gesture of goodwill and friendship between the governments of two countries.

Today you'll see nature in a state of constant change: The glaciers are receding,

the result of global warming, many say. Storms and avalanches have periodically ravaged Going-to-the-Sun Road, the curving, scenic 50-mile road that bisects the park. And fires in 2003 charred more than 100,000 acres of forest, about 10% of the park's total acreage.

If your time is limited, simply drive along Going-to-the-Sun Road, viewing the dramatic mountain scenery. Visitors with more time will find diversions for both families and hard-core adventurers; while some hiking trails are suitable for tykes, many more will challenge those determined to conquer and scale the park's tallest peaks. Glacier's lakes, streams, ponds, and waterfalls are equally engaging. Travelers board cruise boats to explore the history of the area; recreational types can fish, row, and kayak.

However, to truly experience Glacier requires slightly more effort, interest, and spunk than a drive through. Abandon the pavement for even the shortest and easiest hiking trail, and you'll discover a window into Glacier's soul.

1 JUST THE FACTS

GETTING THERE
The closest cities to the park with airline service are **Kalispell,** 29 miles southwest of the park; **Missoula,** 150 miles south; and **Great Falls,** 150 miles southeast.

Glacier Park International Airport, north of Kalispell at 4170 U.S. 2 (© **406/257-5994;** www.glacierairport.com), is serviced by Allegiant, United, Delta, Alaska/Horizon, and Northwest. **Great Falls International Airport** (© **406/727-3404;** www.gtfairport.com) and **Missoula International Airport** (© **406/728-4381;** www.flymissoula.com) are served by these same airlines.

If you're driving, you can reach the park from U.S. highways 2 and 89. Rental cars are available in Kalispell, Great Falls, Missoula, Whitefish, East Glacier, and West Glacier. **Avis, Budget, Hertz,** and **National** all have counters at the above airports.

Amtrak's Empire Builder (© **800/872-7245**; www.amtrak.com), a Chicago-Seattle round-trip route, stops at West Glacier and Essex year-round and East Glacier from May to October.

ACCESS/ENTRY POINTS

There are six paved entrances that provide vehicular access to Glacier National Park, but if you are traveling by car, you will most likely use **West Glacier** and **St. Mary.** These entrances are located at either end of Going-to-the-Sun Road, with West Glacier on the southwest side and St. Mary on the east. From the park's western boundary, you can enter at **Polebridge** to access Bowman and Kintla lakes or enter at the **Camas Creek** entrance and take the Camas Road to Going-to-the-Sun. The **Many Glacier** entrance provides access to the Many Glacier Hotel, Swiftcurrent Lake, and many backcountry trails. The **Two Medicine** entrance is only about 4 miles north of East Glacier Park on Mont. 49, with auto access to Lower Two Medicine Lake and Two Medicine Lake, as well as hiking trails to Pumpelly Pillar and over Pitamakan Pass. Four miles south of the Two Medicine entrance, the **East Glacier** entrance is for hikers only—it is not a paved entry point for cars—for access to trails at the southeastern corner of the park. **Essex** is strictly a backcountry access point to Scalplock Mountain and backcountry campgrounds along Ole Creek and Park Creek. **Cut Bank** is a dirt road, closed in winter, with backcountry access only to Triple Divide Pass and the northern route to Pitamakan Pass.

Caution: Entrance to the park is severely restricted during winter months when the alpine section of Going-to-the-Sun Road is closed. See section 2, "Driving in the Park," below, for more information.

VISITOR CENTERS

To receive information about the park before your trip, contact the superintendent, **Glacier National Park,** West Glacier, MT 59936 (© **406/888-7800;** TDD 406/888-7806; www.nps.gov/glac). The **Glacier Natural History Association** offers numerous publications; for a catalog, contact the association at 12544 U.S. 2 E., P.O. Box 310, West Glacier, MT 59936 (© **406/888-5756;** www.glacierassociation.org).

For up-to-date information on park activities once you arrive, check in at visitor centers located at **Apgar, Logan Pass,** and **St. Mary.** Apgar is open from May through October (and weekends during the winter); Logan Pass from mid-June to late September; and St. Mary from mid-May to mid-October. Park information may also be obtained from the **Many Glacier Ranger Station** or park headquarters in **West Glacier.**

FEES & BACKCOUNTRY PERMITS

Rangers are on duty at most entry points to collect fees, issue backcountry permits, and answer questions.

FEES Admission to the park for up to 7 days costs $25 per vehicle, $20 per motorcycle, or $12 per person for those on foot, bicycles, and motorcycles ($10 in winter). An annual park pass costs $35 and allows unlimited entry to Glacier National Park for an entire year. America the Beautiful passes are also honored (see chapter 3). Camping fees are $10 to $23 per night at the park's drive-in campgrounds. A separate entrance fee is charged for visitors to Waterton Lakes National Park (see "A Side Trip to Waterton Lakes National Park," later in this chapter).

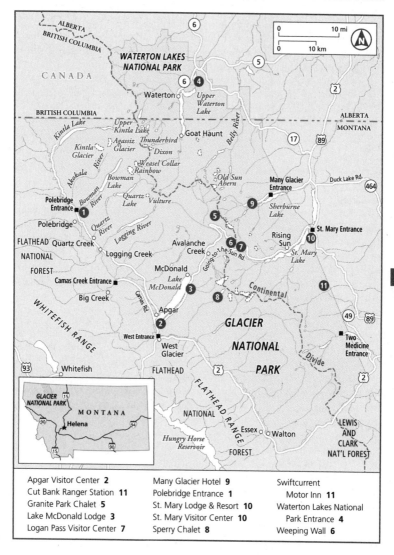

Apgar Visitor Center **2**	Many Glacier Hotel **9**	Swiftcurrent
Cut Bank Ranger Station **11**	Polebridge Entrance **1**	Motor Inn **11**
Granite Park Chalet **5**	St. Mary Lodge & Resort **10**	Waterton Lakes National
Lake McDonald Lodge **3**	St. Mary Visitor Center **10**	Park Entrance **4**
Logan Pass Visitor Center **7**	Sperry Chalet **8**	Weeping Wall **6**

BACKCOUNTRY PERMITS You must obtain backcountry permits in person from the Apgar Backcountry Office, St. Mary Visitor Center, or the ranger stations at Many Glacier, Polebridge, or Two Medicine. Visitors who enter Glacier's backcountry from the Canadian side (at Goat Haunt or Belly River in Waterton) can get a permit at the Waterton Visitor Reception Centre, but only with a credit card. **During summer months,** permits may be obtained no earlier than 24 hours before your visit. There is a $5 per-person per-night charge for backcountry camping. Permits are good only for the prearranged dates and

(Tips) **Traveling Through the Park Without a Car**

In 2007, the park launched a **free shuttle bus service.** Visitors simply park their car at the Apgar Transit Center on the west side or the St. Mary Visitor Center and take the shuttle to about 20 stops throughout the park, most of them on Going-to-the-Sun Road. The shuttles connecting the two lots run from about 7am to 7pm. For detailed information on the schedule and routes, visit the park's website or check the insert in the free *Glacier Visitor Guide* available at all entrances and visitor centers. Additionally, Glacier's signature red **"Jammer"** buses are once more in service. For more information, see "Organized Tours & Activities," below.

locations, with no more than 3 nights allowed at a single campground. Campsites are limited. A single site has a maximum occupancy of four persons. Stoves are required in most areas (no open fires), and pets are not permitted on the trails.

To ensure a spot and avoid the hassle, order a backcountry trip planner from **Backcountry Reservations** (*(C)* **406/888-7800**), GNP, West Glacier, MT 59936; sending them your dates with a check for $30 between June 15 and October 31 will reserve your spot in the wilderness.

Due to lower demand in winter, camping permits are available up to 7 days in advance. A few rules do take effect beginning each November 20, so double-check at visitor centers for details.

SPECIAL REGULATIONS & WARNINGS

Park regulations here are similar to those in other lands administered by the National Park Service, and generally prohibit damaging the natural resources. Pets must be leashed and are not allowed on trails. In addition, RVs and other vehicles longer than 21 feet or wider than 8 feet are prohibited on the 24-mile stretch of Going-to-the-Sun Road between Avalanche Campground and Sun Point on St. Mary Lake. Snowmobiling is prohibited in the park.

WHEN TO GO

Glacier is magnificent at any time of the year, but it's not always easily accessible. Most visitors come in **summer,** and it seems as if they all drive along Going-to-the-Sun Road. The 52-mile two-lane road is generally open from early June to September or October, depending upon the weather and road-construction projects. During summer months, sunrise is around 5am and sunset at nearly 10pm, so there's plenty of time for exploring. The shoulder seasons of **spring and fall** see budding wildflowers and seasonal colors, but these sights can be viewed only from the park's outer boundaries and on a limited stretch of the scenic highway.

In **winter,** road access is limited. Going-to-the-Sun Road is plowed to Lake McDonald Lodge on the west side of the park, 12 miles from West Glacier, but the remainder of the road is closed. Snowmobiles are prohibited. All unplowed roads become trails for snowshoers and cross-country skiers, who rave about the vast wonderland. Guided trips are a great way to experience the park in winter, or you can strap on a pair of snowshoes and explore it on your own. A popular skiing expedition is to go as far up Going-to-the-Sun Road as your energy permits. Wintertime temperatures average between 15°F (–9°C) and

30°F (–1°C), but extreme lows can reach 30°F below zero (–34°C). Average winter snow-fall is almost 12 feet, and it snows about half of the days from November through February.

AVOIDING THE CROWDS

If you want to avoid the crowds, travel in the off season before mid-June, when the park begins to fill, and after Labor Day, when families traveling with youngsters have returned home (Aug is the busiest month). If that's not possible, consider the following: As most people congregate close to the major hotels, find a trail head that is equidistant from two major points and head for the woods.

Going-to-the-Sun Road is nearly always jammed in the summer daylight hours. If you can, make the trip before 8:30am. In July and August, the parking lot at Logan Pass Visitor Center fills to capacity. Try to visit early in the day or late in the afternoon, and make use of the park's free shuttle.

RANGER PROGRAMS

When you enter the park, you'll be given a copy of the *Glacier Visitor Guide,* which lists the naturalist-led programs offered at Glacier and Waterton. There are a wide variety of hikes, boat trips, campfire programs, family programs, and other activities. Many are accessible for those in wheelchairs. There are also presentations given by members of local tribes. Most programs are free, although those including boat trips may have a small fee associated. For schedules, check the park newspapers, or call ℂ **406/888-7800.**

TIPS FOR TRAVELERS WITH PHYSICAL DISABILITIES

Information on facilities and services for those with disabilities is available at any of the visitor centers in the park, although most of the park's developed areas are fully accessible by wheelchair. The park's "Accessibility in Glacier National Park" publication describes current programs and services for visitors with disabilities.

FOR THE VISUALLY IMPAIRED Audiotapes, park brochure recordings, and tactile nature items are available at the Apgar, Logan Pass, and St. Mary visitor centers. All other park facilities—restrooms, restaurants, campgrounds, gift shops—are accessible with some assistance.

FOR THE MOBILITY IMPAIRED The Trail of the Cedars, Oberlin Bend Trail, Goat Lick Overlook Trail, and Running Eagle Falls Nature Trail are wheelchair accessible. A bike path at Apgar also provides magnificent views of the park's scenery. Wheelchairs are available for loan at the Apgar, Logan Pass, and St. Mary visitor centers, and almost all of the park's facilities are fully accessible.

 Especially for Kids

The park has a *Junior Ranger Newspaper* available at the visitor centers that lists seven activities to introduce youngsters between 6 and 12 years of age to the habitats in Glacier. Kids must complete five activities to receive a badge. Children are also welcome on most interpretive activities, but should be accompanied by an adult.

FOR THE HEARING IMPAIRED   Interpreters provide written synopses of most slide and campfire programs. If you plan on hiking, note that five of the park's self-guided nature trails have printed brochures available at the trail head. General park information is available by TDD at © **406/888-7806.** An interpreter may be available to sign at ranger programs. Call © **406/888-7930** 2 weeks in advance to make arrangements.

ORGANIZED TOURS & ACTIVITIES

Glacier Park Boat Co., P.O. Box 5262, Kalispell, MT 59903 (© **406/257-2426;** www. glacierparkboats.com), offers **narrated boat tours** ★★ from Lake McDonald, St. Mary, Two Medicine, and Many Glacier from mid-June to mid-September. These "scenicruises" combine the comfort of an hour-long lake cruise with a short hike or picnic to create an unforgettable experience. Spectacular views of Lake McDonald sunsets, the awe-inspiring Grinnell Glacier, and the panoramic rugged cliffs ringing St. Mary Lake are just a few of the possible photo opportunities you may have while enjoying a cruise. The boats typically depart every hour, usually seven times each day (although schedules are subject to change in late season or if the weather is inclement). Ticket prices top out at $22. Check ahead for a complete listing of prices and departure times. The concessionaire also offers charter service for larger groups and guided hikes in the park.

Unique **"Jammer" coach tours** run along Going-to-the-Sun Road and north to Waterton. Thirty-three classic bright-red coaches from the 1930s, long identified with Glacier, are in service after a restoration project that began in 1999. Drivers provide insightful commentary about the park and its history, and you don't have to worry about how close you may be to the edge of the often-precipitous road! Full-day rates are about $80 for adults and about $40 for children, with tours departing from both sides of the park. Half-day tours (for about half the price) are also available. For schedules, contact **Glacier Park, Inc.** (© **406/892-2525;** www.glacierparkinc.com).

Historical-cultural **25-passenger motorcoach tours** of the Going-to-the-Sun Road conducted by knowledgeable guides from the Blackfeet Nation originate from East Glacier, Browning, and St. Mary. Rates start at $40 for a 4-hour trip. Contact **Suntours** (© **800/786-9220;** www.glaciersuntours.com).

Glacier Guides, P.O. Box 330, West Glacier, MT 59936 (© **800/521-7238** or 406/387-5555; www.glacierguides.com), organizes backpacking trips into the Glacier National Park backcountry. These include a 3-day "taste" of the park for about $450 per person, and an entire week in the wilderness for about $850 per person. The company has been the exclusive backpacking guide service in the park since 1983.

Special Activities

Scenic helicopter tours of Glacier are offered by **Glacier Heli Tours** (© **800/879-9310;** www.glacierhelitours.com) and **Kruger Helicopters** (© **406/387-4565;** www.krugerhelicopters.com). Prices start at about $110 per person for four people for a half-hour trip.

The **Glacier Institute** conducts field classes in the summer that examine Glacier's cultural and natural resources. These 1- to 4-day courses include instruction, transportation, park fees, and college credit. Instructors are highly skilled in their area of expertise, bringing to each course an intimate knowledge of the region and subject matter. The "classroom" is Glacier National Park and other areas in northwest Montana. Courses cover such topics as alpine wildflowers, grizzlies, weather systems, and nature photography. Contact the institute for a copy of its current catalog at 137 Main St., P.O. Box

Vehicle Regulations

Park regulations prohibit vehicles more than 21 feet long or 8 feet wide on the 24-mile stretch of Going-to-the-Sun Road between Avalanche Campground and Sun Point on St. Mary Lake. If you are traveling in a vehicle exceeding the 21-foot limit, park it at one of the parking areas located at Avalanche Campground and Sun Point and let someone else do the driving (see "Traveling Through the Park Without a Car," above).

1887, Kalispell, MT 59903 (© **406/755-1211;** www.glacierinstitute.org). Prices range from $65 to $850 per course.

2 DRIVING IN THE PARK

Because of the massive piles of rock that surround a visitor, it is impossible to drive through Glacier without drawing comparisons to Grand Teton. But at Teton, unless you hit the hiking trails, the mountains keep their distance. In Glacier, as you drive, the mountain peaks envelop you.

GOING-TO-THE-SUN ROAD

If you plan only a day or two in Glacier, the most important thing to do is to drive **Going-to-the-Sun Road,** the 50-mile road that bisects the park between West Glacier and St. Mary. Points of interest are clearly marked along this road, and correspond to the park brochure "Points of Interest Along the Going-to-the-Sun Road," which is available at visitor centers. Bring plenty of film.

The road gains more than 3,400 feet in 32 miles, and is very narrow in places. Visitors with a fear of heights should take a van tour or shuttle. Because of the road's narrowness, oversize vehicles and trailers must use U.S. 2.

As you begin the drive from the West Glacier entrance, you'll pass the largest of the 653 lakes in Glacier—**Lake McDonald.** Numerous turnouts along the way present opportunities to photograph the panoramic views of the lake with its mountainous backdrop. You can see **Sacred Dancing Cascade** and **Johns Lake** after an easy half-mile hike from the roadside through a hemlock and red cedar forest. The trail head for this hike is 2 miles north of the Lake McDonald Lodge along Going-to-the-Sun Road.

The **Trail of the Cedars** is a short, handicap-accessible boardwalk trail through terrain thickly carpeted in vibrant, verdant hues. This is also the beginning of the Avalanche Lake Trail, a 2.1-mile hike (one-way) to the foot of Avalanche Lake, one of the most popular day hikes in the park. The trail head is about 5½ miles north of Lake McDonald Lodge, just past the Avalanche Creek Campground.

Almost exactly halfway along Going-to-the-Sun is the overlook for Heaven's Peak, the massive snow-covered mountain to the south that you've just driven around. This is also the jumping-off point for the **Loop Trail,** which can take you to the Granite Park Chalet. Just 2 miles farther is the **Bird Woman Falls Overlook.** Bird Woman Falls drops in a wondrous bounty of water from a hanging valley above the road. Next along the road is the oft-photographed **Weeping Wall,** which is a wall of rock with water pouring forth.

At the 32-mile mark from West Glacier is **Logan Pass,** one of the park's busiest areas and the starting point for the hike to **Hidden Lake,** likely the park's most popular trail. There's a visitor center here atop the Continental Divide, with a bookstore and a small display about the wildlife, flora, and geology of the area.

As you continue the drive downhill, you'll reach the turnout for **Jackson Glacier,** the most easily recognizable glacier in the entire park; followed by **Sunrift Gorge** and **Sun Point,** which are accessible via two short trails rife with wildlife.

Note: A 20-year construction plan on Going-to-the-Sun Road will cause delays in the summer and early closures in some years.

WINTER ROAD CONDITIONS   Going-to-the-Sun Road is open seasonally, usually from early June to September or October, depending on weather conditions and road construction projects. Call the park at 406/888-7800 to find out when tentative openings and closings are scheduled. During the winter, you may drive Going-to-the-Sun Road for 10 miles from West Glacier along Lake McDonald to the road closure; this is a popular destination for cross-country skiers.

OTHER DRIVES

ALONG THE LOWER EDGE OF THE PARK   Circumnavigating the lower half of the park is easily accomplished in 1 long day. After a leisurely breakfast in West Glacier, you'll be in East Glacier in plenty of time for lunch at the Glacier Park Lodge (see section 6, "Where to Stay," in this chapter) and at St. Mary or Many Glacier for dinner.

The road between West Glacier and East Glacier—approximately 57 miles—is a well-paved, two-lane affair that winds circuitously around the western and southern borders of the park and follows the Middle Fork of the Flathead River. As you descend to the valley floor, you'll travel through beautiful, privately owned Montana ranch and farm land. Shortly after entering the valley, look to the north and admire the park's massive peaks. The **Goat Lick** parking lot, on U.S. 2 just east of Essex, gets you off the beaten path and provides a view down into a canyon carved by the Flathead River. If you have time, take the short hike down to the stream.

Beyond East Glacier, as you head east on Mont. 49 and north toward Two Medicine, you'll notice that the earth appears to fall off. The contrast is inescapable—mountains tower in the west, but to the east the Hi-Line begins, sporting a horizon that extends so far and so flat as to seemingly lend credence and legitimacy to the Flat Earth Society. But round a bend on Two Medicine Road, and suddenly you'll find yourself faced with three mountains (Appistocki Peak, Mount Henry, and Bison Mountain) bare of vegetation but as red as their Southwestern counterparts. Ten miles later, continuing the route northward on U.S. 89, you'll come across a wide panorama of mountain peaks, valleys, ridges, and forested mountains that truly characterizes Glacier's personality. Conclude the bottom half of your long loop by wending downward from these high elevations to the village of St. Mary.

TO POLEBRIDGE   There are two ways to see the park's western boundary and to access the Polebridge area in the north: One is slow and uncomfortable, the other slightly faster and more comfortable. The **North Fork Road** from Columbia Falls takes about an hour to negotiate. It's a sometimes-paved, mostly gravel and pothole stretch that follows the North Fork of the Flathead River. Not much is there besides water and scenery, but the area around Polebridge is a popular place to take in Montana's natural beauty without modern-day distractions like telephones and TVs.

The **Inside North Fork Road,** just north of Apgar, also runs to Polebridge. However, it's totally unpaved, takes an hour longer, and is much harder on the driver, passenger, and equipment. Take the faster route instead, and spend that extra hour relaxing on a riverbank.

3 OUTDOOR PURSUITS

BIKING   Opportunities for biking in the park are limited, since bikes may be ridden only on established roads, bike routes, or in parking areas, and are not allowed on trails. Restrictions apply to the most hazardous portions of Going-to-the-Sun Road during peak travel times from around mid-June to Labor Day; call ahead to find out when the road will be closed to bikers. During low-visibility periods caused by fog or darkness, a white front light and a back red reflector are required. A few shared campsites for bicyclists are held until 9pm at Apgar, Sprague Creek, Fish Creek, Many Glacier, Two Medicine, Avalanche, Rising Sun, and St. Mary campgrounds for $5 per person. Before Logan Pass opens and after it closes, Going-to-the-Sun Road is also popular with bikers, provided it is not knee-deep with snow.

From June 15 to Labor Day, bikes are prohibited between Apgar and Sprague Creek campgrounds between 11am and 4pm in both directions, and from Logan Creek to Logan Pass (eastbound) between 11am and 4pm. It takes about 3 hours and 45 minutes to ride from Sprague Creek to Logan Pass.

BOATING   You can take advantage of some of those 653 lakes with a boat rental at various spots. Motor size is restricted to 10 horsepower on most lakes, and a detailed list of other regulations is available at park headquarters and staffed ranger stations. Park rangers may inspect or board any boat to determine regulation compliance. At Apgar and Lake McDonald, you will find kayaks, canoes, rowboats, and motorboats. Only human-powered or electric motorboats are available at Two Medicine. At Many Glacier you can rent kayaks, canoes, and rowboats. For details, call **Glacier Park Boat Co.** at ☏ **406/257-2426,** or browse **www.glacierparkboats.com**.

FISHING   Glacier's streams and lakes are habitat for whitefish, kokanee salmon, arctic grayling, and five kinds of trout. Try the North Fork of the Flathead to fish for cutthroat and bull trout and any of the park's three larger lakes (Bowman, St. Mary, and McDonald) for rainbow, brook trout, and whitefish. State of Montana fishing licenses are generally not required within the park's boundaries, although you will need one on the North Fork and Middle Fork of the Flathead River. Also, remember that since the eastern boundary of the park abuts the Blackfeet Indian Reservation, you may find yourself fishing in their territorial waters. To avoid a problem, purchase a $10 use permit from businesses in the gateway towns; the permit covers fishing, hiking, and biking in the reservation. Fishing outside the park in Montana waters requires a state license; check in at a local fishing shop to make certain you're within the law. For equipment or sage advice, or to schedule a guided foray ($325 for two people for a half-day), contact **Glacier Anglers** (☏ **800/235-6781;** www.glacierraftco.com) at the Glacier Outdoor Center in West Glacier.

HIKING   Glacier is a park that is best seen on foot. Its 1,600 square miles have more than 150 trails, totaling more than 750 miles. You can hike more than 100 miles along the Continental Divide alone.

Trail maps are available at outdoor stores in Whitefish and Kalispell, as well as at the major visitor centers and ranger stations in the park. Before striking off into the wilderness, however, check with the nearest ranger station to determine the accessibility of your destination, trail conditions, and recent bear sightings. Also note that the trail maps don't show elevation changes or many terrain features beyond lakes and the tallest peaks. If you plan to do any extensive hiking, it is best to purchase a U.S. Geological Survey (USGS) topographic map, available at outdoor sporting goods stores and the USGS website (www.usgs.gov).

The Park Service asks you to stay on trails to keep from eroding the fragile components of the park. Also, don't traverse snowbanks, especially the steeper ones. You should have proper footwear and rain gear, enough food, and, most important, enough water, before approaching any trail head. A can of pepper spray can also come in handy when you're in grizzly habitat. If you're planning to hike in Canada, be sure the bear spray is USEPA approved.

See section 4, "Exploring the Backcountry," below, for information on some of the longer hiking trails and further information on backpacking.

If you plan an extended hike, let someone know your route and your expected time of return. Take a flashlight in case you take longer than you think. Carry a map, rain gear, and extra clothing, and drink lots of water.

Among the park's shorter and easier trails is the **Trail of the Cedars Nature Trail** (.75 miles round-trip; access is across from the Avalanche Campground Ranger Station), an easy, level trail that's wheelchair accessible. It has interpretive signs along the way. The **Hidden Lake Overlook Nature Trail** ★ (3 miles round-trip; accessed from the Logan Pass Visitor Center) is an easy-to-moderate interpretive trail that climbs 460 feet to an overlook of scenic Hidden Lake. It's a popular trail, but by hiking past the overlook to the lake, you'll avoid some of the crowds (and you might even see a mountain goat).

The **Loop** (8 miles round-trip; access is on Going-to-the-Sun Rd., about halfway btw. Avalanche Campground and Logan Pass Visitor Center) offers a moderate hike that climbs to Granite Park Chalet and back. Many people use it as a continuation of the Highline Trail, but this is the section to do if you're not quite so adventurous (the Highline Trail is almost 8 miles long; see "Exploring the Backcountry," below). If you want to spend the night in the chalet, contact **Belton Chalets** for reservations (© **888/345-2649**). See the descriptions of the chalets in section 5, "Camping," below.

The **Sun Point Nature Trail** (1.4 miles round-trip; access is 9 miles west of St. Mary at the Sun Point parking area) is an easy walk on gentle slopes that presents commanding views of Baring Falls. Among the favorite hikes (because of its beautiful scenery) is the **Iceberg Lake Trail** ★★ (9.6 miles round-trip; access at a trail head in a cabin area east of the Swiftcurrent Coffee Shop and Campstore). This is a moderate hike that traverses flower-filled meadows to a jewel of a high lake backed against a mountain wall. Even in summer, there may be snow on the ground and ice floating in the lake. Look for mountain goats or bighorn sheep on the cliffs above. And, as in many of the park's backcountry areas, keep an eye out for the grizzlies.

Swiftcurrent Nature Trail ★ (2.5 miles round-trip; access is at a picnic area half a mile west of the hotel turnoff) is a fun and easy hike along the lake shore, through the woods, and near a marsh, so you may see deer and birds—keep an eye out for blue grouse. If you have time, continue on the trail as it circles Lake Josephine, another easy hike, adding 2.8 miles to the trip. Dramatic Mount Gould towers above the far end of Lake Josephine, and midsummer wildflowers can be spectacular. A longer, 10-mile round-trip trail to Grinnell Glacier, the park's largest, is also accessed from this area.

The very easy **Running Eagle Falls Trail** (.6 mile round-trip; access is 1 mile west of the Two Medicine entrance) winds through a heavily forested area to a large, noisy waterfall. The popular **Twin Falls Trail** (7.6 miles round-trip; accessed from Two Medicine Campground) is an easy hike to scenic Twin Falls. Hikers can walk the entire distance to Twin Falls on a clearly identified trail, or boat across Two Medicine Lake to the foot of the trail head and hike the last mile. The **St. Mary Falls Trail** ★★ (1.6 miles round-trip; accessed from Jackson Glacier Overlook) is a fairly easy walk that takes you to rushing falls of the St. Mary River. The roar of the cascade is prodigious and satisfying.

HORSEBACK RIDING   You can bring your own horses and pack animals into the park, but restrictions apply to private stock. A free brochure detailing regulations regarding horseback riding is available from the National Park Service.

Swan Mountain Outfitters (© **406/888-5121** or 732-4203; www.swanmountain outfitters.com) provides horseback riding at Lake McDonald, Apgar Village, and Many Glacier. The company offers hour-long ($40) to half-day rides ($105) into the nearby wilderness.

MOUNTAIN CLIMBING   The peaks of Glacier National Park rarely exceed 10,000 feet in elevation, but don't let the surveyors' measurements fool you. Glacier has some incredibly difficult climbs, and you must inquire at the ranger station regarding climbing conditions and closures. In general, the peaks are unsuitable, except for experienced climbers or those traveling with experienced guides; park administration does not recommend climbing because of the unstable nature of the rock.

RAFTING & FLOAT TRIPS   Though the waters in the park don't lend themselves to white-water rafting, the boundary forks of the Flathead River are some of the best in the northwest corner of the state. For just taking it easy and floating along in the summer sun, the North Fork of the Flathead River stretching from Polebridge to Columbia Falls and into Flathead Lake is ideal. The same may be said for the Middle Fork of the Flathead, which forms the southern border of the park.

For white-water voyagers, the North Fork of the Flathead River (classes II and III) and the Middle Fork (class III) are the best bets. Flow rates change dramatically as snow melts or storms move through the area; inquire at any ranger station for details and conditions.

The Middle Fork is a little more severe and isn't the sort of river you enjoy with an umbrella drink in hand. The names of certain stretches of the Middle Fork inspire terror in and of themselves (the Narrows, Jaws, Bonecrusher), and to assuage that terror, several outfitters offer expert, sanctioned guides.

Established in 1975, **Glacier Raft Company,** P.O. Box 210, West Glacier, MT 59936 (© **800/235-6781** or 406/888-5454; www.glacierraftco.com), is Montana's oldest raft company. Offerings include half-day trips ($48 adult, $36 child), full-day excursions ($82 adult, $59 child), 2-day trips ($335 adult, $275 child), and 3-day outings ($455 adult, $370 child). Prices include all necessary equipment and food. The company also offers scenic trips, inflatable-kayak rentals, and a number of other services. Other local raft guides include **Great Northern Whitewater,** 12127 U.S. 2 E., P.O. Box 270, West Glacier, MT 59936 (© **800/735-7897;** www.gnwhitewater.com); **Montana Raft Company,** P.O. Box 330, West Glacier, MT 59936 (© **800/521-7238** or 406/387-5555; www.glacierguides.com); and **Wild River Adventures,** P.O. Box 272, West Glacier, MT 59936 (© **800/700-7056** or 406/387-9453; www.riverwild.com).

SNOWSHOEING & CROSS-COUNTRY SKIING   Glacier has numerous cross-country trails, the most popular of which is the **Upper Lake McDonald Trail** to the Avalanche picnic area. This 8-mile trail offers a relatively flat route up Going-to-the-Sun

> **Tips** **Bear Warning!**
>
> To remind you yet again: Glacier is grizzly country. Make noise when you hike, don't cook near where you sleep, and don't sleep in the same clothes you cooked in.

Road with views of McDonald Creek and the mountains looming above the McDonald Valley. For the advanced skier, the same area presents a more intense 11-mile trip that heads northwest in a roundabout fashion to the Apgar Lookout. The most popular trail on the east side is the **Autumn Creek Trail** near Marias Pass. However, avalanche paths cross this area, so inquire about current weather conditions. Yet another popular spot is in Essex along the southern boundary of the park at the Izaak Walton Inn (p. 81). In West Glacier, **Glacier Outdoor Center** (© **800/235-6781**) rents snowshoes and cross-country ski packages for $15 and $18 per day, respectively.

4 EXPLORING THE BACKCOUNTRY

Glacier offers every kind of backcountry experience, from short day hikes to 2-week treks. Consider your fitness level, backcountry experience, and interests, and then get some advice from one of Glacier's rangers. They can provide you with area maps, but a topographical map is highly recommended if you're going for more than a short walk.

Backcountry campgrounds have maps at the entrance to show you the location of each campsite, the pit toilet, food-preparation areas, and, perhaps most important, food-storage areas. If you fish while camping, it's recommended you exercise catch-and-release so as to avoid attracting wildlife in search of food. If you eat the catch, be certain to puncture the air bladder and throw the entrails into deep water at least 200 feet from the nearest campsite or trail. You will need a permit to camp; see "Backcountry Permits," in section 1 of this chapter.

GUIDED BACKCOUNTRY TRIPS   Glacier Guides (© **800/521-7238** or 406/387-5555; www.glacierguides.com) is the exclusive hiking guide service in the park. From May through September, it organizes custom trips and offers weekly departures for 3- and 6-day trips. Prices vary, but you can figure on spending about $150 per person per day. It also rents equipment and can arrange trips where you stay indoors at night.

NOTABLE BACKCOUNTRY HIKING TRAILS

BOWMAN LAKE TRAIL ★★   This especially scenic trail (14 miles to Brown Pass) is similar to the Kintla Lake hike in difficulty, and, like the Kintla Trail, passes a lake on the north. After a hike through the foliage, the trail climbs out of reach of anyone in bad shape, then ascends 2,000 feet in less than 3 miles to join the Kintla Trail at Brown Pass. A left turn takes you to Kintla Lake (23 miles to the Kintla Lake trail head), a right takes you to Goat Haunt at the foot of Waterton Lake (9 miles). To reach the Bowman Lake trail head, go ⅓ mile north of Polebridge, then turn east (right) up the Bowman Creek road. The road ends after 6 miles at the southeast end of Bowman Lake, from which the trails radiate.

DAWSOM-PITAMAKAN LOOP ★ This difficult, 19-mile loop traverses Rising Wolf Mountain; at 9,513 feet, it's the area's most prominent feature. There are backcountry campsites at Old Man Lake and at No Name Lake. The trail offers splendid panoramas of the park's interior and of many alpine lakes. You'll encounter lots of steep ups and downs: The elevation change is 2,400 feet. The trail head is at Two Medicine Campground.

THE HIGHLINE TRAIL This easy-to-moderate 12-mile round-trip hike, which gains only 200 feet in elevation, begins at the Logan Pass Visitor Center and skirts the Garden Wall at elevations of more than 6,000 feet to Granite Park Chalet. Keep an eye on your watch to be certain you'll have enough time for the return hike to Logan Pass. You can continue on from the chalet to "the Loop," the aptly named section of Going-to-the-Sun Road where the trail actually terminates (an additional 3.2 miles), although to make sure you can get back to your car by nightfall, you'll need to plan for a shuttle.

KINTLA LAKE TO UPPER KINTLA LAKE TRAIL This 24-mile round-trip hike skirts the north shore of Kintla Lake above Polebridge for about 7 miles before climbing a couple of hundred feet. This stretch of the hike is a breeze. However, once you hit Kintla Creek, you may want to reconsider going any farther. With 12 miles under your belt at this point, climbing 3,000 feet may not seem like a great idea. The trail, once it breaks into the clear, offers views of several peaks, including Kinnerly Peak to the south of Upper Kintla Lake. The trail head is located 14 miles north of Polebridge after a drive along a gravel road, at the western tip of Kintla Lake.

PIEGAN PASS TO MANY GLACIER If you're looking for a longer, tougher hike from Logan Pass, try this one. You pick up the trail at Siyeh Bend, about 3 miles on the east side of Logan Pass Visitor Center. It's a 13-mile walk up over Piegan Pass, past Grinnell Glacier and Grinnell Lake to Josephine and Swiftcurrent lakes before reaching Many Glacier Lodge. There are many long, steep stretches, going both up and down.

QUARTZ LAKE TRAIL Accessed from the Bowman Creek trail head, the entire loop is 12 miles, running up and over an 1,800-foot ridge and then dropping down to the south end of Lower Quartz Lake. From there it's a level 3-mile hike to the west end of Quartz Lake, then it's 6 miles back over the ridge farther north (and higher up) before dropping back to Bowman Creek. An interesting aspect of this trail is evidence of the Red Bench Fire of 1988, which took a chunk out of the North Fork area.

5 CAMPING

INSIDE THE PARK

Stop at any ranger station for information on closures and availability, and consult the chart below for information on amenities and fees.

There are a variety of camping opportunities here. Campgrounds accessible by paved roads include **Apgar,** near the West Glacier entrance; **Avalanche Creek,** just up from the head of Lake McDonald; **Fish Creek,** on the west side of Lake McDonald; **Many Glacier,** in the northeast part of the park; **Rising Sun,** on the north side of St. Mary Lake; **St. Mary,** on the east side of the park; and **Two Medicine,** in the southeast part of the park near East Glacier. **Sprague Creek,** near the West Glacier entrance, offers a paved road but does not allow towed vehicles. There are also five campgrounds accessed by narrow dirt roads. Though utility connections are not provided at these sites, fireplaces, picnic tables, washrooms (with sinks and flush toilets), and cold running water are located at each campground. Campsites are available on a first-come, first-served basis, payable by cash or check, except for Fish Creek and St. Mary campgrounds, where sites can be reserved by Discover, MasterCard, and Visa through the **National Park Service Reservation System** (① 877/444-6777; www.recreation.gov).

A few shared sites for bicyclists are held until 9pm at Apgar, Sprague Creek, Avalanche, Fish Creek, Many Glacier, Two Medicine, Rising Sun, and St. Mary campgrounds for $5 per person.

THE CAMPGROUNDS

Despite its proximity to the center of the hotel and motel activity, the **Many Glacier Campground** ★★ is a densely wooded campground with more privacy than you'd expect. The campground has adequate space for small motor homes and pickup truck/camper combinations, but space for vehicles pulling trailers is limited. It is a veritable mecca for tent campers. The **Avalanche Campground** is situated in the bottom of the valley near Lake McDonald in a heavily treed area immediately adjacent to the river. The **Two Medicine Campground** ★★ lies in the shadow of the mountains near three lakes and a stream. It is a forested area that has beautiful sites, plenty of shade, and opportunities to wet a fishing line. Two Medicine is a little out of the way of the typical Glacier traveler, and may offer a little more solitude. The **Cut Bank Campground** road is not paved, but it's only 5 miles from the pavement to the ranger station and campground. The road and campground are best suited to recreational vehicles 21 feet or shorter.

CHALETS

Two of the park's most popular destinations, Granite Park and Sperry Chalets—National Historic Landmarks built by the Great Northern Railway between 1912 and 1914—are subjects of an extensive restoration project. The **Granite Park Chalet** is a hiker's shelter only. Guests must bring their own food, water, cooking and eating utensils, flashlights, and sleeping bags. Rooms and beds are provided, as are a kitchen with a cooking stove and dining room. No public water is available, so bring your own. The chalet has 12 rooms (all single bunk beds), and sleeps two to six per room. Cost is about $148 per night for two people, and the kitchen facilities are shared. To get there, you'll have to walk about 3 miles from the Loop trail head off Going-to-the-Sun Road, or about 6 miles on the trail to Swiftcurrent Pass at the end of Many Glacier Road from the east side.

The **Sperry Chalet** is an impressive stone structure in the center of the wilderness. Here you'll get a room (with linens) plus three meals daily, but no bathing facilities except cold water and modern composting toilets located outside. Rates are $285 for two people, and include all meals. To get there, walk about 4 miles from the road, up Snyder Creek, then toward Gunsight Mountain. The trail head is opposite the entrance to Lake McDonald Lodge on the lower portion of Going-to-the-Sun Road.

For reservations at either chalet, contact **Belton Chalets** at (① **888/345-2649;** www.graniteparkchalet.com or www.sperrychalet.com).

Campgrounds in Gateway Communities

During the busy season, it's recommended that you reserve a spot at these campsites at least 1 month in advance.

Campground	# of Sites	Fee	Max RV Length	Flush Toilets	Disposal Stations	Boat Access
Apgar	194	$10–$20	25 sites; up to 40'	Yes	Yes	Yes
Avalanche	87	$20	50 sites; up to 26'	Yes	Yes	No
Bowman Lake*	48	$10–$15	RVs not recommended	No	No	Yes
Cut Bank*	14	$10	RVs not recommended	No	No	No
Fish Creek	178	$23	3 sites; up to 35'	Yes	Yes	No
Kintla Lake*	14	$15	RVs not recommended	No	No	Yes
Logging Creek*	7	$10	RVs not recommended	No	No	No
Many Glacier	110	$10–$20	13 sites; up to 35'	Yes	Yes	Yes
Quartz Creek*	7	$10	RVs not recommended	No	No	No
Rising Sun	83	$20	3 sites; up to 30'	Yes	Yes	Yes
St. Mary	148	$10–$23	25 sites; up to 35'	Yes	Yes	Yes
Sprague Creek	25	$20	No towed trailers	Yes	Yes	No
Two Medicine	99	$10–$20	13 sites; up to 32'	Yes	Yes	Yes

Campgrounds are accessible only by narrow dirt roads. RVs are not recommended.

GLACIER NATIONAL PARK

6

CAMPING

In East Glacier

Y Lazy R   Situated just off U.S. 2, this campground is conveniently located within walking distance of East Glacier and is the closest to town and its laundry facilities. Plan to arrive early if you want to snag one of the few sites with trees. The Y Lazy R is a great value and an ideal place to plant the RV before heading off to explore the region.

Washington St. and U.S. 2, P.O. Box 13, East Glacier, MT 59434. ℂ **406/226-5505**. 10 tent sites, 20 RV sites. $16 tent; $18 water and electric only; $20 full hookup.

In St. Mary

Johnson's of St. Mary   Open April through September (depending on the weather), this is where you want to camp if you can get a spot. The campground is located near the southern end of Lower St. Mary Lake and provides an inexpensive overnight stop with access to the east side of the park and the tourist facilities at the St. Mary Lodge. There are also showers, a Laundromat, and an 18-hole miniature golf course.

HC 72, Box 10, St. Mary, MT 59417. ℂ **406/732-4207**. www.johnsonsofstmary.com. 75 tent sites, 82 RV sites. $23 tent; $32–$35 RV with electricity and water only, $40 full hookup; $26 motor home, no hookup. MC, V.

In West Glacier

Glacier Campground   This campground—1 mile west of West Glacier on U.S. 2—is the closest campground outside the park. Set amid a forested area overgrown with evergreens, it's a quiet, comfortable, shady place to retreat. Most sites have water and electric hookups; the balance is perfect for tent camping. Five rather primitive cabins are also available, but furnishings are modest: sleeping beds with mattresses and electricity, but no plumbing or kitchen facilities. Recreational facilities include volleyball, horseshoes, and a basketball court; also on the premises are an excellent Cajun restaurant, a Laundromat, and a small general store.

P.O. Box 447, 12070 U.S. 2, West Glacier, MT 59936. © **888/387-5689** or 406/387-5689. www.glacier campground.com. 80 tent sites, 80 RV sites, 5 cabins. $19 tent; $22–$27 RV; $40–$50 cabin. AE, DISC, MC, V.

Lake Five Resort   Located 3 miles west of West Glacier and approximately 1 mile from U.S. 2 is this cabin-and-campground arrangement, an alternative to potentially crowded park campgrounds. Situated on a 235-acre lake surrounded by private homes and summer cottages, the resort is far from the madding crowd (though still close to the park itself). Seven of the nine cabins are on the lakefront, all of them equipped with bathrooms and showers. The only distraction may be the sound of powerboats.

540 Belton Stage Rd., West Glacier, MT 59936. © **406/387-5601.** www.lakefiveresort.com. 9 cabins, 6 tipi lodges, 45 sites with electricity and water (14 with sewer hookups). $115–$175 cabin; $50–$60 tipi; $40–$45 site. DISC, MC, V.

BACKCOUNTRY CAMPING

If it's the backcountry you're bent on seeing, Glacier has more than 65 backcountry campgrounds. Fortunately, many are at lower elevation, so inexperienced backpackers have an opportunity to take advantage of them. For an accurate depiction of your itinerary's difficulty, and advice on what may be needed, check with rangers in the area you contemplate visiting. The primary source of danger is bears. Backcountry permits are available at ranger stations, and reservations can be made in person up to 24 hours in advance. There are separate fees for advance reservations ($30) and backcountry camping ($5 per person per night). See "Backcountry Permits," in section 1 of this chapter.

6 WHERE TO STAY

Television reception is limited in the Glacier National Park area, so if TV is important to you, check not only that the lodging facility has in-room TVs, but also call and ask what channels they get.

INSIDE THE PARK

With only one exception, Glacier Park, Inc. (GPI), operates the hostelries in Glacier National Park. Lake McDonald Lodge, Glacier Park Lodge, and Many Glacier Hotel are first-tier properties that have been popular destinations since early in the 20th century. Swiftcurrent Motor Inn is typical of the casual motel-style properties at the other end of the spectrum, providing decent but undistinguished accommodations for less money. Although the lodges have a considerable charm, they don't have spas, air-conditioning, or in-room televisions.

Reserve well in advance. August dates may fill before the spring thaw. For more information on the following properties or to make a reservation, contact **Glacier Park, Inc.,** P.O. Box 2025, Columbia Falls, MT 59912 (© **406/892-2525;** fax 406/892-1375; www.glacierparkinc.com). GPI does not accept pets at any of its facilities.

Apgar Village Lodge   A less expensive alternative to the park's GPI-owned properties, the Apgar Village Lodge is located on the south end of Lake McDonald and is one of two lodgings in Apgar Village. There's a wide variety of lodging available here, but the best places—reserve early—are along Lake McDonald Creek and on the banks of the lake. There are nine river cabins, and several motel rooms overlooking the creek. The cabins are

The Other Gateway Communities

If the convenience of staying on Glacier's back porch is important to you, the places listed on the following pages are your best bets. See "Where to Stay" in the Whitefish, Kalispell, and Columbia Falls sections of chapter 7 for listings of places that might be more in line with your needs if the park is merely a 1- or 2-day part of your vacation.

much nicer than they look on the outside. Five large, two-bedroom cabins have been completely remodeled. Most of them have kitchens with stoves and refrigerators, but some of the small cabins tend to be a little dark.

Apgar Village, P.O. Box 410, West Glacier, MT 59936. ✆ **406/888-5484.** Fax 406/888-5273. www.west glacier.com. 48 units, including 28 cabins. $95–$125 motel room double; $105–$275 cabin. AE, DISC, MC, V. Closed Oct to mid-May. *In room:* TV, kitchens, no phone.

Glacier Park Lodge ★★   Just outside the southeast entrance at East Glacier, this is the park's flagship inn, an imposing timbered lodge that stands as a stately tribute to the Great Northern Railroad and its early attempts to lure tourists to Glacier. The immaculate lawn and ever-blooming wildflowers frame the grounds in colors that rival the mountain backdrop. The interior features massive Douglas fir pillars, some 40 inches in diameter and 40 feet tall. In fact, stand in the middle of the lobby and look up—beams carved from massive trees are the structural supports for the entire building. Skylights, wrought-iron chandeliers, and a desk hewn from a 36-inch-diameter log add to the Old West flavor. Rooms are nicely furnished, but showers are elbow-banging small, and sinks are significantly smaller than those found in today's modern hotels and motels. There's an immaculately groomed executive-style 9-hole golf course, and some evenings, members of the Blackfeet tribe recount their history and culture around the fireplace.

East Glacier, MT 59434. ✆ **406/892-2525.** Fax 406/892-1375. www.glacierparkinc.com. 154 units. $140–$199 double; $299–$449 suite. AE, DISC, MC, V. Closed Oct to late May. **Amenities:** Restaurant; lounge; 9-hole golf course; outdoor pool.

Lake McDonald Lodge, Cabins & Inn ★★   The Lake McDonald Lodge feels like a genuine mountain lodge. Although the two-story building doesn't have the same towering ceilings and open spaces as other park hotels, its wood construction lends it a warm, cozy feel. Lodge rooms, located on the second and third floor (there's no elevator), are pleasantly decorated and have a historical feel. Motel units are simply well-maintained motel rooms. The well-preserved cottages are in multi-unit buildings in a wooded area. Situated on the shore of the park's largest lake, the lodge provides a marvelous central base for exploring the western part of the park. The lodge is a center for boating activity; scenic cruises depart daily, and canoe rentals are popular. Common lounging areas are furnished with heavy couches, sofas, and chairs that surround a stone fireplace. The lodge houses a dining room, gift shop, and lounge; a coffee shop, post office, and sundries store are also on the grounds. The entire lodge is nonsmoking.

Glacier National Park, MT 59936. ✆ **406/892-2525.** Fax 406/892-1375. www.glacierparkinc.com. 62 units in lodge and motel, 38 cottage units. $177 lodge room; $137 motel unit; $124–$177 cottage. AE, DISC, MC, V. Closed late Sept to late May. **Amenities:** 2 restaurants; lounge; post office.

Many Glacier Hotel ★★★   Built in 1915 by the Great Northern Railway, this is the largest hotel in the park and our top choice for a place to stay. The alpine-style hotel may be the most photographed building in the park. When you arrive at Many Glacier after driving along the park's interior road from Babb, it comes slowly into view, as picturesque as a Swiss chalet and almost as inviting as the turquoise blue waters of Swiftcurrent Lake. In August, after the huckleberries ripen, you can almost count on seeing grizzly bears on the nearby mountains. Rooms, decorated in keeping with the hotel's historic roots, are in the main lodge overlooking the lobby or in the adjoining annex. We like the lakeside rooms, for their views of Swiftcurrent Lake; the smaller units without a view are less expensive. A dining room, coffee shop, gift shop, and lounge are in the hotel; evening performances begin midsummer.

Glacier National Park, MT 59936. ✆ **406/892-2525.** Fax 406/892-1375. www.glacierparkinc.com. 216 units. $150–$232 double; $289 suite. AE, DISC, MC, V. Closed mid-Sept to mid-June. **Amenities:** Dining room; coffee shop; lounge.

Rising Sun Motor Inn & Cabins   Located 6½ miles from St. Mary, just off Going-to-the-Sun Road, the Rising Sun is a complex made up of a restaurant, a motor inn, cottages, stores, and a service station. The basic rooms are just that—uninspiring motel rooms that are completely adequate for a good night's rest in an excellent location for those who want to explore the eastern side of the park. The cottage rooms (half of a duplex) are more interesting but a bit on the rustic side. All units here are nonsmoking.

Glacier National Park, MT 59936. ✆ **406/892-2525.** Fax 406/892-1375. www.glacierparkinc.com. 63 units. $121–$137 double; $124 cottage. AE, DISC, MC, V. Closed mid-Sept to mid-June. **Amenities:** Restaurant.

Swiftcurrent Motor Inn ★ (Value)   The Swiftcurrent Motor Inn is located about a mile upstream from Many Glacier Hotel, but it attracts an entirely different crowd. The people who stay here are younger, less well-to-do, and primarily active types interested in spending lots of time exploring the backcountry trails. Like Many Glacier, the inn is set against a mountain backdrop in what is considered a hiker's paradise. Motel rooms here have standard motel decor—functional but nothing special; cabins are a bit more interesting, with one or two bedrooms and perhaps a bathroom (communal facilities are nearby). All units are nonsmoking. The Swiftcurrent was built in 1936 as a motor hotel, the first in the park specifically directed at tourists arriving by car rather than by train. There are three circles of cabins and two motel-style units, all set back in the trees. The inn sits in a wildlife migratory path, so you could see bear, elk, and moose in the parking lot. The Italian Gardens Ristorante serves a mean garlic and artichoke-heart pizza. There's also a camping supplies store on the property.

Glacier National Park, MT 59936. ✆ **406/892-2525.** Fax 406/892-1375. www.glacierparkinc.com. 88 units and cabins; some cabins without private bathroom. $121–$137 double in motor inn; $65–$89 double in cabin. AE, DISC, MC, V. Closed mid-Sept to mid-June. **Amenities:** Restaurant. *In room:* No phone.

Village Inn at Apgar   Not to be confused with Apgar Village Lodge (see above), the Village Inn at Apgar is the smallest of the properties GPI operates in Glacier. Located lakeside in Apgar Village, the inn is near the general store, cafes, and boat docks. Like its counterparts throughout the park, the Village Inn is comfortably outfitted with modest furnishings, making it a cozy and convenient place to stay. Rooms spread over two floors of the inn; 12 of them have kitchenettes. Second-level rooms have the same lake views as those downstairs, but they have less people traffic. Though you won't find a dining room on the property, the restaurants of Lake McDonald and Apgar are all close by. Close to the Apgar corral and the docks of Lake McDonald, not to mention a plethora of hiking trails, Apgar Village bustles with activity during the summer. The entire property is nonsmoking.

Glacier National Park, MT 59936. ✆ **406/892-2525.** Fax 406/892-1375. www.glacierparkinc.com. 36 units. $137–$205 double. AE, DISC, MC, V. Closed early Oct to late May. *In room:* Kitchenette, no phone.

IN GATEWAY COMMUNITIES
East Glacier
Backpacker's Inn　Low-cost, low-end sleeping accommodations for those willing to share bathroom facilities are what you get at this dorm-style hostel.

29 Dawson Ave., P.O. Box 94, East Glacier, MT 59434. ✆ **406/226-9392.** 8 beds in 1 cabin, 2 private cabins. $12 per person in single-sex dorms; $30 for 1 person, $40 for 2 people in private cabin. AE, DISC, MC, V. Closed mid-Oct to Apr. *In room:* No phone.

Brownies Grocery and AYH Hostel (Value)　Reservations are recommended at this popular combination grocery store and hostel, which offers comfortable rooms at extremely affordable prices. Dorm and family rooms are on the second floor of a rustic, older log building with several common rooms for guests to share, including a porch, kitchen, bathrooms, and laundry. Family rooms sleep two to six. A bakery and deli (with Internet access) are in the grocery, there's a restaurant next door, and tent sites ($10) are available out back.

1020 Mont. 49, P.O. Box 229, East Glacier, MT 59434. ✆ **406/226-4426.** 10 units, all with shared bathroom, 1 family room, 2 bunk rooms. Hostelling International members $13 bunk, $28–$33 double private room, $40 family room; nonmembers $16 bunk, $31–$34 double private room, $43 family room. DISC, MC, V. Closed Oct to mid-May, depending on the weather. *In room:* No phone.

Jacobson's Cottages　Located in a nicely wooded area, these quaint cottages are small but comfortable. All have cable TV, and one has a kitchen. Entertainment and good food are nearby, and it's a 12-mile drive to the Two Medicine trail. Reservations are recommended.

1204 Mont. 49, P.O. Box 454, East Glacier, MT 59434. ✆ **406/226-4422.** Fax 406/226-4425. 12 cottages. $70–$90 double. AE, DISC, MC, V. Closed Oct–Apr. *In room:* Cable TV, no phone.

Essex
Izaak Walton Inn ★★ (Finds)　Built in 1939 by the Great Northern Railway, this historic Tudor lodge once served as living quarters for rail crews who serviced the railroad. Located just off U.S. 2 on the southern boundary of Glacier Park, the Izaak Walton is extremely popular with tourists from near and far, many of whom choose to travel by Amtrak train, which stops a mere 100 yards from the front door of the lodge. Both lodge rooms and the converted cabooses offer comfortable and attractive lodging, with wood-paneled walls and various Western touches. And who can pass up the opportunity to sleep in a caboose or the new-in-2009 deluxe locomotive? During the winter, this inn is a popular jumping-off spot for cross-country skiers.

290 Izaak Walton Inn Rd., Essex, MT 59916. ✆ **406/888-5700.** Fax 406/888-5200. www.izaakwaltoninn.com. 33 units, 4 caboose cottages, 1 locomotive lodging. $117–$168 double; $235–$255 suite; $230 cabins and caboose cabins; $299 locomotive lodging. 2-night minimum stay in cabins; 3-night minimum stay in cabooses and locomotive. MC, V. **Amenities:** Restaurant; lounge; sauna; Wi-Fi (free). *In room:* Kitchenette, no phone.

Polebridge

North Fork Hostel and Square Peg Ranch   Formerly part of the Quarter Circle MC Ranch and located inside the park, this lodge was moved to its present location near Polebridge in the late 1960s, and it is ideal for the back-to-nature traveler. It sits within a stone's throw of the North Fork of the Flathead River, right across the river from Glacier National Park. Accommodations are ultrarustic, with a mountain-cabin feel—there is no running water, and heat is from an old-fashioned woodstove. There are separate facilities for men and women, as well as couples' accommodations, washrooms with hot showers, and clean outhouses. There are also several small cabins suitable for families. Hostel guests should bring linens or sleeping bags (sheets are available for rent) and flashlights. The Square Peg Ranch offers two rustic log homes, with decor similar to the hostel's, and a few barebones tipis and campsites for $10 a night. The log homes have solar-heated showers, or guests can use the hostel showers. The hostel and cabins have complete kitchen facilities, and the former has a relaxing 6-foot-long claw-foot bathtub. Equipment rentals are also available.

80 Beaver Dr., Polebridge, MT 59928. ✆ 406/888-5241 or 253-4321. www.nfhostel.com. 12 bunks, 2 cabins, 2 log homes. $20 bunk; $45 cabin; $80 log home, with a 2-night minimum. MC, V. Reservations required in winter. **Amenities:** Communal kitchen; Jacuzzi; Wi-Fi (free). *In room:* No phone.

Polebridge Mercantile and Cabins (Value)   There is no running water in most cabins here, let alone bedding—it's bring-your-own sleeping bag or linens at the Merc. The most expensive "luxury" cabin has a bathroom and running water in the kitchenette. Each cabin has a propane cooking stove and lights, and the views out over the west side of Glacier National Park make the price tag a steal, especially if you brought the kids. This may sound a tad too rough and primitive, but Polebridge is actually a happening spot in the summer when all the river rats and seasonal residents converge for good times and tall tales about the rapids they've run and their mountaineering adventures. There is a great bakery here, too.

265 Polebridge Loop, Polebridge, MT 59928. ✆ 406/888-5105. http://polebridge.tripod.com. 4 cabins. $35–$45 cabin. MC, V. **Amenities:** Wi-Fi (free). *In room:* Kitchenette, no phone.

St. Mary

St. Mary Lodge and Resort ★   Situated at the St. Mary end of Going-to-the-Sun Road, this lodge is one of the few area properties that isn't managed by GPI. The main lodge and rooms are standard Montana fare, with tasteful ironwood furnishings. Lodging is in three different areas near the center of the complex; lodge and motel rooms are nicely done motel-style units that may have two single beds or a queen. The nicest units are the cabins, many of which were built in 2009; they boast living areas with dining tables and queen-size beds in a separate sleeping area, and some have kitchenettes. Most rooms have TVs and air-conditioning. The surrounding complex includes a market, several restaurants, and a lounge.

U.S. 89 and Going-to-the-Sun Rd., St. Mary, MT 59417. ✆ 800/778-6279 or 406/732-4431. Fax 406/732-9265. www.stmarylodgeandresort.com. 136 units, including 28 cabins. $159–$199 double; $229–$269 cabin; $229–$329 suite. AE, DISC, MC, V. **Amenities:** 3 restaurants; 2 lounges; Wi-Fi (free). *In room:* A/C, TV, hair dryer, kitchenette.

West Glacier

Belton Chalets and Lodge   A National Historic Landmark, this facility across from the railroad station has been completely restored to the elegance of an early-20th-century hotel. The rooms are small, simple, and old-fashioned. The bathrooms are also small. But the feel of the place is comfortable, and the staff is very friendly. Many of the rooms have private balconies looking out over the rounded timber foothills of Glacier National Park.

12575 U.S. 2, West Glacier, MT 59936. ℂ **888/235-8665** or 406/888-5000. Fax 406/888-5005. www. beltonchalet.com. 25 rooms, 2 cottages. Early June to early Sept $145–$299; early Sept to early June $120–$225. MC, V. **Amenities:** Restaurant (see "Where to Dine," below); lounge. *In room:* No phone.

Glacier Outdoor Center ★ Built in three stages since 1996, the cabins at the Glacier Raft Company's HQ are delightful, functional, and tasteful, sporting trout, moose, and bears on everything from dishes to lampshades. Backing up to the Flathead National Forest just west of the park entrance on U.S. 2, the cabins are well off the road, nestled around a grassy glen with a picnic area, volleyball court, and a trout pond where casting clinics are held in the summer. Each cabin has a fully equipped kitchen, one to three bedrooms, and a private deck with a barbecue; the two-bedroom units can sleep up to 14 people. There is a full rental/retail/guide operation in the main center, and in the winter, 9 miles of cross-country ski trails.

U.S. 2, P.O. Box 210D, West Glacier, MT 59936. ℂ **800/235-6781** or 406/888-5454. www.glacierraftco. com. 9 cabins. $275–$449 cabin. Lower rates in winter. AE, DISC, MC, V. **Amenities:** Wi-Fi (free). *In room:* Kitchen.

Great Northern Chalets ★ This small, rafting-oriented resort near West Glacier offers log chalets that have balconies facing landscaped flower gardens and a pond, with mountain views in the distance. The largest chalet is a beautifully furnished two-story, two-bedroom unit with a full bathroom upstairs and a half-bathroom downstairs. Smaller chalets have one large bedroom upstairs, and a downstairs level with a full-size sleeper sofa and a kitchen with service for six. There's a pond used for fly-fishing instruction.

12127 U.S. 2, West Glacier, MT 59936. ℂ **800/735-7897** or 406/387-5340. Fax 406/387-9007. www. gnwhitewater.com. 5 units. $200–$300 double. DISC, MC, V. Closed late Oct to Mar. **Amenities:** Wi-Fi (free). *In room:* Kitchen.

Vista Motel Perched atop a hill at the west entrance to Glacier National Park, the Vista boasts tremendous views of the mountains. There's a small heated pool, free Wi-Fi in the lobby, and family-size rooms. Accommodations are not luxurious, but the modern motel rooms are clean and comfortable, the customer service is among the best in town, and it's cheaper than the competition.

12340 U.S. 2 E., P.O. Box 90, West Glacier, MT 59936. ℂ **877/888-5311** or 406/888-5311. www.glacier vistamotel.com. 25 units, including 5 cabins. $80–$140 double. AE, DISC, MC, V. **Amenities:** Seasonal outdoor heated pool. *In room:* No phone.

West Glacier Motel ⓥ Value Formerly the River Bend Motel, this property has two locations. Half of the units are in West Glacier on Going-to-the-Sun Road, about 1 mile from the park entrance, and a second set of units is a quarter-mile away on forested grounds on a bluff above the river. This 1950s-style motel has small rooms and smaller bathrooms, but the prices are considerably lower than what you'll find in the park. The Western-style cabins are better suited for families; they come with two queen-size beds and fully equipped kitchens.

200 Going-to-the-Sun Rd., West Glacier, MT 59936. ℂ **406/888-5662.** www.westglacier.com. 32 units, including 5 cabins. Motel $85–$105 double; cabin $145–$225. AE, DISC, MC, V. Closed late Sept to mid-May. *In room:* TV, kitchen in cabins, no phone.

GLACIER NATIONAL PARK

6

WHERE TO DINE

INSIDE THE PARK

Food options inside the park are primarily limited to dining rooms operated by GPI. Breakfasts range from about $5 to $10, lunch entrees are $6 to $13, and most dinner entrees $10 to $30.

You'll find above-average food served at above-average prices in the dining rooms at the major properties. Glacier Park Lodge has the **Great Northern Dining Room,** which has Western decor and a menu of beef, barbecued ribs, fish, and chicken, plus a full breakfast buffet; and the **Empire Bar and Grill,** which offers a bar menu of sandwiches and appetizers. At Lake McDonald Lodge you'll find **Russell's Fireside Dining Room** ★, which has a hunting lodge atmosphere with rough-hewn beams and hunting trophies, and specializes in American standards, including beef tenderloin, roast duckling, seared mountain trout, roast turkey, Alaskan salmon, and steaks; there's also a full breakfast buffet. Also at Lake McDonald Lodge is **Lucke's Lounge,** which serves a bar menu of sandwiches and appetizers, and **Jammer Joe's,** a pizzeria/family restaurant. Many Glacier Hotel has the **Ptarmigan Dining Room,** which has Swiss decor in keeping with the lodge, emphasizing spectacular mountain views, and serves Continental and Swiss cuisine plus a breakfast buffet. Many Glacier also has the **Swiss Room and Interlaken Lounge,** with a bar menu of sandwiches and appetizers, and **Heidi's,** a fast-food counter known for its huckleberry frozen yogurt. The dining rooms open with the park and close sometime in September, depending on the facility. At each dining room, breakfast is served from 6:30 to 9:30am, lunch from 11:30am to 1:30pm, and dinner from 5:30 to 9:30pm. Coffee and snack shops open either at 7 or 8am and close at 9pm. All of the above restaurants are nonsmoking.

The alternatives include second-tier restaurants close to the hotels, most of which are comparable to chain restaurants in both quality and price. The **Two Dog Flats Grill** at the Rising Sun Motor Inn serves "hearty American fare"; the Swiftcurrent Motor Inn restaurant is the **Italian Gardens Ristorante.** Lunch and dinner feature combinations of salads, sandwiches, pasta dishes, and create-your-own pizzas. At Apgar you'll find a deli and a family dining arrangement.

IN GATEWAY COMMUNITIES
East Glacier & Vicinity

Serrano's MEXICAN   A pretty good Mexican joint, Serrano's is one of the only eateries in town, so don't be surprised if you encounter masses of people in the dining room and on the outdoor deck at the height of summer. You can expect hearty portions of Mexican food, an ample selection of imported beers and microbrews, and a full bar featuring margaritas.

29 Dawson Ave., East Glacier. ⓒ **406/226-9392.** Main courses $9–$18. AE, DISC, MC, V. Daily 5–10pm (until 9pm in early May and late Sept). Closed Oct–Apr.

Two Sisters Cafe ★ Ⓕⁱⁿᵈˢ AMERICAN   This long-standing place serves perhaps the very best pie in the area, with a fun atmosphere and a huge license-plate collection to boot. Susan and Beth Higgins, the eponymous sisters who run the place, specialize in hearty American fare, with a menu that includes dishes like chili cheeseburgers, hand-battered chicken-fried steak, and big brownie sundaes. As for libations, there are margaritas, microbrews, and a non-alcoholic "lemonade of the day."

4 miles north of St. Mary on U.S. 89, Babb. ✆ **406/732-5535.** MC, V. Daily 11am–10pm. Closed Oct–May.

West Glacier

The Belton Tap Room and Grille ★ AMERICAN This restaurant, located in restored buildings that were once the Great Northern Railway Chalet, serves respectable food geared toward American tastes—steaks, buffalo, chicken, ribs, trout, and salmon, as well as some vegetarian selections. A large stone fireplace dominates the taproom, which serves several brands of locally brewed beer.

12575 U.S. 2, West Glacier. ✆ **406/888-5000.** Main courses $9–$30. MC, V. Daily 5–10pm. Bar 3pm–midnight, with a limited menu.

Glacier Highland Restaurant AMERICAN This may be the spot to satisfy your sweet tooth; a baker is on hand, so the pies are well worth the stop, and the cinnamon rolls are immense. The Highland Burger is, by any standard, a great hunk of beef, and fresh trout is a dinner specialty.

U.S. 2, West Glacier. ✆ **406/888-5427.** Breakfast items $4–$9; main courses $5–$10 lunch, $6–$20 dinner. AE, DISC, MC, V. Daily 7am–10pm, with some seasonal variations. Closed mid-Nov to Mar.

ESSENTIAL SERVICES

EAST GLACIER East Glacier has a gas station, post office, several gift shops, a small market with a limited supply of fresh meats and produce as well as beer and wine, and a modest supply of fishing and camping accessories.

WEST GLACIER A gas station, general store, Laundromat, photo shop, rafting companies, post office, gift shop, bar, and restaurant are located just outside the West Glacier entrance to the park.

ST. MARY The **grocery store** (✆ **406/732-4431**) at St. Mary Lodge and Resort will never be confused with a metropolitan-area supermarket, but it's the closest thing you'll find in any of the park's gateway cities except Kalispell, which is 80 miles due west. Fresh produce, canned goods, and beverages, including beer and wine, are found here, but you can expect to pay tourist-town prices. There's also a post office.

8 A SIDE TRIP TO BROWNING & THE BLACKFEET INDIAN RESERVATION

127 miles NW of Great Falls; 69 miles E of West Glacier; 160 miles W of Havre

According to American Indian legend, the Blackfeet were named by white settlers because their moccasins were blackened with soot from fires or paint. Siksika, the "Black-footed People," became their tribal name, and they eventually grew into four bands: the Blackfeet in Montana and the Kaina, Pikuni, and Siksika of Alberta, Canada. Today the Blackfeet maintain a humble existence near the beautiful lands that were once their own, with about half of the tribal enrollment of 14,000 living on the reservation near the east side of Glacier National Park. **Browning,** the tribal headquarters, is a gateway town to Glacier, but many visitors pass through quickly in anticipation of the end of the prairies and the beginning of the mountains.

ESSENTIALS

GETTING THERE To reach Browning, follow U.S. 89 south from St. Mary for 32 miles, or take U.S. 2 east from East Glacier for 12 miles. Browning is about 69 miles east of West Glacier on U.S. 2.

SPECIAL EVENTS Browning holds **North American Indian Days** in mid-July. This 4-day celebration draws visitors from across the region to view American Indian dance competitions, games, and sporting events at the Blackfeet Tribal Campgrounds, which are adjacent to the **Museum of the Plains Indian.**

WHAT TO SEE & DO

The **Museum of the Plains Indian,** U.S. 2 and 89 (© **406/338-2230**), is a fairly modest effort, but it has one of the best collections of Indian garb in the West. It also features some very good art by local Blackfeet artists. Admission is free.

A large and eclectic art collection is on display in the **Blackfeet Heritage Center and Art Gallery** (© **406/338-5661**), at the intersection of U.S. highways 2 and 89. There are historic artifacts alongside contemporary works, as well as a nicely stocked gift shop. The place is open daily May through September and weekdays year-round.

9 A SIDE TRIP TO WATERTON LAKES NATIONAL PARK

190 miles NW of Great Falls; 342 miles S of Edmonton, Alberta, Canada

Waterton Lakes National Park and Glacier are in many ways one park separated by an international boundary. The terrain is much the same. But Canada is a foreign country, and you'll be pleasantly reminded of that in a visit to Waterton, where you can still get British high tea and a biscuit, if you're so inclined.

Waterton is where the Canadian mountains meet the vast rolling prairies, so there's an incredible variety of flowers and animals here. As you travel along the high ridge you'll see meadows and boggy areas that are ideal habitats for moose; later, you'll find yourself surrounded by lakes, as the Canadian Rockies fill the horizon. The area is also a haven for elk, mule deer, and bighorn sheep, and both grizzly and black bears are found in the park.

Compared with its counterparts in the Lower 48, Waterton is a tiny park; the total size is only 203 square miles. However, the park has great historical significance: based on more than 200 identified archaeological sites, historians think that aborigines first populated the area 11,000 years ago.

The parks have been designated the Waterton/Glacier International Peace Park to commemorate the "long history of peace and friendship" between the United States and Canada. Waterton Lakes was made a national park in 1895, with Glacier being designated 15 years later. The joint international designation came in 1932, and in 1995, the peace park became a World Heritage Site.

ESSENTIALS

American and Canadian money is freely accepted in both Glacier and Waterton. Stores provide change in the local currency after adjusting for the current exchange-rate differential.

GETTING THERE From the eastern entrance of Glacier National Park at St. Mary, drive north through Babb until you reach the intersection of Mont. 17—it's very well marked. Head northwest to the Canadian border, where Mont. 17 becomes Alberta 6 (remember that with new regulations, even U.S. citizens need passports). Head down into the valley until you reach the park entrance on your left.

FEES & BACKCOUNTRY PERMITS Park entrance costs about C$8 per person, with a maximum of about C$20 per vehicle. Day hiking does not require a permit, but backcountry overnight trips do; permits cost about C$10 per person per day. Permits may be obtained at the visitor center up to 24 hours in advance of your trip, or they may be reserved by calling © **403/859-2224.**

VISITOR INFORMATION The Visitor Reception Centre is just inside the park, on the same road you used coming in (© **403/859-2224**). Online, visit **www.parkscanada. gc.ca/waterton.**

EXPLORING THE PARK

Unlike most "park villages," Waterton Village actually is a village. As you drive along the perimeter of the lake headed for Waterton Village, you'll pass three large lakes, the habitat of bald eagles that often perch atop the snags of dead trees. The park bears a striking resemblance to Grand Teton National Park in Wyoming in that its attractions spread across a narrow valley floor. But the valley is narrower and three-fourths of it is surrounded by peaks, so the overall effect is cozier, but equally dramatic.

By most standards, it's also windier here—though locals say that they don't acknowledge the wind unless there are whitecaps in the restroom toilets at the Prince of Wales Hotel (see "Where to Stay," below). The Prince of Wales actually does sway noticeably in a high wind, although signs assure you that it is not a concern.

Hiking, biking, and boating on the lake are the most popular pastimes. Most of the 120 miles of trails are easily accessible from town. They range in difficulty from short strolls to steep treks for overnight backcountry enthusiasts.

BIKING All of Waterton's roads are open for bicycling, but because they are shared with automobiles, they are narrow and potentially hazardous. Waterton allows biking on some trails. Check at the visitor center to find out which ones.

HIKING The first thing a lot of people do at Waterton Park is hike the **Bear's Hump Trail** ★★. It is the park's most popular path—but not necessarily the easiest. The trail starts at the visitor center. Only about .75 mile long, it gains 700 feet in elevation from bottom to top. You'll be rewarded with a panoramic view of the park. The hike is called Bear's Hump because of the shape of the mountain, not because you're likely to run into bears—though, of course, you never know.

Right at the edge of Waterton Park, at **Cameron Falls,** Cambrian rocks are exposed from the period 600 million years ago when life exploded on earth. This is the oldest exposed formation in the Rocky Mountains. The falls are spectacular, too.

The 11-mile **Crypt Lake Trail** ★★★ has been rated as one of Canada's best hikes—except for those prone to seasickness, since the trail head is reached by taking a 2-mile boat ride across Upper Waterton Lake. Contact **Waterton Shoreline Cruise Company** (© **403/859-2362;** www.watertoncruise.com) for details regarding the boat shuttle. After that, the trail leads past Hellroaring Falls, Twin Falls, and Burnt Rock Falls before reaching Crypt Falls and a passage through a 60-foot rock tunnel. The elevation gain is 2,300 feet, but the hike is doable in 3 hours, one-way.

A second extended tour starts at the marina and heads south across the international boundary to **Goat Haunt,** Montana, an especially popular trip because of the sightings of bald eagles, bears, bighorn sheep, deer, and moose, as well as numerous unusual geologic formations.

The **International Peace Park Hike** is a free guided trip held on Saturdays from the end of June to the end of August. Participants meet at the Bertha trail head at 10am and spend the day on an 8.5-mile trail that follows Upper Waterton Lake. At the end of the trail, hikers return via boat to the main dock.

There is a wonderful nature trail in **Red Rock Canyon,** a short, easy trek through time—.7 mile, 65 million years—to when the shallow sea that once lay here exposed and then oxidized mudstone rock to the color of a merlot. The rocks are banded with white slashes—portions that didn't oxidize because they were not exposed to the air from the receding and returning sea. The Red Rock Canyon Road is also an area of fairly frequent bear sightings.

WHERE TO STAY

Although the Prince of Wales Hotel is clearly the flagship in these woods, a worthwhile alternative is the **Waterton Lakes Lodge Resort** (🔿 **888/985-6343** or 403/859-2150; www.watertonlakeslodge.com), with a great location in the heart of Waterton Village. The lodge offers lake and mountain views, and some rooms have fireplaces, whirlpool tubs, and kitchenettes. Other facilities include a health-center spa and indoor pool. Basic lodge doubles start at C$185 in summer.

The Prince of Wales Hotel   The Prince of Wales compares with the finest park hostelries in Montana and Wyoming. Built in 1927 by the Great Northern Railway, the hotel boasts soaring roofs, gables, and balconies that convey the appearance of a giant alpine chalet. Rooms, though small, have aged well, with dark-stained, high-paneled wainscoting and heavily upholstered chairs. Bathrooms have European-style tubs with wraparound curtains; one look at the washbasins, and you'd surmise that guests were Lilliputian size when the hotel was first constructed.

The lobby, like those in many of the old railroad hotels, is wood, wood, and more wood—in this case accented by tufted furniture and carpeting. Two-story-high windows overlook the lake and village, only minutes away by footpath. If you don't spend the night at the Prince of Wales, at least stop in for a traditional British high tea, served daily from 2 to 5pm.

Waterton Lakes National Park, AB T0K 2M0. 🔿 **403/859-2231** or 406/892-2525 in winter. Fax 403/859-2630. www.glacierparkinc.com. 87 units. C$235–C$278 double; C$857 suite. AE, DISC, MC, V. Closed mid-Sept to mid-June. **Amenities:** Restaurant; lounge; gift shop.

Camping

At the west end of the village is **Townsite Campground ★**, a Parks Canada–operated facility with 235 sites that's an especially popular jumping-off spot for campers headed into the park's backcountry. Prices range from roughly C$16 to C$38; half of the sites have electricity and sewage disposal. Also available on the premises are kitchen shelters, washrooms, and shower facilities. The site perches right on the lake, so views are excellent and trails await evening strollers.

There are also a number of designated **wilderness campgrounds** with dry toilets and surface water, some of which have shelters.

All of the village's restaurants and retail outlets are within a 4-block area around Waterton Avenue (which the locals call Main St.). So despite the fact that many buildings aren't numbered, you'll have no problem finding places to eat or shop.

The **Royal Stewart Dining Room** in the lobby of the Prince of Wales Hotel (*C* **403/859-2231**) serves Continental and English fare at breakfast, lunch, and dinner. At Waterton Lakes Lodge Resort, the casual **Vimy's Ridge Lounge and Grill** (*C* **403/859-2150**) serves three meals a day in a room with spectacular views.

7

Missoula, the Flathead & the Northwest Corner

The northwest corner of Montana is the mythological Montana, the one you probably envisioned when you set out for the Big Sky. This is the country of snow-capped mountains and dense forests and crystal lakes. It's a land of barely explored wilderness and steel-toed lumberjacks, a land peopled with the ghosts of trappers, mountain men, and Blackfeet Indians.

It's also a booming recreational area. The geographic center of the region is Flathead Lake, which boasts the somewhat cumbersome distinction of being the "largest natural freshwater lake west of the Mississippi." The lake was gouged during the last glaciation about 12,000 years ago. It is very deep in places—386 feet out toward the middle—with 128 miles of shoreline, much of it taken up by vacation homes. Anglers will appreciate the fact that trophy trout, salmon, perch, and whitefish populate the lake's depths. And vacationers seeking a quiet getaway will be

pleased by the fact that despite the busy summer season on Flathead Lake, it doesn't feel crowded, and there are plenty of places to get out of earshot of everyone.

Besides the lake, the area from White-fish to Missoula offers plenty of opportunities for hiking, biking, fishing, boating, golf, parasailing, and nearly every other outdoor activity known to man. In winter, you'll find fine alpine ski areas, excellent cross-country skiing, snowshoeing, snow-boarding, and inner-tubing.

Also here is the nation's largest wilderness complex, the **Bob Marshall–Great Bear–Scapegoat Wilderness,** which includes some of the most rugged, beautiful, untrammeled country in the Lower 48 states. The magnificent Chinese Wall, a vast monolith on the spine of the Continental Divide, is a symbol of wilderness in Montana, as is the grizzly bear, the king of the wild even when humans venture in for a visit.

1 SCENIC DRIVES

Two major cross-country routes intersect in the northwest corner: U.S. 93, which runs north to south, and U.S. 2, which runs east to west. Mont. 200, one of the state's most scenic drives, bisects the lower section of the region.

U.S. 93 heads north from the Bitterroot Valley south of Missoula to the Canadian border. Much of the road slices beneath jagged peaks poking at the skyline. It's especially pretty early in the morning or early evening, when the light softens the rugged landscape. North of Missoula in the Flathead Valley near St. Ignatius and the spectacular Mission Mountains, the valley opens. At **Polson,** you've reached the southern portion of Flathead Lake, which stretches 28 miles to the north. In some places it is 8 miles wide. North of the lake are Kalispell, Whitefish, and Columbia Falls, gateway towns to nearby Glacier National Park. The last oasis in Montana is the border village of Eureka, just minutes south of the Canadian border.

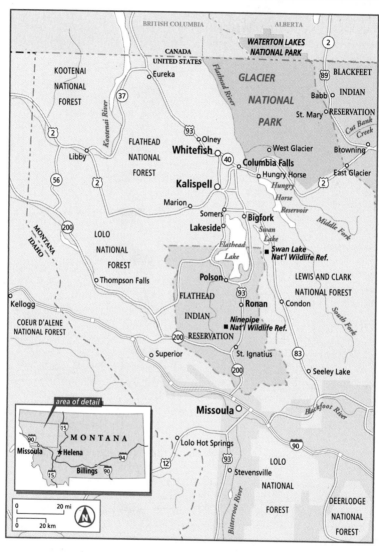

2 MISSOULA ★

200 miles E of Spokane, Washington; 213 miles NE of Lewiston, Idaho; 339 miles W of Billings; 115 miles NW of Helena; 115 miles S of Kalispell

Missoula has been growing by leaps and bounds, and the reason is clear: The city is in a beautiful valley along the Clark Fork River, with a relatively mild climate more influenced by the Pacific Northwest than by the high Rockies. One could say the same about the local culture.

Because this is the home of the University of Montana, the crowds in Missoula's vibrant downtown are usually either young and Birkenstocked or grizzled and cowboy-booted. Also in the mix are many prominent Western writers who live in or near the city; the result is an intellectual and cultural outpost.

The great outdoors—be it fly-fishing on Rock Creek, skiing at Snowbowl, hiking in the Selway-Bitterroot or the Rattlesnake Wilderness, or cross-country skiing on Lolo Pass—is probably what most attracts these types to the area. The outdoors figures heavily in area politics as well, with a strong pro-environment sentiment among the populace.

ESSENTIALS

GETTING THERE **Alaska/Horizon** (© 800/547-9308), **Allegiant** (© 702/505-8888), **Delta** (© 800/221-1212), **Northwest** (© 800/225-2525), and **United** (© 800/864-8331) all have flights into the **Missoula International Airport** (© 406/728-4381; www.flymissoula.com), northwest of downtown off U.S. 93.

I-90 leads into Missoula from the west (Washington State and Idaho) and the east (Billings and Bozeman). From Salt Lake City, I-15 leads up through Idaho and intersects with I-90 at Butte. For information on **road conditions** in Missoula, call © 406/728-8553 or **511** for road conditions statewide. Avalanche information can be obtained by calling the **West Central Montana Avalanche Center** (© 800/281-1030 or 406/549-4488).

The **bus terminal,** 1660 W. Broadway (© 406/549-2339), is served by **Greyhound** (© 800/231-2222; www.greyhound.com) for national travel and **Rimrock Stages** (© 800/255-7655; www.rimrocktrailways.com), which serves intrastate Montana travelers with daily transportation from Missoula to Whitefish.

VISITOR INFORMATION The **Missoula Convention and Visitors Bureau,** 1121 E. Broadway, Ste. 103, Missoula, MT 59802 (© 800/526-3465 or 406/532-3250; www.missoulacvb.org), has brochures, city maps, and area maps for outdoor activities, shopping, dining, and tours for most of northwestern Montana.

GETTING AROUND Several rental-car agencies, including **Avis** (© 800/230-4898), **Budget** (© 800/527-0700), **Hertz** (© 800/654-3131), and **National** (© 800/227-7368), maintain counters at the airport; or try **Rent-a-Wreck,** 1905 W. Broadway (© 877/877-0700). **Airport Shuttler** (© 406/543-9416) operates a transit service to and from the airport.

Missoula's city bus line is **Mountain Line Transit** (© 406/721-3333; www.mountainline.com). It doesn't run late at night or on Sundays.

Taxi service is available 24 hours a day through **Yellow Cab** (© 406/543-6644) and **Green Taxi** (© 406/728-8294).

ORIENTATION Missoula's layout is a tad confusing, so make sure you have a good city map. Remember that downtown is bisected by the Clark Fork River, and become acquainted with the locations of the three bridges, which provide access to the university and points south. Trails alongside the river are suitable for strolling, though you'll share them with runners and bikers.

SPECIAL EVENTS The **International Wildlife Film Festival** ★, founded by internationally known bear biologist Dr. Charles Jonkel in 1977, recognizes scientific accuracy, artistic appeal, and technical excellence through a juried competition. Highlights of the 1-week festival, held annually in early to mid-May, include four daily screenings,

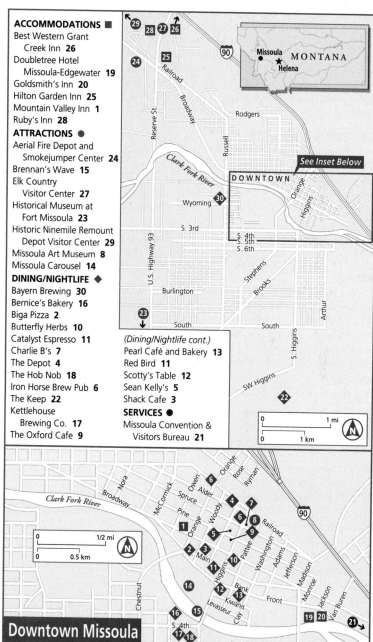

ACCOMMODATIONS ■
Best Western Grant
   Creek Inn **26**
Doubletree Hotel
   Missoula-Edgewater **19**
Goldsmith's Inn **20**
Hilton Garden Inn **25**
Mountain Valley Inn **1**
Ruby's Inn **28**

ATTRACTIONS ●
Aerial Fire Depot and
   Smokejumper Center **24**
Brennan's Wave **15**
Elk Country
   Visitor Center **27**
Historical Museum at
   Fort Missoula **23**
Historic Ninemile Remount
   Depot Visitor Center **29**
Missoula Art Museum **8**
Missoula Carousel **14**

DINING/NIGHTLIFE ◆
Bayern Brewing **30**
Bernice's Bakery **16**
Biga Pizza **2**
Butterfly Herbs **10**
Catalyst Espresso **11**
Charlie B's **7**
The Depot **4**
The Hob Nob **18**
Iron Horse Brew Pub **6**
The Keep **22**
Kettlehouse
   Brewing Co. **17**
The Oxford Cafe **9**

(Dining/Nightlife cont.)
Pearl Café and Bakery **13**
Red Bird **11**
Scotty's Table **12**
Sean Kelly's **5**
Shack Cafe **3**

SERVICES ●
Missoula Convention &
   Visitors Bureau **21**

MONTANA

Missoula
Helena

See Inset Below

DOWNTOWN

0   1 mi
0   1 km

N

(Downtown inset)

Clark Fork River

Broadway

0   1/2 mi
0   0.5 km

N

90

Downtown Missoula

workshops and panel discussions, a wildlife photo contest, and various wildlife art displays. Contact the festival (© 406/728-9380; www.wildlifefilms.org) for details. **Out to Lunch at Caras Park** and **Downtown ToNight** (© 406/543-4238; www.missoula downtown.com) are popular summer series featuring live entertainment and numerous food vendors from 11am to 1:30pm every Wednesday and Thursday from 5:30 to 8:30pm June through August. The **Farmers' Market** ★ (© 406/777-2636) at Market Plaza (located at the north end of Higgins Ave., where it meets with Railroad and Alder sts.) is the place to be during summer for organic vegetables, fresh flowers, and assorted culinary pleasures. It's open Saturday from 9am to noon May through late October, as well as Tuesday from 5:45 to 7:15pm in July and August.

GETTING OUTSIDE

When you look up in Missoula, it is hard to miss the giant "M" on Mount Sentinel. The trail to the M is a popular hike, a steep zigzag that rewards the determined hiker with panoramic views of the valley. Mount Sentinel is also a favorite spot for hang gliding. You can obtain information and maps of recreation areas before leaving town at the **Bureau of Land Management,** 3255 Fort Missoula Rd. (© 406/329-3914).

ORGANIZED ADVENTURES   **Lewis & Clark Trail Adventures,** 912 E. Broadway (P.O. Box 9051), Missoula, MT 59807 (© 800/366-6246 or 406/728-7609; www. trailadventures.com), offers guided hiking, biking, and paddling trips in the area.

Biking

The best place to cycle is at the **Rattlesnake National Recreation Area and Wilderness** (© 406/329-3750). To get there, drive northeast on Van Buren to Rattlesnake Drive. Be sure to consult one of the free trail maps available at bike shops before setting out. Bikes are prohibited in the wilderness portion of the recreation area. **Montana Snowbowl** ski area also has trails for the serious mountain biker. For information, contact © 406/549-9777. To rent bikes, contact **Missoula Bicycle Works,** 708 S. Higgins Ave. (© 406/721-6525; www.missoulabicycleworks.com). Rentals run $18 for a half-day and $25 for a full day.

Cross-Country Skiing

There are hundreds of square miles of cross-country ski terrain within 30 miles of Missoula. In nearby Garnet, the absence of gold turned a once-prosperous mining town into a ghost town that's now become a magnet for cross-country skiers at the **Garnet Resource Area.** With more than 50 miles of trails and a remote location, this area offers a delightful backcountry experience. And while out there, many like to stay in Garnet's **old-fashioned miner's cabins** (see "Where to Stay," below). Getting there can be an arduous task in winter. Take I-90 east to Mont. 200, turn east for 5 miles to Garnet Range Road, and then go south along the Forest Service Road.

   There are 150 miles of marked cross-country ski trails scattered through the **Lolo National Forest** (© 406/329-3750). Popular areas include **Pattee Canyon, Seeley Lake,** and **Lolo Pass.** The Pattee Canyon Complex, 5½ miles south of town, offers several groomed trails that range in difficulty from a short 1-mile trail to a longer 3.4-mile trail, but the snow level varies from year to year. At Lolo Pass, there's a National Forest information center at the top of the pass with maps and permit sales. To get there, take U.S. 12 west from Lolo for about 30 miles.

   Twenty miles from Missoula, the **Lubrecht Experimental Forest** (© 406/244-5524), operated by the University of Montana's forestry department, has six ski trails and numerous logging roads. To reach Lubrecht from Missoula, take I-90 east to exit 109 and follow Mont. 200 northeast to Greenough. Turn right just past the post office, and less than a half-mile down that road is the Lubrecht camp.

Downhill Skiing

Montana Snowbowl   Snowbowl has a vertical drop of 2,600 feet, much of it in the form of steep runs suitable only for experts. There's not a lot of terrain for beginners here, but the hard-core skier will have a ball. Eighty percent of the runs are for intermediate, expert, and advanced skiers, with another 500 acres for the extreme skier. Snowbowl has reasonably priced rooms for rent during the winter, with and without private bathrooms. Rentals and instruction are also available.

Snowbowl Rd., P.O. Box 8107, Missoula, MT 59807. (C) **406/549-9777.** www.montanasnowbowl.com. Full-day lift tickets $39 adults, $36 students and seniors, $18 children 6–12, free for children 5 and under; half-day rates available. Late Nov to early Apr 9:30am–4pm (Fri–Sun only in off-peak). From I-90, exit at Reserve St.; head north on Grant Creek Rd., and turn left on Snowbowl Rd.

Fishing

The **Clark Fork River,** which runs through town, has had its share of environmental problems and concerns over the years. A cleanup effort that began in the 1970s has helped, but it's never going to be an angler's first choice. The **Bitterroot River** and **Rock Creek** are better bets. Though Rock Creek has been known as a blue-ribbon trout stream, the Bitterroot is also a good spot for those who want to pull in a trout or two, and it has multiple public-access areas near the highway. The Missoula office for the **Montana Department of Fish, Wildlife, and Parks** ((C) **406/542-5500**) will direct you to some fine fishing spots, including Siria, a more remote site 30 miles up Rock Creek Road.

Whether guiding you along Missoula's Clark Fork River or helping you pick out the perfect fly, **Grizzly Hackle,** 215 W. Front St. ((C) **800/297-8996** or 406/721-8996; www.grizzlyhackle.com), can help you with your fly-fishing vacation. Seasoned guides lead you to fishing holes along the Lower Clark Fork, the Bitterroot, the Missouri, and the Blackfoot rivers, as well as Rock Creek, in search of native rainbow, Westslope cutthroat, and brown trout. The company also runs the **Lodge on Butler Creek,** not far from Missoula, where rooms rent for $165 per night for two, and other overnight accommodations. Grizzly Hackle advocates barbless hooks and catch-and-release fishing, donating heavily to river restoration projects and angling-oriented charities.

Golf

Farther north, there are a number of great golf courses, but in Missoula the golf is only average. The 9-hole **Highlands Golf Club,** located at 102 Ben Hogan Dr. ((C) **406/721-4653**), is a short, hilly, public course with wickedly gyrating greens. A round runs $12 to $15. There's also the par-29 executive **Linda Vista,** 4915 Miller Creek Rd. ((C) **406/251-3655**), with greens fees of $10, and another 9-hole course on the **University of Montana** campus ((C) **406/728-8629**), with greens fees of $13 to $15. The **Larchmont Golf Course,** 3200 Old Fort Rd. ((C) **406/721-4416**), an 18-hole public course within city limits, is a long, fairly tough track that the big hitters will like. Greens fees are $26 to $28 for 18 holes. A more expensive 18-hole option is the **Ranch Club,** 8501 Ranch Club Rd. ((C) **406/532-1018;** www.ranchclub.com), with peak summer greens fees of $95 to walk and $115 to ride. Nonmember access is limited to six rounds a year.

Hiking

Named for a late local newspaper columnist, the **Kim Williams Trail** follows either side of the Clark Fork River for 2.5 miles through downtown. Just north of town is the **Rattlesnake National Recreational Area and Wilderness** (© 406/329-3750). To get there, drive northeast on Van Buren to Rattlesnake Drive. The Rattlesnake covers 60,000 acres, 33,000 of which are congressionally designated wilderness. Camping is prohibited within 3 miles of the road because of the heavy use the area receives. Drive northeast on Van Buren to Rattlesnake Drive.

There are two state parks in the Missoula area: **Beavertail Hill** (© 406/542-5500; fwp.mt.gov/parks) is located on the Clark Fork and is open May through September, with excellent river access and shady cottonwood trees lining the riverbanks. There is a day-use charge of $5 for nonresidents; campers pay $15 per night. **Council Grove State Park** (© 406/542-5500; fwp.mt.gov/parks) is where the Hellgate Treaty establishing the Flathead Indian Reservation was signed. Open for day use only (free), the park has interpretive displays and picnic facilities. Take the Reserve Street exit from I-90 and drive 2 miles south, then 10 miles west on Mullan Road.

Southwest of town, the **Lolo Trail** is an interesting hike. This trail was created by the constant use of the Nez Perce, Salish, and other tribes that lived in the area and moved back and forth across Lolo Pass.

You can explore a half-mile section of the original trail at Howard Creek, 18 miles west of the intersection of U.S. 93 and U.S. 12 in Lolo. Or hike a 5-mile section of the trail from Lee Creek Campground to the Idaho border. The campground is about 26 miles west of the highway intersection in Lolo.

Snowmobiling

The areas around Missoula have more than 500 miles of groomed snowmobile trails in a number of popular areas. In Lolo Pass, for instance, there are 150 miles of groomed trails connecting the Lolo and Clearwater national forests. There are four other nearby designated areas—Superior, Skalkaho Pass, Seeley Lake, and Lincoln—each with approximately as many miles of groomed trails. For a guide to area snowmobiling, contact the **Missoula Convention and Visitors Bureau** (© 800/526-3465).

White-Water Rafting & Kayaking

Lewis & Clark Trail Adventures, 912 E. Broadway (© 800/366-6246 or 406/728-7609; www.trailadventures.com), offers no-nonsense white-water rafting on the Salmon River during excursions through the heart of the Frank Church No Return Wilderness. The main trip is on a 120-mile stretch of Idaho white water, where you can expect to see mountain goats, bighorn sheep, elk, deer, eagles, and otters. Other excursions take in the Lochsa River, the Alberton Gorge of the Clark Fork River, and the Missouri River (through areas in which Lewis and Clark made their famous trek). Trips run May through September. Hiking, biking, and historical tours on the Lolo Trail are also available. Six-day trips on the Salmon River start at $995 per adult. One-day trips on the Lochsa or through Alberton Gorge range from $75 to $115 per adult. Guided hikes on the Lolo Trail are between $139 (1 day) and $675 (3 days) per adult. Children's rates are about 30% lower.

The Clark Fork, Bitterroot, and Blackfoot rivers are the settings for white-water adventure with **10,000 Waves** ★ (© 800/537-8315 or 406/549-6670; www.10000-waves.com). Half-day and full-day floats feature thrilling white-water rapids along high mountain rivers and through steep, narrow canyons. Half-day trips are $70 per person;

full-day floats cost $85 (includes a great lunch), and dinner trips run $87. The company uses self-bailing rafts, which enable the paddler to focus on the sport, not survival. If you want an even bigger thrill, consider a guided kayak trip with instruction. Rates are $159 for a full day, or $243 for a 2-day beginner clinic.

Montana River Guides (© 800/381-7238 or 406/273-4718; www.montanariver guides.com) is another good option, offering paddling instruction as well as rafting expeditions. Half-day trips run $45; full-day and dinner trips are $75. The most gonzo approach is a guided "riverboarding" trip—akin to sledding on the river on a board designed for the purpose—for $85 to $129.

In town, **Brennan's Wave** is a white-water kayaking park on the Clark Fork in the shadows of the Higgins Avenue Bridge. Named for late local kayaking legend Brennan Guth, the park is open to the public and busy with paddlers nearly every day of the year.

SEEING THE SIGHTS

You can organize your own tour and check out the architectural highlights of the "Garden City" by contacting the **Missoula Historic Preservation Office** (© 406/258-4706) or downloading a map from **www.historicmissoula.org**.

Aerial Fire Depot and Smokejumper Center   This is the nation's largest training base for smokejumpers—firefighters who parachute into remote areas of national forests to combat wildfires. This facility offers a fascinating look at the life of a Western firefighter, beginning with the days when pack animals were an important part of backcountry firefighting, through the 1939 advent of the smokejumper, up to today's heroes. The Aerial Fire Depot Visitor Center features murals, educational videos, a reconstructed lookout tower, and exhibits of firefighters that illustrate the lives and history of these rescue workers. The center also talks about the important role of fire in forest ecology.

5765 W. Broadway, adjacent to Missoula International Airport. © 406/329-4934. Free admission. Daily 8:30am–5pm. Tours available on the hour beginning at 10am; no tours noon–2pm; last tour begins 4pm. Closed Labor Day to Memorial Day weekend.

Elk Country Visitor Center ★ (Kids)   Though a relatively young conservation organization, the Rocky Mountain Elk Foundation has made a large contribution to conserving elk and elk habitat. Its visitor center does that contribution proud: Encompassing ecology, biology, game management, and hunting, the center does a nice job telling the story of elk in North America, from their peak population of 10 million to their overhunted low point of just 90,000 (ca. 1900), to their rebound to about a million head today. The exhibits are interactive, covering everything from the unusual elk bugle to conservation legends, and many of them are geared toward children. Many visitors come simply to see the world-record antler racks on display here—one of them measures 448 inches in all, adding up every last fork and tine. There is a short nature trail on the property. Allow 1 hour.

5705 Grant Creek Rd. (just north of I-90, exit 101). © 406/523-4545. www.rmef.org. Free admission. May–Dec Mon–Fri 8am–6pm, Sat–Sun 9am–6pm; Jan–Apr Mon–Fri 8am–5pm, Sat 10am–5pm.

Historical Museum at Fort Missoula   Fort Missoula, one of Montana's first military posts, was established in 1877, the year Chief Joseph of the Nez Perce led his tribe toward Canada. Now the home of the National Guard and Reserve units, Fort Missoula has as its main attraction this museum, which houses displays that detail the fort's history and rotating exhibits in its indoor galleries. Outside, the campus is also home to several historic buildings moved to the site, including a one-room schoolhouse, a homestead cabin, an 1863 church, and other buildings.

Building 322, Fort Missoula Rd., entrance on South Ave. ✆ **406/728-3476.** www.fortmissoulamuseum. org. $3 adults, $2 seniors, $1 students, free for children 5 and under; $10 maximum per family. Memorial Day to Labor Day Mon–Sat 10am–5pm, Sun noon–5pm; rest of year Tues–Sun noon–5pm.

Historic Ninemile Remount Depot Visitor Center   This visitor center, along with the Smokejumper Center (above), will educate you in the early methods of rugged firefighting in the northern Rockies. Listed on the National Register of Historic Places, the depot appears today much as it did when the Civilian Conservation Corps constructed it in the 1930s, complete with live pack mules. All tours are self-guided.

20325 Remount Rd., Huson, MT 59846. ✆ **406/626-5201.** Free admission. Daily 9am–5pm. Closed Labor Day to Memorial Day weekend. Drive 22 miles west of Missoula on I-90, then 4 miles north of exit 82.

Missoula Art Museum ★   Located downtown in the historic Carnegie Library (1903) and a new wing (2006), this museum's permanent collection includes about 600 works by about 200 artists, with a special emphasis on contemporary works by Montana and Native-American artists. Changing exhibits feature regional, national, and international art and photography; recent displays showcased works by the late Freeman Butts and Missoula's Donna Loos. Associated programs include films, concerts, lectures, tours, and children's events.

335 N. Pattee St. ✆ **406/728-0447.** www.missoulaartmuseum.org. Free admission; donations suggested. Wed–Fri noon–6pm; Sat–Sun 10am–3pm.

SHOPPING

The **Fair Trade Store,** 519 S. Higgins Ave. (✆ **406/543-3955;** www.jprc.org), is a project of the Jeannette Rankin Peace Resource Center, selling jewelry, clothing, and musical items from communities around the world. **Butterfly Herbs,** 232 N. Higgins Ave. (✆ **406/728-8780**), features an eclectic collection of items, including jewelry, coffee mugs, teapots, and handmade paper and candles. If you begin to feel the bohemian spirit and suddenly want your own pair of Birkenstocks, just go next door to **Hide & Sole,** 236 N. Higgins Ave. (✆ **406/549-0666**), for reshodding.

   Pipestone Mountaineering, 129 W. Front St. (✆ **406/721-1670;** www.pipestone mountaineering.com), has an excellent range of outdoor gear for serious climbers, river runners, and campers. The **Trail Head,** 221 E. Front St. (✆ **406/543-6966;**

Ⓚⁱᵈˢ   Especially for Kids

A remarkable community effort, the **Missoula Carousel** (✆ **406/549-8382;** www.carrousel.com) was a project begun with nothing more than unrealistic optimism. During planning, funding, and assembly stages of the project, Missoula relied on the kindness of others to make it happen. The hand-carved and -painted horses are the result of thousands of hours of labor from volunteer workers, most of whom were novices trained in the art of carving and painting. It's a treat for kids, and adults will also marvel at this merry-go-round by the river at downtown's **Caras Park,** which is located at the spot where Higgins Avenue crosses the Clark Fork River. The carousel is open daily year-round, with 50¢ rides for children 16 and under and seniors 55 and over, and $1.50 rides for adults. Immediately west of the carousel building is another fun community project: a fantasy-themed playground dubbed Dragon Hollow.

www.trailheadmontana.net), is another good outdoors store, with gear for snowshoers, kayakers, and just about everybody in between.

Missoula is home to an impressive literary community, and the city's bookstores are among the state's best, including **Fact and Fiction,** 220 N. Higgins Ave. (© 406/721-2881). Vintage, rare, and first-edition books are available from **Bird's Nest Books** (© 406/721-1125) at 219 N. Higgins Ave.

If you're looking for clothes, the **Macy's,** 110 N. Higgins Ave. (© 406/542-6000), is an old standard and Missoula's only downtown department store.

Monte Dolack is one of the best-known artists in Montana. His often-humorous posters and prints are available at 139 W. Front St. in the **Monte Dolack Gallery** (© 406/549-3248; www.dolack.com). The gallery also features works of other prominent Montana artists, including Mary Beth Percival. Other top Missoula galleries include Larry Pirnie's **Pirnie Art Showroom,** 337 E. Broadway (© 406/543-2713; www.pirnieartshowroom.com), and the **Montana Museum of Art and Culture** in the PAR/TV Building on the campus of the University of Montana (© 406/243-2019).

WHERE TO STAY

You won't find a whole lot of lodging variety within Missoula's city limits: It's dominated by chains, with a smattering of independents and Victorian-era B&Bs. For a distinctive night's sleep, try roughing it in a historic cabin. Information on rental of **old-fashioned miner's cabins** at the ghost town of Garnet is available by contacting the **Garnet Preservation Association,** 3255 Fort Missoula Rd., Missoula, MT 59804 (© 406/329-3883; www.garnetghosttown.net). The cabins are available for $30 to $40 a night from December through April, when they are typically accessible only on skis, snowshoes, or snowmobiles. Rustic cabins and lookouts are also available for rent through the **National Forest Service,** 200 E. Broadway (P.O. Box 779), Missoula, MT 59807 (© 406/329-3511) and the National Recreation Reservation Service (© 877/444-6777; www.recreation.gov). Get information on camping at Missoula's **Bureau of Land Management,** 3255 Fort Missoula Rd., Missoula, MT 59804 (© 406/329-3914; www.blm.gov/mt).

Hotels & Motels

Best Western Grant Creek Inn ★ Situated close to a freeway offramp (I-90, exit 101), this Best Western is a solid choice in Missoula. The quality of the rooms and services is what you'd normally associate with a higher-priced chain, with a business center, flatscreen TVs, and near-constant upgrading. There is a good variety of options here. Deluxe suites have a fireplace, a dining area, a desk, a closet, and a nice city view. Conventional rooms are bright and cheery, with two queen-size beds or one king-size bed.

5280 Grant Creek Rd., Missoula, MT 59808. © **888/543-0700** or 406/543-0700. Fax 406/543-0777. www.bestwestern.com/grantcreekinn. 126 units. $105–$159 double; $149–$199 suite. Rates include hot breakfast buffet. AE, DC, DISC, MC, V. **Amenities:** Exercise room; Jacuzzi; indoor pool; sauna. *In room:* A/C, TV, hair dryer, Wi-Fi (free).

Doubletree Hotel Missoula-Edgewater ★★ This is the premier hotel facility in Missoula. Located on the north bank of the Clark Fork, the upper-end rooms offer a good deal of space with a beautiful view of the river and the University of Montana. Rooms on the second level have balconies, some overlooking the swimming pool. The property is geared toward business travelers, with meeting rooms and a 24-hour business center. The lobby area is nicely finished, with a gift shop that sells Western souvenirs, clothing, and trinkets. The Finn and Porter restaurant, specializing in steaks, seafood, and chops, is just off the lobby. The wooden deck outside the lounge is a fine spot for a cocktail over the Clark Fork River.

100 Madison St., Missoula, MT 59802. ✆ **800/222-8733** or 406/728-3100. www.missoulaedgewater. doubletree.com. 171 units. $89–$275 double; $185–$275 suite. AE, DISC, MC, V. **Amenities:** Restaurant; lounge; free airport transfers; exercise room; outdoor Jacuzzi; outdoor heated pool. *In room:* A/C, TV, hair dryer, Wi-Fi (free).

Goldsmith's Inn ★   This beautiful 1911 brick building is Missoula's only riverside B&B, right on the Clark Fork River just across from the University of Montana. The home is the relocated former residence of Clyde Duniway, the second president of the University of Montana. Four of the seven rooms are suites with private sitting rooms, and all rooms have private bathrooms and attractive Victorian furnishings. Some also have fireplaces or reading nooks. Request the Clark Fork Suite for your own Japanese soaking bath, complete with a view of the river.

809 E. Front St., Missoula, MT 59802. ✆ **866/666-9945** or 406/728-1585. www.goldsmithsinn.com. 7 units. $89–$139 double. Rates include full breakfast. DISC, MC, V. *In room:* A/C, TV, fridge, hair dryer, Wi-Fi (free).

Hilton Garden Inn ★★   The newest and most comprehensive lodging on Missoula's west side, the six-story Hilton Garden Inn is a convention-oriented facility with terrific rooms. There's more than a hint of "New West" inspiration in the clean and sleek design, and a choice of two queen-size beds or one king. Some feature whirlpool tubs. Facilities include a pair of restaurants (including a good lunch-and-dinner place in the Blue Canyon Kitchen and Tavern), an indoor pool, and easy access to both I-90 and downtown.

3720 N. Reserve St., Missoula, MT 59808. ✆ **800/222-8733** or 406/532-5300. Fax 406/532-5305. www. hiltongardeninn.com. 146 units, including 1 suite. $129–$189 double; $350–$439 suite. AE, DISC, MC, V. **Amenities:** 2 restaurants; lounge; exercise room; indoor Jacuzzi; indoor heated pool. *In room:* A/C, TV, hair dryer, Wi-Fi (free).

Lolo Hot Springs Lodge ⓕ**Finds**   This hot-springs resort, 25 miles west of Lolo and only 7 miles from the Montana-Idaho border, is an especially popular winter destination—the cross-country skiing on Lolo Pass is excellent, as is the snowmobiling. There are 18 modern rooms and a large, inviting lobby in the lodge and 15 in a motel-style unit. The lodge is called the Fort because the design is reminiscent of the fort in the 1948 John Wayne film *Fort Apache*. The motel rooms are large and less expensive than those in the lodge, but they are spare in the decor department. Since the adjacent fabled **Lolo Hot Springs Pool** (www.lolohotsprings.com) is a separate operation, there's a fee to soak in them, but there are two 20-person hot tubs for guest use.

38600 W. U.S. 12, Lolo, MT 59847. ✆ **406/273-2201.** www.lololodge.com. 33 units. $49–$99 double. DISC, MC, V. **Amenities:** Restaurant; lounge; 2 indoor Jacuzzis; Wi-Fi (free). *In room:* A/C, no phone.

Mountain Valley Inn ⓥ**Value**   This one-time chain property has evolved into a first-rate independent, as new ownership has poured money back into the place. Rooms are fresh and clean, with small bathrooms with tub/shower combos; two nicely renovated family suites are available. There's also a small exchange library and guest lounge on the property.

420 W. Broadway, Missoula, MT 59802. ✆ **800/249-9174** or 406/728-4500. www.mountainvalleyinn missoula.com. 60 units, including 1 suite. $69–$72 double; $119 suite. Rates include complimentary cookies and full breakfast. AE, DISC, MC, V. **Amenities:** Exercise room. *In room:* A/C, TV, hair dryer, Wi-Fi (free).

Ruby's Inn ★ (Kids)   Just south of I-90 at the west end of town, Ruby's is hard to miss—just look for the big neon lips. The gaudy sign belies a top-notch independent motel, run by Ruby Erck for more than 25 years, with fresh, clean rooms and a full slate of amenities. Executive rooms are twice as big, and the honeymoon suite has a king-size bed and a two-person hot tub. The best feature might be the "backyard" along Grant Creek with fishing access (and grills to cook your catch) and a creek-side Jacuzzi.

4825 N. Reserve St., Missoula, MT 59808. ☎ **800/221-2057** or 406/721-0990. Fax 406/721-0990. 126 units. $79–$99 double; $125–$149 suite. Complimentary afternoon refreshments and hot breakfast buffet. AE, DC, DISC, MC, V. Pets accepted ($10 fee). **Amenities:** Free airport transfers; exercise room; outdoor Jacuzzi; seasonal outdoor pool. In room: A/C, TV, hair dryer, kitchenette, Wi-Fi (free).

WHERE TO DINE

Thanks to the university and a relatively cultured populace, Missoula is blessed with an excellent variety of restaurants, ranging from organic vegetarian to full-blown carnivorous. In addition to the options discussed below, I suggest the **Hob Nob,** 531 S. Higgins Ave. (☎ **406/541-4622**), for great breakfasts such as homemade corned beef hash, sourdough flapjacks, and *migas* (a breakfast taco). Also reliable for a scrumptious breakfast and lunch, **Catalyst Espresso,** 111 N. Higgins Ave. (☎ **406/542-1337**), cooks frittatas and scrambles for breakfast and soups, salads, and sourdough for lunch. The historic **Shack Cafe,** 222 W. Main St. (☎ **406/549-9903;** www.theshackcafe.com), is another local favorite, serving huge omelets known as "buffalo pies" for breakfast and a wide variety of lunch entrees, as well as dinners on Saturday and Sunday nights.

Expensive

The Depot ★★ STEAKS/SEAFOOD   A Missoula institution, the Depot is known for its upscale atmosphere and good food. The decor is along the contemporary cowboy and Western theme, with an inviting brick bar that looks out onto an active rail yard and more than 20 colorful paintings by Larry Pirnie. You might try the scallop casserole: scallops and mushrooms in white wine, Swiss cheese, and cream sauce. The beef menu features prime rib, New York strip, and filets; specialties include the garlic-roasted filet and a fresh range veal chop served with fresh mushrooms and heavy cream. There is a huge wine list, including some hard-to-find bordeaux. There's also a more casual pub area called the **Deck,** serving a less expensive array of burgers, sandwiches, and pizzas ($8–$15).

201 W. Railroad Ave. ☎ **406/728-7007.** Reservations recommended. Main courses $13–$35. AE, DC, DISC, MC, V. Daily 5:30–10pm; shorter hours fall-spring. Bar open later.

The Keep ★ STEAKS/SEAFOOD   After the landmark Greenough Mansion at the Highlands Golf Club burned to the ground in 1992, this castlelike restaurant, serving some of the area's best food, took its place on the very same foundation. Positioned on the bluffs of southeast Missoula, the Keep has a terrific ambience, heightened by the 30-foot ceiling in the bar and the panoramic views of the city and surrounding mountains. The Keep is known for its rack of lamb and salmon, as well as its rich and decadent desserts. The lounge and terrace offer a more casual setting and a menu of appetizers, salads, and small plates.

102 Ben Hogan Dr. ☎ **406/728-5132.** www.thekeeprestaurant.com. Main courses $23–$50. AE, DISC, MC, V. Daily 5–10pm.

Pearl Café and Bakery ★★ STEAKS/SEAFOOD/NEW AMERICAN Named for chef/owner Pearl Cash, this swank new eatery opened in summer 2004 and immediately rose into the upper echelon of Missoula's culinary landscape. Cash, who has operated several acclaimed restaurants in the area since the 1970s, delivers a sumptuous menu of creative regional standards, such as grilled filet mignon with a port-roquefort sauce, and duckling with pomegranate-cherry sauce and truffle-shiitake-chèvre flan. Located in half of the historic former Missoula Mercantile Warehouse, Pearl has three distinct dining areas: a sleek but casual bar area out front that takes only walk-ins; a first-floor dining room with warm peach and brick walls; and an upstairs mezzanine with wrought-iron railings and an air of elegance. The wine list is excellent.

231 E. Front St. ☎ **406/541-0231.** www.pearlcafeandbakery.com. Reservations recommended. Main courses $18–$33. AE, MC, V. Mon–Sat 5–9pm.

Red Bird ★★ NEW AMERICAN The small, intimate Red Bird is tucked in the alley on the ground floor of the Art Deco Florence Building. Chef Jim Tracey changes the menu monthly, but the entrees are fresh and superbly prepared year-round. One of Tracey's personal favorites is grilled bison tenderloin with goat cheese–corn sauce and smoked tomato mashers, which makes for remarkable presentation. Other dishes include hand-cut beef and lamb plates, as well as killer homemade desserts. A wine bar serves a different menu that includes a gourmet cheeseburger (sharp white cheddar, grilled onions, and shiitake mushrooms) for $12.

111 N. Higgins St., Ste. 100. ☎ **406/549-2906.** www.redbirdrestaurant.com. Reservations recommended. Main courses $22–$35. AE, DISC, MC, V. Tues–Sat 5–9:30pm. Wine bar Mon–Sat 5–10:30pm.

Scotty's Table ★★ NEW AMERICAN/MEDITERRANEAN A chic, upscale bistro just north of the Higgins Avenue Bridge, Scotty's Table uses organic and local ingredients in large part in its menu, which is the perfect balance of Montana and Mediterranean cuisine. The former is characterized by plenty of excellent local beef, served in non-Montanan presentations that respectively include creamy polenta and a blue corn crepe; the latter includes creative spins on French, Italian, and Moroccan standards. Owner-chef Scott Gill moved the eatery to a slick space on the ground level of the historic Wilma Building after a long run south of the river.

113 S. Higgins Ave. ☎ **406/549-2790.** Reservations recommended. Main courses $19–$28. AE, MC, V. Mon–Sat 11am–2:30pm; daily 5–9:30pm. Closed Mon fall–spring.

Moderate & Inexpensive

Bernice's Bakery ★ BAKERY Bernice's has been one of Missoula's most beloved culinary spots since the late 1970s. This small, out-of-the-way place, known for its delicious baked goods, is a great place for breakfast of the continental variety. In addition to an outstanding soft homemade granola, Bernice's sells buttery croissants filled with flavored cream cheeses, an excellent complement to the freshly brewed organic coffee that's also a staple. Organic juices and teas are available, too. This is also a great dessert spot— the cream puffs are out of this world—and a good choice for lunch as well.

190 S. 3rd St. W. ☎ **406/728-1358.** www.bernicesbakerymt.com. Most items $2–$5. DISC, MC, V. Daily 6am–8pm.

Biga Pizza (Kids) PIZZA Biga Pizza cooks up gourmet pies using what's in season locally. The tables are in view of a central open kitchen featuring a colossal brick oven. Among the seasonal options on the menu: in the winter months, the cherry chutney and sausage, and in summer the Sicilian, with Italian sausage, caramelized onions, and goat **103** cheese.

241 W. Main St. ☏ **406/728-2579**. www.bigapizza.com. Pizzas $12–$19; salads and sandwiches $5–$10. MC, V. Mon–Fri 11am–3pm; Mon–Thurs 5–9:30pm; Fri–Sat 5–10pm.

The Oxford Cafe AMERICAN Even if you don't eat at the Ox, as it's known, you really should go in and look around. Established in 1883, this distinctly Montanan cafe is a Missoula institution, adorned with beer signs, a long bar, a breakfast counter, a bison head, and an endless stream of eccentrics, cowboys, and bikers. Chicken-fried steaks are the specialty of the house; the Ox had sold more than 185,000 at last count (the record-keeping has admittedly gotten a bit shaky in recent years). Other restaurants come and go, but the Ox endures, a testament to overflowing breakfast plates, keno, and bottled American beer. As the late proprietor Ralph Baker once put it, "The place hasn't closed in so long, we don't even know where the keys are."

337 N. Higgins Ave. ☏ **406/549-0117**. www.the-oxford.com. Breakfast $3–$13; lunch $3–$8; dinner $6–$13. AE, DISC, MC, V. Daily 24 hr.

MISSOULA AFTER DARK
Watering Holes for Any Taste
There are plenty of watering holes in Missoula, whether your buzz of choice is alcohol or caffeine induced. **Sean Kelly's**, 130 W. Pine (☏ **406/542-1471**), serves Irish pub–style food—bangers and mash, pot roast, Irish stew—in addition to your alcoholic beverage of choice. The weekend jazz is wonderful, and there are also pool tables in the back. **Iron Horse Brew Pub**, 501 N. Higgins Ave. (☏ **406/728-8866**), has one of the city's best selections of Montana-brewed beer and myriad TVs to watch the game. Bold, bawdy, and bedecked with black-and-white photos of regulars, **Charlie B's**, 428 N. Higgins Ave. (☏ **406/549-3589**), is one of the best dives in the northwest, serving a cross section of Missoula: blue-collar types, professionals, and college kids. The exterior doesn't have a sign; just follow the laughter and chatter.

There are a number of good breweries in town, with taprooms where they can pour customers a maximum of 48 ounces of beer a day due to Montana state laws. My favorite is the **Kettlehouse Brewing Co.** ★★, 602 Myrtle St. (☏ **406/728-1660**; www.kettlehouse.com), a neighborhood brewery that supplies excellent craft beer to many local restaurants. Its taproom—open Monday through Saturday from noon to 9pm—is a funky hangout with old couches and a jovial atmosphere. A second location opened in 2009 at 313 N. 1st St. W. **Big Sky Brewing Company** has a taproom near the airport at 5417 Trumpeter Way (☏ **406/549-2777**; www.bigskybrew.com), open Monday through Friday from 11am to 6:30pm and Saturday from 11am to 6pm. Touting itself as the only German brewery in the Rockies is **Bayern Brewing**, 1507 Montana St. (☏ **406/721-1482**; www.bayernbrewery.com), with taproom hours of 10am to 8pm Monday through Friday and noon to 8pm Saturday and Sunday.

The Performing Arts
The **Montana Repertory Theater,** located at the University of Montana campus (☏ **406/243-6809**; www.montanarep.org), is the state's only Equity company, performing new and classical works. The **Missoula Children's Theater** is the largest touring children's theater in the United States, performing original musical productions and featuring hundreds of talented children from communities across the States, Canada, and the Pacific Rim. The theater season starts early in June and continues through the end of

March. The **MCT Community Theater** provides a year-round calendar of family enter-tainment. Both the Children's Theater and the Community Theater are located at 200 N. Adams St. (© **406/728-1911;** www.mctinc.org).

The **Missoula Symphony Orchestra and Chorale,** 320 E. Main St. (© **406/721-3194;** www.missoulasymphony.org), is composed of university students, Missoula resi-dents, and other regional musicians, who often perform with featured guests in the University Theater on campus. The **String Orchestra of the Rockies,** P.O. Box 8265, Missoula, MT 59807 (© **406/493-2990;** www.sor-montana.org), a statewide profes-sional string ensemble, is based in Missoula and performs almost exclusively there. At the University of Montana's **Music Recital Hall** (© **406/243-6880**), the school's music department often brings in outstanding musicians to perform. Regularly scheduled recit-als include solo and ensemble performances by faculty and students.

3 A DETOUR INTO THE BITTERROOT VALLEY ★

Extends 89 miles S of Missoula to the Idaho border

Although in part a bedroom community for Missoula, the Bitterroot Valley has become a booming second-home and retirement paradise for folks who have fallen in love with the Missoula-area mountains, but not with the Missoula-area traffic. Though not as well known as other areas of the state, the fly-fishing in the Bitterroot River is excellent, mak-ing it a preferred destination for anglers in the know.

The Bitterroot has the reputation as Montana's banana belt because the microclimate in the valley offers a long growing season. A lot of Missoula-area golf fanatics head to Hamilton in February because the golf course there greens up for play much earlier than the ones even a few miles farther north.

GETTING AROUND & VISITOR INFORMATION   For maps, brochures, and sage advice about the area and its happenings, consult the **Bitterroot Valley Chamber of Commerce,** 105 E. Main St., Hamilton, MT 59840 (© **406/363-2400;** www.bv chamber.com).

DRIVING TOURS

If you'd like to take a driving tour through the area (see the "Southwestern Montana" map, in chapter 8), travel south on U.S. 93 to Florence, then cross the Bitterroot River and travel south on Mont. 203/263 through a 32-mile area filled with interesting land-marks, reconnecting with U.S. 93 at Hamilton. On your trip back, take U.S. 93 south through Hamilton, Victor, Darby, and Sula. As an alternative, continue south beyond Sula to Mont. 43, the road that leads to Wisdom. Doing so will take you winding through the valley and canyons of the Bitterroot Mountains, and you'll finally emerge at the Big Hole Battlefield.

If you are feeling very brave, and you don't mind getting your car beaten up on a rough dirt road, take the Skalkaho Pass Road to the east of Hamilton. Pick up Mont. 38 just south of Hamilton—up Skalkaho Creek. The pavement runs out after a few miles, and you'll drive over a rocky, pitted, narrow road up through the Sapphire Mountains. Go slowly; the drop-offs here are as extreme as those along Going-to-the-Sun Road in Glacier National Park, but without the guardrails. The views of forested hills are unsurpassed. It takes about

GETTING OUTSIDE

The Bitterroot Valley runs south along the Bitterroot River between the Bitterroot Range to the west and the Sapphire Mountains to the east. The Bitterroot Range is the site of the Selway-Bitterroot Wilderness, which at 1.3 million acres is one of the nation's largest wilderness areas. Numerous trail heads are located off major highways between Lolo and Darby. You can get information about hiking in the wilderness from the Bitterroot National Forest's **Darby Ranger District Office,** 712 N. Main St., Darby, MT 59829 (© **406/821-3913;** www.fs.fed.us/r1/bitterroot), open Monday through Friday from 8am to 4:30pm.

The **Lake Como Recreation Area** is a popular day-use and camping area with swimming, hiking, and boating. To get there, go 4 miles north from Darby on U.S. 93. Turn west on Lake Como Road and go about 2½ miles to the area. There are 22 camping units in two different campgrounds for $8 to $14 a night and a "rustic" cabin on the lake for $60 per night. Reservations for the cabin are available through the National Recreation Reservation Service (© **877/444-6777;** www.recreation.gov); the campgrounds are first-come, first-served.

If it's fly-fishing you're seeking, check out **Chuck Stranahan's Flies and Guides,** 105 State St. (P.O. Box 594), Hamilton, MT 59840 (© **406/363-4197;** www.chuck-stranahan.com), one of the longest-running acts in the Montana guiding business. Owner Chuck Stranahan is a nationally known fly-tier, with a number of his patterns chosen for the Jack Dennis fly-tying book, the bible of the business. He excels in instruction. His company customizes trips for its customers, with an emphasis on the Bitterroot River, though trips also go to other rivers in western Montana. Guided trips cost $365 to $450 per day for one or two people; personal instruction is $165 per person for a full day.

SEEING THE SIGHTS

The west side of the valley has fishing access as well as places to shop, eat, and stay. The historic section of the valley is on the east side of the river, and is accessible at Florence, Stevensville, Victor, Pinesdale, and Hamilton.

Following are a lot of the attractions you'll come across if you start driving at the north end of Mont. 203/269 and head south.

Eight miles south of Florence on Mont. 203, you'll hit the **Lee Metcalf National Wildlife Refuge** (© **406/777-5552;** leemetcalf.fws.gov), which is free and open daily from dawn to dusk. This wetland habitat is the result of dikes and dams that impound the water of several streams. It has helped to improve migratory waterfowl habitats and has created a nesting success, but a number of other species benefit as well, including osprey and deer. A short loop trail, open from mid-July to mid-September, leads around several ponds and blinds in the refuge's southwest corner. The picnic area is open year-round and has 2½ miles of nature trails. Hunting for waterfowl is permitted on designated ponds during the fall duck-hunting season. Bow hunting for deer is also permitted, as is fishing, during their respective seasons. Near the entrance is the well-preserved exterior of the 1885 **Whaley Homestead,** an excellent example of vernacular frontier architecture. You can drive around the refuge on the dirt road and come out in Stevensville, the next stop on the tour.

Stevensville is the oldest town in Montana, the result of the early missionary work of the indefatigable Jesuit Father Pierre DeSmet, who founded **St. Mary's Mission** in 1841. Capped with a bell tower, the mission is a small structure paneled with logs and white boards and an important place in the development of Montana—it was the first permanent structure in the state to be built by European Americans. John Owen bought the mission from the Jesuits in 1850 and established a trading post, Fort Owen. Though the issue of who first found gold in Montana will doubtless never be completely settled, in Owen's diary in 1852 he wrote: "Hunting gold. Found some."

From here, continue south on Mont. 203 to Hamilton and the Marcus Daly Mansion. Montana copper king Marcus Daly never did anything on a small scale, and his house is no exception. The **Marcus Daly Mansion,** 251 Eastside Hwy. (© 406/363-6004; www.dalymansion.org), is a spectacular Georgian Revival mansion with classical porticoes. It occupies 24,000 square feet on three floors, with 25 bedrooms, 15 bathrooms, and 7 fireplaces. The mansion was finished in 1910, after Daly's death, and his widow, Margaret, lived there in the summers until her death in 1941. It's typically open 10am to 4pm daily from May through October, as well as on weekends and December. Admission costs $8 for adults, $7 for seniors, and $5 for kids 6 to 17 (free for 5 and under).

On the opposite side of the river, the village of Hamilton, several blocks long and 4 blocks wide, is worth a leisurely stroll since most of the businesses here are small, locally owned, and interesting. For outdoor gear, head to **Bob Ward & Sons,** 1120 N. 1st St. (© 406/363-6204), for a good selection of fishing, skiing, camping, and hunting equipment. Nearby is **Robbins,** 209 W. Main St. (© 406/363-1733), a nice shop that sells home furnishings, crystal, china, and gourmet kitchen accessories. The **Chapter One** bookstore, 252 W. Main St. (© 406/363-5220), featuring new and used books and periodicals, adjoins the unusually capitalized **JitterZ,** which sells all manner of espresso drinks. Also worth a look are **Big Sky Candy,** 319 W. Main St. (© 406/363-0580; www.bigskycandy.com), **Art City,** 407 W. Main St. (© 406/363-4764), and **CT's Bazaar,** 111 S. 3rd St. (© 406/363-3473) for "collectible things and rare finds."

WHERE TO STAY

Hamilton Super 8, 1325 N. 1st St., Hamilton, MT 59840 (© 800/800-8000 or 406/363-2940), is a clean, typically budget-minded motel with a location central to the Bitterroot Valley. The same holds true for the **Best Western Hamilton Inn,** 409 S. 1st St., Hamilton, MT 59840 (© 800/426-4586 or 406/363-2142), though the advantage here is the presentation of an excellent breakfast buffet and the fact that some rooms are equipped with microwaves and refrigerators. Double rooms at both properties typically run $65 to $95 per night. Southwest of town, the **Lost Horse Creek Lodge,** 100 Lost Horse Rd., Hamilton, MT 59840 (© 406/363-1460; www.losthorsecreeklodge.com), abuts national forest land with its 22 cabins and lodge featuring a restaurant and a thoroughly Western 1890s saloon. Double rates in summer are $45 to $90.

Triple Creek Ranch ★★★ This is one of the most elegant, and expensive, guest ranches in the West. The ranch is an adults-only resort that encourages guests to relax and do things according to their own schedules. The luxury cabins have a sitting area, king-size log-frame bed, complimentary wet bar, wood-burning fireplace, and double steam shower. Tennis rackets, Orvis fly-fishing gear, and horses are available to guests. The ranch is the only Montana property to meet the Relais & Châteaux standards. The

Wall Street Journal called a stay here "roughing it Robin Leach style." New cabins went up in 2007, and they were definitely in keeping with the previous high standard. The on-site **Triple Creek Dining Room** serves gourmet cuisine for breakfast, lunch, and dinner. It's open to the public, but during the summer season, it's filled with resort guests, and it's difficult to get a dinner reservation—try to stop for lunch instead.

5551 W. Fork Rd., Darby, MT 59829. (℃ **800/654-2943** or 406/821-4600. Fax 406/821-4666. www.triple creekranch.com. 23 cabins. $650–$2,500 per couple per night. Rates include meals, drinks, and activities. AE, DISC, MC, V. **Amenities:** Restaurant; bikes; concierge; exercise room; outdoor Jacuzzi; outdoor heated pool; room service; outdoor tennis court. *In room:* A/C, TV, hair dryer, kitchenette, minibar, Wi-Fi (free).

WHERE TO DINE

The **Bitterroot Brew Pub,** 101 Marcus St. (℃ **406/363-7468;** www.bitterrrootbrewing. com), serves pub fare, burgers, tacos, and burritos, as well as its own excellent beers. The **Spice of Life Cafe,** 163 S. 2nd St. in Hamilton (℃ **406/363-4433;** www.thespicein hamilton.com), has creative offerings ranging from a Bitterroot strip steak to Thai curry noodles. A classic diner, the **Kitchen,** 102 S. 2nd St. (℃ **406/363-0903**), is a local favorite for breakfast and lunch. If all your outdoor activities have you craving a juicy steak, try **Bradley O's Steakhouse,** 1831 U.S. 93 S. (℃ **406/375-1110**).

A SIDE TRIP: SKIING & HOT SPRINGS AT LOST TRAIL PASS

Lost Trail Pass is a remote and undiscovered corner of Montana about 80 miles south of Missoula on the Idaho border. This area is heavily timbered but not heavily populated. It's also off the beaten path because most travelers use I-15. This corner of the state is very pretty—with pine-covered peaks replacing the forbidding rock crags that dominate the skyline farther north.

With Lost Trail Powder Mountain, Lost Trail Hot Springs, and Camp Creek Inn, this pass area is an unforgettable winter vacation destination for those who loathe big crowds and the attendant ski scene.

Lost Trail Powder Mountain ski area recently expanded into a long, steeper area adjacent to the original hill, with five lifts in all. Overall, the runs are mostly intermediate, with lots of light powder. If you like to ski the bumps but aren't a fanatic about it, the moguls develop on the intermediate runs in the afternoon, just in time to wear you out completely. The full-day lift ticket prices are an excellent value at $34 adults, $25 seniors 60 to 69, and $24 children 6 to 12; kids 5 and under ski free and seniors 70 and over are $10. For more information, contact Lost Trail Powder Mountain, P.O. Box 311, Conner, MT 59827. Ski reports are available during the season at ℃ **406/821-3211** or online at **www.losttrail.com.** The ski area is 90 miles south of Missoula at the Montana-Idaho border, a quarter-mile from U.S. Hwy. 93.

Just down the hill to the north from the ski area is the unpretentious lodge and hot springs, **Lost Trail Hot Springs Resort,** 8221 U.S. 93 S., Sula, MT 59871 (℃ **800/825-3574** or 406/821-3574; www.losttrailhotsprings.com). The lodge arranges summer raft trips, horseback riding, and fishing. It isn't fancy by urban standards, but the food in the restaurant, which overlooks the hot-springs pool, is good, especially if you enjoy basic American grub—burgers and pizzas. Nightly rates are $65 to $200 for lodge rooms and $80 to $210 for cabins. If you come just to soak, it's $7 for adults, less for seniors and children.

4 THE FLATHEAD INDIAN RESERVATION & THE MISSION VALLEY

42 miles N of Missoula; 75 miles S of Kalispell

The Confederated Salish & Kootenai tribes make their home on the Flathead Indian Reservation, with tribal headquarters for the 1.3-million-acre reservation in Pablo. The tribes, however, own only slightly more than 50% of the land within reservation boundaries.

The change in culture for the tribes came quickly when fur traders, homesteaders, and the missionaries of the Catholic Church headed west. Founded in the early 1850s by Jesuit priests, the town of **St. Ignatius** (located 32 miles north of Missoula on U.S. 93) is nestled in the heart of the Mission Valley. One of the valley's larger small towns, St. Ignatius has a modest Flathead Indian Museum and trading post on the highway.

Wildlife conservation and land management have played big parts in the lives of the tribal members. The **Mission Mountains Tribal Wilderness** was the first wilderness area officially designated as such by a tribe in the United States. Hiking in the wilderness area requires the purchase of a tribal permit from the **Flathead Reservation Confederated Salish & Kootenai Tribes,** 42487 Complex Blvd., Box 278, Pablo, MT 59855 (© **406/675-2700;** www.cskt.org). The Mission Mountains Wilderness is located in the Mission Mountain Range, east of U.S. 93. Numerous gravel roads lead up to the trail heads.

The **St. Ignatius Mission,** 300 Beartrack Ave., P.O. Box 667, St. Ignatius, MT 59865 (© **406/745-2768**), was established in 1854 as an offshoot of the missionary work of the famous Jesuit Father Pierre DeSmet. A Father Hoecken began the mission in a small log cabin, which is still on the premises and serves as the visitor center. In 1891, the mission added this magnificent brick church in its ministry to the Indians. The ceiling is decorated with 58 murals, depicting scenes from the Old and New Testaments, by Brother Joseph Carignano, an Italian Jesuit without formal art training. The mission is 2 blocks off U.S. 93.

The **National Bison Range** ★ (© 406/644-2211; www.fws.gov/bisonrange/nbr), just west of St. Ignatius on reservation land, is 7 miles southwest of Charlo on County Road 212. The 18,500 acres here contain between 350 and 500 bison, the remnants of a national bison herd that once totaled 60 million. The visitor center has a small display about the history and ecology of bison in America. The 19-mile Red Sleep Road goes through four different habitat types—grasslands, riparian, montane forest, and wetlands. In addition to the bison, you'll see deer, bighorn sheep, antelope, and maybe an occasional coyote or black bear. There's a trail here for people with physical disabilities. Gates are open from 7am to dusk daily year-round; the visitor center is open from 8am to 6pm weekdays, 9am to 6pm weekends in summer, and 8am to 4pm weekdays in winter. Cost is $5 per car (free in winter).

If you're more interested in feathers than in fur, check out the **Ninepipe National Wildlife Refuge** (© 406/644-2211; www.fws.gov/bisonrange/ninepipe), which is next to U.S. 93, 5 miles south of Ronan. Established in 1921, the refuge has more than 2,000 acres of water, marsh, and grassland for the double-crested cormorant and the great blue heron, among other migrating birds. The refuge is open daily from dawn to dusk, although portions are closed during the fall and early winter hunting season and the bird-nesting season in spring and early summer. Admission is free. Fishing is permitted in some areas of the adjacent Pablo Reservoir, but a tribal permit is required. For information on tribal fishing regulations, call © 406/675-2700.

WHERE TO STAY & DINE The **Ninepipes Lodge,** 41000 U.S. 93, Charlo, MT 59824 (© **406/644-2588;** www.ninepipes.com), across from the Ninepipe National Wildlife Refuge, is a pleasant motel, with 25 rooms decorated with lodgepole furniture and a wildlife/nature theme. Your choice of king-size, queen-size, double, or twin beds is offered, and all units have TVs and telephones. Double rates are $70 to $92. There is also a restaurant on the premises, offering American selections for all three meals. Also adjacent and under the same management is the **Ninepipes Museum of Early Montana** (© **406/644-3435**), which contains early Western art, American-Indian beadwork, wildlife displays, a life-size diorama of an Indian camp scene, and other displays on the area's history. Admission costs $4 for adults, $3 for students, and $2 for children 6 to 12, and is free for children 5 and under. Call for current hours; the museum is closed in winter.

A SIDE TRIP TO HOT SPRINGS

Hot Springs is a funky little town of hand-painted signs and potholed streets, tucked into a cul-de-sac of low Montana mountains. Lots of visitors swear by the local waters' therapeutic qualities, especially as a palliative for arthritis. Situated southwest of Polson, just off Mont. 28, the tiny community is about 1½ hours from Flathead Lake.

The 1928 **Symes Hotel** ★, 209 Wall St. (© **888/305-3106** or 406/741-2361; www. symeshotsprings.com), is a vaguely pink, Alamo-like structure that aspires to be Art Deco. You can rent rooms or just tubs in stalls that can be filled with the famous waters. Some rooms have their own tubs, and there are two small pools and a large soaking tub outside ($7 adult). Rooms run from $49 to $133 a night, in a bewildering combination of options (you get claw-foot tubs and the occasional TV, but no phones). There's also a day spa, a yoga studio, and a restaurant on the property. A funky 1935 motel with housekeeping apartments, **Alameda's Hot Springs Retreat,** 308 N. Spring St. (© **406/741-2283;** www.alamedashotsprings.com), is a better option. Many of its rooms have soaking tubs; rates range from $45 to $75, including continental breakfast.

Wild Horse Hot Springs (© **406/741-3777**), 5 miles northeast of town, offers a rather primitive soak in blue concrete tubs. This place is located several miles down a dirt road. The private rooms are each outfitted with a "plunge" (private pool), toilet, shower, steam room, and furniture that your grandmother would have found old-fashioned. But some people swear by the place and come back every year. There are only two kitchenette rooms to sleep in here, priced at $75 to $95 a night. A soak costs $6 an hour per person.

For more information, contact the **Hot Springs Chamber of Commerce,** P.O. Box 580, Hot Springs, MT 59845 (© **406/741-2662;** www.hotspringsmtchamber.org).

5 THE FLATHEAD LAKE AREA: SOMERS, POLSON & BIGFORK ★★

Bigfork: 92 miles N of Missoula; 15 miles SE of Kalispell

This is one of the most beautiful areas in Montana. Glacier National Park's towering peaks rise from the valley floor on the east, and the mountains of the Flathead National Forest define the edge of the valley to the west. This is a land of forests, cattle, and alfalfa—with a velvet-green valley floor, green and granite mountains, and, on a sunny day, a dramatic deep-blue ceiling.

This part of Montana seems to offer something for everyone, whether your interests lie indoors or out. There are watersports on the lake and hikes that lead to sparkling mountain streams with views. But if you want to shop or see a play, you can easily spend your day inside the boutiques, galleries, and theater of Bigfork.

With much of this area lying within the tribal lands of the Salish & Kootenai, there is also a long-standing American-Indian heritage.

ESSENTIALS

GETTING THERE   Bigfork is located near the northeastern shores of Flathead Lake, 15 miles southeast of Kalispell by car, at the intersection of Mont. 35 and Mont. 83. Polson is at the southern tip of the lake, 33 miles southwest of Bigfork via Mont. 35 and 60 miles north of Missoula via U.S. 93. The nearest airports are **Glacier Park International** (© 406/257-5994; www.iflyglacier.com), north of the lake between Kalispell and Columbia Falls, and the **Missoula International Airport** (© 406/728-4381; www.fly missoula.com) in Missoula. Bigfork is just a little more than a 30-minute drive from Glacier Park International; Polson is roughly midway between the two airports. For rental cars, **Avis** (© 800/230-4898), **Budget** (© 800/527-0700), **Hertz** (© 800/654-3131), and **National** (© 800/227-7368) maintain counters at each airport.

VISITOR INFORMATION   Your best bet for information on the south end of the lake is the **Polson Chamber of Commerce,** 418 Main St., Polson, MT 59860 (© 406/883-5969; www.polsonchamber.com). For goings-on north, contact the **Bigfork Chamber of Commerce,** P.O. Box 237, Bigfork, MT 59911 (© 406/837-5888; www.bigfork. org). The **Flathead Convention and Visitor Bureau** (© 800/543-3105 or 406/756-9091; www.fcvb.org), **Travel Montana** (© 800/847-4868; www.travelmt.com), and **Glacier Country** (© 800/338-5072; www.glaciermt.com) can supplement this information.

GETTING OUTSIDE

The Flathead is one of those rare places where you see the serious golfer and the serious backpacker in the same spot, sometimes in the same body. The golfing is excellent on several courses, and the backpacking, hiking, and fishing are even better. Fishing, boating, and yachting are popular sports for those who can afford to practice them. If your plans take you to one of the lakes or trails on the Salish & Kootenai Reservation, don't forget to buy a tribal permit.

Biking

Rentals and guided tours are available from **Mountain Mike's,** 417 Bridge St., Bigfork (© 406/837-2453).

Boating

With Flathead Lake being the largest natural freshwater lake west of the Mississippi River, you can bet that this is a big boating destination. Boat rentals are available at the **Kwa Taq Nuk Resort** in Polson (© 800/882-6363), and to the north at **Bigfork Marina and Boat Center** (© 406/837-5556), **Bayview Resort and Marina** (© 406/837-4843), and **Marina Cay Resort** (© 406/837-5861).

A sailboat excursion is available from **Averill's Flathead Lake Lodge** (© 406/837-5569) on two classic racing sloops designed by L. Francis Herreshoff. Fewer than a dozen

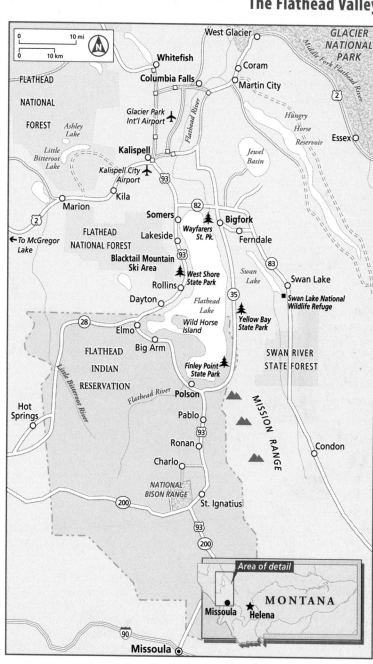

of these 51-foot "Q-Boats" remain in the world. There are a couple of 2-hour cruises daily from late May to mid-October. Fixed-keel sailboats can be launched at the state parks around Flathead Lake. Big Arm, Yellow Bay, and Somers have fishing access. Because winds may blow hard during the afternoon, only ballasted boats are recommended on the main portion of the lake.

The Montana Department of Fish, Wildlife, and Parks has designated a **Flathead Lake Marine Trail,** showing point-to-point campsites and landing points that a human-powered craft like a canoe or kayak can reach in 1 day. You can obtain a brochure on the trail from the **MFW&P** (© **406/752-5501;** www.fwp.state.mt.us) or from the **Flathead Convention and Visitor Bureau** in Kalispell (© **406/756-9091**).

Cruises

Excursion cruises are a good way for visitors to check out Flathead Lake. The 65-foot *Far West* (© **406/857-3203**) is one of the area's oldest, with daily scenic cruises and occasional Sunday brunch cruises. **Pointer Scenic Cruises** (© **406/837-5617**) offers charter rides on high-speed powerboats that cruise to ancient pictographs viewable only by boat; this company also offers explorations of Wild Horse Island, dinner cruises, and custom tours. The *Shadow* cruise boat (© **406/883-3636**) takes a 3-hour tour, leaving the Kwa Taq Nuk resort marina in the early afternoon and making a loop around Wild Horse Island before heading back. The boat also takes a shorter bay tour in the morning, or if it's a Montana sunset you're after, take a sunset cruise, departing in the late afternoon, and look west.

Fishing

Fishing the southern half of Flathead Lake requires a Salish & Kootenai tribal permit, which you can purchase at stores in Polson or at the tribal headquarters in Pablo. The brochure *Fishing the Flathead* is available from the **Flathead Convention and Visitor Bureau** (© **406/756-9091**). It provides information on 14 different fishing opportunities, as well as an outline of the licensing and catch-and-release regulations. This brochure includes information on Whitefish, Flathead, and Swan lakes, and several lesser-known lakes where you can catch fish but avoid crowds. To increase your odds of snagging something besides a log, contact **Glacier Fishing Charters** (© **406/892-2377**). **A-Able Fishing** (© **406/844-0888;** www.aablefishing.com) will also outfit a fishing trip with guides who know the area.

Golf

There are two golf courses—one terrific, the other just pretty good—overlooking the shores of Flathead Lake. In Polson, the 27-hole **Polson Bay Golf Club** public course is the pretty good one, situated just off the lake on U.S. 93 (© **406/883-8230;** www.polsonbaygolf.com). A round of 18 holes is $30 to $40. The course is fairly short—just more than 7,000 yards from the tips and about 6,000 from the white tees—but it's very pretty and beautifully maintained.

The terrific course is **Eagle Bend Golf Club** (© **800/255-5641** or 406/837-7310; www.golfmt.com), a challenging Jack Nicklaus–designed track with views of Flathead Lake and the surrounding mountains, located in Bigfork just off the highway on Holt Drive. The 18-hole course is about 6,300 yards from the white tees, but it's extremely challenging. There are 27 excellent holes of golf here. Greens fees range from $35 to $92 for 18 holes, depending on the time of year. *Golf Digest* has called this one of the country's top 50 courses. Be sure to call ahead for a tee time.

There are several other courses in the area. Contact the **Flathead Valley Golf Association** (© **800/392-9795;** www.golfmontana.net) for a free visitor's guide and information regarding all of the courses.

Hiking

This is bear country, and hikers should work to avoid confrontations by making noise and being watchful. Don't surprise them and they won't surprise you.

Besides strolling by the lake at one of the marinas or state parks, the best bet for trekking is in the **Jewel Basin,** a designated hiking area north of Bigfork. More than 30 miles of trails make it a great place for day hiking as well as overnights. Before dropping into the actual basin, you'll get a great look at the Flathead Valley and Flathead Lake. For free maps of some of the more popular trails, inquire locally at one of the **Forest Service** offices in Kalispell (© **406/758-5200**) or Bigfork (© **406/837-7500**). To reach the head of the hiking area, take Mont. 83 from either Bigfork or Somers, turn north onto Echo Lake Road, and follow the signs.

A short hike, not far from Bigfork and about 45 minutes from the trail head, will take you to **Estes Lake.** Take County Road 209 out of Bigfork. Turn south at the Ferndale fire station. When the road forks, take the right fork, County Road 498. It's about a 7-mile drive from there to the parking area.

A slightly more ambitious, but still short, hike goes up to **Cold Lakes** in the **Mission Mountains Tribal Wilderness.** Take Mont. 83 south to County Road 903. Turn right (west), then follow the road to the trail head. The hike is about an hour each way.

Rafting

The **Flathead Raft Company** (© **800/654-4359** or 406/883-5838; www.flatheadraftco. com) runs half of its outfit from Polson at Riverside Park on U.S. 93 and half from Bigfork. Tours go down the South Fork of the Flathead River and include a swing through the Buffalo Rapids and Kerr Dam. Half-day white-water trips are $39 to $45, and full-day scenic trips range from $65 to $80. Meals and overnight trips are also available, as are guided kayaking expeditions.

Skiing

The **Blacktail Mountain Ski Area** (© **406/844-0999;** www.blacktailmountain.com) is working hard to make the Flathead Lake region a full-blown year-round resort area. There's an average annual snowfall of 250 inches, which ought to be enough. The area is on more than 1,000 acres of national forest, served by two double chairs, a triple lift, and a handle tow. The hill is excellent for beginner and intermediate skiers, with 1,440 vertical feet of drop. Beginner terrain makes up 15% of the runs, 70% are rated intermediate, and 15% are black diamonds. There are two restaurants, a lounge, ski rental, a ski school, and a terrain park. Lift tickets for adults cost $36 full day, $30 half-day; children ages 13 to 17 cost $25 full day, $21 half-day; ages 8 to 12 are $16 for full day, $13 half-day; seniors 70 and older are $16 half- or full day; and children 7 and younger are free. Lifts open at 9:30am and close at 4:30pm Wednesday through Sunday and holidays (closed Mon–Tues). The area is located 14 miles west of Lakeside on Blacktail Mountain Road.

EXPLORING THE AREA

Bigfork Museum of Art and History   This small but nicely staged museum in the village center offers a downstairs gallery with rotating art exhibits and an upstairs primer on the area's history. The art in the gallery is often local and changes on a monthly basis; the historical exhibits include a nice collection of black-and-white photographs and cover the region's cherry farming, the log-rolling laborers that were known as "river pigs," lake ice harvests, and of course wild huckleberries.

525 Electric Ave., Bigfork. © **406/837-6927**. www.bigforkmuseum.org. Free admission. Tues–Sat 10am–5pm.

Bigfork Summer Playhouse   For over 50 years, Bigfork has earned a fine regional reputation for its summer stock theatrical productions, performed by rising college-age stars. Performances of Broadway shows are scheduled from the end of May until early September. Recent productions include *The Wiz, The Best Little Whorehouse in Texas*, and *Singin' in the Rain*.

526 Electric Ave., Bigfork. © **406/837-4886** for showtimes and reservations. www.bigforksummerplay house.com. Ticket prices vary, but are usually around $25.

Miracle of America Museum   This eccentric but often interesting museum contains an extensive collection of odds and ends dedicated to explaining the development of America, with specific attention to the Constitution and the Bill of Rights. Like most of these efforts, the place is heavily weighted toward the military side of the story, with plenty of guns, uniforms, and battle memorabilia. But unlike a lot of the roadside museums, there is at least some effort to explain what you're looking at. There's also a collection of antique Harley-Davidsons, dating as far back as 1912, and odds and ends ranging from comic books and Bibles to a two-headed calf trophy and a statue of a winged monkey.

58176 U.S. 93, Polson. © **406/883-6804**. www.miracleofamericamuseum.org. $5 adults, $4.50 seniors, $2 for children 3–12, free for children 2 and under. Summer daily 8am–8pm; rest of year Mon–Sat 8am–5pm, Sun 1:30–5pm.

The Mission Mountain Winery   Montana's only winery is located here on Flathead Lake, producing award-winning merlot along with chardonnay and pale ruby champagne. Tours of the small facility are free and take about 15 minutes. The winery produces 6,500 cases of wine a year. Although most of the wines produced here are white, the winery considers the reds to be the finer vintages. The pinot noir grapes are grown in vineyards around Flathead Lake.

82420 U.S. 93, Dayton. © **406/849-5524**. www.missionmountainwinery.com. May–Oct tastings daily 10am–5pm.

SHOPPING

Bigfork's main street, Electric Avenue, is littered with a variety of galleries, gift shops, boutiques, and bookstores—and it's only 4 blocks long. **Twin Birch Square,** 459 Electric Ave., is a two-level, pine-log shopping mall where you'll find **Artisans** (© **406/837-2789**), featuring functional art from all over the country.

The **Eric Thorsen Sculpture Gallery,** 547 Electric Ave. (© **406/837-4366**), handles artwork from the well-known sculptor. He is best known for the sculptures he has created for Trout Unlimited, the Wild Turkey Federation, and Ducks Unlimited (at last count more than 12,000 fundraising pieces in total). His two-level gallery is a display case for bronze and wood creations; on the second level is the artist's studio, where visitors are encouraged to observe the artist at work. Doors away is the gallery of **Ken Bjorge** (© **877/837-3839**), 603 Electric Ave., who also creates life-size studies of wildlife in bronze. Don't be surprised to find yourself standing next to a 6-foot-tall crane or eagle while he works his craft in your presence.

(Moments)   **A Visit to Wild Horse Island**

Wild Horse Island, one of the largest islands in the inland United States at 2,000 acres, is run as a wildlife preserve by the Montana Department of Fish, Wildlife, and Parks (© **406/752-5501;** fwp.mt.gov). It contains one of the last remnants of Montana's endangered Palouse prairie plant and provides a habitat for bighorn sheep, mule deer, coyotes, and a few wild horses. The island was originally created more than 17,000 years ago as a result of heavy glacial activity that formed the entire area. Sensitivity by the human visitors who visit this unusual environmental preserve is essential—please leave no traces of your visit. The park is open for day use only, and can be reached only by boat. Take your own or rent one from the **Kwa Taq Nuk Resort** (© **406/883-3636**). Several boat tours go to Wild Horse Island as well. You can take one from Bigfork with **Pointer Scenic Cruises** (© **406/837-5617**). **Note:** There are no visitor services on the island.

Across the street from Bjorge's studio is **Two River Gear** (© **406/837-3474**), which deals in fly-fishing equipment and info, and Patagonia wear. **Artfusion,** 471 Electric Ave. (© **406/837-3526**), is an eclectic gallery that represents more than 60 contemporary Montana artists and craftspeople. Around the corner at **Bay Books & Prints,** 350 Grand Dr. (© **406/837-4646**), there are rare books and first editions. The owners carry an extensive collection of books about the explorers Lewis and Clark, some very rare and in good condition.

If you're looking for an authentic yet unusual gift item with a Western theme, visit **Electric Avenue Gifts** (© **406/837-4994**), 459 Electric Ave. For delectable jams and syrups, try **Eva Gates Homemade Preserves,** 456 Electric Ave. (© **406/837-4356**), which has been in the business since 1949.

Shopping in **Polson** at the other end of Flathead Lake is less of an upscale experience, but **Three Dog Down,** 48841 U.S. 93 (© **800/364-3696**) sells comforters, coats, pillows, duvets, and other cold-weather gear. Owner Robert "Bronco Bob" Ricketts is a former opera singer who moved from Cincinnati to Polson to start a low-key dream business. Prices for high-quality down goods are lower here than in more fashionable metropolitan stores.

WHERE TO STAY

There are five campgrounds in **Flathead Lake state parks,** each located at a different point around the lake: Big Arm (© **406/849-5255**) and West Shore (© **406/844-3044**) on the west side of the lake; and Finley Point (© **406/887-2715**), Yellow Bay (© **406/982-3034**), and Wayfarers (© **406/837-4196**) on the east shore. The phone numbers are operational only in summer. You can also call © **406/752-5501** for information on any of these state park campgrounds, most of which are open May through September, charging $15 per night.

Accommodations on and near the lake include guest ranches, water-oriented resorts with the gamut of recreational opportunities, and basic motels that offer clean but modest rooms. Of the last category, a good option is **America's Best Value Port Polson Inn,** 502 U.S. 93 E., Polson, MT 59860 (© **888/315-2378** or 406/883-5385; www.port posoninn.com), with an excellent view of the lake. Rates run $89 to $129 double room and $300 to $350 for a family apartment with a kitchenette; rates are lower in winter.

Averill's Flathead Lake Lodge ★★★ (Kids) This is the best all-around vacation experience on the lake. A beautiful log lodge surrounded by thousands of acres of forest serves as your home base for all activities, which include horseback riding, boating, and fishing. The Western dude-ranch experience is done right at this place, complete with sing-alongs, campfires, and barn dances. The location and the atmosphere of this place (the Averills perfectly combine a ranching lifestyle with the summer vacation experience) make this one of the top picks in the state. Scattered around the property are 20 two- and three-bedroom cabins, featuring simple Western-style furnishings. Inside the lodge are 19 guest rooms, just as woodsy but smaller, which sleep up to four and have queen-size beds and a pair of twin beds in a loft. Meals are served family style in the main lodge—the food is top-notch.

P.O. Box 248, Bigfork, MT 59911. ⓒ **406/837-4391.** Fax 406/837-6977. www.flatheadlakelodge.com. 19 lodge rooms, 20 cabins. $3,200 per adult per week (based on 1-week minimum stay); $1,340–$2,400 children 3–18; $170 children 2 and under. Rates include all meals and ranch activities. AE, MC, V. **Amenities:** Babysitting; children's program; 4 tennis courts; extensive watersports equipment; Wi-Fi (free). In room: No phone.

Best Western Kwa Taq Nuk Resort ★ This Best Western affiliate is a top-draw resort managed and owned by the Salish & Kootenai Indian tribes. It's the nicest property on the Polson end of the lake and offers a restaurant, marina, and art gallery. It's also the best decorated, with interesting and artful American-Indian works on the walls. Lakeside rooms have commanding views, enhanced by decks furnished with chairs and cocktail tables. All the rooms are large and amply furnished. The main lobby level is home to both a lounge and an indoor-outdoor restaurant, with stunning lakeside views. The lower level has a large, comfortable sitting area with a large-screen cable television, swimming pool, and casino. This is the most expensive property on this end of the lake, but the amenities make it worth the extra money.

303 U.S. 93, Polson, MT 59860. ⓒ **800/882-6363** or 406/883-3636. Fax 406/883-5392. www.kwataqnuk. com. 112 units, including 1 suite. $129–$159 double; $159–$209 suite. Lower rates fall–spring. AE, DC, DISC, MC, V. **Amenities:** Restaurant (steakhouse); lounge; concierge; Jacuzzi; indoor and outdoor pools; watersports rentals. In room: A/C, TV, hair dryer, Wi-Fi (free).

Bridge Street Cottages ★★ Nestled into a nicely wooded area adjacent to the Swan River, these relatively new cottages (2003) are very clean and comfortable, sporting original art, granite countertops, and terrific attention to detail. The units sleep from two to six guests, ranging from hotel-like "cottage suites" to charming "river cottages," with full kitchens, laundry rooms, and porches fronting the river. All in all, this is a terrific base for couples and families alike, and the nicely landscaped property balances privacy with easy walking access to the village center.

309 Bridge St., Bigfork, MT 59911. ⓒ **888/264-4974** or 406/837-2785. www.bridgestreetcottages.com. 12 units. Summer $185–$325 double; rest of year $95–$245 double. AE, DISC, MC, V. In room: A/C, TV w/ VCR or DVD, Internet (free), kitchen.

The Candlewycke Inn ★ (Finds) Tucked away on 10 acres of pine forest at the foot of the Swan Mountains in dinky Ferndale, this luxurious and large B&B is a modern home that innkeepers Megan and Steve Ward converted into a first-rate inn. The parlor, with 30-foot ceilings and an exposed pine staircase, draws you into a comfortable living space bedecked with an attractive selection of folk art. The large rooms have private bathrooms (two have jetted tubs) and range from the somewhat frilly Botanical (with a canopied king-size bed, large bathroom, and private entry) to the rugged Wilderness (adorned with animal hides and two queen-size beds). There's a trail system on the property, an immaculate lawn, and all sorts of little touches—such as antlers converted to backscratchers. The breakfasts, anything from orange-cheese blintzes to spinach-artichoke-mushroom Italian eggs, are tailored to the tastes of guests.

311 Aero Lane, Bigfork, MT 59911. © **888/617-8805** or 406/837-6406. www.candlewyckeinn.com. 5 units. $135–$185 double; $265 suite. Rates include full breakfast. AE, MC, V. **Amenities:** Outdoor Jacuzzi. *In room:* A/C, TV, fridge, hair dryer, Wi-Fi (free).

Marina Cay Resort ★ Boasting the most protected harbor on the lake, Marina Cay is a nice resort right on the water on the outskirts of Bigfork. The recently remodeled rooms are very large, and most open to a view on the water. The place attracts a few celebrities, including actress Jodie Foster, basketball legend Shaquille O'Neal, and writer Stephen King. Rooms here are sizable, and there is a wide variety to choose from, but the walls in the older buildings are on the thin side and noise carries from room to room. The restaurant, **Champs,** serves food year-round, with a sports-bar atmosphere; it will also cook the fish you catch from the lake or nearby rivers. The summer-only **Tiki Bar** serves drinks by the pool under flaming gas lamps.

180 Vista Lane, Bigfork, MT 59911. © **800/433-6516** or 406/837-5861. Fax 406/837-1118. www.marina cay.com. 125 units. $135–$210 double; $249–$379 condo. Lower rates in off season. AE, DC, DISC, MC, V. **Amenities:** Restaurant (American); lounge; concierge; 2 Jacuzzis; outdoor pool; extensive watersports rentals. *In room:* A/C, TV, hair dryer, kitchenette.

Mountain Lake Lodge ★★ Unlike many of its peers, Mountain Lake Lodge focuses on accommodations, not recreation, and its single-mindedness shows. The highlights of the hotel, located 5 miles south of Bigfork, are the idyllic courtyard—with a pool, waterfall, and the best view on the lake—and the rooms, each with a sitting area, fireplace, lake view, and deck or patio. Located in one of five buildings, all have a king-size bed in an imposing log frame and a queen-size sofa sleeper; many have Jacuzzis. The restaurant, **Terras,** serves steak and seafood, or you can grab a wood-fired pizza in the pub. The entire property is nonsmoking.

1950 Sylvan Dr., Bigfork, MT 59911. © **877/823-4923** or 406/837-3800. Fax 406/837-3861. www.mountainlakelodge.com. 30 units, including 15 suites. $219–$229 double; $229–$285 suite. Lower rates in off season. AE, DISC, MC, V. **Amenities:** Restaurant; lounge; exercise room; outdoor Jacuzzi; seasonal outdoor pool. *In room:* A/C, TV, fridge, hair dryer, kitchen, Wi-Fi (free).

Swan River Inn ★ Located in the heart of Bigfork, the Swan River Inn has a decidedly European feel, injected with a fair amount of whimsy to boot. Each of the eight rooms is quite distinctive. The large log-cabin suite is decorated to resemble, well, a log cabin. The Arabian suite is an Aladdin-style fantasy come to life. The Art Deco suite hearkens back to the 1920s. All have beautifully restored bathrooms. Upstairs, the **Swan River Dinner House** serves steak, pork loin, rack of lamb, and a number of chicken and pasta dishes. The second dining room (served from the same kitchen), the **Grotto,** is a lounge transformed into a beautiful French-inspired facility complete with heavy wood furniture, stucco walls, and wrought-iron fixtures.

360 Grand Ave., Bigfork, MT 59911. © **406/837-2220.** Fax 406/837-2327. www.swanriverinn.com. 8 units. $145–$265 summer; $115–$165 fall–spring. DISC, MC, V. **Amenities:** Restaurant; bar; rooftop garden cafe. *In room:* A/C, TV, fridge.

WHERE TO DINE

7

Bigfork has cornered the market on fine dining on the lake. Flathead residents from Whitefish and Kalispell routinely make their way to Bigfork to eat and take in a play at the Bigfork Summer Playhouse. Aside from the options below, the restaurant at the **Swan River Inn** (see above) is also recommended.

Invite American Kitchen & Bar ★★ AMERICAN   Comfort food done with a creative flair is the specialty at this swank second-story bar and grill in the village center. The menu offers selections like fish and chips and bacon-wrapped meatloaf all day long, and expands into pricier game dishes and steaks come dinnertime. Favorites include cedar-planked scallops and a chargrilled elk filet with a red wine–currant sauce and Parmesan-sage potatoes. The presentation and atmosphere are both a cut above the norm. There is a long and varied cocktail menu that includes a surprisingly tasty mango-jalapeño margarita.

459 Electric Ave., Bigfork. ✆ **406/837-2786.** www.invitemontana.com. Reservations recommended. Lunch $8–$12; dinner $8–$32. AE, DISC, MC, V. Summer daily 11:30am–10:30pm; fall–spring daily noon–10pm.

La Provence ★★ FRENCH/MEDITERRANEAN   Marc Guizol, the affable chef/owner of La Provence, made his way to Bigfork after his culinary career took him to the Ritz-Carlton in Naples and Caesars Palace in Las Vegas. In his own eatery, Guizol's experience shines. The dinner menu is filled with lovingly prepared French standards, from escargot on a potato cake to roasted duck and grilled filet mignon. He also seasonally mixes in a few game dishes and classic European desserts. The room itself is an airy, pleasant space with a simple country French flair. For lunch, the restaurant's deli serves light fare: quiche, pastries, and sandwiches.

408 Bridge St., Bigfork. ✆ **406/837-2923.** www.bigforklaprovence.com. Reservations recommended. Lunch $7–$9; dinner $17–$29. AE, MC, V. No credit cards at lunch. Mon–Sat 11am–2pm; daily 5–9pm. Closed Sun–Mon in winter.

ShowThyme ★★ NEW AMERICAN   When you ask locals what the best restaurant in town is, they'll more often than not tell you ShowThyme—the restaurant that's located next to the summer playhouse. The atmosphere is a little bit New York, a little bit Montana. With a chef named Blu Funk and a manager named Rose Funk, you know the food has to be colorful. And it is: The Funks serve up everything from rack of lamb to sirloin steaks to *chiles rellenos*, plus nightly specials, all with a touch of creative flair. The king salmon is excellent, as is the seared sea scallop with seaweed salad.

548 Electric Ave., Bigfork. ✆ **406/837-0707.** www.showthyme.com. Reservations recommended. Main courses $14–$28. AE, DISC, MC, V. Summer Tues–Sat 5–10pm; fall–spring Tues–Sat 5–9pm. Often closed for several weeks in Jan and/or Feb.

Tiebuckers Pub and Eatery AMERICAN   Located in the old railroad depot in the sleepy town of Somers, Tiebuckers is a good restaurant that is prized by the locals. The fresh fish and steamed clams keep the crowds coming, but the menu also offers a good variety of beef and pasta. The ribs in Grandpa's Sauce (a family secret) are also excellent. There's also a selection with sandwiches and other inexpensive dishes.

75 Somers Rd., Somers. ✆ **406/857-3335.** Reservations recommended for parties of 6 or more. Main courses $6–$22. DISC, MC, V. Tues–Sat 5–9pm. Closed Nov.

Extends 91 miles S of Bigfork; southern end: 33 miles E of Missoula; 90 miles W of Helena

The 50-mile stretch of Mont. 83 from Columbia Falls to Swan, Condon, and Seeley lakes is isolated from Flathead Lake's tourist attractions. Though less traveled, the road boasts vistas even more lovely than those seen from U.S. 93, its federal cousin to the west. Opportunities for watching wildlife are quite good, and Seeley, Summit, and Alva lakes—all excellent recreational areas—lie close to the highway.

Swan Valley seems more authentically "Montana" than other, busier areas, perhaps because the area isn't developed for tourists. Though some think the timber industry clear-cuts are an eyesore, the remainder of this thinly populated area is crowned with snowcapped mountains and accessible lakes. Swan Valley seems remote compared to the nearby larger towns—an hour from Missoula, 2 hours from Helena—and it looks like it will remain relatively undiscovered for some time. In winter, snowmobiling, cross-country skiing, and even sled-dog mushing are the sports of choice in this out-of-the-way wonderland. Be sure to watch out for deer year-round along Mont. 83, especially at dawn and dusk—and remember, they usually travel in small groups.

Seeley Lake is one of the places where you can see loon. Henry David Thoreau described the bird's call as a "long-drawn, unearthly howl, probably more like that of a wolf than any other bird." The loon is a symbol of north-country wilderness, and an appropriate one for this quiet and beautiful area.

ESSENTIALS

GETTING THERE Other than being air-dropped, the only way to get into the Swan Valley is by motor vehicle via Mont. 83. The airports near **Kalispell** (© **406/257-5994**) and in **Missoula** (© **406/728-4381**) are almost equidistant from the Swan. The town of Seeley Lake is 48 miles from Missoula. Take Mont. 200 east from Missoula 33 miles to Mont. 83 north. It's 42 miles from Kalispell to Swan Lake in the northern portion of the valley. Take U.S. 93 south to Mont. 82 east, then Mont. 83 south. For weather reports, call © **800/226-7623** or 511 (mobile) for road conditions statewide.

VISITOR INFORMATION The Swan Valley isn't exactly a self-promoter. Though several businesses rely on tourists, the valley-wide tendency is to remain small. The **Seeley Lake Chamber of Commerce,** P.O. Box 516, Seeley Lake, MT 59868 (© **406/677-2880;** www.seeleylakechamber.com), can send you information on local happenings. For general information about Glacier Country, which includes the Swan Valley, call © **800/338-5072,** or check out **www.glaciermt.com**.

GETTING OUTSIDE

Densely forested and marked by a sparkling chain of lakes, the Seeley–Swan Valley offers a variety of activities for the outdoor enthusiast, with a vast network of Forest Service trails providing year-round recreational opportunities for hiking, mountain biking, fishing, cross-country skiing, and snowmobiling. The **Seeley Lake Ranger District,** 2583 Mont. 83, Seeley Lake (© **406/677-2233;** www.fs.fed.us/r1/lolo), will provide you with a detailed map of these trails upon request. The district office is 3 miles north of Seeley Lake near mile marker 18 of Mont. 83. One of the most popular summer activities is the **Clearwater River Canoe Trail,** a 3½-mile leisurely run down the river to the north end of Seeley Lake. The put-in is at the end of Forest Service Road 17597 and ends at the canoe landing at the ranger station.

The Forest Service publishes a brochure that outlines a number of hikes in the national forest and wilderness areas. You can pick up a copy at the Lolo National Forest ranger district office, located at 3583 Mont. 83 just north of the town of Seeley Lake, or request one by phone (✆ **406/677-2233**). For a fairly short and interesting family hike, try the **Morrell Falls Trail,** a 2.5-mile hike from the trail head to a series of cascades, the largest of which drops 90 feet. From Clearwater Junction, travel north on Mont. 83 for 15 miles. Turn east on Cottonwood Lakes Road 477 and go 1¼ miles. Turn north on West Morrell Road 4353, then go 6 miles. Turn east on Pyramid Pass Road 4364 and go a quarter-mile. Turn north on Morrell Falls Road 4364 and go a mile to the trail head.

OUTFITTERS & GUIDES   Swan Valley is home to several experienced guides who know parts of this vast territory like the toughened backs of their leathery hands. Guided pack trips on horseback usually run from $175 to $250 per person per day, with a normal trip into the Bob Marshall Wilderness usually lasting a week. **Buck Creek Guide Service** (✆ **406/754-2471**; www.buckcreekguideservice.com) offers trips that focus on natural history and local culture, as well as big-game-hunting expeditions. **JM Bar Outfitters** (✆ **406/825-3230**; www.jmbaroutfitters.com) offers trail rides and fishing trips in the summer and hunting trips in the fall and winter. Call for prices. In Clearwater, **Monture Crick Outfitters** (✆ **888/420-5768** or 406/244-5763; www.montanaoutfitter.com) offers summer backpacking trips, hunting, and fishing in the Bob Marshall Wilderness.

WHERE TO STAY

The Lodges on Seeley Lake ★ (Finds)   One of only two lodges right on Seeley Lake, this 1920 lodge-and-cabins operation is secluded and offers plenty of space to stretch out. The cabins are spacious and beautifully decorated, complete with upholstered chairs and queen-size beds. All the rooms have televisions, kitchens, fireplaces, and private bathrooms; some have in-room Jacuzzis. Fortunately, the modern conveniences have been added without sacrificing the rustic feeling of the lodge. The best thing here, though, remains the peaceful views of the lake from the beachfront and of the wilderness beyond. The lodges have complimentary boats for guests to take out for fishing or recreation.

2156 Boy Scout Rd., P.O. Box 568, Seeley Lake, MT 59868. ✆ **800/900-9016.** Fax 406/677-3806. www. lodgesonseeleylake.com. 15 units. $139–$208 double. MC, V. **Amenities:** Watersports equipment; Wi-Fi (free). *In room:* TV, kitchen, no phone.

Swan River Lodge (Value)   This is a good budget option in the Swan Valley. The rooms are fairly ordinary, though the setting is spectacular. And the building is pretty, a two-level log structure that doesn't look like your typical roadside motel. Several restaurants are nearby, and you can also arrange accommodations for your horse.

Btw. mile markers 46 and 47 on Mont. 83, P.O. Box 1278, Condon, MT 59826. ✆ **877/588-7926** or 406/754-2688. www.theswanriverlodge.com. 22 units. $56–$65 double. Rates include continental breakfast. AE, DC, DISC, MC, V. Dogs accepted (free). **Amenities:** Wi-Fi (free). *In room:* TV.

Guest Ranches & Resorts

Double Arrow Lodge ★   Double Arrow is 2 miles south of Seeley Lake off of Mont. 83, near the Bob Marshall Wilderness Area. The resort has just about any activity that a Montana-bound vacationer could want—golf, fishing, horseback riding, hiking, and mountain biking. There are also guided fly-fishing and float trips available on the Blackfoot River. In the winter, there's cross-country skiing, snowmobiling, and sleigh riding. You can get accommodations suited to nearly any taste, from relatively inexpensive rooms in the main lodge, to cabins, to a full-size, four-bedroom lodge all to yourself. The cabins are large and comfortably furnished, with sitting areas featuring upholstered chairs and sofas. Rides to trail heads in the wilderness area offer opportunities for guests to explore Clearwater Valley, Horseshoe Hills, and the Morrell Falls National Recreation Trail. Two all-weather tennis courts and an enclosed pool with a hot tub keep guests busy afterward. There's also an 18-hole golf course.

East of Mont. 83, P.O. Box 747, Seeley Lake, MT 59868. © **800/468-0777** or 406/677-2777. Fax 406/677-2922. www.doublearrowlodge.com. 26 units. $100–$200 double; $200–$800 2- to 4-bedroom lodges. Call for off-season rates. AE, DISC, MC, V. **Amenities:** Restaurant; lounge; golf course; indoor Jacuzzi; indoor pool; watersports equipment; Wi-Fi (free). *In room:* Kitchen, no phone, Wi-Fi (in some).

The Lodge at Lake Upsata ★ Finds

This family-oriented lodge is secluded along the southern border of the Bob Marshall Wilderness Area in the grand setting of the Blackfoot Valley. You stay in trim, woodsy cabins that have shower-only bathrooms (no tubs) and plenty of charm. Hiking is the number-one activity here, although kayaks and canoes are available for guests. The seclusion is second to none; the most noise you'll hear is the loons calling out to you across the lake.

201 Lower Lakeside Lane, P.O. Box 6, Ovando, MT 59854. © **800/594-7687** or 406/793-5890. Fax 406/793-5894. www.upsata.com. 8 cabins. $120 double. Rates include full breakfast. MC, V. Pets accepted (free). **Amenities:** Dining room; outdoor hot tub; watersports equipment; Wi-Fi (free). *In room:* Fridge.

The Resort at Paws Up ★★

Opened in 2005—199 years after Meriwether Lewis climbed Sentinel Rock on the property—this cattle ranch-turned-ultraposh-resort is situated along 7 miles of the Blackfoot River on 37,000 pristinely rugged acres. Lavish accommodations come in several varieties, ranging from smallish timber duplexes to guest homes, including the historic 1908 Morris Ranch House next to Elk Creek, which sleeps eight. With 300-thread-count linens, outdoor hot tubs, lifelike dog sculptures, and DVD libraries among the standard amenities, the common thread is luxury, which even extends into Paws Up's eco-resort "Tent City," where roughing it includes feather beds, electricity, and running water. It's certainly not cheap, but Paws Up's rate includes just about every imaginable recreational activity, and then some: hiking on the resort's 25 miles of trails; horseback riding; sport shooting; ATV rides; boating and watersports; and snowmobiling, cross-country skiing, and sleigh rides in winter. There are special packages for anglers, couples, and equestrians.

40060 Paws Up Rd., Greenough, MT 59823. © **800/473-0601.** Fax 406/244-5201. www.pawsup.com. 26 cabins. $540–$2,450 per person per night. Rates include all meals and activities. AE, DC, DISC, MC, V. About 30 miles east of Missoula via Mont. 200. **Amenities:** 2 restaurants; concierge; exercise room; room service; spa; extensive watersports equipment; Wi-Fi (free). *In room:* A/C, TV/DVD, movie library, hair dryer, kitchenette.

Tamaracks Resort ★ Finds

Tamaracks started out as a homestead in 1916 and became a resort in 1930. It is right on Seeley Lake with 1,700 feet of lakefront. The resort has a 1940s feel to it, with lots of room between the cabins, screened-in porches, and an attached campground (sites run $30 a night). The cabins are clean and comfortable, and there is also a trio of full-fledged log homes for those needing more space (the largest is 2,500 sq. ft.). Every cabin and home has a full kitchen. The resort offers boat, canoe, and kayak rentals (as well as launch and moorage facilities), a basketball court, horseshoe pits, and volleyball in the summer, and cross-country ski, skate, and snowmobile rentals in winter.

Mont. 83, mile 17, P.O. Box 812, Seeley Lake, MT 59868. © **800/477-7216** or 406/677-2433. Fax 406/677-3503. www.tamaracks.com. 17 cabins, including 4 log homes. $119–$305 cabin; $225–$450 log home. Lower rates Oct–May. MC, V. **Amenities:** Watersports equipment. *In room:* TV/VCR or DVD, kitchen, no phone, Wi-Fi (some units, free).

In Seeley Lake, the locals' choice for breakfast or lunch is the **Filling Station Restaurant and Bar,** 3183 Mont. 83 N. (✆ 406/677-2080), and the best fried takeout option is undoubtedly the **Chicken Coop,** 645 Pine Dr. (✆ 406/677-2980). **Littlebird's Schoolhouse,** 110 Larch Lane (✆ 406/677-3663), serves breakfast, lunch, and coffee drinks every day but Sunday and gourmet dinners on Fridays and Saturdays. Both restaurants are in the heart of town. In Swan Lake, try the restaurant at the **Laughing Horse Lodge** on Mont. 83 (✆ 406/886-2080), which serves hearty meals and uses fresh, locally grown ingredients. The lodge also has double rooms for $85 to $185 in summer.

Lindey's Prime Steak House ★ STEAKS   A carbon copy of a sister restaurant in Minnesota that has achieved national acclaim, Lindey's makes ordering easy: There are only three dinner choices—chopped sirloin, prime sirloin, and special sirloin—all of which are accompanied by the restaurant's excellent greaseless hash browns plus a tossed green salad. Seating is in a comfortable glass-enclosed space with views overlooking the lake and the seaplane landing area. Bay Burgers is the lunch outlet, serving juicy burgers and little else.

Mont. 83, Seeley Lake. ✆ 406/677-9229. Main courses lunch $5–$8, dinner $13–$30. DISC, MC, V. May–Sept daily 11am–10pm; Oct to mid-Apr Thurs–Mon 11am–3pm and 5–9pm. Closed mid-Apr to late Apr.

---

7 THE BOB MARSHALL WILDERNESS COMPLEX ★★

45 miles S of Big Fork; 78 miles NE of Missoula; 80 miles W of Great Falls

The Bob Marshall Wilderness Complex is the largest wilderness area in the Lower 48 states, covering 1.5 million acres, or about 2,400 square miles. I hate to keep picking on Rhode Island for these comparisons, but the Bob, as it is usually called, is more than twice the size of that state.

The complex includes the Bob Marshall Wilderness proper, and the Great Bear and Scapegoat wilderness areas. It abuts Glacier National Park, creating a huge area of relatively untouched country extending nearly half the width of Montana from the Canadian border. Marshall himself was one of the earliest advocates of wilderness for its own sake in the U.S., and the wild lands that bear his name were among the areas designated by the federal Wilderness Act of 1964. The Great Bear and Scapegoat areas were set aside in the 1970s.

Just south of Glacier National Park, the complex occupies nearly the entire territory that lies between the boundaries of U.S. 2 to the north, Mont. 83 to the west, Mont. 200 to the south, and U.S. highways 287 and 89 to the east. Access points along these roads occur infrequently and are poorly marked, so keep your eyes peeled.

The wilderness area has become very popular with hikers and horse-packers over the years, leading to a curious pattern of trail deterioration. Federal budget austerity allows the U.S. Forest Service little funding for trail maintenance, and while heavy traffic on the most popular trails has led to their erosion, many of the secondary trails have virtually disappeared. Quite a few trails that are marked on topographical maps of the area are faint or nonexistent on the ground. You should know fundamental trail-finding and direction skills—how to read a topo map—in case a trail dies out or is covered by snowbanks.

(**Tips**) **Advice for Day-Trippers**

Day hiking is best done near **Holland Lake.** Take Mont. 83 south 61 miles from Bigfork, or north 20 miles from Seeley Lake, to reach the **Holland Lake Lodge** ((**877/925-6343** or 406/754-2282; www.hollandlakelodge.com) and the trails. Trail 42 from the north side of Holland Lake connects with Trail 110 to reach the Necklace Lakes just inside the Wilderness boundaries. To reach the Holland Lake Falls and Upper Holland Lake before crossing the Wilderness boundary at Gordon Pass, take Trail 415 a short way until it joins Trail 35. This trail, taken to its end, stretches from the western boundary into the center of the park near the South Fork of the Flathead River (not a day hike). Rooms at the lodge run $145 to $185 per person, double occupancy, all meals included.

EXPLORING THE AREA

For information, maps, and advice about traveling in the Bob Marshall Wilderness Complex, contact one of the ranger stations monitoring the wilderness. In the **Lewis and Clark National Forest:** Rocky Mountain Ranger District, 1102 Main Ave. NW, Box 340, Choteau, MT 59242 ((**406/466-5341;** www.fs.fed.us/r1/lewisclark). In the **Flathead National Forest:** the Glacier View and Hungry Horse Ranger Districts, 8975 U.S. 2 E., Hungry Horse, MT 59919 ((**406/758-5376**). In the Swan Lake Ranger District, 200 Ranger Station Rd., Bigfork, MT 59911 ((**406/837-7500;** www.fs.fed.us/r1/flathead). In the **Lolo National Forest:** Seeley Lake Ranger District, HC 31 P.O. Box 3200, Seeley Lake, MT 59868 ((**406/677-2233;** www.fs.fed.us/r1/lolo). In the **Helena National Forest:** Lincoln Ranger District, 1569 Mont. 200, Lincoln, MT 59639 ((**406/362-4265;** www.fs.fed.us/r1/helena). The **Bob Marshall Wilderness Foundation,** P.O. Box 190688, Hungry Horse, MT 59919 ((**406/387-3808;** www.thebmwf. org), is a good resource as well.

The most popular destination in the Bob is the **Chinese Wall,** a striking rock formation that stands more than 1,000 feet tall and stretches for 22 miles through the wilderness on the western boundary of the **Sun River Game Preserve.** One of the more well-traveled trails and easy accesses to the Chinese Wall is along the South Fork of the Sun River on the Holland Lake–Benchmark Trail (see below). From the east, reach the Chinese Wall by taking Trail 202 at Benchmark for 5 miles to Trail 203, then continue on this trail for roughly 11 miles before taking the Indian Creek Trail, Trail 211, to the south end of the Chinese Wall at White River Pass, elevation 7,590 feet. The Chinese Wall is unmistakable and is one of the most recognizable geologic formations in Montana. The USGS topographical maps for the trip are Slategoat Mountain, Prairie Reef, and Amphitheatre Mountain.

The high meadows at the base of the wall are very fragile, and overnight camping is prohibited along the base between Cliff and Salt mountains, so plan your trip to allow time to reach a camping area away from this section of the wall.

Towering peaks run great lengths through the Bob and stand as some of the tallest, and certainly the most dramatic, sites in the northwest part of the state outside Glacier National Park. **Holland Peak,** just north of Holland Lake on the wilderness area's western boundary, is a spectacular 9,356-foot giant that can be seen from afar but cannot be accessed directly. A short day hike is available from the Holland Lake Lodge (see "Advice for Day-Trippers," above, for directions to the lodge) into the wilderness to **Holland Falls.** The distance from the trail head to the falls is only about 1.5 miles, an easy hike with only 240 feet of elevation gain. This trail is designated for hikers only; bikes, horses, and other pack animals are prohibited.

Once inside the wilderness area, **Big Salmon Lake** is a wonderful destination for photographers, capturing the length and the beauty of Holland Peak's east face. To reach Big Salmon Lake, take Trail 42 from the Holland Lake Lodge on the west side of the Bob to Trail 110. It's a very long day hike, and a reasonable 2-day hike through the Swan Range to Big Salmon Lake.

Located one-third of the way in on the **Holland Lake–Benchmark Trail** (a 60-mile trail across the midsection of the Bob that, following a series of shorter trails, takes roughly a week to traverse), Salmon Lake is simple purity without sight or sound of civilization. This trail also runs just south of the Chinese Wall.

North, in the Great Bear, is the impressive **Great Northern Mountain.** This 8,705-foot peak towers over the northeast part of the Great Bear Wilderness and can be viewed from many different points along the roadsides near the wilderness areas. You'll need a couple of vehicles if you don't have someone who can pick you up where you exit the Bob at the end of your journey. Park at Holland Lake if you plan on making it your terminus, or at Benchmark, west of Augusta, if you plan on ending there.

If you begin on the east side, the Holland Lake–Benchmark Trail follows the South Fork of the Sun River on trails 202 and 203 before moving west along Indian Creek on Trail 211. This takes you to the south end of the Chinese Wall at White River Pass. From there, you'll take Trail 138 along the South Fork of the White River until you reach the White River and Trail 112. This trail takes you to the South Fork of the Flathead River at White River Park. Across the river, you'll find Murphy Flats and Trail 263 along the river to Trail 110. This long trail takes you along Big Salmon Lake and the Swan Range, and then to Holland Lake outside the Bob's western boundary.

To reach the summit of Great Northern, you'll have to do some off-trail hiking—8 miles, if you make a round-trip. From Martin City, just northeast of Columbia Falls on U.S. 2, take the East Side Reservoir Road (38) for just more than 15 miles to Highline Loop Road (1048). Take this road for just more than a half-mile across the bridge to the trail head. Start along the left side of the creek until the landscape opens up. Trudge up to the ridge, then along it, to Great Northern's summit.

The majestic **Scapegoat Mountain** is the dominating jewel of the Scapegoat Wilderness Area. Surrounded by cliffs, this 9,200-foot summit is easily the most prominent feature in the southern part of the wilderness complex.

Wildlife abounds in the Bob, with grizzly bears being the most feared and the most difficult to spot. Moose and deer are common. Elk gather each fall for mating at the base of the Chinese Wall in the Sun River Game Preserve on the wilderness's east side. There are lots of birds, including the ptarmigan, a brown quail-like bird that changes the color of its plumage each winter to snow white.

HELPFUL TIPS Some things to remember when camping: Before you set out, consult a ranger at one of the district ranger stations mentioned above about distances, the wisdom of your itinerary, and restrictions. You can also pick up a topographical map. Carry plenty of water and water containers. Remember when loading up your pack that this is the weight you'll likely endure for a week or so. Restrictions are few. No vehicles are allowed in the area, including bicycles. To get around in the Bob you either walk or ride on an animal's back. It might also help to remember, too, that hunting is allowed in many

Fun Facts **Ericaceae Vaccinium: The Huckleberry**

The key ingredient in everything from vinegar to fudge to jelly beans in Montana's northwestern corner, the wild huckleberry grows in similar climates around the world. In Montana, it was a sweet and tart staple for Native Americans and early settlers, and remains a favorite of the grizzly bear to this day. Humans harvest them from the state's public lands—the plants can't be commercially cultivated—and no permit is necessary. Harvest season begins in July at lower elevations (around 3,000 ft.) and continues into September (at elevations around 7,000 ft.). Look for blueberry-like berries on bushes with oval leaves—and try to resist eating them until the picking is done.

areas, making backpacking in the Bob a little less inviting in the fall. Wear bright colors and make lots of noise.

A RECOMMENDED OUTFITTER　A Montana native, Choteau-based Bill Cunningham has been guiding backpacking expeditions into the Bob Marshall Wilderness since 1973, and that makes his **High Country Adventures** the oldest backpacking guide company in the country. It's also the Bob's only licensed backpacking outfitter, where there are dozens of licensed horse-packing guides. Cunningham goes on every trip, as does his wife, Polly. The company organizes three or four trips per summer that cover about 10 miles of trail in an average day, ranging from a week to 12 days. Breaking up the hiking are good meals, good company, and a layover day for a little fishing or mountain climbing. Contact High Country Adventures (© **406/466-5699;** www.hcamontana.com) for reservations. Trips start at $875 per person per week. Rates include shuttle from airport, food, and community gear.

8 KALISPELL ★

115 miles N of Missoula; 249 miles E of Spokane, Washington

Located smack-dab in the center of Montana's primary vacation and tourism region, Kalispell isn't as much a destination for recreational visitors as are Whitefish and Bigfork, but it is a good base for exploring the area and has a number of attractions in its own right. The city, which is also a business and industrial center, is in a beautiful setting and conveniently located for visits to Flathead Lake, skiing in Whitefish, or hiking and touring in Glacier National Park. If you come to Kalispell after visiting Glacier or the Bob Marshall Wilderness, it will seem positively urban. It has all the modern inconveniences, including a crowded mall and long waits at traffic lights. But it has managed to preserve a good deal of its historical character, and has a colorful arts-and-dining scene.

ESSENTIALS

GETTING THERE　**Glacier Park International Airport** (© **406/257-5994;** www. flyglacier.com) is located north of town at 4170 U.S. 2. **Alaska/Horizon** (© **800/547-9308**), **Allegiant** (© **702/505-8888**), **Delta** (© **800/221-1212**), **Northwest** (© **800/225-2525**), and **United** (© **800/864-8331**) provide service.

U.S. 2 will get you here from the east or west. From Missoula, U.S. 93 leads north into town on a scenic 120-mile route that takes you past Flathead Lake. The drive usually takes a solid 2½ hours, no matter what the season. RVs amble along the gradually curving road during summer to the frustration of most other drivers, and icy conditions warrant added caution and reduced speeds during the winter.

Amtrak (© **800/872-7245;** www.amtrak.com) stops at the Whitefish depot, just 15 miles north of Kalispell. The bus terminal is located at 1301 S. Main St. (© **406/755-4011**).

VISITOR INFORMATION The **Flathead Convention and Visitor Bureau** is located at 15 Depot Park, Kalispell, MT 59901 (© **800/543-3105** or 406/756-9091; www.fcvb. org), and not only offers practical information concerning Kalispell, but provides information on year-round lodging, activities, and attractions, including Glacier National Park, Whitefish Mountain Resort, and Flathead Lake.

GETTING AROUND Rental-car companies **Avis** (© **800/831-2847**), **Budget** (© **800/527-0700**), **Hertz** (© **800/654-3131**), and **National/Alamo** (© **800/227-7368**) maintain counters at the airport.

For taxi service, call **Kalispell Taxi and Airport Shuttle** (© **406/752-4022**) or **Flathead-Glacier Transportation** (© **406/892-3390**).

GETTING OUTSIDE

Kalispell itself isn't exactly a destination for the person looking for outdoor recreation, but its location between Glacier National Park and Flathead Lake makes it a good home base for those exploring this region during both the summer and ski seasons.

BIKING Since motor vehicle traffic on U.S. 2 or U.S. 93 makes them less than ideal for bike riding, cyclists usually head to the back roads. **Whitefish Stage Road** runs parallel to U.S. 93 (from U.S. 93, go east on Reserve St. to reach it) and offers some great views of the mountains in a bucolic environment. For area information, as well as all kinds of bicycle accessories, try **Wheaton's,** 214 1st Ave. W. (© **406/257-5808**).

FISHING There is good fishing on the main Flathead River between Columbia Falls and Kalispell for trout and whitefish. There is good shore access at Pressentine, which is 5 miles north of Kalispell on U.S. 2 (follow the fishing access signs). Or you can float from Pressentine downriver to Old Steel Bridge.

GOLF **Buffalo Hill** (© **888/342-6319** or 406/756-4530; www.golfbuffalohill.com), just off U.S. 2 north of town at 1176 N. Main St., is an older course that's very hilly, with lots of trees and lots of memorable holes that can have serious golfers brushing up on their cursing. Cost is $42 to $58 for 18 holes, depending on the month and time of day. Carts are $28 to $34.

HIKING **Lone Pine State Park** (© **406/755-2706;** fwp.mt.gov) is an attractive park with a few hiking trails. Go west on U.S. 2. At the intersection with Meridian, you'll see signs for the park sending you left (south). Take this road for about 5 miles (in the curve to your right, the road becomes Foys Lake Rd.) to the park. Once you're there, take in the views of the valley below or hike on the trails. The day-use fee is $5.

SEEING THE SIGHTS

Woodland Park, on the east edge of town at Woodland Park Drive, is a little spot that offers visitors a place to sit down in the sun and relax if they want to kill a few hours outside without killing themselves. There's a lagoon with ducks and a swimming pool.

Walking tracks skirt the park. Another worthwhile attraction is the **Museum at Central School,** 124 2nd Ave. E. (© **406/756-8381;** www.yourmuseum.org), dedicated to preserving Kalispell's history. Admission is $5 adults, $4 seniors, and kids are free.

Conrad Mansion Museum ★ This 26-room Victorian mansion takes up most of a city block. Built in 1895 by Missouri River freighter Charles E. Conrad, the mansion has been beautifully restored and outfitted with the original furnishings. All tours of the mansion are guided and last about an hour; tour guides are dressed in Victorian costume and explain the history of Conrad and his palatial home. Some highlights: an amazing collection of dolls and toys from three generations of the Conrad family, meticulously kept clothing from the 19th century, and the annual Christmas bazaar in late October. The beautiful grounds also make for a peaceful locale for a short walk or a picnic.

330 Woodland Ave. © **406/755-2166.** www.conradmansion.com. Tours $8 adults, $7 seniors, $3 children 11 and under. Mid-May to mid-Oct daily 10am–5pm; Christmas tours offered in Dec Wed–Sun 1–4pm. Last tour begins an hour before closing. Located 6 blocks east of Main St.

Hockaday Museum of Art ★ The charming Hockaday contains art formerly located in the Carnegie Library. The museum focuses on the works of Montana artists, both contemporary and historic, including Russell Chatham, Ace Powell, and Robert Scriver. There are tours, a gift shop, and an "Arts in the Park" program each July. The Hockaday has a very fine regional reputation for the quality of its programs.

302 2nd Ave. E. © **406/755-5268.** www.hockadaymuseum.org. $5 adults, $4 seniors, $2 students, free for children 11 and under. Tues–Sat 10am–5pm.

SHOPPING

Although not a major shopping destination, Kalispell has enough to offer if your money is burning a hole in your pocket. The **Kalispell Center Mall,** 20 N. Main St. (© **406/751-5052**), has more than 40 stores and restaurants. Just up the street, downtown Kalispell has a few stores of its own. **Norm's News,** 34 Main St. (© **406/755-5466**), has the latest newspapers from around the globe as well as a comprehensive magazine rack and espresso bar. **Books West** (© **406/752-6900**) is the downtown bookshop on 101 Main St. The **Western Outdoor Store,** 48 Main St. (© **406/756-5818**), has a vast collection of Western gear for sale—4,000 pairs of cowboy boots, sterling silver Western belt buckles, and, for the wannabe dude, cowboy hats in all sizes and shapes. There's also an antiques store in the basement. The **Rocky Mountain Outfitter,** 135 Main St. (© **406/752-2446**), has all the gear you'll need for hiking nearby trails and scaling the peaks. You can also rent kayaks and canoes if you want to head out on the water on your own. **Mark Ogle Gallery,** 101 E. Center St. (© **406/752-4217**), features a selection of wildlife paintings and prints by its same-named owner.

WHERE TO STAY

Beyond the choices listed below, there are a number of reliable chain properties in Kalispell, including **Travelodge,** 350 N. Main St., Kalispell MT 59901 (© **800/578-7878** or 406/755-6123), with summer rates of $80 to $105 double; and **Holiday Inn Express & Suites,** 275 Treeline Rd., Kalispell MT, 59901 (© **888/465-4329** or 406/755-7405; www.kalispellhie.com), with rates of $99 to $199 double.

Hampton Inn ★ A top-flight chain property, Kalispell's Hampton Inn is an attractive three-story brick structure surrounded by lovely landscaping. The fairly large rooms have one king-size bed or two queen-size. The lobby has a comfortable sitting area in front of a large dome fireplace, enhanced by colorful log furniture with leather cushions. A business center provides a personal computer, fax-modem lines, copy machines, and a printer for guests.

1140 U.S. 2 W., Kalispell, MT 59901. © **800/426-7866** or 406/755-7900. Fax 406/755-5056. 120 units. $110–$180 double; $175–$250 suite. Rates include continental breakfast. AE, DISC, MC, V. **Amenities:** Exercise room; indoor Jacuzzi; indoor pool. *In room:* A/C, TV, fridge, hair dryer, Wi-Fi (free).

The Kalispell Grand Hotel ★   The Kalispell Grand is a historic hotel (1912) done in the Old West tradition. Located downtown, the hotel has been beautifully remodeled, right down to the pressed-tin ceiling and elegant oak staircase. By today's standards the rooms are small, as are the bathrooms, but the historical ambience and fresh feel more than compensate for the lack of space. The lobby is the hotel's centerpiece, with cherry-wood walls, a small art gallery, and an air of Victorian elegance.

100 Main St., Kalispell, MT 59901-4452. © **800/858-7422** or 406/755-8100. Fax 406/752-8012. www. kalispellgrand.com. 40 units. June–Sept $100–$150 double; Oct–May $80–$125 double. Rates include continental breakfast. AE, DC, DISC, MC, V. Pets accepted (free). **Amenities:** Restaurant; lounge. *In room:* A/C, TV, hair dryer, Wi-Fi (free).

WHERE TO DINE
Moderate

Capers ★★ NEW AMERICAN   Recently renamed after a long run as Cafe Max, Capers brings a dash of big city–style culinary glitz to the Flathead Valley. Owned by Doug and Vonnie Day, the place is small, stylish, and popular. The food is excellent, elegantly prepared and presented by Doug, the chef, who broadened his menu a bit with the name change. While the menu changes often, two standbys are the wild Alaskan salmon with a champagne-shallot sauce and the grilled filet mignon. (The rack of lamb also gets high marks.) There are also some soup entrees, such as Montana buffalo with barley and shrimp and roasted red-pepper bisque, as well as one of the Flathead Valley's best cheeseburgers. The restaurant serves beer and wine only, but its eclectic wine list is one of Kalispell's best.

121 Main St. © **406/755-7687.** www.capersmontana.com. Reservations recommended. Main courses $14–$29. AE, MC, V. Tues–Sun 5–9pm. Closed Sun in winter.

North Bay Grille ★ STEAKS/SEAFOOD   A relatively new entry in the Kalispell dining landscape, this restaurant is easily one of the city's best. Thanks to a diverse menu that focuses on steaks and seafood, but also includes jambalaya and chicken Marsala, the Grille has quickly become a local favorite. The approach is to bring in fresh seafood and excellent beef, and prepare it with more flair than the Kalispell norm. For lunch, we recommend an entree salad or the Thai stir-fry, with more than a pound of veggies. The dinner specialties are the signature mixed grill (Alaskan King crab, mango duck breast, and a petite filet mignon) and the salmon, marinated in teriyaki and grilled on an open wood fire. There is a full bar and a long and varied martini list.

138 1st Ave. W. © **406/755-4441.** Reservations recommended. Lunch $8–$16; dinner $15–$33. AE, DISC, MC, V. Mon–Thurs 11:30am–9pm; Fri–Sat 11:30am–11pm; Sun 4–9pm. Bar open later.

Inexpensive

Alley Connection CHINESE   The best place in the valley for Chinese cuisine, the Alley Connection took several years to reach its current state of grace. What started out as a small, one-room operation has become two tastefully but simply decorated dining rooms that serve up excellent fare. Meals of chow mein, sweet-and-sour pork, and

Szechuan chicken may be ordered separately or in the more popular family style. Lunch is a great deal for less than $6, and service is always quick and dependable.

22 1st St. ☎ **406/752-7077.** Reservations recommended. Lunch $3.75–$6; dinner $8–$13. AE, DISC, MC, V. Mon–Sat 11:30am–2:30pm; Mon–Thurs 5–9pm; Fri–Sat 5–9:30pm.

The Knead Café ★ (Finds) STEAK/SEAFOOD/NEW AMERICAN A funky, bohemian bakery, the Knead Café is a great breakfast and lunch spot. The brightly decorated walls are covered with the work of local artists, and the entire place has an arty, breezy atmosphere. The food is tasty and designed to please meat-eaters and vegetarians alike. Breakfast includes tasty breakfast burritos and eggs Benedict. Lunch runs the gamut from falafel to Thai chicken curry burritos and buffalo burgers. The Knead also has a stellar weekend brunch.

25 2nd Ave. W. ☎ **406/755-7510.** Reservations accepted for large parties only. Breakfast $6–$10; lunch $8–$12. AE, MC, V. Mon–Sat 8am–4pm; Sun 9am–3pm.

Norm's News (Kids) BURGERS Established in 1938, Norm's is a classic old-fashioned soda fountain, with racks of magazines and newspapers and an assortment of 300 kinds of candy, which should perk up the kids after a long day. It's quite a sight, from the Rockola jukebox to the ornate back bar carved by Mediterranean cypress. The menu is as basic as it gets: burgers, hot dogs, pork chop sandwiches, and french fries, plus a wide variety of sundaes, shakes, ice-cream sodas, and hard-packed ice cream.

34 Main St. ☎ **406/755-5466.** Reservations not accepted. Most items $3–$6. DISC, MC, V. Mon–Sat 9am–6pm; Sun 11am–5pm; slightly shorter hours fall–spring.

9 WHITEFISH ★★

15 miles N of Kalispell

Whitefish has boomed as a resort community, attracting people from all over the country and making it Montana's fastest-growing area. Longtime residents have feared it will become another Aspen or Jackson Hole, but that hasn't quite happened yet. In fact, Whitefish is still relatively sedate.

Whitefish is almost two different towns—the town itself and the Whitefish Mountain ski area. The busy season in town is the summer, and room rates are correspondingly higher there during warm weather. This may seem odd for a ski town, but Glacier National Park attracts about two million visitors a year, while the ski area brings in only about 300,000.

Up on the mountain, however, the peak season is winter, especially during Christmas vacation time. So if you don't mind the winding 5-mile drive up (or down) the road to Whitefish Mountain Resort, you can find slightly less expensive accommodations in the appropriate season.

ESSENTIALS

GETTING THERE Whitefish is easier to get to than virtually any other Montana vacation town. From Kalispell, it's a quick drive north on U.S. 93. For the local weather forecast, call ☎ 406/755-4829.

Glacier Park International Airport (☎ 406/257-5994; www.flyglacier.com) is 10 minutes away between Columbia Falls and Kalispell at 4170 U.S. 2. **Alaska/Horizon**

(© 800/547-9308), **Allegiant** (© 702/505-8888), **Delta** (© 800/221-1212), **Northwest** (© 800/225-2525), and **United** (© 800/864-8331) offer service.

The **Amtrak** (© 800/872-7245; www.amtrak.com) station on North Central Avenue, with two trains daily—one eastbound and one westbound—is shared with **Burlington Northern** at the edge of downtown in a renovated and charming depot. The bus terminal is also located at the train depot, with daily service to and from Missoula from **Rimrock Stages** (© 406/755-4011).

VISITOR INFORMATION The **Whitefish Convention and Visitors Bureau** (© 877/862-3548 or 406/862-3501; www.explorewhitefish.com) is located at the chamber downtown at 520 E. 2nd St. Here you'll find just about everything you need in the way of brochures, area maps, and travel information. The chamber is open Monday through Friday from 9am to 5pm.

GETTING AROUND **Avis** (© 800/230-4898), **Budget** (© 800/527-0700), **Hertz** (© 800/654-3131), and **National/Alamo** (© 800/227-7368) maintain counters at Glacier Park International Airport. Other companies renting cars in Whitefish include **Dollar** (© 800/800-3665) and **Enterprise** (© 800/261-7331). **Flathead Glacier Transportation** can be reached at © 406/892-3390.

SPECIAL EVENTS Whitefish is home to the **Winter Carnival** ★ (© 406/862-3501), a wild and woolly event held annually since 1960. The early February carnival includes a parade, children's events, a dance party, a snow-sculpting competition, and a battle of the bands at local bars. Of special note is the Penguin Plunge, where a group of brave locals take a dip in frigid Whitefish Lake in the name of charity.

GETTING OUTSIDE

Whitefish is truly a paradise for outdoors enthusiasts, with ski slopes, hiking trails, watersports opportunities, and Glacier National Park just down the road. For all kinds of outdoor equipment or apparel, check out **Sportsman & Ski Haus** at the Mountain Mall (© 406/862-3111). The **Wave,** 1250 Baker Ave. (© 406/862-2444; www.whitefishwave.com), is a first-rate new aquatic and fitness facility, with several pools, weight machines and free weights, massage therapists, and much more.

Biking

Although there are some road-biking opportunities here, biking in Whitefish really means mountain biking. The same old logging roads that make the hiking only average (see below) make the mountain biking excellent. Whitefish Mountain Resort has 20 miles of single-track bike trails. The trails are free, but the area offers a ride to the top on the chairlift for you and your bike for $13 to $19 for two rides. The **Whitefish Mountain Resort** (© 406/862-2900; see "Downhill Skiing," below) offers five graded mountain-biking trails, the longest of which, graded as intermediate, is 8 miles. There's also a short half-mile trail for beginners and two expert trails of about a mile each. The resort also offers full-day passes ($16–$24) and bike rentals ($19–$39 per day).

For a less challenging ride, you can make the 20-mile round-trip on paved roads from downtown Whitefish to the head of Whitefish Lake. Most of the route follows East Lakeshore Drive and offers views of the lake. **Glacier Cyclery and Fitness,** 326 E. 2nd St. (© 406/862-6446; www.glaciercyclery.com), provides excellent service and maintenance as well as rentals ($19–$39 per day), area maps, and up-to-date information for the serious mountain biker. This outfit has been ranked among the 100 best cycle shops in a pool of 6,800 independent dealers.

Boating & Swimming

The boating is excellent on Whitefish Lake, and the lifeguard-staffed City Beach abuts the west side of town. You can rent water-skiing boats, fishing boats, paddle boats, and personal watercraft from the marina at the **Lodge at Whitefish Lake** (© **406/863-4000;** see "Where to Stay," later in this section) between mid-May and mid-September. Options range from a canoe or kayak to a water-ski boat. There are also sunset yacht cruises on many evenings. For kayaking clinics ($60 per person for 3 hr.), kayak rentals ($35–$45 per day), and kayak tours of Whitefish Lake or Flathead Lake ($80 per person for 6 hr.), contact **Whitefish Sea Kayaking** (© **406/862-3513**).

Cross-Country Skiing

The **Whitefish Mountain Resort** (see "Downhill Skiing," below) offers 7.5 miles of very challenging cross-country trails. The **Glacier Nordic Club** (www.glaciernordicclub. wordpress.com) maintains about 6 miles of trails on the Whitefish Lake Golf Course (see "Golf" below) near the Grouse Mountain Lodge. These provide an excellent outing on the hilly golf course. A small donation allows skiers to enjoy both sides of the street, and yearly passes are available. For information, contact the **Grouse Mountain Lodge** (© **406/862-3000**). The **Flathead Convention and Visitor Bureau** (© **406/756-9091**) provides a free outline of trails in or near Whitefish, as well as a list of equipment sales and rental operations.

Dog-Sledding

Dog-Sled Adventures (© **406/881-2275;** www.dogsledadventuresmontana.com) lets you explore the mountains around Whitefish "at the speed of dog." The guided 12-mile rides in two-person or family-size sleds run through Stillwater State Forest, 2 miles north of Olney. Each trip takes about 1½ hours and the sleds are equipped with blankets to keep you warm. Many of the dogs pulling the sleds were rescued by the owners from unwanted homes or animal shelters and trained as sled dogs. A sled ride costs about $90 per adult, $45 for kids 13 and under, and includes a cup of hot chocolate and homemade cookies at the end of your ride.

Downhill Skiing

Whitefish Mountain Resort ★★ (Finds) Formerly known as Big Mountain, this resort offers lots of powder, lots of skiing in the trees, and plenty of runs for every level of skier. With an annual snowfall of 300 inches, a vertical drop of 2,353 feet, three terrain parks, and virtually no lines, Whitefish Mountain Resort is one of the best ski areas in the northwestern United States. More than half the mountain is geared to intermediate skiers, but there is plenty of terrain for experts and beginners. The expert runs are pretty steep—not as steep as those at Wyoming's Jackson Hole Ski Area, but steep enough. There are never any crowds at Whitefish, even in the holiday seasons, so although the prices have gone up a bit over the years, you can still spend your time skiing rather than waiting in lift lines.

Ski school options include 2-hour group lessons for kids 7 to 12 ($55) and half-day private sessions for adults ($275). A 2-day learn-to-ski program is a bargain at $69. There's also a full-service ski-rental shop.

For après-ski food and entertainment, Whitefish Mountain Resort holds its own, with 10 restaurants in the village or on the hill. Your choice for food and beverage at the mountain is **Ed & Mully's Smokehouse,** a casual restaurant and bar with a menu chock-full of Memphis-style barbecue. **Summit House** is a cafeteria that dishes up burgers and the like during the daytime; dinner is also offered several nights a winter on "Moonlight Dine and Ski" evenings. The **Hellroaring Saloon** serves both lunch and dinners in a typical après-ski atmosphere. The **'Stube** is the mountain's rowdiest watering hole, with good burgers and pizza.

In summer, you can take gondola rides to the top of the mountain ($10 per person), ride an alpine slide ($20 for four rides) or take a zip line tour ($69 for 3 hr.), or mountain bike on the trails (bike rentals are available). A new warm-weather diversion is **Walk-in-the-Treetops** ($54 for 3 hr.), a harnessed adventure that goes 70 feet aboveground into the forest's canopy. There are also some popular summer concerts and special events.

P.O. Box 1400, Whitefish, MT 59937. © **800/858-3930** or 406/862-2900. Snow reports 406/862-7669. www.skiwhitefish.com. Lift tickets $61 adults, $49 seniors 65–69, $52 ages 13–18, $32 ages 7–12, free for children 6 and under. Beginner and night rates available. AE, DISC, MC, V. Daily late Nov to Apr. 12 miles north of Whitefish on Big Mountain Rd. From Whitefish, head north on Baker Ave. over the viaduct to Wisconsin Ave. for 3 miles until you see the flashing yellow light. Turn right on Big Mountain Rd. and proceed 8 miles to Whitefish Mountain Resort Village.

Fishing

It's not the Madison Valley, but Whitefish does have some hot spots for anglers wanting to try their hand. **Tally Lake** is a deep hole (Montana's deepest lake, actually) located north of Whitefish off U.S. 93. Five miles north of town, turn left onto the Tally Lake Road (signs will direct you). You can expect cutthroat, rainbow, kokanee, brook trout, and whitefish.

In town, across the viaduct toward Whitefish Mountain Resort, lies **Whitefish Lake.** If you can handle the summer bustle, the lake offers some pretty good lake trout. Northern pike can be found here, and rainbow and cutthroat can be nabbed on dry flies in the evening. The **Lakestream Flyshop,** 334 Central Ave. (© **406/862-1298;** www.lakestream.com), is the best resource in town for information about fly-fishing the Flathead River and local streams. It's also a great spot for a fly-fisherman to construct a wish list, since the store sells all types of fly-fishing equipment, clothing, books, flies, dust catchers, and memorabilia. The staff here provides full-service fly-fishing, tying, and rod-building services, in addition to clinics and good advice. Guided trips are $449 a day, $299 for a half-day.

Golf

The **Whitefish Lake Golf Club** ★, U.S. 93 N. (© **406/862-4000;** www.golfwhitefish.com), is the only 36-hole golf course in the state. Built in the 1930s, the golf club's trees have grown up considerably in the time since.

While not especially long, the course offers a wide variety of shots that will require you to use all the clubs in your bag (and maybe some you forgot). Almost all the fairways are lined with trees. There are few fairway bunkers, but they have strategic placement around the greens. Both 18-hole setups measure a little more than 6,500 yards from the tips. There is also a driving range and putting green. This course may not be as good as Meadow Lake (see the "Golf" section in the Columbia Falls section, later in this chapter), but it is a very fun track. Greens fees are $32 to $49 for 18 holes, $21 to $26 for 9 holes. Carts rent for $30 for 18 holes, $18 for 9.

Hiking

The hiking in the immediate Whitefish area is not great. For the most part, trails either stay in the woods so that you don't see anything except trees, or they go along old logging roads—which make for good mountain biking, but less interesting hiking. The most popular trail in town is the **Danny On Trail** to the summit of the Big Mountain. Named for a Forest Service ecologist who was killed in a ski accident on the Big Mountain in 1979, it begins in the mountain village and ascends over 2,500 feet up the south face of the mountain on four different paths. There's about a 4-mile trek from the top of the lift along the ridge to Flower Point and back. It takes about 2 hours. The most demanding walk is 5.75 miles from the base of the ski area to the top of the hill and then along the ridge. You can ride the lift back down. Snow can be a problem in late spring and even the early months of summer. In progress is Whitefish's "A Trail Runs Through It" project, which will eventually connect downtown Whitefish with a network of trails hikers can take into beautiful state forest land.

Snowboarding

Snowboarders will find kindred spirits—as well as an extensive line of boards and apparel—at **Stumptown Snowboards** (℃ **406/862-0955**) at 128 Central Ave. The staff here will fill you in on the local snowboarding scene at Whitefish Mountain Resort (where the shop has a smaller annex) and other spots in the Flathead Valley. Locals love the **White Room Mountain Shop,** 130 Lupfer Ave. (℃ **406/863-7666**), offering tuning and waxing, gear, and advice.

Snowmobiling

Contact the **Flathead Snowmobile Association** (www.flatheadsnowmobiler.com) for current conditions and advice. The **Flathead Convention & Visitors Bureau** (℃ **406/756-9091**) prints a brochure, "Snowmobiling Montana's Flathead Valley," with information on guides, trails, and snowmobile-friendly accommodations. For rentals contact **J&L RV Rentals** in Columbia Falls (℃ **406/892-7666;** www.jandlrvrentals. com).

SHOPPING

The main shopping area of Whitefish is on Central Avenue and stretches for 3 blocks. For a ski town, the shopping frenzy is fairly subdued. The largest bookshop in town is **Bookworks,** 244 Spokane Ave. (℃ **406/862-4980**), which stocks the best in nature books, regional writing, and children's literature; it's also the source of current hardcover and paperback bestsellers. **McGough and Company,** 131 Central Ave. (℃ **406/862-9199**), has a large selection of Indian-made jewelry. The **Bear Mountain Mercantile,** 237 Central Ave. (℃ **406/862-8382**), is chock-full of gimcracks, knickknacks, and souvenirs, many with a bear theme. There are 12 art galleries in Whitefish that participate in a "First Thursdays" program on the first Thursday night of each month from July to October. On Tuesday evenings, head to the downtown farmer's market.

For a behind-the-scenes look at some of the local farms and their offerings, contact **FarmHands** (℃ **406/862-5356;** www.whoisyourfarmer.org) for a free map of Flathead Valley farms that produce everything from goats to garlic and also welcome visitors.

WHERE TO STAY
In & Around Town

Whitefish might just have the best range of accommodations in all of Montana, with everything from mom-and-pop motels to graceful inns to slope-side condos. There's a **Super 8,** 800 Spokane Ave. (℃ **800/800-8000** or 406/862-8255), with double rates of about $100 nightly in peak season. The **Pine Lodge,** 920 Spokane Ave. (℃ **800/305-7463** or 406/862-7600; www.thepinelodge.com), is a good independent option, with doubles and suites for $145 to $230 in summer, less during other times of year.

Best Western Rocky Mountain Lodge ★ Located on the U.S. 93 commercial strip just south of downtown, this is a very nice Best Western, with an emphasis on Western. The rooms are sunny and nicely maintained, with balconies and Jacuzzis in the higher-priced options. The larger rooms have their own wet bars and fireplaces. This is an especially good option for those passing through on their way to or from Glacier and aren't concerned with proximity to downtown Whitefish or the ski resort. The outdoor year-round pool is a nice perk.

6510 U.S. 93 S., Whitefish, MT 59937. © **800/862-2569** or 406/862-2569. Fax 406/862-1154. www.rocky mtnlodge.com. 79 units. $88–$139 double; $97–$189 suite. Pets accepted on 1st floor ($15–$20 one-time fee). Rates include continental breakfast. AE, DC, DISC, MC, V. **Amenities:** Exercise room; outdoor Jacuzzi; outdoor heated pool. *In room:* A/C, TV, hair dryer, Wi-Fi (free).

Duck Inn ★★ (Finds) This stylish and modern B&B is one of the better values in the Whitefish area. The building is a block off the U.S. 93 strip, overlooking the Whitefish River on the south end of town. The handsome guest rooms are large, every one with a fireplace and a private bathroom with a deep soak tub, and many of them have log-framed beds and great views of the river and surrounding scenery. There is a lovely lobby area, a broad-windowed room overlooking the river. Even though it's right in town, the location gives the illusion of the serene, quiet countryside. The owners also own a car-rental agency, and guests at the inn are met at the train station with their rentals.

1305 Columbia Ave., Whitefish, MT 59937. © **800/344-2377** or 406/862-3825. www.duckinn.com. 10 units. $94–$199 double. Rates include continental breakfast. AE, DISC, MC, V. *In room:* A/C, TV, hair dryer, Wi-Fi (free).

The Garden Wall Inn ★★★ (Finds) While it's right on the main Whitefish drag, the Garden Wall Inn is a world of its own. Owners Rhonda Fitzgerald and Chris Schustrom clearly take pride in providing all of the little luxurious extras. The inn is full of country charm—it was built in 1923, and all of the furnishings are period antiques, including claw-foot tubs and Art Deco dressers, depending on your room. Every detail is just about perfect, right down to the towels, which are large and fluffy enough to dry two adults. Since Rhonda and Chris are both trained chefs, breakfast is a gourmet event with an emphasis on local ingredients (the wild huckleberry crepes are a standout), and afternoons end with hors d'oeuvres and beverages. They're also avid outdoorspeople: Ask them for tips before you head out on that excursion to Glacier or Whitefish Mountain Resort.

504 Spokane Ave., Whitefish, MT 59937. © **888/530-1700** or 406/862-3440. www.gardenwallinn.com. 4 units. $145–$195 double; $255 suite. Rates include full breakfast and afternoon refreshments. AE, MC, V. *In room:* No phone, Wi-Fi (free).

Good Medicine Lodge ★★ The Good Medicine Lodge is an excellent place that is continually improving itself. Two of the best rooms have gas-log stoves and new furnishings. Several second-floor rooms have beautiful views of the Big Mountain, and ground-floor rooms have porches with access to the remarkable backyard, featuring plenty of green grass, a great deck, and all sorts of swings, benches, and chairs. Rooms are large, modern, and clean, and decorated with various themes including golf, Western, and Native American. One suite has a private yard and accepts pets; another features an eight-headed shower. Breakfasts include a delectable smoked trout cake on a savory corn pancake with a poached egg and dill sauce.

537 Wisconsin Ave., Whitefish, MT 59937. © **800/860-5488** or 406/862-5488. Fax 406/862-5489. www.
goodmedicinelodge.com. 9 units, including 3 suites. $150–$200 double; $200–$250 suite. Lower rates
fall–spring. Rates include full breakfast. AE, DISC, MC, V. Pets accepted in 1 suite. **Amenities:** Outdoor
Jacuzzi. *In room:* A/C, hair dryer, Wi-Fi (free).

Grouse Mountain Lodge ★★

Immediately adjacent to the 18th hole of one of
Whitefish Lake's two golf courses, Grouse Mountain Lodge has been one of Montana's
premier vacation lodge properties since 1984. The lodge combines luxury accommodations, fine service, and good food to provide a memorable experience. Standard hotel-like
rooms are called executive rooms, with vaulted ceilings and a wet bar, and overlook the
golf course from the third floor. The loft rooms have a king-size bed, fridge, and microwave downstairs, and a staircase leading to the loft, featuring a TV room and an area with
two twins. The restaurant has two places to eat: a dining room and a nice patio.

2 Fairway Dr., Whitefish, MT 59937. © **800/321-8822** or 406/862-3000. Fax 406/862-0326. www.grouse
mountainlodge.com. 145 units, including 12 lofts. $205–$265 double; $275–$449 loft. Lower rates fall–
spring. AE, DISC, MC, V. **Amenities:** Restaurant; concierge; golf course; 2 outdoor Jacuzzis; indoor pool;
sauna. *In room:* A/C, TV, Wi-Fi (free).

Hidden Moose Lodge ★★ (Finds)

Striking a nice balance between the service of a
B&B with the privacy of a hotel, this small, independent, moose-adorned property is
centered on a vaulted, high-ceilinged great room with an impressive river-rock chimney
fireplace. The comfortable rooms are nicely done as well, with a mellow Montana vibe
and bathroom mirrors appointed with handmade ironwork. Guests can savor their gourmet breakfast (including some seriously tasty huckleberry waffles and *huevos rancheros*)
on their own decks if they wish. The lodge is located about 1½ miles from town on the
road to Whitefish Mountain Resort and has a small trail system on its property that connects with trails into the surrounding mountains.

1735 E. Lakeshore Dr. (on the road to Whitefish Mountain Resort), Whitefish, MT 59937. © **888/733-
6667** or 406/862-6516. Fax 406/862-6514. www.hiddenmooselodge.com. 12 units. $99–$199 double
depending on season. Rates include full breakfast. AE, DISC, MC, V. **Amenities:** Outdoor Jacuzzi. *In room:*
TV/DVD player, movie library, fridge, Wi-Fi (free).

The Lodge at Whitefish Lake ★★

Inspired by the classic lodges in the national
parks of the West, this bold building opened just before New Year's 2006 and instantly
became the primo spot to hang your hat on the shores of Whitefish Lake. Lodge rooms
and suites are attractively decorated, with slate tile floors, rock fireplaces, and private
balconies. The preexisting resort condos include a very large tiled kitchen, a dining area,
a deck overlooking Whitefish Lake and the marina, and a large loft bedroom, as well as
a downstairs bedroom. In summer, there is a full-service marina with boat rentals. The
Boat Club restaurant has a popular lakefront deck that attracts a boisterous cocktail
crowd for summer sunsets.

1380 Wisconsin Ave., Whitefish, MT 59937. © **877/887-4026** or 406/863-4000. Fax 406/863-2750. www.
lodgeatwhitefishlake.com. 63 units, including 18 condos. $220–$329 double; $406–$1,050 suite; $449–
$549 condo. Lower rates fall–spring. AE, DISC, MC, V. **Amenities:** 2 restaurants; lounge; exercise room;
outdoor Jacuzzi; outdoor pool; spa; watersports rentals; Wi-Fi (free). *In room:* A/C, TV, hair dryer, Internet
(free), kitchen.

North Forty Resort (Finds)

Nestled in the pines along Mont. 40 between Whitefish
and Columbia Falls, the North Forty is a great place to stay if you don't like being in town
but still want to be close. Even the smaller duplex cabins all have large living areas, fireplaces, kitchens, front porches, and barbecue grills. North Forty is located in a serene and

quiet area off the main highway, and there is a hiking/cross-country skiing trail located at the north end of the property.

3765 Mont. 40 W., P.O. Box 4250, Whitefish, MT 59937. © **800/775-1740** or 406/862-7740. Fax 406/862-7741. www.northfortyresort.com. 30 units. Summer $199 double; fall–spring $119–$139 double. AE, DISC, MC, V. Pets accepted ($10/night). **Amenities:** Outdoor Jacuzzi. *In room:* TV, kitchen, Wi-Fi (free).

At Whitefish Mountain resort

Whitefish Mountain Resort is a full-service ski area, attracting local skiers, Canadian and American vacationers, and families. It provides a wide variety of accommodations to fit almost every pocketbook. Be sure to ask about discounted lift and lodging packages. If you're looking for a house or condo instead of a hotel, inquire at **Whitefish Mountain Resort Lodging** (© **800/858-4152;** www.skiwhitefish.com/lodging). Most are available for rent on a nightly basis, although some require longer stays. You can get a low-end condo or house for as little as $150 a night, or a glorious ski home during the holiday season for as much as $1,250. A video-lending library is available, as is a heated indoor pool for certain condos.

Edelweiss (Kids) The Edelweiss has some very nice large rooms, all with kitchens, full bathrooms, and fireplaces, and configurations ranging from basic studios to condo units with lofts and two bathrooms. Many of the rooms have panoramic views of the valley below, and all of them have a small balcony or patio. Convenient to the lifts, the Edelweiss has a large hot tub and a Finnish dry-heat sauna. Residents also have access to an indoor swimming pool.

3840 Big Mountain Rd., Whitefish, MT 59937. © **800/858-5439** or 406/862-5252. Fax 406/862-0586. www.skiwhitefish.com/lodging. 50 units. $130–$170 double. AE, MC, V. **Amenities:** Indoor Jacuzzi; sauna. *In room:* TV/VCR, kitchen.

Hibernation House (Value) This is the least expensive place on the hill, popular with high school and college groups, ski teams, and families on budgets. And if you'll be on the slopes all day and just want a clean bed, this will do just fine. All of the rooms are exactly alike: pretty small with a queen-size bed and a set of bunk beds. Each room has its own television—a relatively recent development—but people still like to congregate in the lobby, where there is a large-screen TV. You can ski right to the back door on a groomed trail, and it is only a short walk to a lift in the morning. Another perk: The complimentary buffet breakfast is quite good.

3812 Big Mountain Rd., Whitefish, MT 59937. © **800/858-5439** or 406/862-1982. Fax 406/862-1956. www.skiwhitefish.com/lodging. 42 units. $70–$95 double. Rates include full breakfast. AE, DISC, MC, V. **Amenities:** Outdoor Jacuzzi. *In room:* TV.

Kandahar Lodge ★ Kandahar combines the genteel ambience of a European inn with the requirements of an upscale modern ski hotel. The rooms are large and elegantly appointed, featuring pine walls, leather furnishings, and down comforters. About a third of the units are outfitted with kitchenettes, and the large loft bedrooms have vaulted ceilings. Overall, the lodge is one of the best (and priciest) lodging options at Whitefish Mountain Resort. Likewise, the Cafe Kandahar is the best restaurant on the mountain (see "Where to Dine," below).

3824 Big Mountain Rd., Whitefish, MT 59937. © **800/862-6094** or 406/862-6098. Fax 406/862-6095. www.kandaharlodge.com. 50 units, including 11 suites. $129–$339 double; $289–$599 suite. Lower rates summer and fall. AE, DISC, MC, V. Closed May and Oct–Nov. **Amenities:** Restaurant; lounge; exercise room; outdoor Jacuzzi; spa. *In room:* A/C, TV, kitchenettes (in some), fridge, Wi-Fi (free).

Kintla Lodge ★   A grand native log-and-stone lodge that echoes the architecture in Glacier National Park, Kintla is one of the newest accommodations on the mountain, opening in 1998. It is very upscale, and has an elevator serving its four floors. (That's something people appreciate more than you might think after a day of skiing.) But it's not cheap: A three-bedroom, three-bathroom unit goes for $600 a night in peak holiday season (mid-Dec through New Year's). All units have wood-clad French doors opening onto a patio, stone flooring in the entry and kitchens, individual ski storage, and tastefully simple pine furnishings. Best of all, Kintla is only 20 feet from Whitefish Mountain Resort's Tenderfoot lift. There is no restaurant on the premises, but the village's tonier shops are located on the ground level outside.

Whitefish Mountain Resort Village, Whitefish, MT 59937. ℭ **800/858-4157** or 406/862-1960. Fax 406/862-2955. www.skiwhitefish.com/lodging. 14 units. $150–$450 1- to 3-bedroom unit. AE, DISC, MC, V. **Amenities:** Outdoor Jacuzzi; sauna. *In room:* TV/VCR.

Morning Eagle Lodge ★★   The newest lodging option at Whitefish Mountain Resort, Morning Eagle welcomed its first guests during the 2003–04 ski season and immediately entrenched itself as the most posh address on these slopes. The units range from studios to lavish three-bedroom affairs, all with similar contemporary, mildly Western decor: granite countertops, checkered Berber carpet and slate flooring, large tiled bathrooms, and fully equipped kitchens. The studios here are about 500 square feet, whereas the largest three-bedroom, three-bathroom units are about three times that size. The rooms have great views, pullout sleeper sofas, washer/dryer units, and private balconies. There is a ski room downstairs and a rooftop deck—a great perk, featuring outdoor heaters, a barbecue, and a 10-person hot tub.

Whitefish Mountain Resort Village, Whitefish, MT 59937. ℭ **800/858-4157** or 406/862-1960. Fax 406/862-2955. www.skiwhitefish.com/lodging. 49 units. $175–$475 1- to 3-bedroom unit. AE, DISC, MC, V. **Amenities:** Outdoor Jacuzzi; sauna. *In room:* TV/DVD player, hair dryer, kitchen.

Ptarmigan Village ★   This is an extensive condo setup that is spread over a lower portion of the Whitefish Mountain Resort. The individually owned units are pretty snazzy, featuring vaulted ceilings, fireplaces, fully equipped kitchens, and some unexpected touches: woodstoves, grills, CD players, and spiral staircases. The decks overlook a woody area where signs warn about increased black bear activity in the summer—there's a hiking trail here, too, if the bears don't scare you off. There's also a nice fishing pond where kids can spy out the turtles hiding in the reeds in summer.

3000 Big Mountain Rd., P.O. Box 458, Whitefish, MT 59937. ℭ **800/552-3952** or 406/862-3594. Fax 406/862-6664. www.ptarmiganvillage.com. 50 units. $112–$230 condo. AE, DISC, MC, V. **Amenities:** Indoor and outdoor pools; indoor Jacuzzi; sauna; tennis courts. *In room:* TV/VCR, CD player, kitchen.

Camping

Whitefish Lake State Park is tucked on the outskirts of town in a nicely wooded area on Whitefish Lake. A campsite runs $13 nightly. Call the **Department of Fish, Wildlife, and Parks** (ℭ **406/752-5501;** www.fwp.mt.gov) for additional information. The **Whitefish KOA Kampground** (ℭ **800/562-8734** or 406/862-4242; www.glacierpark koa.com) is a comprehensive RV park about 2 miles south of town on U.S. 93 and has RV and tent sites (about $20–$60 each) and cabins ($50–$150).

WHERE TO DINE

A good cup of organic coffee and a selection of baked goods are available at the **Montana Coffee Traders,** located at 110 Central Ave. (ℭ **406/862-7667**), which also houses a nifty store (selling kitchen gadgets, food, and gifts) and a nice place to read a book. **Loula's Café,** located downstairs at 300 E. 2nd St. (✆ **406/862-5614**), serves traditional American breakfasts and salads and sandwiches for lunch in an attractive setting. The **Buffalo Cafe,** 514 3rd St. (✆ **406/862-2833**), is Whitefish's best breakfast spot—try their legendary bacon-and-egg-filled pies. Bagels and coffee are the orders of choice at the **Bean Hive,** 10 Baker Ave. (✆ **406/862-6383**). And for inexpensive but tasty Mexican fare for lunch and dinner, try **La Hacienda,** 130 Central Ave. (✆ **406/862-6111**), in the Remington Casino.

Cafe Kandahar ★★★ FRENCH/NEW AMERICAN   Chef Andy Blanton has raised the stakes in the Whitefish culinary scene by reinventing the restaurant at Kandahar Lodge since he took it over with his family in 2006. The appealing room, highlighted by bay windows looking down the mountain and historical photos of the area, is an excellent setting for his handiwork in the kitchen. Patrons can choose off two menus, one that changes nightly, another that lasts a season. Inspired by French and Creole traditions but more than willing to experiment, Blanton uses as much local produce and meats as he can in such creations as seared elk roulade with forest mushrooms, grilled buffalo tenderloin, and beef *tournedos* with oyster mushroom and smoked shallot bordelaise; he also experiments with far-flung influences in a number of creative seafood and pasta dishes. The wine list and the desserts—including a decadently rich molten chocolate soufflé with raspberry-huckleberry *coulis*—are also excellent.

3824 Big Mountain Rd., at Kandahar Lodge, Whitefish Mountain Resort. ✆ **406/862-6247.** www. cafekandahar.com. Reservations recommended. Main courses $8–$14 breakfast, $20–$36 dinner. AE, DISC, MC, V. Daily 7:30–10:30am and 5:30–9:30pm. Closed May and Oct–Nov.

Ciao Mambo ITALIAN   A dimly lit *ristorante,* Ciao Mambo is otherwise hard to miss. The color scheme and the music are both loud—the bright walls are multicolored and the stereo blasts Sinatra, Louis Prima, and Dean Martin—but it complements the rich Italian fare quite nicely. For an appetizer, you can't miss with the Italian Tootsie Rolls: egg wrappers stuffed with ricotta, mozzarella, and pesto. Cooked in an open central kitchen, main courses range from crackly crust pizza to Papa Biagio's Bolognese (ribbon noodles baked with meat sauce and mozzarella) and Pollo Con Formaggio (two breaded chicken cutlets dripping with four cheeses).

234 E. 2nd St. ✆ **406/863-9600.** www.ciaomambo.com. Reservations accepted weekdays only. Main courses $11–$27. AE, DISC, MC, V. Mon–Thurs 5–9pm; Fri–Sat 5–10pm.

Pescado Blanco ★ MEXICAN   Located in the pine-clad ground floor of a split-level building in downtown Whitefish, Pescado Blanco puts a creative spin on Mexican food—chef/owner David Lewis dubs this cuisine "Mountain Mexican." Favoring local ingredients and fresh seafood, Lewis plates up such savory and spicy dishes as enchiladas (bison, pheasant, or seafood), elk chorizo tacos, and tortilla-crusted halibut. The daily seafood specials are standouts, with creative Mexican-inspired preparations like chili-seared ahi with roasted red pepper. The salsa bar is one of Montana's best; beer, wine, and wine-based margaritas are served.

235 1st St. ✆ **406/862-3290.** www.pescadoblanco.com. Main courses $13–$22. AE, DISC, MC, V. Daily 5–10pm (until 9pm fall–spring).

The Red Caboose ★ AMERICAN/DINER   This new eatery caters to rail travelers with its always-open hours and railroad-themed decor. The menu offers a creative spin on traditional diner fare, with appetizers such as crab cakes and deep-fried artichoke hearts, hearty egg dishes for breakfast, po'boys and burgers for lunch, and steaks, catfish, meatloaf, and other American standards for dinner. Kids will love the paper chef's hats **139** for coloring. Beer, wine, and a limited selection of liquors are available.

101 Central Ave. (C) **406/863-4563**. www.redcaboosediner.com. Breakfast items $5–$10; lunch and dinner main courses $6–$19. AE, DISC, MC, V. Summer Sun–Thurs 7am–11pm, Fri–Sat 7am–2:30am; winter Sun–Thurs 7am–10pm, Fri–Sat 7am–2:30am.

Rising Sun Bistro ★ (Finds) FRENCH/AMERICAN

This pleasant, sunny cafe in a converted house just north of downtown Whitefish is decked out with French maps and photos and a nice variety of seating options on the hardwoods. The food, likewise, has its Gallic influences: croissants and parfaits for breakfast, great quiches and crepes (as well as juicy burgers) for lunch, and classic dishes like steak frites and short ribs as well as nightly vegetarian specials for dinner. Beer and wine are available.

549 Wisconsin Ave. (C) **406/862-4979**. Main courses $4–$12 breakfast and brunch, $7–$11 lunch, $13–$20 dinner. AE, DISC, MC, V. Tues–Sat 9am–9pm; Sun 9am–2pm.

The Tupelo Grille ★★ CONTINENTAL/CAJUN

The Tupelo is downtown Whitefish's best restaurant, especially for those with a taste for spicy New Orleans–style food. Creole chicken and dumplings in a rosemary-tomato cream sauce and a Cajun Creole combo (a platter of shrimp Creole, crawfish étouffée, and chicken and sausage jambalaya) are specialties. The menu is full of creative variations on staples from both North and South (for instance, rack of lamb with citrus-rosemary yogurt, low-country shrimp and grits, and blackened ahi), and the atmosphere is pleasant and mildly contemporary, with big, comfortable booths and tables.

17 Central Ave. (C) **406/862-6136**. www.tupelogrille.com. Reservations recommended for large parties. Main courses $17–$32. AE, MC, V. Daily 5:30–10pm. Closed at 9:30pm and Sun in off season.

Wasabi ★★ SUSHI

Few locals thought that a sushi joint in Whitefish would fly, but it turned out to be a match made in heaven. The contemporary space is a real eye-catcher, with purple walls, an orange ceiling, and a large mirror—displaying the chefs hard at work—above checkerboard floors. The menu runs the whole gamut of sushi, from California rolls to six-fish rainbow rolls to quinoa-based rolls, and also includes a nice selection of Asian-influenced beef, poultry, and seafood. There's beer, wine, and six varieties of sake, but no liquor. The establishment also encompasses the adjacent **Ginger Grill,** a casual East-meets-West eatery. The desserts, including Key lime pie and huckleberry ice cream, are delectable.

419 E. 2nd St. (C) **406/863-9283**. www.wasabimt.com. Reservations recommended. Sushi $6–$15 per order; main courses $10–$30. AE, MC, V. Daily 5–9:30pm. Closed Mon fall and spring.

Whitefish Lake Restaurant ★ CONTINENTAL

There are Montanans who consider this the best restaurant in the state. Located at the public golf course, it is generally conceded to be the best restaurant in the Whitefish area. It's housed in a building that was constructed in 1936 as a WPA project. The dining room has an almost churchlike atmosphere: dark and quiet, with large log beams and a large stone fireplace providing warmth on chilly evenings. The menu for the evening meal covers the culinary landscape, from vegetable napoleon to 12-ounce prime rib, rack of lamb, and roast duckling; fresh seafood may include lobster, king crab, halibut, or Pacific salmon. The wine list is impressive, as is the bar's martini menu. As formal as a golf club ever gets, it's the only place in Whitefish that approaches dressy.

U.S. 93 N. (at the Whitefish Lake Golf Course). (C) **406/862-5285**. www.whitefishlakerestaurant.com. Reservations recommended. Lunch $7–$10; dinner $17–$38. AE, DISC, MC, V. Summer daily 11am–3pm and 5:30–10pm; winter Sun–Thurs 5:30–9pm, Fri–Sat 5:30–9:30pm.

Tips   **The Yaak**

Remote and wild to say the least, the **Yaak Valley** is nestled in far northwestern Montana on Mont. 308 and is home to the only rainforests in the state. It's devastatingly beautiful in some places and devastated by clear-cut logging in others. And as a tourist destination, it's certainly not for everyone. I can't recommend any of the few lodging or eating/drinking establishments in the valley—unless you're desperate for a beer or an earful from a gun-toting, anti-government survivalist—but I can recommend some of its campgrounds and hiking trails. I like both the tranquil, two-site Caribou Campground, just northwest of the town of Yaak on Mont. 308 (no fee), and the Vinal–Mt. Henry–Boulder National Recreational Trail, just west of the campground. Take caution, however: Not only is this wolf and grizzly country, but many of the trails are favored by armed drug smugglers and would-be terrorists entering the U.S. from Canada. Contact the **Kootenai National Forest,** 31374 U.S. 2, Libby, MT 59923 (© **406/293-6211;** www. fs.fed.us/r1/kootenai), for more information. And stock up on groceries and other supplies in Whitefish or Kalispell before you go—the shopping in these parts leaves something to be desired.

WHITEFISH AFTER DARK

The summer-only **Alpine Theatre Project** (© 406/862-7469; www.alpinetheatre project.org) and the year-round **Whitefish Theatre Company** (© 406/862-5371; www. whitefishtheatreco.org) stage musicals and dramas at the O'Shaughnessy Center and Whitefish Performing Arts Center in downtown Whitefish. There's also a pretty good bar scene: Start at the **Black Star Draught House** at the Great Northern Brewing Company, 2 Central Ave. (© 406/863-1002), serving plump sandwiches and beers that are brewed on premise. Follow that with a timeout at **Casey's,** 101 Central Ave. (© 406/862-8150), a bit seedy but not lacking character; this is Whitefish's oldest structure. A third stop could be at the **Great Northern Bar and Grill,** 27 Central Ave. (© 406/862-2816), which is more upscale. This place is jumping on weekend nights. Your final stop: the **Bulldog Saloon,** 144 Central Ave. (© 406/862-5636). Not just a bar, the Bulldog turns out a pretty mean garlic burger, too.

10 COLUMBIA FALLS

11 miles N of Kalispell; 9 miles E of Whitefish

Columbia Falls gets a bad rep not only for being the home of the Plum Creek plant, a smoke-billowing institution seen for miles even at night, but also for its not-so-subtle image as a tourist trap. And unlike Great Falls, where the falls are out of town and (gasp!) dammed, Columbia Falls goes one better by not having any falls at all. The redeeming features and equalizers are the town's proximity to Glacier National Park, and lodging rates that are relatively inexpensive—it's a good fallback location if you have trouble finding a room in Whitefish. Residents here are real Montanans, something of a rarity in an area being inundated with out-of-staters setting up house.

GETTING THERE **Glacier Park International Airport** (© **406/257-5994;** www.fly glacier.com) is 10 minutes away between Columbia Falls and Kalispell at 4170 U.S. 2. **Alaska/Horizon** (© **800/547-9308**), **Allegiant** (© **702/505-8888**), **Delta** (© **800/221-1212**), **Northwest** (© **800/225-2525**), and **United** (© **800/864-8331**) offer service. The closest **Amtrak** station is in Whitefish, 10 miles to the northwest.

VISITOR INFORMATION The **Columbia Falls Area Chamber of Commerce,** P.O. Box 312, Columbia Falls, MT 59912 (© **406/892-2072;** www.columbiafallschamber. com), can provide you with pertinent area information. The chamber and the **U.S. Forest Service** jointly operate an information cabin in Maranette Park on U.S. 2 near the center of town. You can also get Columbia Falls information from the **Glacier Country Regional Tourism Commission** (© **800/338-5072;** www.glaciermt.com).

GETTING AROUND **Dollar,** 5506 U.S. 2 W. (© **406/892-0009**), and **Thrifty,** 4785 U.S. 2 W. (© **406/257-7333**), both have car-rental offices in Columbia Falls.

GETTING OUTSIDE

Two of the best-kept secrets in this part of the state are the **North** and **South Lion lakes.** To find them, follow the signs to the west side of the Hungry Horse Reservoir. Less than 5 miles after turning off of Mont. 40, you will come to a cutoff to the North Lion Lake and, within a hundred yards, arrive at South Lion Lake. Both are well protected, quiet, and for the most part undiscovered by tourists—excellent for camping, picnicking, fishing, or swimming.

There is a road around **Hungry Horse Reservoir,** a 110-mile round-trip that you can start from the town of Hungry Horse. Hungry Horse is 9 miles south of West Glacier or 6 miles east of Columbia Falls on U.S. 2. This is an excellent drive for seeing wildlife. You're almost certain to see at least an elk, and maybe a moose or bear. It's also a great place for fishing.

Golf

Columbia Falls is home to one of Montana's best golf courses, **Meadow Lake** (© **406/892-2111;** www.meadowlakegolf.com) at the Meadow Lake Resort; see "Where to Stay," below. About 6,700 yards from the back tees, the course is very challenging, especially the greens, which are "speed sensitive" and have lots of nearly invisible breaks in them. The fairways are fairly wide but lined with intimidating large trees. Greens fees are $35 to $60 for 18 holes, depending on the time of year and day. Carts rent for $16 per rider.

Hiking

Columbia Mountain, Glacier National Park, and the Jewel Basin are nearby, but the **Great Northern** is the grandpappy of 'em all in these parts. If you want a leisurely stroll with moderate difficulty, stick to the Danny On Trail on the Big Mountain in Whitefish. If you want 8 hours of hardship, then the Great Northern is for you. To get there, take U.S. 2 to Martin City, then turn onto the East Side Reservoir Road for 15 miles. At that point, turn east to Highline Loop Road, and from here you should be able to see the approach route. The hike goes up the 8,705-foot-high Great Northern Mountain in the Great Bear Wilderness. While there's not an official trail, enough people have beaten a path to the summit that one is clear enough to make out. This isn't a leisurely walk, nor is it the most publicized hike in the area, but it is the most rewarding for those willing to make the effort. The views of Glacier and the Hungry Horse Reservoir are remarkable.

Remember when your dad used to drive the family to the ocean or the mountains for the annual family vacation? Whenever you passed the Tent of Miracles or the Cave of 10,000 Rattlesnakes or the Fabulous Mystery House, you'd beg Dad to stop. He always ignored you and drove on as if you hadn't spoken. Columbia Falls offers you the chance to find out what attractions like these are all about.

Montana's largest waterslide park, the **Big Sky Waterpark,** at the junction of U.S. highways 2 and 206 (℘ **406/892-5026;** www.bigskywp.com), is a good place to cool off. The **Amazing Fun Center,** at U.S. 2 E., Coram (℘ **406/387-5902;** www.amazingfun center.com), offers myriad opportunities to stay dry *and* have some fun. Like rats hunting for an odorless cheese, tourists often enter the Fun Center's maze and emerge hours later. If mazes aren't your bag, the place also has go-carts and other games. The **House of Mystery,** 7800 U.S. 2 E., Columbia Falls (℘ **406/892-1210;** www.montanavortex. com), offers a vortex (you'll just have to go in to find out) and other bewilderments.

WHERE TO STAY

Bad Rock Country Bed and Breakfast ★ (Finds)

This is a great choice for those who want to use Columbia Falls as a base for visiting both Glacier and Whitefish but want to avoid the hustle and bustle of being right on the highway. Nestled in a beautifully landscaped meadow at the base of the Swan Mountains, this is a very good B&B with three rooms in the main house and five cabin units on the grounds. The cabins are newer, built with square-cut pine logs and furnished with custom lodgepole-pine trappings and fridges, microwaves, and coffeemakers. In the main house, the best room is the Columbia Mountain Suite, with a four-poster queen-size bed, Asian art on its red walls, and a private balcony perfect for watching the sunset. The Bad Rock is known for its lavish breakfasts; you might have bacon-wrapped polenta or Montana potato pie.

480 Bad Rock Dr., Columbia Falls, MT 59912. ℘ **888/892-2829** or 406/892-2829. www.badrock.com. 3 main house units, 5 cabin units. Summer $185–$225 double; fall–spring $125–$150 double. Rates include full breakfast. AE, DC, MC, V. *In room:* A/C, fridge (in some), hair dryer, microwave (in some), Wi-Fi (free).

Glacier Park Motel and Campground (Value)

This well-maintained low-cost hostelry offers clean, comfortable accommodations with prices to match their modesty. Single rooms come with one queen-size bed and double rooms have two queen-size beds. The accommodations are no better or worse than those found in a typical low-cost national chain. Also available for rent are 13 RV campsites (about $25 each) and four tipis ($65).

7285 U.S. 2 E. (at U.S. 206), Columbia Falls, MT 59912. ℘ **406/892-7686.** Fax 406/892-4575. www.glacier parkmotelandcampground.com. 25 units, including 4 suites and 3 cabins. $75–$115 double; $65 cabin; $175 suite. Lower rates fall–spring. Rates include continental breakfast. AE, DISC, MC, V. **Amenities:** 2 indoor Jacuzzis; outdoor heated pool. *In room:* TV, kitchenettes, Wi-Fi (free).

Meadow Lake Resort ★

Meadow Lake offers a wide variety of excellent accommodations in a modern-resort style. Development focuses on the golf course, which is one of the best in the state. Rooms are stylish in the modern sense, and many of the condo units have jetted tubs. The resort has a recreation center with Nautilus weight machines and aerobic equipment. There are large indoor and outdoor pools and hot tubs. The inn features standard-size hotel rooms with a king-size bed, double sleeper sofa, a large bathroom with double vanity sinks, and a veranda or patio. The condos come in suites (a single room with partial kitchen, bathroom, and, usually, a Jacuzzi), or one- and two-bedroom versions, which all have fireplaces, full kitchens, convenient washer and dryer access, private deck with barbecue, VCR or DVD player, and stereo. Even if you haven't come for golf, this is still the best place in town to spend the night.

100 St. Andrews Dr., Columbia Falls, MT 59912. ℭ **800/321-4653** or 406/892-8700. Fax 406/892-8731. www.meadowlake.com. 24 units in inn plus a wide variety of condos and rental homes. $139–$159 at inn; $139–$475 condo or home. AE, DC, MC, V. **Amenities:** Restaurant; lounge; children's program; 18-hole golf course; exercise room; Jacuzzi; indoor and outdoor heated pools; sauna; spa. *In room:* A/C, TV/VCR or DVD player, kitchen.

WHERE TO DINE

The Back Room of the Nite Owl (Value) AMERICAN   This old-fashioned roadside eatery is just off the main drag in Columbia Falls. You'll be pleasantly surprised by what the joint has to offer—the roasted chicken, spareribs, and country ribs (small chunks cooked in barbecue sauce) are all delicious and reasonably priced. Fry bread is the house specialty and comes with meals instead of standard bread items. The Sunday pizza, fried chicken, and salad buffet is a bargain for about $10. Up front, the Nite Owl itself is one of the busiest restaurants in the region, serving three hearty American meals daily from 5:30am to 12:45am.

U.S. 2 E. (near the intersection with 4th Ave.). ℭ **406/892-3131.** www.niteowlbackroom.com. Most items $6–$15. AE, DISC, MC, V. Mon–Wed 4–9pm; Thurs–Sat 4–9:30pm; Sun 2–9pm. Shorter hours in winter.

Helena & Southwestern Montana

This is where Montana came of age, changing in a few short years from an isolated outback of fur traders and rugged explorers to a series of bustling, boisterous mining camps, where fortunes were made and lost overnight. Butte was once the "Richest Hill on Earth," and gold strikes were also made at Helena's Last Chance Gulch and Virginia City's Alder Gulch. Bannack, another gold-mining boom-town, was the first territorial capital.

The area has calmed down somewhat since then. Butte's Berkeley Pit, full of toxic water, is a Superfund site. The Ana-conda copper smelter is shut down, and the Old Works, formerly a Superfund site itself, is now a golf course. Helena is the

businesslike state capital, the seat of Mon-tana's politics.

But in the Big Hole Valley, you can still see some ranching and farming done the old-fashioned way. There are plenty of fishing and outdoor opportunities all over the mountains that cloak southwestern Montana.

While signs of modern American life are now rampant, many cross sections of this region's storied past have been meticu-lously preserved. The old prison at Deer Lodge can give you an eye-opening per-spective on frontier justice, and the pre-served mining towns of Nevada City and Virginia City provide a taste of the boom-town, mining-camp life.

1 SCENIC DRIVES

Two high-speed highways—interstates 90 and 15—intersect in the region, but the best roads to take are the well-maintained back roads: state and county highways that follow unlikely and out-of-the-way paths. Traveling from Anaconda to Dillon could be done via the interstate in just over an hour. But a better, less-frequented route through the Big Hole Valley runs east of the Continental Divide and the Anaconda-Pintler Wilderness Area. A good stopping point is Wisdom, which has the dubious distinction of being one of the coldest towns in the Lower 48, and the turnoff for the Big Hole National Battle-field. Driving farther south on Mont. 278 takes you to Jackson, then Bannack State Park, before ending at I-15 south of Dillon. From Dillon, drive north on Mont. 41 to Twin Bridges and the junction with Mont. 287. This road runs south through the Old West towns of Sheridan, Laurin, Alder, Nevada City, and Virginia City, before ending in Ennis at the junction with U.S. 287.

DRIVING TOUR 1: THE BIG HOLE VALLEY

This short loop tour takes you through the Big Hole Valley, nicknamed "Land of 10,000 Haystacks." Begin in Dillon, the largest of the towns in this area, and keep your eye out for white-tailed and mule deer in the morning and early evening. Travel north on I-15 to Divide, then take Mont. 43 southwest to Wisdom. This is a tiny town with little other than its residents and the scenery to recommend it, but the Big Hole National Battlefield

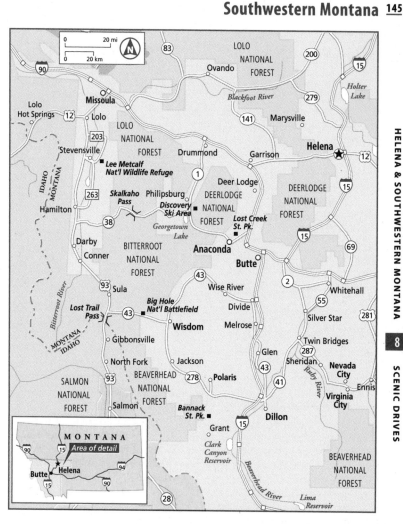

(described in detail later in this chapter) is a short drive west on Mont. 43 and is well worth the trip.

Then head back to Wisdom and take Mont. 278 south toward Dillon. Along the way, stop in Jackson for a soak in the hot springs, or tour Montana's territorial capital city, Bannack, in Bannack State Park (see section 6, later in this chapter) just 28 miles farther, off Mont. 278. As you stroll the boardwalks you'll discover the ease with which you can lose yourself in the state's early history—a microcosm that reflects the entire Old West. This drive is great during the summer, when haystacks fill the fields and the Bannack Days celebration re-creates early events in Montana's history. It's not so tame during winter months, though, when roads are icy and caution is required.

This tour is best enjoyed during summer, when area attractions open their doors to visitors and long summer days extend daylight hours.

This scenic route takes you from the mining city of Anaconda on a loop tour with ghost towns, historic buildings, and wildlife. Starting in Anaconda—where you can visit the copper-smelting display at the Copper Village Museum or admire an old Art Deco theater, the **Washoe,** which was ranked fifth in the nation by David Naylor *(American Picture Palaces)* for its architectural value—you'll head on little-traveled roads into a mountainous area that rivals any in the state.

Northwest of Anaconda on Mont. 1 lies **Georgetown Lake,** a popular tourist destination in both summer and winter, when anglers and skiers flock to the lake and nearby ski area, **Discovery.** There are dog-sled races here on winter Sundays. Next stop is the charming historic town of **Philipsburg,** a good place for lunch or even an overnight stay. Continue on Mont. 1 to Drummond, known as the "Bull Shipper's Capital of the World."

Heading southeast on I-90 will take you to **Deer Lodge,** home to the state prison, historic **Grant-Kohrs Ranch,** and the **Montana Auto Museum,** which features a slightly depleted collection of 120 antique automobiles—restored, original models from the early 1900s to the 1960s. County Road 273 takes you back to Anaconda.

2 HELENA ★

64 miles N of Butte; 115 miles SE of Missoula; 89 miles S of Great Falls

Cradled in the foothills of the Montana Rockies, Helena is the focal point of the state's politics. During the week, it's a bustling community of elected officials, lobbyists, and bureaucrats. On the weekends, however, it seems they all turn into outdoors fanatics, heading to the lakes and mountains. Helena is also a haven for artists and other creative types, evidenced by the galleries that dot the streets once dominated by mining-era saloons and houses of ill repute.

In its early days, Helena was a wild-and-woolly boomtown, built on gold mining. Last Chance Gulch was named when four miners said they had one last chance to hit it big in the West—and they did. The town boomed in the gold rush of 1865. During the height of this prosperity, only Manhattan could boast more millionaires than the small Montana city. And along the way, the town recorded an alarming number of murders and robberies. Then, in 1935, earthquakes devastated the town. Beginning October 3, more than 2,000 tremors rocked the city, causing millions of dollars in damage.

After Helena took state capital rights from Virginia City in 1875, Marcus Daly, the Butte copper king with more than just a bystander's interest in the capital's location, decided to steal it away from Helena and move it to Anaconda, 25 miles from Butte. As we all now know, Daly's efforts proved unsuccessful, but he started a political war that echoes throughout the state even today.

GETTING THERE **Alaskan/Horizon** (℃ 800/252-7522), **Northwest/Pinnacle** (℃ 800/225-2525), **SkyWest/Delta** (℃ 800/221-1212), and **United** (℃ 800/864-8331) provide commuter links to larger airports in Montana and other Western states from **Helena Regional Airport** (℃ 406/442-2821; www.helenaairport.com), northeast of the city on Skyway Drive off U.S. 15.

HELENA & SOUTHWESTERN MONTANA

8 **HELENA**

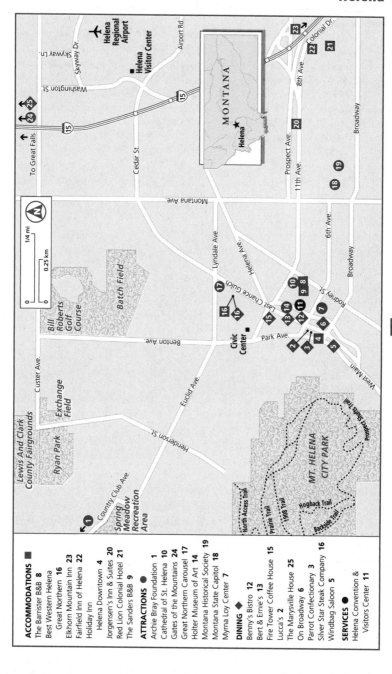

ACCOMMODATIONS ■

The Barrister B&B **8**
Best Western Helena
  Great Northern **16**
Elkhorn Mountain Inn **23**
Fairfield Inn of Helena **22**
Holiday Inn
  Helena Downtown **4**
Jorgensen's Inn & Suites **20**
Red Lion Colonial Hotel **21**
The Sanders B&B **9**

ATTRACTIONS ●

Archie Bray Foundation **1**
Cathedral of St. Helena **10**
Gates of the Mountains **24**
Great Northern Carousel **17**
Holter Museum of Art **14**
Montana Historical Society **19**
Montana State Capitol **18**
Myrna Loy Center **7**

DINING ◆

Benny's Bistro **12**
Bert & Ernie's **13**
Fire Tower Coffee House **15**
Lucca's **2**
The Marysville House **25**
On Broadway **6**
Parrot Confectionary **3**
Silver Star Steak Company **16**
Windbag Saloon **5**

SERVICES ●

Helena Convention &
  Visitors Center **11**

The **bus depot** is located at 630 N. Last Chance Gulch (© **406/442-5860**), with service on **Rimrock Stages,** a Trailways affiliate (© **800/255-7655;** www.rimrocktrailways.com) that links with Greyhound.

Driving from the east or west, take I-90; turn north on I-15 and head toward Helena. From the north or south, I-15 leads right into town.

VISITOR INFORMATION　A good starting point for local activities and area maps is the **Helena Convention and Visitor's Bureau** at 225 Cruse Ave., Ste. A, Helena, MT 59601 (© **800/743-5362** or 406/447-1530; www.helenacvb.visitmt.com). There is an information office run by the chamber out near the airport at Cedar Street off I-15. Another source is **Gold West Country** (a branch of Travel Montana, the mother lode for brochures and information about the region and the state), 1105 Main St., Deer Lodge, MT 59722 (© **800/879-1159** or 406/846-1943; www.goldwest.visitmt.com).

GETTING AROUND　Car-rental agencies at the airport include **Avis** (© **800/230-4898**), **Hertz** (© **800/654-3131**), and **National** (© **800/227-7368**). **Enterprise** (© **800/261-7331**) is in town at 3015 Prospect Ave.

GETTING OUTSIDE

Just beyond the city limits, the area is chock-full of recreational opportunities, with blue-ribbon trout streams, downhill ski areas, and millions of acres of public land.

Fishing

There are several stretches of prime fishing along the upper stretch of the Missouri River. The section from **Toston Dam** downstream to **Canyon Ferry Lake** offers brown and rainbow trout in the 2- to 10-pound class. Floating with large streamers, wet flies, and lures is the most popular and productive way to catch these fish as they make their way upriver to spawn. The fishing gets progressively better from late spring to fall. The section below **Hauser Dam** to **Beaver Creek** offers a chance for really big trout. Other popular fishing areas include **Park Lake** 15 miles southwest of Helena, **Lake Helena,** and the **Smith River** to the east of the Big Belt Mountains.

Pro Outfitters, P.O. Box 621, Helena, MT 621 (© **800/858-3497** or 406/442-5489; www.prooutfitters.com), offers customized fly-fishing trips on the Smith River, considered in fishing circles one of the best in the state, and in the world. The company offers all-inclusive 3-day trips ($2,050 per person) and 5-day trips ($2,850 per person) from mid-May to mid-July, as well as day trips ($450 for one or two anglers) on the Missouri River.

Hiking

Mount Helena City Park covers 628 acres on Mount Helena, a 5,468-foot peak that looks out over the city. Nine trails cover the park, the easiest of which, the **1906 Trail,** follows the base of the limestone cliffs past Devil's Kitchen to the 5,468-foot summit. To reach the 1906 Trail, take W. Main south of downtown and turn right on Reeder's Village Drive. Drive up the hill to the dead end and you're at the trail head. **Hogback Trail** is a rough and rocky hike that leads from the peak to the exposed Hogback Ridge. Contact the Helena Convention and Visitor's Bureau (see above) for information.

There are more than 700 miles of trails in the Helena National Forest. The **Trout Creek Canyon Trail** offers a spectacular view of Hanging Valley. Helena is also the gateway to the **Gates of the Mountains Wilderness.** For a serious hike in the wilderness area, you can go to **Mann Gulch,** the site of a forest fire in August 1949. Sixteen firefighters parachuted into Mann Gulch at about 6pm on August 5. Within 2 hours, all but three

had perished. The incident is the subject of Norman Maclean's book, *Young Men and*
Fire. You can get more information about hiking into Mann Gulch from the Helena
Ranger district, with offices in Helena at 2001 Poplar St. (© **406/449-5490;** www.fs.fed.
us/r1/helena).

Rockhounding
Helena was founded on gold mining, and the area is still rightly famous for its gemstones,
particularly Montana sapphires. Sapphires, a variety of the mineral corundum, are harder
than any natural stone except a diamond. The Helena area has several commercial areas
that allow visitors to dig for sapphires. Diligent treasure seekers can also uncover garnets,
moss agates, fossils, and hematite. The **Spokane Bar Sapphire Mine & Gold Fever
Rock Shop,** 5360 Castles Rd. (© **406/227-8989;** www.sapphiremine.com), south of
Hauser Lake lets groups dig buckets for $60. The record sapphire taken from here was
155 carats.

Skiing
Great Divide Ski Area   Great Divide is primarily a local ski hill, not a destination
resort, but the resort has added a half-pipe and night lights while expanding to 1,600
acres. With a 1,500-foot vertical drop, it is also pretty tough (15% beginner, 40% intermediate, and 45% advanced), although the Lower Mountain offers wide-open runs that
cater to novice and intermediate skiers. There are a total of 139 trails on a trio of mountains served by five double chairs and a surface tow.

There is also the Backyard Beginner Slope with a free lift and free ski-instruction sessions for entry-level skiers every day and three terrain parks for snowboarders. Private
lessons are also available through the ski school.

P.O. Box SKI, Marysville, MT 59640. © **406/449-3746.** Snow reports © 406/447-1310. www.skigd.com.
Lift tickets $36 adults, $16–$28 kids 6–18, free for children 5 and under with adult; hourly tickets available
for $8. Mid-Nov to early Apr Wed–Fri 10am–4pm, Sat–Sun 9am–4pm, with some Fri night skiing. Take exit
200 off I-15, then go west on Mont. 279 to Marysville Rd.

Snowmobiling
Three major trail systems are within a 30-minute drive of Helena. The Minnehaha-
Rimini area grooms 120 miles of trails, and the Marysville and Magpie-Sunshine areas,
with views into the Gates of the Mountains Wilderness, each groom 45 miles of trails.
For details on these trails, as well as special event information, contact the **Helena Snow-
drifters Snowmobile Club** (www.helenasnowdrifters.org).

Watersports
Canyon Ferry Lake Recreation Area, managed by the Bureau of Reclamation
(© **406/475-3921**), is a 25-mile-long lake within 20 minutes of Helena. In the spring,
summer, and fall, the lake is primarily a rainbow trout fishery, but it does have numerous
campgrounds, picnic areas, and boat ramps. The lake is especially popular with water-
skiers, jet-skiers, and water-tubers, though you'll see sailboats racing as well. This is also
a prime bird-watching area.

Watersports fans also head to two Helena-area state parks that are centered on man-
made lakes: **Spring Meadow Lake** (day use only) and **Black Sandy** at Hauser Reservoir
(campsites are $13–$15). Spring Meadow is a 30-acre, spring-fed lake on Helena's western edge, noted for its clarity and depth. Open to nonmotorized boats only, the lake is
popular for swimming and fishing. To reach Spring Meadow Lake, take U.S. 12 west,
then head north on Joslyn to Country Club. One of the only public parks on the shores

of Hauser Reservoir, Black Sandy is an extremely popular weekend boating, fishing, and water-skiing takeoff point. To get to Hauser Reservoir, drive 7 miles north of Helena on I-15, then 4 miles east on Route 453, then follow signs 3 miles north on a county road. Information on both is available by calling the regional office (© **406/495-3270;** http://fwp.mt.gov) and each sports a $5 per vehicle day-use fee.

SEEING THE SIGHTS

A walking tour of the city will give you a capsule of the history of the Old West. For pointers on where to explore, contact the **Helena Convention and Visitor's Bureau** (© **800/743-5362** or 406/442-1530) and request one of the excellent walking tour brochures by the Montana Historical Society.

Last Chance Gulch was so named because a quartet of gold-seeking prospectors declared the spot to be their "last chance" to strike it rich. It came to be one of the richest gold-producing areas in the world and remains one of Helena's main streets. Located downtown, this historic area combines Helena's colorful past with a contemporary freshness. Architecturally significant buildings, many of which are listed on the National Register of Historic Places, house espresso shops and boutiques, while ultramodern sculptures depict historical events. Interpretive markers are scattered along the pedestrian mall, with historical information relating to period construction.

In Jefferson City, 15 miles south of Helena via I-15, the **Tizer Botanic Gardens & Arboretum,** 38 Tizer Rd. (© **406/933-8789;** www.tizergardens.com), is the only botanic garden in the vicinity, a peaceful display of bulbs, perennials, roses, and other plants crisscrossed by paths. It's open May through September and by appointment other times of year; admission is $4 (free for kids 5 and under).

Archie Bray Foundation   Archie Bray, a Helena resident and enthusiastic supporter of the arts, established this artistic colony for potters in 1951 at the brickyard and kilns of the Western Clay Manufacturing Company. Over the years it has become a premier testing ground for ceramic artists working together to share ideas and techniques. Various playful sculptures dot the lawns. Of special note are several larger, free-standing monuments by Robert Harrison, including *A Potter's Shrine,* dedicated to Bray and incorporating some materials up to 100 years old; *Tile-X,* stacked drain tiles in the shape of a pyramid; and *Aruina,* a monument of brick and tile whose four arches frame the surrounding Helena landscape. Because of the intimate nature of each individual resident's art-making process, visitors are asked to respect their privacy. Ceramic art is also for sale during gallery hours. Allow 1 to 2 hours.

2915 Country Club Ave. © **406/443-3502.** www.archiebray.org. Free admission. Gallery Mon–Sat 10am–5pm; also in summer Sun 1–5pm. Visitors may take a self-guided walking tour of the grounds during daylight hours.

Cathedral of St. Helena   Completed in 1924, the Cathedral of St. Helena was modeled on a church in Vienna, Austria. Its beautiful twin 230-foot spires seem ready to soar heavenward on their own, filigreed and light. The cathedral is decorated with magnificent Bavarian stained-glass windows, hand-carved oak pews, hand-forged bronze light fixtures, and Carrara marble statues. At one time it was open to all who wandered by, but there are now times when the cathedral is left unattended and the doors are locked. So if you want to see the inside, it is best to call ahead. Masses are held here daily.

530 N. Ewing. © **406/442-5825.** www.sthelenas.org. Open to public; hours vary, typically 6:30am–6pm. Call to arrange a free guided tour.

Gates of the Mountains Boat Tours   Meriwether Lewis coined the name "Gates of the Mountains" while plying this portion of the Missouri with his party. At almost every bend in the waterway, the towering rock formations seemed to block their passage, only to magically open up as they drew closer. Visitors can have an experience similar to Lewis's through a boat tour of this scenic river on the *Pirogue*, the *Sacajawea II*, or the *Hilger Rose*. The 105-minute excursions take you through the mountain "gates," past prehistoric pictographs on the limestone rocks, to a picnic area where wildlife-viewing opportunities abound. You can choose to return on a later boat and take a hike into the nearby Gates of the Mountains Wilderness Area. There are also dinner cruises on many Friday nights; call for details.

P.O. Box 478, Helena, MT 59624. ☎ **406/458-5241.** www.gatesofthemountains.com. $14 adults, $12 seniors, $8 children 4–17, free for children 3 and under. Memorial Day to late Sept; call or visit website for cruise schedule departures and returns. From Helena, drive 18 miles north on I-15 to exit 209 (Gates of the Mountains).

Holter Museum of Art ★   Considered one of the premier galleries in the state, the Holter displays artwork in 7,200 square feet and features 10 to 14 different shows each year, all of which include an intriguing diversity of mediums and styles. Specializing in contemporary art of the Northwest region, the museum provides exhibition space for local as well as nationally prominent artists, and is definitely worth a couple hours of your time. The museum also runs a summer arts-education program for youngsters and adults and is home to a slick gift shop.

12 E. Lawrence St. ☎ **406/442-6400.** www.holtermuseum.org. Free admission. Tues–Sat 10am–5:30pm; Sun noon–4pm.

Last Chance Tours Train   A train engine on wheels pulls you around Helena on a tour of its historic sites, including the Atlas Block, the Montana Club, and the old governor's mansion. This is an excellent way to get oriented in Helena and learn a few things about the city at the same time. The tours last 1 hour.

Tours leave from the Montana Historical Society Bldg., 225 N. Roberts. ☎ **888/423-1023** or 406/442-1023. www.lctours.com. Tickets $7.50 adults and teenagers, $6 children 4–12, free for children 3 and under. Mid-May to mid-Sept; tour times vary seasonally.

The Montana Historical Society Museum ★   The Montana Historical Society maintains a library and archives, as well as a museum. The **Montana Homeland Gallery** displays the history of Montana going back more than 11,000 years. A long-term exhibit, **Neither Empty nor Unknown,** covers Lewis and Clark. The **Mackay Gallery of Russell Art** has a permanent display of original Charles Russell masterpieces—from a collection of more than 200 artworks, including oils, watercolors, sculptures, and Russell's famous illustrated letters—that showcase one of the West's most remarkable artists. The **Northeast and Haynes galleries** house seasonal exhibits. The mounted hide of Big Medicine, a sacred, rare white bison that lived on Montana's National Bison Range from 1933 to 1959, is on display on the second-floor mezzanine.

Guided tours of the original **governor's mansion** ($4 adults, $1 children 5–18, $10 maximum per family; combination museum-mansion tickets available), located at 304 N. Ewing, are also available through the society. This Queen Anne–style mansion with a distinctive checkerboard background was constructed in 1888 for entrepreneur William A. Chessman and his family. The state acquired the mansion in 1913 and governors resided here for half a century, during which time the mansion lost much of its original historical flavor. However, a major restoration of the building was undertaken beginning in 1969, and much of its allure has been recovered. Tours operate on the hour from noon to 4pm Tuesday through Sunday (Oct–Apr Sat only). Allow about 2 hours.

225 N. Roberts St. © **406/444-2694.** www.montanahistoricalsociety.org. $5 adults, $1 children 5–18, free for children 4 and under; $12 maximum per family. Summer Mon–Sat 9am–5pm; winter Mon–Sat 10am–5pm. Library and archives Tues–Fri 9am–5pm; Sat 9am–1pm.

Montana State Capitol   Several years ago Montana's beautiful state capitol building underwent extensive renovations, revitalizing the historic grandeur that was lost during construction in the 1960s. Situated on 14 acres, the building was designed by architects Charles Bell and John Kent in the late 1800s. It's decorated in the French Renaissance style with frescoes, a grand stained-glass dome, and murals. The dome, faced with copper, rises 165 feet. Inside are murals by noted Montana artists Charles Russell, Edgar Paxson, and Ralph DeCamp, including Russell's famed *Lewis and Clark Meeting Indians at Ross' Hole.* The grounds and flower gardens of the state capitol building in Helena are a designated state park, visited by thousands of people each year.

1301 E. 6th Ave. © **406/444-4789.** www.montanacapitol.com. Free admission; no charge for tours. Building Mon–Fri 8am–5pm. Daily tours on the hour May–Sept Mon–Sat 9am–3pm, Sun noon–4pm; rest of year (even-numbered years only) tours on the hour Sat 10am–2pm.

SHOPPING

Last Chance Gulch is a 4-block-long pedestrian mall. Though it is not exclusively a shopping area, the office buildings are liberally interspersed with boutiques, restaurants, pubs, and places for the kids to play. Informational kiosks are located in the center of this walking mall and at its north end. The **Atlas Block** is a group of historically significant architectural structures in Last Chance Gulch. As Helena's main areas were leveled several times in the last 125 years or so, once by earthquakes (in 1935) and several times by fire in the 19th century and again in 1928, builders of the Atlas Block carved images of salamanders, which, in medieval European mythology, are impervious to fire.

Lasso the Moon, 25 S. Last Chance Gulch (© **406/442-1594**), is a classic toyshop, featuring rack after rack of unique toys that aren't stocked by the mass-market retailers. Next door at 21 S. Last Chance Gulch, is the **Ghost Art Gallery** (© **406/443-4536**), which features art on Western and nature themes. Another good gallery is **Upper Missouri Artists,** 7 N. Last Chance Gulch (© **406/457-8240**).

The attractive **Great Northern Town Center** is an emerging retail area just west of the intersection of Lyndale Avenue and Last Chance Gulch. Here, **Cobblestone Clothing,** 828 Great Northern Blvd., Ste. 103 (© **406/449-8684**), sells upscale women's apparel with a hint of the New West; **Grand Junction Mercantile,** 825 Great Northern Blvd. (© **406/442-6210**), is the place for gifts. There is also a new eight-screen movie theater here.

ESPECIALLY FOR KIDS

Great Northern Carousel (**Kids**)   Privately built by the developer of the Great Northern Town Center, this new carousel is an enchanting work of art with a definitive Montana spin—there are hand-carved bison, grizzly bears, dinosaurs, otters, and bighorn sheep alongside the horses, frogs, and pigs. There is also the **Painted Pony Ice Cream Parlor** and a gift shop on-site.

924 Bicentennial Plaza (at the Great Northern Town Center). © **406/457-5353.** www.gncarousel.com. 50¢ kids 16 and under and seniors, $1.50 adults. Memorial Day to Labor Day Sun–Thurs 10am–9pm, Fri–Sat 10am–10pm; shorter hours rest of year.

The Parrot Confectionery (Kids) Kids and adults alike will love this colorful candy store, established in 1922. The Parrot serves its original cherry phosphates and caramel-cashew sundaes from the soda fountain, beneath its charming collection of ceramic elephants. Family owned, the Parrot has provided gourmet chocolate and candy to Helena for more than 80 years, and loyal customers attest that the place and its products haven't changed a bit over time. In addition to its Helena clientele, the Parrot supplies candy to chocoholics from nearly every state in the union. It's known for its signature parrot confection, chocolate-covered caramels, and many other candies. They also have a "secret recipe" chili for lunch.

42 N. Last Chance Gulch. (C) **406/442-1470.** Most sundaes and candies $3–$8. AE, DISC, MC, V. Mon–Sat 9am–6pm (soda fountain until 5:30pm).

WHERE TO STAY

There's no shortage of good accommodations in Helena, with a bevy of historic inns and a number of business-oriented hotels and motels that cater to traveling politicos of all stripes. Aside from the options discussed below, you might try the **Holiday Inn Helena Downtown,** 22 N. Last Chance Gulch ((C) **406/443-2200**), a seven-story brick edifice with double rates of $119 to $199. The **Fairfield Inn of Helena,** 2150 11th Ave. ((C) **800/228-2800** or 406/449-9944), is another good option, with doubles for $85 to $120 and an indoor pool. **Elkhorn Mountain Inn,** 1 Jackson Creek Rd., Montana City, at I-15, exit 187 ((C) **866/442-6625** or 406/442-6625; www.elkhorninn.com), is a top-drawer mom-and-pop just south of Helena with a double rate of $65 to $75.

The Barrister Bed & Breakfast ★ Located directly across the street from the Cathedral of St. Helena, the Barrister is one of many elegant homes near the original governor's mansion. Built in 1874 and listed on the National Register of Historic Places, this Queen Anne–style gem was renovated in 1992 and opened as a B&B in 1993. The rooms are large and elegantly furnished with antiques. Each has a private bathroom—though some are across the hall. A nice touch is that each room has a black-and-white photo of what it looked like in the 19th century, courtesy of the Montana Historical Society. Most of the rooms are somewhat frilly, aside from the manly Captain's Suite, with a rich red carpet and a nautical theme. The third floor is a two-bedroom apartment that rents for $175 per night but is usually leased on longer term, by the week or the month. The common areas include a parlor, sun porch, den, TV room/library, laundry room, and office with a guest computer.

416 N. Ewing St., Helena, MT 59601. (C) **800/823-1148** or 406/443-7330. Fax 406/442-7964. http://the barristermt.tripod.com. 5 units. $119–$134 double. Rates include full breakfast and evening wine and hors d'oeuvres. AE, DC, DISC, MC, V. Pets accepted. *In room:* A/C, TV w/VCR or DVD player, movie library, hair dryer, Wi-Fi (free).

Best Western Helena Great Northern ★ Helena's newest hotel has rich, somewhat masculine rooms with two queen-size beds or a king-size, high ceilings, railroad-themed art, and a striking red contrast wall. Six of the rooms open up to both the hall and the indoor pool. The hotel is the anchor of the new Great Northern Town Center development, and is adjacent to a steakhouse on one side and a health club on the other. It's a bit outside of walking distance to downtown Helena, but worth the short drive because of the rooms' freshness and comfort, which overshadow the downtown Holiday Inn. There's a restaurant attached, the **Silver Star Steak Company** (see "Where to Dine," below), that is under different ownership but will deliver to your room. The entire property is nonsmoking.

835 Great Northern Blvd., Helena, MT 59601. ℂ **800/829-4047** or 406/457-5500. www.gnhotelhelena. com. 101 units. $135–$159 double; $169 suite. AE, DC, DISC, MC, V. **Amenities:** Restaurant; lounge; exercise room; indoor Jacuzzi; indoor pool; room service. *In room:* A/C, TV, fridge, hair dryer, Wi-Fi (free).

Jorgenson's Inn & Suites (Value) Jorgenson's has been a Helena institution since the 1950s, and offers a relative bargain. As you might expect in an older place, the rooms are a little smaller than those in most newer motels, but they have been religiously renovated, modernized, and refurbished throughout the years; some have microwaves and fridges. Guests also have access to the fully equipped fitness center across the street.

1714 11th Ave., Helena, MT 59601. ℂ **800/272-1770** or 406/442-1770. Fax 406/449-0155. 115 units. www.jorgensonsinn.com. $64–$129 double. AE, DC, DISC, MC, V. **Amenities:** Restaurant; lounge/casino; access to nearby fitness center; small indoor pool. *In room:* A/C, TV, Wi-Fi (most rooms, free).

Red Lion Colonial Hotel This is a fairly upscale property, with a spiral stairway inside that you might expect Scarlett O'Hara to come sweeping down at any moment. The rooms are huge by any standard, and the location right by the interstate is convenient for travelers. Some rooms also offer panoramic views of the valley and mountains beyond. The suites include king-size beds, refrigerators, and microwaves; some have private Jacuzzis.

2301 Colonial Dr. (just off I-15 at U.S. 12), Helena, MT 59601. ℂ **800/733-5466** or 406/443-2100. Fax 406/449-8815. www.redlion.com/colonial. 149 units. $115–$179 double. AE, DC, DISC, MC, V. **Amenities:** Restaurant; lounge; indoor Jacuzzi; indoor and outdoor heated pools; room service. *In room:* A/C, TV, hair dryer, Wi-Fi (free).

The Sanders B&B ★★★ One of the state's oldest and best B&Bs, the Sanders is a lesson in Montana history all on its own. Built and owned by Wilbur Fisk Sanders in 1875, the B&B has been beautifully restored by Bobbi Uecker (no relation to former ballplayer Bob) and Rock Ringling (a fourth-generation descendant of the famous circus family). Sanders was Montana's first U.S. senator and made his reputation by vigorously prosecuting the infamous Plummer gang in Virginia City. Guests sleep on beds from 1875 and look at the same pictures that Sanders did. (One was painted by his wife, an important Western suffragette in her day.) Our favorite accouterment is the elephant "bridle" in the Sanders Suite, marked with a big round disc reading "The Greatest Show on Earth." Wonder where they got that? Bobbi's enthusiasm shows in every detail, from the savory breakfasts, where she's willing to accommodate every kind of dietary restriction, to the advice she can offer on Helena's restaurants and attractions.

328 N. Ewing, Helena, MT 59601. ℂ **406/442-3309.** Fax 406/443-2361. www.sandersbb.com. 7 units. $115–$150 double. Rates include full breakfast and afternoon refreshments. AE, MC, V. *In room:* A/C, TV, hair dryer, Wi-Fi (free).

Camping

Twenty miles west of town, **Kim's Marina and RV Resort,** 8015 Canyon Ferry Rd., Helena, MT 59601 (ℂ **406/475-3723;** www.kimsmarina.com), has a complete resort facility that includes comfortable cabins situated on the lakefront. Canoes, deck boats, and paddle boats are for rent on a daily basis. You'll find rental cabins ($90 nightly) along with 50 tent and 60 RV sites ($15–$27), as well as tennis, horseshoes, and boat rentals.

For more primitive sites, the Bureau of Reclamation and Bureau of Land Management jointly run several campgrounds between Townsend in the south and Helena along U.S. 287 at Canyon Ferry Lake. From south to north, they are: **Indian Road Recreation Area** (1 mile north of Townsend on U.S. 287, mile marker 75), Silos (7 miles north of Townsend on U.S. 287, mile marker 70), and **White Earth Campground** (13 miles

ation Area offers a fishing pond for children and visitors with disabilities.

WHERE TO DINE

Fire Tower Coffee House, 422 N. Last Chance Gulch (✆ **406/495-8840;** www.firetower coffee.com), is a nice place to sit in an overstuffed chair and have a cup of coffee, muffin, or sandwich. Wagon ride dinners are available for $76 per person through **Last Chance Ranch,** 2884 Grizzly Gulch (✆ **406/442-2884;** www.lastchanceranch.biz).

Benny's Bistro ★★ NEW AMERICAN   This breezy cafe has a jazz theme, with horns and woodwinds on the brick walls and a piano—played during dinner on Fridays—and big windows that face the street. The open kitchen in the back specializes in crepes for dinner, stuffing them with everything from curried shrimp to smoked salmon to veggies and brie. Beyond the delectable crepes, the dinner menu includes "localvore" specialties with pork, chicken, and lamb, as well as excellent steaks (this is Montana, after all). Lunches consist of gourmet sandwiches on house-baked bread and big salads. This is the spot to eat downtown if you're looking for casually upscale, but not stuffy.

108 E. 6th Ave. ✆ **406/443-0105.** www.bennysbistro.com. Main courses $6–$9 lunch, $12–$22 dinner. AE, MC, V. Mon–Fri 11am–3pm; Wed–Sat 5:30–9pm.

Bert & Ernie's AMERICAN   A stalwart bar and grill in downtown Helena since 1974, Bert & Ernie's has occupied its present Last Chance Gulch location (a former clothing store) since 1990 and remains a good, reliable pick for a casual lunch or dinner. The fun atmosphere with the requisite clutter hanging from the walls (stuffed animals, neon signs, stained glass, and such) is a good match for the menu, a mix of sandwiches, burgers, Mexican fare, and dinner entrees such as fajitas, pasta, jambalaya, and steaks. Attached and under the same ownership is the intimate **Sommeliers,** an upscale wine bar that serves appetizers and desserts.

361 N. Last Chance Gulch. ✆ **406/443-5680.** www.bertanderniesofhelena.com. Reservations accepted. Main courses $7–$25. AE, DISC, MC, V. Sun–Thurs 11am–9pm; Fri–Sat 11am–10pm.

Lucca's ★★ ITALIAN   Recently moving to Last Chance Gulch, Lucca's is a swank and dim restaurant specializing in good steaks and good wine. The kitchen also plates up a nice selection of pork, lamb, and pasta dishes, including an excellent sausage-and-mushroom lasagna and a spicy shrimp *fra diavolo* with angel-hair pasta and a red-pepper cream sauce. The dining room is classic but contemporary, fronted by windows displaying a cornucopia of wine corks.

56 N. Last Chance Gulch. ✆ **406/457-8311.** Reservations recommended. Main courses $15–$32. AE, DISC, MC, V. Wed–Sun 5pm–close, usually around 9:30pm.

The Marysville House ★ STEAKS/SEAFOOD   Every Rocky Mountain state has a barely surviving ghost town with a still-great steakhouse. Marysville, an 1870 gold-mining town, once boasted a population of 4,000—now it's 70. And the Marysville House is the steakhouse that's still going strong, reportedly selling the most lobster of any eatery in the state. Located in what was once a train depot, the Marysville House serves steaks, crab legs, and cold, smooth beer in a rustic setting. The no-nonsense meals come with corn on the cob and beans. Guests have their choice of dining inside or out. And how's this for low-key Americana: Meals are served on paper plates, horseshoes and a marshmallow-roasting fire pit can be found outside, and you can eat at a picnic table on the deck.

153 N. Main St., Marysville. ℭ **406/443-6677**. www.marysvillemontana.com. Reservations accepted for groups of 10 or more only. Dinner $18–$40. MC, V. Wed–Sun 5–9pm (call first, as hours vary with seasons); closed Sun fall–spring. From Helena, take U.S. 15 N. to exit 200, Mont. 279. Go north on Mont. 279 for 23 miles; turn left at the sign for Marysville for 6 miles to find this living ghost town; it's a 45-min. drive from Helena.

On Broadway ★★ ITALIAN   Located in a historic brick building near Last Chance Gulch, On Broadway is a longtime standout in Helena. It's got a warm atmosphere, brick walls contrasting with ferns, two levels of dining, and exceptional food, with artful combinations of meats and vegetables, fresh herbs, and pasta highlighting the menu. A local favorite is the Chicken alla Broadway, a chicken breast topped with fresh mushrooms and cheese, then baked in a Mornay sauce with mozzarella. The fish menu is the most imaginative, headed up by blackened tuna and oven-roasted salmon.

106 Broadway. ℭ **406/443-1929**. www.onbroadwayinhelena.com. Reservations not accepted. Main courses $14–$26. AE, DISC, MC, V. Mon–Sat 5:30pm–close, usually around 9:30pm.

Silver Star Steak Company ★ STEAKS/SEAFOOD   The culinary anchor of the new Great Northern Town Center development, the Silver Star is an intimate, contemporary space with hints of the new West and a traditional menu. While the menu changes regularly, the food is quite good, with a nice selection of steaks—all USDA-certified Angus beef—and seafood. The latter includes halibut stuffed with brie and crab, and roasted salmon. There is a less expensive menu served in the bar, with burgers and other dishes running $9 to $16. Lunch includes salads, sandwiches, and pasta dishes.

833 Great Northern Blvd. ℭ **406/495-0677**. www.silverstarsteakco.com. Reservations recommended. Lunch $7–$15; dinner $17–$30. AE, DISC, MC, V. Mon–Sat 11:30am–2:30pm; daily 5–10pm. Bar open later.

Windbag Saloon ★ AMERICAN   Helena residents love this restaurant like you'd love an eccentric aunt: She's the most interesting relative you have and you always have a great time at her place. Who cares if she has a checkered past? This former bordello continues the location's tradition as a focal part of Helena's nightlife. Try one of a long list of microbrews (including Bag Bitter, brewed exclusively for the saloon by the local Blackfoot River Brewing Company), or order something from the extensive collection of appetizers before moving on to the Little Ida, 10 ounces of ground sirloin with peppers and onions, and fries so thick you'll barely be able to finish a serving. Seafood is flown in twice weekly, steaks are hand-cut on the premises, and the daily quiches are top of the line.

19 S. Last Chance Gulch. ℭ **406/443-9669**. Lunch $8–$19; dinner $10–$27. AE, DISC, MC, V. Mon–Thurs 11am–2pm and 5:30–9:30pm; Fri 11am–2pm and 5:30–10pm; Sat 2–10pm.

NIGHTLIFE & THE PERFORMING ARTS

Make it a point to visit the state-of-the-art **Myrna Loy Center for the Performing and Media Arts ★**, 15 N. Ewing St. (ℭ **406/443-0287**; www.myrnaloycenter.com). Formerly the county jail, the Myrna Loy (named after the silver-screen legend who was one of Helena's most famous residents) is today a multidisciplinary cultural center. Within its castlelike facade are a 55-seat cinema and a 250-seat performance hall, along with a gallery that focuses on regional art. Other playgoing opportunities include productions by **Grandstreet Theatre,** 325 N. Park Ave. (ℭ **406/447-1574**; www.grandstreet.net), and the **Montana Shakespeare Company** (ℭ **406/431-1154**; www.montanashakespeare. org), which takes to the stage June through August at Tizer Botanic Gardens and Arboretum.

Of the Queen City's watering holes, we like **Miller's Crossing,** 52 S. Park Ave.
(© **406/442-3290**), for the live music, neighborhood atmosphere, and Blackfoot River
Brewing suds on tap, and the popular **Brewhouse Pub & Grille,** 939½ Getchell St.
(© **406/457-9390**), atop the Lewis & Clark Brewing Company in the Great Northern
Town Center area. The **taproom** at Blackfoot River Brewing Company, 66 S. Park Ave.
(© **406/449-3005**), is another good option, open daily from 2 to 8pm with free tasters
and a three-beer limit.

---

3 BUTTE

64 miles S of Helena; 120 miles SE of Missoula; 82 miles W of Bozeman; 150 miles NW of West Yellowstone

Butte may not be most people's idea of a vacation destination, but in many ways the city
is the hidden soul of Montana. Butte's emergence in the 19th century as a hell-raising,
wide-open mining town drew a lot of people to the state, including a variety of racial and
ethnic groups. Butte has always been a strong union town in a state and region that
disdain union activity. This union and socialist tradition from the rip-roaring days has
made a lasting contribution to a strong progressive political tradition.

Butte used to be called "the richest hill on earth" for its production of copper, silver,
and other precious metals, and during the 1880s, Butte was the world's largest copper
producer. In 1955, the world's richest hill became the beginning of one of the world's
largest holes, the Berkeley Pit, which provided more cost-efficient open-pit mining of
copper. The pit grew and grew and almost swallowed the town. But after the mine closed
in the 1980s, groundwater seeped up through the maze of tunnels below, creating a
gigantic pollution problem. The town's drinking water—and very survival—was threatened by this toxic sea, but the problem is now being addressed by a $20-million water
treatment plant that opened in 2003.

If you can look past the signs of decline that remain from the end of the mining era,
Butte is full of rich history, colorful citizens, and a sort of blue-collar San Francisco–style
charm. Physically, Butte is built along the sides of steep hills, which provides a great
vantage point on the valley below. It also boasts Montana Tech, an arm of the University
of Montana system and one of the top-rated engineering schools in the country.

Sister city Anaconda was the "company town" formed when copper king Marcus Daly
extended his copper empire 24 miles west. The community was spared the name "Cop-
peropolis."

ESSENTIALS

GETTING THERE   The **Bert Mooney Airport** (© **406/494-3771;** www.butteairport.
com) is served by **Delta/SkyWest** (© **800/221-1212**). The **Greyhound** station in Butte
is located at 1324 Harrison Ave. (© **406/723-3287;** www.greyhound.com). For current
weather conditions on the highways, call © **406/721-3939** or 511.

VISITOR INFORMATION   The **Butte Convention and Visitors Bureau Information
Center,** 1000 George St., Butte, MT 59701-7901 (© **800/735-6814** or 406/723-3177;
www.buttecvb.com), is located off exit 126 near the intersections of I-15 and I-90. The
center is a user-friendly facility just off the freeway, close to a wetlands area where you
can take a breather from driving and watch wild ducks, geese, and muskrats go about
their business. It's also the home of the bronze statue of the locally legendary canine, the
Auditor, until he is relocated to a permanent home at the Berkeley Pit (see "Seeing the

Sights," later in this section). The Auditor was the mysterious dreadlocked dog that wandered the desolate moonscape around the Berkeley Pit for 17 years until his passing in 2003.

The **Anaconda Chamber of Commerce,** 306 E. Park, Anaconda, MT 59711 (© **406/563-2400;** www.anacondamt.org), can give you information on Butte's sister city. For brochures devoted to area attractions and driving tours, contact **Travel Montana's Gold West Country** (© **406/846-1943**).

GETTING AROUND   Car-rental agents at the airport are **Avis** (© **800/230-4898**), **Budget** (© **800/527-0700**), **Enterprise** (© **800/261-7331**), and **Hertz** (© **800/654-3131**).

The **Butte–Silver Bow Transit System** city buses run from 6:45am to 6:15pm Monday through Friday and 8:45am to 4:45pm on Saturday; for information on fares and stops, call © **406/497-6515. Mining City Taxi** (© **406/723-6511**) provides local transportation 24 hours a day.

SPECIAL EVENTS   Butte's thick Irish heritage from its days as a mining boomtown shines brightly (maybe a bit too brightly) on **St. Patrick's Day** ★, when this mining museum of a town throws a shamrock-tinted bash that is the big event of the year—even the banks shut down. The March 17 celebration is one of the biggest St. Patrick's Day parties outside of New York City, but be forewarned: It tends to be very rowdy and very drunk.

If you want a more family-friendly Irish festival, try **An Ri Ra** (www.mtgaelic.org), an annual 3-day tradition in mid-August. Another fun annual event—which began in 2002—is **Evel Knievel Days** (www.knieveldays.com), held in late July in honor of the late daredevil and Butte native, featuring motorcycle stunt shows and a parade. Contact the **Butte CVB** (see above) for the dates and times of these activities.

GETTING OUTSIDE

Lost Creek State Park (© **406/542-5500**), a few miles outside of Anaconda, is a great place to camp, hike, or simply sit and admire the scenery. At the end of the road into the park, a short path will take you to pretty Lost Creek Falls, which tumble over a 50-foot drop. There are also mountain goats and bighorn sheep in residence. Several hiking trails lead off from the road. Among the most interesting things here are the rocks. Exposed on the tops of some cliffs is the 1.3-billion-year-old Newman Formation, a Precambrian rock that's among the oldest exposed rocks in the Lower 48 states. This is a primitive park without services (and without charge). There are 25 campsites, suitable mostly for tents and car campers. To get to the park, drive 1½ miles east of Anaconda on Mont. 1, then 2 miles north on County Road 273, then 6 miles west on Lost Creek Road.

Golf

The **Old Works** ★★, 1205 Pizzini Way, Anaconda (© **406/563-5989;** www.oldworks. org), is a golf course, a work of landscape art, and a symbol of environmental reclamation. The course is built on a Superfund site that had been a blight on the landscape since 1884, when the upper works began to process 500 tons of copper ore daily under Marcus Daly's voracious eye. By 1887, the lower works were necessary because of the demand. The Old Works closed in 1902, when the new Washoe Smelter—the big tower you can see from anywhere in the valley—took over all the processing. Jack Nicklaus designed the golf course, a tough but fair layout that even eight-handicappers are willing to play from the white tees. The black sand traps, the old processing works, and the vast, forbidding

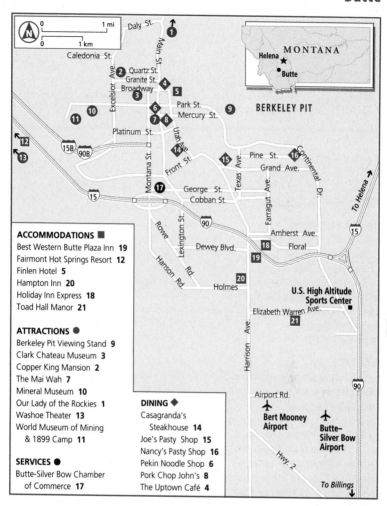

ACCOMMODATIONS ■
Best Western Butte Plaza Inn **19**
Fairmont Hot Springs Resort **12**
Finlen Hotel **5**
Hampton Inn **20**
Holiday Inn Express **18**
Toad Hall Manor **21**

ATTRACTIONS ●
Berkeley Pit Viewing Stand **9**
Clark Chateau Museum **3**
Copper King Mansion **2**
The Mai Wah **7**
Mineral Museum **10**
Our Lady of the Rockies **1**
Washoe Theater **13**
World Museum of Mining
  & 1899 Camp **11**

SERVICES ●
Butte-Silver Bow Chamber
  of Commerce **17**

DINING ◆
Casagranda's
  Steakhouse **14**
Joe's Pasty Shop **15**
Nancy's Pasty Shop **16**
Pekin Noodle Shop **6**
Pork Chop John's **8**
The Uptown Café **4**

black tailings piles are all worked beautifully into the layout of the course. This is one of the finest courses not just in Montana, but in America. To reach the course, which is open from mid-May to the end of October, take Commercial Street to North Cedar Street, turn north, then east (right) on Pizzini Way. Greens fees are $29 to $50 for 18 holes per person, depending on the day of week and time of year; cart rentals are $14 per person.

There's also an 18-hole course ($29–$43) at nearby **Fairmont Hot Springs Resort** (see "Where to Stay," later in this chapter). **Highland View Golf Course** (© **406/494-7900**), at Stodden Park in Butte, has two separate 9-hole courses: a par 3 ($10) and a regulation ($13).

Tips   **Butte Touring Tips**

From June through September, the **Butte Trolley** tour leaves from the Butte Visitor Center for a 1¹/₂-hour tour of the city's key attractions. Driver/tour guides are chosen for their knowledge of the town's history. Fares are $10 for adults and $5 for kids 5 to 18. Call © **406/723-3177** for schedules and other information. Year-round **Old Butte Historical Tours** (© **406/498-3424;** www.buttetours.info) offers historic walking tours, covering old speak-easies, brothels, hotels, and more ($10 adults, $5 kids).

Rock Climbing

Spire Rock and the Humbug Spires are the two most popular routes for rock climbers. The **Bureau of Land Management** (© **406/533-7600**) can refer guides and provide other climbing information.

Rockhounding

From the Continental Divide east of Butte through the mountains to the south, diligent rockhounders can find smoky quartz, amethyst, epidote, and tourmaline. Ask the curator at the **Mineral Museum** (see "Seeing the Sights," below) on the Montana Tech campus for leads on local hot spots. The **Butte Mineral and Gem Club,** P. O. Box 4492, Butte, MT 59702, has mining claims on **Crystal Park** about 70 miles southwest of Butte that are free and open to the public. From Butte go south on I-15 and west on Mont. 43; just past Wise River, turn south on the Pioneer Mountains Scenic Byway and drive about 20 miles to Crystal Park.

Skiing

In addition to **Discovery Ski Area,** Butte visitors are within range of **Maverick Mountain** (see section 4, "Dillon & the Big Hole," later in this chapter).

Discovery Ski Area   This is another Montana ski resort that falls somewhere in the middle of the pack if you make a list ranking them for nearly any category. The 67 runs on 2,400 patrolled acres here are nicely spread among beginner, intermediate, and expert runs. Three miles of groomed trails will satisfy the Nordic skier, a terrain park offers thrills for snowboarders, or you can blaze your own trail through untracked snow.

While the scenery equals or exceeds that of other areas in the state, the real plus here is the proximity to **Fairmont Hot Springs Resort** (see "Where to Stay," below), a four-season facility where soaking and swimming are year-round favorites. Ski rentals and instruction are available (private lessons are $40 per hour) as well as cafeteria-style food. There are no hotels at the ski area; the nearest accommodations are at Fairmont Hot Springs or in Butte and Anaconda.

P.O. Box 221, Anaconda, MT 59711. © **406/563-2184.** www.skidiscovery.com. Full-day lift tickets $35 adults, $18 children 12 and under and seniors; adult half-day $27 beginning at 12:30pm. From Anaconda, drive west on Mont. 1 for 20 miles to Georgetown Lake. Turn right (north) at the DISCOVERY SKI AREA sign. Continue north for 4¹/₂ miles to the ski area.

Snowmobiling

Call the Butte office of the **Beaverhead-Deerlodge National Forest** (© **406/494-2147;** www.fs.fed.us/r1/b-d) for information on nearby trails, most of which explore the

Georgetown Lake area. The four major trail systems are Carp Ridge, which terminates at the Anaconda-Pintler Wilderness boundary; Echo Lake, at the midpoint of Georgetown Lake and Discovery Ski Area; Peterson Meadows, a popular spot for cookouts and picnics; and Red Lion Racetrack Lake, with ridge-top views of surrounding peaks.

SEEING THE SIGHTS

For information on the **Pintler Scenic Route,** a driving tour that begins in Butte, see section 1 of this chapter.

The **Berkeley Pit** is rumored to be visible from the moon. It is located just off the Continental Drive in Butte. Starting in 1955, nearly 1.5 billion tons of material were removed from the pit—including more than 290 million tons of copper ore—before mining ceased in 1982. A short walk through a dimly lit tunnel (fully accessible for those with disabilities) takes you to an observation deck where you can view the pit, which is doggedly filling with groundwater. Unfortunately, the water flows through several thousand miles of underground pit tunnels through the mineralized zones and becomes heavily acidic en route to the surface. In 2003, a newly built water treatment plant began processing the polluted water, sidestepping the possibility that the toxic water would seep into the city's drinking water and render the town pretty much uninhabitable. The viewing stand is at the east end of Mercury Street on the fringes of the downtown area, and is open to the public ($2 admission) during daylight hours May through September. It's free at other times of year, weather permitting. A good online resource is **www.pitwatch. org.** As the Pit is Butte's most-visited attraction, the viewing area underwent a recent face-lift, including a rest area and other new facilities.

The 585-foot **Anaconda Smelter Stack,** just off Mont. 1 on the outskirts of Anaconda, is one of the tallest standing brick structures in the world and is designated a Montana State Park, though there is no public access to the structure. Once considered the largest copper-smelting stack in the entire world, all 58 stories of the desolate shaft rise starkly to meet the Montana sky. A few interpretive displays detail the smelter stack's history and construction.

Clark Chateau Museum ★ Built in 1898 for Charles Clark, son of copper king William A. Clark, the Clark Chateau is an impressively restored mansion and art gallery. Stained-glass windows, beveled glass, ornate wrought iron, and intricately

HELENA & SOUTHWESTERN MONTANA

8

BUTTE

ⓘ Tips Anaconda Touring Tips

You can take the **Vintage Bus Tour of Historic Anaconda** from the Anaconda Chamber of Commerce, 306 E. Park St. (ⓒ **406/563-2400**), Monday through Saturday at 10am and 2pm, from mid-May to mid-September. The cost is $8 adults, $4 children 6 and under. The tour includes a stop and inside tour of the fabulous Washoe Theater, which is usually open only at 8pm. The chamber also has a historical walking tour brochure for $2, but you won't see the inside of the Washoe unless you get lucky. For a different perspective, take a train ride on the historic **Copper King Express,** 300 W. Commercial Ave., Anaconda (ⓒ **877/563-5458** or 406/563-5458; www.copperkingexpress.com), from Anaconda through rugged Durant Canyon to Ramsay and back, a 3-hour round-trip. Tickets are $25 adults, $20 seniors, $18 students, and $5 kids 5 and under.

detailed woodwork contribute to the mansion's early-20th-century elegance. The home's magnificent staircase leads to a second-story museum, filled with period furniture, and the gallery, which houses traveling displays by Montana artists in a much more modern setting. The two galleries have exhibits that change every 6 weeks. Other highlights include the fourth-floor ballroom, which replicates a grand hunting lodge, and the first-floor gift shop, with hundreds of made-in-Montana items for sale. Under the same umbrella is a coffee shop, the **Venus Rising Espresso House,** 124 S. Main St. (✆ **406/491-4476**), with a gallery, an arts store, and regular films and musical entertainment.

321 W. Broadway, Butte. ✆ **406/723-7600.** www.bsbarts.org. $4 adults, $3 seniors, $2 children, $10 family of 4. Summer daily noon–5pm; winter by appointment. Tours available.

Copper King Mansion   This combination museum and bed-and-breakfast inn is an ideal choice for those who want to savor the historical ambience of one of the most lavish homes of the late 19th century. The huge home was built for mining magnate William A. Clark in 1888 for $260,000. There are 34 rooms on three floors, decorated in a lush "modern Elizabethan" style. While the inn's exterior has seen better days, the interior features remarkably intricate woodwork and a large number of opulent pieces of period furniture collected by the inn's owners. There are even a few original items from the period of Clark's ownership. In the third-floor ballroom, there's an 814-pipe Estey organ as well as a private collection of clothing and memorabilia dating from the late 1800s; a small chapel is discreetly located to the side.

The guest rooms ($65–$115 nightly) are in general spacious and furnished with antiques. There are parquet floors downstairs, and the octagon-shaped reception room, the billiard room, and the library all reflect Clark's love of luxury. Antique lamps and chandeliers, ornate frescoed ceilings, and etched amber transoms complement the rooms' original furniture, including two matching African mahogany sleigh beds. If you stay at the B&B, you can sleep in the copper king's room, but you have to get up early and leave when the tours begin at 9am.

219 W. Granite St., Butte, MT 59701. ✆ **406/782-7580.** www.thecopperkingmansion.com. $7 adults, $3.50 children. Summer daily 9am–4pm; rest of year by appointment.

The Mai Wah ★   Adjacent to China Alley, the Mai Wah and Wah Chong Tai buildings stand as tributes to Butte's early Chinese population, which numbered 400 in 1890. With a first-floor mercantile and second-floor noodle parlor, the Mai Wah provided a segment of the city's ethnic community with jobs after the mines were exhausted. Today the buildings house exhibits and memorabilia honoring the rich Asian history of the area. The Mai Wah's permanent exhibit, "The Butte Chinese Experience," tells this fascinating story with artifacts, images, and interpretive displays.

17 W. Mercury St., Butte. ✆ **406/723-3231.** www.maiwah.org. $3 adults, free for children. June–Sept Tues–Sun 11am–5pm.

Mineral Museum   This museum displays only a small percentage of the mineral specimens that belong to Montana Tech's geology department, though that still makes for a pretty impressive mineral display. The explanation of the minerals consists of their identification and place of origin. One display features a comprehensive display of fluorescent minerals, starkly illuminated by ultraviolet lights. One of the area's most exciting discoveries, a 28-ounce gold nugget found in the Highland Mountains south of Butte, is also on display.

Montana Tech Campus. ℂ **406/496-4414.** www.mbmg.mtech.edu. Free admission. Mid-June to mid-Sept daily 9am–5pm; rest of year Mon–Fri 9am–4pm. From the center of Butte, take Park St. west to the Montana Tech Campus and follow the signs to the museum.

Our Lady of the Rockies   When you look up to the eastern heights above Butte, you'll see the large white statue of "Our Lady of the Rockies" in a notch at the top of a hill. The 90-foot statue was built "in the likeness of Mary, Mother of Jesus," and is dedicated to all women, especially mothers. Private cars are not allowed up to the site, but you can get a close-up view of the statue on 2½-hour bus tours. If you don't have time for a tour but are interested in learning more about "Our Lady of the Rockies," visit the information center and gift shop for a look at a panoramic mural of the statue. There is also a 30-minute video detailing the construction: 400 tons of concrete were used just for the statue's base.

Butte Plaza Mall, 3100 Harrison Ave., Butte. ℂ **800/800-5239** or 406/782-1221. www.ourladyofthe rockies.com. Free admission to information center and gift shop. June–Sept daily 9am–6pm; winter limited hours. Tours depart daily during summer at 10am and 2pm. $15 adults, $13 seniors 55 and over, $11 ages 13–17, $7 ages 5–12, $2 ages 4 and under.

Washoe Theater ★   The Washoe shares the distinction with New York City's Radio City Music Hall of being the last two theaters done in the Art Deco style, and the Washoe is actually the more impressive. The brick exterior is unremarkable, and when you see it you'll wonder what all the fuss is about. But inside, this is a true movie palace. Considered one of the most architecturally significant theaters in the country, it's a work of art in cerulean, salmon, beige, and yellow, with a fabulous curtain. If you arrive at midday, the theater is usually closed—it's still a working first-run movie theater and doesn't open until evening. But if someone is there, he'll turn on the lights and let you look around. Or you can take a trolley tour through the Anaconda Chamber to get a guaranteed peek.

305 Main St., Anaconda. ℂ **406/563-6161.** Showtimes and ticket prices vary; call for current information.

World Museum of Mining & 1899 Mining Camp ★   This popular museum is a re-creation of the 1899 Hellroarin' Gulch mining town. It's on the site of the Orphan Girl mine, which, though not a blockbuster by Butte standards, managed to produce 7.6 million ounces of silver, along with lead and zinc. The mining town is set up with typical businesses and buildings of the mining era here, with explanations of each of their functions in the community. Underground tours of the first 65 feet of the 2,700-foot-deep Orphan Girl Mine are offered three times daily in summer and less frequently other times of year for an additional fee. There's also a hard-rock mining hall with tools of the trade and examples of types of framing timbers used underground.

155 Museum Way, P.O. Box 33, Butte. ℂ **406/723-7211.** www.miningmuseum.org. Admission $7 adults, $6 seniors, $5 ages 13–18, $2 ages 5–12, free for ages 4 and under. Underground mine tours $10 adults, $8 seniors and ages 13–18, $3 ages 5–12, not recommended for ages 4 and under. Combination passes available. Apr–Oct daily 9am–6pm; shorter hours rest of year. From the center of Butte, take Park St. west to the Montana Tech Campus. Continue on Park through the campus and make a left at Museum Way.

WHERE TO STAY

Beyond the options listed below, we recommend the **Holiday Inn Express,** 1 Holiday Park Dr. (ℂ **800/465-4329** or 406/494-6999), with rates of $94 to $109 double and suites for $115 to $135, and the **Hampton Inn,** 3499 Harrison Ave. S. (ℂ **800/426-7866** or 406/494-2250), with double rates of $109 to $139.

Best Western Butte Plaza Inn ★ This property is the best motel in the area because of its facilities, services, and location next to the freeway. Rooms, with modern decor, are small but quiet and clean, all with either king- or queen-size beds. The breakfast buffet, included in the room price, includes scrambled eggs and bacon, fresh fruit, muffins, hot or cold cereals, and juices and coffee. On-site, **Hops** is a pub and casino decorated in the style of an English pub.

2900 Harrison Ave., Butte, MT 59701. ☎ **800/543-5814** or 406/494-3500. Fax 406/494-7611. www.best western.com/butteplazainn. 134 units, including 1 suite. $85–$135 double; $150–$200 suite. Rates include breakfast buffet. AE, DISC, MC, V. Pets accepted ($50 deposit). **Amenities:** Restaurant; lounge; exercise room; indoor Jacuzzi; indoor pool; room service; sauna. *In room:* A/C, TV, hair dryer, Wi-Fi (free).

Fairmont Hot Springs Resort ★ (Kids) This oasis between Butte and Missoula is a great place for families, with a 350-foot water slide and a pair of Olympic-size pools, a small wildlife zoo, and a playground. Parents will enjoy the wide range of activities as well, from golf and tennis to cross-country skiing in the winter. Plus, of course, the soothing hot springs (there are two soaking pools), and the fact that Discovery Ski Area is only 30 minutes away. The standard rooms are fairly typical, hotel-style accommodations, but they all have balconies, and the suites are as large and snazzy as one could want, sleeping as many as eight guests. Many of the suites also have fully equipped kitchens, and, by resort standards, the cost is modest.

1500 Fairmont Rd., Fairmont, MT 59711. ☎ **800/332-3272** or 406/797-3241. Fax 406/797-3337. www. fairmontmontana.com. 152 units. Summer $149–$159 double; $299–$385 suite. Higher holiday rates. Lower rates fall–spring. AE, DC, DISC, MC, V. Exit 211 off I-90. **Amenities:** 2 restaurants; lounge (w/casino); 18-hole golf course; 2 indoor and 2 outdoor hot-springs pools; room service; 2 steam rooms; tennis courts; Wi-Fi (free). *In room:* A/C, TV, hair dryer, kitchen (suites only).

Finlen Hotel Butte's most historic hotel, the 1924 Finlen was modeled after New York's Astor Hotel after its mining-era predecessor was razed. The lobby is elegant—with soaring copper-accented columns, crystal chandeliers, and marble walls—inside an attractive nine-story, brick facade. Some rooms are nicer than others, but they are clean and well-maintained, with small bathrooms and a typical motel feel (lacking historical ambience). There is also a motel-style annex with slightly lower rates that represents more than half of the rooms.

100 E. Broadway, Butte, MT 59701. ☎ **800/729-5461** or 406/723-5461. www.finlen.com. 53 units, including 3 suites. $56–$74 double; $86 suite. AE, DISC, MC, V. **Amenities:** Lounge; Wi-Fi (free). *In room:* A/C, TV.

Toad Hall Manor ★ In 2003, Glenn and Jane Johnson opened their palatial, 11,000-square-foot home on the 16th hole of the Butte Country Club to guests as a splendid B&B. The 1993 home has a more historical feel than you'd think, and a quartet of whimsical guest rooms named for characters in the children's classic *The Wind in the Willows*. We like Mr. Mole's Hide-away, with its great mountain views and stately walnut furnishings, but for a splurge, Sir Badger's Suite might be the best room in the city, with two bedrooms, a walk-in closet, and a two-person Jacuzzi, occupying the entire fifth floor. The breakfasts are unique, with such dishes as Toad's Extravagant Omelet and breakfast strudel.

1 Green Lane, Butte, MT 59701. ☎ **866/443-8623** or 406/494-2625. Fax 406/494-8025. www.toadhall manor.com. 4 units. $115–$140 double; $175 suite. Rates include full breakfast. AE, DC, DISC, MC, V. *In room:* TV, hair dryer, Wi-Fi (free).

Butte's ethnic tradition is most evident in its food, with pasties (pronounced *pass*-tees, or *pah*-stees if you're British) ranking high on the list. If you've never tried one of these Cornish meat-filled pastries, you're in for a treat. Try **Joe's Pasty Shop,** 1641 Grand Ave. (© **406/723-9071**), or **Nancy's Pasty Shop,** 2810 Pine St. (© **406/782-7410**). Another local delicacy that should not be missed is a $3.25 breaded pork chop sandwich from **Pork Chop John's,** 8 W. Mercury St. (© **406/782-0812**). This barebones, blue-collar diner is a Butte landmark, and the sandwiches, wrapped in wax paper and topped with pickles, mustard, and onions, are the best deal in town.

Casagranda's Steakhouse ★ STEAKS/ITALIAN   The industrial exterior of this former warehouse belies an excellent dinner destination, with a menu that runs the gamut from *cioppino* to ribs to duck. The dining room is at once casual and intimate, with many of the old warehouse trappings still in place. There is also a nice selection of seafood and pasta dishes and a good wine list.

801 S. Utah Ave., Butte. © **406/723-4141.** Reservations recommended. Main courses $13–$25. AE, DISC, MC, V. Daily 5–10pm (9pm in winter).

Pekin Noodle Parlor (Finds CHINESE   Operated by the same family since 1916, the Pekin Noodle Parlor is a time capsule from the days when its neighborhood was a bustling Chinatown. Featuring curtained pink booths that are former brothel stalls (the old opium den is in the basement), the Pekin does a decent job with Chinese standards such as chow mein and chop suey, and also serves a few American standards (burgers, steaks, and egg plates), but the historical ambience outshines the food.

117 S. Main St., Butte. © **406/782-2217.** Reservations accepted for large parties only. Dinner $6–$14. MC, V. Sun–Mon and Wed–Thurs 5–10:30pm; Fri–Sat 5pm–midnight or later. Closed Tues.

The Uptown Café ★★ NEW AMERICAN   The Uptown Café is a white-tablecloth restaurant in a no-tablecloth town. Despite the fact that the restaurant is one of the city's finest, it's also unpretentious, as longtime owners Barb Kornet and Guy Graham present five-course meals built around Montana beef and fresh seafood flown in from the Pacific Northwest. The favorite starter is Clams Maison—succulent clams prepared with white wine, chives, and butter. Other choices include soup—gazpacho if you're lucky—plus several types of salads, a pasta or vegetable dish, and the main course. We recommend the salmon or halibut, when they're available, but we wouldn't turn down a steak either. Every night until 6:30pm, the cafe also serves an early dining special: cheese ravioli with artichokes and roasted red peppers or chicken Dijon, for example, always with a Caesar salad and French bread for only $14. It makes you wonder if this is really Butte.

47 E. Broadway, Butte. © **877/723-4735** or 406/723-4735. www.uptowncafe.com. Reservations recommended. Lunch $6.50–$11; dinner $17–$30. AE, DISC, MC, V. Mon–Fri 11am–2pm; Mon–Sat 5–9 or 10pm; Sun 4–8pm.

BUTTE AFTER DARK

No trip to Butte is complete without a visit to the **M&M Cigar Store,** 9 N. Main St.— providing that it's open. The cigar store/saloon/diner/casino that Jack Kerouac said was "the end of my quest for an ideal bar" was continuously open, 24 hours a day, for more than a century after it went into business in 1890, but found itself boarded up in 2003. Then director Wim Wenders fixed up the M&M when he used it as a location for *Don't Come Knocking*. The renovations made the place a more attractive investment, and it reopened—with Governor Brian Schweitzer hand-delivering the liquor license just

Philipsburg: Off the Beaten Path

Located southwest of Butte on the Pintler Scenic Route (Mont. 1), Philipsburg is one of the best little towns in the state, complete with a vibrant and historic downtown and outdoor recreation in every direction. Many of the historic storefronts are impeccably kept and painted in every color of the rainbow; instead of housing brothels, gambling dens, and saloons as they did in the mining heyday of "P-burg," they now are more likely occupied by boutiques and galleries. Officially designated a town in 1867, Philipsburg boomed until World War II, at which time the population began to decline. Today the town is livelier than it's been in many decades, as retirees and tourists discover the area. Besides a fair number of B&Bs and other lodgings, there are several restaurants, a theater company, and the **Sweet Palace,** 109 E. Broadway (© 406/859-3353), a confectionery that makes its own fudge, taffy, and caramel on-site. For more information, contact the **Philipsburg Chamber of Commerce** (© 406/859-3388; www.philipsburgmt.com).

before he took a shot of whiskey in time for St. Patrick's Day 2005. "May she never close," Schweitzer remarked on that day. Then she closed again. At press time, locals expected it to reopen under new ownership in the future. Call the **Butte CVB** (© 800/735-6814) for current information.

A SIDE TRIP TO DEER LODGE

Deer Lodge is home to Montana's state prison, which isn't ordinarily a recommendation for a tourist destination. And we won't recommend any places to stay, because you probably won't want to spend the night. But there is a collection of museums here that makes Deer Lodge worth a morning's stop—especially if you're a car buff or a fan of ranching life.

As you enter Deer Lodge from the west on County Road 275, you'll pass the **Grant-Kohrs Ranch National Historic Site** ★ (© 406/846-2070; www.nps.gov/grko), another of the National Park Service's marvelous facilities. The site preserves the rich history and traditions of ranch life in the West. The ranch itself was founded in the late 1850s when Johnny Grant, a Canadian trader, moved here, eventually building up a herd of several hundred cattle. After a few years, he sold it to legendary cattleman Conrad Kohrs, and the ranch became the headquarters for a vast cattle empire scattered across the open range of Montana, Idaho, and Wyoming. Today the site includes 90 structures, 26,000 artifacts, and a 1,500-acre cultural landscape maintained as a small-scale working ranch. Rangers lead tours of the 1862 Kohrs manor on an hourly basis. Wagon tours are offered Thursday through Monday in summer for $5 per person or $15 per family. Admission is free, but donations are appreciated. It's open to the public daily 9am to 5:30pm in summer (9am–4:30pm winter) except Thanksgiving, Christmas, and New Year's Day.

Gold was discovered near Deer Lodge in 1862. This was an early precursor of the gold rush that reached full bloom with the discoveries at Bannack and Virginia City. One of the consequences of this gold rush is downtown—the castlelike **Old Montana Prison,** at 1106 Main St. (© **406/846-3111;** www.pcmaf.org). Vigilantes initially dealt with the thievery and lawlessness that prevailed during the gold rush, but the need for a real jail was eventually solved by the construction of this prison, which took in its first prisoner in 1871. It was used until 1979, when another facility was built about 5 miles from here. You can take a self-guided tour of the prison. Cellblocks, maximum-security areas, turreted guard towers, and the imposing arches of the "Sally Port" gate are the attractions here, as well as a tribute to officers killed in the line of duty at the **Montana Law Enforcement Museum.**

The Old Prison and the Law Enforcement Museum are only two of a collection of museums in Deer Lodge, which are all covered under one admission fee ($8 adults, $4 kids 10–15, and free for kids 9 and under, with lower rates in the winter). The prison complex also houses the **Montana Auto Museum,** the **Powell County Museum,** the **Frontier Montana Museum,** and **Yesterday's Playthings.** The complex is open to the public daily year-round: from Memorial Day to Labor Day, 8am to 8pm, and 9am to 5pm or 10am to 4pm the rest of the year; not all of the museums stay open during the off season. Some of the museums have different hours different times of the year; call © **406/846-3111** or visit www.pcmaf.org for current information.

The newest exhibit is **Cottonwood City,** a re-creation of an Old West town, with a blacksmith, cabins, a church, a schoolhouse, and a mortuary (you can get your photo taken in a casket). There's a working blacksmith's shop as well. The **Montana Auto Museum** houses more than 120 exquisitely restored automobiles—mostly classic Fords and Chevys, but also vintage firetrucks, motor homes, and motorcycles. The **Frontier Montana Museum** has a collection of the tools that were used to win the West. There is a nice exhibit on Colt "peacemakers" and their effect on the keeping of the peace. There are also saddles, spurs, and Desert John's Saloon, with one of the largest bottle and whiskey-memorabilia collections in the country.

The vast weapons collection at the **Powell County Museum,** 1193 Main St., includes long guns and handguns from 1776 to 1956. **Yesterday's Playthings,** 1017 Main St., is a doll and toy museum. The collections of Harriet Free and Pat Campbell are displayed here, with dolls, toys, and antiques of all descriptions: mohair teddy bears, carriages and cradles dating from 1835, clown dolls, and various reproductions.

For additional information on these and other activities in Deer Lodge, contact the **Powell County Chamber of Commerce,** 1109 Main St., Deer Lodge, MT 59722 (© **406/846-2094;** www.powellcountymontana.com), or **Gold West Country,** 1105 Main St., Deer Lodge, MT 59722 (© **800/879-1159;** goldwest.visitmt.com).

4 DILLON & THE BIG HOLE

Dillon: 65 miles S of Butte; 141 miles N of Idaho Falls, Idaho

In early Western parlance, a "hole" was a valley surrounded by steep mountains. And Big Hole is, well, a big "hole," in this old sense of a valley. It is a vast expanse of hay meadows, sagebrush flats, and ranch land ringed by towering mountains in the distance. These hay meadows have also given the Big Hole its nickname of the "valley of 10,000 haystacks," which may be a rare case of Rocky Mountain understatement.

While there are plenty of haystacks, there aren't many people. This region is the least densely populated area in western Montana. Beaverhead County, which is as large as

Connecticut and Rhode Island combined, has only about 9,000 residents, and most of those live in Dillon, the county's largest town.

Dillon is primarily an agricultural center, still dependent on local farmers and ranchers rather than tourism or industry. The population temporarily jumps from 5,000 to roughly 20,000 people around Labor Day during the event known as **"Montana's Biggest Weekend."** Among the draws are a county fair, which is wrapped around a PRCA Rodeo that draws some of the country's best cowboys, as well as national musical acts. If you plan on attending, book a room at least 3 months in advance.

The scenic loop that takes you around this valley is one of the state's more popular driving tours, and is described in section 1 of this chapter.

ESSENTIALS

GETTING THERE The **Dillon Airport** is located at 2400 Airport Rd. and has paved runways for light planes. See Butte "Essentials," earlier in this chapter, for information on the closest airport to the Big Hole Valley, car rentals, and train and bus service. Dillon is located on I-15, about 65 miles south of Butte and 78 miles from Anaconda.

This area is also a popular destination for snowmobilers, and visitors are encouraged to call the **avalanche advisory line** (✆ 406/587-6981) before setting out on a snowmobiling excursion. For **current road conditions,** call ✆ 800/226-7623; for current **weather information,** call ✆ 406/721-3939.

VISITOR INFORMATION The **Dillon Visitor Information Center** (operated by the Beaverhead Chamber of Commerce) is located in the Camp Fortunate Interpretive Center at 10 W. Reeder St., Dillon, MT 59725 (✆ 406/683-6731; www.beaverhead chamber.org).

GETTING OUTSIDE

Beaverhead County has several natural hot springs, including **Jackson Hot Springs Lodge** (see "Where to Stay," below) and **Elkhorn Hot Springs,** which is located about 10 miles off Route 278 on a newly paved road. Go west of Dillon on 278 about 30 miles, then turn north toward Polaris at the sign. Follow the road through Polaris to Elkhorn Hot Springs, about 5 miles farther. These waters provide a therapeutic complement to various winter activities, most notably snowmobiling, downhill skiing, and cross-country skiing.

Outfitters & Organized Trips

Montana High Country, 35 miles west of Dillon at 7501 Pioneer Mountain Scenic By-way, Polaris, MT 59746 (✆ 406/834-3469; www.mhct.com), is operated by sixth-generation Montanan Russ Kipp. The company offers year-round guiding services, including fly-fishing, horseback riding, big-game hunting, and snowmobiling. Whether you're a sportsman looking to bag that elusive elk or a family longing for some quality time together, Kipp has plenty of experience in arranging a unique outdoor adventure. His most popular trips center on southwest Montana's classic trout streams, picturesque limestone canyons, and stunning mountain ranges. Prices range from $900 for a 3-day, 4-night snowmobiling package to around $3,500 for a 6-day moose-hunting trip. Kipp also operates an Orvis-endorsed guest lodge with rates starting at $150 per person per night, meals included.

Great Divide Wildlands Institute (✆ 406/683-4669; www.greatdividetours.com) offers a variety of scenic and historical tours, with a special emphasis on the route of Lewis and Clark and the Nez Perce through the area. Starting at $250 for two people,

the packages include day trips to where Lewis first met the Shoshone and other customized historical and scenic tours in the Big Hole.

Fishing

The Big Hole, Beaverhead, and Poindexter rivers are all within easy reach of Dillon, and
Jefferson is only half an hour away by car. The fishing season begins early in the year
when other streams may still be clearing, and extends into October. Big Hole fishermen
can find several trout species, including eastern brook, brown, and golden. The **Clark
Canyon Reservoir** provides good fishing for rainbow trout. Arctic grayling, ling, and
whitefish also populate the waters of the Big Hole Valley. The **Beaverhead-Deerlodge
National Forest,** 420 Barrett St., Dillon, MT 59725 (© **406/683-3900;** www.fs.fed.us/
r1/b-d), can provide you with information on the lakes and streams in the forest.

For licenses, equipment, and advice on hot fishing spots, check with the locals in Dillon at **Frontier Anglers,** 680 N. Montana St. (© **800/228-5263;** www.frontieranglers.
com). You can arrange a trip on any of the local rivers with **Tom Smith's Backcountry
Angler,** 426 S. Atlantic St., Dillon, MT 59725 (© **406/683-3462;** www.backcountry
angler.com). Smith has been guiding in Montana since 1983, and he also has a pair of
kitchenettes and a private log home on the Beaverhead River available for rent (call for
details). In Twin Bridges (just up Mont. 41), your best bet for fishing equipment and
outfitting services is the **Four Rivers Fishing Co.,** 205 S. Main St. (© **888/474-8377;**
www.4riversmontana.com). Aficionados of the fishing world should stop at the **R. L.
Winston Rod Co.,** also in Twin Bridges, at 500 S. Main St. (© **406/684-5674;** www.
winstonrods.com), for a look at some of the finest fly rods in the world. Free tours of the
company facility are given each weekday at 11am; a showroom/museum is open weekdays from 8am to 4:30pm.

Hiking

Hike along the **Continental Divide National Scenic Trail** in the **Anaconda-Pintler
Wilderness** for interesting geologic discoveries, fabulous scenery, and views of wildlife:
Elk, moose, mule deer, antelope, and even black bears are all indigenous to the region.
Covering parts of the Bitterroot and Beaverhead-Deerlodge national forests, this
158,500-acre wilderness spans 40 miles along the Continental Divide over four counties.
Highways with access to the area are U.S. 93 on the west, Mont. 38 and Mont. 1 from
the north, and Mont. 43 from the east and south. The **Wise River Ranger District,** P.O.
Box 100, Wise River, MT 59762 (© **406/832-3178**), can direct you to the area's most
traveled trails. You can also obtain a recreation directory, which describes many of the
trails in the forest. The guide is available for free from **Beaverhead-Deerlodge National
Forest,** 420 Barrett St., Dillon, MT 59725 (© **406/683-3900;** www.fs.fed.us/r1/b-d).

Horseback Riding

Diamond Hitch Outfitters, 3405 Ten Mile Rd., Dillon, MT 59725 (© **800/368-5494**
or 406/683-5494; www.diamondhitchoutfitters.com), offers 1½-hour rides, half-day
trips, and full-day trips in the Pioneer Mountains. As an alternative, evening horseback
rides include a campfire cookout. More adventurous overnight and extended backcountry rides are also available. Rates range from $30 per 1½-hour ride to $1,050 for a 5-day
trip.

Skiing

In addition to **Maverick Mountain,** discussed below, Dillon is fairly close to **Lost Trail
Powder Mountain** (see "A Detour into the Bitterroot Valley," in chapter 7).

Maverick Mountain   Located 35 miles west of Dillon in the Beaverhead National Forest, Maverick Mountain is a small, inexpensive area that attracts mostly local skiers. It remains crowd-free, yet to become a destination ski resort. There are 24 runs with 2,020 vertical feet of skiing. Most of the runs are rated for the intermediate skier. There are some wide-open bowls, meadows, winding runs, and steep chutes. The area gets enough snow—200 inches yearly—to offer some good powder days. Rentals and lessons are available for downhill skis and snowboards. There's a child-care facility, but call ahead to reserve a spot. There are no lodging facilities at the ski area, although there are some nice accommodations nearby. Cafeteria-style meals are available at the base lodge, or you can grab a hot toddy at the Thunder Bar.

Maverick Mountain Rd. (P.O. Box 475), Polaris, MT 59746. ✆ **406/834-3454.** www.skimaverick.com. Full-day lift tickets $30 adults, $20 children, $15 preschooler with lesson. Mid-Dec to mid-Apr Thurs–Sun and holidays 9:30am–4pm. Take Mont. 278 west off U.S. 15 to Polaris Rd. for 13 miles.

Snowmobiling

The Wise River trail system features 150 miles of groomed trails in the Big Hole Valley area, including **Anderson Meadows**—which leads to backcountry lakes and a rental cabin—and **Lacy Creek,** with 10 miles of groomed and ungroomed trails to five high-mountain lakes. The Beaverhead-Deerlodge National Forest's **Wise River Ranger District,** P.O. Box 100, Wise River, MT 59762 (✆ **406/832-3178**), is a good source of information.

NATURE PRESERVES & WILDERNESS AREAS

One of the Bureau of Land Management's Backcountry Byways, the **Big Sheep Creek Canyon** offers the opportunity to observe the majestic bighorn sheep in their spectacular natural habitat. The 50-mile byway begins in Dell, Montana, on I-15, 24 miles north of the Montana-Idaho border, and passes beneath the high rock cliffs of Big Sheep Canyon to the head of Medicine Lodge Creek. From here, it's just a short drive down to the Medicine Lodge Valley to Mont. 324, just west of Clark Canyon Dam.

Clark Canyon Recreation Area, a man-made lake 20 miles south of Dillon on I-15, is a popular spot for water-skiing or trout fishing. Lewis and Clark's Camp Fortunate is located on the northwestern shore of the reservoir, where camping and boat-launching facilities are also available.

Two Dillon-area landmarks are designated state parks because of the historical significance attached to them as a result of the Lewis and Clark expedition. **Clark's Lookout** (✆ 406/834-3413; www.fwp.mt.gov) provided the explorers with a vantage point from which to view their route and is reached by taking the Dillon exit from I-15 and then following the signs. **Beaverhead Rock,** 14 miles south of Twin Bridges on Mont. 41 (✆ 406/834-3413), was a tribal landmark recognized by expedition scout Sacajawea. Both parks have no admission charge and are day-use only.

SEEING THE SIGHTS

Based in Dillon or elsewhere in the valley, you can branch out to see **Big Hole National Battlefield;** see section 5 of this chapter for details.

The **Pioneer Mountain Scenic Byway** is a 4-mile drive that begins on Mont. 278 west of Dillon or along Mont. 43, south of the Wise River. Only the northern 28 miles of the road are paved. Driving between the east and west Pioneer Mountain Ranges, you'll experience alpine meadows, jagged peaks, and ghost towns with numerous opportunities to

Red Rock Lakes National Wildlife Refuge: A Haven for the Trumpeter Swan

Though well off the beaten path in the Centennial Valley, 28 miles east of Monida (about an hour south of Dillon), the **Red Rock Lakes National Wildlife Refuge** is often called the most beautiful wildlife refuge in the United States. The refuge was established in 1935 to protect the rare trumpeter swan, and it is here that the endangered species has been brought back from near extinction after a century of being hunted for their meat and feathers (quill pens were a hot item in the 1800s). It was feared that these beautiful creatures, which have wingspans of 7 to 8 feet, had been completely wiped out, until biologists discovered several dozen here in 1933. (They're also found along the Pacific coast and in Alaska.)

This is the largest population in the Lower 48 states—300 to 500 of the rare birds winter in the area, with about 100 calling the refuge home. They mate for life and often return to the exact same nest each year to tend their eggs and cygnets. The best place to view the trumpeters is in the open areas near Upper Red Rock Lake, from late April to the end of September.

In addition to the swan population, the 40,000-acre refuge is home to moose, deer, elk, antelope, foxes, great blue herons, sandhill cranes, ducks, and geese; more than 50,000 ducks and geese may be seen during times of migration.

The multiuse refuge is a popular spot for hiking, mountain biking, and canoeing; check with the refuge (© **406/276-3536;** http://redrocks.fws.gov) for regulations concerning these activities within refuge boundaries. To reach the refuge, take I-15 to the town of Monida, then drive east on a gravel-and-dirt road 28 miles to the refuge entrance. If you are coming from West Yellowstone, travel west on U.S. 20 for about 12 miles to Mont. 87. Travel northwest on Mont. 87 for 5 miles and turn south at the Sawtell historical marker. Follow the paved road around the west shore of Henry's Lake for approximately 5 miles and then turn right at Red Rock Pass Road (an improved dirt road), following it west for about 25 miles to the refuge entrance.

camp, fish, or watch wildlife. Near Coolidge (as you drive south) you'll see the old railroad bed of the Montana Southern Railway. Built to serve the Elkhorn mine, this was the last narrow-gauge railroad built in the U.S.

Beaverhead County Museum The Beaverhead County Museum is located in the center of town. It's housed in the old Union Pacific Railroad Depot and an 1870s settler's cabin moved to the spot. Inside there is a little bit of everything from the pioneer era—clothes, tools, cooking utensils, furnishings, and typewriters. Like a lot of small-town museums in the West, though, this one seems more interested in preserving the names of the families that donated items than in telling a coherent historical story.

15 S. Montana St., Dillon. © **406/683-5027.** $3 adults, $2 seniors, free for children; $6 maximum per family. Summer Mon–Fri 9am–5pm; shorter hours rest of year.

8

University of Montana Western Art Gallery/Museum The most exciting exhibit at this gallery and museum is the Seidensticker Wildlife Collection of big-game trophies, featuring animals from the far-flung locales of Africa and Asia as well as North American game. The museum also houses a small permanent regional collection and seasonally rotating exhibits, including student artwork.

Main Hall, 710 S. Atlantic St., Dillon. © **406/683-7331**. Free admission. Daily 9am–4:30pm.

WHERE TO STAY

In addition to the hotels listed below, two other chain options in Dillon are at I-15 exit 63. The **Comfort Inn,** 450 N. Interchange (© **800/442-4667** or 406/683-6831), has double rates from $79 to $109, and the **Super 8 Motel,** 550 N. Montana St. (© **800/800-8000** or 406/683-4288), has double rates from $69 to $104. Of the less expensive independents, I like the **Sundowner Motel,** 500 N. Montana St. (© **800/524-9746** or 406/683-2375), with double rates of $45 to $55.

Best Western Paradise Inn The Paradise Inn is a comfortable two-story facility set back from one of Dillon's busier streets. The standard rooms are cozy and appointed with an eye for efficiency, if a bit dated, but the penthouse suites are well worth the price, with huge bathtubs and large living areas. For families, there is one two-bedroom unit.

650 N. Montana St., Dillon, MT 59725. © **800/528-1234** or 406/683-4214. Fax 406/683-4216. 65 units. $100 double; $125 suite. Lower rates fall–spring. Rates include continental breakfast. AE, DISC, MC, V. **Amenities:** Restaurant; exercise room; indoor Jacuzzi; indoor pool. *In room:* A/C, TV, hair dryer, Wi-Fi (free).

Jackson Hot Springs Lodge ★ (Finds) A frequent comment from new arrivals at this lodge, when they enter the lobby and look up at the collection of animal heads on the wall, is "This is what you really expect a lodge to look like." The establishment effortlessly combines the trappings of a classic mountain lodge with an informal, cowboy-style atmosphere. The accommodations are in a series of attractive cabins, which are large, with pine-framed beds. There's also an RV park and campground on-site ($25 per site per night). The grounds are landscaped with attractive gardens. On the other hand, you would not be too surprised to see a cowboy ride his horse up to the bar and order a drink—for the horse. The large hot-springs pool—75×30 feet—is free to guests and available to others for a $5 fee. Don't go on Wednesdays, though, because that's when it's emptied and cleaned, and it takes all day to fill up again. There is a small restaurant on the premises, with a menu that changes seasonally. Dinner goes for $15 to $35.

Main St. (P.O. Box 808), Jackson, MT 59736. © **888/438-6938** or 406/834-3151. Fax 406/834-3157. www. jacksonhotsprings.com. 12 cabins. $80–$135 cabin. AE, MC, V. Pets accepted ($10 per pet per night). **Amenities:** Restaurant; lounge; outdoor hot-springs pool; massage. *In room:* No phone.

A Fishing Lodge

Craig Fellin Outfitters and Big Hole Lodge ★★ (Finds) This is one of the finest fly-fishing lodges in the West. You can catch every species of trout—rainbow, brown, cutthroat, grayling, and brook. The Big Hole River is the only river in the Lower 48 that still has native grayling in it, and the fine guides at Fellin's will help you find them; they also take guests to a private spring creek under lease to the operation. The food is excellent and the accommodations are comfortable, though not luxurious, and well-suited for the angler. Deer often loiter in front of the lodge in the evening. Fellin's is best for the experienced angler, but the guides are very patient and give beginners casting lessons at

the lodge before hitting the streams. Craig is also an avid golfer, and he's installed a 300-
foot par-3 golf hole on the property. You can practice your putting and casting, and then combine a half-day of fishing with a round of golf at the Old Works course in nearby Anaconda (see section 3, earlier in this chapter).

36894 Pioneer Mountains Scenic Byway (P.O. Box 156), Wise River Rd., Wise River, MT 59762. © **406/832- 3252.** www.flyfishinglodge.com. 3 cabins. $3,300 per person per 6-night, 5-day package double occupancy; single occupancy and shorter-stay packages available. Rates include all meals, drinks, fishing guide, and boat. AE, MC, V. **Amenities:** Lounge; activities desk. *In room:* No phone, Wi-Fi (free).

Camping

Under new ownership, the year-round **Dillon KOA,** 735 W. Park St., Dillon, MT 59725 (© **406/683-2749**), is right in town. Campers here will find 60 sites for RVs and 35 tent campsites. In addition to the usual bathhouse, there is a seasonal swimming pool, small grocery store, fishing supplies, propane, and an RV dump station. Rates are $28 to $38 for RV sites and $21 to $28 for tent sites. There are also four camping cabins (which share the campground's bathhouse) at $40 to $50 double.

WHERE TO DINE

Sweetwater Coffee has freshly brewed coffee, some pastries, and light lunch fare. It's located downtown at 26 E. Bannack (© **406/683-4141**). Another recommended option is **Stageline Pizza,** at 531 E. Poindexter St. in the University of Montana-Western student union building (© **406/683-9004**). Order takeout and head down to the riverbank to enjoy a beautiful Montana sunset.

Big Hole Crossing Restaurant ★ Finds AMERICAN   This is a neat little restaurant in the dinky mountain town of Wisdom, with a blue-tiled counter seating area, knotty-pine furnishings, a roaring fireplace, and wildlife art on the walls. The food is good yet inexpensive, and runs toward beef (prime rib on Sat), chicken, and seafood, and excellent house-made soups. It's popular with the Forest Service and BLM types for breakfast and lunch, which is usually a good sign, because they tend to work up quite an appetite wrestling mountain lions, corralling grizzly bears, and arguing with ranchers about riparian habitat improvements. The pies, cinnamon rolls, and bagels are all baked in-house and are especially good. While nobody's quite sure what it is, the bumbleberry pie is excellent. (If you'd like to stay the night, ask about the restaurant's rental cabin; a night goes for $60 for two in summer and $100 for two in ski season, lift tickets included.)

105 Park St., Wisdom. © **406/689-3800.** www.bigholecrossing.com. Breakfast main courses $4–$11; lunch $6–$10; dinner $8–$25. AE, DISC, MC, V. Summer daily 7am–9pm; winter Thurs–Mon 8am–8pm, Tues–Wed 8am–2pm.

Blacktail Station ★ STEAKS/SEAFOOD   Located in the basement below a local watering hole called Mac's Last Cast, Blacktail Station used to be the Mine Shaft, and some of the decorations from its past life still remain—like the trophy heads. But generally it's a more upscale place than you'd expect in agricultural Dillon; prints by Montana artist Larry Zabel now adorn the walls as well as the hard-rock mining detritus. The food is very traditional and very good. The steak almost melts in your mouth, and the twice-baked potato is very popular. For dessert, the chefs crank out a killer bread pudding.

26 S. Montana St., Dillon. © **406/683-6611.** www.blacktailstation.com. Main courses $9–$38. DISC, MC, V. Summer daily 5–10pm; winter Mon–Sat 5–9pm.

Las Carmelitas MEXICAN   Located across the street from the old depot, Las Carmelitas focuses on traditional Mexican cuisine. The menu includes standards like nachos, salads, enchiladas, burritos, and tacos; evening meals include *chiles rellenos, mole* chicken or beef, and other south-of-the-border standbys. The atmosphere is very basic, with square tables and metal chairs. Cold beer is available, as are wine-based margaritas, because the establishment's liquor license does not allow for a full bar.

220 S. Montana St., Dillon. ℂ **406/683-9368.** Main courses $7–$13. AE, DISC, MC, V. Daily 11am–2pm and 4:30–9pm.

Papa T's (**Kids**) PIZZA   Papa T's is Dillon's version of Chuck E. Cheese's, only better. It's a converted saloon where the kids can run around without getting on anyone's nerves. There are video games lining one wall, and a kiddies' carousel for the tykes. The food is basic American: burgers (consisting of local organic beef), chicken, Philly cheese steaks, and pizza. The formula has worked for more than 20 years. The family-owned restaurant is named for founder and patriarch Tom Lohman, whose kids all call him "Papa."

10 N. Montana St., Dillon. ℂ **406/683-6432.** Main courses and pizzas $5–$20. MC, V. Daily 11am–10pm; shorter hours in winter, call for details.

Sparky's Garage AMERICAN/BARBECUE   As its name suggests, Sparky's sports a garage theme, with petroliana of all kinds hanging above the red-and-green checkerboard floors. The aroma of gasoline, however, is nowhere to be smelled; instead, the scent of barbecue wafts from the kitchen. The sauce is sweet and slathered all over everything from pork ribs to chicken to pulled pork, with more than respectable results. There are also burgers, steaks, and baskets of fried shrimp and catfish. Beyond dinner, Sparky's is a reliable choice three meals a day near the University of Montana-Western campus, and has beer and wine only.

420 E. Poindexter St., Dillon. ℂ **406/683-2828.** Reservations not accepted. Breakfast $5–$9; lunch and dinner $7–$21. DISC, MC, V. Mon–Thurs 6:30am–9:30pm; Fri–Sat 6:30am–10pm; Sun 6:30am–9pm.

TWIN BRIDGES

28 miles from Dillon, just up Mont. 41, a faded billboard proclaims Twin Bridges to be the platinum capital of the Western world, an odd designation for a town that seems to be much more famous regionally for great fishing. "Floating Flotillas & Fish Fantasies" is the name given to the tiny town's annual summer festival, held in late July or early August, with highlights that include the extremely popular floating parade on the Beaverhead, dances, and a barbecue. Locals are even given the chance to show their skills at fly-casting, and there's a tug of war over the river. For additional information about the Twin Bridges area and scheduled activities, visit the Greater Ruby Valley Chamber of Commerce's website at **www.rubyvalleychamber.com**.

Where to Stay & Dine

The Old Hotel ★ (**Finds**)   This excellent inn and restaurant is right on the highway in an out-of-the-way spot, serving gourmet meals out of a beautifully restored brick building decorated with a Scottish motif. While the menu changes weekly, you'll always find a creative assortment of main courses, including fresh seafood, vegetarian, and game dishes; past selections have included Cajun-spiced Hawaiian mahimahi and rack of lamb with raspberry-chipotle sauce. Dinner main courses run about $20 to $25. Sunday brunch is also available, as is Saturday brunch in summer. An excellent wine cellar features French, Italian, Australian, and California labels. The second level has been

converted to a two-suite B&B: Accommodations are tailored to the needs of the angler;
omelets, oatmeal, and salmon and eggs are among the breakfasts served.

101 E. 5th Ave., Twin Bridges, MT 59754. ℂ **406/684-5959.** www.theoldhotel.com. 2 units. $150 double. Lower rates in winter. Rate includes full breakfast. DISC, MC, V. **Amenities:** Restaurant. *In room:* TV, Wi-Fi (free).

5 BIG HOLE NATIONAL BATTLEFIELD ★★

76 miles W of Dillon; 106 miles S of Missoula

The flight of the Nez Perce across Montana in 1877 is among the most heroic and epic stories of the Indian Wars period. About 800 nontreaty Nez Perce left the Wallowa area of Idaho in June 1877. In an attempt to join Sitting Bull in the relative safety and freedom of Canada, the Nez Perce eluded the pursuing forces of the United States until early October, when they surrendered—not so much from military defeat but from exhaustion and starvation. On October 5, 1877, only 431 remained.

The **Big Hole National Battlefield** commemorates the flight of the Nez Perce over 1,200 miles of some of the roughest land in the Lower 48 states, through Yellowstone National Park, across Montana's high plains, all the while outwitting and outfighting the U.S. Cavalry. There were several battles along the way, but by far the largest skirmish took place here. Between 60 and 90 members of the band were killed. Only 12 of the dead were warriors—the rest were women, children, and seniors. The U.S. military suffered 29 dead and 40 wounded.

The Nez Perce had traditionally lived in eastern Washington, Idaho, and Oregon. They had always maintained good relations with the white explorers, assisting Lewis and Clark in 1805 by caring for the expedition's members when they arrived in their country sick, tired, and low on provisions. They gave them food, two dugout canoes, and guides. The Nez Perce were also the subjects of the first major Protestant mission effort among the Indians, when the stern and domineering Eliza Spaulding—an associate of the later-martyred Marcus Whitman—urged them to give up their traditional ways in return for eternal salvation.

The Nez Perce's problems multiplied in 1860, when gold was discovered. Most were sent to reservations, but Joseph—known as "Young Joseph"—led a nontreaty band to live on his traditional homeland in the Wallowa Valley. Pressure from settlers eventually led to an order forcing Joseph's band onto a reservation.

In the summer of 1877, several Nez Perce braves ignored advice from the tribal elders and attacked and killed four white settlers in Oregon to exact revenge for the earlier murder of the father of one of the braves. This attack raised the ire of settlers, and the cavalry was called in to hunt down the Nez Perce. On June 1, 1877, Joseph's band joined four other Nez Perce groups and crossed the swollen Snake River, fleeing to Canada.

Battles erupted in Idaho before the Nez Perce entered Montana, fleeing from U.S. Army troops under the leadership of Gen. Oliver O. Howard. When the Nez Perce reached the Big Hole Valley, they decided to make camp, thinking all the while that they left their troubles behind them in Idaho.

However, in addition to Howard's troops behind them, a second group of soldiers, under the command of Col. John Gibbon, was advancing up the Bitterroot Valley toward the unsuspecting tribe. On the morning of August 9, 1877, Gibbon's soldiers, along with a contingent of local volunteers, attacked the sleeping tribe in what is today known as the

Battle of the Big Hole. Less than 48 hours after they'd set up camp, the remaining Nez Perce once again found themselves fleeing for their lives and their freedom. They headed toward Canada, but the U.S. Army troops caught up to them at Bear Paw, only 40 miles from the Canadian border. The capture of Joseph's tattered band was the last major military effort of the Indian Wars period.

The Battle of the Big Hole is somewhat unusual among Indian fights in that a number of descriptions of the battle exist, many from the Indian point of view. André Garcia, a scout and adventurer, married a Nez Perce woman, In-who-lise, who was wounded in the battle. In his marvelous book *Tough Trip Through Paradise,* he says that he visited the battlefield 2 years later and human bones and skulls were still scattered everywhere.

Begun as a military reserve in 1883, the area became a national monument in 1910 and was designated a national battlefield in 1963. Today, the National Park Service maintains an interpretive center, where rangers help visitors understand the significance of the battle that occurred at Big Hole. Guided tours, a museum, exhibits, a bookstore, movies, and three self-guided walking trails are available.

Trails begin at the lower parking lot and lead to several points of interest. The **Nez Perce Camp,** where soldiers surprised the sleeping tribe, is considered sacred ground. The **Siege Area** marks the place where soldiers were besieged for nearly 24 hours as the Nez Perce fought to save their families from certain death. A fairly steep walk will lead you to the **Howitzer Capture Site,** where soldiers suffered a heavy blow as Nez Perce warriors captured and dismantled the military weapon. This spot affords a spectacular view of the battlefield and surrounding area.

The Big Hole Battlefield represents only a small fraction of the Nez Perce's tragic flight across the West. The 1,200-mile Nez Perce (Nee Me Poo) National Historic Trail follows the entire route of the Nez Perce War, from Wallowa Lake in northwestern Oregon to Bear Paw Battlefield in north-central Montana (see chapter 9). Crossing four states, the trail features several Nez Perce war sites with interpretive markers telling the story of the tribe's fight for freedom. The trail is administered by the U.S. Forest Service, and the Beaverhead-Deerlodge National Forest (see "Visitor Information," below) can provide you with an excellent map of the four-state area.

GETTING THERE From Missoula, you can reach the Big Hole National Battlefield by going south on U.S. 93 through the Bitterroot Valley 80 miles to Lost Trail Pass. Then turn east on Mont. 43 and drive 16 miles to the site. From Butte, go south on I-15 20 miles to Mont. 43, west for 51 miles to Wisdom, then continue west on Mont. 43 for about 10 miles to the site. From Dillon, take Mont. 278 west to Wisdom, then go west on Mont. 43 for 10 miles.

VISITOR INFORMATION Located 10 miles west of Wisdom on Mont. 43, the **Big Hole National Battlefield Visitor Center,** 16245 Mont. 43 W., P.O. Box 237, Wisdom, MT 59761 (© 406/689-3155; www.nps.gov/biho), is open daily (except on Thanksgiving, Christmas, and New Year's Day) with summer hours from 9am to 6pm, fall hours of 9am to 5pm, and winter/spring hours from 10am to 5pm. Admission is free. Picnic tables are located at the lower parking lot, though there are no camping or overnight facilities on the premises. Fishing is allowed within the battlefield's boundaries and adjacent national forest, but there are restrictions on the private land adjoining the battle site.

You can obtain a pamphlet with an auto tour of the flight of the Nez Perce through the Big Hole, Horse Prairie, and Lemhi valleys from the **National Park Service, Big Hole National Battlefield** (see above), or the **Beaverhead-Deerlodge National Forest,** 420 Barrett St., Dillon, MT 59725 (© 406/683-3900).

The nearest facilities—restaurants, gas stations, grocery stores, and lodgings—are located in Wisdom, 10 miles to the east.

6 THE OLD MINING TOWNS: VIRGINIA CITY, NEVADA CITY & BANNACK ★★

Virginia City and Nevada City: 72 miles SE of Butte; 67 miles S of Bozeman; 84 miles NW of West Yellowstone. Bannack: 90 miles SW of Butte, 21 miles SW of Dillon.

Virginia City and nearby Nevada City have both a boisterous and colorful past and present. They are old towns, but Virginia City never turned into a ghost town; in fact, it's one of the oldest continuously occupied towns in the West.

In 1863, a group of miners led by Bill Fairweather took $180 in their first day of gold panning from a creek, which they later named Alder Gulch after the trees growing on the bank. A gold rush soon followed and a mining town grew. The nation was in the midst of the Civil War, and the Southern sympathizers in the crowd wanted to name the new city Varina after Jefferson Davis's wife. But G. G. Bissell, a Northerner and a miners' judge, said, "I'll see you damned first." He wrote "Virginia" on the founding document instead, a sort of compromise, but since Virginia housed the capital of the Confederacy, no one complained.

The restoration of Virginia City began in 1946 when Charles and Sue Bovey began the painstaking task of preserving and restoring many of the structures you see in town today. Most of the buildings were erected during Virginia City's heyday as the state's second territorial capital. In the mid-1950s, Bovey also began to rebuild Nevada City, then a true ghost town, by bringing in buildings he'd acquired from around the West.

In 1991, following the deaths of Sue and Charles, son Fred Bovey determined that he was unable to continue to operate the properties and attractions. He decided to sell the whole kit and caboodle, including millions of dollars of antiques (Sotheby's estimate: $60 million). The state of Montana and Montana Historical Society attempted to have the area designated a national park, but to no avail. Even the National Trust for Historic Preservation got into the act, declaring Virginia City an endangered historic site.

Finally, partly because of a public outcry and due to the efforts of Governor Marc Racicot, the 1997 Montana legislature took dramatic fiscal measures and agreed to fund the $6.5-million purchase (such a bargain), and added $3 million for operational expenses. Today, the cities operate under the supervision of the Montana Historical Society and its foundation.

The dusty main drag of Bannack also pays tribute to the mining era. The town grew up quickly after the state's first big gold strike occurred here in 1862, but the vein was a shallow one, and Bannack quickly turned into a ghost town. Despite its short life, Bannack has a colorful history. One writer said, "It is probable that there never was a mining town of the same size that contained more desperadoes and lawless characters than did Bannack during the winter of 1862 to '63."

GETTING THERE Virginia City and Nevada City are 13 miles west of Ennis on Mont. 287. From Bozeman, take Mont. 84 west to Norris, then go south on U.S. 287 to Ennis, then west on Mont. 287 to the sites. From Butte, take I-90 east to the Whitehall exit (Mont. 55), then go south 27 miles to Twin Bridges. From Twin Bridges, take Mont. 287 east 30 miles to the sites. They are only about a mile apart, with Nevada City being the farther west.

Bannack is reached by driving about 15 miles west of Dillon on Mont. 278, then south on a gravel road at the sign for Bannack State Park.

VISITOR INFORMATION   There are remains of many other Montana ghost towns in this part of the state; it's just that information about them is often hard to find and the towns themselves even harder. Your best bet: Contact the **Virginia City Chamber of Commerce,** P.O. Box 218, Virginia City, MT 59755 (✆ **800/829-2969;** www.virginia citychamber.com), and **Gold West Country,** 1155 Main St., Deer Lodge, MT 59722 (✆ **800/879-1159;** www.goldwest.visitmt.com). These two agencies can provide you with free information about the historic ghost towns of Montana. While you're at it, request copies of two brochures that will enhance your visit to the area: *Walking Tour,* a historical, block-by-block guide to Virginia City; and *A Walking Tour of Nevada City, Montana.*

Most attractions in Virginia City (and all of them in Nevada City) are run by the **Montana Heritage Commission,** P.O. Box 338, Virginia City, MT 59755 (✆ **406/843-5247;** www.montanaheritagecommission.com and www.virginiacitymt.com), and they're open only during the peak summer season, from Memorial Day to Labor Day.

VIRGINIA CITY

As Virginia City boomed after Bill Fairweather discovered gold, it became the site of a dramatic ordeal of Western lawlessness and revenge that has fueled a thousand cowboy movie plots. Much of Virginia City's history was driven by the vigilante movement, and the town launched the career of Wilbur Fisk Sanders, who eventually went to Washington as Montana's first U.S. senator.

By 1864, when the Montana Territory was created by President Abraham Lincoln, nearly 30,000 people were living along the gulch's 8 miles. Virginia City was named territorial capital in 1865—taking that title from Bannack, virtually a ghost town by then—and held the position until 1875. For many years after its founding, the only currency acceptable to Virginia City merchants was gold dust.

As the town boomed, the incidence of robberies and murders increased. Many of the robberies depended on inside information by people usually called "road agents." The miners' sheriff, Henry Plummer, who had "persuaded" the sheriffs in Bannack, Nevada City, and Virginia City to turn over their duties to him, turned out to be the leader of the road agents. As sheriff, he knew the timing of the gold movements.

No legal relief was possible, because the nearest officials to administer an oath were 400 miles away. In 1863, when a popular miner, Dutchman Nicholas Thiebalt, was murdered for $200, the other miners were outraged. The killer, George Ives, was captured and tried by a miners' court, then hanged. The site of his hanging is preserved in Nevada City. The local residents formed "vigilance committees" to capture and bring the road agents to justice. They hanged at least 21 more of the road agents—including Plummer—and some order was restored to the area.

Virginia City is the larger of the two towns; Nevada City is entirely a ghost town, a collection of original and transplanted buildings from the period. A pair of beautifully **restored trains** makes numerous round-trips daily between the two ($6–$15 round-trip, free for children 5 and under).

Seeing the Sights

Virginia City has a number of operating commercial enterprises interspersed with the historical stuff. Along the main thoroughfare you'll find the village centerpieces: the **Fairweather Inn,** the **Wells Fargo Overland Company building,** and the **Virginia City**

Historical Museum. One of the oldest structures, the **Montana Post Building,** once housed the state's first newspaper; the paper's original press is still used locally for menus, playbills, and placards.

You should start your visit to Virginia City at the **Visitor Center and Museum Store,** at the end of Main Street. The center has photos, a brief explanation of the history of the town, and a friendly staff of volunteers. The government shut down gold mining for good in 1942, and a few years later the Boveys began buying up the property.

The **Virginia City Players** have been an entertainment staple in town since 1949, operating out of the Smith and Boyd Livery Stable (1900). The players are Montana's oldest professional acting company. For information on showtimes, prices, and days for the Virginia City Players, call ℃ **800/829-2969,** or visit **www.virginiacityplayers.com.**

A little farther up the hill is the **Hangman's Building.** On January 4, 1864, the building was still being constructed, and a stout beam was exposed in the unfinished structure. The vigilantes took advantage of this situation to hang four road agents. The history-oriented **J. Spencer Watkins Memorial Museum** (℃ **406/843-5500**), also on the main street, has some photos of the vigilantes on exhibit and a nice collection of period clothing.

Up above the town, looking down over the main street, is **Boot Hill,** the last resting place of several road agents, who required hasty burial after they died with their boots on.

If you *really* want to see the Old West come to life, check out a **Brewery Follies** production. Famous statewide for its funny cabaret-style revues and entertaining period melodramas, the company performs nightly during the summer. The Brewery Follies have a loyal following. For information on showtimes and prices, call ℃ **406/843-5218,** or visit **www.breweryfollies.net.**

Where to Stay

Fairweather Inn   This small hotel, located right in the middle of downtown Virginia City, has a great upstairs porch that's a fun place to sit and people-watch. Though most of the rooms are tastefully decorated in an Old West theme, a few of them are distinguished by odd combinations of bright paint and mismatched quilts. Only 6 of the hotel's 14 rooms have private bathrooms; the rest are rooming house style.

305 W. Wallace St. (P.O. Box 205), Virginia City, MT 59755. ℃ **800/829-2969** or 406/843-5377. www.aldergulchaccommodations.com. 14 units, 8 with shared bathroom. $70–$82 double. MC, V. *In room:* No phone.

Gingerbread House   The candied Victorian exterior of this charming B&B has been a landmark on Idaho Street since C. W. Rank built the two-story house in 1898. There are two rooms in the main house that share a bathroom and the rustic Karen's Cabin out back, with a private bathroom. All feature queen-size beds and antique furnishing; the cabin has a loft and a kitchenette. The back patio and yard have plenty of space to stretch out and offer terrific mountain views.

201 E. Idaho St., Virginia City, MT 59755. ℃ **877/424-4012** or 406/843-5471. 3 units (2 with shared bathroom), including 1 cabin. $85–$110 double. Rates include full breakfast. DISC, MC, V. *In room:* No phone.

Stonehouse Inn   Built in 1884 by a local blacksmith/rancher/miner, this Gothic Revival–style B&B is a cozy place to hang your hat while in town for a night. Clad in locally quarried stone, the gray exterior is softened by a few brightly painted accents and a sweeping porch with a rocking chair. Your options range from a masculine room, embellished with antique snowshoes and a NO SPITTING sign, to a romantic upstairs room with stained glass, a private balcony, and lace-laden decor. All of the rooms have brass beds, predominately full-size. While the bathrooms are shared, they are exceptionally spacious and feature antique commodes, showers, and tubs.

306 E. Idaho St., Virginia City, MT 59755. (C) **406/843-5504.** 5 units, none with private bathroom. $85 double. Rates include full breakfast. MC, V. *In room:* No phone.

Camping

The **Alder/Virginia City KOA,** 2280 Mont. 287, Alder, MT 59710 ((C) **800/562-1898** or 406/842-5677; www.koa.com), has over 100 RV sites and 50 tent sites, and is open from March to November. The campground has a dump station, propane sales, store, a playground, and a fishing pond. Tent sites are $24, RV sites $36, cabins $59.

Where to Dine

In season, there are a few decent restaurants in Virginia City: **Banditos,** 320 Wallace Ave. ((C) **406/843-5556;** www.banditosmontana.com), a bar/restaurant specializing in Southwestern dinners, and the **Virginia City Café,** 210 Wallace Ave. ((C) **406/843-5311**), serving sandwiches for lunch and Irish fare for dinner.

NEVADA CITY

The distance between Nevada City and Virginia City is only a mile or so, but back in the days before the vigilance committees formed, it was a dangerous mile. Miners dared not go between the two cities after dark. A robber waylaid one miner known as Dutch Fred. When the highwayman found that Fred had only $5 with him—and paper money, not gold dust, at that—the bandit cursed and told him, "If ever you come this way again with only $5, I'll shoot you." The robber shot Dutch Fred anyhow, wounding him in the arm.

Nevada City is the site of the resurgence of law and order in these Montana mining camps. Two thousand people reportedly came to town to watch the trial of George Ives for the murder of Nicholas Thiebalt. Emotions were running high on both sides, and it was in the face of these feelings that Wilbur Fisk Sanders began his place in Montana history by courageously prosecuting Ives before the crowd. The spot where Ives was hanged is marked in town.

Today Nevada City is a tourist attraction—a collection of historic wooden buildings, including an open-air museum depicting the gold-mining and settlement period of the area's turbulent history. Nevada City also exists as the result of Charles Bovey's diligence and dedication to the preservation of history. In the mid-1950s, Bovey began to re-create an authentic Western town with buildings he'd accumulated around the West. The buildings are authentic, though their setting may not be. It looks like a perfect cowboy movie set, though, and has in fact been used for a couple of oaters, including *Missouri Breaks, Little Big Man,* and *Return to Lonesome Dove.*

Admission to the Nevada City site costs $8 adults, $6 for kids 6 to 16, and free for those 5 and under; the site is open Memorial Day to Labor Day daily from 9am to 6pm. For information, call (C) **800/829-2969** or 406/843-5247.

Seeing the Sights

With your walking-tour booklet in hand, begin your excursion behind the **Nevada City Hotel,** where you can view the state's only double-decker outhouse, and stroll along the streets to see what a Western mining town might have looked like. Boardwalks pass barbershops, homes, a schoolhouse, and even an Asian section. Some of the buildings are closed, but many include period furnishings and wares.

When you hear a cacophony of horns and whistles, follow the noise to the **Nevada** **City Music Hall,** located next door to the hotel. There you can see the "famous and obnoxious horn machine from the Bale of Hay Saloon!" A sign on the machine begs visitors not to miss hearing "the machine that has driven 28 change-makers, 72 bartenders, and near a million tourists to the brink of insanity!" The music hall is a fascinating place to spend an hour listening to the many music machines and reading about their history. It's one of the largest collections of its kind on display in the United States today. The building was originally the Canyon Lodge Recreation Hall in Yellowstone.

Across the street is the railroad museum, where you can board the steam-powered **Locomotive No. 12** for the short train ride to Virginia City (the railroad depot there is at the west end of town). The museum has an observation car once used by Calvin Coolidge and the last "Catholic chapel car" in the world. The train runs every hour, and costs $6 to $15 round-trip (free for children 6 and under).

Another local attraction is the **Alder Gulch River of Gold Mining Museum,** 1552 Mont. 287 (② **406/843-5402**), featuring myriad historic mining tools and vehicles, including the Mount Vernon Dredge (1935), one of the few gold-dredging boats on display anywhere, and gold-panning for visitors. It's open Memorial Day to Labor Day daily 10am to 6pm and admission is free.

Where to Stay & Eat

You can believe the claim of the **Star Bakery Restaurant and Emporium,** 1585 Mont. 287 (② **406/843-5525**), that it has the best biscuits and gravy in town, because it's also the *only* restaurant in town. Best known for its breakfasts, the cozy country restaurant serves three meals a day. The restaurant dates from 1865 and has an old-fashioned soda fountain and a gift shop. The specialty of the house, believe it or not, is fried pickles. The restaurant is closed Labor Day to Memorial Day.

Just an Experience Bed and Breakfast If you want something more modern than the Nevada City Hotel and Cabins (see below), this B&B is your only other choice in Nevada City proper (dare we say, downtown Nevada City?). Two of the rooms in the house share a bathroom, and one has a private bathroom. The rooms are large, with iron-post beds, but the cabins are larger, with enough room for six people, and include loft bedrooms for the kids, color TVs with VCR/DVD player combos, and full kitchens. The original log house here was built in 1864, but it has been remodeled and incorporated into a modern cedar-sided home. Pets are permitted outdoors only.

1570 Mont. 287, Virginia City, MT 59755. ② **866/664-0424** or 406/843-5402. www.justanexperience. com. 3 units, 3 cabins. $90–$130 double. Rates include full breakfast; other meals optional ($10–$25/ person). AE, DISC, MC, V. **Amenities:** Jacuzzi. *In room:* TV/VCR or DVD, movie library, kitchen (cabins only), no phone, Wi-Fi (free).

Nevada City Hotel and Cabins Entering this hotel is like taking a step back in time. Constructed in the 1860s, it was originally a stage stop near Twin Bridges, and still has the cool, musty smell of a mining-camp hotel. Most of the rooms are small and spare, but the upstairs Victorian suites are huge, furnished in rough but exquisite Victorian style, complete with polished burl-wood furniture and private bathrooms. If you rent a cabin, be sure to lock your door—many tourists mistake the cabins for museum exhibits and may come exploring.

Mont. 287 (P.O. Box 205), Virginia City, MT 59755. ② **800/648-7588** or 406/843-5377. Fax 406/843-5402. www.aldergulchaccommodations.com. 29 units, including 2 suites and 17 cabins. $85 double; $100 suite; $90 double cabin. MC, V. Closed Oct to mid-May. *In room:* No phone.

Bannack was the site of the state's first big gold strike in 1862. With more than 60 of the town's original buildings preserved, the tumbledown town is a stark reminder of the heyday of the frontier: vigilantes stalking road agents stalking prospectors, in a place where the rivers yielded gold dust.

Born out of the discovery of placer gold in 1862, Bannack quickly grew to a town of 3,000 people, largely composed of those hoping to strike it rich. Blacksmiths, bakeries, stables, restaurants, hotels, dance halls, and grocery stores rapidly sprang up to complement an expanding mining industry.

Bannack became the first territorial capital and the site of the first territorial legislative session in 1864. But the placer veins in Grasshopper Creek were thin. Only a few years later, it was a ghost town, and the boosters of the capital movement had turned their attention to Virginia City and the richer mines at Alder Creek.

Notorious Henry Plummer killed his first local man in Bannack in Goodrich's saloon. The victim was Jack Cleveland, who had threatened another man about a debt, which the other man had already paid. Cleveland bragged that he wasn't afraid of him. Plummer, apparently a bystander, got to his feet, cursed Cleveland, roared, "I'm tired of this," and commenced to shooting. Cleveland got the worst of it, dying 3 hours later.

Plummer was an enigmatic outlaw. He was considered a "gentleman" by the standards of the era. He married a schoolteacher, though she left him after only 10 weeks of wedded bliss. Only a few weeks before he was hanged (see the section on Virginia City, above), Plummer held an elaborate dinner for territorial officials, including the governor and some of the vigilantes, for which he had ordered a $60 turkey from Salt Lake City. His guests apparently saw nothing unusual about enjoying the hospitality of a man they had already decided to hang.

VISITOR INFORMATION   Designated a state park in 1954, Bannack is open year-round. Summer hours are daily from 8am to 9pm; winter hours 8am to 5pm. There is a seasonal visitor center, as well as camping and picnic grounds, a group-use area, and hiking trails. Other lodging facilities are available in nearby Dillon (see section 4 of this chapter). Day-use fees are $5 per vehicle ($3 for bikes or walk-ins) and $15 for a campsite ($13 in the off season). There are also rental tipis for $25 (available May–Sept).

To get to Bannack from Dillon, drive 3 miles south on I-15 to Mont. 278. Head west 17 miles on Mont. 278, then south 4 miles when you see the sign. For additional information, call © **406/834-3413,** or visit **www.bannack.org.**

A SPECIAL EVENT   **Bannack Days,** staged annually during the third weekend in July, is a 2-day event commemorating the history and heritage of Montana's early pioneers, with activities centering around frontier crafts, music, pioneer food, and dramas. A black-powder muzzleloader shoot, Sunday church services, and horse-and-buggy rides bring the "toughest town in the West" to life and are fun for the entire family.

The Hi-Line & North-Central Missouri River Country

This part of Montana is classic cattle and wheat country, the domain of the authentic American cowboy. The vast northern plains of Montana were once a wilderness of tallgrass, rolling in the wind like the sea, home to millions of pronghorn and buffalo.

Lewis and Clark reported vast herds of the latter, but that wasn't all they saw here. When the adventurers entered Montana in 1805, just past the confluence of the Yellowstone and Missouri rivers, they saw their first grizzly bear, and Lewis made the first extensive description of the animal for science.

As you travel through this region, you'll likely be closely following the trail of Lewis and Clark to the portage of the Great Falls. In the city of Great Falls, take time to visit the Lewis and Clark National Historic Trail Interpretive Center and experience vicariously one of the great American adventures. This portion of the state is also the landscape that Charles Russell memorialized in his famous Western paintings and bronzes.

But the region isn't all history and vanished mythology. There's plenty of outdoor activity, including fishing and boating on Fort Peck Lake, bird-watching at the Charles M. Russell National Wildlife Refuge, rafting on the wild and scenic Missouri River, and both downhill and cross-country skiing.

1 SCENIC DRIVES

DRIVING TOUR 1: KINGS HILL SCENIC BYWAY

The Kings Hill Scenic Byway is a 71-mile stretch of U.S. 89 through the Little Belt Mountains and the Lewis and Clark National Forest. You pick it up about 22 miles southeast of Great Falls, where U.S. 87 and U.S. 89 divide. Take U.S. 89 south toward the towns of Monarch and Neihart. From the south, take U.S. 89 north from just east of Livingston on I-90. For a leisurely tour, you can watch the wildlife and the scenery, then visit the ghost towns at Castle Town and Hughesville, and the historic mining site at Glory Hole. For a more active trip, go to **Sluice Boxes State Park,** just north of Monarch (© **406/454-5840;** http://fwp.mt.gov), to hike along the abandoned rail line there, or fish in Belt Creek. In winter there are cross-country skiing at the Silver Crest Trail System (just north of Showdown Ski Area; see below) and snowmobiling at Kings Hill. Memorial Falls has a nature trail that is accessible to visitors with disabilities. Primitive backcountry camping sites (free, but you must camp a half-mile or more from the trail head) and national forest access points are at numerous spots along the highway.

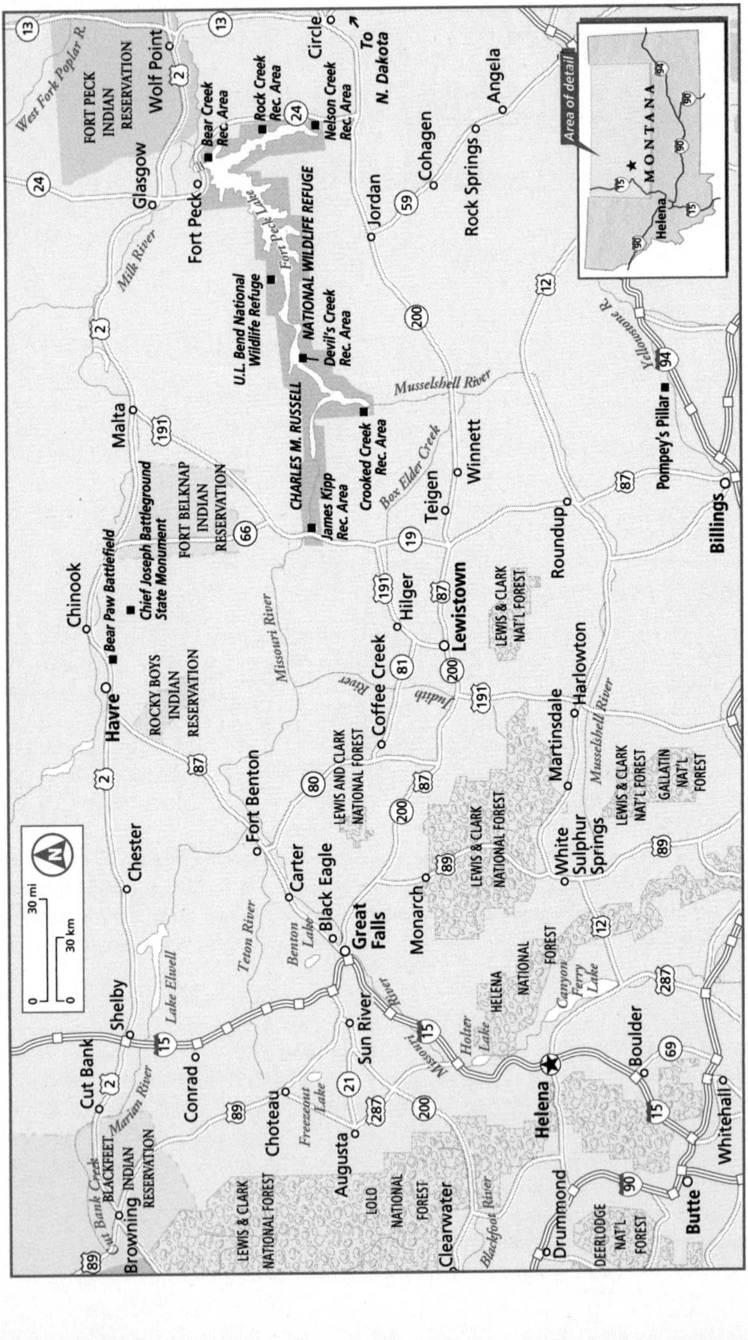
0 30 mi
0 30 km
N
FORT PECK INDIAN RESERVATION
West Fork Poplar R.
Wolf Point
Glasgow
Milk River
Fort Peck
Bear Creek Rec. Area
Rock Creek Rec. Area
Nelson Creek Rec. Area
Circle
To N. Dakota
Fort Peck Lake
CHARLES M. RUSSELL NATIONAL WILDLIFE REFUGE
U.L. Bend National Wildlife Refuge
Devil's Creek Rec. Area
Crooked Creek Rec. Area
James Kipp Rec. Area
Jordan
Cohagen
Rock Springs
Angela
Musselshell River
Malta
Chinook
Bear Paw Battlefield
Chief Joseph Battleground State Monument
FORT BELKNAP INDIAN RESERVATION
ROCKY BOYS INDIAN RESERVATION
Havre
Missouri River
Box Elder Creek
Teigen
Winnett
Hilger
Lewistown
Coffee Creek
Judith River
Roundup
Harlowton
Martinsdale
LEWIS & CLARK NAT'L FOREST
Pompey's Pillar
Billings
Yellowstone R.
Area of detail
MONTANA
Helena
Chester
Fort Benton
LEWIS AND CLARK NATIONAL FOREST
Carter
Black Eagle
Great Falls
Benton Lake
Teton River
Monarch
LEWIS & CLARK NATIONAL FOREST
White Sulphur Springs
GALLATIN NAT'L FOREST
Shelby
Lake Elwell
Cut Bank
Marias River
Conrad
Sun River
Missouri River
HELENA NATIONAL FOREST
Canyon Ferry Lake
Holter Lake
Boulder
Whitehall
Butte
Choteau
Freezeout Lake
Augusta
BLACKFEET INDIAN RESERVATION
Cut Bank Creek
Browning
LEWIS & CLARK NATIONAL FOREST
LOLO NATIONAL FOREST
Clearwater
Blackfoot River
Drummond
DEERLODGE NAT'L FOREST

The Judith Basin inspired the work of one of the West's seminal artists, Charles M. Russell. This drive on U.S. 87/Mont. 200 between Great Falls and Lewistown provides an intimate glimpse at the unsettled West through Russell's eyes. The drive is lovely in a pastoral way, but it helps to have a copy of the interpretive guide of the trail from Travel Montana's **Russell Country** (© 800/527-5348; www.russell.visitmt.com), if you want to get the full experience. The guide uses Russell's art to illuminate the history of the basin.

These highways were designated the Russell Trail by the Montana legislature. The scruffy cowhands and toughened Indians that Russell painted have been replaced by carefully tended fields of grain, but with the help of Russell's art and a little imagination, you can put yourself back in the saddle in 1880s Montana.

From Great Falls, you go southeast through the towns of Raynesford, Geyser, and Moccasin, taking in the history of the Blackfeet, the infamous last wolves of the basin in Stanford, and the role of the railroads in Hobson. Spring and fall are the best times to match Russell's color palette with that of the scenery.

There are roadside turnouts along the highway for many of the 25 interpretive sites, including the settings for two of Russell's best-known paintings, *Buffalo in Winter* and *Paying the Fiddler.*

2 GREAT FALLS

89 miles N of Helena; 219 miles NW of Billings

Great Falls, named for a series of waterfalls on the Missouri River, is a city of about 55,000, making it Montana's third largest (after Billings and Missoula). An important cog in the U.S. military strategy, it is the home of Malmstrom Air Force Base, which several times has been threatened with closure (which would devastate the city), but it has thus far avoided that fate.

But the country around Great Falls looks much as Charles Russell found it and painted it at the end of the 19th century. Russell made Great Falls his home, and did much of his painting in his studio there.

Nearly a century before Russell's day, Lewis and Clark came through with the Corps of Discovery in 1805, making an 18-mile portage around the falls. It is a somewhat sad sign of Great Falls's progress that it is now known as "the Electric City," because the falls that Lewis and Clark marveled at have been tamed by a series of dams to provide electric power.

ESSENTIALS

GETTING THERE   Great Falls serves as the hub for north-central Montana east of the Rockies. The **Great Falls International Airport** (© 406/727-3404; www.gtfairport. com) has daily service from **Alaska/Horizon** (© 800/547-9308), **Allegiant** (© 702/505-8888), **Delta** (© 800/221-1212), **Northwest** (© 800/225-2525), and **United** (© 800/864-8331). Shelby, 88 miles northwest, provides the closest **Amtrak** service (© 800/872-7245; www.amtrak.com).

Great Falls is located on I-15, which runs north from Butte, where the highway intersects with I-90, passing through Helena and then Great Falls. From Missoula, you can take Mont. 200 east, or you can take I-90 a little southeast, pick up U.S. 12, and go east to Helena, then north to Great Falls. Mont. 200 is more scenic. From Billings, you can take Mont. 87 north to Lewistown and then west to Great Falls. Or you can go west on I-90 to Livingston, then take Mont. 89, which includes the Kings Hill Scenic Byway (see the driving tour above), northwest to Great Falls. From Bozeman, take U.S. 287 north at Three Forks, then I-15 to Great Falls.

VISITOR INFORMATION Request tour information from **Russell Country,** P.O. Box 3166, Great Falls, MT 59403 (© **800/527-5348** or 406/761-5036; www.russell.visitmt. com). The **Great Falls Convention and Visitors Bureau** is at 1106 9th St. S., Great Falls, MT 59405 (© **800/735-8535** or 406/761-4434; www.greatfallscvb.visitmt.com). There is a visitor center at the Broadwater Overlook at 15 Upper River Rd., right under the tall flagpole.

GETTING AROUND The best way to explore Great Falls and environs is by car. Rental franchises in town include **Avis** (© **800/230-4898**), **Hertz** (© **800/654-3131**), **National** (© **800/227-7368**), and **Thrifty** (© **800/847-4389**).

Great Falls Transit System (© 406/727-0382; www.gftransit.com) offers bus service Monday through Saturday from early morning to early evening (no service Sun and holidays). Fare is $1 adults, 75¢ students, and 50¢ seniors; kids 5 and under are free.

ORGANIZED TOURS To see the town, take the 2-hour **Great Falls Historic Trolley** tour (© **888/707-1100** or 406/771-1100; www.greatfallshistorictrolley.com). Tickets are $22 for adults and $5 children 2 to 12, with one stop at the Rainbow Falls. You pick up the tour at the visitor information center at Broadwater Overlook Park. The company also does a Lewis and Clark tour, a parks tour, and custom trips.

A SPECIAL EVENT Great Falls hosts the **Lewis and Clark Festival** each year in June. Events include history workshops, tours, food booths, and children's activities. For information and tickets, call © **406/452-5661** or visit **www.lewisclarkia.com.**

GETTING OUTSIDE
Fishing & Boating
Great Falls is the unofficial dividing line for cold- and warm-water fish. You can fish for trout from Giant Springs, or take one of the many tours available on the Missouri. For half- to 7-day fishing and white-water trips on the Missouri, try **Montana River Outfitters,** 923 10th Ave. N., Great Falls (© **800/800-8218** or 406/761-1677; www. montanariveroutfitters.com). You can also paddle the Upper Missouri in 34-foot *voyageur*-style canoes with **River Odysseys West** (© **800/451-6034;** www.rowadventures. com), which offers tours in the style of the fur trappers (but with first-class tenting accommodations). Price for a 5-day trip on the Missouri is $1,390 to $1,485 per adult and $1,245 to $1,390 per child (16 or younger).

Golf
The city offers two public golf courses: **Anaconda Hills,** on Smelter Hill in Black Eagle northeast of town at 2315 E. Smelter Ave. (© **406/761-8459**), with greens fees of $23 to $26 for 18 holes and $14 to $16 for 9, and the **Eagle Falls Golf Club** at 25th Street and River Drive North (© **406/761-1078**), with greens fees of $26 to $29 for 18 holes and $15 to $16 for 9.

Hiking & Biking
The 30-mile **River's Edge Trail** (www.thetrail.org), along the Missouri River, starts downtown at the Oddfellows Park and runs out past Rainbow Dam and Crooked Falls,

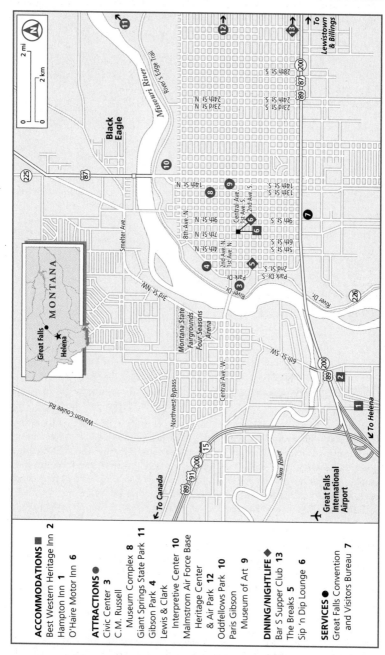

ACCOMMODATIONS ■
Best Western Heritage Inn **2**
Hampton Inn **1**
O'Haire Motor Inn **6**

ATTRACTIONS ●
Civic Center **3**
C.M. Russell
    Museum Complex **8**
Giant Springs State Park **11**
Gibson Park **4**
Lewis & Clark
    Interpretive Center **10**
Malmstrom Air Force Base
    Heritage Center
    & Air Park **12**
Oddfellows Park **10**
Paris Gibson
    Museum of Art **9**

DINING/NIGHTLIFE ◆
Bar S Supper Club **13**
The Breaks **5**
Sip 'n Dip Lounge **6**

SERVICES ●
Great Falls Convention
    and Visitors Bureau **7**

out to the "Great Falls of the Missouri," below Ryan Dam. The trail is ideal for hiking, biking, running, walking, and roller skating. The **Great Falls Convention and Visitors Bureau** (see above) can provide you with information and trail maps.

Winter Sports

Showdown Ski Area   Although relatively undiscovered, this is a full-service ski area, with 34 trails, three chairlifts, a surface lift, and a 1,400-foot vertical drop. The area is perfect for beginning and intermediate skiers (30% beginner, 40% intermediate, 30% expert), with long, uninterrupted runs and lots of dry, light powder. The total average snowfall is 240 inches annually. There are ski rentals and a restaurant and bar. Family-oriented perks include a day-care center and a children's program. Adjacent to Showdown is the **Silver Crest Trail System** for cross-country skiing.

65 miles southeast of Great Falls on U.S. 89, near Neihart. ℭ **800/433-0022** or 406/727-5553. For snow conditions, call ℭ **406/771-1300.** www.showdownmontana.com. Full-day lift tickets $35 adults, $25 seniors 70 and over, $20 children 6–12, free for 5 and under. Early Dec to early Apr Wed–Sun 9:30am–4pm. Closed Christmas, Martin Luther King, Jr., Day, and Presidents' Day.

SEEING THE SIGHTS

Gibson Park, located 1 block north of the Civic Center along Park Drive, is quite nice, with a large pond, playgrounds, flower gardens, and picnic areas. This is a good place to pick up the trail system along the Missouri River. A grizzly bear chased Meriwether Lewis into the Missouri River near here in 1805.

Benton Lake National Wildlife Refuge   Established in 1929 by President Herbert Hoover, the refuge is physically unimpressive, a small lake in a broad, open, treeless plain. But the 12,383 acres are some of the country's most important nesting grounds for waterfowl, especially mallards, pintail, teal, and canvasback. Bird-watching for waterfowl and prairie species is best early in the morning or in the evening. There's a 9-mile auto-tour route that takes about an hour, marked with signs to provide information about what you're seeing, but Mother Nature is constantly changing the refuge attractions.

922 Bootlegger Trail, Great Falls, MT 59404. ℭ **406/727-7400.** www.fws.gov/bentonlake. Free admission. Open daily during daylight hours. Go 1 mile north of Great Falls on Mont. 87, take a left on Bootlegger Trail, then proceed about 9 miles north to well-marked entrance.

C. M. Russell Museum Complex ★★   You can divide the world into two kinds of people—those who like cowboy art, and those who don't. It is a measure of Charles Russell's greatness that, although he was a cowboy artist, almost everybody likes his work. This facility, which includes tours of Russell's studio and home, is one of the high points of any trip to Montana, and it's worth going out of your way to see.

Russell and the dime novelists practically invented the West. But the power of his work is that the personality of everyone and everything portrayed—American Indians, cowboys, even the landscape—shines through. Much modern "Western art" concentrates on the scenery and fierce animals without making much of a statement. Conversely, Russell had something to say about a celebrated but passing way of life, and he said it powerfully.

The museum houses the largest collection of Russell's work on the planet, hung in chronological order—starting with a trio of paintings he did when he was 13. From there, visitors get to see an amazing evolution in his vivid, self-taught style, from early watercolors, to statues made of wax and plaster and later bronze, to Christmas cards and sketches, all the way to his final, most renowned oil period before his death in 1926. The studio contains some of Russell's personal belongings, including many of the Indian artifacts he collected to help maintain his art's authenticity. A number of other excellent Western artists are shown to good advantage in the museum; besides the permanent display of works by Russell protégé Olaf Seltzer and another permanent exhibit on bison art, exhibits change several times a year. You can spend an hour or all day here.

400 13th St. N. ℰ **406/727-8787.** www.cmrussell.org. $9 adults, $7 seniors, $4 students (age 6 or older), free for kids 5 and under. May–Sept daily 9am–6pm; Oct–Apr Tues–Sat 10am–5pm, Sun 1–5pm. Tours May–Sept Mon–Fri 10am and 2pm; Sat–Sun 2pm. Closed major holidays.

Giant Springs State Park ★

Lewis and Clark came upon and described the Giant Springs, purportedly the largest freshwater spring in the world. The spring now also feeds a fish-breeding facility nearby. It burbles out of the 250-million-year-old Madison Formation, a large water-bearing formation that provides a lot of groundwater throughout the northern West. The springs send out more than 100,000 gallons a minute into the 201-foot-long Roe River, credited as one of the two shortest rivers in the world. The entire park covers 218 acres and has about 2 miles of trails.

The Great Falls that gave Lewis and Clark so much trouble have been dammed, but you can see a few remnants of their former glory from overlooks. In the spring, especially, you can see the power of the river flowing through the spillways at Rainbow Dam, spewing mist hundreds of feet into the air, creating the rainbows in the sunshine that so entranced the explorers. Lewis called Rainbow Falls "one of the most beautiful objects of nature." The Montana Department of Fish, Wildlife, and Parks also operates a fish hatchery and visitor center nearby (Mon–Fri 8am–5pm), where visitors can purchase hunting and fishing licenses.

4600 Giant Springs Rd. ℰ **406/454-5840.** http://fwp.mt.gov. $5 per vehicle ($3 per bicycle or pedestrian). Open daily during daylight hours. Take River Dr. east along the Missouri River to Giant Springs Rd. Turn left and drive about ¼ mile, just past the Lewis & Clark Interpretive Center.

Lewis & Clark National Historic Trail Interpretive Center ★★

Located on a bluff overlooking the Missouri River, this facility is, hands down, the best Lewis and Clark exhibit between St. Louis and the Pacific Ocean. The facility is cleverly arranged to follow the adventurers' path to each major point along the way. You start at Monticello with Thomas Jefferson's instructions to the Corps of Discovery. Then you go from one high point to the next along the journey. You visit a Mandan earth lodge, see the grizzlies, and feel the voyagers sweat as they pull their 3,000-pound boat along the 18-mile portage of the Great Falls. Of this portage Clark wrote: "To state the fatigues of this party would take up more of this journal than other notes which I find scarcely time to set down." An excellent facility, it will take several hours to see properly. The docents are wonderfully informed and entertaining. Interpretive programs are held year-round, outdoors at a "River Camp" setting during the summer months.

4201 Giant Springs Rd. ℰ **406/727-8733.** www.fs.fed.us/r1/lewisclark/lcic. $8 adults, free for children 15 and under. Memorial Day to Sept daily 9am–6pm; Oct to Memorial Day Tues–Sat 9am–5pm, Sun noon–5pm. Closed major holidays.

Malmstrom Air Force Base Heritage Center and Air Park

The air park has a number of aircraft from various eras, primarily from the 1950s and 1960s, but the real attractions here are the implements of nuclear weaponry: a Minuteman III ICBM and its transporter erector. Inside, amid scads of military equipment and uniforms and a reconstruction of a World War II–era barracks, is the old command center that once controlled the base's nuclear missiles. Interpretation of the exhibits is minimal, unfortunately.

Malmstrom Air Force Base, east end of 2nd Ave. N. past 57th St. ℂ **406/731-2705.** Free admission; civilian passes are available at the base's visitor center. Air park: Daily during daylight hours. Museum: Mon-Fri 10am–4pm. Closed holidays.

Paris Gibson Square Museum of Art ★   Located in a national historic landmark building that served as Great Falls's first high school, Paris Gibson Square is now the cultural and art center of the city. The changing art shows display the works of artists from around the Northwest, as well as pieces from the permanent collection. The selection includes both contemporary and historical exhibits in a comfortable, beautifully restored space. Among the newest works are Len Steen's "outsider art," stick-figure statues that once graced Montana's roadsides.

1400 1st Ave. N. ℂ **406/727-8255.** www.the-square.org. Free admission. Mon–Fri 10am–5pm (Tues also 7–9pm); Sat noon–5pm.

SHOPPING

There are at least 19 antiques stores in Great Falls, and the chamber of commerce can give you a map of their locations. The terrific **Dragonfly Dry Goods,** 504 Central Ave. (ℂ **406/454-2263**), specializes in home decor, clothing, gifts, and things Western. **Hoglund's,** 306 1st Ave. S. (ℂ **406/452-6911**), has an awe-inspiring selection of cowboy boots and hats. You can find Montana-made souvenirs or gifts at the **Blue Ribbon of Montana,** 3400 10th St. S. (ℂ **406/761-1233**).

WHERE TO STAY

Aside from the properties listed below, we also recommend the **Hampton Inn,** 2301 14th St. SW (ℂ **406/453-2675**), with rates of $99 to $139 double and $199 for a whirlpool suite.

Best Western Heritage Inn   The hotel is located on a sedate street just off the main drag, and is the preferred business stop-off in Great Falls, located a little closer to the interstate than downtown. The rooms are comfortable, a notch above your typical chain, and many of them adjoin the central gardened atrium where the pool is located. It has the largest convention center in Great Falls, with a latte bar to boot.

1700 Fox Farm Rd., Great Falls, MT 59404. ℂ **800/548-8256** or 406/761-1900. Fax 406/761-0136. www. bestwestern.com/heritageinngreatfalls. 233 units. $100–$120 double. AE, DC, DISC, MC, V. **Amenities:** Restaurant; lounge/casino; free airport transfers; exercise room; indoor Jacuzzi; indoor pool; sauna. *In room:* A/C, TV, hair dryer, Wi-Fi (free).

O'Haire Motor Inn ⟨Value⟩   A solid independent motel centered on an interior parking lot, this is my lodging of choice in downtown Great Falls, with all of the trappings for a perfect break from the highways en route to Glacier or points beyond. The hotel, built in 1962 and recently updated, is well-kept and clean, a cut above the normal independent. The restaurant, **Clark & Lewie's,** is a more than respectable diner with personality and microbrew on tap, serving hearty breakfasts and a pub menu for lunch and dinner. The **Sip 'n Dip Lounge** (see "Great Falls After Dark," below) must be seen to be believed. Besides the usual amenities, rubber duckies come with the rooms.

17 7th St. S. Great Falls, MT 59405. ℂ **800/332-9819** or 406/454-2141; 800/543-9819 in Canada. Fax 406/454-0211. www.ohairemotorinn.com. 69 units. $72–$90 double; $110 suite. AE, DC, DISC, MC, V. **Amenities:** Restaurant; lounge; exercise room; indoor pool. *In room:* A/C, TV, Wi-Fi (free).

WHERE TO DINE

Bar S Supper Club ⟨Finds⟩ STEAKS/SEAFOOD   Authentic cowboy steakhouses have become endangered with the expansion of national chains in recent years, but you'll find the real deal at the Bar S, about 5 miles east of Great Falls city limits. The place has a rustic charm, with brands on the walls, lots of red vinyl and wood, and the requisite beer signs. While lunches are primarily burgers and sandwiches, the dinner menu focuses almost exclusively on Montana choice beef, ranging from a 10-ounce tenderloin to a 30-ounce rib-eye, and there is also a fair amount of seafood and a smattering of poultry. Some locals come every Saturday night, and nobody leaves hungry.

8535 U.S. 89. © **406/761-9550.** Reservations recommended. Main courses $6–$10 lunch; $20–$50 dinner. AE, DISC, MC, V. Tues–Sun 11am–2pm and 5–10pm.

The Breaks Ale House & Grill ★ CONTINENTAL/FUSION   The Breaks opened in 2004 in a renovated brick building that was a Model T factory in the 1920s before settling in as a Sears warehouse. Today, the space would be unrecognizable to its former occupants: Now, it's an industrial-chic eatery with plenty of exposed brick, contemporary light fixtures, and colorful artwork. Patrons can sit in the dim bar area or in an airier dining room with booths and tables. The food is also creative for staid Great Falls, with good homemade soups and such dishes as lobster won tons and buffalo T-bones. Lunches are sandwiches, salads, and other light fare (including crepes stuffed with salmon, garlic chicken, or beef).

202 2nd Ave. S. © **406/453-5980.** Main courses $7–$10 lunch, $11–$35 dinner. AE, DISC, MC, V. Mon–Thurs 11am–9:30pm; Fri–Sat 11am–10pm. Bar open later (usually until 2am).

GREAT FALLS AFTER DARK

The bar scene in Great Falls is fairly sedate and typical for a city its size, with one outrageous exception: the **Sip 'n Dip Lounge** at the O'Haire Motor Inn, 17 7th St. S. (© **406/454-2141**), an authentic tiki bar, clad in bamboo and loaded with South Seas paraphernalia of all kinds. The sip in the moniker refers to the cocktails served by the bar. The dip, however, is quite unusual: Windows behind the bar make for a view of a pool where actresses in mermaid garb swim on Wednesday through Saturday nights. Then you've got "Piano Pat" Sponheim tickling the ivories, as she has since 1963, delivering unusual covers of Neil Diamond, Sinatra, and Elvis tunes. This is one of the kitschiest, wackiest, and flat-out coolest nightspots, not just in Montana, but in the entire West.

Beyond the Sip 'n Dip, another nightspot worth checking out is **Machinery Row,** a vast basement club under the Breaks Ale House & Grill (see "Where to Dine," above).

A SIDE TRIP TO FORT BENTON

Thirty-six miles north of Great Falls on Mont. 87, you can drop down to the historic town of Fort Benton. The town faces the Missouri River, which formed its destiny. There is a pleasant waterfront park with an interesting series of murals detailing the town's history.

The Lewis and Clark expedition made a critical decision a short distance downstream from Fort Benton, where the Marias River enters the Missouri. The expedition was divided on which was the main branch of the Missouri. The vote was 30-to-2 for the Marias being the main branch. The two who went for the other branch were Lewis and Clark. Had they chosen the Marias branch, there is a good chance that the expedition would have failed, because they would not have been able to get over the Rockies before winter. A statue of the explorers at this decisive point dominates one end of Front Street in Fort Benton. A small visitor center at the Bureau of Land Management (BLM) office on Front Street offers some information about this event.

Next to the Lewis and Clark statue is the **Keelboat Mandan,** a full-scale replica 62 feet long and 13 feet wide built for the movie *The Big Sky.* In the heyday of keelboating, broad-shouldered men could push a boat upstream at a pace of about 2 miles a day. There is also a monument on the riverfront to Shep, a dog whose master died and was sent East by train for burial. After that, Shep met every train in Fort Benton from 1936 until 1942, waiting for his master's return, until—hard of hearing and arthritic—the old dog met his end one wintry morning on the tracks.

The first steamboat reached Fort Benton in 1850, and 600 of them stopped here from 1859 to 1870. Furs, goods, and gold were all shipped through the town. The **Museum of the Northern Great Plains,** 1205 20th St. (© **406/622-5316;** www.fortbenton.com/museums), tells the story of settlement. There is a vast collection of farming equipment here, testifying to the fortitude and ingenuity of the settlers on the Great Plains. The **Museum of the Upper Missouri,** at Old Fort Park and Front Street (© **406/622-5316;** www.fortbenton.com/museums), has an excellent historical collection, including the rifle that Nez Perce Chief Joseph surrendered at the Bear Paw battle, and the history and personality of Fort Benton as expressed by the artist Charles Russell, the preacher Brother Van, and the infamous "Madame Mustache," the woman who reputedly introduced Calamity Jane to prostitution. Both museums are open late May to late September Monday to Saturday 10am to 4pm and Sunday noon to 4pm. Adult admission is $5 for one museum or $10 for both (which includes access to three other attractions in town), and kids 12 and under are $1.

The BLM manages 149 miles of the Missouri here as a federally designated Wild and Scenic River, and canoeing and keelboating are both good ways to take in the landscape. Contact the **Fort Benton Chamber of Commerce** (© **406/622-3864;** www.fortbenton.com) for a list of river outfitters.

For lodging, you can't beat the **Grand Union Hotel** ★★, 1 Grand Union Sq. (P.O. Box 1119), Fort Benton, MT 59442 (© **888/838-1882** or 406/622-1882; www.grandunionhotel.com), right on the river. Built in 1882 at a cost of $50,000, it was completely restored to its original splendor in 1999. Said to be Montana's oldest operating hotel, the Grand Union has 26 luxurious guest rooms in a range of sizes (with modern conveniences: phones, free Wi-Fi, and TVs), a top-notch restaurant in the **Union Grille** (dinner entrees, such as roasted chicken and grilled beef tenderloin, are $19–$30), and a pub. The three suites are largest. During the high summer season, rates start at $115 for a double and go up to $190 for the suites; rates include a deluxe European breakfast.

3 THE ROCKY MOUNTAIN EASTERN FRONT ★

53 miles W of Great Falls

The eastern front of the Rockies is an isolated, sparsely populated section of Montana, but it is no less beautiful than the peaks and valleys to the west. A great paleontological mystery was solved here. Scientists had discovered many dinosaur fossils in the far-eastern part of the state, but no nests or eggs. When fossilized dinosaur eggs turned up along the Rocky Mountain Eastern Front—the shoreline of a shallow sea 65 million years ago—paleontologists learned that the beasts had migrated to this area to lay their eggs.

There are two towns with distinctive personalities on the front: Choteau and Augusta. Choteau bills itself the gateway to the Rockies. Named for the president of the American

> **(Tips) Rental-Car Tip**
>
> A reliable four-wheel-drive vehicle is strongly recommended for touring the back roads of the Rocky Mountain Eastern Front. Many are gravel roads that turn into a slippery mush, locally known as "gumbo," during rainy weather. Car-rental companies in Great Falls and other nearby cities keep such vehicles in stock, but requests should be made weeks in advance.

Fur Co., who brought the first steamboat up the Missouri, it is one of the oldest towns in Montana.

Tiny Augusta is a cheerful, friendly community. Unlike a lot of small Western towns, it is not hustling to turn itself into something else. It's only about 2 blocks long, with weathered wood exteriors on the buildings. Folks are out and about and everybody's on a first-name basis with just about everybody else. The pace picks up a bit the last weekend in June when the rodeo hits town.

ESSENTIALS

GETTING THERE   The closest airport is in Great Falls, about 53 miles from Choteau (see the "Great Falls" section, earlier in this chapter, for airport information). From the airport, take I-15 north to the U.S. 89 exit (about 13 miles), then go west on U.S. 89 for 40 miles to Choteau.

To reach the area by car from the northwest, drive on U.S. 2 along the southern border of Glacier National Park. At Browning, go south on Mont. 89 to Choteau. From Choteau, go southwest on U.S. 287. Two miles past the junction of Mont. 21 and U.S. 287, Augusta lies 40 miles due west of Great Falls.

VISITOR INFORMATION   For an information packet, contact the regional tourism office for **Travel Montana's Russell Country,** P.O. Box 3166, Great Falls, MT 59403 (© **800/527-5348;** www.russell.visitmt.com). In Choteau, write to the **Choteau Chamber of Commerce** at 815 Main Ave. N. (P.O. Box 897), Choteau, MT 59422 (© **800/823-3866** or 406/466-5316; www.choteaumontana.com). For hunting and fishing info, contact the **Montana Department of Fish, Wildlife, and Parks** (4600 Giant Springs Rd., Great Falls, MT 59406; © **406/454-5840;** http://fwp.mt.gov).

GETTING AROUND   The only way to travel this country is to drive. The closest car-rental agencies are in Great Falls (see earlier in this chapter).

OUTFITTERS & ORGANIZED TRIPS

Also see **Pine Butte Guest Ranch** and **JJJ Wilderness Ranch** (see "Where to Stay," below) for learning vacations covering the region's ecology and natural history, backpacking, and horse-packing trips.

Timescale Adventures (Kids)   Timescale Adventures runs some popular dinosaur field programs, designed for all ages and levels of interest. The 3-hour seminar is a walk along the Rocky Mountain Eastern Front covering identification of dinosaur bones and eggs, and what to do when you find one. The 2-day seminar includes a dig and instruction in fossil-preservation techniques. All of the programs originate from the **Two Medicine Dinosaur Center** in the town of Bynum, 14 miles north of Choteau on U.S. 89. The center, open daily from 9am to 6pm from Memorial Day to Labor Day, or by appointment the rest of the year, houses displays on the various dinosaurs the organization has excavated. Admission is $5 for adults, $4 for seniors, $3 children 3 to 11, and free for kids 2 and under.

P.O. Box 786, Bynum, MT 59419. (C) **800/238-6873** or 406/469-2211. www.timescale.org. 3-hr. day tour $50 per person; 1-day program $120 per person; longer programs about $120 per person per day. Advance registration is required; space is limited.

A SCENIC DRIVE

The beautiful **Sun Canyon Drive** on Sun Canyon Road starts out along the plains west of Augusta, and then weaves up the canyon past a 1913 Bureau of Reclamation dam. During the time of Lewis and Clark, the Blackfeet called the river that carved the canyon the Medicine River, but it is now known as the Sun River. The canyon, a gray-granite jumble with snowcapped peaks in the distance, is a weekend getaway spot for residents all along the front. There are opportunities for fishing, boating, hiking, and four-wheeling in the area. The road up here is an easily navigable gravel track for the most part, but it can be rugged in portions, especially if they've been trying to fix it. After you get to the national forest, however, the road is paved. Go figure.

SHOPPING

Latigo and Lace, 124 Main St. in Augusta ((C) **406/562-3665**), is an eclectic shop overflowing with the work of Montana artists and craftspeople, plus books, cups of cappuccino, and an array of "made in Montana" collectibles.

WHERE TO STAY

The Bunkhouse Inn (Value) This is the cowboy way. Housed in a building that dates from 1912 and is constantly under renovation, the Bunkhouse is sort of a bed-and-breakfast without the breakfast. Proprietor Terry Taillon sends his guests to Mel's Diner across the street. Taillon says that Mel doesn't rent rooms, so he won't serve food. That's the sort of town this is. The rooms are small and basic; there are no phones or televisions (except for one in the common room), but instead of staring at the idiot box, you can sit out on the second-floor porch watching the slow-paced bustle on Main Street. On Memorial Day weekend, you'll have a front-row seat to Montana's smallest parade as the gray-haired American Legionnaires march to the strains of Sousa marches played on a boombox carried by two of the ladies' auxiliary.

122 Main St. (P.O. Box 294), Augusta, MT 59410. (C) **800/553-4016** or 406/562-3387. 10 units. $48 double. MC, V. *In room:* No phone, Wi-Fi (free).

JJJ Wilderness Ranch ★ The Triple J is a guest ranch located in the extraordinary Sun Canyon along the Rocky Mountain Eastern Front. Run by the Barker family for three generations, the ranch offers everything the outdoorsy type could want—horseback riding, hiking, fishing, pack trips into the Bob Marshall Wilderness Area (at an extra charge), and pure and simple relaxation. Nestled in a forest of aspen and spruce, the rustic cabins accommodate a total of 20 guests, so you're never crowded. Though there are few amenities, it's not due to an oversight: Those who come here don't want phones and televisions.

80 Mortimer Rd., P.O. Box 310, Augusta, MT 59410. (C) **406/562-3653.** Fax 406/562-3836. www.triplej ranch.com. 7 cabins. $1,900 per adult per week, $1,550–$1,700 per child 6–17 per week, double occupancy with a 1-week minimum stay. Rates include all meals and ranch activities (except pack trips). AE, DISC, MC, V. Closed Oct–May. **Amenities:** Children's programs; free transportation from and to the Great Falls airport; outdoor Jacuzzi; Wi-Fi (free). *In room:* Fridge, no phone.

Pine Butte Guest Ranch ★ (Finds) Located deep in the Sawtooth Range along the Rocky Mountain Eastern Front, Pine Butte Guest Ranch is the property of the Nature Conservancy, a national land-preservation organization. Since a few endangered grizzly bears have made the 15,500-acre Pine Butte Swamp Preserve their home, the Conservancy saw fit to buy it to protect the delicate ecosystem. The preserve is the only place left in the Lower 48 states where grizzlies use both the mountain and prairie ranges as they did before settlement drove them to the remnant habitat in the mountains.

Pine Butte was first homesteaded in the 1930s, but it has always been a guest ranch, not a cattle ranch, which accounts in part for the largely undisturbed habitat. (Relentless winter winds have also helped keep development to a minimum.) Today the ranch focuses on education, running numerous workshops on topics ranging from grizzly bears to wildflowers. As well as visits to local dinosaur dig sites, guests can also take part in the usual dude-ranch activities—riding, hiking, swimming, and the like. Each of the ranch's handsome, rustic log cabins has a river-rock fireplace and is comfortably equipped with handmade furniture.

351 S. Fork Rd., HC 58, P.O. Box 34C, Choteau, MT 59422. ℂ **406/466-2158.** Fax 406/466-5462. www. nature.org/montana. 10 cabins. Summer $1,800 per adult per week double; children 13–17 $1,500 per week; children 6–12 $1,300 per week; children 5 and under free. Rates include all meals, riding, ranch facilities. AE, MC, V. **Amenities:** Free transportation from and to Great Falls airport, outdoor heated pool. *In room:* No phone.

WHERE TO DINE

Buckhorn Bar STEAKS/AMERICAN   The Dellwo family has run this bar in the same location for more than 50 years, serving a selection of steaks, chicken, and burgers. If you've got a serious appetite, your best bet is a charbroiled 16-ounce rib steak with a salad and potato for $17. The portions are remarkably large and moderately priced, the atmosphere classic woody Western, complete with dozens of antler racks overhead, cowboy-hatted patrons, and gaming machines.

Main St., Augusta. ℂ **406/562-3344.** All dishes $3.25–$17. MC, V. Daily 8am–2am. (After 11pm, only pizzas are available.)

Mel's Diner AMERICAN   Everyone in town will send you to breakfast at Mel's, a tiny place with four booths and two tables. You'll get good food at good prices: bacon and eggs, hot cakes, and biscuits and gravy for breakfast; fish and chips and burgers for lunch and dinner. You can also take your pick of ice-cream treats, shakes, and malts. The hours depend on how business is doing.

Main St., Augusta. ℂ **406/562-3408.** All dishes $2–$10. MC, V. Daily 6am–7pm (until 6pm in winter).

4 LEWISTOWN

105 miles E of Great Falls; 128 miles N of Billings

The hub of a vast agricultural region, Lewistown is not right on the way to any particular tourist destination, so if you find yourself here, you probably meant to come. The town is blessed with great downtown architecture, stately homes, and modest citizens. And there is some notable recreation here—especially hunting and fishing. Located in the center of the Judith Basin, Lewistown is surrounded by three mountain ranges—the Big and Little Snowies, the Moccasin, and the Judith. While Charles Russell lived in

Great Falls later, the Judith Basin is where he worked as a cowboy and where he fell in love with Montana.

ESSENTIALS

GETTING THERE   **Great Lakes Airlines** (© 800/554-5111; www.greatlakesav.com) provides daily commuter airline service to **Lewistown Municipal Airport** (© 406/535-3264; www.lwtairport.com) on a route that flies to Worland, Wyoming, then Denver.

Lewistown is connected to other Montana cities by two-lane U.S. highways that radiate from the town. From Billings, go north 92 miles, then west 31 miles on U.S. 87. From Great Falls, Lewistown is 105 miles east on U.S. 87.

VISITOR INFORMATION   The **Lewistown Chamber of Commerce** has its offices at Symmes Park at 408 NE Main St. (© 866/912-3980 or 406/535-5436; www.lewistown chamber.com and www.destinationlewistownmontana.com). Local maps, and maps from the Bureau of Land Management, the U.S. Forest Service, and the C.M. Russell Wildlife Refuge are all available. Information about Lewistown is also available from **Travel Montana's Russell Country** (© 800/527-5348; www.russell.visitmt.com).

GETTING AROUND   Rental cars are available from **Sparks Rent-a-car** (© 406/535-7701).

SPECIAL EVENTS   The **Chokecherry Festival,** held on the Saturday following Labor Day, honors that smarter-than-the-average-berry, the chokecherry, one of the few indigenous fruits of the prairie. Generally overlooked by poets and songwriters—no one has ever been the chokecherry of someone's eye, nor has life ever been a bowl of chokecherries—Lewistown attempts to place the chokecherry on its proper pedestal with parades, bake sales, pie cook-offs, and even a pit-spitting contest.

Lewistown's other big annual event is the **Montana Cowboy Poetry Gathering** ★. Each year in mid-August, cowboys, ranchers, large-animal vets, and other swaybacked and bowlegged Montana literati gather to swap lies and poems. Those who may have considered the term "cowboy poetry" an oxymoron are usually pleasantly surprised to find a relentless rhyming vitality to the poetry, along with a lot of humor, and an honest and healthy appreciation of fellow poets. For details on these events, call the **Lewistown Chamber of Commerce** at © 866/912-3980.

GETTING OUTSIDE

For information on activities in the national forest lands in this area, contact the **Lewis and Clark National Forest** (© 406/791-7700).

Cross-Country Skiing

If you're here in the winter, there is good cross-country skiing in any of the three mountain ranges that ring the valley. There are a number of trails accessible by car in the Judith Mountains north of town, on old logging and mining roads. Head north on U.S. 191 to the Maiden Canyon sign, then take a left and follow the road for 5 miles to the trails.

Fishing

High in the Big Snowy Mountains is **Crystal Lake,** about 35 miles southwest of Lewistown. This is a popular and somewhat remote recreational area that offers good fishing, hiking, and camping. You have to travel about 25 miles on gravel road to get there. Take U.S. 87 west of town for 8 miles, then turn south at the sign for Crystal Lake. After about 16 miles it runs into Forest Service Road 275, which you should follow for another 9 miles to the lake. Motorized boats are prohibited, but overnight RV and tent camping is available. For good trout fishing closer to town, try **Big Spring Creek,** which begins south of Lewistown and flows north through town to join the Judith River. You can easily access Brewery Flats on Big Spring Creek about 2 miles outside of town on Mont. 238. Flatwillow Creek in the Forest Grove area of the Little Snowies provides some rainbow and cutthroat fishing. For **flat-water fishing,** try Upper and Lower Carter's Pond, man-made ponds 6½ miles north of Lewistown on U.S. 191. There are picnic facilities and overnight camping as well. The **James Kipp Recreation Area,** 78 miles north of town on the Missouri River in the Charles M. Russell National Wildlife Refuge, also has fishing, camping, hiking, and a boat ramp. Take U.S. 191 northeast until it intersects with Mont. 19, then go north about 35 miles. Camping is $12 a night. Contact the **Bureau of Land Management** (© **406/538-1900**) for more information.

Golf

The 18-hole **Judith Shadows Golf Course,** 464 Rifle Range Rd. (© **406/538-6062;** www.judithshadows.com) is an alternative-spikes-only facility located at the end of Marcella Avenue in the northeast corner of Lewistown. Greens fees are $16 for 9 holes, $28 for 18. Carts are $12 for 9 holes, $24 for 18 holes. **Pine Meadows Golf Course,** on the south side of Lewistown at 320 Country Club Lane ([tel **406/538-7075;** www.pine meadowslewistown.org), has 9 holes and charges $15 to $18 in greens fees and $12 for a cart rental.

Hiking

At **Crystal Lake** (see "Fishing," above), there are numerous trails into the Lewis and Clark National Forest, including the Crystal Lake Loop National Recreation Trail. There is also good hiking along the Wild and Scenic Missouri River from the James Kipp Recreation Area. The **Bureau of Land Management** (© **406/538-1900**), can give you information on additional hiking trails.

SEEING THE SIGHTS

Operated by the local chamber of commerce (and perhaps a little too cutely named), the **Charlie Russell Chew-Choo Dinner Train** (© **866/912-3980** or 406/535-5436; www. montanacharlierussellchewchoo.com) runs from Lewistown to Denton and back every Saturday from the beginning of June through the end of September, with special holiday trains. On the 56-mile round-trip ride, the train crosses three large trestles and navigates a 2,000-foot tunnel during its 3½-hour run through the Judith Basin. The schedule varies, so call ahead. A regular summer trip with dinner is $90 per adult, $50 for children 12 and under.

The **Central Montana Museum,** next to the Lewistown Chamber of Commerce in Symmes Park at 408 NE Main St. (© **406/535-3642**), displays historical artifacts from the late 1800s to modern day, including a facial reconstruction of Rattlesnake Jake, an outlaw who shot the town up on July 4, 1884, before being gunned down himself. The museum is open daily in summer from 10am to 4pm and by appointment the rest of the year. Admission is free; donations accepted.

Big Spring, located 7 miles south of Lewistown on County Road 466, is the third-largest freshwater spring in the world. The spring is the water source for the town, and is considered one of the purest in the nation. It is bottled by the Big Spring Water Company and sold at stores in the west-central part of the U.S. The spring also feeds the Montana State Fish Hatchery nearby.

Lewistown became a regional commercial center after a ranching and mining boom in the early part of the 20th century. The industry barons built large homes in a range of styles, primarily Gothic and Victorian. The first to build was J. T. Wunderlin, a gold miner and organizer of the Empire Bank & Trust. Others soon followed, creating a neighborhood of elegant homes. They lived in the **Silk Stocking District,** which is just northeast of downtown on Boulevard. (Not the section of Boulevard near Symmes Park; if you're there, you're lost.) The Lewistown Chamber of Commerce (see above) can provide information on self-guided tours. The homes, however, are private residences and not open to the public. At 220 W. Blvd., there is a plaque outside the Symmes-Wicks House (see below) describing the area. At the top of the hill overlooking the Silk Stocking District, check out the **Fergus County Courthouse** (7th Ave. and Main St.), a gold-domed mission-style courthouse built in 1906.

WHERE TO STAY

Pheasant Tales Bed-and-Bistro ★   While the nearby Symmes-Wicks House (see below) offers an early-20th-century experience, Pheasant Tales is a modern, newly remodeled guesthouse with some unique touches. Proprietors Chris and Rick Taylor are both avid pheasant hunters and anglers. After Chris began preparing gourmet meals with local pheasant, hunters told the couple that if they opened a bed-and-breakfast, they would stay there on hunting trips. Chris instead opened a bed-and-bistro (Pheasant Tales's guests still get breakfast) specializing in eclectically prepared game birds, with impressive results. The inn is done in reddish pine, and the large rooms are comfortably furnished and have a full kitchen or kitchenettes. With advance reservations, Chris can often prepare a gourmet dinner in the evening (starting at $35 per person). The Taylors also breed English setters, so there is almost always a brace of puppies providing entertainment. There's an extensive deck, plenty of space, and good fishing nearby as well.

1511 Timberline Rd., Lewistown, MT 59457. ℂ **406/538-2124.** Fax 406/538-6244. www.pheasanttales. biz. 6 units. $75–$120 double; $150–$120 suite. Rates include full breakfast. AE, MC, V. Located 4 miles south of Lewistown. Pets accepted ($10/night). *In room:* Kitchenette, no phone, Wi-Fi (free).

The Symmes-Wicks House Bed & Breakfast ★★   Charles and Carole Wicks have beautifully restored this 1909 shingle-style, Arts and Crafts home, which sits right in the heart of the Silk Stocking District. Though you can easily see the stately exteriors of all of the surrounding homes, a stay here provides the unique opportunity to view the inside of one, replete with rich hardwoods, Tiffany glass, and period antiques. Upstairs, the guest rooms are tastefully decorated, one with masculine tones, a sleigh bed, and a bathroom that's a wooden work of art. The room facing northeast has a more feminine touch. The bathroom isn't so much a separate room as it is a tasteful area partitioned off from the main room, with a green-marble shower as its centerpiece. In the early 20th century, there was an influx of Croatian stonecutters to Lewistown. Some of their work can be seen on this house, as well as on other buildings in the area.

220 W. Blvd., Lewistown, MT 59457. ℂ **406/538-9068.** Fax 406/538-5331. www.symmeswickshouse. com. 3 units. $80 double. Rates include full breakfast. AE, MC, V. *In room:* A/C, hair dryer, no phone, Wi-Fi (free).

Yogo Inn ★   Once a train depot, the Yogo is now a very good independent hotel and the primary convention center for Montana's midsection, with clean, quiet rooms and a hint of rustic elegance. There is a well-kept, interior courtyard that catches the sun and features a stage taken by musicians throughout the summer. The Yogo is popular with business travelers, and everything is functional but not fancy. The indoor pool is next to a marker signifying that the spot is the exact geographic center of the state. It's also the locus of the annual Montana Cowboy Poetry Gathering every August, and it books up pretty quickly for the event.

211 E. Main St., Lewistown, MT 59457. ✆ **800/860-9646** or 406/535-8271. www.yogoinn.com. 123 units. $85–$124 double. AE, DISC, MC, V. Pets accepted ($10 per night). **Amenities:** 2 restaurants; lounge/ casino; indoor Jacuzzi; indoor pool. *In room:* A/C, TV, Wi-Fi (free).

WHERE TO DINE

Harry's Place (Kids) STEAKS/AMERICAN   A rock-clad A-frame decorated with memorabilia from the local high school sports teams, Harry's Place is the best place for a good meal in Lewistown. With excellent homemade soups—such as chicken corn chowder—burgers, wraps, and other sandwiches (including six varieties made with prime rib), Harry's is a good bet for lunch and grills the best steaks in town pretty much any day of the week. However, the restaurant truly goes all out on Friday nights, with prime rib, corn fritters, and homemade honey butter. Beer and wine are served, but liquor is not.

631 NE Main St. ✆ **406/538-9310.** Reservations recommended on Fri night. Main courses $6–$9 lunch, $6–$24 dinner. AE, DISC, MC, V. Mon–Thurs 11am–9pm; Fri–Sat 11am–10pm.

5 THE HI-LINE: U.S. 2

Havre: 115 miles NE of Great Falls; Fort Belknap: 46 miles E of Havre; Glasgow: 279 miles N of Billings

If you're not from Montana and find yourself on the Hi-Line, you're probably on the way somewhere else. There isn't a great deal of anything up here, except for wheat, birds, lots of ground squirrels, and the occasional pronghorn.

There are a number of National Wildlife Refuges along this drive: the gigantic **Charles M. Russell NWR,** and the smaller **Black Coulee, Bowdoin,** and **Medicine Lake**—the latter on the far-eastern border of the state. Like most of the refuges nationwide, they are managed primarily for the benefit of birds, especially migratory waterfowl. This is a good place to bring your field guide: Even if you don't leave your car, you'll be able to identify many species, possibly including the Franklin's gull with its telltale black wingtips, the melodious western meadowlark, or the marsh hawk (or harrier, not a true hawk). The latter flies low to the ground, flapping its wings more often than the gliding hawks, and is gray when mature, brown when young, with a white bar across its rump.

Caution: The roadsides here are dotted with white crosses—memorials to people who have died in auto accidents. Maintained by friends and family, many are decorated with flowers, flags, and ribbons. There are a lot of them. Don't be fooled by the long, straight stretches of road. Drive carefully.

Call the **Havre Area Chamber of Commerce,** 130 5th Ave., Havre, MT 59501 (✆ **406/265-4383;** www.havremt.com), for further information about the area.

FROM HAVRE TO FORT BELKNAP

Havre probably isn't anyone's idea of a vacation spot, but it has its moments. There are some interesting historic sites, including the nearby **Bear Paw Battlefield** (see "Bear Paw Battlefield: The Nez Perce Surrender," below), the site of the last major battle of the Indian Wars. For both cultural and natural history, the best place to start is the **H. Earl Clack Museum,** 1753 U.S. 2 in the Holiday Village Shopping Center (✆ **406/265-4000**). The museum is open Monday through Saturday from 10am to 6pm and Sunday noon to 5pm from mid-May until Labor Day. Admission is free. Southeast of Havre lies

Bear Paw Battlefield: The Nez Perce Surrender

One of the most remarkable events of the Indian Wars culminated at the Bear Paw Battlefield (☏ 406/357-3130), a unit of the Nez Perce National Historic Park (www.nps.gov/nepe), located 26 miles south of Chinook on County Road 240.

In 1877, in what is now northeast Oregon, the Army tried to force a band of Nez Perce Indians under the leadership of Chief Joseph onto a reservation far from their native lands. The Nez Perce decided to escape, trying to reach Canada where they hoped to join Sitting Bull's Lakota, who had already found homes there.

Joseph led 800 of his tribal members on a 1,700-mile flight through Yellowstone National Park and eventually north to this site, a mere 45 miles south of the Canadian border and freedom.

The U.S. Army under Gen. Oliver O. Howard pursued the tribe as it fled. A Civil War hero known as "the praying general," Howard, a deeply religious Christian, developed considerable hostility toward some of the Nez Perce leaders because he considered them heathens. Through a series of brilliant maneuvers, Joseph and his band of warriors, women, children, horses, and cattle escaped or defeated the army at every turn. Even Howard was forced to admit in his memoirs about the chase, "The leadership of Chief Joseph was indeed remarkable. No general could have chosen a safer position or one that would be more likely to puzzle and obstruct a pursuing foe."

They fought several battles along the way, but Col. Nelson A. Miles finally caught Joseph and his band in a snowstorm at Bear Paw, a rolling, grassy landscape achingly close to the freedom promised by the Canadian border. After a 6-day fight, Joseph surrendered on October 5, 1877. The chief's rifle is now in the Museum of the Upper Missouri in Fort Benton.

Chief Joseph is believed to have delivered this famous speech, translated by an interpreter:

the home of 2,000 Chippewa and Cree Indians on this rather small plot of land at the Western Front of the Bear Paw Mountains. The **Rocky Boy Powwow** is held near Box Elder the first weekend of every August. Call ☏ **406/395-4478** for more information.

Start your driving tour of the region just south of Havre on U.S. 87, coming up from Great Falls. Drive north to Havre until you reach the junction with U.S. 2. Take U.S. 2 east until it converges with Montana's version of Route 66, a state highway running south through the Fort Belknap Indian Reservation. Take 66 through the reservation to the intersection of U.S. 191. Turn left (northeast) and drive about 57 miles until the road joins U.S. 2 again.

Seeing the Sights

Fort Assinniboine This well-preserved fort was established in 1879, after it was already obsolete. It was intended to protect settlers from Indian attacks, but all the tribes had already been defeated. After the defeat of Chief Joseph in the nearby Bear Paw Battle,

"Tell General Howard I know his heart. What he told me before, I have in my heart. I am tired of fighting. Our chiefs are killed. Looking Glass is dead. Toohoolhootze is dead. The old men are all killed. It is the young men who say yes or no. He who led the young men is dead. It is cold and we have no blankets. The little children are freezing to death. My people, some of them, have run away to the hills, and have no blankets, no food; no one knows where they are—perhaps freezing to death. I want time to look for my children and see how many of them I can find. Maybe I shall find them among the dead. Hear me, my chiefs. I am tired; my heart is sick and sad. From where the sun stands now, I will fight no more forever."

That night, White Bird and 200 of his followers slipped away to Canada. Of the 431 remaining, 21 died by the end of spring. The survivors moved to a reservation in Oklahoma, where another 47 of Joseph's people died and many more became ill. Finally, in 1885, 118 Nez Perce who agreed to convert to Christianity were allowed to relocate to the Lapwai Agency near Lewistown, Idaho. The rest, including Joseph, were settled on the Colville Reservation in Nespelem in northeast Washington State.

Joseph never gave up hope of a return to his homeland in the Wallowa Valley. He met with Pres. William McKinley in 1897, and tried unsuccessfully to purchase the land in 1900. He died at Colville in 1904 at age 64. Even in death, he wasn't returned to the Wallowa Valley, but was buried at Nespelem.

For more insight into the flight of Chief Joseph and the Nez Perce, stop at the **Blaine County Museum,** 501 Indiana St., Chinook (© **406/357-2590**), and take a look at the interpretive displays and the 20-minute film *Forty Miles from Freedom*. Admission is free.

the Fort Assinniboine troops didn't have much to worry about. After the fort closed, much of the land around it was turned into the Rocky Boys Reservation. Only guided tours are permitted because the fort is now run by Montana State University as an agricultural research station.

3 miles south of Havre on U.S. 87. © **406/265-4000** or 265-8336. $6 adults, $5 seniors, $3 students, free for children 5 and under. June–Aug guided tours only, originating from the H. Earl Clack Museum in Havre daily at 5pm.

Havre Beneath the Streets ★ This tour of Havre's boisterous history as a railroad and cowboy town provides an interesting look at the past. When a devastating fire in 1904 destroyed Havre's business district, the labyrinth of tunnels and basements under the town served as a subterranean "shopping mall." Many local businesses of the last century were located here. Their products included legal representation, food, and laundry service—not to mention honky-tonk music, gambling, opium, and prostitution. There is also an aboveground railroad museum focusing on the area's rail history.

9

120 3rd Ave., Havre. (C) **406/265-8888.** $10 adults, $9 seniors, $7 children 6–12, free for children 5 and under. Reservations recommended. Summer daily 9am–5pm, tours 9:30am–3:30pm; winter Mon–Sat 10am–4pm, tours 10:30am–2:30pm.

Wahkpa Chu'gn Bison Kill   From a steep cliff above the Milk River called Wahkpa Chu'gn, the Assinniboine drove bison to their deaths to provide food for the tribe. Indians used the jump from 2,000 years ago until the 15th century. The hour-long guided tours are very informative, in part because this is one of the largest and most studied buffalo jumps in existence. Visitors are also given the opportunity to try their skill with an *atl-atl,* or throwing stick.

Behind the Holiday Village Shopping Mall on U.S. 2 W. (C) **406/265-6417** or 265-4000. www.buffalojump. org. Tour info available at H. Earl Clack Museum. $6 adults, $5 seniors, $3 students, free for children 5 and under. June to Labor Day weekend, tours daily 9am–2pm; tours at other times (including winter) available by reservation, weather permitting.

Where to Stay

El Toro Inn, 521 1st St. ((C) **800/422-5414** or 406/265-5414), is a reliable roadside motel charging $60 to $75 for a double. Rooms are well kept but basic, although they do have refrigerators and microwaves. On Route 2 in the eastern part of town there is a pleasant campground called the **Havre RV Park,** 1415 1st St. ((C) **800/278-8861** or 406/265-8861). There are showers, a saloon, a casino, laundry, and a store. Cost is about $36 for an RV, $18 for a tent.

Best Western Great Northern Inn ★   This is our pick of the Havre lodging scene, and it's a relatively new and upscale place. The rooms have a tad more square footage than your typical Best Western, and they have more extensive facilities than anyplace else in Havre. There is also a bridal suite with an in-room hot tub and a corporate suite. While the hotel lacks a restaurant, you can charge your meal to your room at the restaurant across the street. The 24-hour business center has fax, copying, and computer capabilities, and "business plus" rooms are available, with big desks, ergonomic chairs, and expanded amenities. Single rooms also have microwave ovens and fridges.

1345 1st St., Havre, MT 59501. (C) **888/530-4100** or 406/265-4200. Fax 406/265-3656. www.bestwestern. com/greatnortherninn. 75 units. $95–$115 double; $135–$159 suite. Lower rates fall–spring. Rates include continental breakfast. AE, DC, DISC, MC, V. **Amenities:** Lounge/casino; exercise room; indoor Jacuzzi; indoor pool; steam room. *In room:* A/C, TV, fridge (in some), hair dryer, microwave (in some), Wi-Fi (free).

Where to Dine

PJ's AMERICAN   You're out on the Hi-Line, driving through Havre, so you might as well eat in a typical Montana place. PJ's is across the street from the railway station; there's a poker game in the corner with the clickety-clack of chips, and the *boop-boop-boop* of the electronic games of chance. The food isn't bad at all, from a menu of sandwiches for lunch and steaks and seafood for dinner, and you can play keno while you wait.

15 3rd Ave. (C) **406/265-3211.** Breakfast and lunch $4–$7; dinner $7–$20. MC, V. Sun–Thurs 6am–9pm; Fri–Sat 6am–10pm.

Wolfer's Diner (Kids) AMERICAN   Wolfer's is my lunch pick in Havre. The basic dining room sports a 1950s theme, complete with pictures of Elvis, Marilyn, and James Dean hanging alongside a hula hoop and a leather jacket. The kitchen makes good sandwiches—I like the Denver, with scrambled eggs, green peppers, ham, and onion on

Texas toast (very thick toast)—as well as steaks and shrimp baskets for dinner. Better yet are the hand-dipped shakes, sundaes, freezes, and whips.

126 3rd Ave. © **406/265-2111.** Main courses $5–$9. MC, V. Mon–Sat 11am–8pm.

FORT BELKNAP RESERVATION

Established in 1888, the Fort Belknap Reservation is home to the Gros Ventre and Assinniboine tribes. It was named for William W. Belknap, who was secretary of war under Pres. Ulysses S. Grant. The Gros Ventre call themselves the A'ani, or White Clay People. They had lived in North Dakota's Red River Valley from A.D. 1100 to 1400, gradually being pushed west by competition from other tribes. After coming to the Missouri River country in about 1730, they split into two tribes, and the southern branch became known as the Arapaho.

The Assinniboine split from the Yanktonai Sioux in the early 1600s, supposedly over a squabble. (Two of the first ladies of the tribe fought about a local delicacy, a buffalo heart.) They call themselves the Nakota, the Generous Ones. There is also a branch of the tribe at the Fort Peck Reservation to the east.

There is a small **museum** and visitor center at the intersection of Mont. 66 and U.S. 2 (© **406/353-2205** or 353-8473; www.fortbelknap-nsn.gov). From here you can arrange a tour of the tribe's herd of more than 800 buffalo and learn a little bit about the tribe's culture (about $50; summer only; reservations recommended).

Nearby Snake Butte was often used as a site of vision quests, where individuals sought supernatural powers or medicine. These powers came with a price. It was said few who had them lived long lives. The Army Corps of Engineers quarried Snake Butte for stone to build the dam at Fort Peck in the 1930s.

If you head south from here to Hays, then turn to the east, you'll come to **St. Paul's Mission,** a solid stone structure established by Jesuit missionaries in 1886. Next to it is a tiny chapel built in 1931 that is dedicated to Our Lady of the Little Rockies. A local devotee has carved a statue practically identical to the supposedly miraculous one at Einsiedeln in Switzerland. To get here, take Mont. 66 south from U.S. 2 at Fort Belknap for about 40 miles to the sign for Hays. Turn left (east). Once you get to Hays, follow the road south after it turns to gravel. The mission is on the left (east) side of the street about a quarter-mile after the road turns south.

Up the road is Mission Canyon, a steep, narrow, cool gash in the otherwise open landscape. Just after entering the canyon, you'll see a natural stone arch. The very brave can climb nearly to the top, and there are several ledges where you can pose for the photographer.

FROM GLASGOW TO THE FORT PECK INDIAN RESERVATION & THE C. M. RUSSELL WILDLIFE REFUGE

People moving through the northeast extremes of Montana can find themselves a little disoriented by the sheer vastness of the horizons that stretch unbroken all the way to the Dakotas. Although this is mostly wheat country, it's not totally flat. In fact, it is sharply rolling and canyon-scored country, but it's open to the eye in all directions.

In 1879, Robert Louis Stevenson rode an immigrant train through here and later wrote: "What livelihood can repay a human creature for a life spent in this huge sameness? He is cut off from books, from news, from company, from all that can relieve existence but the prosecution of his affairs. A sky full of stars is the most varied spectacle he can hope. He may walk 5 miles and see nothing; ten, and it is as though he had not moved; twenty, and he is still in the midst of the same great level, and has approached no nearer to the object within view, the flat horizon which keeps pace with his advance."

There is a story, usually attributed to an area just over the border in western North Dakota, but in the same sort of landscape, of a lone Indian who watched patiently as a recently arrived farmer plowed into the virgin earth, turning the soil with its deep and tangled roots to begin the civilization of the already vanishing native prairie. After some time, the Indian came over to the farmer, pointed to the plowed earth, and said, "Wrong side up."

The story is probably another in the long chain of myths on which the West is built in the American imagination. But there are two contrasting sentiments made tangible here that illustrate the conflicting impulses of America: progress and preservation.

The first and easiest to spot is the Fort Peck Dam and Lake. Construction of the dam began in 1933, at the height of the Great Depression, as a way to put men to work and to provide inexpensive water to the growing agricultural area.

The dam is the largest hydraulically earth-filled dam in the world, nearly 5 miles across, backing up a lake that is 134 miles long with 1,600 miles of shoreline—more shoreline, it is said, than the entire coast of California. The dam is one of the many Corps of Engineers projects that have turned the cantankerous Missouri River that Lewis and Clark navigated into a tame and regulated lake from the Mississippi River to the Rockies.

Seven thousand men and women went to work on the dam in 1933, and at the peak of employment nearly 11,000 were employed here. Locally, the attitude toward the dam was ambivalent, as the residents were losing their homes to the slowly rising water. On the other hand, they could appreciate the need for jobs, for irrigation water, for electric power, even for a large recreational lake. The story of the dam is told at the **Fort Peck Powerhouse Museum** (✆ **406/526-3493**). The powerhouse looms over the landscape like a chunky Art Deco skyscraper that somehow got lost on its way to Des Moines. Admission is free; it is open daily 9am to 5pm from Memorial Day to Labor Day weekend, and by reservation in winter. Tours of the plant are offered at 9 and 11am, and 1 and 3pm. The powerhouse is located on Mont. 24 at Fort Peck Dam. Tours start at the **Fort Peck Interpretive Center and Museum** ★, on Yellowstone Road (✆ **406/526-3493;** www.fortpeckpaleo.com), which houses a fine collection of dinosaur fossils and displays on the area's history in an impressive new facility that opened in 2005. The big attraction is a frightening, fleshed-out replica of the most complete Tyrannosaurus rex skeleton ever found, unearthed nearby in 1997, but there are also dioramas populated by taxidermy, live fish in aquariums, a look at terrifying aquatic dinosaurs, and the region's human history. It's open year-round Monday to Friday, 9:30am to 5pm May to September, and varied hours in the off season.

SPECIAL EVENTS   **Fort Peck Lake,** backed up by the dam, is the best spot in Montana for walleye fishing. An annual competition, the **Governor's Cup,** takes place there each spring. Contact the **Glasgow Area Chamber of Commerce** (✆ **406/228-2222;** www.glasgowmt.net) for the schedule and details.

Seeing the Sights

The tiny town of Fort Peck is Montana's only planned community, the result of its heyday as the housing base for the workers at the dam in the 1930s. It started out as a trading post in 1867, then grew with the dam, then faded when construction was finished. It is testimony to the remoteness of this region that in 1934, months after the U.S. Army Corps of Engineers had begun construction of this $100-million project (big money during the Depression), a New York supplier asked the New York army headquarters how to address some equipment it was sending out to Montana. The army solemnly replied that there was no such place as Fort Peck—it had been abandoned in the 1880s.

The **Fort Peck Theatre** (© 406/526-9943; www.fortpecktheatre.org) is a large former cinema built in the 1930s for the workers. The surprisingly beautiful theater seats 900 people, and its season runs approximately from the last week of June to the last week of August.

Surrounding the many miles of shoreline at Fort Peck Lake is the **Charles M. Russell Wildlife Refuge,** named for the famous Western wildlife cowboy artist Charles Russell. Born in 1864 in St. Louis, Russell was a working Montana cowboy at the age of 16 and drew much of his artistic inspiration from those years. He greatly admired the region's American Indians, and deplored the plowing of the grasslands. Russell knew that destroying the native grass would destroy the habitat for the animals, the bison would be lost, the Indian conquered. Russell didn't like seeing the West civilized, and he had little use for "settlers."

Turnoffs and campsites are located all along the perimeter of the refuge, as are boat ramps for anglers. Flat Creek, Rock Creek, and Nelson Creek boat ramps are easy to reach, located just off Mont. 24, which skirts the eastern side of the lake. There are 15 campgrounds scattered along the lake margin. The camping varies from rugged to semicivilized. Only two campgrounds—the West End Campground and Downstream Campground—have flush toilets and showers; both are located near the dam. Contact the Corps of Engineers (© 406/526-3411) for information.

The **Fort Peck Indian Reservation** is home to the Assinniboine and the Sioux. The Sioux, who had been on the reservation by themselves, were joined by the Assinniboine nation after smallpox killed more than half of the tribe farther west along the Missouri River and again threatened the tribe after it resettled near Fort Belknap. The escape from the deadly disease brought them to Fort Peck. Now the reservation is home to many non-Indians, with American Indians possessing less than half of the actual reservation.

This has been an extremely important area for the study of dinosaurs. The world's first Tyrannosaurus rex remains were discovered in 1902, just south of where the lake is in Garfield County. The **Garfield County Museum** (© 406/557-2517 or 406/557-2226) in Jordan has replicas of the T. rex skull there, along with a duckbill dinosaur and triceratops. It is open June to September daily from 1 to 5pm. Jordan is located at the intersection of Mont. 59 and Mont. 200 in the plains south of Fort Peck Lake. From Miles City, drive north on Mont. 59 for 83 miles. From Glendive, take Mont. 200 west 111 miles. From Fort Peck Dam, take Mont. 24 south 59 miles to Mont. 200, then take Mont. 200 west 36 miles.

Where to Stay

The Cottonwood Inn & Suites   This motel and convention center is far and away the nicest place in Glasgow: modern and clean, if a little small in the lobby. The rooms are conventional motel rooms, with queen- or king-size beds and, for the most part, refrigerators. The restaurant, the **Willows,** is the most popular one in town. It specializes in homemade soups, bread, and pies, all made from scratch. The motel has complimentary wireless Internet access and valet and room service, unusual out here in Hi-Line Country. There's also an adjacent RV park under the same ownership; RV sites are $27 to $30 nightly in summer and lower in winter.

U.S. 2 E. (P.O. Box 1240), Glasgow, MT 59230. ℂ **800/321-8213** or 406/228-8213. Fax 406/228-8248. www.cottonwoodinn.net. 124 units, including 15 suites. $70–$90 double; $80–$110 suite. AE, DISC, MC, V. Pets accepted (free). **Amenities:** Restaurant; lounge/casino; exercise room; indoor Jacuzzi; indoor pool; room service. *In room:* A/C, TV, hair dryer, Wi-Fi (free).

Fort Peck Hotel ⟨Finds⟩   A stone's throw from U.S. 2, this registered historic site is an intimate, old-fashioned hotel. Built in 1939—5 years after the completion of the dam— the establishment harks back to a slower way of life in Montana. There are no televisions or telephones in the rooms, a situation that tends to usher people out into the bar in the lobby for (gasp!) conversation. There is a good restaurant that serves three meals a day and summertime dinner buffets that cater to visitors holding tickets to a play at the Fort Peck Theatre. The rooms are small but serviceable, with high ceilings and spare furnishings reminiscent of the 1930s and 1940s.

Missouri Ave. (P.O. Box 168), Fort Peck, MT 59223. ℂ **800/560-4931** or 406/526-3266. Fax 406/526-3472. 33 units. $54 double with shared bathroom; $69 double with private bathroom; $105 for 2 adjoining rooms. Rates include continental breakfast (except summer weekends). DISC, MC, V. Closed Dec–Apr. **Amenities:** Restaurant; lounge; Wi-Fi (free). *In room:* No phone.

10

Bozeman, South-Central Montana & the Missouri Headwaters

Relatively pristine, south-central Montana is a world-class playground for the outdoor recreation enthusiast. Its biggest draws are the mountains that are a haven for hikers and campers, and the fly-fishing waters of the four major rivers that run through its valleys—the Madison, Jefferson, Gallatin, and Yellowstone.

During the winter, downhill skiing takes over at Bridger Bowl, Big Sky, which boasts the largest vertical drop of any hill in the United States (4,350 ft.), and the relatively new Moonlight Basin resort. The region is also excellent for cross-country skiing—Lone Mountain Ranch and Bohart Ranch are two of the best Nordic skiing facilities in the state.

Booming Bozeman, home of Montana State University, provides the hip, intellectual charm and culture of a college town—good bookstores and restaurants, charming shops, a lively bar scene—as well as cultural events that appeal to both the cosmopolitan and cowboy cultures. The Livingston Rodeo, one of the best in the region, complements Bozeman's Sweet Pea Festival, a celebration of music and the performing arts.

A few years ago, the area around Bozeman bounded by the Bridger, Gallatin, Madison, and Tobacco ranges seemed like an undiscovered bargain for real estate opportunists. Those times have changed; the communities of Bozeman, Livingston, and Belgrade experienced a boom as newcomers moved in, attracted to the easygoing Montana lifestyle and the wide range of outdoor activities. It's also been discovered by a number of Hollywood types, such as Peter Fonda and Glenn Close, who have purchased real estate in the area. Media mogul Ted Turner is another famous part-time resident.

1 A SCENIC DRIVE

The Bozeman–Livingston–Three Forks area is one large intersection. **Interstate 90** runs east to west through this region, and from it, three valley highways extend south or north. The westernmost of these highways, **U.S. 287,** passes through Three Forks, and runs 120 miles south along the Madison Valley to the town of Ennis (a fishing mecca) and West Yellowstone, the western gateway to Yellowstone National Park. From Bozeman, **U.S. 191** parallels U.S. 287 down the Gallatin Valley, past the resort community of Big Sky, to West Yellowstone.

The third highway, **U.S. 89,** runs 57 miles south from Livingston through the Paradise Valley to Gardiner and the north entrance of Yellowstone. Though the area is populated primarily by ranchers and there are few developed attractions, it's a beautiful drive, especially through Yankee Jim Canyon.

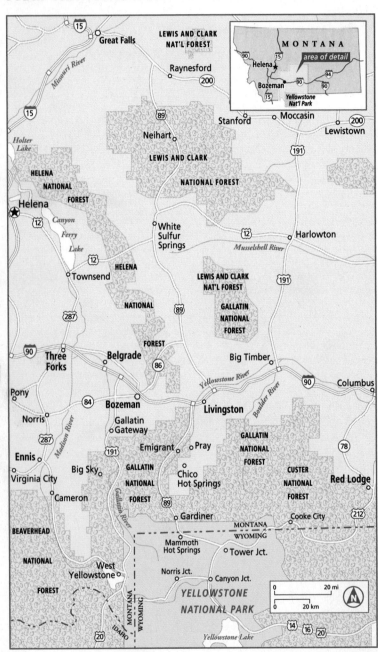

Great Falls

LEWIS AND CLARK
NAT'L FOREST

Raynesford

200

Missouri River

15

MONTANA

Helena

area of detail

Bozeman

Yellowstone
Nat'l Park

90

15

94

90

200

Stanford

Moccasin

Lewistown

89

Neihart

191

LEWIS AND CLARK

Holter
Lake

HELENA

NATIONAL

FOREST

NATIONAL FOREST

Helena

12

Canyon

Ferry

White
Sulfur
Springs

12

Harlowton

Musselshell River

Lake

12

HELENA

Townsend

LEWIS AND CLARK
NAT'L FOREST

NATIONAL

287

89

GALLATIN

NATIONAL

FOREST

191

FOREST

90

Three
Forks

Belgrade

86

Big Timber

Yellowstone River

Boulder River

90

Columbus

Pony

84

Bozeman

Livingston

Norris

Gallatin
Gateway

287

191

Emigrant

Pray

GALLATIN

NATIONAL

78

Ennis

Big Sky

GALLATIN

FOREST

CUSTER

Virginia City

NATIONAL

Chico
Hot Springs

NATIONAL

Red Lodge

Cameron

FOREST

89

FOREST

Gardiner

Cooke City

MONTANA

212

BEAVERHEAD

WYOMING

NATIONAL

West
Yellowstone

Mammoth
Hot Springs

Tower Jct.

FOREST

Norris Jct.

Canyon Jct.

YELLOWSTONE

0   20 mi

0   20 km

N

20

NATIONAL PARK

Yellowstone Lake

14

16

20

Madison River

Gallatin River

MONTANA

IDAHO

WYOMING

to exit 408 at Columbus and heading south on Mont. 78 through Absarokee and Roscoe
for 48 miles.

THE BEARTOOTH SCENIC BYWAY

This loop drive takes you to altitudes of almost 11,000 feet, taking in the sights that led
Charles Kuralt to call this the most scenic road in America.

Begin in Livingston. Drive south on U.S. 89, following the Yellowstone River through
Paradise Valley, 53 miles to Gardiner, and then into Yellowstone National Park. Once
inside the park, you can stop off at Mammoth Hot Springs, a geothermal wonderland
just inside the park's northern boundary. Then, take the road from Mammoth Hot
Springs east to Tower Junction, continuing east to the park's northeast entrance at Silver
Gate to pick up U.S. 212 (this is the Beartooth Byway). From here, the road begins to
wind upward along the Montana and Wyoming border for nearly 40 ear-popping miles
until it reaches the Beartooth Pass (elevation 10,947 ft.). From that spectacular altitude,
you'll see miles and miles of mountains across both Wyoming and Montana. The road
then drops for 24 miles as the byway continues on to Red Lodge. From Red Lodge, drive
north on Mont. 78 down into the high plains before heading back to the mountains of
Bozeman, west on I-90. The entire trip takes between 6 and 8 hours, depending on the
time of day you choose to drive it and the condition of the roads. *Note:* The Beartooth
Byway is especially subject to the whims of Mother Nature; mudslides have closed the
road regularly in recent history. For current information, contact the **Montana Department of Transportation** (© **406/444-6200**; www.mdt.mt.gov).

2 BOZEMAN ★★

82 miles E of Butte; 142 miles W of Billings; 91 miles N of West Yellowstone

A college town and tourism hot spot with a friendly, semibohemian vibe, Bozeman was
first settled in the 1860s as a farming hub. Today, its cowboy edge has been mostly
chipped away, revealing a sophisticated Western chic in the form of a vibrant downtown
strip filled with independent shops and restaurants. The area bustles all year long—whatever the season, the locals are always out and about. The city has also become the unofficial capital of Montana environmental politics, with several nationally important
nonprofits based here.

Bozeman has experienced its greatest growth since 1990, and it shows little sign of
slacking off. In fact, longtime residents worry that the town may be getting a little too
hip. But it's easy to see the city's appeal. The university, Montana State, is a good one,
and the downhill skiing at nearby Bridger Bowl is excellent and free of lift lines. The fact
that Bozeman is less than 100 miles from Yellowstone certainly doesn't hurt, either.

But Bozeman hasn't always been a hotbed of activity. In the 1930s, for instance, local
ordinances prohibited dancing anywhere in town after midnight, and in beer halls at any
time. It was illegal to drink beer standing up, so all the bars had plenty of stools.

ESSENTIALS

GETTING THERE Bozeman's **Gallatin Field Airport** (© **406/388-8321**; www.
gallatinfield.com) serves a wide region in this part of the state. Daily service is available
from **Delta** (© 800/221-1212), **Northwest** (© 800/225-2525), **Alaska/Horizon**

(© 800/547-9308), **Frontier** (© 800/432-1359), **United Express** (© 800/241-6522), and **Allegiant** (© 702/505-8888).

Bus service is available through **Greyhound,** with a terminal at 1205 E. Main St. (© **406/587-3110;** www.greyhound.com). **Rimrock Stages** (© **800/255-7655**) operates intrastate service.

By car, Interstate 90 handles most of the traffic. It is 140 miles along I-90 from Billings to the east and 202 miles from Missoula to the west. For **statewide road reports,** call © **800/226-7623.**

VISITOR INFORMATION The **Bozeman Convention and Visitors Bureau** is located at 2000 Commerce Way (© **800/228-4224** or 406/586-5421; www.bozemancvb.com). Information is also available at the **Downtown Bozeman Visitor Center** (© **406/586-4008;** www.downtownbozeman.com) at 224 E. Main St. The chamber publishes an extensive visitors guide, as well as maps detailing the area's farms and historic hot spots. Call © **406/556-8680,** or check out their website at **www.yellowstonecountry.net.**

GETTING AROUND There are a number of car-rental agencies in Bozeman, including **Budget** (© **800/527-0700**), **Enterprise** (© **800/261-7331**), **Hertz** (© **800/654-3131**), and **National** (© **800/227-7368**). For taxi service, call **All Valley Cab** (© 406/388-9999).

With retro designs inspired by vintage Yellowstone buses, the free **Streamline Bus** (© 406/587-2434; www.streamlinebus.com) connects downtown Bozeman with the Montana State campus and points beyond (namely the airport and Belgrade). Buses run from weekdays 7am to 6:30pm and Saturdays 8:30am to 5:30pm, with later service (8:30pm–3am) Thursday through Saturday for the bar crowd.

SPECIAL EVENTS Held the first full weekend each August, the **Sweet Pea Festival,** at Lindley Park and throughout Bozeman (© **406/586-4003;** www.sweetpeafestival. org), is a music, arts, and sports festival, with a parade, bands from rock to reggae, dance, art, and even a little Shakespeare. Unspooling over 6 days in early October, **Hatch** (© 406/586-2635; www.hatchfest.com) is an audiovisual arts festival that includes film screenings, workshops, filmmaker Q & As, and live music after dark.

GETTING OUTSIDE

Many of the outdoor activities discussed in this section take place in the **Gallatin National Forest.** For additional information, including current road and trail conditions, contact the Bozeman Ranger District, 3710 Fallon St., Ste. C, Bozeman, MT 59718 (© **406/522-2520** or 587-6701; www.fs.fed.us/r1/gallatin).

Organized Adventures

Yellowstone Safari Company ★★ (© **866/586-1155** or 406/586-1155; www. yellowstonesafari.com) specializes in wildlife-biologist-guided trips in Montana, at Yellowstone and Grand Teton national parks, and along the Lewis and Clark Trail. Founded by biologist Ken Sinay—he's been described as "Vesuvian in his enthusiasm"—the company offers guide services for both individuals and groups. Using specially adapted vehicles and boats, their activities include single- and multiday safari-style expeditions to observe wildlife and explore the natural and cultural history of the area. Full-day trips include guides, transportation, binoculars, spotting scopes, food, and beverages. Rates depend on group size and the kind of tour, with full-day rates varying from $650 for one or two people to about $160 per person for seven people. A half-day safari is $99 per person. Advance reservations are required, the earlier the better.

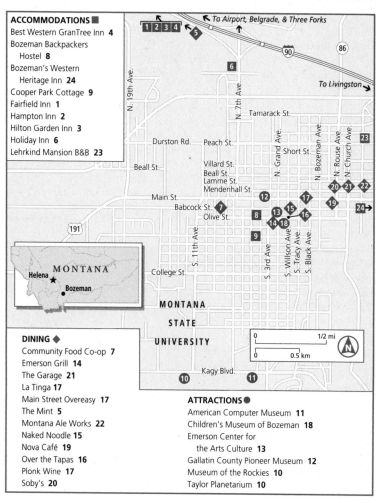

ACCOMMODATIONS ■
Best Western GranTree Inn **4**
Bozeman Backpackers
  Hostel **8**
Bozeman's Western
  Heritage Inn **24**
Cooper Park Cottage **9**
Fairfield Inn **1**
Hampton Inn **2**
Hilton Garden Inn **3**
Holiday Inn **6**
Lehrkind Mansion B&B **23**

DINING ◆
Community Food Co-op **7**
Emerson Grill **14**
The Garage **21**
La Tinga **17**
Main Street Overeasy **17**
The Mint **5**
Montana Ale Works **22**
Naked Noodle **15**
Nova Café **19**
Over the Tapas **16**
Plonk Wine **17**
Soby's **20**

ATTRACTIONS ●
American Computer Museum **11**
Children's Museum of Bozeman **18**
Emerson Center for
  the Arts Culture **13**
Gallatin County Pioneer Museum **12**
Museum of the Rockies **10**
Taylor Planetarium **10**

Founded by Susan Eckert in 1982 and the first of its kind, **AdventureWomen,** 300 Running Horse Trail, Bozeman (© **800/804-8686** or 406/587-3883; www.adventure women.com), offers customized trips to just about anywhere in the world for active and adventurous women ages 30 and older. In Montana, the company guides hiking trips as well as skiing and guest-ranch trips. Rates for the weeklong outings start at $2,495 per woman.

In the guiding business since 1985, **Off the Beaten Path,** 7 E. Beall St., Bozeman (© **800/445-2995;** www.offthebeatenpath.com), is another top-notch local guiding outfit. The company offers about a dozen trips throughout Wyoming and Montana each year, with an emphasis on Yellowstone and Grand Teton, with expeditions that run the gamut from family outings to wolf-watching. The trips range from 4 to 10 days in length, and prices typically run between $300 and $500 per day.

Biking

There are plenty of biking opportunities here, mostly off-pavement. Some of the best mountain biking is in the Gallatin National Forest—check with the Bozeman Ranger District office (see "Getting Outside," above) for tips on where to go.

Cross-Country Skiing

If you want to explore on your own, many drainages provide excellent skiing around Bozeman. Some local favorites are the 10-mile, moderately difficult **Bozeman Creek to Mystic Lake Trail** that gains 1,300 feet of elevation over its course (go south of S. 3rd St. for 4 miles to Nash Rd., then east on Nash Rd. for a mile to Bozeman Creek Rd., then 1 mile south to the parking area), and the **Hyalite Reservoir Ski Loop**, a 4-mile, relatively flat track around the Hyalite Reservoir, also rated moderately difficult (see the "Hiking" section, below). The road may not be plowed or maintained in winter. Two ski mountaineering routes for the adventurous are the 14-mile **Hyalite Ski Loop** and the 5½-mile **New World Gulch to Mystic Lake Trail.** Check with the Bozeman Ranger District office (see "Getting Outside," above) for directions.

   Bohart Ranch, 16621 Bridger Canyon Rd., Bozeman, MT 59715 (ⓒ **406/586-9070;** www.bohartranchxcski.com), next to the Bridger Bowl downhill area, offers 16 miles of groomed and tracked trails for all levels of skiers. There are a biathlon range, a ski school, and ski rentals. Located in Bridger Canyon, 17 miles northeast of Bozeman on U.S. 86, it's open in winter daily from 9am to 4pm, and summer daily from dawn to dusk. Cost is $15 for adults, $8 for children 7 to 12, and free for seniors and kids 6 and under.

Downhill Skiing

The nonprofit **Bridger Bowl** is just 16 miles north of town, on Mont. 86 (15795 Bridger Canyon Rd., Bozeman, MT 59715; ⓒ **800/223-9609** or 406/587-2111; www.bridger bowl.com). Although not as steep as Teton Village in Jackson Hole, Bridger Bowl is plenty steep for most of us, and a great hill for good skiers. There is a lot of advanced and extreme terrain (50%), tempered by 50% beginner and intermediate terrain. Full-day lift tickets cost $45 adults, $37 seniors 65 to 71, $16 children 7 to 12, and free for those 6 and under or 72 and over; half-day rates are available. The fixed-grip quad, two triple, and five double chairs can haul people up the hill at the rate of 7,600 an hour. With almost 30 feet of snowfall annually, Bridger sees a lot of powder days. It's usually open from the second Friday in December to early April, daily from 9am to 4pm. There is limited lodging on the mountain; a free shuttle runs from Bozeman. And there are seldom any lift lines. For more downhill skiing in the Bozeman area, see Big Sky and Moonlight Basin in the Gallatin Valley section, later in this chapter.

Fishing

The **River's Edge,** 2012 N. 7th Ave. (ⓒ **406/586-5373;** www.theriversedge.com), is a highly professional fly-fishing specialty shop "in the heart of Montana's blue-ribbon trout streams." They offer guided fishing trips year-round—including float fishing and walking or wading trips, plus equipment rental and shuttle service. A full-line Orvis shop, **Montana Troutfitters,** 1716 W. Main St. (ⓒ **800/646-7847** or 406/587-4707; www. troutfitters.com), offers guided float, walk and wade, and tube trips to rivers, lakes, and streams; plus 2- and 4-day fly-fishing schools. The Troutfitters are especially good at teaching youngsters the basics of the sport. The **Bozeman Angler,** 23 E. Main St. (C 800/886-9111 or 406/587-9111; www.bozemanangler.com), provides guided trips in the Madison, Gallatin, Yellowstone, Jefferson, and Missouri rivers plus numerous creeks, reservoirs, and lakes. Anglers can choose float trips in hard-sided drift boats, walk and wade, or backcountry fishing trips. From all three, full-day guided trips typically run $400 to $500 for two people, a price that includes lunch.

Golf

Bridger Creek Golf Course, 2710 McIlhattan Rd. (C **406/586-2333;** www.bridger creek.com), offers a scenic and challenging 18-hole layout, 6,400 yards from the back tees. It costs $33 for 18 holes on the weekend, $31 during the week. Carts are $28 for two people. **Cottonwood Hills Golf Course,** 8955 River Rd. (C **408/587-1118;** www. cottonwoodhills.com), has an 18-hole course and a par-3 executive 9-hole course. Greens fees run $24 to $40 at the former ($28 for carts) and $10 to $14 at the latter ($14 carts).

Hiking

There's a beautiful and popular hiking area near Bozeman, known as the **Hyalite drainage,** in the Gallatin National Forest (see "Getting Outside," above, for contact information). The area includes Hyalite Canyon and reservoir, Palisades Falls Trail, and many trail heads for access to the national forest. A lot of the trails here are steep and difficult, though. An excellent introductory hike to get the lay of the land is the .5-mile **Palisades Falls National Recreation Trail.** From Bozeman, take 19th Avenue south for 7½ miles to the Hyalite Canyon Road, and follow the road to the reservoir. Continue east around the reservoir for 2 miles to the East Fork Road, and proceed to the Palisades Falls parking area. The trail gains 540 feet in a little more than .5 mile, which makes it very steep and gives it a rating of "most difficult" for a recreational trail.

Hyalite Reservoir itself contains cutthroat and grayling, and there are two campsites here. The **Grotto Falls Trail** is a steep 1.25-mile graveled trail to Grotto Falls located 13 miles up the West Fork Road in Hyalite Canyon. For a longer hike, go the 7.25 miles up the **Hyalite Peak Trail** to the peak. There is a 3,300-foot elevation gain on this hike.

The Gallatin Valley Land Trust's **"Main Street to the Mountains"** project has connected downtown Bozeman with a 50-mile network that connects with the surrounding communities and mountain ranges. For more information, visit **www.gvlt.org/trails. html**.

If you're interested in combining a little **bird-watching** with your hiking, try the Kirk Hill nature preserve in the foothills transition zone, where you might spot a colorful western tanager or a great gray owl. Take South 19th Street south for 5 miles until the road curves west. The entrance to the preserve is on the left.

White-Water Rafting

Montana Whitewater (C **800/799-4465** or 406/763-4465; www.montanawhitewater. com) can get you sprayed in the face by the waters of both the Yellowstone and the Gallatin rivers. You paddle the raft as you fly through the nearly continuous rapids of the Gardiner section of the upper Yellowstone or through the dauntingly named rapids of Snake Bite and Mother Eater on the Gallatin. In addition to the white-water trips, the company offers more sedate scenic trips and "saddle and paddle" outings in which the morning is spent riding and the afternoon rafting. Half-day trips on the Gallatin cost $51 adults, $41 ages 12 and under; on the Yellowstone it's $39 and $29, respectively. Full-day Gallatin trips cost $84 adults and $68 ages 12 and under, and on the Yellowstone $75 and $55, respectively. "Paddle and saddle" jaunts that mix rafting and horseback riding range from $92 to $140 per adult per day, and $82 to $130 for kids 12 and under. **Wild West Whitewater Rafting** (© 800/862-0557; www.wildwestrafting.com) offers similar trips on Yellowstone River, including half- and full-day rafting tours ($38–$75 adults; $28–$55 kids 6–12).

WHERE TO FIND EQUIPMENT & SUPPLIES

It's easy to find whatever outdoor recreation equipment you need for your particular adventure. Among the rental outlets I recommend are **Panda Sports Rentals,** 621 Bridger Dr. (© 406/587-6280), which rents skis and snowboards; **Chalet Sports,** 108 W. Main St. (© 406/587-4595), a full-line sporting goods store that sells skis as well as rents bikes, in-line skates, skis, and snowboards; and **Northern Lights Trading Co.,** 1716 W. Babcock (© 866/586-2225), a high-end store selling gear for everything from kayaking to Telemark skiing, and renting canoes, rafts, and kayaks. These stores are also great sources for advice.

SEEING THE SIGHTS

American Computer Museum ★
Now located near the MSU campus, this unique museum traces the history of computing technologies from the abacus to the Apple. In an hour or so, you can catch up on more than 4,000 years of computing history and gain a newfound respect for the speed of innovation during the past few decades. Though you won't find any T. rexes here, you can view computing's dinosaurs: slide rules and room-size computers with a mere fraction of the power of today's superpowered miniatures.

2023 Stadium Dr., Unit 1-A. © 406/582-1288. www.compustory.com. $5 adults, $4 students and seniors 65 and over, free for children 5 and under. June–Aug daily 10am–4pm (Thurs until 8pm); Sept–May Tues–Sun noon–4pm. Closed major holidays.

Children's Museum of Bozeman (Kids)
This converted warehouse space is now the only museum of its kind in the Gallatin Valley. Exhibits include arts-and-crafts tables, a "bubble wall" that allows kids to make a barrier from suds, a 110-gallon aquarium with native Montana fish, and other displays designed to educate and entertain young minds.

202 S. Willson Ave. © 406/522-9087. www.cmbozeman.org. $5 per person. Mon–Sat 10am–5pm (Fri until 8pm). Closed Sun and major holidays.

The Emerson Center for the Arts & Culture ★
Once a home for schoolchildren, this historic building (ca. 1918) was converted in 1993 into an arts and cultural center. The nonprofit organization hosts a variety of professional and contemporary art exhibits, offers a fine-arts education program, and provides retail and studio space for more than 80 artists in converted schoolrooms. The Emerson also hosts free community events such as Lunch on the Lawn in summer, with live music and food vendors every Wednesday afternoon; special holiday activities in December; and other concerts, events, and activities year-round. There is also a restaurant (the **Emerson Grill;** see "Where to Dine," below), and a theater and ballroom for a variety of programs.

111 S. Grand Ave. © 406/587-9797. www.theemerson.org. Free admission. Building daily 8am–10pm; galleries Tues–Sat 11am–5pm.

Gallatin County Pioneer Museum (Kids)
Located in the old county jail, which was in use until 1982, this museum features county history, focusing in part on law enforcement (as you might expect), the area's military history, and local daily life of the past. There's a display and memorabilia from actor Gary Cooper, known as Frank in the days

he grew up in Bozeman and Helena, and the lowdown on town founder John Bozeman. The museum also contains a cell from its days as the jail. There's also a collection of 11,000 historical photos and a research library devoted to Lewis and Clark. Expect to spend about an hour here if you want to dig deep.

317 W. Main St. (© **406/522-8122.** www.pioneermuseum.org. $5 adults, free for children 12 and under. Memorial Day to Labor Day Mon–Sat 10am–5pm; rest of year Tues–Sat 11am–4pm.

Museum of the Rockies ★★ This first-class museum explains the history, geology, wildlife, and people of the Rocky Mountains all the way back to the Big Bang. The centerpiece of the museum is the world-class Siebel Dinosaur Complex, which is one of the premier paleontology attractions in the world. The **Hall of Horns and Teeth** is centered on a life-size torosaurus model, next to the actual 9-foot skull (the biggest land-animal noggin ever unearthed) that served as a blueprint; other displays offer an in-depth look into dinosaur biology, ecology, and theoretical behavior. The **Hallway of Growth and Behavior** provides a look beyond the bones, and the **Mesozoic Media Center** allows visitors to get a closer look at dig sites via interactive touch screens. The **Hall of Giants** is populated with lifelike dinosaur models, including a diorama of velociraptor-like deinonychs taking down a much larger sauropod. Visitors can also watch fossil preparers as they clean recently discovered bones.

But that's not all: In the **Martin Discovery Room,** young children can learn through play. The **Taylor Planetarium** is a state-of-the-art, 40-foot domed multimedia theater, with a computer graphics simulator that provides the illusion of flying through space in three dimensions. Outside, the **Living History Farm** is an early-20th-century homestead with costumed interpreters, as well as the interactive **Lewis & Clark Challenge Course.** There's also a restaurant and gift shop on-site.

600 W. Kagy Blvd. (on the Montana State University campus). (© **406/994-3466.** www.museum oftherockies.org. Museum $10 adults, $9 seniors, $7 children 5–18, free for children 4 and under. Planetarium shows included in admission. Mid-June to early Sept daily 8am–8pm; mid-Sept to early June Mon–Sat 9am–5pm, Sun 12:30–5pm. Living History Farm mid-June to early Sept daily 9:30am–5pm. Closed Thanksgiving, Christmas, and New Year's Day.

SHOPPING

Main Street offers an Old West feel and New West selection, starting at about 7th Avenue and running out to I-90. Among our favorite stops here are **Vargo's Jazz City and Books,** 6 W. Main St. (© **406/587-5383**), which sells an eclectic mass of new, used, and out-of-print books, CDs, and LPs (or the elusive, vanishing vinyl); **Schnee's Powder Horn Outfitters,** 35 E. Main St. (© **406/587-7373**), which sells high-end Western wear and all sorts of outdoor gear; the **Montana Gift Corral,** 237 E. Main St. (© **406/585-8625**), which offers a wide selection of made-in-Montana gifts, in case you need a moose clock to take home; **Thomas Nygard Gallery,** 135 E. Main St. (© **406/586-3636**), which specializes in pre-1950 artwork from the Northern Plains; the **Country Bookshelf,** 28 W. Main St. (© **406/587-0166**), a terrific bookstore; and **Barkenhowell's,** 777 E. Main St. (© **406/586-6160**), a chic dog boutique. The **Gallatin Valley Mall,** 2825 W. Main St. (© **406/586-4565**), has department and specialty stores, art galleries, and a food court.

WHERE TO STAY

Bozeman has a full complement of chain motels, most just off I-90. In addition to the places listed below, you can stay at the **Best Western GranTree Inn,** 1325 N. 7th Ave., Bozeman, MT 59715 (© **800/624-5865** or 406/587-5261); the **Fairfield Inn,** 828

Wheat Dr., Bozeman, MT 59715 (✆ **406/587-2222**); and the **Hampton Inn,** 75 Baxter Lane, Bozeman, MT 59715 (✆ **406/522-8000**). The above are all at I-90 exit 306, and have rates for two in the $80-to-$150 range. Newer is the **Hilton Garden Inn,** 2023 Commerce Way (✆ **877/782-9444** or 406/582-9900), south of I-90, exit 305, with double rates of $99 to $179. The lodge-inspired accommodations feature thoughtful amenities such as in-room exercise kits and a lobby pantry. I also like **Bozeman's Western Heritage Inn,** within walking distance of downtown, 1200 E. Main St. (✆ **800/877-1094** or 406/586-8534), with double rates of $60 to $120. Another option is the cozy 1920s **Cooper Park Cottage,** 401 S. 5th Ave. (✆ **406/586-2012**), which rents for $100 to $125 double.

Bozeman Backpackers Hostel (Value) Located in a funky Victorian that Hollywood legend Gary Cooper once called home, these bunkhouse accommodations are in a quiet residential neighborhood near downtown. The bunkrooms are coed, allowing couples to stay together, and there are also two private rooms available. The downstairs public area has a homey feel; to encourage conversation, there is no Wi-Fi. A full kitchen and a telephone are available to guests. The hostel also has a great library/book exchange and rents bicycles for $10 a day.

405 W. Olive St., Bozeman, MT 59715. ✆ **406/586-4659.** www.bozemanbackpackershostel.com. 16 bunks, 2 private rooms. $20 per person dorm bed; $42 private room. No credit cards. *In room:* No phone.

Holiday Inn The largest hotel in town, the Holiday Inn opened in 1969 when there was virtually nothing else in the immediate vicinity. It's now surrounded by other chain motels and hotels, but it remains the best. The big, open lobby has a sort of a lodge feel, with a fireplace, contemporary artwork, and two complimentary high-speed Internet terminals in a small business center, and there's a big TV in the adjacent bar that's usually surrounded by a crowd watching a ballgame. The rooms are well kept and nicely furnished, and a few of them have terrific mountain views.

5 Baxter Lane, Bozeman, MT 59715. ✆ **800/366-5101** or 406/587-4561. Fax 406/587-4413. www.hi bozeman.com. 179 units, including 1 suite. $99–$179 double; $129–$229 suite. Lower rates fall and winter. AE, DC, DISC, MC, V. From I-90, take exit 306. **Amenities:** Restaurant; lounge/casino; exercise room; high-speed Internet (free); indoor Jacuzzi; indoor pool. *In room:* A/C, TV w/pay movies, hair dryer, Wi-Fi (free).

Lehrkind Mansion Bed & Breakfast ★★★ German-born brewer Julius Lehrkind shunned the tonier neighborhoods on Bozeman's south side and built a stately Queen Anne mansion right next door to his brick brewery in 1897. Former national park rangers Jon Gerster, Jr., and Chris Nixon turned "the house that beer built" into a bed-and-breakfast 99 years later, with the original woodwork, plumbing, and floor plan intact. The ornate abode still sticks out in the quasi-industrial but up-and-coming Historic Bozeman Brewery District. Surrounded by breweries that are slated to become lofts and other vestiges of the neighborhood's beery past, the Lehrkind Mansion looks like something out of a fairy tale inside and out. Gerster and Nixon have done a remarkable job capturing the house in 1890s amber: Everything, from the rare 1897 Regina music box in the parlor to the many original fixtures in the bathrooms to the amazingly preserved original carpet in the Audubon Suite, is from Lehrkind's day. In 2004, Gerster and Nixon bought, moved, and restored a Victorian farmhouse that had been abandoned outside of town as a five-bedroom counterpart to the four-bedroom mansion.

719 N. Wallace Ave., Bozeman, MT 59715. ✆ **800/992-6932** or 406/585-6932. www.bozemanbedand breakfast.com. 9 units. $139–$169 double; $189 suite. Lower rates in winter. Rates include full breakfast. AE, DISC, MC, V. **Amenities:** Outdoor Jacuzzi. *In room:* Hair dryer, no phone, Wi-Fi (free).

Camping

The **Bozeman KOA** (© 406/587-3030) is the area's largest campground, with sites for 100 RVs and 50 tents. It is adjacent to a natural hot-springs pool (which charges a separate fee), laundry, store, and a variety of other amenities. It is located 7 miles south of Belgrade on U.S. 191, with sites from $27 to $45 and basic cabins for $63 to $73 double. There are also numerous places to camp in the **Gallatin National Forest;** contact the Bozeman Ranger District, 3710 Fallon St., Ste. C, Bozeman, MT 59718 (© **406/522-2520;** www.fs.fed.us/r1/gallatin), for details.

WHERE TO DINE

Beyond the restaurants that follow, I'm a firm believer in the restorative powers of the breakfast burritos at **Soby's,** in the Bozeman Hotel at 321 E. Main St. (© **406/587-8857),** a favorite student haunt for breakfast and lunch. For a burger and a beer on an outdoor deck, you can't beat the **Garage,** 451 E. Main St. (© **406/585-8558).** In the winter, the place compensates for the cold weather with the **Soup Shack,** serving seven hot soups and an array of toppings, from a space that houses the ice-cream-oriented **Scoop Shack** in summer. **La Tinga,** 12 E. Main St. (no phone), serves up authentic Mexican burritos, tacos, and tostadas using homemade tortillas and salsa. The **Community Food Co-op,** 909 W. Main St. (© **406/587-4039),** is a locally beloved market, with a great deli, salad bar, and seating area upstairs.

The Emerson Grill ★★ ITALIAN   Intimate and artsy, this dinky eatery in the Emerson Center for Arts and Culture has emerged as a local favorite, and it's an equally good bet for a romantic dinner. The kitchen uses locally produced organic ingredients more often than not, creating terrific Italian fare: The menu includes flatbread *pizze,* spaghetti and meatballs, and risotto as well as grilled bison and Idaho trout. Only beer and wine are available, but the selection is excellent. Next door is the Grill's sister wine bar, the **Emerson Grill North.**

207 W. Olive St., in the Emerson Center for Arts and Culture. © **406/586-5247.** www.emersongrill.com. Reservations recommended. Main courses $15–$33. AE, MC, V. Mon–Wed 5–9pm; Thurs–Sat 5–10pm. Emerson Grill North: Thurs–Sat 5–9pm.

Main Street Overeasy AMERICAN   Chef Erik Carr opened this restaurant in 1998, and it has been a local favorite ever since, winning "Bozeman's Best Breakfast" from the weekly *Tributary* every year since 2000. The place packs 'em in for breakfast with such dishes as biscuits and gravy, chicken-fried steak, and cinnamon bread pudding with warm vanilla sauce. Or have the "Bobcat Benedict," which is two fried eggs atop chicken-fried steak and biscuits and gravy. Lunches consist of gourmet sandwiches and salads.

9 E. Main St. © **406/587-3205.** Breakfast $5–$10; lunch $6–$10. AE, DISC, MC, V. Tues–Sun 7am–2pm. Closed Mon.

The Mint ★★ Finds AMERICAN   Few places meld upscale and cowboy as well as the historic Mint in downtown Belgrade, about 8 miles west of Bozeman. A local landmark since 1904, the interior is lined with black-and-white photos of cowboys, and a stuffed Hereford head guards the entrance, but the blonde wood and sleek details make it a tad more formal than your typical Montana roadhouse. The superlative specialties will rouse the carnivore in most anybody: buffalo tenderloin, a 14-ounce New York strip, and half a cast-iron-roasted chicken. There are also daily specials, including a pasta dish and a seafood plate, and a great bar menu running the gastronomic gamut from burgers to crab cakes. The wine list is one of the best within a 100-mile radius.

27 E. Main St., Belgrade. ⓒ **406/388-1100**. www.themintmt.com. Reservations recommended. Dinner $9–$47. AE, DISC, MC, V. Tues–Sun 4–10pm. Bar open later.

Montana Ale Works ★ AMERICAN   A casual, social place to see and be seen, Montana Ale Works is a relatively new standby, a great place to unwind over hearty portions and cold libations or catch a ballgame. I like the Montana Meatloaf, a spicy slab of buffalo, beef, and pork, but other favorites include fish tacos, barbecued ribs, and plenty of steaks. After a long period of dormancy, the former railroad warehouse became a restaurant in 2000. The place hangs on to a bit of its past in the form of industrial chic decor, with brick walls and an exposed ceiling framing a vast room with plenty of nooks and crannies to find a seat. There are also pool tables, but no cigarette smoke. In the center of it all is a full bar with plenty of seating and, of course, plenty of ale: Of the 40 beers on tap, about half are brewed in Montana.

611 E. Main St. ⓒ **406/587-7700**. www.montanaaleworks.com. Reservations accepted. Main courses $8–$30. AE, DISC, MC, V. Mon–Thurs 4–10pm; Fri–Sun 4–11pm. Bar open later.

Naked Noodle ⟨Value⟩ NOODLES   If you like to sample from several cuisines, or everybody in your group wants something different, this is the perfect choice. At this casual eatery in a brick- and funky art-clad space just off Main Street, you can get noodles of all kinds, from soba noodles in Thai green chile curry to Italian fettuccine Alfredo to good old American mac and cheese, with four varieties of the latter. The signature dish is the Gaucho: cavatappi pasta topped with chipotle cream sauce, black beans, and tortilla chips. Also on the menu are a number of filling salads with the same international variety, as well as gluten-free and kids' options.

27 S. Willson Ave. ⓒ **406/522-0800**. www.nakednoodle.com. Most items $6–$10. AE, MC, V. Mon–Sat 11am–9pm; Sun 11–8pm.

Nova Cafe ★ AMERICAN   A colorful diner with blue tabletops, vintage concert posters, and a health-oriented menu, the Nova is a great breakfast spot. The menu includes dozens of scrambles, omelets, Benedict variations (like Eggs Argyle with salmon standing in for the bacon), and other egg dishes as well as turkey hash, pancakes, sausages du jour, and all-you-can-eat waffles (for $8.50 on Wed mornings only). Breakfast is served whenever the place is open; lunchtime also brings a selection of creative salads and sandwiches. There's a kids' menu, and espresso and smoothies are available.

312 E. Main St. ⓒ **406/587-3973**. www.thenovacafe.com. Reservations not accepted. Main courses $5–$13 breakfast and lunch. AE, DISC, MC, V. Daily 7am–2pm.

Over the Tapas ★ TAPAS/MEDITERRANEAN   A new favorite since opening in early 2007, the basic room of black tables and booths is one of the few midprice options downtown, and the long lines on weekend nights reflect that. The small plates are excellent, ranging from meatless cheese and olive samplers to grilled lamb chops. Most of the items are Spanish standards, like paella and spinach croquettes. Beer and wine (mostly Spanish and South American) are available, but liquor is not.

19 S. Willson Ave. ⓒ **406/556-8282**. www.bozemantapas.com. Reservations not accepted. Most tapas $3–$10 lunch and dinner. AE, DISC, MC, V. Mon–Sat 11am–10pm.

Plonk Wine ★★★ CONTEMPORARY/WINE BAR   A dimly lit hot spot that feels more San Francisco than Bozeman, Plonk (Euro-slang for ordinary table wine) took over the space that housed the Stockman's Bar from 1921 to 1971 (and a Hallmark shop until 2003) and molded it into an eatery that oozes with a hip, urban atmosphere. The menus

selection of wine, cheese, and decadent desserts. The dinner menu always features ravioli (its stuffing changes); you might also find bison tamales, Thai green curry with black tiger shrimp, or braised rabbit. Across from the well-stocked shelves of vino, there is a full bar, above which hangs a restored brand-laden mural that dates from Plonk's Stockman's Bar era. There is a full bar with house-infused liquors; DJs entertain the crowd on Friday nights.

29 E. Main St. (C) **406/587-2170.** www.plonkwine.com. Reservations not accepted. Lunch $8–$10; dinner $15–$25. AE, DISC, MC, V. Daily 11:30am–10:30pm. Bar open later (usually until 2am).

BOZEMAN AFTER DARK

Bozeman is a college town, so there are lots of places to get a casual drink accompanied by loud music. Popular watering holes include the Irish-themed **Pub 317,** 321 E. Main St. ((C) **406/582-8898**), the vintage **Crystal Bar,** 123 E. Main St. ((C) **406/587-2888**), and the **Zebra,** 321 E. Main St. in the old Bozeman Hotel ((C) **406/585-8851**), ground zero for the local live music scene. If it's the college bars you are after, the somewhat grungy **"Barmuda Triangle"** consists of the **Haufbrauhaus,** the **Molly Brown,** and the **Scoop,** conveniently positioned within stumbling distance of one another near the intersection of 8th Avenue and Main Street. Another fun option (with a limit of 48 oz. per customer per day) is the **Bozeman Brewing Company's** bustling taproom, 504 N. Broadway ((C) **406/585-9142;** www.bozemanbrewing.com), It's open Monday through Saturday from 4 to 8pm, pouring the brewery's popular Bozone-brand beers.

Bozeman is also home to coffee shops galore, including the **Leaf and Bean,** 35 W. Main St. ((C) **406/587-1580**), **HomePage Internet Cafe,** 242 E. Main St. ((C) **406/582-9388**), **Wild Joe's Coffee,** 18 W. Main St. ((C) **406/586-1212**), and, near the MSU campus, **Daily Coffee Bar & Bakery,** 1013 W. College St. ((C) **406/585-8612**). **Lindley Perk** ((C) **406/582-9800**) is a coffee shop in the beloved new library at 626 E. Main St.

Montana Shakespeare in the Parks ((C) **406/994-3901;** www.montana.edu/shakespeare) is a professional touring company that was formed in 1973. Based in Bozeman, the troupe of 10 to 12 actors produces more than 60 performances during the summer at communities throughout Montana, Wyoming, and Idaho—often in a different town each day. Some summer weekends find them at their Bozeman stage—located on the MSU campus on 11th Avenue near the corner of Grant Street—for "Shakespeare Under the Stars." Parking is available just north of the MSU field house. Call for the schedule. Performances are always free.

For edgy and experimental fare, one-act-play festivals, and the stylings of a local comedy troupe, head to the **Equinox Theatre,** 2304 N. 7th Ave. ((C) **406/587-0737;** www.equinoxtheatre.com).

3 THE MADISON RIVER VALLEY: THREE FORKS & ENNIS ★★

Ennis: 54 miles SW of Bozeman; 71 miles N of West Yellowstone

The Madison Valley is an almost mythical place surrounded by spectacular mountain scenery where anglers from all over gather to fish. The main attraction is the Madison River, which flows through the valley at the base of the Madison Range, a stretch of peaks that runs toward Yellowstone Park.

Besides the phenomenal fishing, the Madison Valley has tourist-worthy historical sites. The **Missouri Headwaters State Park** is at the confluence of the Jefferson, Madison, and Gallatin rivers, where Lewis and Clark paused to take shelter; **Lewis and Clark Caverns State Park,** with its spectacular underground peaks, is just up the road; and **Madison Buffalo Jump State Park** is nearby.

ESSENTIALS

GETTING THERE The Bozeman airport, **Gallatin Field** (discussed earlier in this chapter), is the closest airport to the valley.

Greyhound stops at the Sinclair station in Three Forks at 2 Main St.

Three Forks is located on I-90, 30 miles from Bozeman, 170 miles from Billings, and 173 miles from Missoula. Three Forks is 66 miles from the capital in Helena. Ennis is 45 miles south of Three Forks on U.S. 287.

VISITOR INFORMATION Contact the **Three Forks Chamber of Commerce,** P.O. Box 1103, Three Forks, MT 59752 (© **406/285-4753;** www.threeforksmontana.com), or the **Ennis Chamber of Commerce,** P.O. Box 291, Ennis, MT 59729 (© **406/682-4388;** www.ennischamber.com). **Yellowstone Country** (© **406/556-8680;** www.yellowstonecountry.net) is the Travel Montana tourism office for the region.

GETTING AROUND If you're flying into Bozeman, pick up a car at the airport (see "Getting Around," in section 2, for more information). For **statewide road reports,** call © **800/226-7623** or 511 on your mobile phone.

GETTING OUTSIDE

There is plenty of fishing water along the road from Three Forks to Quake and Hebgen lakes along U.S. 287. The first fishing access is **Cobblestone,** just a few miles south of Three Forks on the right side of U.S. 287. If you plan to base yourself in Ennis, the **Valley Garden, Ennis Bridge, Burnt Tree,** and **Varney Bridge** fishing accesses are within minutes of town along U.S. 287. Between Ennis and Quake Lake, the accesses begin popping up frequently. **McAtee Bridge, Wolf Creek, West Fork,** and **Reynolds Pass** are all accessible from the roadside. Hebgen Lake, just south of the dam, and Quake Lake are also great fishing spots.

On Ennis's Main Street, it seems that every second door houses a fly-fishing outfitter. The **Madison River Fishing Company,** 109 Main St. (© **800/227-7127** or 406/682-4293; www.mrfc.com), has a good stock of fishing supplies and a guide service. Guided trips, for one or two people, cost $325 for a half-day and $425 for a full day; full-day trips include lunch. They also offer a free brochure that contains a map of fishing spots and various facilities along the way. Other guide services, with similar rates, include **Clark's Guide Service** (© **406/682-7474**); **Howard Outfitters** (© **406/682-4834**); and the **Tackle Shop Outfitters,** 127 Main St. (© **800/808-2832** or 406/682-4263; www.thetackleshop.com).

SEEING THE SIGHTS

Lewis & Clark Caverns State Park ★ These lovely limestone caverns are named for the famous explorers, but there is no evidence that their party ever saw or visited them. Discovered in the late 19th century, these caverns are a succession of vaulted chambers and passageways, thickly decorated with stalactites and stalagmites, as well as other underground formations such as massive, gleaming organ pipes; silky, delicate soda straws; intricate filigrees; and weirdly hung draperies. Plan at least 2 hours for the 2-mile guided tour through the caverns; and aboveground there are hiking trails, several picnic areas, and a large campground (see "Camping," below). A Christmas candlelight tour is held on 2 weekends in December. Reservations should be made in early December for one of the 200 or so spots available. There is a campground as well as three cabins on the premises with electric heat; rates are $40 in summer.

Located 19 miles west of Three Forks (midway btw. Butte and Bozeman) on Mont. 2. *C* **406/287-3541.** www.fwp.mt.gov. Entrance fee $5 per car. Cave tours $10 adults, $5 children 6–11; no children 5 and under allowed. Park and campground open daily year-round. Guided cave tours May to mid-June daily 9am–4:30pm; mid-June to mid-Aug daily 9am–6:30pm; mid-Aug to Sept daily 9am–4:30pm. Tours leave as required by demand. Closed Oct–Apr (except for Christmas event).

Madison Buffalo Jump State Park   This is one of a few buffalo jumps, or *pishkun*, that have been excavated. Prior to the advent of the horse, the Northern Shoshone and the Bannock drove the bison off this steep cliff to their death on the rocks below. Long rows of rocks funneled the animals to the cliff. There is a well-worn trail up to the base of the cliff, making for a short but steep hike.

Located 23 miles west of Bozeman, off I-90 exit 283. *C* **406/994-4042.** www.fwp.mt.gov. Entrance $5 per car. Daily 24 hr. From the Logan exit off I-90, 7 miles south on Buffalo Jump Rd.

Missouri Headwaters State Park ★★   You can easily spend an hour just exploring the interpretive signage at this historic state park. Begin by following the Missouri River out from Three Forks. The headwaters themselves are no great shakes—just another river—but the sunsets from the bank of the river are breathtaking. From the headwaters, drive back toward Three Forks where, on the opposite side of the road, you'll see a parking area with interpretive markers. Allow plenty of time to read about Lewis and Clark and Sacajawea, the young Shoshone guide, as well as early American Indians, trappers, traders, and settlers. Camping and RV sites are available as well as access to hiking, boating, and fishing.

Located 4 miles northeast of Three Forks. *C* **406/994-4042.** www.fwp.mt.gov. Entrance $5 per car. Daily 24 hr. Drive east on C.R. 205, then north on C.R. 286; follow signs.

National Fish Hatchery   The Ennis National Fish Hatchery, constructed in 1931, is probably the only place in America where you can observe two genetic mutants of ordinary rainbow trout: albino and blue. (These fish are not released into the wild trout population.) Some of the trout in the hatchery ponds weigh more than 20 pounds and are more than 5 years old. The hatchery cultivates seven different strains of rainbow trout. You can learn about the operation in the small exhibit area and tour the facility. When some of those huge adults are past their use as brood stock, they too are released into lakes and streams to test fishermen.

180 Fish Hatchery Rd., Ennis. *C* **406/682-4847.** www.fws.gov/ennis. Free admission. Daily 7:30am–5pm. The hatchery is 12 miles southwest of Ennis. Take U.S. 287 south from town to R.R. 249 and go west to Call Rd. Turn left (south), then left (east) on Fish Hatchery Rd. after 1/2 mile.

Norris Hot Springs ★ (Finds)   You'll be hard-pressed to find a more scenic spot for a soak, or a better soaking pool with live music, or a better place to work away the aches and pains induced by outdoor recreation than Norris Hot Springs, about a 45-minute drive west from Bozeman. The year-round hot springs-fed pool, which is lined with wood, sits adjacent to a saloon (serving beer, wine, and light fare) and a geodesic dome that provides musicians with shelter.

Mont. 84, Norris, 16 miles north of Ennis and 34 miles west of Bozeman. © **406/685-3303.** www.norris hotsprings.com. Admission $5. Year-round Wed–Sun, typically 4–9 or 10pm; call or check website for current calendar.

Quake Lake   Just before midnight on August 17, 1959, a massive earthquake measuring 7.5 on the Richter scale jolted Yellowstone and the Madison River canyon, sending large chunks of mountain into the river. A campsite just below the mountain was covered with rubble and 19 people were buried alive. The rubble that collapsed into the river created a dam and the aptly named Quake Lake. The ghostly fingers of trees that died when they were swamped still poke skyward from the lake. The visitor center on the north side of the highway offers exhibits, a video every half-hour, and an observation area from which you can see the massive slides. The area around Yellowstone and Quake Lake is still very seismically active, and southwest Montana is second only to California in terms of earthquake frequency. The visitor center has a great deal of information about the area's seismic activity and hypotheses of how it got this way.

Off U.S. 287, 27 miles northwest of West Yellowstone and 43 miles south of Ennis. © **406/682-7620** or 823-6961. Visitor center $3 per car; $1 per person on foot or bike. Memorial Day to mid-Sept daily 8:30am–6pm.

WHERE TO STAY

In addition to the properties discussed below, the **Rainbow Valley Motel,** 1 mile south of Ennis on U.S. 287 (P.O. Box 26), Ennis, MT 59729 (© **800/452-8254** or 406/682-4264; www.rainbowvalley.com), offers large, well-maintained cabin-style rooms, with rates for two people of $80 to $120. There are also a couple of large cabin homes for $175 to $220 a night.

El Western Cabins & Lodges ★   It's a little hard to categorize this place, which has some inexpensive log duplex-style cabins as well as large, expensive two- and three-bedroom lodges, and uniformly well-maintained rooms. The original portion, built in 1948, is done with knotty-pine interiors and built-in wooden cabinets. The newest lodge is the Eagle's Loft, a three-bedroom, three-bathroom, two-story cabin with a vaulted ceiling and rock fireplace, plus a whirlpool tub and washer and dryer. Every unit enjoys spectacular views of the Madison Range, including Fan Mountain and the Spanish Peaks. You can't go wrong here, and the overnight cabins are as affordable as anything in the valley. There's no restaurant or lounge associated with the property, but a new conference center with a large, inviting deck and picture windows serves both business and family groups.

4787 U.S. 287 N., P.O. Box 487, Ennis, MT 59729. © **800/831-2773** or 406/682-4217. Fax 406/682-5207. www.elwestern.com. 29 units. $80–$105 double; $135–$150 creek-side kitchen cabin; $190–$285 deluxe mountainside kitchen cabin; $275–$475 lodge. Lower rates fall–spring. AE, DISC, MC, V. From the town of Ennis, drive south 1 mile on U.S. 287. *In room:* TV, kitchen, hair dryer, Wi-Fi (free, most rooms).

Wade Lake Cabins (Finds   This secluded cabin resort, which consists of five cabins, is located in a picture-perfect forested canyon on Wade Lake. The cabins are fairly primitive, with only a refrigerator, running water, heat, a gas stove, and a gas barbecue grill. A shared modern bathhouse is out back. There aren't any electric outlets to plug in your computer, which I consider a major plus, just power for the fridge and the lights. Bring food to cook because the nearest restaurant is 11 miles back up the road. The area is very beautiful, though—Wade has been designated a Montana Wildlife Viewing Site. A hiking and mountain-biking mecca in summer and a cross-country skiing destination in winter, the area is rich in wildlife, with eagles and osprey nesting on the lake, and moose, elk, bear, and other locals dropping in occasionally. It also helps you remember what real quiet and real darkness are like.

P.O. Box 107, Cameron, MT 59720. © **406/682-7560.** www.wadelake.com. 5 cabins. Summer $75–$100 double; fall–spring $100 double, 3-night minimum. No credit cards. Drive 40 miles south of Ennis to the Wade Lake turnoff, marked by a sign. Turn west on the bumpy, gravel Wade Lake Rd. and follow the signs about 6 miles to Wade Lake. *In room:* Kitchen, no phone.

Camping

Lewis & Clark Caverns State Park (see "Seeing the Sights," above; © **406/287-3541**) has 40 campsites ($13–$15), showers, a dump station, and fishing access on a river, plus hiking trails and interpretive programs. **Missouri Headwaters State Park** (see "Seeing the Sights," above; © **406/994-4042**) has a year-round campground ($12) with 20 sites and basic cabins ($25) scattered along the river, plus numerous hiking trails and plenty of fishing access. Maximum trailer length is 25 feet; there's a boat ramp and dump station. Those wanting RV hookups and the usual commercial campground amenities should head to **Camp Three Forks,** on U.S. 287, 1 mile south of I-90 exit 274 (© **866/523-1773** or 406/285-3611; www.campthreeforks.com), which has a pastoral setting as well as a clean bathhouse, swimming pool, rec room, and playground. It's open May through September, with sites for both tents and RVs at rates of $20 to $36, and basic cabins for $45 to $50.

WHERE TO DINE
Near Three Forks

Wheat Montana Bakery and Deli, 1-90 and U.S. 287 (© **406/285-3614**), is a popular breakfast and lunch spot where Montana-grown wheat is turned into bread, and just the smell of bread baking makes it worth the stop.

Willow Creek Café and Saloon ★ (Finds) AMERICAN   This place is a find, if you can find it—it's located 7 miles southwest of Three Forks on the Old Yellowstone Trail. It's worth the search, though, because Willow Creek is the best restaurant in the area (don't let the bullet holes in the ceiling scare you off). It began as the Babcock Saloon around 1916, and continues as a remarkable reflection of what's best in Montana: hearty meals and friendly people. The ever-popular baby back pork ribs draw repeat customers from around the country, but the local cowboys know that the beef is tops here, so the hand-pounded chicken-fried sirloin steak is their recommendation. The pasta dishes are very good and the homemade soups really taste homemade. The weekend-only lunches are also recommended.

21 Main St., Willow Creek. © **406/285-3698.** Dinner reservations recommended in summer. Lunch $4–$8; dinner $8–$25. AE, DISC, MC, V. Tues–Fri 4–10pm; Sat–Sun 11am–10pm.

Ennis

20° Below ★ AMERICAN   Located in the rear of the Longbranch Saloon, 20° Below is pure Western steakhouse. Our choice is the chicken-fried steak with country gravy, but pork chops, Cornish pasties, and sirloin are also on the menu. There are also burgers, loaded baked potatoes, panini, and homemade soups. Lunch is sandwiches and variations on the dinner entrees.

125 E. Main St. © **406/682-5300.** Lunch $6–$9; dinner $7–$20. MC, V. Mon–Sat noon–3pm and 4–10pm; hours vary in winter.

Big Sky: 53 miles S of Bozeman; 48 miles N of West Yellowstone

According to legend, the Sioux and Nez Perce once engaged in a bloody battle in the lower Gallatin Valley. On the third day of the fighting, the sun was blotted out and a booming voice told the warriors to forget old wrongs and stop fighting because they were in the Valley of Peace and Flowers.

These days, the sun mostly shines around here, and the only booming voices heard are those calling you for your tee time or your dinner reservation. The transition of Big Sky from peace and flowers to year-round resort was not entirely without dissension, however. When legendary NBC newsman Chet Huntley—a Montana native—proposed the Big Sky ski resort, there was an outcry from the budding environmental movement. But Huntley's dream was realized in 1973, and the resort has blossomed into a world-class facility, with a second ski area—Moonlight Basin—opening in 2003.

The valley is a narrow, shining slice of Montana edged by the Absaroka and Gallatin ranges to the east and the Madison Range on the west. The Big Sky Resort covers two of the western peaks—Lone Mountain, elevation 11,186 feet, and Andesite Mountain, 8,800 feet. Moonlight Basin's runs are also on Lone Mountain, and connect with those of Big Sky.

There are several distinct "villages" in Big Sky. The **canyon area** along U.S. 191 has a haphazard collection of motels, taverns, restaurants, gas stations, and whatnot. The **Meadow Village,** 2 miles west of the highway, includes a community of condos, a few overnight lodging places, and the golf course. The main base area for the ski resort is at the **Mountain Village,** 8 miles west of the highway, with condos, restaurants, and hotels. The Moonlight Basin development is just above Mountain Village.

The valley's summers bring excellent fly-fishing, horseback riding, and white-water rafting. This beautiful scenery may seem familiar—the Gallatin River was the setting for the film *A River Runs Through It.*

ESSENTIALS

GETTING THERE Big Sky is about 53 miles south of Bozeman's **Gallatin Field Airport** on U.S. 191. From the airport, you can ride to the ski area with **Karst Stage** (© **800/845-2778** or 406/556-3500; www.karststage.com), a company that has a transportation fleet of sturdy four-wheel-drive vehicles. The ride is about $80 round-trip per adult and $40 per child 3 to 12 in winter. Or you can take a van or town car provided by **Shuttle to Big Sky** (© **406/995-4895**) for about $140 one-way.

GETTING AROUND A car gives you the greatest flexibility in getting around this area. For service between condominiums, hotels, restaurants, and activities within the ski area, take Big Sky's free local shuttle-bus system, which operates daily during the ski season.

GETTING OUTSIDE
Biking
Big Sky Resort rents mountain bikes and offers bike rental/lift ticket combos. Call © **406/995-5840** for details.

Cross-Country Skiing
Big Sky Resort (see below) offers some groomed trails for cross-country skiing. But for the real deal, go to **Lone Mountain Ranch ★★★** (P.O. Box 160069, Big Sky, MT

59716; ☎ **800/514-4644** or 406/995-4644; www.lmranch.com), which has 50 miles of cross-country trails over terrain that will challenge every level of skier. Near the ranch headquarters, in the meadows, lies some flat terrain that beginners might appreciate. There's also a steeper portion to practice your Telemark technique, and 12 miles of snow-shoe trails. Intermediate trails with more hills make up about 60% of the area, and expert trails provide plenty of challenging downhill runs. Ski and snowshoe rentals are also available. Full-day trail passes cost $20 for adults, $15 for seniors 60 to 69, and free for kids 12 and under and seniors 70 and over. The entrance to Lone Mountain Ranch is off Lone Mountain Trail (the main road to the Big Sky Resort), about 4 miles west of its intersection with U.S. 191 and 2 miles east of the Meadow Village.

Downhill Skiing

In 2005, Big Sky and Moonlight Basin connected their trail systems, making for a com-bined 5,512 acres of terrain—the largest ski area in the country. Skiers and snowboarders can buy the **"Biggest Skiing in America" ticket** for a day of unlimited access to both resorts' runs for $94 adults, $84 seniors 70 and over and college students, and $74 for juniors 11 to 17 (free for kids 10 and under).

Big Sky Resort ★★   Tennis, golf, and rock climbing are all very nice, but the real reason to come to Big Sky is to ski. It's a huge hill, with more than 3,812 acres of terrain and 85 miles of trails. You can ski for nearly a vertical mile from the top of the tram at 11,150 feet elevation to the bottom of the Lone Moose lift, at 6,800 feet, the second-longest vertical drop of any U.S. resort. There is terrain here for everybody, with 60% for advanced and expert skiers, 26% for intermediate, and 14% beginner. Big Sky gets 400 inches of snowfall, offering plenty of powder days. There's an ambitious children's pro-gram, offering lessons for kids as young as 3, and day care for kids who don't want to ski. Full ski-rental packages are available. New in the winter is a zipline operated by the ski school.

P.O. Box 160001, Big Sky, MT 59716. ☎ **800/548-4486** or 406/995-5750; 406/995-5900 for snow condi-tions; 406/995-5743 for ski school. www.bigskyresort.com. Lift ticket $79 adults, $69 seniors (70 and over), $59 college students with ID and juniors 11–17, and free for children 10 and under. Late Nov to mid-Apr daily 9am–4pm.

Moonlight Basin ★   The first new destination ski resort in the U.S. in more than 20 years, Moonlight Basin opened in 2003 to rave reviews from hard-core skiers, but its long, steep runs may be a bit challenging for neophytes. (This makes the "Biggest Skiing in America" ticket, above, a safe bet if you're on the fence about your abilities.) Seven lifts (a high-speed six-passenger lift, three quads, one triple, one double, and a conveyor) serve 1,900 acres of terrain crisscrossed by about 90 trails—with a precipitous 4,150-foot drop. Most of the terrain is for the advanced skier, but there are some easier runs. Like Big Sky, the resort gets more than 400 inches of snow a year. It also features a spa, snow sports school, kids' programs, and other outdoor activities. But the folks behind this infant of a resort look like they're just getting started. Coming in 2010: a private Jack Nicklaus–designed golf course.

P.O. Box 160040, Big Sky, MT 59716. ☎ **877/822-0430** or 406/993-6000; 406/993-6666 for snow condi-tions. www.moonlightbasin.com. Lift ticket $55 adults; $45 seniors (70 and over), college students with ID, and juniors 11–17; free for children 10 and under. Late Nov to mid-Apr daily 9am–4pm.

Fishing

According to an Indian legend, folks who drink the water of the Gallatin River will return to the valley before they die, but of course you should no longer drink untreated water out of even high mountain streams, because of the possibility of giardia, an intestinal microbe that you don't want traveling back home with you. We're not sure if eating the fish that live in the water counts toward the legend, but it's worth a try. Several guides offer trips for prices ranging from about $250 to $300 for a half-day for two to $350 to $500 for a full day. For details contact **Lone Mountain Ranch** (© 406/995-4644), **Gallatin Riverguides** (© 406/995-2290; www.montanaflyfishing.com), or **East Slope Anglers** (© 406/995-4369; www.eastslopeoutdoors.com).

Golf

Big Sky Golf Course, Meadow Village (© 406/995-5780), is a striking Arnold Palmer design that is fairly short, fairly open, and harder than it looks on the card. A few of the holes wander next to the West Fork of the Gallatin River, which runs through the property. Cost, which includes the cart fee, is $36 to $65 for 18 holes, $30 to $45 for 9. Tee times can be reserved up to a week in advance.

Hiking

As you might expect in an area surrounded by three mountain ranges and two national forests, there is an abundance of hiking opportunities not far from Big Sky. An easy, 4-mile hike to **Porcupine Creek** is accessible nearby. Go south 2¾ miles on U.S. 191 from the intersection with the mountain village road. Turn left at the sign that announces Porcupine Creek, and go about a half-mile to the trail head. The first mile of the hike wanders along Porcupine Creek, and then offers a choice of either a north or a south fork. The left (north) fork goes up into the foothills, offering a view of the creek below.

If you want more of a workout, try the **Lava Lake** trail, which begins about 13 miles north of the intersection of the mountain village road and U.S. 191 on the highway. Take the Lava Lake turn. The trail climbs steeply, without much relief, for 3 miles to an alpine lake in the shelter of three mountains.

Yellowstone National Park is only about 40 miles south of Big Sky, and you can hike there for a lifetime.

WHERE TO STAY

Big Sky Resort, P.O. Box 160001, Big Sky, MT 59716 (© 800/548-4486 or 406/995-5000; www.bigskyresort.com), handles a wide variety of lodgings—from economy to full-fledged luxury scattered among nearly 70 properties. The three-story **Huntley Lodge,** with 205 units, was the beginning of late NBC newsman Chet Huntley's original vision for Big Sky. It offers rooms that can sleep up to four, and several loft rooms that can accommodate six. The 97-unit **Shoshone Condominium Hotel** combines the living quarters of a condo with the amenities and services of a hotel, with sleeping for four to six. Weight-training centers, saunas, an outdoor pool, gift shops, and ski storage are included at both places. The **Summit at Big Sky** ★, with 213 luxury condominiums, offers European sophistication in a Western style, and hosted President Obama in August 2009. All three properties are slopeside and offer ski-in/ski-out convenience. Winter rates start around $160 a night double and top out at more than $1,000.

Moonlight Basin, P.O. Box 160040, Big Sky, MT 59716 (© 877/822-0430 or 406/993-6000; www.moonlightbasin.com), offers properties ranging from condos to private residences to luxurious penthouses. The **Moonlight Lodge and Spa** ★★ (© 800/845-4428) is a magnificent mountain lodge offering luxurious penthouse suites and secluded mid-mountain cabins; plus a sophisticated yet down-home restaurant, a relaxed-atmosphere bar, and a deli. There's also a full-service spa with treatment rooms, complete fitness center, steam rooms, heated pool, and a cascading waterfall hot tub; a concierge ready and able to organize everything from fly-fishing trips, to backcountry skiing, to dog-sled adventures; and even an ice-skating rink just outside in winter. Winter rates start at about $225 a night double during the ski season and top out well over $1,000.

In the Big Sky area, rates vary with the season and within the ski season. The highest rates are during Christmas vacation, the lowest in the spring and fall "shoulder" seasons.

Buck's T-4 Lodge ★   Begun in 1946 as a hunting camp, Buck's T-4 came to the valley before electricity did. It has grown quite a bit over the years. Buck's still offers a woody, Western ambience on the highway about 10 miles away from the ski resort lodgings, with large, comfortable rooms in a wide variety of floor plans, all with nice views and tasteful decor. The current lodge is modern, including two hot tubs large enough for the kids to swim in, a game room, and all of the other amenities you want in ski- and Yellowstone-area accommodations. The best thing about the place, though, is the restaurant, reviewed below. Standard rooms, suites, and suites with kitchenettes are available. Ask about ski packages and vacations when making reservations.

P.O. Box 160279, U.S. 191, Big Sky, MT 59716. ✆ **800/822-4484** or 406/995-4111. Fax 406/995-2191. www.buckst4.com. 72 units, including 3 suites. $129–$149 double; $199–$299 suite. Lower rates spring and fall. Rates include hot buffet breakfast. AE, DC, DISC, MC, V. About ¹/₂-mile south of the intersection of U.S. 191 and Lone Mountain Trail. Pets accepted ($10). **Amenities:** Restaurant; lounge; 2 outdoor Jacuzzis. In room: TV, fridge, hair dryer, kitchenette (suite only), MP3 player docking stations, Wi-Fi (free).

Gallatin Gateway Inn ★   The Gallatin Gateway Inn is a model of historical elegance from the days of luxury railroad travel. The hotel opened in the summer of 1927, as visitors were beginning to come to Yellowstone in large numbers. With lavish appointments that include Polynesian mahogany woodwork, decoratively carved beams, and high arched windows, the Spanish-style building recalls pre–World War II elegance, and you almost expect to see Teddy Roosevelt and Buffalo Bill Cody relaxing side-by-side on the porch. The spacious guest rooms provide a tastefully understated balance to the regal lobby. They maintain the refined historical feel, but have been updated with light colors, providing a more open and airy feeling than you usually find in hotels of this vintage. Serving dinner only, the **Porter House** restaurant's seasonally changing menu includes regional specialties showcasing ingredients from local growers; combinations are imaginative and portions generous.

76405 Gallatin Rd. (U.S. 191), P.O. Box 376, Gallatin Gateway, MT 59730. ✆ **800/676-3522** or 406/763-4672. Fax 406/763-4777. www.gallatingatewayinn.com. 33 units, including 6 suites. $149 double; $197–$200 suite. Lower rates in winter. Rates include continental breakfast. AE, DISC, MC, V. 28 miles north of Big Sky on U.S. 191. **Amenities:** Restaurant; lounge; outdoor Jacuzzi; outdoor pool. In room: A/C, TV, Wi-Fi (free).

Lone Mountain Ranch ★★★ (Kids)   Before there was even a community of Big Sky there was Lone Mountain Ranch. Started in 1926 as a working cattle ranch, Lone Mountain rapidly blossomed into a year-round destination as a guest ranch and cross-country ski area. In the summer, the ranch blends traditional guest-ranch activities—riding, hiking, fishing, and eating—with naturalist programs that will improve your understanding of Yellowstone. Lone Mountain prides itself on a family atmosphere and has separate activities for children, including animal tracking and camp-outs. In winter the ranch is a cross-country skiing and snowshoeing destination, with 50 miles of trails.

Accommodations here vary from small, woodsy cabins to the large, modern Ridgetop Lodge, which can host an entire family reunion. Some of the cabins are quite old—from the original ranch—while the new lodge was built in the 1990s. All are spacious with private bathrooms and attractive pine interiors.

The restaurant is excellent, and in the winter there is a sleigh ride and dinner at the ranch's North Fork cabin. There is a buffet breakfast and lunch each day. Call *C* **406/995-2782** after 3pm for dinner reservations.

P.O. Box 160069, Big Sky, MT 59716. *C* **800/514-4644** or 406/995-4644. Fax 406/995-4670. www. lmranch.com. 23 cabins, 1 house, 6 rooms in Ridgetop Lodge. Winter: cabin or lodge room $2,245–$3,085 1st person, $1,405 each additional person; Douglas Fir House $4,385 1st person, $1,405 each additional person. Lower rates for children 12 and under. Rates include 7 nights' lodging, 3 meals daily, an 8-day trail pass with unlimited access to the ranch's trail system, evening entertainment, a sleigh-ride dinner, a trail buffet lunch, and airport transfers. Summer rates are slightly higher. DISC, MC, V. From Bozeman, head south on U.S. 191 about 45 miles. **Amenities:** Restaurant; lounge; children's program; outdoor Jacuzzi. *In room:* Hair dryer, no phone, Wi-Fi (free).

320 Guest Ranch Kids   Bordered by the Gallatin River, the 320 Guest Ranch dates from 1898 and is one of the few cowboy-oriented accommodations in Montana that takes guests by the night (and not the week) year-round. With a full slate of activities—horseback riding, fishing in the river or a trout pond on-site, hayrides, and plenty more in the winter—the ranch is self-contained, but also offers a good base for skiing Big Sky's slopes or Yellowstone's wildlands. Accommodations come in the form of seven lodge rooms and 52 cabins and log homes on the extensive grounds (320 acres, thus the name) that range from small and fairly basic to two-bedroom log cabins on the river to even larger guest homes. The furnishings are unremarkable but fitting, and the campfire out front roars every night for marshmallows and cowboy poetry.

205 Buffalo Horn Creek, Gallatin Gateway, MT 59730. *C* **800/243-0320** or 406/995-4283. Fax 406/993-4694. www.320ranch.com. 59 units, including 52 cabins and log homes. $135–$388 double. Lower rates in winter. AE, DISC, MC, V. 15 miles south of the turnoff to Big Sky Resort on U.S. 191. **Amenities:** Restaurant; lounge. *In room:* TV, kitchen, Wi-Fi (free).

WHERE TO DINE

There are almost two dozen eateries at Big Sky, so you know you won't go hungry. But the closer you are to the slopes, the more expensive the food is. Restaurants range from simple snack bars to the upscale **Huntley Lodge Dining Room** (*C* **406/995-5783**), which has a good breakfast buffet in the morning and fine dining in the evening. Big Sky also has more than a dozen nightspots.

In the **Meadow Village** area, there are about a dozen restaurants, including the **Blue Moon Bakery** (*C* **406/995-2305**), which is open for all three meals and has good sandwiches and fresh-baked pastries, along with salads, soups, and pizza, and free delivery after 5pm. The local's favorite is the **Corral Bar and Steakhouse,** 42895 U.S. 191 about 5 miles south of the turnoff to Big Sky (*C* **406/995-4249**), serving primarily steaks—including buffalo T-bone—and seafood. Main courses run $10 to $35 at dinner.

Buck's T-4 Restaurant ★★ NEW AMERICAN   Buck's offers an adventurous menu of "Montana cuisine," with about a half-dozen wild game dishes, including pan-seared elk chops (a bone-in pork chop, chargrilled and served with raspberry-chipotle sauce), pan-roasted pheasant breast, and the New Zealand red deer sirloin. Our choice here, though, is any of the chargrilled steaks, served with hand-smashed potatoes and a daily vegetable. Of special note is the old bar, part of the original building here and still sporting the same well-worn bar and Technicolor vinyl-tile flooring.

U.S. 191, Big Sky. ℂ **406/993-5222.** www.buckst4.com. Reservations recommended. Entrees $18–$32. **229**
AE, DC, DISC, MC, V. About ½-mile south of its intersection with Lone Mountain Trail. Daily 6–9:30pm.
Closed mid-Apr to mid-June and early Oct to late Nov.

5 LIVINGSTON & THE PARADISE VALLEY ★★

Livingston: 26 miles E of Bozeman; 110 miles W of Billings; 58 miles N of Mammoth Hot Springs in Yellowstone National Park

Livingston is caught between very cowboy and very hip. As the largest community in the Paradise Valley, it has been discovered by the Hollywood set who want to get away from it all, but unfortunately still bring some of it with them. Peter Fonda has a ranch here. You might see Dennis Quaid or Tom McGuane. Robert Redford and Anthony Bourdain are also big fans of the area.

The Paradise Valley is the product of the Yellowstone River, the largest undammed river in the Lower 48. Along with the two valleys paralleling it to the west—the Gallatin and Madison—this portion of Montana is a fly-fishing paradise. There are lots of fishing guides and tackle shops, and millions of acres to wander in and wonder at.

ESSENTIALS

GETTING THERE   The nearest airport is Bozeman's **Gallatin Field,** 26 miles west along I-90. It's also possible to fly into Billings's **Logan Airport,** 116 miles east along I-90.

The Gardiner entrance to Yellowstone National Park is 53 miles south on U.S. 89. For local road reports, call ℂ **406/586-1313.** Greyhound and Rimrock Stages provide bus service. The bus depot is at 1404 E. Park St. (ℂ **406/222-2231**).

VISITOR INFORMATION   The **Livingston Area Chamber of Commerce** is located at 303 E. Park St. (ℂ **406/222-0850;** www.livingston-chamber.com). For information on **Yellowstone Country,** Travel Montana's region including Livingston and the Paradise Valley, call ℂ **800/736-5276** or 406/556-8680 (www.yellowstonecountry.net).

GETTING AROUND   Car-rental agents in the area include **Budget** (ℂ **800/527-0700**), **Enterprise** (ℂ **800/261-7331**), **Hertz** (ℂ **800/654-3131**), and **National** (ℂ **800/227-7368**). All are at Gallatin Field Airport in Bozeman.

GETTING OUTSIDE

Much of the outdoor recreation in this area takes place in the **Gallatin National Forest.** Check with the Livingston Ranger District, 5242 U.S. 89 S., Livingston, MT 59047 (ℂ **406/222-1892;** www.fs.fed.us/r1/gallatin). Another good source of information on hiking, mountain biking, cross-country skiing, and snowshoeing, as well as equipment rentals and sales, is **Timber Trails Outdoors Co.,** 309 W. Park St. (ℂ **406/222-9550**).

Cross-Country Skiing & Snowshoeing

The most popular spots are in the national forest. For specific locations and current conditions, check with the Livingston Ranger District or Timber Trails Outdoors Co. (see above).

Fishing

Montana has the best trout fishing in the country, and the area around here is the best trout fishing in Montana. Livingston is the gateway to classic Montana fly-fishing in the blue-ribbon Madison River, the Paradise Valley, and the Yellowstone River. **Dan Bailey's Fly Shop,** 209 W. Park St. (© **800/356-4052;** www.dan-bailey.com), in business since 1938, offers all manner of fishing tackle for sale or rent. Bailey's can give you some tips on where to fish on your own, or provide a guide for about $400 a day for one angler or $425 for two. **Hatch Finders Fly Shop,** 113 W. Park St., no. 3 (© **406/222-0989;** www.hatchfinders.com), can tie your custom flies and also provide outfitters almost anywhere in the state. A full-day guided trip in the Yellowstone River area is $450 for two anglers (plus Montana fishing licenses), or $475 in Yellowstone proper.

About a quarter-mile south of town at 5256 U.S. 89 S., **George Anderson's Yellow-stone Angler** (© **406/222-7130;** www.yellowstoneangler.com) is another fully equipped equipment store and guide service ($425 a day for two). Anderson also offers a fly-fishing school. About 20 miles south of Livingston in the town of Pray is **Knoll's Yellowstone Tackle and Fly Shop,** 104 Chicory Rd. (© **406/333-4848;** www.knolls.us). Here you can learn how to cast and how feathers mysteriously become fishing flies, or purchase a handcrafted rod or reel. Take U.S. 89 south to Emigrant then east and northeast on County Road 540 to Pray.

Early-season fishing before runoff starts—in late April and early May—offers excellent dry fly-fishing. In late May and June, the water on most of the rivers is running high and muddy, but the Firehole River in Yellowstone National Park has a heavy early hatch, and the fishing is good. All fishing in the park is catch and release. The rivers drop in July and August, and there are hatches daily for good fishing.

Hiking & Biking

This area is nearly surrounded by the **Gallatin National Forest,** which has several thousand miles of hiking and biking trails, including more than 800 miles of hiking trails in two designated wilderness areas—the Lee Metcalf and Absaroka-Beartooth. Popular trails that are relatively easily accessible include **Pine Creek Falls** south of town off the East River Road. The falls themselves are a short walk from the campground at the end of the access road, and Pine Creek Lake is about 4 miles farther along. **Livingston Peak** (or Mount Baldy Trail) is east of town off Swingley Road, and the **Big Timber Canyon Trail** is north of the town of Big Timber. The Livingston Ranger District of the U.S. Forest Service and Timber Trails Outdoors Co. (see "Getting Outside" above) can provide information about trails and access routes to them. Timber Trails also rents mountain bikes starting at about $25 per day.

Horseback Riding

Chico Hot Springs (© **406/333-4933**), about 22 miles south of Livingston off U.S. 89 to the east, also offers horseback riding. **Wilderness Pack Trips,** 209 K St. (© **406/848-9953** or 701/523-4907 in winter; www.wildernesspacktrips.com), offers 5- to 10-day horse-packing trips into Yellowstone National Park. Rates are about $2,000 to $3,000. Call or check their website for their current schedule and availability.

Rafting

Both scenic and white-water rafting and kayaking are available on the Yellowstone River throughout the Paradise Valley. **Rubber Ducky River Rentals,** 4 Mount Baldy Dr. (© **406/222-3746;** www.riverservices.com), provides guided trips June through September, or will rent boats and equipment and provide river shuttles. Call for current schedules and rates.

The main attractions in downtown Livingston are its three museums (www.livingston museums.org), all of which contain gift shops.

International Fly Fishing Center   You'll find some 10,000 flies on display here, plus exhibits on the history of fly-fishing, displays showing the evolution of the fishing rod, fishing-related art, and two aquarium rooms—one containing warm-water species, the other with cold-water fish. Owned and operated by the Federation of Fly Fishers, the center also offers fly-casting lessons (call for times).

215 E. Lewis St. (℃ **406/222-9369.** www.livingstonmuseums.org. $3 adults, $2 seniors, $1 children 7–14, free for children 6 and under. June–Sept Mon–Sat 10am–6pm, Sun noon–5pm; Oct–May Mon–Fri 10am–5pm.

Livingston Depot Center ★   This is a beautifully restored 1902 Northern Pacific railway depot, built in handsome Italianate style, that is one of the most stunning railroad stations I've ever seen (it was designed by the same architects that designed Grand Central Station in New York City). The depot houses a museum with exhibits that concentrate on the history of the railroad and how it contributed to the development of the area. There are videos and interactive displays in this thoroughly modern look at the olden days, and the museum also hosts changing exhibits on some aspect of local history, such as explorers Lewis and Clark (the depot is a designated stop on the Lewis and Clark Trail) or the story of Montana's railroads.

200 W. Park St. (℃ **406/222-2300.** www.livingstonmuseums.org. $3 adults, $2 seniors and students, free for children 5 and under. June–Sept Mon–Sat 9am–5pm; Sun 1–5pm. Closed Oct–May.

Yellowstone Gateway Museum of Park County   Located in a historic school, this museum offers artifacts from Livingston's early days—including an 1889 train caboose and a Yellowstone National Park stagecoach—and exhibits of the prehistoric people who lived in this area some 10,000 years ago.

118 W. Chinook St. (℃ **406/222-4184.** www.livingstonmuseums.org. $4 adults, $3.50 seniors, $3 children 6–12, free for kids 5 and under. June–Aug daily 10am–5pm; Sept Tues–Sat 11am–4pm; open by appointment rest of year.

ART GALLERIES

Livingston is a center of Western art and artists, and there are about a dozen galleries in town. For Western wildlife and fly-fishing art, try the **Visions West Gallery** at 108 S. Main St. (℃ **406/222-0337;** www.visionswestgallery.com), with woodcarvings, bronzes, and original oils. You'll find the work of Russell Chatham, a Livingston artist known for his oils and lithographs of Western landscapes, at the **Chatham Fine Art Gallery,** 120 N. Main St. (℃ **406/222-1566;** www.russellchatham.com). The **Danforth Gallery,** 106 N. Main St. (℃ **406/222-6510;** www.pcfadanforth.org), is a nonprofit gallery of contemporary Western art that changes its exhibits every month in the summer.

WHERE TO STAY

Right across from Livingston's downtown depot, the **Murray Hotel,** 201 W. Park St. (℃ **406/222-1350;** www.murrayhotel.com), opened in 1904 and has since put up everyone from director Sam Peckinpah to the queen of Denmark. Off the lobby, there's a good restaurant and a classic Western bar. Double rates are $89 to $119; suites are $139 to $229. Among the chains in town: **Rodeway Inn,** 102 Rogers Lane (℃ **406/222-6320**), a woodsy motel with a candy shop on-site and double rates of $69 to $119; and the **Best Western Yellowstone Inn and Conference Center,** 1515 W. Park St. (℃ **800/770-1874** or 406/222-6110; www.theyellowstoneinn.com), with a long list of facilities and amenities and rooms for $89 to $129 double.

Chico Hot Springs Resort ★★   Rambling over 150 magnificent acres in the Paradise Valley, just 30 miles north of Yellowstone National Park, Chico offers a taste of gentility, cowboy style. The hot springs were discovered in 1876. The lodge opened in June 1900 and has been going strong ever since. There's a bewildering variety of lodgings from small rooms that share a bathroom to deluxe rooms, plus rustic log cabins, a stand-alone caboose-turned-lodging, and a five-bedroom, two-bathroom private house. The three-story original Main Lodge is furnished mostly with antiques, and houses the casually elegant restaurant. Two open-air mineral hot-springs pools are just outside and are open daily from 6am to midnight year-round. Most rooms have high-speed Internet access. In the film *Rancho Deluxe*—screenplay by local resident Tom McGuane—Sam Waterston and Jeff Bridges soak in Chico's hot pool in their cowboy hats.

1 Chico Rd., Pray, MT 59065. (✆ **800/468-9232** or 406/333-4933. Fax 406/333-4964. www.chicohotsprings.com. 110 units. $115–$125 double; $49–$89 double with shared bathroom; $169–$225 suite; $79–$209 cabin; $169–$345 private house. AE, DISC, MC, V. Pets accepted ($20 per pet per stay). **Amenities:** 2 restaurants (see "Where to Dine," below); saloon; 2 outdoor hot-springs pools; Wi-Fi (free). *In room:* High-speed Internet (in most), kitchen (in some), no phone.

Mountain Sky Guest Ranch ★★ **Kids**   This guest ranch sits among 5,000 acres and is just 30 miles from the north entrance of Yellowstone and about an hour's drive from Bozeman. Weeklong stays focus on outdoor activities such as white-water rafting, riding, and hiking. Summers are popular with families (couples would do better coming in fall or spring), and the kids camp program keeps the young ones busy. Individual log cabins come in various one-, two- or three-bedroom configurations; the two-bed/two-bathroom Granite is popular, as is P3, with its big living room, three bedrooms, and view over the property. Yoga and massage are offered, but keep in mind that the latter fills up quickly, so sign up for your time slots when you check in. Dining is community style, so if you don't know anyone at the start of your trip, you'll be sure to leave with at least a few new friends.

P.O. Box 1219, Emigrant, MT 59027. (✆ **800/548-3392** or 406/333-4911. www.mtnsky.com. 32 cabins. Weekly rates mid-June to late Aug adults $3,235–$3,895, ages 7–12 $2,740–$3,235, ages 18 months–6 $2,130–$2,490, and ages 17 months and under $650; early May to early June and late Aug to mid-Oct adults only $300–$335 double. Rates include all meals, beverages, gratuities, and on-ranch activities such as hiking, horseback riding, and pond fishing. MC, V. Closed mid-Oct to late Apr. From Bozeman, take I-90 east, then U.S. 89 south; ranch is 7 miles past Emigrant. No pets. **Amenities:** Restaurant; bar; children's programs; fitness center; Internet (free); outdoor Jacuzzi; heated outdoor pool; sauna; tennis court. *In room:* A/C, fridge, hair dryer, no phone.

Camping

There are plenty of camping opportunities in the Gallatin National Forest, including **Pine Creek** and **West Boulder** campgrounds to the south of town toward Yellowstone National Park. For information, contact the Livingston Ranger District, 5242 U.S. 89 S., Livingston (✆ **406/222-1892;** www.fs.fed.us/r1/gallatin).

Nine miles south of Livingston is the **Livingston KOA,** 163 Pine Creek Rd. (✆ **800/562-2805** or 406/222-0992). Open from May to mid-October, the facility boasts an indoor heated pool, a snack bar, liquefied petroleum (LP) gas sales, and a bathhouse. The campground is situated along the Yellowstone River, with shady sites that cost $25 to $30 for tents and $26 to $41 for RVs. Cabins range from $60 to $150 a night. **Yellowstone's Edge,** 3502 U.S. 89 S., Livingston (✆ **800/865-7322** or 406/333-4036;

to mid-October, it has both pull-through sites and back-in sites along the river for RVs, plus grassy tent sites and a lodge with a store, game room, laundry room, and bathhouse. There's also a dump station and LP gas available. RV sites cost $42 to $47. A fully furnished cabin, the River Suite, rents for $150 for the first night and $120 each additional night.

WHERE TO DINE

The Chico Dining Room ★ NEW AMERICAN   The Chico Hot Springs Resorts is 35 miles north of Gardiner, but if you're in the area, stop here for some of the best food in the Greater Yellowstone Ecosystem and a soak in this resort's hot springs. The carnivorous traveler will enjoy the selection of top-drawer beef, the pine nut–crusted Alaskan halibut is a seafood aficionado's dream, and wine lovers won't be disappointed one bit by the award-winning list. Many of the incredibly fresh veggies originate in the resort's garden and greenhouse, and the menu always includes a vegetarian selection. You'll want to linger over the food, so consider a night's stay.

Old Chico Rd., Pray. ✆ **406/333-4933.** Reservations recommended. Main courses $25–$30. AE, DISC, MC, V. Summer daily 5:30–10pm; winter Sun–Thurs 5:30–9pm, Fri–Sat 5:30–10pm; Sun brunch 8:30–11:30am. Located 35 miles north of Gardiner.

Grand Hotel ★ LAMB/SEAFOOD   This beautiful restaurant is located in downtown Big Timber, about 30 miles east of Livingston, in an 1890 hotel that has been beautifully restored. The ingenious menu lists starters such as elk *rellenos* and calamari tempura, before giving way to main dishes such as herb-roasted racks of lamb, "butterknife" filets, and mountain morel-crusted chicken breasts. The restaurant has won the *Wine Spectator* award of excellence numerous times for its all-American wine list.

139 McLeod St., Big Timber. ✆ **406/932-4459.** www.thegrand-hotel.com. Lunch and brunch $5–$12; dinner $16–$29. DISC, MC, V. Sun–Fri 11am–2pm; daily 5–9pm.

Second Street Bistro ★★ FRENCH/AMERICAN   This slick, stylish eatery, in the lobby of the Murray Hotel since 2004, is the cream of the Livingston culinary crop, serving a creative, simple menu of French-inspired plates. All of the produce in summer comes from Chef Brian Manges's garden in town, and much of it comes from a greenhouse in winter. Appetizers include escargot, fried brie, and of course french fries, while main courses include individual gourmet pizzas and hearty American standards (meatloaf and pork chops) as well as steaks, pastas, and salads. There is a sommelier to help with the voluminous wine list, as well as a full bar.

123 N. 2nd St., in the Murray Hotel, Livingston, MT. ✆ **406/222-9463.** www.secondstreetbistro.com. Reservations recommended. Main courses and pizzas $10–$20. AE, DISC, MC, V. Daily 5–9pm; Sun also 10am–2pm. Closed Mon in winter.

6 RED LODGE & THE ABSAROKA-BEARTOOTH WILDERNESS

60 miles SW of Billings; 62 miles NW of Cody, Wyoming

Nestled in a steep valley at the edge of the Absaroka-Beartooth Wilderness and surrounded by the spectacular Beartooth Mountains, the community of Red Lodge is not quite a tourist town, not quite a destination ski resort, but still not the sleepy little town it once was, either. It has elements of all three, giving it a homey and still busy feel. While it is slowly losing its small-town identity in favor of a resort persona, this hasn't happened completely.

Founded as a coal-mining community in the late 1880s, it did fairly well until the mines closed in the 1930s. Today it's the beautiful scenery and outdoor activities around Red Lodge that attract us. It doesn't hurt that the town sits at the northern end of the Beartooth National Scenic Byway, which the late Charles Kuralt called the most beautiful road in America.

ESSENTIALS

GETTING THERE   To reach Red Lodge, you'll have to fly into Billings's **Logan International Airport** (© **406/247-8609;** www.flybillings.com). From Billings, take I-94 west to Laurel, about 16 miles, then go south on U.S. 212/310. The route diverges after about 12 miles at the small town of Rockvale. Follow U.S. 212 southwest 44 miles to Red Lodge. Rental cars are plentiful at Billings's airport (see section 1 in chapter 11). For **road conditions** concerning the Red Lodge area and closures of the Beartooth National Scenic Byway, call © **800/226-7623.**

VISITOR INFORMATION   Contact the **Red Lodge Area Chamber of Commerce,** P.O. Box 988, Red Lodge, MT 59068 (© **888/281-0625** or 406/446-1718; www.red lodge.com).

GETTING OUTSIDE

Many of the outdoor activities in these parts take place in the Custer National Forest. For information, contact the **Beartooth Ranger District Office** of the Custer National Forest, at the south end of town along U.S. 212 (HC 49, P.O. Box 3420, Red Lodge, MT 59068; © **406/446-2103;** www.fs.fed.us/r1/custer). The office is open daily from 8am to 5pm in summer, and Monday through Friday 8am to 4:30pm in winter.

Golf

The **Red Lodge Mountain Golf Course** (© **406/446-3344**) is notorious for swallowing golf balls. Water comes into play on 13 of the 18 holes. The signature hole is the 238-yard, par-3 no. 15, where you hit to an island green from an elevated tee about 80 feet above the hole. Adult greens fees are $29 to $39 for 18 holes. Carts are $24 for two riders playing 18 holes.

Hiking

There are some popular and challenging day hikes not far from Red Lodge. Drive south on Route 212 about 10 miles to County Road 2346, then 2 miles down that road to the **Lake Fork of Rock Creek.** From here you can do a full loop of 19 miles to the West Fork of Rock Creek trail head (or do it as an overnight backpacking trip), or just walk up a few miles to some great fishing in the streams and lakes along the way and return.

Other popular hikes leave from the trail head at the **West Fork of Rock Creek.** Head west on Red Lodge Mountain Resort's access road, known locally as Ski Run Road. When the road forks, stay left and continue for several miles past a number of campgrounds. The road turns to gravel and ends at the West Fork trail head. The hike from here to Timberline Lakes is a moderate 9 miles round-trip. If you're not feeling that energetic, you can hike for about a mile to a picturesque waterfall. The fishing in Lake Mary near the trail is very good.

And They're Off . . . to the Pig Races?

Bored with the rodeo? Horse racing seems ho-hum? Just head down to the **Bear Creek Saloon & Steakhouse** (© **406/446-3481;** www.redlodge.com/bearcreek); behind the bar is Bearcreek Downs, site of the famed local pig races.

After the famous fires in Yellowstone in 1988 created a slow tourist season, the Bear Creek Saloon & Steakhouse owners decided that a **pig race** might generate some visitor interest. There was some question over whether the races were legal, but the Montana legislature stepped in and said pig races were okay by them, provided the proceeds went to charity. So Bearcreek Downs porkers are sending Carbon County students to college—more than $75,000 has gone for scholarships so far. Pig races are held Thursday through Sunday at 5pm, from Memorial Day to Labor Day.

Even if you don't come for the races, the Bear Creek Saloon & Steakhouse is a great place to eat. It's an authentic Western tavern, and the grub is mostly beef. Prices range from $8 to $27, and food is served Thursday through Sunday from 5 to 10pm. The saloon is 7 miles east of Red Lodge on County Road 308.

The **Absaroka-Beartooth Wilderness area** is a 950,000-acre wilderness that extends from the boundary of Yellowstone through two national forests. It's some of the most spectacular country in the Lower 48 states. Because of its proximity to the park, it is heavily used. There are lots of great hikes, incredible vistas, and pristine lakes with excellent trout fishing. **Granite Peak,** at 12,799 feet, is the tallest mountain in Montana, but it's only one of the 28 mountains topping 12,000 feet in the Absaroka-Beartooth.

For information about the above trails, contact the **Beartooth Ranger District Office** (see "Getting Outside," above).

Skiing

Red Lodge Mountain Resort (P.O. Box 750, Red Lodge, MT 59068; © **800/444-8977** or 406/446-2610; www.redlodgemountain.com) is a relatively small, family-oriented ski area. But it's growing: The skiable terrain includes 1,600 acres of mountain, with a vertical drop of 2,400 feet. There are about 70 trails, with 45% of the mountain rated for intermediate skiers, 17% for beginners, and 38% for advanced and expert. Of the eight lifts, two are high-speed quads. An average of 250 inches of snow falls each year, plus Red Lodge has one of the largest snowmaking operations in the Rockies. Lift tickets cost $47 for adults, $39 for seniors 65 to 69, $40 for juniors 13 to 18, and $17 for children 6 to 12 (free for kids 5 and under and seniors 70 and over); half-day tickets are also available. The season usually runs from late November to early April, with hours of 9am to 4pm.

SEEING THE SIGHTS

When it's open, the **Beartooth National Scenic Byway,** a 64-mile stretch of U.S. 212 from Red Lodge to Cooke City, is an incredible road that takes you to almost 11,000 feet elevation. Make sure a camera is handy when Pilot Peak comes into view, just outside Cooke City.

Beartooth Nature Center The Beartooth Nature Center is the only nature center in Montana that provides a home exclusively for animals that have been injured, orphaned, or too accustomed to humans to be returned to the wild. Residents, about 60 at a recent count, include mountain lions, wolves, coyotes, black bears, bison, eagles, and other animals native to Montana.

615 2nd Ave. E., Red Lodge. (✆ **406/446-1133.** www.beartoothnaturecenter.org. $6 adults, $5 seniors 55 and older, $2.50 children 5–15, free for children 4 and under. May–Oct daily 10am–5pm; Nov–Apr daily 10am–2pm.

Carbon County Historical Society Museum Highlights of this well-run and interesting museum include a simulated coal mine that recalls Red Lodge's underground past, and the Greenough Collection of cowboy and rodeo gear. There's also a Crow Indian tipi, a mountain man camp, and pioneer displays. This is the place to find out more about "Liver Eatin'" Johnston, who got his name because . . . no, it's too repulsive. You'll have to find out for yourself.

224 N. Broadway at 8th Ave., Red Lodge. (✆ **406/446-3667.** www.carboncountyhistory.org. $5 adults, $3 students, free for children 5 and under. Memorial Day to Labor Day Mon–Sat 10am–6pm, Sun 11am–3pm; rest of year Thurs–Fri 10am–5pm, Sat 11am–3pm.

WHERE TO STAY

In addition to the properties discussed below, I recommend the **Comfort Inn of Red Lodge,** 612 N. Broadway, Red Lodge, MT 59068 (✆ **888/733-4661** or 406/446-4469), which charges $140 to $160 double in peak season.

Chateau Rouge The Chateau Rouge offers excellent accommodations at a very reasonable price, especially for families. Though run like a motel, the Chateau Rouge is actually a collection of privately owned condominiums. Most are two-story, two-bedroom affairs with a living room (with a fireplace) and kitchen on the first floor and the sleeping rooms upstairs. The two-story condos have large, fully appointed kitchens, while the studios have small but complete kitchens. All are attractively decorated and maintained. The only drawback—a minor one in our opinion—is that they are not air-conditioned, which can be uncomfortable on those rare summer days when the mountain temperatures reach the 90s (30s Celsius).

1505 S. Broadway, Red Lodge, MT 59068. (✆ **800/926-1601** or 406/446-1601. Fax 406/446-1602. www. chateaurouge.com. 24 units. $89 double studio; $125 double 2-bedroom condo. Lower rates in spring and fall. AE, DC, DISC, MC, V. **Amenities:** Indoor Jacuzzi; indoor pool. *In room:* TV, kitchen/kitchenette, Wi-Fi (free).

The Pollard ★★ Built in 1893 by the Rocky Fork Coal Company at an initial cost of $20,000, the Pollard has undergone a magnificent restoration a century later, integrating modern conveniences with historical character and elegance. It has been a stopover for a number of Old West celebrities, including Buffalo Bill Cody, Calamity Jane, and Jeremiah "Liver Eatin'" Johnston. The Pollard has a three-story gallery with a wood-burning fireplace. No two rooms are exactly alike, but most are large, done with manly oak furniture and ladylike flower-print comforters. Six have balconies overlooking the lobby; many have Jacuzzi tubs. The entire operation is first-class. For fine dining in Red Lodge, the **Pollard Hotel Dining Room** is a solid choice. The food is excellent—we suggest the steaks, grilled over a wood fire. Reservations are recommended. Breakfast and dinner are served daily.

2 N. Broadway, Red Lodge, MT 59068. *℃* **800/765-5273** or 406/446-0001. Fax 406/446-0002. www.the pollard.net. 38 units. $90–$200 double; $270–$295 suite. Lower rates spring and fall. Rates include full breakfast. AE, DISC, MC, V. **Amenities:** 2 restaurants; lounge; health club; indoor Jacuzzi; room service; sauna. *In room:* A/C, TV/VCR, hair dryer, Wi-Fi (free).

Rock Creek Resort ★★   This property was built in 1963 as a dormitory for members of an international ski-racing camp founded by owner Pepi Gramshammer. Rock Creek retains much of the ski atmosphere that produced it, although the ski hill is a good 5 miles away, plus it's got all sorts of warm-weather recreation (a stocked trout pond, horseshoe pits, and a soccer field). The cedar-sided Beartooth Lodge, the main building, boasts a huge fireplace made of river rock and windows that offer mountain views. A wide variety of accommodations decorated in a Western theme are available, from mountain lodge-style units with lots of wood to luxurious condominiums and three-bedroom town houses. Many units have wood-burning stoves or fireplaces, patios or balconies, or a private hot tub. It would be hard to find a room here without a wonderful view.

6380 U.S. 212 S., Red Lodge, MT 59068. *℃* **800/667-1119** or 406/446-1111. Fax 406/237-9851. www. rockcreekresort.com. 87 units. $140–$375 double. AE, DC, DISC, MC, V. From Red Lodge, drive 5 miles south on U.S. 212. **Amenities:** 2 restaurants; 2 lounges; bike rental; weight room; Jacuzzi; indoor pool; sauna; 4 tennis courts; volleyball court. *In room:* TV, hair dryer, kitchenette, Wi-Fi (free).

Camping

There are 16 Forest Service campgrounds available in the Red Lodge area, with sites for more than 700 campers. Many of the larger campgrounds accept reservations through the **National Recreation Reservation Service** (*℃* **877/444-6777;** www.recreation.gov), and the rest are first-come, first-served. For information, contact the **Beartooth Ranger District Office** of the Custer National Forest, at the south end of town along U.S. 212 (*℃* **406/446-2103**).

Those seeking commercial campgrounds, with all the usual RV hookups and other amenities, can head to the **Red Lodge KOA,** 7464 U.S. 212 (*℃* **406/446-2364**). It has grassy and shady sites, a heated outdoor pool, and a convenience store, and charges $27 to $34 for tents, $27 to $35 for RVs, and $55 to $60 for basic cabins. It's typically open from mid-May through September.

WHERE TO DINE

In addition to the restaurants discussed below, see the box "And They're Off . . . to the Pig Races?," above, for information on the **Bear Creek Saloon & Steakhouse,** and the "Where to Stay" section above for information on the excellent restaurant the **Pollard. Bogart's,** 11 S. Broadway (*℃* **406/446-1784**), offers pizza, sandwiches, and Mexican fare. A good bet for a burger, a bowl of chili, a beer, or a ballgame (or any combination thereof) is **Foster and Logan's Pub and Grill,** 17 S. Broadway (*℃* **406/446-9080**).

Bridge Creek Backcountry Kitchen and Wine Bar NEW AMERICAN   Bridge Creek is a local favorite, with a widely varied, moderately priced menu. Lunches include wraps, salads, sandwiches on fresh-baked breads, and homemade soups, including an excellent clam chowder. At dinner you'll find fish, chicken, steaks, chops, and pasta. The house salad with huckleberry-balsamic vinaigrette is a must. The wine bar is a small, bright room with an extensive wine list that for several years has received the *Wine Spectator* award of excellence. The atmosphere is casual, sort of California cafe with a Western flavor. Open at 11am daily, a Starbucks coffee bar here serves a wide selection of espresso, cappuccino, latte, mocha, and iced drinks, plus freshly baked pastries, and offers free Wi-Fi. There is also a wine shop and specialty market up front.

116 S. Broadway Ave. © **406/446-9900.** www.eatfooddrinkwine.com. Lunch main courses $8–$19; dinner $8–$33. MC, V. Sun–Thurs 11am–9pm; Fri–Sat 11am–10pm. Closed Sun–Mon fall–spring.

Old Piney Dell ★★ (Finds SWISS/AMERICAN   Located in a former homesteader's cabin on the banks of Rock Creek, this is where locals come for a special evening. If you like Wiener schnitzel, this place is for you—the veal is lightly breaded and delicately pan-fried to perfection. The tenderloin, with port wine and blue cheese sauce, practically melts in your mouth, and the seared rainbow trout is also excellent. Chicken and lamb are also on the menu, with prime rib on Fridays and Saturdays. Ask about the nightly specials, created from the best find of the day.

In Rock Creek Resort. © **406/446-1111.** www.rockcreekresort.com. Reservations recommended. Dinner main courses $16–$27. AE, DC, DISC, MC, V. Mon–Thurs 5:30–9pm; Fri–Sat 5:30–10pm; Sun 9am–1pm. Closed Sun–Wed Nov–May. From Red Lodge, drive 5 miles south on U.S. 212.

11

Billings & Eastern Montana

The plains of eastern Montana offer a more subtle beauty than the rugged mountains to the west. A land of rolling hills, dusty bluffs and badlands, and the occasional rock-walled canyon, this is classic cattle and wheat country, with grass thick and green in spring, brown and dry by fall, and blanketed by snow in winter. Temperatures can be extreme; hot in the summer under a blazing sun, and bitter cold in the winter, dipping below zero for long stretches.

Eastern Montana's history is rich: Lewis and Clark trekked along the Missouri River, and one of the most famous battles of the American West, the Battle of the Little Bighorn, was fought here.

In the old days, travel in eastern Montana was defined by the railroads. Virtually every town with 300 people and a tavern could be reached by either the main line or a spur. But the romantic days of rail travel have been replaced by the automobile, and interstates have triumphed over the rails. I-94 sweeps across the state west to east, I-15 cuts through the Rockies from Idaho to the Canadian border, and I-90 dips south from near Billings to the Crow Reservation in Sheridan, Wyoming.

1 BILLINGS

104 miles W of Cody, Wyoming; 123 miles N of Sheridan, Wyoming; 142 miles E of Bozeman; 339 miles E of Missoula

The most populous city in Montana with over 100,000 residents, Billings might well be the most urban place in Montana or Wyoming. You'll find real shopping malls here, along with the occasional 5 o'clock traffic jam and the tallest free-standing brick building in the world (the 23-story Crowne Plaza). Since its 1880s development by Frederick Billings as a railroad town, the city has evolved into the economic and industrial hub for the entire region.

Once a booming oil town, as well as a crossroads for the railroads, Billings has now positioned itself as the progressive medical center for all of eastern Montana, the Dakotas, and Wyoming. The economy is still based on cattle and grain, but downtown Billings boasts new banks and contemporary business centers, with many historic buildings enjoying restorations since the turn of the 21st century. Billings also has its share of scenic splendor: From the rimrocks surrounding the city you can see the Pryor Mountains, the Bighorns, and the majestic Beartooths to the west.

ESSENTIALS

GETTING THERE Billings's **Logan International Airport** (© **406/238-3420;** www. flybillings.com) is the state's busiest, located about 2 miles north of downtown. Service is provided by **Alaska/Horizon** (© 800/547-9308), **Allegiant Air** (© 702/505-8888), **Delta/SkyWest** (© 800/221-1212), **Frontier** (© 800/432-1359), **Northwest** (© 800/225-2525), and **United** (© 800/864-8331).

If you're traveling by car, I-90 connects Billings to Bozeman, Butte, and Missoula in the west before crossing into Idaho; I-90 east heads southeast into Wyoming. I-94 branches off I-90 10 miles east of town and runs northeast through Miles City and Glendive before reaching North Dakota. U.S. 87 heads north out of Billings to Roundup, and U.S. 310 goes south to Lovell, Wyoming.

VISITOR INFORMATION   The **Billings Chamber of Commerce & Visitors Bureau,** 815 S. 27th St. (P.O. Box 31177), Billings, MT 59107 (✆ **800/735-2635** or 406/252-4016; www.billingscvb.visitmt.com), has brochures, maps, and area information. Travel Montana's **Custer Country** (✆ **800/346-1876;** www.custercountry.com) is another information source.

GETTING AROUND   Billings's downtown street system might be a bit confusing at first, but can be mastered if you remember that Montana Avenue is the dividing line between north and south. Numbered avenues run parallel to Montana, starting with 1st Avenue North and 1st Avenue South, which are located 1 block away on each side of it, and increasing from there. The numbered streets run perpendicular to Montana, their names changing from North to South as they cross it, and increase numerically from east to west. The heart of downtown lies north of Montana and is relatively compact. Its boundaries are North 27th and North 29th streets and 1st and 6th avenues North.

To access downtown from I-90, which skims the southern edge of the city, take exit 450 and go north on 27th Street; the Business Loop follows Montana Avenue between exits 446 and 452. Coming from the north, from Roundup, U.S. 87 turns into a four-lane road before heading west into the Heights, the northeastern part of the city. Follow this road into downtown, or turn right on Airport Road to reach Logan International Airport.

The best way to see Billings is to drive. Car-rental companies at the airport include **Alamo/National** (✆ **800/227-7368**), **Enterprise** (✆ **800/261-7331**), **Hertz** (✆ **800/ 654-3131**), and **Thrifty/Dollar** (✆ **800/847-4389**).

The city bus service is **MET Transit** (✆ **406/657-8218**), with buses running from 5:50am to 6:40pm weekdays and 8:10am to 5:45pm Saturdays. Fare is $1.25. Taxi service is available from **City Cab** (✆ **406/252-8700**), **Yellow Cab** (✆ **406/245-3033**), and **Montana Custom Tours** (✆ **406/860-7439;** www.montanacustomtours.com).

GETTING OUTSIDE

Montana Fun Adventures Tours (✆ **406/254-7180;** www.montanafunadventures. com) offers historical tours of Billings and vicinity, as well as 2-day packages into Yellowstone National Park. **Total Transportation** (✆ **800/698-1778** or 406/252-1778; www.mttotaltransportation.com) offers trolley, carriage, and bus tours.

Fishing

Though the Yellowstone River runs through the city, it is wide, busy, and often muddy. The best nearby fishing is in the **Bighorn Canyon National Recreation Area** (see section 3, later in this chapter), 83 miles southeast of town. Fishing guides come and go pretty often in the Billings area; to find a local one, the best bet is to ask at the **Base Camp,** 1730 Grand Ave. (✆ **406/248-4555;** www.thebasecamp.com).

Golf

Lake Hills Golf Club (✆ **406/252-9244;** www.lakehillsgolf.com), **EagleRock Golf Course** (✆ **406/655-4445;** www.eaglerockgolfcourse.com), and the **Peter Yegen, Jr., Golf Club** (✆ **406/656-8099;** www.yegengolfclub.com) are the three 18-hole public

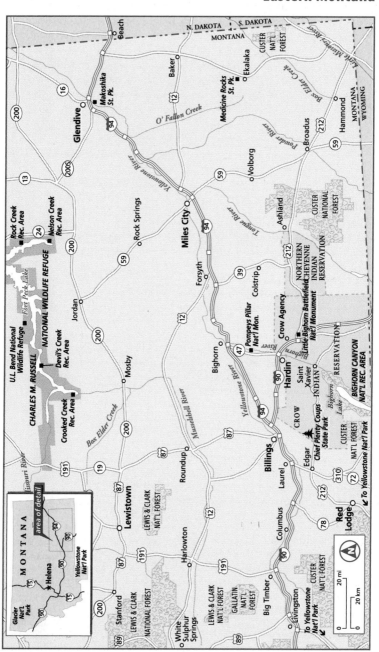

Black Otter Trail Scenic Drive

The Black Otter Trail Scenic Drive, following about 3 miles along the edge of the sheer rimrock overlooking Billings, affords a spectacular view of the city and the three mountain ranges in the distance. To get there, take Montana Avenue east to U.S. 87 and turn left (north). After you pass the MetraPark arena complex on your right, turn left onto Airport Road, and shortly thereafter, left again onto Black Otter Trail. Boot Hill Cemetery is at this end of the road, and contains 40 of the unlucky residents of the town of Coulson, most of whom "died with their boots on." It's also the final resting place of the famous scout Yellowstone Kelly, who asked to be buried here above the land he scouted.

golf courses in Billings, with greens fees of $25 to $42, not including carts. The par-3, 9-hole **Exchange City Golf Course** (© **406/652-2553**) has greens fees of $10.

Nearby Parks & Nature Preserves

In town, there is a good **multiuse trail system** popular with joggers, walkers, and bikers. Contact **Billings Parks & Public Lands** (© **406/657-8371;** www.prpl.info) for information.

An unusual side trip is to **Pictograph Cave State Park** (© **406/247-7342;** www. pictographcave.org), where you can see cave paintings made by prehistoric people more than 4,500 years ago. There are more than 100 pictographs, in red and black pigments made from ashes, clay, and animal fat. The meaning of the designs is continually debated—were they ceremonial, or perhaps celebrations of a successful hunt or battle (there are many images of shield-bearing warriors)? A short, but fairly steep, interpretive trail leads up to the caves, which are more like large stone alcoves than caves in the usual sense. They lie in a classic, sheer, broad sandstone canyon inhabited by rabbits and an occasional rattlesnake—so stay on the trail. From Billings, take I-90 east to exit 452 and follow the signs for 6 miles. The park is open May 1 to September 30 daily from 9am to 7pm with shorter hours the rest of the year and an entrance fee of $5 per vehicle.

Locals go to nearby **Lake Elmo State Park,** 10 miles north of Billings on U.S. 87 (© **406/247-2955;** www.fwp.mt.gov), for picnicking, swimming, windsurfing, fishing, and volleyball. Boat rentals and windsurfing lessons are available in the summer; gas-powered boats are prohibited. Entrance fee is also $5 per vehicle.

SEEING THE SIGHTS

To view some modern artists' contributions to decorating the West, drive the **Avenue of the Sculptures** along 27th Street (from I-90 exit 450 to the airport) for an outdoor art show. The first work, *The Cattle Drive Monument,* is right outside the chamber of commerce's visitor center. *The Sheriff Webb Memorial Marker* is on the courthouse lawn, and finally, in front of the airport is the *Range Rider of the Yellowstone,* posed for by silent-screen cowboy actor William Hart. Also around downtown, visitors will spot more public art in the form of a number of colorful equines from 2002's "The Horse, Of Course!" fundraiser for the Billings Depot restoration.

Kids will enjoy **Geyser Park,** 4910 Southgate Dr. (© **406/254-2510;** www.geyser park.net), featuring video games, a climbing wall, a laser tag arena, and a pizzeria.

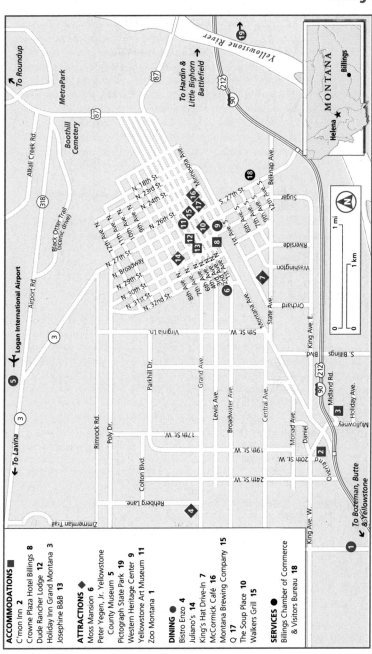

ACCOMMODATIONS ■
C'mon Inn **2**
Crowne Plaza Hotel Billings **8**
Dude Rancher Lodge **12**
Holiday Inn Grand Montana **3**
Josephine B&B **13**

ATTRACTIONS ◆
Moss Mansion **6**
Peter Yegen, Jr. Yellowstone
County Museum **5**
Pictograph State Park **19**
Western Heritage Center **9**
Yellowstone Art Museum **11**
Zoo Montana **1**

DINING ●
Bistro Enzo **4**
Juliano's **14**
King's Hat Drive-In **7**
McCormick Café **16**
Montana Brewing Company **15**
Q **17**
The Soup Place **10**
Walkers Grill **15**

SERVICES ●
Billings Chamber of Commerce
& Visitors Bureau **18**

(Kids) Especially for Kids: Animals, Animals

The only wildlife and botanical park within 500 miles of Billings, ambitious **ZooMontana** ★ covers 70 acres and is continually changing and growing. The zoo concentrates on northern plains wildlife, some of which you may see on your trip through the state. There are nature trails meandering among the natural habitats of red pandas, eastern gray wolves, Manchurian sika deer, bald eagles, great horned owls, and the North American river otter; there's a petting zoo in a farm and ranch setting.

The zoo is also home to 2 of the 300 Siberian tigers remaining in the world, as well as to the retirees from a captive breeding program for black-footed ferrets, North America's rarest mammal. A new state-of-the-art grizzly bear habitat opened in 2008.

Take exit 443 north off I-90, head northwest on King Avenue to Shiloh Road, and then south (© **406/652-8100;** www.zoomontana.org). Admission is $6 adults, $3 children 3 to 15, and $4 seniors 65 and over. May through late September, the zoo is open daily 10am to 5pm; late September through April daily 10am to 4pm.

Moss Mansion ★   This massive red-sandstone mansion, built in 1901 for Billings banker Preston B. Moss, was designed by prominent New York architect Henry Janeway Hardenbergh. It has many European influences, including a Moorish entry, a Shakespearean library, and a French Louis XVI parlor. Oak and mahogany millwork gives an elegant feel to the upstairs bedrooms. The mansion, listed on the National Register of Historic Places, has been used in various TV miniseries and Hollywood films, and was featured on A&E's *America's Castles* in 1997. Visitors view a short video about Moss and early Billings before taking the 1-hour guided tour of the home. The Moss Mansion also hosts various events during the spring and summer months, and is elaborately decorated for Christmas.

914 Division St. © **406/256-5100.** www.mossmansion.com. $7 adults, $5 seniors and students with ID, $3 children 6–12, free for children 5 and under. Summer guided tour every hour on the hour Mon–Sat 9am–4pm, Sun 1–3pm; winter daily 1–3pm with expanded holiday hours from mid-Nov to Dec. Closed Thanksgiving, Christmas, and New Year's Day.

Peter Yegen, Jr., Yellowstone County Museum   Located next to the airport, this collection is housed in a century-old cabin, which has had such eminent visitors as Teddy Roosevelt and Buffalo Bill Cody. Rotating exhibits describe the history and diverse cultures of Montana and the Yellowstone River Basin, from prehistory through the 1950s. Changing exhibits of contemporary local and national artists are in the Landmarks Gallery. Also on the grounds: a vintage steam engine and a stuffed two-headed calf. The view of Billings and the surrounding countryside from the museum's deck is terrific.

1950 Terminal Circle, adjacent to Logan International Airport. © **406/256-6811.** www.pyjrycm.org. Free admission. Mon–Fri 10:30am–5pm; Sat 10:30am–3pm. Closed Sun and national holidays.

Western Heritage Center   A lot of Western museums are just vast collections of dusty reminders of bygone eras. But this facility, an affiliate of the Smithsonian Institution, has done an excellent job of interpreting and editing its extensive collection, making the panoramic history of Western settlement accessible to casual visitors. In addition to the usual exhibits of the area's settlement by white people, the Heritage Center includes sensitive displays on the Crow tribe and on Japanese and other minority settlers. Interactive presentations include videos and recorded memories of three Yellowstone County homesteaders.

2822 Montana Ave. © 406/256-6809. www.ywhc.org. $5 adults, $3 students and seniors, $1 children 11 and under. Tues–Sat 10am–5pm.

Yellowstone Art Museum ★★ Montana art aficionados are justifiably proud of the Yellowstone Art Museum, a leader in the contemporary Western art movement. The museum showcases the best the new West has to offer, from Deborah Butterfield's ranch sculptures to Russell Chatham's gauzy landscapes to Rudy Autio's colorful, erotic ceramics. Additionally, the museum's permanent collection—more than 3,000 pieces— includes the largest public gathering of the drawings, paintings, books, and memorabilia of cowboy illustrator Will James, plus paintings and drawings by other historic regional artists such as J. H. Sharp and Charles M. Russell. Changing exhibitions have recently spotlighted prints by Roy Lichtenstein and large-scale woodcuts by Bozeman's Tom Buck. Expect to spend up to 2 hours.

401 N. 27th St. © 406/256-6804. www.artmuseum.org. $5 adults, $4 seniors, $3 students and children 6–18, free for children 5 and under. Tues–Sat 10am–5pm (Thurs–Fri until 8pm); Sun 11am–4pm.

SHOPPING

In the downtown area, the shopping district covers about 4 blocks on North 29th Street, Broadway, and 1st and 2nd avenues North. The area is heavy in the antiques line, but it also has a few boutiques and independent bookshops. **Granny's Attic,** 2804 Minnesota Ave. (© 406/256-5455), is the first stop for antiquers. You can find just about anything in this cavernous downtown space. For contemporary art, try the **Toucan Gallery,** 2505 Montana Ave. (© 406/252-0122), in the city's historic district, offering prints, oils, handmade furniture, and ceramics. The fashion conscious can find clothing from around the world at the **Cactus Rose,** 202 N. 29th St. (© 406/252-9126). Open since 1919, the classic Western department store, where lots of real cowboys get their gear, is **Lou Taubert Ranch Outfitters** (© 406/245-2248), at 123 Broadway. Another Western standby, carrying everything from feed to fine art, is **Shipton's Big R,** with locations at 216 N. 14th St. (© 406/252-0503) and 2600 Gabel Rd. (© 406/652-9118). If you're in the market for a top-of-the-line custom cowboy hat, call **Rand's Custom Hats,** 2205 1st Ave. N. (© 800/346-9815; www.randshats.com). For outdoor clothing and equipment, check out the **Base Camp** (© 406/248-4555) at 1730 Grand Ave.

WHERE TO STAY

In addition to the properties discussed below, you might consider the **Holiday Inn Grand Montana,** 5500 Midland Rd. (I-90 exit 446; © 877/554-7263 or 406/248-7701), with double rates of $129 to $149; or the **C'mon Inn,** 2020 Overland Ave. (I-90 exit 446; © 406/655-1100), with double rates of $75 to $150.

Crowne Plaza Hotel Billings ★★ Declared the world's tallest free-standing brick building by the Brick Institute of America, this 23-story tower is like a beacon in the heart of downtown—you can see it from just about everywhere. Renovated from top to bottom since the Crowne Plaza flag went up in 2006, the rooms are stylish and chic, with comfortable beds, plush chairs, and the best views around, and the list of amenities is comprehensive. The hotel caters to the business traveler—there's a 24-hour business center, rates are lowest on weekends, and the desks are huge—but it fits the bill for anyone who wants quick access to downtown. The restaurant on the 20th floor, **Montana Sky,** has great steaks and the best views in town.

27 N. 27th St., Billings, MT 59101. ✆ **800/465-4329** or 406/252-7400. Fax 406/252-2401. www.crowne plaza.com. 282 units, including 3 suites. $149–$169 double; $500 suite. Lower weekend rates. AE, DC, DISC, MC, V. **Amenities:** Restaurant; lounge; concierge; exercise room; room service; 2 saunas. *In room:* A/C, TV, hair dryer, Wi-Fi (free).

Dude Rancher Lodge (Value)
The Dude Rancher has been offering real Western hospitality since it opened in 1949. The rooms, which surround an inner courtyard, are comfortable and quiet, with ranch oak furniture and king- and queen-size beds. Many have fridges and microwaves, so request one if you are in need. The motel's downtown location puts you within walking distance of numerous restaurants, shopping, banks, the library, and the Alberta Bair Theatre.

415 N. 29th St., Billings, MT 59101. ✆ **800/221-3302** or 406/259-5561. www.duderancherlodge.com. 57 units. $48–$80 double. AE, DISC, MC, V. **Amenities:** Restaurant; room service. *In room:* A/C, TV, fridge (in some), hair dryer, microwave (in some), Wi-Fi (free).

The Josephine Bed & Breakfast ★
The Josephine is housed in a 1912 Victorian built by a wealthy rancher to give his children access to schools in Billings. Named for a steamboat that once plied the waters of the Yellowstone between here and St. Louis, the inn is located within walking distance of downtown, offering a quiet retreat amid Billings's urban bustle. Owners Bobbi and Harvey Bybee have installed high-speed Internet access, and there's a modern whirlpool tub in one room, but most rooms feature the classic claw-foot tubs familiar to Western movie buffs. The Captain's Room offers a masculine feel, from the pipes on the night table (but don't light one up; the entire inn is nonsmoking) to the four-poster bed. The other rooms have more feminine touches. There are a library, parlor, and dining room for breakfast, and a wraparound porch outside. Breakfasts are memorable: Harvey makes a terrific caramel-pecan French toast and his sourdough pancakes aren't bad at all.

514 N. 29th St., Billings, MT 59101. ✆ **800/552-5898** or 406/248-5898. www.thejosephine.com. 5 units. $95–$170 double. AE, DISC, MC, V. *In room:* A/C, TV, Wi-Fi (free).

WHERE TO DINE

For breakfast and lunch, we like the **McCormick Café,** 2419 Montana Ave. (✆ **406/255-9555**), and its offerings of eggs, crepes, sandwiches, pizza, and numerous vegetarian dishes. A classic drive-in known for its pork chop sandwiches and trademark UFO-shaped "flying burgers," **King's Hat Drive-In,** 105 S. 37th St. (✆ **406/259-4746**), is open Tuesday through Saturday; credit cards are not accepted. New to downtown is the **Soup Place,** 106 N. Broadway (✆ **406/294-7687**), which makes homemade soup (as well as sandwiches and soup-and-sandwich combos) with gumbo, Brunswick stew, and Cincinnati-style chili on the dinner menu.

Bistro Enzo ★ MEDITERRANEAN
The diverse and creative menu at this high-ceilinged restaurant on Billings's west side melds influences from not only the Mediterranean, but Asia and the Rockies as well: Entrees include Kobe burgers, Moroccan couscous, and Asian vegetarian pasta as well as a rib-eye and good old macaroni and cream-Parmesan cheese. There is a seating area with booths and a bar on the main floor and a quieter upstairs loft. Homemade desserts include crème brûlée and a decadent

"Molten Chocolate Cake" with caramelized bananas, a gooey marshmallow, and toasted walnuts. Beer and wine are available, but liquor is not.

1502 Rehberg Lane. ☎ **406/651-0999.** www.bistroenzobillings.com. Reservations accepted. Main courses $12–$28. AE, DISC, MC, V. Tues–Sun 5–9pm.

Juliano's ★★ NEW AMERICAN   One of the best restaurants in Montana, Juliano's serves excellent, original food in a casually elegant atmosphere. It's a little hard to categorize the food here. Chef Carl Kurokawa is a native of Hilo, Hawaii, and his menu describes the cuisine as "Fun American with European and Asian influences." The menu changes monthly, but you can depend on it having the fresh Hawaiian fish that Kurokawa insists on flying in. For dinner you might get locally raised lamb or Rocky Mountain elk, or maybe chicken-fried, almond-crusted calamari. At lunch there are salads—if you're feeling adventurous, try the crispy chicken and grapefruit salad—plus sandwiches and pasta dishes. The building was originally the stable of the sandstone "castle" next door, built in 1902. A pressed-tin ceiling with Bacchus hoisting a glass covers one of the dining rooms, and there is an outdoor patio for nice days. There is an extensive wine list—call for the dates of special wine dinners.

2912 7th Ave. N. ☎ **406/248-6400.** Reservations recommended. Lunch $7–$9; dinner main courses $19–$30. AE, DC, DISC, MC, V. Mon–Fri 11:30am–2pm; Wed–Sat 5:30–9pm. Closed Mon Jan–Feb.

Montana Brewing Company ★ **Kids** MICROBREWERY   A bustling bar and grill, Billings's downtown microbrewery has won a number of medals at the Great American Beer Fest, and it's easy to taste why. Their beers, brewed in vats behind the dining room, include Custer's Last Stout, Stillwater Rye, and several seasonal beers; nine are always available on draft. The food is pretty good, too, including pizza, chicken potpie, enchiladas, and a gamut of burgers and sandwiches—including bison burgers and a burger served on a pretzel bun. Despite the noisy bar area and adjacent casino, this is a pretty good place for families, and there's a kids' menu to boot.

113 N. Broadway. ☎ **406/252-9200.** Reservations accepted for large parties only. Main courses $5–$10. AE, DISC, MC, V. Daily 11am–11pm. Bar open later.

Q ★★ MEDITERRANEAN/CONTEMPORARY   An anchor in the ongoing revitalization of Historic Montana Avenue, Q is the brainchild of Suzy Schaer, for whom it is named. (Suzy Q, get it?) In sharp contrast to its peers in Billings, this eatery is very sleek and very hip, and feels more California than Montana. The room combines historic details—an original pressed-tin ceiling, for one—with contemporary design—suede wall panels, custom veneers, and striking yellow lamps. The menu meshes Mediterranean and Asian influences with a contemporary American slant: Entrees include pastas, steaks, salmon, and a few vegetarian dishes. The restaurant is attached to the **Carlin Martini Bar and Nightclub,** equally hip and serving a mean kamikaze martini.

2503 Montana Ave. ☎ **406/245-2503.** www.qcuisine.com. Reservations recommended. Main courses $13–$24. AE, DC, DISC, MC, V. Mon–Sat 4:30–10pm.

Walkers Grill ★★ AMERICAN BISTRO   Longtime Billings stalwart Walkers moved into posh new digs in 2004, taking over the first floor of a new brick loft building in the heart of downtown. Featuring the work of 26 different artists, the space itself is a masterwork of contemporary Western design, marked by barbed-wire chandeliers, wheat-field-inspired carpeting, a host stand made from a hitching post, and a bar made from a cattle guard. The food is also excellent: The menu, which changes several times a year, offers a bit of the exotic (such as house-made salmon pastrami) along with plenty of creative interpretations of local standards. You might find grilled buffalo sirloin with shiitake mushrooms, poblano peppers, and pomegranate demi-glace. A tapas menu of gourmet pizzas, Asian appetizers, and small versions of main courses is also served. The wine list is extensive, including many French wines—often difficult or impossible to find on the plains.

2700 1st Ave. N. (C) **406/245-9291.** www.walkersgrill.com. Reservations recommended. Main courses $13–$28; tapas $5–$11. AE, DISC, MC, V. Daily 5–10pm. Tapas bar Mon–Fri 4–11pm; Sat–Sun 5–11pm.

BILLINGS AFTER DARK

Playing host to productions and live music of all kinds, the **Alberta Bair Theater,** Broadway and 3rd. Ave. ((C) **877/321-2074** or 406/256-6052; www.albertabairtheater.org), is the prime performing arts venue in Billings, recently hosting Crystal Gayle and a touring production of *Cats.* The **Rainbow Bar,** 2403 Montana Ave. ((C) **406/259-0047**), has a reputation for stiff drinks; other diversions include shuffleboard and live music. **Hooligan's,** 109 N. Broadway ((C) **406/294-3495**), is a good sports bar with an Irish theme. Beyond the **Montana Brewing Company** (see "Where to Dine," above), there are three breweries with tasting rooms—**Carter's Brewery,** 2526 Montana Ave., unit B ((C) **406/252-0663**), **Yellowstone Valley Brewing Company,** 2123 1st Ave. N., unit B ((C) **406/245-0918**), and **Angry Hank's,** 2405 1st Ave. N. ((C) **406/252-3370**)—within easy walking distance of one another.

A SIDE TRIP TO POMPEYS PILLAR NATIONAL MONUMENT

A 150-foot-high sandstone butte 29 miles east of Billings holds the only concrete evidence left along the way of the famous journey of Lewis and Clark through the Louisiana Purchase. On July 25, 1806, Capt. William Clark carved his name and the date on the side of the rock. He noted in his famous journals for that day, "The nativs [sic] have ingraved [sic] on the face of this rock figures of animals & near which I marked my name and the day of the month and year." Clark then walked to the top and described the panoramic view of the river and plains that can be captured from that vantage. Clark had to scramble up through the yucca and sagebrush, but visitors now are aided by stairways and enthusiastic and informative volunteer guides who will point out the historic sites and wildlife—from ant lions to eagles' nests.

Halfway up a 120-foot stairway, Clark's name is now locked under a protective glass cabinet, but many others have added their names. The pillar was originally called Pompy's Tower by Clark, using the nickname he'd given the youngest member of their expedition, little Baptiste Charbonneau, the son of Sacajawea and Touissant Charbonneau, the expedition guides. The boy traveled in Clark's dugout, and the captain called him "my boy Pomp." Continue up to the top of the stairway for incredible views and photo opportunities.

The monument, operated by the Bureau of Land Management, is open from Memorial Day to Labor Day, daily from 8am to 8pm; then into late September (and sometimes later, weather permitting) from 9am to 4pm; after that you have to park a half-mile away and walk in. The fee is $7 per carload during the season, free at other times. The interactive multimedia exhibits at the modern visitor center are worth an hour of your time. There is also a film on Lewis and Clark regularly playing in the visitor center's theater.

For more information, call the visitor center (© **406/875-2400**), or visit **www.pompeys** **pillar.org**. To get there, go 29 miles east of Billings to I-94 exit 23. The signage is somewhat confusing: Don't turn right to go to the town of Pompeys Pillar; go straight over the bridge to Pompeys Pillar National Monument.

2 THE CROW RESERVATION

54 miles E of Billings

The beautiful Crow Reservation—the Crow People call themselves the Apsáalooke, "Children of the Large-Beaked Bird"—encompasses over 9 million acres in southeastern Montana. It consists of seven main communities, of which Crow Agency, on I-90, is the hub of tribal management and government.

One of the main Indian Nation events of the summer-long powwow trail is **Crow Fair,** held here the third week in August. Powwows are social gatherings featuring traditional food, dress, and dances. Visitors are welcome at powwows, but flash photography is not allowed during contests, and you should always ask dancers for permission before taking their photographs. For more information, contact the **Tribal Headquarters,** P.O. Box 159, Crow Agency, MT 59022 (© **406/638-3700**), or visit **www.crow-fair.com**.

The most famous historic site here is the **Little Bighorn Battlefield National Monument** (see section 4, below), a somewhat ironic inclusion on this reservation. The Crow scouted for Custer, and the Little Bighorn is the site of the cavalry's most infamous defeat at the hands of the Indians.

A good place to learn about the Crow culture is at **Chief Plenty Coups State Park** (© **406/252-1289;** www.fwp.mt.gov). The tribe's last traditional chief, Chief Plenty Coups, deeded his home and lands as a memorial to the Crow Nation, and the museum houses many of the Crow leader's personal items plus interpretive displays about the Crow people. From Billings, drive about 25 miles south on Montana highways 416 and 418 to Pryor, then go a mile west, following signs. There are picnic facilities but no overnight camping. The grounds are open May through September daily from 8am to 8pm, and the museum is open from 8am to 5pm (by appointment in the off season). Access to the grounds is free, but the museum's admission is $3 per adult, $2 for children 6 to 12, and free for kids 5 and under.

3 BIGHORN CANYON NATIONAL RECREATION AREA

Fort Smith: 83 miles SE of Billings

Over aeons, the Bighorn River carved a steep, sheer canyon out of the rolling plains of present-day southeastern Montana and into northwestern Wyoming. The construction of the Yellowtail Dam—named for Crow chairman Robert Yellowtail—near Fort Smith on the Crow Reservation, not only provides power and irrigation, but also marvelous recreational opportunities on and around 71-mile-long Bighorn Lake. Established on October 15, 1966, the Bighorn Canyon National Recreation Area encompasses more than 120,000 acres and straddles the Montana-Wyoming border.

The lake and recreation area are remote and not easy to get to, requiring long drives on winding roads through small towns. The Wyoming and Montana portions of the recreation area are not connected by a road, although a boater can cruise easily up and down the reservoir. But it's worth the effort to get here: Steep walls soar above the deep waters, and there's superb water fun, some hiking, and tremendous photo opportunities.

ESSENTIALS

ACCESS POINTS   There are two portions of the recreation area and two different access points. On the **Montana** side, from Billings, exit I-90 at Hardin and follow Route 313 south to Fort Smith and Yellowtail Dam.

The **Wyoming** section is accessed about 3 miles east of Lovell. From I-90 north of Sheridan, head west on U.S. 14 and turn north on Wyo. 37. The route is well marked.

FEES   The daily entrance fee is $5 per vehicle.

VISITOR INFORMATION   Contact **Bighorn Canyon National Recreation Area,** P.O. Box 7458, Fort Smith, MT 59035 (© 406/666-2412; www.nps.gov/bica).

Bighorn Canyon has visitor centers with exhibits and a descriptive film in each of its sections. Near Lovell, Wyoming, the **Cal S. Taggart Bighorn Canyon Visitors Center,** 20 Hwy. 14A E., Lovell, WY 82431 (© 307/548-2251), is open daily from 8am to 6pm in the summer and from 8:30am to 4:30pm Thursday through Monday in the winter. The **Yellowtail Dam Visitor Center** (© 406/666-3218) in Montana is open 9am to 5pm daily from Memorial Day to Labor Day as well as Thursday through Monday in early May and late September.

For additional information, contact the **Lovell Area Chamber of Commerce,** 287 E. Main St., Lovell, WY 82431 (© 307/548-7552; www.lovellchamber.com).

REGULATIONS & WARNINGS   The park has a number of black bears, which are not generally as dangerous to people as grizzlies, but can cause problems when they learn that humans carry food. Therefore, *never* feed the bears, not only for your safety but for theirs as well.

GETTING OUTSIDE

Bighorn Canyon is primarily a flat-water recreation area with excellent boating and fishing, plus swimming, water-skiing, and scuba diving. There are limited hiking trails and scenic drives.

Fishing regulations are tricky in these parts since the Crow Reservation encompasses nearly all of the Montana portion of the canyon. A state fishing license from whichever state you'll be fishing in is needed, and unless you are certain which it will be, it's best to get both. The visitor center has information on limits, regulations, and fishing conditions.

On the Montana Side

A park ranger can help you find the **Om-Ne-A Trail,** which stretches for 3 steep miles one-way along the canyon rim. The **Beaver Pond Trail** is a short trip from the visitor center along Lime Kiln Creek.

On the Wyoming Side

The south side of the park offers some of the more sensational canyon views and is a prime viewing spot of some of the last wild horses to run free in North America. The **Horseshoe Bend** area, on Wyo. 37, has a full-service marina (© 307/548-7230), typically open from Memorial Day to Labor Day.

Leaving Horseshoe Bend, you'll pass burgundy-colored hills and enter the **Pryor Mountain National Wild Horse Range,** which has been home to wild mustangs—the virtual emblem of the West, along with the buffalo—for more than a century. Sometimes, you can catch a glimpse of a few from the road. If you want more information, there is a new **Pryor Mountain Wild Mustang Center** (© 307/548-9453; www.pryor mustangs.org) in Lovell. Just across the Montana border is the **Devil Canyon Overlook,** offering a view of the river as it winds through a steep canyon of gray limestone and orange shale.

At the end of the highway is **Barry's Landing,** with a boat ramp and fishing access, and the focus for most of the recreational opportunities in the southern part of the park.

The self-guided **Canyon Creek Nature Trail** (.5 mile), which starts at Loop C of the campground at Horseshoe Bend, and the trail from **Barry's Landing** to the campground at Medicine Creek (2 miles), are the only hikes on this side of the park.

WHERE TO STAY

There are five park-service campgrounds in the recreation area; sites are free and first-come, first-served. Accommodations on the south side of the park are available in **Lovell,** 3 miles west of the intersection of Wyo. 37 and U.S. 14A (Alt. 14).

Forrester's Bighorn River Resort ★ (© 800/665-3799 or 406/666-9199; www.forrester-travel.com) is an outfitting company owned and run by former wildlife biologist Nick Forrester and his wife, Francine, a Manhattan-trained chef. There are seven rustic but very comfortable private cabins and a lodge with a massive river-rock fireplace in the living room, cigar loft, pro shop, and dining room where Francine serves meals to soothe weary fishermen. Located about a half-mile north of Fort Smith, the cabins sit on a bluff overlooking the Bighorn River. The Forresters offer hunting and fishing packages that include all meals and lodging starting at about $600 per person per day.

4 LITTLE BIGHORN BATTLEFIELD NATIONAL MONUMENT

56 miles E of Billings

Perhaps there is no phrase in the English language that serves as a better metaphor for an untimely demise than "Custer's Last Stand." It was on this battlefield, on the dry sloping prairies of southeastern Montana, that George Armstrong Custer met his end. Though the details of the actual battle that took place on June 25, 1876, are sketchy at best, much remains for the visitor to explore and ponder in this mysterious place. The **Little Bighorn Battlefield National Monument** chronicles the history of this world-famous engagement, offering a coherent look at how the battle developed, where the members of Custer's contingent died, and how it might have looked to the swarming warriors.

ESSENTIALS

GETTING THERE   The monument is located 56 miles east of Billings. Take I-94 east to I-90 south; just past Crow Agency, take exit 510 for U.S. 212. The battlefield is located a few hundred yards east.

ADMISSION & HOURS   The park and visitor center are open daily 8am to 9pm from Memorial Day through July, 8am to 8pm from August through Labor Day, 8am to 6pm in spring and fall, and 8am to 4:30pm in winter. The visitor center is closed on

Christmas, New Year's Day, and Thanksgiving. Admission costs $10 per vehicle or $5 for those on foot or motorcycle.

VISITOR INFORMATION At the **visitor center** just inside the park entrance, you'll see actual uniforms worn by Custer, read about his life, and view an eerie reenactment of the battles on a small-scale replica of the battlefield. For advance information, contact the Superintendent, Little Bighorn Battlefield National Monument, P.O. Box 39, Crow Agency, MT 59022-0039 (© **406/638-2621;** www.nps.gov/libi).

TOURING THE MONUMENT It's possible to view the site in less than a half-hour, but you'll shortchange yourself with that approach. Instead, plan to spend enough time to explore the visitor center, listen to interpretive historical talks presented by rangers there, and then tour the site. You'll leave with a greater appreciation for the monument and an understanding of the history that led up to the battle.

After stopping at the **visitor center,** drive 4½ miles to the **Reno-Benteen Monument Entrenchment Trail,** at the end of the monument road, and double back. Interpretive signs at the top of this bluff show the route followed by the companies under Custer, Benteen, and Reno as they approached the area from the south, and the positions from which they defended themselves from their Indian foes.

As you proceed north along the ridge, you'll pass **Custer's Lookout,** the spot from which the general first viewed the Indian village. This was the spot where Custer sent for reinforcements, though he continued marching north.

Capt. Thomas Weir led his troops to **Weir Point** in hopes of assisting Custer but was immediately discovered by the Indian warriors and forced to retreat to the spot held by Reno.

The **Medicine Trail Ford,** on the ridge, overlooks a spot well below the bluffs in the Medicine Trail Coulee on the Little Bighorn River, where hundreds of warriors who had been sent from the Reno battle pushed across the river in pursuit of Custer and his army.

Farther north, the Cheyenne warrior Lame White Man led an attack up **Calhoun Ridge** against a company of the Seventh Cavalry that had charged downhill into the coulee. When Indian resistance overwhelmed the army, troops retreated back up the hill, where they were killed.

As you proceed to the north, you will find detailed descriptions of the events that occurred on the northernmost edges of the ridge, as well as white markers that indicate the places where army troops fell in battle. The bodies of Custer, his brothers Tom and Boston, and nephew Autie Reed, were found on Custer Hill.

Indian casualties during the rout are estimated at 60 to 100 warriors. Following the battle, which some say began early in the morning and ended within 2 hours, the Indians broke camp in haste and scattered to the north and south. Within a few short years they were all confined to reservations.

The survivors of the Reno-Benteen armies buried the bodies of Custer and his slain army where they fell. In 1881, the graves that could be located were reopened, and the bones reinterred at the base of a memorial shaft found overlooking the battlefield. Custer's remains were eventually reburied at the U.S. Military Academy at West Point in 1877.

The adjacent **National Cemetery,** established in 1879, incorporates a self-guided tour to some of the more significant figures buried there. In 2003, there was a dedication for a new Indian memorial, a sculpture garden dubbed "Peace Through Unity." There are also three **walking trails** within the monument for visitors wishing to explore the battle in greater depth.

A SPECIAL EVENT The **Hardin Area Chamber of Commerce** (I-90 exits 497 and 503) sponsors **Little Bighorn Days** around June 25 each year (in town, not at the monument). The events include a reenactment of Custer's Last Stand, parade, symposiums, and, of course, food. For information, call ℂ **406/665-1672.**

5 MILES CITY ★

145 miles E of Billings; 70 miles SW of Glendive

Miles City gets its name from Col. Nelson A. Miles—the commander of the Fifth Cavalry who was ordered to return bands of Indians to reservations in the summer of 1876. As the world moves on around it, Miles City has retained its Western flair for more than a century. In the early days, as portrayed in Larry McMurtry's novel *Lonesome Dove,* Miles City was a cowboy town on the verge of becoming a leading cattle market; the market came with the arrival of the Northern Pacific Railroad in 1881.

Today, Miles City maintains its cowboy traditions with its annual Bucking Horse Sale—which attracts rodeo stock contractors from all over the country—and the Range Riders Museum, a thorough collection of photographs and firearms from the old days. It's where remote ranchers come when they need barbed wire or tractor axles, and still boasts a traditional Main Street with a saloon and lunch counter. Residents take an active pride in the town's lack of parking meters—a vestige of its civility and small population.

ESSENTIALS

GETTING THERE It's an easy 145-mile drive on I-94 from Billings. Miles City's **Frank Wiley Field** (ℂ **406/234-1296**) is serviced by **Great Lakes Airlines** (ℂ **800/554-5111;** www.greatlakesav.com), with connecting flights to Billings, Denver, and other regional destinations.

VISITOR INFORMATION The **Miles City Area Chamber of Commerce,** at 511 Pleasant St., Miles City, MT 59301 (ℂ **406/234-2890;** www.mcchamber.com), provides maps and guides to the town. Or get an area vacation guide from **Custer Country** (ℂ **800/346-1876;** www.custercountry.com).

GETTING OUTSIDE

There's an attractive municipal swimming facility at the west end of Main Street.

Fishing & Boating

Miles City isn't classic Montana fishing country, but there is plenty of access to the Yellowstone and Tongue rivers for walleye, sauger, catfish, crappie, and, occasionally, the unusual paddlefish (see "Paddlefishing," in section 6, below). Fishing throughout the area is best in late spring and early fall. **Twelve-Mile Dam,** 11 miles south of Miles City on Mont. 59, then 1 mile south on Tongue River Road, has camping facilities, a boat launch, and a handicapped-accessible fishing platform.

Luring in floaters with Yellowstone River access, **Pirogue Island State Park** (ℂ **406/234-0926;** www.fwp.mt.gov) is just north of Miles City. Go 1 mile north on Mont. 59, then 2 miles east on Kinsey Highway, then 2 miles south on an unnamed county road (look for a sign for the park). Stop by **Red Rock Sporting Goods,** 700 S. Haynes Ave. (ℂ **406/232-2716**), for gear and information.

11

The World-Famous Miles City Bucking Horse Sale

Since 1914, rodeo contractors—the men who supply the animals for the West's rodeos—have been meeting in Miles City and lining up their stock. This gathering, which began as an informal event, has now become the "World-Famous Miles City Bucking Horse Sale," held every third weekend in May. More than 200 horses are sold at auction, from untried stock to spoiled saddle horses. There are parimutuel horse races, a parade, a trade show, and rodeos, as well as wild-horse racing. The downtown area is virtually closed down at night, bands play on the streets, and beer is swilled and spilled while the city's open-container ordinances are suspended inside the "people corral." Tickets cost $12 to $17. For the current schedule, call the **Miles City Area Chamber of Commerce** (© 406/234-2890), or visit **www.buckinghorsesale.com**.

Golf

Miles City has the **Town and Country Club golf course** (© 406/234-1500) running along the banks of the Tongue River southeast of town. It's relatively short—3,280 yards. Greens fees are $27 to $32 for 18 holes; carts are $14 per rider.

SEEING THE SIGHTS

Custer County Art and Heritage Center ★★ (Kids)

The old city water plant, built between 1910 and 1924, has been reincarnated as an art-and-history museum, with one-time water tanks now filled with art. There are changing exhibits of traditional and contemporary art from the museum's permanent collection, plus national and regional touring exhibits. Listed on the National Register of Historic Places, the museum building is actually an attraction itself. In 1979, it was awarded the governor's trophy for best adaptation of a historic structure. The art center hosts an annual "Quick Draw" event on the third weekend in May and an art auction each year in late September.

Waterplant Rd. off W. Main St. (just west of town). © 406/234-0635. www.ccac.milescity.org. Free admission. May–Sept Tues–Sun 9am–5pm; rest of year Tues–Sun 1–5pm.

Range Rider Museum ★

The amazing thing about this collection is its size—the Western memorabilia collection fills 11 buildings and includes a frontier town, an art gallery that includes the work of Charles Russell, and a gun collection of more than 400 firearms, including an elephant gun, all on the site once occupied by Fort Keogh. Items on display also include American-Indian artifacts and French sabers. There are 500 photos of local celebrities in the Wilson Photo Gallery, and a replica of Old Milestown—as the town was originally called—of 1877. Of particular interest are the excellent photos of Cheyenne tribal members taken in the 1890s.

U.S. 12 (on Main St., just west of town at I-94 exit 135). © 406/232-6146 or 232-4483. $5 adults, $4 seniors, $1 high school and college students, 50¢ elementary and middle school students, free for children 5 and under. Apr–Oct daily 8am–6pm. Closed Nov–Mar.

WHERE TO STAY & DINE

There are several properties at I-94 exit 138 in Miles City. The **Holiday Inn Express,** 1720 S. Haynes Ave. (© 888/700-0402 or 406/234-1000), is a well-maintained facility with 52 units. There's a pool and whirlpool; rooms have wireless Internet access, irons and boards, hair dryers, and coffeemakers. Rates are $89 to $129 double, and include an expanded continental breakfast. The **Best Western War Bonnet Inn,** 1015 S. Haynes Ave. (© **800/528-1234** or 406/234-4560), has 54 units, including three suites with microwaves and refrigerators; plus there's an indoor pool, hot tub, and sauna. Double rates start at $75. Open mid-April through October, the **Miles City KOA Campground,** 1 Palmer St., Miles City, MT 56301 (© **406/232-3991**), is shaded by more than 70 cottonwoods and has full RV hookups, tent sites, a pool, and a store. Campsite rates range from $18 to $28; basic cabins are $36.

For a small Montana town, Miles City offers several pretty good restaurants. The **Stagecoach Station,** 3020 Stower St. (© **406/234-2288**), offers steak, seafood, great barbecue, and pasta (dinner items are in the $10–$20 range) with Old West hospitality and atmosphere to match—from the boot upholstery to "old Gabby" greeting you at the door. It's open daily from 6:30am to 10pm (Fri–Sat until 11pm). For fine dining, visit **Club 519,** 519 Main St., on the second floor of the Professional Building (© **406/232-5133**), a softly lit, quiet, comfortable restaurant serving very good steaks and seafood, with dinner prices in the $10-to-$30 range. It's open daily from 5 to 10pm. For a vintage Montana diner and corresponding grub, look no farther than the **600 Cafe,** 600 Main St. (© **406/234-3860**), with hearty American standards for breakfast and lunch, a well-worn breakfast counter, and maroon booths. Menu items are $3 to $9.

MILES CITY AFTER DARK

The cowboys in their dress hats come out after dark in Miles City, mostly in the bars. The historic **Montana Bar** ★, 612 Main St. (© **406/234-5809**), has a Montana map for a sign, with Miles City marked by a check. Built in 1893, this is where stockmen gathered. It was enlarged and received a new facade in 1914, but has changed little since, and is known as one of the most authentic Western bars in the state. It has a multicolored tile floor, antique back bar, pressed-tin ceiling, and a bullet hole in one leaded-glass panel. Patrons used to have to stand up to the bar and "drink like a man," but bar stools have been added for the modern tippler.

6 GLENDIVE

222 miles E of Billings; 196 miles W of Bismarck, North Dakota

A cattle town in the 1880s, Glendive has gradually become a farming community, producing mostly sugar beets and wheat. The city's most curious attraction is paddlefishing—dropping a line in the Yellowstone River in hopes of hooking a prehistoric monster (the state record is 142 lb.).

GETTING THERE   It's a 222-mile drive on I-94 from Billings, or you can fly **Great Lakes Airlines** (© **800/554-5111**) to **Dawson Community Airport** (© **406/687-3372;** www.glendiveairport.com).

VISITOR INFORMATION   The **Glendive Area Chamber of Commerce and Agriculture,** 808 N. Merrill Ave., Glendive, MT 59330 (© **406/377-5601;** www.glendive chamber.com), provides brochures and maps.

Thousands of anglers come every year to try to snag one of these prehistoric spoonbill sturgeons from the bottom of the Yellowstone River. The season is from May 15 to whenever the annual quota is met or June 30, whichever comes first, and the best fishing spot is at the intake diversion dam on the Yellowstone, 17 miles northeast of town on Mont. 16. Thought to be extinct until an angler snagged one here in 1962, these monsters (adults generally weigh 60–120 lb.) are "snagged"—caught on treble hooks dragged along the bottom of the river—and the limit is one fish per fisherman. Interestingly, local nonprofits accept paddlefish roe as a donation, and they sell the caviar to raise funds. You'll need both a Montana fishing license and a special tag, which several places in town sell; a concessionaire rents poles and lures. There are 30 campsites ($12, or $7 with valid Montana fishing license) at the intake. Call the chamber (© **406/377-5601**) for additional information.

MAKOSHIKA STATE PARK

Montana's largest state park, at 11,531 acres, **Makoshika State Park** ★★ (© **406/377-6256;** www.fwp.mt.gov) is a few blocks from town via the railroad underpass. The name is Lakota, and means "bad earth" or "bad land." Erosion has done wonders with the park's upper and most malleable layer, forming magnificent spires in some places and coulees that cut deep into the multicolored valleys in others. Ponderosa pine trees are scattered over much of the park. The amazing thing about this state park is not necessarily the uncanny resemblance to Badlands National Park in South Dakota, but the abundance of dinosaur bones that have been removed from under the loess. Among the exhibits in the visitor center is the actual skull—not a replica or cast—from a young triceratops uncovered in the park. For more on the region's prehistory, pay a visit to the **Makoshika Dinosaur Museum** 111 W. Bell St. in downtown Glendive (© **406/377-1637;** www.makoshika.com). Admission is $5 adults, $3 students and seniors, and free for kids 5 and under.

A paved road—steep and narrow even by Montana mountain standards—winds about 4 miles to an overlook that provides a wonderful view of the badlands. From there, the road becomes gravel and continues for another 3½ miles before maintenance ends. There are also 5 miles of hiking trails (with 10 more to come at some point), along with a number of off-trail backpacking routes. The visitor center (daily 10am–6pm Memorial Day to Labor Day; Mon–Sat 9am–5pm the rest of the year) has a fine display of the history, prehistory, and geology of the park. There is also a "folf," or Frisbee golf, course and several hiking trails. The day-use fee is $5 per vehicle; campsites are $12 to $15.

WHERE TO STAY & DINE

Lodging here includes the historic **Best Western Glendive Inn,** 222 N. Kendrick Ave. (© **888/453-6348** or 406/377-5555), with rates of $75 to $110 double; and **Days Inn,** 2000 N. Merrill Ave. (© **800/329-7466** or 406/365-6011), which charges $65 to $75 double, with lower rates in winter. For lunch or dinner, we like the family-friendly beer-and-pizza joint, the **Gust Hauf,** 300 W. Bell St. (© **406/365-4451**), featuring a video arcade and casino and a big kitschy beer stein out front.

Charley Montana Bed & Breakfast ★★   An impeccable restoration of a majestic neoclassical mansion, Charley Montana is a top-flight B&B in what was once the palatial, 26-room abode of rancher Charles Krug. Built in 1906, the house has been restored to its original condition, with impeccable attention to the woodwork inside and out. The five guest rooms include the Charles Room, the old master bedroom with the leather-bound encyclopedia from the Krug family library, as well as the Annie Suite, named for Krug's wife, with an impressive wardrobe and separate sitting area with heirloom arm-chairs. The 8,000-square-foot inn is located on the outskirts of downtown Glendive, cater-cornered to an old silo and a stone's throw from the old Bell Street Bridge across the Yellowstone River, now reserved for pedestrians and bicyclists.

103 N. Douglas St. (P.O. Box 1192), Glendive, MT 59930. ℂ **888/395-3207** or 406/365-3207. www. charley-montana.com. 5 units. $95–$110 double; $135 suite. Rates include full breakfast. AE, DISC, MC, V. *In room:* A/C, TV, hair dryer, Wi-Fi (free).

A SIDE TRIP TO FORT UNION

Strictly speaking, the **Fort Union Trading Post National Historic Site** is in North Dakota. The Montana–North Dakota border bisects the parking lot, and the fort itself is a few paces east. But Fort Union was so important to Montana's development that it should be part of any trip through the eastern part of the state.

For 30 years after 1828, Fort Union was the edge of the frontier—the most important trading post in John Jacob Astor's beaver pelt and buffalo robe empire in the Northern Plains. This National Park Service site has been spectacularly reconstructed from pictures and descriptions. The main gate of the glistening, whitewashed wooden stockade over-looks the wide Missouri, and two tall stone bastions stand sentinel over the river at the fort's corners.

Lewis and Clark camped near here on their trip to the Pacific, on April 25 and 26, 1805. Lewis commented in his journals on the "wide and fertile vallies" and how ideal the site would be for a fort. The Bourgeois House has been converted into a modern visitor center, and contains excellent exhibits detailing the life and times of the fur trad-ers. Artist George Catlin visited in 1832, as did Karl Bodmer in 1833, and John James Audubon in 1843. In 1867, the U.S. Army acquired the fort, and its lumber was used to expand nearby Fort Buford and fuel steamboats.

GETTING THERE & VISITOR INFORMATION   From I-94 exit 213 at Glendive, take Mont. 16 northeast to the North Dakota border, then North Dakota 58 north to the fort (it's about 75 miles). Contact **Fort Union Trading Post National Historic Site,** 15550 N. Dak. 1804, Williston, ND 58801 (ℂ **701/572-9083** or 572-7622; www.nps.gov/ fous). Admission is free and the park is open daily from 8am to 8pm during the summer and 9am to 5:30pm in winter.

12

Yellowstone National Park

For all the epic wonder of the geysers and the antlered elk and the towering waterfalls, visitors to our nation's first national park often bring home memories more subtle and personal: the fine grades of pastel colors in a small hot spring, or the flight of an osprey above the river, or a spider web sagging with steam droplets in the early morning light. Yellowstone isn't just about beauty. At every turn it raises questions about the mysteries of nature, awakening a curiosity you might have thought died during that long-ago biology exam.

After the initial reaction of wordless awe to a bubbling mud pot or a meadow of brightly colored wildflowers, it's human nature to want to know how it all works. And only in Yellowstone can you observe firsthand how wolves wander amid an elk herd seeking prey, or smell the sulfurous vapors venting from the volcanic caldera beneath the plateau, or touch the fireweed and pine seedlings sprouting within the forests burned by the 1988 fires.

It was a prescient move in 1872 when Congress set aside 2.2 million acres of the West as a geothermal and wildlife preserve and "pleasuring ground for the benefit and enjoyment of the people." Since then, Yellowstone has been the model for the creation of parks around the world. For Americans, it's become a kind of national touchstone to our wilderness past, visited by more than three million pilgrims a year.

Despite all we get out of Yellowstone, not nearly as much has been put back. There is a backlog of work to be done, from road repair to sewer improvements, and there are also issues of ecological health. Imported Mackinaw trout are crowding out the native cutthroat in Yellowstone Lake, and increasing traffic congestion interferes with the wildlife.

But there are success stories, too, such as the reintroduction of wolves to the Yellowstone ecosystem, and the devoted work of park scientists and managers. People who know the park well remain optimistic that our mistakes will not dislodge nature's plan. For 600,000 years, since the last time the Yellowstone caldera blew its top, the forces of nature have been reshaping Yellowstone and populating it with flora and fauna. These things take time. Likewise, as much time as you and your family can invest here will be richly rewarded.

1 THE GATEWAY TOWNS: WEST YELLOWSTONE, GARDINER & COOKE CITY

West Yellowstone: 91 miles SW of Bozeman; 30 miles W of Old Faithful; 320 miles NE of Salt Lake City. Gardiner: 79 miles SE of Bozeman; 163 miles SW of Billings. Cooke City: 127 miles SW of Billings

WEST YELLOWSTONE

By making itself the headquarters for snowmobilers who want to travel the park's roads in winter, **West Yellowstone**—just outside the park's west gate—has created a year-round tourist economy and attracted an ever-growing number of big hotel chains. The quiet fly-fishing town that once was is no more: The shops are chock-full of curios, and the streets are clogged with tour buses and, in the winter, rumbling snow machines.

One could argue that West Yellowstone made its Faustian bargain with tourism long ago, when the Oregon Short Line's *Yellowstone Special* train first arrived in 1909. Originally called Riverside, then Yellowstone, the town was grudgingly renamed West Yellowstone in 1920 when Gardiner residents complained that tourists would mistakenly believe the town was the park. Name aside, this place is more about shopping than about nature, and its biggest attraction is the zoolike Grizzly & Wolf Discovery Center.

Essentials

GETTING THERE   The **West Yellowstone Airport,** U.S. 191, 1 mile north of West Yellowstone (© **406/646-7631**), provides commercial air service, June through September only, on Delta's **SkyWest Airlines.** If you're driving the 91 miles from Bozeman to West Yellowstone, take U.S. 191 south (a pretty journey along the Gallatin River) to its junction with U.S. 287 and head straight into town. From Idaho Falls, take I-15 north to U.S. 20, which takes you directly into West Yellowstone, a 53-mile drive.

VISITOR INFORMATION   Contact the **West Yellowstone Chamber of Commerce,** 30 Yellowstone Ave., P.O. Box 458, West Yellowstone, MT 59758 (© **406/646-7701;** www.westyellowstonechamber.com).

GETTING AROUND   At the West Yellowstone Airport, **Avis** (© **800/230-4898** or 406/646-7635; www.avis.com) and **Budget** (© **800/527-0700** or 406/646-7882; www. budget.com) offer car rentals. **Yellowstone Taxi** (© **406/646-1118;** www.yellowstone taxi.com) provides local service.

Getting Outside

Most people arrive here on their way to the park, but there is no fence along the park's boundary, so some of the best wild country is actually to the west. If you like fishing, the rivers—the Gallatin and the Madison, particularly—are among the best in the country. The following tackle shops offer the full gamut of guided fishing trips and instruction: **Arrick's Fly Shop,** 37 Canyon St. (© **406/646-7290**); **Bud Lilly's Trout Shop,** 39 Madison Ave. (© **406/646-7801**); **Jacklin's,** 105 Yellowstone Ave. (© **406/646-7336**); and **Madison River Outfitters,** 117 Canyon St. (© **406/646-9644**).

Come winter, **cross-country skiers** hit the trails (see section 7, "Winter Sports & Activities"). Ski rentals are available in West Yellowstone at **FreeHeel and Wheel,** 40 Yellowstone Ave. (© **406/646-7744**), or **Bud Lilly's,** 39 Madison Ave. (© **406/646-7801**).

Despite a push for a ban and a new quota system in the park, **snowmobiling** is a huge draw in West Yellowstone, where sleds are more common than cars on snowpacked winter streets. In addition to driving the machines on the snowpacked roads of Yellowstone—where speed limits are strictly enforced—you can take the trails in surrounding national forests with fewer restrictions. There are tricks to riding on backcountry snow, so if you're inexperienced, rent a guide as well as a machine. All the major hotels and motels in West Yellowstone arrange snowmobile rentals that include gear, and there are numerous independent operations offering rentals and guides, including **Yellowstone Arctic/Yamaha,** 208 Electric St. (© **406/646-9636**), and **Yellowstone Adventures,** 131 Dunraven Ave. (© **800/231-5991**).

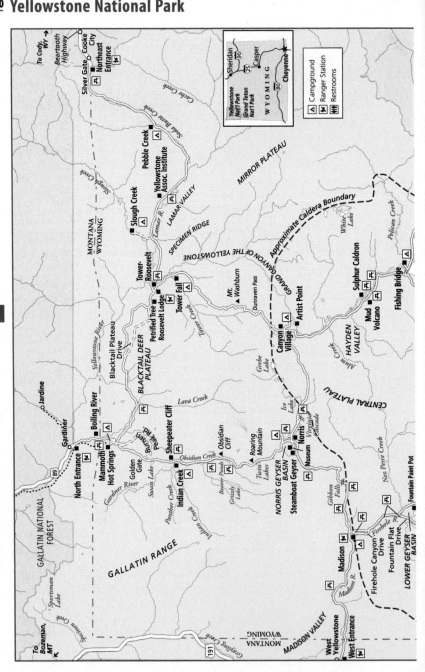

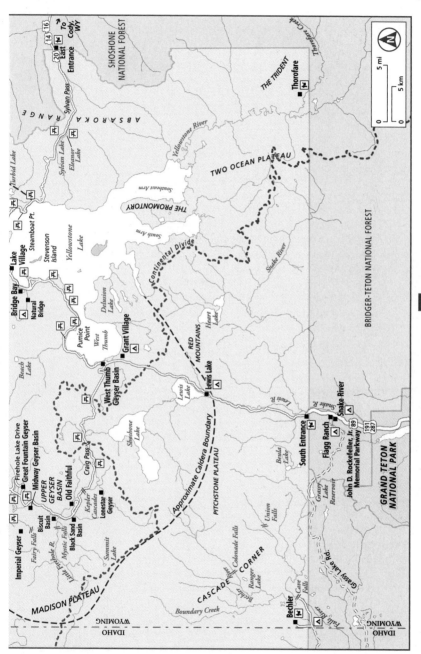

(Moments) **Frommer's Favorite Yellowstone Experiences**

Witness the World's Most Famous Geologic Alarm Clock. Old Faithful is known for its reliability, but it's slowing down a little with age. Still, about once every 90 minutes, give or take, you can watch her blow, making her the most predictable geyser on the planet. While you're there, get a good look at the beautiful and historic Old Faithful Inn. See section 4, "Seeing the Highlights."

Escape to the Backcountry. If the packed benches at Old Faithful give you the impression that Yellowstone is overrun, venture into the backcountry for a dose of true wilderness. It will restore your spirits and perhaps your belief in national parks. Get advice from a ranger on how to travel safely in bear country, and then have it mostly to yourself—most of the three million annual park visitors rarely leave the roadways. See section 8, "Hiking."

Get Hooked on Yellowstone Trout. There is some fine fly-fishing water in and near the park. Try the Madison, the Gibbon, and the Firehole rivers, or troll the lakes for cutthroat, brown, rainbow, and brook trout. When a big trout slaps the twilight surface of the Yellowstone River, Izaak Walton smiles in fly-fishing heaven. See section 6, "Summer Sports & Activities."

Have a Howling Good Time at Lamar. Since wolves were reintroduced in Yellowstone in 1994, they have surprised biologists by making frequent morning and late-afternoon appearances along Slough Creek and in other parts

Expect to pay $225 to $250 per day per snowmobile, plus about $225 for a guide (required), and unless you have a helmet and winter gear to protect you from subzero wind chill, plan on spending another $25 for clothing. Also popular are **snowcoach tours,** offered in vans equipped with tanklike treads to travel on snow. Check with **Yellowstone Alpen Guides Co.,** 535 Yellowstone Ave. (✆ **800/858-3502**), or with snowmobile outfitters, who often offer snowcoach rides as well.

Seeing the Sights

Grizzly and Wolf Discovery Center   Those who haven't the patience to search out and observe the free-ranging wildlife of Yellowstone might want to try this not-for-profit educational center. The interpretive center gives a detailed explanation of these animals' history in this country, along with the difficult and controversial efforts to revive them in the wild. This is a closer look than you'll likely get with animals in the wild, but did you really come to Yellowstone to look at grizzlies imported from Alaska in an enclosure? 201 S. Canyon St. in Grizzly Park. ✆ **800/257-2570** or 406/646-7001. www.grizzlydiscoveryctr.org. $11 adults, $9.75 seniors, $5.50 children 5–12, free for children 4 and under. Summer daily 8:30am–8:30pm; shorter hours in winter.

Yellowstone Historic Center ★   Located in the historic 1909 Union Pacific depot, this is the only museum that focuses on Yellowstone's cultural history, providing an interesting snapshot into the ways of the park's first tourists, with scads of memorabilia,

of Lamar Valley. This especially untamed area in the northeast corner of Yellowstone is loaded with wildlife: bison, elk, coyotes, and grizzly bears. See section 8, "Hiking."

Make Like Teddy and Be a Rough Rider. At Roosevelt Lodge, visitors relive the Old West by taking organized rides on horseback, stagecoach, or wagon. A more adventurous alternative is the Old West cookout; you will arrive by either horseback or wagon for hearty meat-and-potatoes grub. See section 11, "Where to Dine in the Park."

Learn Something at the Yellowstone Association Institute. You can take classes on everything from bears to butterflies at the Yellowstone Association Institute, which inhabits the old Lamar Buffalo Ranch in the park's northeast corner. It's a friendly, communal way to get a more intimate knowledge of the ecosystem. See section 3, "A Park Primer."

Sleep on a Historic Pillow in the Park. Old Faithful Inn, dating from 1904, is a log cathedral within view of the geyser. Relax with a drink on the second-floor terrace, or climb the timber lattice that holds up the great roof. Original rooms may not all have private bathrooms, but it's still the nicest place to stay in the park. Ask for suite no. 3014 or room no. 229 to watch the geyser erupt from your room. See section 10, "Where to Stay in the Park."

postcards, and concessionaire ephemera. There are also displays on the Yellowstone ecosystem, covering epochal events such as the 1959 earthquake that created Quake Lake and the 1988 fires, along with a mounted grizzly bear known in his animate days as "Old Snaggletooth."

At Yellowstone Ave. and Canyon St. ☏ **406/646-1100.** www.yellowstonehistoriccenter.org. $5 adults, $4 seniors, $3 children 3–18 and students, free for children 2 and under. Families receive 20% discount. Mid-May to mid-Oct daily 9am–9pm. Closed rest of year.

Yellowstone IMAX Theater   This theater is next door to the Grizzly and Wolf Discovery Center and, together, they form the centerpieces of a real estate development on the edge of the park, which includes several new hotels. Regardless, the IMAX concept works pretty well here—there are things an airborne camera can show you on a six-story-tall screen that you'll never see on your own two feet. A film called *Yellowstone* plays fairly often, with sweeping views of the canyon and falls and other sights.

101 S. Canyon St. ☏ **406/646-4100.** www.yellowstoneimax.com. $9 adults, $8.50 seniors, $6.50 children 3–12, free for children 2 and under. Summer daily 8:30am–9pm; shorter hours rest of year; call for exact showtimes.

Where to Stay

Make your reservations early if you want to visit in July or August, or if you're going to spend Christmas to New Year's here. If you're smart, you'll come in the fall, when there are plenty of empty rooms and better rates, and spend your days fishing the Henry's Fork or one of the other great streams in the vicinity. Rates for rooms often reflect the seasonal traffic, and prices fluctuate. Unless noted, all these establishments are open year-round.

You'll find chains like **Comfort Inn,** 638 Madison Ave. (℃ **406/646-4212;** www. comfortinn.com), with summertime doubles for $79 to $199; and **Days Inn,** 301 Madison Ave. (℃ **800/548-9551** or 406/646-7656; www.daysinn.com), with summer rates of $119 to $199 for a double. There are three **Best Western** affiliates, ranging from about $100 to $170 a night for a double during the summer (℃ **800/528-1234;** www. bestwestern.com). **One Horse Motel,** 216 N. Dunraven St. (℃ **800/488-2750** or 406/646-7677; www.onehorsemotel.com), is a top-notch independent across the street from City Park, with doubles for $90 to $100 a night. Another good inexpensive option (with more character than the chains, to boot), the 1912 **Madison Hotel,** 139 Yellowstone Ave. (℃ **800/838-7745** or 406/646-7745; www.madisonhotelmotel.com), has historic rooms for $59 to $89 for a double or $30 for a bunk in a dormitory, and newer motel doubles for $79 to $139. Another option with historic cachet—and a one-time favorite of broadcasting legend Charles Kuralt—is the **Parade Rest Guest Ranch,** 10 miles north of West Yellowstone at 1279 Grayling Rd. (℃ **800/753-5934** or 406/646-7217; www.paraderestranch.com), in a serene setting near Hebgen Lake. Rates are about $190 for adults and $110 to $150 for kids, all meals and horseback riding included.

Bar N Ranch ★★   One of the oldest brands in Montana, the Bar N is an excellent new lodging option in West Yellowstone, operating a spiffed-up lodge and cabin complex since 2004. Located on 200 acres of unsullied ranchland with 2 miles of the Madison River and a fishing pond, the lodge is an image of the New West, with a great river-rock fireplace and a knotty pine banister leading up to the rooms upstairs. The lodge rooms mix equal parts Ralph Lauren and Old West, exuding a simple but rich style with antler lamps, hardwood floors, and jetted tubs. The cabins are one- and two-bedroom units arranged in a half-circle around the lodge, with decor that echoes that of the lodge; all of them have fireplaces and private outdoor hot tubs. The staff can arrange for guides to take guests fishing, rafting, or horseback riding for an extra fee.

890 Buttermilk Creek Rd. (P.O. Box 250), West Yellowstone, MT 59758. ℃ **406/646-0300.** Fax 406/646-0301. www.bar-n-ranch.com. 15 units, including 8 cabins. Lodge rooms $223–$238 double; cabins $273–$345 double; 4-bedroom cabin $500–$600; lower rates Oct–June. AE, DC, DISC, MC, V. **Amenities:** Restaurant; Jacuzzi; small outdoor pool; Wi-Fi (free). *In room:* TV/DVD, fridge, no phone.

Holiday Inn West Yellowstone ★   This is the town's best modern hotel. The rooms are sizable and comfortable, well maintained, and regularly updated. At the tour desk, you can arrange fishing and rafting trips, bike and ATV rentals, and chuckwagon cookouts. The Iron Horse Saloon serves regional microbrews, and the Oregon Short Line

---

(Tips)   **Superintendent's Advice**

"People have trouble grasping the enormity of our park," says Yellowstone Superintendent Suzanne Lewis. So do your homework. "Really spend time on our website," Lewis suggests. "If you don't have Internet access, go to the public library. It's also important to tell folks, if you come between June and mid-September, you'll be sharing the park with a lot of people."

Restaurant serves Western cuisine including game and seafood dishes. At the center of the restaurant sits the restored railroad club car that brought Victorian gents to Yellowstone a century ago.

315 Yellowstone Ave. (P.O. Box 470), West Yellowstone, MT 59758. © **800/646-7365** or 406/646-7365. www.doyellowstone.com. 123 units. $99–$209 double; $119–$299 suite. AE, DISC, MC, V. **Amenities:** Restaurant; lounge; bikes; children's program; health club; Jacuzzi; large indoor pool; sauna. In room: A/C, TV, fridge, hair dryer, Wi-Fi (free).

Moose Creek Cabins ★ (Finds)   A 1950s motel complex that got a slick revamp in 2004, Moose Creek Cabins offers comfortable and stylish rooms and cabins in the heart of West Yellowstone. The one-time Ranger Motel—which spent 2 decades as employee housing before becoming Moose Creek—is a good value and one of the better-maintained properties in town. There are stand-alone kitchenette cabins (good for families) and cabin-style motel rooms with queen-size beds; both are laden with pine and charming individual themes. The proprietors also own a good motel, the Moose Creek Inn, a few blocks away with double rooms for $69 to $92.

220 Firehole Ave., West Yellowstone, MT 59758. © **406/646-9546.** www.moosecreekcabin.com. 13 units and cabins. $92–$170 double; $170 cabin. MC, V. In room: TV, kitchenette, no phone, Wi-Fi (free).

Three Bear Lodge ★ (Kids)   Rebuilt from the ground up after a 2008 fire, this woodsy, family-friendly inn is located less than 3 blocks from the park entrance. Those familiar with the old Three Bear will be hard-pressed to recognize the slick new incarnation, featuring recycled wood, a striking lobby with a monolithic stone fireplace and scads of taxidermy, and stylish guest rooms. Some rooms are family suites that sleep up to eight people. About half of the rooms survived the fire, but were updated as the main lodge was rebuilt. The Three Bear offers snowmobile and snowcoach tours in the winter, as well as van tours in the summer.

217 Yellowstone Ave. (P.O. Box 1590), West Yellowstone, MT 59758. © **800/646-7353** or 406/646-7353. Fax 406/646-4567. www.threebearlodge.com. 87 units, including 8 family suites. $95–$219 double. AE, DISC, MC, V. **Amenities:** Restaurant; lounge; exercise room; indoor Jacuzzi; outdoor heated pool (seasonal); sauna. In room: TV, hair dryer, Wi-Fi (free).

Where to Dine

West Yellowstone is a good place to stop for a quick bite on your way into the park. For coffee and baked goods, visit the espresso bar at the excellent **Book Peddler** in Canyon Square (© **406/646-9358**). **Morning Glory Coffee,** 129 Dunraven St. (© **406/646-7061**), roasts its own beans on-site and offers a low-key atmosphere for getting going.

Beartooth Barbecue ★ BARBECUE   A bustling and funky space that plates up some mean Texas-style barbecue, this is my pick for a casual meal in West Yellowstone. At the bar or at a table in the bric-a-brac-laden room (hanging from the walls are sleds, *ristas*, a traffic light, and sports memorabilia), order a plate of St. Louis–cut spareribs or beef brisket for lunch or dinner (or a sandwich with brisket, sausage, or chicken), and plenty of tangy sauce. The bar has Montana-micro beer on draft and serves wine by the glass, but no liquor is served.

111 Canyon St. © **406/646-0227.** Lunch and dinner $10–$27. MC, V. Daily 11:30am–10pm.

The Canyon Street Grill (Value) AMERICAN   It's hard not to like an establishment whose slogan is "We are not a fast-food restaurant. We are a cafe reminiscent of a bygone era when the quality of the food meant more than how fast it could be served." With checkerboard floors and shiny red booths, this delightful 1950s-style spot serves hearty food for breakfast, lunch, and dinner. Hamburgers and chicken sandwiches are popular, accompanied by milkshakes made with hard ice cream or their famous root beer float.

22 Canyon St. ☎ 406/646-7548. Main courses $4–$11. MC, V. May–Nov Mon–Sat 11am–10pm; shorter hours rest of year. Closed Apr.

Eino's Tavern (Finds AMERICAN   Locals snowmobile out from West Yellowstone to Eino's (there's a trail that follows U.S. Hwy. 191) to become their own chefs at the grill here. It's a novel concept, and it keeps patrons coming back to this casual restaurant with a fine view of Hebgen Lake time and time again. There's usually a line out the door, but it's fun to peruse the walls, plastered with dollar bills and other currency as well as bras and funny photos, while you wait. After placing your order for a steak, teriyaki chicken, hamburger, or hot dog, keep a straight face when you're handed an uncooked piece of meat. Go to the grill, slap it on, and stand around, drink in hand, shooting the breeze with other patrons until your food is exactly the way you like it. Steaks and chicken come with your choice of a salad (or the place's trademark "hot potatoes" in winter), and hamburgers come with chips.

155 Eino's Loop (9 miles north of West Yellowstone on U.S. Hwy. 191). ☎ 406/646-9344. Main courses $5.50–$26. No credit cards; ATM on premises. Winter daily 9am–9pm; rest of year daily noon–9pm. Closed Thanksgiving to mid-Dec.

The Outpost Restaurant (Kids AMERICAN   Tucked away in a downtown mall, this rustic restaurant laden with Western bric-a-brac serves old-fashioned home-style fare, such as hearty beef stew with fork-size chunks of carrots and potatoes. There's also salmon, steak, trout, liver, and an excellent salad bar. For breakfast, if you're really hungry, you can't beat the Campfire Omelette, smothered in homemade chili, cheese, and onions. The menu isn't all that adventurous, and there's none of the vices you'll find in the local taverns (no video poker, beer, wine, liquor, or smoking); but it offers solid fare in a quiet, family-friendly atmosphere. The desserts include pie and a wild huckleberry sundae.

115 Yellowstone Ave. (in the Montana Outpost Mall). ☎ 406/646-7303. Breakfast $5–$16; lunch $6–$14; dinner $9–$25. AE, DISC, MC, V. Daily 6:30am–10:30pm. Closed mid-Oct to mid-Apr.

Sydney's Mountain Bistro ★★ CONTEMPORARY AMERICAN   The most upscale option in a meat-and-potatoes town, Sydney's offers an intimate setting, an excellent wine list, and a menu that balances seafood and vegetarian fare with beef, poultry, and pork. With interesting preparations—such as flash-fried calamari for starters and entrees including sweet-chili salmon and a porterhouse pork chop with butternut squash—and a breezy patio complementing the upscale atmosphere inside, this is my pick for a special meal in West Yellowstone. Lunches include sandwiches, panini, and burgers, as well as a quiche of the day and a savory pear-walnut salad.

38 Canyon St. ☎ 406/646-7660. Brunch and lunch $5–$9.50; dinner $14–$26. MC, V. Daily 11am–3pm and 5–10pm.

GARDINER

Of all the towns that stand sentry on the roads into Yellowstone, Gardiner is the prototype gateway community. This is partly due to the historic stone Roosevelt Arch that marks the entrance through which the earliest visitors passed into the park. This is the only park entrance that's open to auto traffic year-round, in order to keep a connection open to Cooke City, which in winter can be reached only through the north entrance.

Gardiner sits at the junction of the Gardner and Yellowstone rivers (the town's eight-letter name has been attributed to a 19th-c. spelling error), still looking like the gritty little mining town it once was. Nobody puts on airs in the coffee shops and bars, and nobody raises an eyebrow when a bison or deer wanders through town.

GETTING THERE From Bozeman (the nearest jet-service airport), take I-90 26 miles east to Livingston, then take U.S. 89 south 53 miles to Gardiner.

VISITOR INFORMATION Contact the **Gardiner Chamber of Commerce,** 222 Park St., P.O. Box 81, Gardiner, MT 59030 (✆ **406/848-7971;** www.gardinerchamber.com). Across from the landmark Roosevelt Arch is the slick new headquarters of the **Yellowstone Association** (✆ **406/848-2400;** www.yellowstoneassociation.org), a restored historic building by renowned architect Robert Reamer, complete with a terrific store and visitor center.

Getting Outside

Gardiner is the spot to go for white-water rafting on the Yellowstone River. Several outfitters take guests on half- and full-day trips on routes skirting the park's northern boundary; the best of the bunch is the **Yellowstone Raft Company,** U.S. Hwy. 89 (✆ **800/858-7781** or 406/848-7777; www.yellowstoneraft.com), with half-day trips for $37 and full days for $80; children get on the boat for $27 half-day or $60 full day. While not a **snowmobiling** hub on the magnitude of West Yellowstone, a few motels here rent snowmobiles or offer snowcoach tours. **Hiking** and **fishing** opportunities are bountiful in every direction from town.

Where to Stay

Dinky, personable, and a bit eccentric, Gardiner has long had ultrafriendly lodging—thin-walled motels where, if you show up late, they've gone to bed and left a key in the door. These days it also has some newer, chain-affiliated properties, built to accommodate the ever-increasing traffic to the park. As with all the gateway towns, make your reservations early if you're coming during the peak season. The steep off-season decline in traffic results in discounts that can be considerably less expensive than the high-season rates quoted below, so be sure to ask.

Inexpensive motels are moving in and filling up during the summer months: the **Yellowstone Park Travelodge,** 109 Hellroaring Rd. (✆ **406/848-7520**), and **Super 8,** 702 U.S. Hwy. 89 (✆ **800/800-8000** or 406/848-7401; www.super8.com), are open year-round with rates during the high season between $120 and $140 for a double. The **Best Western by Mammoth Hot Springs,** on U.S. Hwy. 89 (✆ **800/828-9080** or 406/848-7311; www.bestwestern.com), is another option, with doubles for $99 to $189. Of the independents, I like **Yellowstone River Motel,** 14 E. Park St. (✆ **406/848-7303**) with doubles for $60 to $100 in peak season.

Absaroka Lodge ★★ Every room in this lodge has its own furnished balcony with jaw-dropping views of the Yellowstone River and the mountain scenery beyond it. The lodge's riverbank location—with a nice slope of lawn overlooking the river gorge—is just a few blocks from the village center, and the rooms are well appointed with queen-size beds. Suites with kitchenettes cost a little more; there is also a pair of cabins without balconies. Like most other properties in town, the lodge has staff ready and able to assist in arrangements with outfitters for fly-fishing, rafting, and, in the fall, hunting.

U.S. Hwy. 89 at the Yellowstone River Bridge (P.O. Box 10), Gardiner, MT 59030. ✆ **800/755-7414** or 406/848-7414. Fax 406/848-7560. www.yellowstonemotel.com. 41 units. Summer $110–$125 double; winter $45–$60 double. AE, DC, DISC, MC, V. *In room:* A/C, TV, kitchenette, Wi-Fi (free).

Comfort Inn   This log cabin–style hotel looks like it belongs here, unlike a lot of chain operations. The centerpiece is a 3,000-square-foot rustic lobby decorated with wild-game trophies, and a large second-floor balcony that offers views of Yellowstone scenery and passing wildlife. Family rooms that sleep six and luxurious suites with hot tubs are also available. The Antler Pub and Grill here serves Italian and American dinners in summer only.

107 Hellroaring Dr. (P.O. Box 268), Gardiner, MT 59030. ℂ **800/424-6423** or 406/848-7536. Fax 406/848-7062. www.yellowstonecomfortinn.com. 77 units. Summer $140–$200 double; winter $50–$100 double. AE, DISC, MC, V. **Amenities:** Restaurant; bar/casino; 2 indoor Jacuzzis. *In room:* A/C, TV, hair dryer, Wi-Fi (free).

Yellowstone Suites Bed and Breakfast ★ (Finds)   This quiet B&B on the south bank of the Yellowstone River is a good alternative to the motels that line U.S. Hwy. 89. Originally built in 1904, legend has it that the second story's quarried-stone exterior is actually a leftover from the Roosevelt Arch. The rooms are frilly and cozy, with a teddy-bear motif in the Roosevelt Room and a Victorian theme in the Jackson Room; the Yellowstone Suite has satellite television and a kitchenette. The real perks here are the impeccably gardened backyard and the breakfasts, which might feature cinnamon rolls or cheese blintzes.

506 Fourth St. (P.O. Box 277), Gardiner, MT 59030. ℂ **800/948-7937** or 406/848-7937. www.yellowstone suites.com. 4 units. Summer $112–$158 double; winter $80–$105 double. Rates include complimentary full breakfast. MC, V. **Amenities:** Outdoor Jacuzzi. *In room:* A/C, kitchenette, no phone, Wi-Fi (free).

Where to Dine

An indication that Gardiner has kept in touch with its mining-town roots is the relative dearth of fancy restaurants—you'll find mostly steakhouse fare, hearty breakfasts, and travelers' food. A few upscale eateries have come and gone in recent years, but the dish-clattering local color of the park-side coffee shops is hard to beat.

The Corral Drive-In AMERICAN   Okay, so it's not much to look at, and the menu's most adventurous item is a basket of fried shrimp. But since 1960, the place's reputation has rested on burgers that are nothing short of colossal. With a half pound of meat (beef, elk, or buffalo), several slices of American cheese, bacon, and all the usual veggies, these burgers have been known to measure a full 7 inches from bun to bun. The monstrous things garnered the nickname "Helen's Hateful Hamburgers" after a dissatisfied customer wrote a letter to the local paper dubbing them just that. Corral founder Helen Gould ran with it, using the intended insult as a sarcastic slogan in promotions and on T-shirts. Ice cream and an assortment of fried goods round out the menu.

U.S. Hwy. 89 at Yellowstone St. ℂ **406/848-7627.** Menu items $4–$14. No credit cards. May–Sept daily 11am–11pm. Closed Oct–Apr.

Pedalino's ★★ ITALIAN   Gardiner's culinary standout, Pedalino's serves reliably tasty Italian dishes in a woodsy room on the main drag, decked out with exposed rough-hewn logs and historical photos of the area. The menu features a number of pasta dishes—including the signature spicy penne *pazze*—"crazy"—as well as a selection of steaks, seafood, and barbecued ribs. There is a kids' menu and a full bar.

200 W. Park St. ℂ **406/848-9950.** www.pedalinositalian.com. Main courses $14–$26 dinner. AE, DISC, MC, V. Wed–Mon 5–9pm.

Sawtooth Deli ★ DELI/AMERICAN   This stalwart eatery on Park Street is a reliable spot for hearty American breakfasts and plump subs. I like the burritos in the morning for breakfast (especially before a big hike) and the Philly cheese steaks and veggie subs for lunch (especially after a big hike). With a basic main room and a breezy patio, there is both wait service and a to-go counter. Beer and wine are served, but not liquor.

222 W. Park St. © **406/848-7600.** Main courses $5–$8 breakfast and lunch. MC, V. Summer Tues–Sat 8am–4pm; shorter hours rest of year.

COOKE CITY

If little ol' Gardiner seems just a little too connected to the civilized world, you ought to spend a winter in tiny Cooke City or even tinier Silver Gate, just outside Yellowstone National Park's northeast entrance. In the winter, when the cloud-scraping Beartooth Pass closes to the north, supplies for these towns have to come through the park. Better to visit in the summer and take the breathtaking drive north over the pass (U.S. 212 toward Red Lodge) or south along the scenic Chief Joseph Highway (Wyo. 296). For 100 years, the lifeblood of this town was mining gold, platinum, and other precious metals, but now there is only park tourism, which seems a little anemic by comparison. Fewer than 100 residents live year-round in the town today, and Silver Gate, right next to the park entrance, has perhaps a dozen hardy year-round residents. Contact the **Colter Pass/ Cooke City/Silver Gate Chamber of Commerce** at P.O. Box 1071, Cooke City, MT 59020 (© **406/838-2495;** www.cookecitychamber.org), for information. The chamber operates a visitor center at 109 Main St. that is open daily from 11am to 6pm in summer.

GETTING THERE From Billings, Montana, drive west on I-90 to Laurel, then south on U.S. 212 to Red Lodge, a total distance of 60 miles; then continue another 67 miles south over spectacular Beartooth Pass, dipping into Wyoming and back up into Montana at Cooke City.

WHERE TO STAY & DINE A room for the night will be less expensive than in other gateway towns, typically from $60 to $120 a night. The **Soda Butte Lodge,** 209 Main St. (© **406/838-2251;** www.cookecity.com), is the biggest motel in Cooke City, and it includes the **Prospector Restaurant** and a small casino; or, you can go to the cheaper, barebones **Alpine Motel,** 105 Main St. (© **888/838-1190** or 406/838-2262; www. cookecityalpine.com). The newest property is a woodsy **Super 8,** 303 Main St. (© **877/ 338-2070** or 406/838-2070; www.cookecitysuper8.com). For a bite to eat and a great selection of beers, try the funky **Beartooth Cafe** (© **406/838-2475**), also on Main Street. I also like the sandwiches and barbecue plates at **Buns 'N' Beds,** 201 Main St. (© **406/838-2030**). In Silver Gate, the **Log Cabin Café and B&B** (© **406/838-2367**) is a rustic-meets-refined eatery specializing in trout dinners.

2 JUST THE FACTS

BEFORE YOU GO

To obtain maps and information about the park prior to arrival, contact **Yellowstone National Park,** Yellowstone National Park, WY 82190 (© **307/344-7381;** www.nps. gov/yell). Information regarding lodging, some campgrounds, tours, boating, and horse-back riding in Yellowstone is available from **Xanterra Parks & Resorts,** P.O. Box 165, Yellowstone National Park, WY 82190 (© **866/439-7375** or 307/344-7311; www. travelyellowstone.com). For information regarding educational programs at the **Yellowstone Association Institute,** contact **Yellowstone Association,** P.O. Box 117,

Yellowstone National Park, WY 82190 (📞 **406/848-2400;** www.yellowstoneassociation. org). The association operates bookstores in park visitor centers, museums, and information stations, and the old Lamar Buffalo Ranch in the park's northeast corner is the Institute's primary campus. They also have a catalog of publications you can download from the website or order by mail.

GETTING THERE

If interstate highways and international airports are the measure of accessibility, then Yellowstone is as remote as Alaska's Denali National Park or the Serengeti Plains of Africa. But three million people make it here every year, on tour buses, in family vans, on bicycles, and astride snowmobiles, even from the other side of the world.

The closest airport to Yellowstone is in **West Yellowstone,** Montana, which sits just outside the park's west entrance. For information on flying into West Yellowstone, see "Essentials" in section 1 of this chapter.

Visitors can reach the park from the south by flying into **Jackson,** Wyoming (only 14 miles from the southern entrance to Grand Teton), then driving 56 miles through Grand Teton to the southern entrance of Yellowstone. **American** (📞 800/433-7300; www. aa.com), **Delta** (📞 800/221-1212; www.delta.com), **Northwest** (📞 800/225-2525; www.nwa.com), and **United** (📞 800/241-6522; www.united.com) all have flights to and from **Jackson Hole Airport** (📞 307/733-7682; www.jacksonholeairport.com).

To the north, **Bozeman,** Montana, is 87 miles from the West Yellowstone entrance on U.S. Hwy. 191. Or you can drive east from Bozeman to Livingston, a 20-mile journey on I-90, and then south 53 miles on U.S. Hwy. 89 to the northern entrance at Gardiner. Bozeman's airport, **Gallatin Field** (📞 406/388-8321; www.gallatinfield.com), provides daily service via **Delta, Northwest,** and **United** (see phone numbers and websites above), as well as **Horizon** (📞 800/547-9308; www.horizonair.com) and **Frontier** (📞 800/431-1359; www.frontierairlines.com).

Also to the north, **Billings,** Montana, is 129 miles from the Cooke City entrance. Billings is home to Montana's busiest airport, **Logan International** (📞 406/247-8609; www.flybillings.com), which is 2 miles north of downtown. Daily service is provided by **Allegiant Air** (📞 702/505-8888; www.allegiantair.com), **Delta, Frontier, Horizon, Northwest,** and **United** (see phone numbers above). From Billings, it's a 65-mile drive south on U.S. Hwy. 212 to Red Lodge, and then 30 miles on the Beartooth Highway to the northeast entrance to the park. Keep in mind that the Beartooth Highway (U.S. 212), which takes you on a high, twisting journey over a spectacular pass, is open only from Memorial Day weekend until late October.

From **Cody,** Wyoming, it's a gorgeous 53-mile drive west along U.S. Hwy. 14/16/20 to the east entrance of the park. Cody's **Yellowstone Regional Airport** (📞 307/587-5096; www.flyyra.com) serves the Bighorn Basin as well as the east and northeast entrances of Yellowstone National Park with year-round commercial flights via **Delta** and **United** (see phone numbers above).

Airfares to the small airports surrounding the parks can be pricey, so if you like to drive, consider flying in to **Salt Lake City,** Utah, and driving about 300 miles to Grand Teton National Park, a drive that has some nice scenic stretches. Even **Denver,** a drive of roughly 500 miles, is an alternative, although the route is not nearly as scenic.

Most of the major auto-rental agencies have operations in the gateway cities.

Yellowstone has five entrances. The **north entrance,** near Mammoth Hot Springs, is located just south of Gardiner, Montana, and U.S. 89. In the winter, this is the only access to Yellowstone by car.

The **west entrance,** just outside the town of West Yellowstone on U.S. 20, is the closest entry to Old Faithful. Inside the park, turn south to see Old Faithful or north to the Norris Geyser Basin. This entrance is open to wheeled vehicles April through November, and during the winter to snowmobiles and snowcoaches.

The **south entrance,** on U.S. 89/191/287, brings visitors into the park from neighboring Grand Teton National Park and the Jackson area. As you drive north from Jackson, you'll get a panoramic view of the Grand Tetons. Once in the park, the road winds along the Lewis River to the south end of Yellowstone Lake, at West Thumb and Grant Village. It is open to cars May through November and to snowmobiles and snowcoaches December through March.

The **east entrance,** on U.S. 14/16/20, is 52 miles west of Cody, Wyoming, and is open to cars May through September and to snowmobiles and snowcoaches December through March. The drive up the Wapiti Valley and over Sylvan Pass is especially beautiful.

The **northeast entrance,** at Cooke City, Montana, is closest to the Tower-Roosevelt area, 29 miles to the west. This entrance is open to cars year-round, but beginning on October 15, when the Beartooth Highway closes, until around Memorial Day, the only route to Cooke City is from Gardiner through Mammoth Hot Springs. When it's open—or not blockaded by landslides, as it was during the summer of 2005—the drive from Red Lodge to Cooke City is a grand climb into the clouds.

Regardless of which entrance you choose, when you enter the park you'll be given a good map and up-to-date information on facilities, services, programs, fishing, camping, and more.

Note: Check **road conditions** before entering the park by calling for a road report (© **307/344-7381**). There always seems to be major road construction in one part of the park or another, so be forewarned.

VISITOR CENTERS & INFORMATION

There are five major visitor and information centers in the park, and each has something different to offer. Unless otherwise indicated, summer hours are from 8am to 7pm daily.

The **Albright Visitor Center** (© **307/344-2263**), at Mammoth Hot Springs, is the largest and is open year-round. It provides visitor information and publications about the park, has exhibits depicting park history from prehistory through the creation of the National Park Service, and houses a wildlife display on the second floor.

A new, state-of-the-art **Old Faithful Visitor Center** (© **307/545-2750** or 344-2751 for a recording of Old Faithful eruption predictions) is slated to open in 2010, showing a film on Yellowstone's thermal features throughout the day and featuring exhibits focusing on the park's thermal features and underlying volcanism. Rangers also post projected geyser-eruption times here.

The **Canyon Visitor Center** (© **307/242-2550**), in Canyon Village, reopened in 2007 after a renovation and is the place to go for books and an informative display about the park's geology, with a focus on the underlying volcanism. It's staffed with friendly rangers used to dealing with crowds.

The **Fishing Bridge Visitor Center** (☎ 307/242-2450), near Fishing Bridge on the north shore of Yellowstone Lake, has an excellent display that focuses on the park's bird life. You can get information and publications here as well.

The **Grant Visitor Center** (☎ 307/242-2650) has information, publications, a video program, and a fascinating exhibit that examines the role of fire in Yellowstone.

Helpful staff and park literature can also be found at several small information stations: the **Madison Information Station** (☎ 307/344-2821); the **Museum of the National Park Ranger** (no phone; daily in summer 9am–5pm) and the **Norris Geyser Basin Museum and Information Station** (☎ 307/344-2812; daily in summer 10am–5pm), both at Norris; the **West Thumb Information Station** (no phone; daily in summer 9am–5pm); and the **Visitor Information Center** at the West Yellowstone Visitors Information Center, 100 Yellowstone Ave. (☎ 307/344-2876). In Gardiner (but also within Yellowstone boundaries) is the **Yellowstone Heritage and Research Center** (☎ 307/344-2664), housing a library, archives, and other resources available to the public. It is open year-round Monday to Friday 9am to 4pm, but because it is a research center, it is not equipped to handle standard visitor inquiries about camping and hiking and such.

FEES & PERMITS

Entrance for up to 7 days costs $25 per vehicle and covers both Yellowstone and Grand Teton national parks. A snowmobile or motorcycle pays $20 for 7 days, and visitors on bicycles, skis, or on foot pay $12. You can buy an **annual permit** for $40, but the various national park passes are the best deal (see chapter 3).

BACKCOUNTRY PERMITS   Backcountry permits are free, but you have to have one for any overnight trip, on foot, on horseback, or by boat. Camping is allowed only in designated campsites, many of which are equipped with food-storage poles to keep wildlife away. These sites are primitive and well situated, and you won't feel at all like you're in a campground. If designated campsites in a particular area have already been reserved, you're out of luck. So while you can make a reservation as few as 48 hours before beginning a trip, you would be wise during peak season to make a reservation well in advance (you can contact the park for reservations for the upcoming year beginning Apr 1), although it costs $20. The **Yellowstone Backcountry Office** (P.O. Box 168, Yellowstone National Park, WY 82190) will send you the useful "Backcountry Trip Planner" brochure with a detailed map showing where the campsites are. Call the office for more information at ☎ 307/344-2160.

Pick up your permit in the park within 48 hours of your departure, at one of the following visitor ranger stations any day of the week during the summer: Bechler, Canyon, Mammoth, Old Faithful, Tower, West Entrance, Grant Village, Lake, South Entrance, and Bridge Bay. Boating permits for motorized craft can be obtained at only the last four ranger stations.

BOATING PERMITS   Any vessels used on park waters must have a permit. For motorized craft, the cost is $20 for annual permits and $10 for a 7-day pass. Fees for nonmotorized boats are $10 for annual permits and $5 for 7-day permits. Rivers and streams are closed to boats of any kind, except for the stretch of the Lewis River between Lewis and Shoshone lakes, which is restricted to hand-propelled craft. Coast Guard–approved personal flotation devices are required for each person boating.

FISHING PERMITS   Permits are required for anglers 16 and over; the permit costs $15 for 3 days, $20 for 7 days, and $35 for the season. Youths 12 to 15 years of age also must have a permit, but it's free. Children 11 and under may fish without a permit. Permits are available at any ranger station, visitor center, Yellowstone General Store, and most fishing shops in the gateways. The season usually begins on the Saturday of Memorial Day weekend and continues through the first Sunday in November. Exceptions to this rule are Yellowstone Lake, its tributaries, and sections of the Yellowstone River. In the search for ecological equilibrium, the regulations have two key wrinkles: Any nonnative lake trout caught within the park must not be released alive and cutthroat trout are catch-and-release only.

REGULATIONS

You can get more detailed information about these rules from a park ranger, at a park visitor center, or at the park's website (www.nps.gov/yell).

BICYCLES   Bicycles are not allowed on the vast majority of the park's trails or any of the boardwalks, but the park is a popular destination for pavement cyclists. Because of the narrowness of park roads and the presence of large recreational vehicles with poor visibility, it's recommended that you wear helmets and bright clothing. There are some designated off-pavement bicycling areas; contact the park for more information.

CAMPING   In any given year, a person may camp for no more than 30 days in the park, and only 14 days during the summer season. Food, garbage, and utensils must be stored in a vehicle or container made of solid material and suspended at least 10 feet above the ground when not in use.

CLIMBING   Because of the loose, crumbly rock in Yellowstone, climbing is discouraged throughout the park and prohibited in the Grand Canyon of the Yellowstone.

DEFACING PARK FEATURES   It's illegal to pick wildflowers or collect natural or archaeological objects. Only dead-and-down wood can be collected for backcountry campfires.

FIREARMS   Licensed guns are allowed in the park. The specifics of the law is based on the state, be it Wyoming or Montana.

LITTERING   Littering in the national parks is strictly prohibited—remember, if you pack it in, you have to pack it out. Throwing coins or other objects into thermal features is illegal.

MOTORCYCLES   Motorcycles, motor scooters, and motorbikes are allowed only on park roads. No off-road or trail riding is allowed. Operator licenses and license plates are required.

PETS   Pets must be leashed and are prohibited in the backcountry, on trails, on boardwalks, and in thermal areas. If you tie up a pet and leave it, you're breaking the law.

SMOKING   There is no smoking in thermal areas, visitor centers, ranger stations, or any other posted public areas.

SNOWMOBILING   After a push for an all-out ban, the snowmobile quota was 540 per day in the 2010–11 season; all trips are required to be guided. Snowmobilers must have a valid driver's license, stay on the designated unplowed roadways, and obey posted speed limits.

Impressions

[W]e beheld one of the grandest displays of the kind we had ever beheld—a perfect geyser—an immediate volume of clear, hot water projected into the air one-hundred and fifty vertical feet, attended with dense volumes of steam rising upward for many hundred feet, and floating away in clouds...

–Edwin Stanley, from *Rambles in Wonderland*, 1878

SWIMMING   Swimming or wading is prohibited in thermal features or in streams whose waters flow from thermal features in Yellowstone. (An exception is Boiling River near Mammoth, where visitors can take a warm soak btw. daybreak and dusk except during spring runoff.) Swimming in Yellowstone Lake is discouraged because of the low water temperature and unpredictable weather. Bathing suits are required.

WILDLIFE   It is unlawful to approach within 300 feet of a bear or within 75 feet of other wildlife. Feeding any wildlife is illegal. Wildlife calls such as elk bugles or other artificial attractants are forbidden.

WHEN TO GO

During the quiet "shoulder" seasons of spring and fall, there are more bison and elk around than autos and RVs. Before the second week in June, you'll be rewarded by the explosion of wildflowers as they begin to bloom, filling the meadows and hillsides with vast arrays of colors and shapes. After that, roads become progressively busier. Traveling before peak season has economic advantages, as well, since rates at gateway-city motels are lower, as are the costs of meals. After Labor Day weekend, crowds begin to thin again and the roads become less traveled. In addition to wildlife and improved fishing conditions in some areas, the fall foliage transforms the area to a calendar-quality image.

In the winter, Yellowstone has a storybook beauty, as snow and ice soften the edges of the landscape and shroud the lumbering bison. Geyser basins appear even more dramatic, the frigid air temperature in stark contrast to the steaming, gurgling waters. Nearby trees are transformed into eerie "snow ghosts" by frozen thermal vapors. Wildlife clusters at the thermal areas to take advantage of the softer ground and more accessible vegetation. Lake Yellowstone's surface freezes to an average thickness of 3 feet, creating a vast ice sheet that sings and moans as the huge plates of ice shift.

The other winter sound is made by the herds of snowmobiles that roam the roads and are at the center of a contentious issue of late. (For more information on the snowmobile issue, see the box, "Snowmobiling: To Ban or Not to Ban," on p. 292, and the section "Snowmobiling," above.)

You can also enter the park in snowcoaches, the tracked vehicles that deliver visitors to the beautifully rebuilt Old Faithful Snow Lodge and tour the park. From the lodge or Mammoth—which also stays open to cars during the winter—you can ski, snowmobile (assuming regulations still permit it), or visit the thermal areas. The only road within the park open for automobile traffic is the Mammoth Hot Springs–Cooke City Road.

Seasons

Natives of the region describe weather in the Yellowstone ecosystem as predictably unpredictable. Because of the region's high elevations and changing weather systems, the park is characterized by long, cold winters and short, though usually warm, summers.

into April and May (and even June), though temperatures generally warm up by then. The average daytime readings during spring are 40°F to 50°F (4°C–10°C), gradually increasing to 60°F to 70°F (16°C–21°C) by early June. Yellowstone is never balmy, but temperatures during the middle of the summer are typically 75°F to 85°F (24°C–30°C) in the lower elevations, and are especially comfortable because of the lack of humidity. Even during the summer months, nights will be cool, with temperatures dropping into the low 40s (4°C–7°C). No matter how warm you expect it to be, it's a good idea to bring a warm jacket, rain gear, and water-resistant walking shoes. And, because this is high altitude, bring plenty of sunscreen and a wide-brimmed hat to protect yourself in the thin atmosphere. As summer thunderstorms are common, a tarp and an umbrella are also recommended.

During winter months temperatures hover in the single digits, and subzero overnight temperatures are common. You should bring long underwear, heavy shirts (fast-drying synthetic fabrics, not cotton), vests and coats, warm gloves and hats, and warm, wicking socks. The lowest temperature recorded at Yellowstone was a dangerously chilly –66°F (–54°C) in 1933.

Avoiding the Crowds

One of the things you'll discover when you venture down a trail is that the majority of Yellowstone's three million annual visitors aren't going to follow you. (Only about 10% of visitors wander beyond the trail heads.) Some are afraid of grizzly bears, some are in a hurry, and others just don't want the exercise. Regardless, Yellowstone rewards those who expend a bit of shoe leather: A mere half-mile from the traffic jams, you'll find few people and much better opportunities to smell the wildflowers.

If you really want a Yellowstone experience that's all your own, head for the backcountry. This is some of the deepest, most exquisite wilderness in the country, and you definitely won't be fighting a mob. While visitation at Yellowstone increases yearly, backcountry permits do not—they've actually declined a bit in the last 30 years. My favorite areas are the Thorofare region, in the park's southeast corner at the headwaters of the Yellowstone River, and the shores of Shoshone Lake, the largest backcountry body of water in the Lower 48, but there's so much wilderness here that it's hard not to find views of your own.

EDUCATIONAL PROGRAMS

Yellowstone offers free **ranger-led educational programs** ★★ that will significantly enhance a visitor's understanding of the area's history, geology, and wildlife. Most programs run from early June through late September. Detailed information on location and times is listed in the park newsletter, which is distributed at the entrance gates. On a more informal basis, you'll run into ranger-naturalists roaming the geyser basins and along the rim of the Grand Canyon of the Yellowstone, and in areas where wildlife gather in both parks, leading informative walks and answering the questions of inquisitive visitors.

Evening campfire programs are presented nightly in the summer at Mammoth, Norris, Madison, Old Faithful, Bridge Bay, Grant, and Canyon. Many of these activities are accessible to those with disabilities. It's a good idea to bring a flashlight, warm clothing, and rain gear. Rangers also conduct free walking, talking, and hiking programs throughout the park, including half-day "Adventure Hikes."

As one would expect, there are more tours and evening programs in the **Old Faithful** area than anywhere else in the park. The topics of the guided walks, which can run as long as 1½ hours, usually focus on the geysers, their fragile plumbing, and their role in the Yellowstone ecosystem. A slide-show program is held in the auditorium in the evening.

Beginning in June, daily hikes in the **Canyon** area head out to the Hayden Valley and the rim of the Grand Canyon; a ranger talk on the art inspired by the falls is held several times a day at the lower platform of Artist Point. An explanation of the origins of the hot pools and mud pots is conducted daily beginning in June at the **Grant** area as part of a walk of the Lakeshore area of the West Thumb Geyser Basin. The **Lake/Fishing Bridge** agenda includes walking tours of the Mud Volcano area and along the shores of Yellowstone Lake. There is an afternoon talk at the Fishing Bridge Visitor Center about managing wildlife like grizzlies and wolves, and a discussion of fisheries management is held on the west end of the Fishing Bridge. For a full schedule, consult the park newsletter distributed at the entrance gates.

Mammoth Hot Springs is host to several interesting ranger-led programs, including talks on the park's natural and cultural wonders and a historical tour of the original site of Fort Yellowstone, established more than 100 years ago. There is also a guided tour of the hot springs terraces. The hottest, most dynamic, and oldest geyser basin in the park is at **Norris,** where a popular 1½-hour tour begins at the Norris museum on a daily basis in season.

The ranger/naturalist programs are one of several activities that make up the **Junior Ranger** program. For $3, kids can pick up an activity paper at one of the visitor centers, and then follow its guidelines for hiking and learning about the park. When they complete the program, their enrollment as Junior Rangers is announced to the public with great fanfare.

Many changes are made annually in these presentations; consult the park newspaper, *Yellowstone Today,* for locations and times.

Astronomers from the **Museum of the Rockies** in Bozeman, Montana, often bring their telescopes and stories to a series of stargazing sessions throughout the park—contact the museum at ✆ 406/994-3466 for a schedule.

The **Yellowstone Association Institute** ★★★ (✆ 406/848-2400; www.yellowstone association.org/institute) offers a slew of guided classes, including daylong hikes to multiday backcountry adventures, often with a historical or scientific bent. The Institute has teamed with Xanterra Parks & Resorts to offer visitors days spent exploring trails with guides and nights at the comfortable lodgings throughout the park. These **Lodging and Learning** packages are excellent options for those who want to delve into the park without too much of the traditional "roughing it." Rates (starting at about $600 per person) include box lunches, breakfast, and in-park transportation. Contact **Xanterra Parks & Resorts** (✆ 866/439-7375; www.travelyellowstone.com).

In September, the Institute takes over **Roosevelt Lodge** with the **Roosevelt Rendezvous,** a series of 4-day educational experiences with a daily menu of different field trips led by park experts. There are also evening programs. Rates start at $679 per person, which includes tuition, a cabin, and three meals a day.

SERVICES & SUPPLIES

Independent of Xanterra, Yellowstone General Stores is the concessionaire behind the bulk of the park's retail operations. The company operates **stores** throughout the park, including Old Faithful, Mammoth Hot Springs, Lake, Fishing Bridge, and Grant Village, which feature gift shops, grocery supplies, and soda fountains. Depending upon the location, you may find a limited supply of fresh veggies and canned goods (as at the Canyon store), plus fishing supplies, souvenirs, and, of course, ice cream. **Service stations** are located at major visitor areas: Old Faithful, Canyon, Mammoth Hot Springs, and Grant Village. Exact locations of all services and stores are listed in the park newspaper you receive at the entrance gates.

If you have medical problems while visiting the park, Yellowstone Park Medical Services provides help at the **Lake Hospital** (℗ 307/242-7241), an acute-care facility; the **Old Faithful Clinic** (℗ 307/545-7325); and the **Mammoth Clinic** (℗ 307/344-7965), the only year-round facility of the three.

ORGANIZED TOURS & ACTIVITIES

A number of tour companies offer bus and van tours of the park originating in gateway communities: **Yellowstone Alpen Guides** (℗ 800/858-3502; www.yellowstoneguides. com) takes travelers around the park from West Yellowstone; rates run about $50 per person for a 4-hour tour. Salt Lake City–based **AdventureBus** (℗ 888/737-5263; www. adventurebus.com) takes groups to Yellowstone and Grand Teton between June and August; weeklong tours run about $1,000 per person. I highly recommend **Escape Adventures** (℗ 800/596-2953; www.escapeadventures.com), which offers supported 6-day road biking tours of Yellowstone and Grand Teton for about $1,500 if you camp or $2,300 if you stay in the park's accommodations. If you are looking for specialized guided trips—such as photo safaris—contact the chamber of commerce in the gateway community where you want to begin.

Within the park, the hotel concessionaire, **Xanterra Parks & Resorts** (℗ 866/439-7375; www.travelyellowstone.com), has a variety of general and specialized tours. Five different motorcoach tours are available from all of Yellowstone's villages. For about $70, you can explore the **Circle of Fire** (Old Faithful, Yellowstone Lake, the Hayden Valley); or you can do the **Yellowstone in a Day** tour. These are full-day tours, with stops at all the sights and informative talks by the guides. In 2007, eight restored **Old Yellow Buses** that roamed the Yellowstone roads here in the first half of the 20th century went back into service for Xanterra. Tours in the buses range from 1 to 4 hours ($15–$81). Other specialty trips include custom van tours, photo safaris, wildlife trips up the Lamar Valley, and Yellowstone Lake sunset tours in historic buses from the 1930s.

At Bridge Bay Marina, 1-hour **Scenicruiser tours** (℗ 866/439-7375; www.travel yellowstone.com) depart throughout the day from June to the end of September for a trip around the northern end of giant Yellowstone Lake. You view the Lake Yellowstone Hotel from the water and visit Stevenson Island while a guide fills you in on the history, geology, and biology. Fares are $14 for adults and $9 for children ages 2 to 11. Guided fishing trips on 22-foot and 34-foot cabin cruisers are also available at Bridge Bay ($152 and $196 for 2 hr., respectively), and you can rent smaller outboards and rowboats.

Buses are replaced in the winter by **snowcoach tours.** These are closer in size to a van than a bus, mounted on tank treads with skis in front for steering. The snowcoach can pick you up at the south or west entrances, or at Mammoth, and take you all over the park. You can spend a night at Old Faithful and then snowcoach up to Mammoth the next night, or do round-trip tours from the gates or wherever you're staying in the park. One-way and wildlife-watching trips range from roughly $30 to $60, while round-trips cost $110 to $130. **Yellowstone Alpen Guides** (℗ 800/858-3502; www.yellowstone guides.com) offers snowcoach trips and tours from West Yellowstone for $110 per person and up.

Guided horseback trail rides lasting from 1 to 2 hours are available at Roosevelt Lodge and Canyon Village. Children must be at least 8 years old and 48 inches tall; adults cannot exceed 240 pounds. Tour prices are $35 for a 1-hour ride and $54 for a 2-hour ride (no discount for children). Check any activity desk for times and dates. Reservations are recommended and can be made at **Xanterra Parks & Resorts** activity centers in the hotels, although not before you leave home.

FOR TRAVELERS WITH DISABILITIES

In recent years, both parks have become increasingly user-friendly for travelers with disabilities. People who are blind or who have permanent disabilities can obtain an **Interagency Access Pass,** which costs nothing and allows lifetime access to all national parks and other federal fee areas. All passes are available at any entrance point to Yellowstone or Grand Teton. The Interagency Access passes must be purchased in person.

Accessible accommodations are located in the Dunraven and Cascade lodges and Western cabins at Canyon Village; in Grant Village; in the Old Faithful Inn and Snow Lodge and Cabins; and in the Lake Yellowstone Hotel. For a free *Visitors Guide to Accessible Features in Yellowstone National Park,* write to the **Park Accessibility Coordinator** (© 307/344-2314; www.nps.gov/yell), P.O. Box 168, Yellowstone National Park, WY 82190, or pick up the guide at the gates or visitor centers. There are accessible campsites at Fishing Bridge, Bridge Bay, Madison, Canyon, and Grant campgrounds, which you can reserve by calling © **307/344-7311.**

Accessible restrooms with sinks and flush toilets are located at all developed areas except West Thumb and Norris. Accessible vault toilets are found at West Thumb and Norris, as well as in most scenic areas and picnic areas.

Many of Yellowstone's roadside attractions, including the south rim of the Grand Canyon of the Yellowstone, West Thumb Geyser Basin, much of the Norris and Upper Geyser basins, and parts of the Mud Volcano and Fountain Paint Pot areas, are negotiable by wheelchair.

Visitor centers at Old Faithful, Grant Village, and Canyon are wheelchair accessible, as are the Norris Museum and the Fishing Bridge Visitor Center. The Albright Visitor Center at Mammoth is also accessible via a rear entrance.

Accessible parking is available at Old Faithful, Fishing Bridge, Canyon, Norris, and Grant Village, although you'll have to look for it; at some locations, it is near a Yellowstone General Store.

3 A PARK PRIMER

A BRIEF HISTORY

A trip to Yellowstone has changed considerably since the days of George Cowan: When he visited the park in 1877, he set a new standard for "roughing it." Cowan was kidnapped from his horse-packing camp and shot by the Nez Perce Indians, then subsisted on roots and coffee grounds as he dragged his paralyzed body for days through the wilderness.

Let's just say the United States government had a bit to learn about how to run the world's first national park. It still does, but it's getting better all the time. For more than 125 years, the National Park Service has been directing traffic at this complex intersection of wilderness and tourism, juggling the protection of powerful natural wonders

while allowing for civilized comforts. And if anyone complains that the roads are potholed or the coffee is cold . . . well, George Cowan would not be sympathetic.

Yellowstone was never known as a hospitable place. Nomadic Indian bands crossed the plateau but never settled there, except for a small group of Shoshone known as "Sheep eaters." The first white explorer to lay eyes on Yellowstone's geothermal wonders was probably John Colter, an explorer who broke away from the Lewis and Clark expedition in 1806 and spent 3 years wandering a surreal landscape of mud pots and geysers. When he described his discovery on his return to St. Louis, no one believed him, and he settled down to life as a farmer. Later, miners and fur trappers followed in his footsteps, occasionally making curious reports of a sulfurous world still sometimes called "Colter's Hell."

The first significant exploration of what would become the park took place in 1869, when a band of Montanans led by David Folsom completed a 36-day expedition. Folsom and his group traveled up the Missouri River, then into the heart of the park, where they discovered the falls of the Yellowstone, mud pots, Yellowstone Lake, and the Fountain Geyser. But it was an 1871 expedition led by U.S. Geological Survey Director Ferdinand Hayden that brought back astonishing photographs of Yellowstone's wonders by William Henry Jackson.

Crude health spas and thin-walled "hotels" went up near the hot springs. A debate soon followed over the potential for commercial development and exploitation of the region. Many people take credit for the idea of creating the national park—members of the Folsom party later told a story about thinking it up around a campfire in the Upper Geyser Basin. In any case, the idea caught on as Yellowstone explorers hit the lecture circuit back East. In March 1872, President Ulysses S. Grant signed legislation declaring Yellowstone a national park.

No one had any experience in managing a wilderness park, and many mistakes were made: Superintendents granted favorable leases to friends with commercial interests in the tourism industry; poachers ran amok, decimating the wildlife population; a laundry business near Mammoth cleaned linens in the hot pool.

By 1886, things were so bad that the army took control of the park; its firm-fisted management practices resulted in new order and protected the park from those intent upon exploiting it, although the military participated in the eradication of the plateau's wolf population. By 1916, efforts to make the park more visitor-friendly began to bear fruit: Construction of the first roads had been completed and guest housing was available in the area. Stewardship of the park was then transferred to the newly created National Park Service.

THE PARK TODAY

It has long been difficult for park managers to both provide the public with a good vacation and protect the natural wonders of the parks. One challenge is to make the parks accessible to three million annual visitors, many with different, even contradictory, expectations of a wilderness excursion. This brings about the construction of new facilities and ongoing road maintenance and repair. At the same time, the parks are wild preserves, and the National Park Service must cope with the impact of six million feet on the forests, meadows, and thermal areas, as well as on the day-to-day lives of the millions of animals that inhabit the area.

It's a tough balancing act. Some of the pivotal issues in the parks today include the impact of snowmobiles; the reintroduced wolves and the resulting livestock losses of

Wildlife & Where to Spot It

Biologists consider Yellowstone one of the most important wildlife habitats in the world. You'll find all sorts of creatures here, from the dramatic bald eagle to the less-publicized reptiles of the thermal areas. What particularly distinguishes this collection of wildlife is that the elk, bison, and all their brethren are free-roaming.

Bison (buffalo) are right at home here, wandering along the main thoroughfares without much regard for their human spectators. They are easy to view in the summer months, often seen munching grass, wallowing in dust pits, and even wrestling sumo-style for mates in the Lamar, Hayden, and Pelican valleys; the Bechler River area; and in the geyser areas near the Firehole River. *Caution:* They have poor eyesight and cranky dispositions, and, like moose, they can move with sudden speed (up to 35 mph) to batter anyone who invades their personal space.

Biologists have trouble agreeing on how many **bears** there are in Yellowstone, but most will acknowledge that their numbers are on the rise. (However, car-bear accidents were on the rise as well.) Their food supplies seem to have stabilized a bit with the wolf reintroduction (more carcasses) and pro-cutthroat fishing regulations. In the Greater Yellowstone Ecosystem there are probably about 1,000 black bears and 600 grizzlies, but estimates vary. Grizzlies were delisted as an endangered species in 2007, but conservationists argue the move was premature.

Decades ago, bears foraged in open-pit garbage dumps near the lodges, or tourists hand-fed bears who begged along the park roads. When the dumps were closed in the 1970s and bear feeding was prohibited, the population of bears plummeted. Diminishing habitat around the park also had an impact. However, bears are creative omnivores, they tend to gravitate toward elk and bison (either the very young or the very old) and wolf kills, but their diet has been assessed as being about three-quarters vegetarian.

Black bears are most commonly sighted in the spring, sometimes with cubs, in the Canyon, Tower, Madison, and Old Faithful areas, where they feed on green grass and herbs, berries, ants, and carrion. The more aggressive grizzly's unpredictable behavior makes them the likely suspect in the rare instances of bear attacks on humans, but blacks have demonstrated that they also are capable in this regard.

Odds of seeing a grizzly are best during May and June, in the Lamar and Hayden valleys, before they retreat into the backwoods for the summer. Backcountry travelers often see bears in the remote Thorofare Country on the park's southeast border, where bears (and avid anglers) journey to the Yellowstone River headwaters for the spawning cutthroat trout in the spring.

It is estimated that about 40,000 **elk** (wapiti) populate the entire ecosystem, although numbers have been on the decline in park boundaries in recent years, in large part because of predation by wolves. You should have no problem telling elk from deer or antelope by their size (typically 900 lb.); the males have large antler racks, chestnut-brown heads and necks, and a distinctive tan patch on their rumps. One herd can usually be located around **Mammoth Hot Springs;** others are often seen in the meadows between Old Faithful and Madison Junction.

During winter months, the northern Yellowstone herd heads to a winter grazing area near Gardiner as the southern herd descends to the National Elk Refuge near Jackson. Listen in the fall for the distinctive bugling of the males, a throaty gargle that slips into a piercing, high whistle.

Moose are grumpy loners and not very patient with the tourists. They usually appear in alder thickets and marshes around streams, particularly around Canyon and near Shoshone Lake in the backcountry. They are recognizable by their dark coats, massive antlers, and the fleshy dewlap that hangs beneath their necks like a bell. A moose is capable of traveling at 30 mph; cows will charge any perceived threat to a calf, and bulls become particularly ornery in the fall. Give them a wide berth.

The **pronghorn,** usually labeled antelope (though unrelated to the true African antelope), is often sighted grazing near the northern entrance to Yellowstone. These fleet and flighty animals have excellent vision, and they'll take off at 45 mph when photographers try to get near. However, the park's population of pronghorn has plummeted in recent years. The pronghorn is identified by its short, black horns, tan-and-white body, and black accent stripes.

For a long time, the **coyote** has been the predator most often spotted by park visitors, but the arrival of wolves has taken its toll on the smaller canine. Coyotes may be seen alone or in small packs—they're particularly visible in winter—with brown to gray coats that grow silvery after the snow falls. They prey on small animals like squirrels and rabbits, or larger ungulates like elk and deer that have grown old or ill. They'll also scavenge the leftovers of other predators. Biologists estimate there are around 500 coyotes in the park. You'll see them out in the open meadows of the Hayden Valley, and you might get lucky and see the interaction between wolves and coyotes in places like Slough Creek.

Gray wolves from Canada were reintroduced to the park in 1995. There are more than 1,500 wolves in the Northern Rockies today, but the number in the park dropped to about 125 in 2008 due to a bout with distemper. The Lamar Valley is where they were first released, and patient observers at dawn and dusk can sometimes see the Druid Peak pack along the river or the Rose Creek pack on the slopes above Slough Creek. Look for ranger Rick McIntyre—he's there most of the summer—or one of the many dedicated wolf trackers on hand in springtime, and ask for advice, or check at the east gate or Mammoth Visitor Center for the best sighting opportunities.

ranchers in and around the parks; the inadequacy of the park's infrastructure to cope with three million annual human visitors; invasive nonnative species, such as lake trout and zebra mussels; and the reduction of habitat surrounding the parks, coupled with a growing population of elk and bison seeking forage beyond park boundaries and possibly infecting domestic animals with a disease called brucellosis. And that's the short list.

Possible solutions are often "too little, too late," layering complex management strategies on an ecosystem that might do better if it were simply allowed to work things out naturally. The problem is, Grand Teton and Yellowstone have already been altered significantly by humans, so "natural" becomes a relative concept.

A good example is the reintroduction of a natural predator of the overpopulated elk: gray wolves, which were eliminated in the 1920s. These days, ranchland surrounds the parks, so the Defenders of Wildlife set up a trust to pay anyone who loses a calf to a wolf—and ranchers do because wolves haven't read the management plan. And wolves from Yellowstone have migrated south into Grand Teton and beyond; besides the packs that den in and around the Gros Ventre area, a lone wolf was spotted at the Wyoming-Colorado border, and two others turned up dead in Colorado in 2004 and 2009.

Yellowstone's artificial boundaries also cause problems for bison. The state of Montana now allows hunters to shoot bison when they stray outside the park. Ranchers fear bison because of brucellosis, a disease that, when transmitted to cattle, causes cows to abort fetuses. A full 1,400 animals were killed when they left the park for low country in Montana in 2008 alone, although so far there are almost no documented cases of bison infecting livestock.

As for the proliferation of snowmobiles and cars, most agree that there must be changes as visitation continues to grow. Currently, snowmobilers flock to the park as soon as the snow starts falling and remain until late February. While the popularity of the sport has had a positive effect on the tourism industry in the gateways of West Yellowstone, Jackson, and Gardiner, park officials are studying the long-term environmental impact of the machines. In their opinion, the snowmobiles create their own types of problems. The machines are noisy, and engine emissions create air pollution, which some say presents a health hazard. While better technology has reined in the noise and smog to a large degree, the snowmobiles still share narrow trails with wildlife during months when the animals' energy levels are depleted by bad weather and a lack of food. As a consequence, a 3-year phase-out of snowmobiles was agreed upon in 2000 but it was overturned before park policy could be changed. The compromise resulted in a quota system that limits the number of snowmobiles in the park to 540 per day.

Then there's the traffic issue. Park roads are narrow and twisty, so the intrusion of 30-foot-long motor homes and pickup trucks towing trailers creates congestion, especially during the peak summer months. There have been studies of transportation alternatives to unclog park roadways, even a costly monorail that would wind through Yellowstone, but no decisive action has been taken.

Recently, park scientists have battled to protect the native cutthroat trout in Yellowstone Lake from the impact of lake trout introduced by man. They have also recognized the enormous value of the microbes evolving in Yellowstone's super-hot thermal areas, and scientists are using them in new technologies ranging from nano-circuitry to industrial bleaching products. As the world awakens to the accelerating loss of vital species in shrinking wild habitat, it becomes ever more imperative to find ways in which to preserve the relatively unspoiled ecosystems, like that of Greater Yellowstone.

The large mammals may be the stars of Yellowstone National Park, but flower lovers will find plenty to enjoy here among the park's 1,200 native plants. Flowers and shrubs broadcast bright shades of blues, purples, yellows, and oranges throughout the park, providing a colorful accent to the forests and meadows.

The plateau's volcanoes, fires, and glaciers have created a series of tumultuous changes that have had an enormous impact on plant life. At one site in the Lamar Valley, the inspection of petrified tree stumps exhumed by erosion resulted in the identification of 27 distinct layers of forests, one atop the other.

The plants have evolved with the ever-changing Yellowstone environment. Forests once populated with hardwoods, such as maple, magnolia, and sycamore, are now filled with conifers, the most common of which are pine, spruce, and fir. A smattering of cottonwood and aspen thrive in the cool park temperatures.

Vegetation zones tend to reflect altitude: Lower-elevation valleys tend to be dry and grassy, with sagebrush and few trees; forests of fir dominate between about 6,000 and 7,500 feet, followed by lodgepole pine stands and then spruce and more fir up to the timberline, with open meadows where wildflowers explode in the spring. At high elevations, shrubs and carpetlike vegetation take over, and you have to lean over to examine the tiny blossoms.

Attempts by park officials to manage the ecosystem have had an impact, too. Climax forests—a plant succession leading to conifers that create a shady canopy and block the growth of seedlings—had a prolonged reign in Yellowstone because of fire suppression, which contributed to the ferocity of fires in the dry summer of 1988. However, once the fires were allowed to burn, it became clear that fire was crucial in the life cycle of lodgepole pine. Since its cones release seeds only after a burn, many of the areas that were "ravaged" in 1988 are now carpeted by dense juvenile forests.

4 SEEING THE HIGHLIGHTS

This is a wonderland you can return to again and again, sampling a different pleasure each time. All the sites mentioned here are easily accessible along the loop tours detailed in section 5, "Driving the Park." The farther you get from the pavement, and the farther from July and August you schedule your visit, the more private your experience will be.

I've organized this list geographically, following the roadways that form a figure eight at the heart of the park. We'll begin in the north, then move south, first along the east side, then the west. Get out the oversize map you receive at the gate or by mail, and follow along.

MAMMOTH HOT SPRINGS

At the park's north entrance, 5 miles south of Gardiner, Mammoth Hot Springs is home to spectacular limestone terraces, historic park buildings, and the Mammoth Hot Springs Hotel. It's one of the older park settlements, with stone buildings dating from the late 19th century, when the army was stationed here at Fort Yellowstone.

There are no geysers at **Mammoth Hot Springs Terraces ★★**, but this cascading staircase of hillside hot pools, among the oldest in the park, offers a boardwalk tour of gorgeous pastels in shades of white, yellow, orange, and green, the unintentionally artistic work of microscopic bacteria in the sediments. The mineral-rich springs constantly

---

Moments   **Hot Springs Hot Spot**

Once upon a time, travelers in Yellowstone bathed, cooked, and laundered their clothes in the hot springs, but such activities are illegal nowadays. There is one spot on the east side of the road to the north entrance, however, where the public is allowed to take a dip. Called **Boiling River** ★★, the hot springs here run into the Gardner River and create a series of temperature-graded (around 100°F/38°C) pools. This was once a late-night skinny-dipping secret, but you can't do that anymore: There's a parking lot, gate, and posted hours (daybreak–dusk, closed during times of high runoff). Regardless, this is just about the best possible way to cap off a day of touring and hiking: sitting in Mother Nature's hot tub, surrounded by beautiful scenery.

---

bubble to the surface, depositing travertine as the water cools in contact with the air. It's a vivid illustration of the park's unusual geological situation: a rare geologic hot spot of seismic activity in the middle of the continent, where molten rock nearly makes it to the earth's surface.

Whether or not you spend the night at the **Mammoth Hot Springs Hotel**—not the most distinguished lodging in the park, but it has historic character—you should drop by the **Albright Visitor Center.** This building once housed Fort Yellowstone's bachelor officers, but you won't find a pool table here today; rather, you'll find displays on park history, wildlife and photography exhibits, helpful rangers dispensing advice, and numerous park publications and maps. For more information, call 💲 **307/344-2263.**

TOWER-ROOSEVELT AREA

East of Mammoth Hot Springs you enter a delicious mix of high plains, deep forest, and twisting rivers. Toward the northeast corner lies one of the most beautifully serene valleys in the Rockies, the **Lamar Valley** ★★★. This glacier-carved swath of grassy bottom and forested flanks sits apart from the vehicular chaos at the center of the park, a good thing because the traffic here is not automobiles, but the bison, bears, wolves, and elk whose presence has earned the valley the nickname, "the Serengeti of the United States." If you continue east and leave Yellowstone via the park's northeast entrance, you'll be heading up to the spectacular views of the **Beartooth Highway.**

The area around the Tower-Roosevelt Junction was once a favorite spot of U.S. President Theodore Roosevelt. At **Roosevelt Lodge,** visitors can enjoy the kind of simple accommodations that fit the tastes of the Bull Moose himself: those with the rustic flavor of the Old West. This is the most relaxed of the park's villages, and a great place to take a break from the more crowded attractions. Get into the cowboy spirit by taking a **guided trail ride,** a **stagecoach ride,** or a **wagon ride.** You can skip the dining room and ride out for an **Old West cookout,** served from a chuckwagon to patrons who arrive by either horseback or wagon. The nearby 132-foot **Tower Falls** ★ is named for the looming volcanic pinnacles at its brink and provides an excellent photo opportunity. While in the area, take time to view the petrified forests on **Specimen Ridge,** where a wide variety of fossilized plants and trees date back millions of years. All things considered, Roosevelt is a great place to escape the hordes.

Farther south, **Pelican and Hayden valleys** are the two most prominent remnants of large, ancient lakebeds in the park. They are now vast, subalpine meadows, thriving with plant life that provides feed for sizable bison and elk populations. You might see a bear here, too.

THE GRAND CANYON OF THE YELLOWSTONE RIVER

Hayden Valley flanks the featured attraction of the park's center: the **Grand Canyon of the Yellowstone River** ★★★, a colorful, 1,000-foot-deep, 24-mile-long gorge that some can't resist comparing to its larger counterpart in Arizona. Okay, then: This canyon is greener, the water clearer, the air cooler, and it has two dramatic waterfalls, the big one taller than Niagara. As it drops through this gorge, the Yellowstone River in some places moves at 64,000 cubic feet of water per second.

Volcanic explosions and glaciers surging and receding shaped the canyon. The geological story is told in the canyon itself, where hard lava flows formed the lip of the falls next to softer quartz-rich rock that gave way, allowing the river to cut deeply through the layers of red, orange, tan, and brown hue. Plumes of steam pinpoint vents along the canyon's rock spires, where viewing opportunities are extensive and varied. There are many hikes along and down into the canyon, which is 24 miles long and up to 1,200 feet deep, and you'll be surprised at how few people you encounter away from the parking areas. Many do trek down to a view of the Lower Falls on **Uncle Tom's Trail** ★★ (which is actually a 328-step staircase bolted to the canyon wall) from the South Rim, and a short path from a parking area for Upper Falls View also offers breathtaking views. Two other favorite trails are **Inspiration Point** and **Artist Point;** both are wheelchair accessible.

Canyon Village has a sprawling 1950s look, which puts off some visitors, but the architecture is starting to come back in vogue. It's usually crowded, but you can find many useful services there, and some of the newer lodging is an improvement.

NORRIS GEYSER BASIN

If you travel south from Mammoth on the west side of the park, you pass some interesting rock formations, **Obsidian Cliff** and **Roaring Mountain,** before coming to **Norris Geyser Basin** ★★. Norris is not nearly as famous as the Mammoth terraces or the crowd of geysers around Old Faithful, but there's a lot going on here, from the steaming pools

YELLOWSTONE NATIONAL PARK

12

SEEING THE HIGHLIGHTS

(Finds) **Petrified Wood**

With so many hot pots, mountain peaks, geysers, and bison to gawk at, it's not surprising that many visitors to Yellowstone miss some of the finest examples of petrified forest found anywhere. The trees were preserved, scientists believe, when their organic matter was replaced by volcanic material during one of the many eruptions on the plateau. Some of the tree trunks still stand, particularly in the Specimen Ridge area in the northeast area of the park, and they are a monument to the region's warmer, swampier past: sycamore, magnolias, and dogwoods are all preserved in stone. Check at the Tower Ranger Station for maps showing you where to find petrified wood. This is not a renewable resource: Don't touch or take.

of the **Porcelain Basin** to the eruptions of **Echinus Geyser.** If you're the patient type, you can sit by the blowhole of **Steamboat Geyser** and hope that this, the largest of park geysers with a maximum height of 400 feet, will erupt. But be prepared to wait: It erupted eight times between 2000 and late 2009, but blew its top only twice during the preceding 12 years and not at all between 1911 and 1961. This is one of the hottest, most active thermal areas on the plateau, at the intersection of three faults in the earth's crust; when they shift, new geysers pop up and old ones disappear. The **Norris Geyser Basin Museum** explains geothermal features, and the nearby **Museum of the National Park Ranger** tracks the history of the park's stewards.

OLD FAITHFUL

About a quarter of the world's geysers are crowded into hills, valleys, and riverbanks around **Old Faithful ★★**, where the hot pools and spouts are divided into three areas: the **Lower, Midway,** and **Upper geyser basins.** Here you'll find burbling mud pots, radiant pools like **Chromatic Spring,** and geysers with a variety of tricks, from the angled shots of **Daisy Geyser** to the witches' cauldron of **Crested Pool.**

But the grand old dame of geysers, the star of the show, is **Old Faithful.** Over the past 100 years, its eruptions have been remarkably consistent, blowing 15 to 23 times daily with a column averaging about 134 feet and a duration of about 40 seconds. Recent seismic activity has elongated the intervals (to about 92 min.) between eruptions a tad, but it's still the most predictable geyser in the world. Estimates posted at the visitor centers are give-or-take 10 minutes; if the last eruption was a long one, you might have to wait 2 hours for the next burst. (No big deal—there's plenty else to see here.)

Since the geyser is one of the key park attractions, the **Old Faithful Visitor Center** (© 307/545-2750) is larger than most of its counterparts. A film describing the park's geothermal features is shown throughout the day in an indoor auditorium that provides relief from hot July afternoons. Various park publications and an informative seismographic exhibit are added attractions. You will also want to check the information board for estimated times of geyser eruptions, and plan your time accordingly. (At press time, the visitor center was housed in a temporary structure near Old Faithful Lodge with construction underway on a cutting-edge facility that will better blend into the architectural motif of the Old Faithful Inn and Snow Lodge; park officials hope to open the new building in Aug 2010.)

A National Historic Landmark, the shingled, steep-roofed **Old Faithful Inn** was built of local stone and hand-hewn timber, including a pair of interior balconies above the lobby floor. See section 10, "Where to Stay in the Park," later in this chapter, for a full description and review.

YELLOWSTONE LAKE

West of Old Faithful, over Craig Pass, or south of Canyon, through the wildlife-rich **Hayden Valley,** is gigantic **Yellowstone Lake ★★**, another natural wonder unique to Yellowstone. At 20 miles long, 14 miles wide, and more than 300 feet deep in places, it's the largest lake on the continent above 7,000 feet in elevation. If you took a dip in the frigid water (not recommended), you could hardly guess that the caldera underneath the lake is filling with hot liquid magma, actually tilting the lake northward at a measurable pace. The caldera is the sunken remainder of a huge volcanic blast 600,000 years ago, and another about 700,000 years before that. Experts believe it's due to blow again some time in the next 100,000 years—any day now, at least in geologic time. Volcanic underpinnings aside, grizzlies work the tributary streams in the spring when fish spawn (some

osprey.

The lake has long been a favorite fishing spot, but recent regulations have made cutthroat trout a catch-and-release species park-wide. This is part of a desperate attempt by park biologists to help the cutthroat come back against the planted Mackinaw or lake trout, which dine on small cutthroat and therefore are not to be released alive. You'll see some big sailboats braving the quirky winds of the lake, and experienced paddlers may want to **kayak** or **canoe** into the south and southeast arms of the lake, which are closed to motorboats. These deep bays are true wilderness, and great areas to fish and view wildlife. When you pick up a boating permit, you'll also get a stern warning from rangers to watch out for the changeable weather if you get out on the lake's open water. They're right to urge caution; even the best paddlers risk their lives in a sudden afternoon storm.

Lake Village, on the north shore of the lake, offers a large range of amenities, including fine restaurants at either the rustic cabins at **Lake Lodge** or the Victorian majesty of **Lake Yellowstone Hotel.** This historic lodging has Greek columns and a spacious solarium overlooking the lake, the best place for a cocktail or a romantic dinner within park boundaries. It's very different from the Old Faithful Inn, but a rival for its beauty and history. Just south of Lake Village is **Bridge Bay Marina,** the park's water-activity center. Here you can obtain guided fishing trips, small-boat rentals, and dock rentals; there's also a store and tackle shop.

WEST THUMB & GRANT VILLAGE

On the south end of the lake, at **West Thumb,** the boiling thermal features extend out into the lake. You can see steaming cones and churning water created by the action of the underwater hot springs. **Fishing Cone** is rumored to be the place where fishermen once used the "hook and cook" method, immediately tossing their catch into a hot pot for instant meal preparation. Don't try it—it's illegal to drop anything into a thermal feature, and the geyser water has traces of mercury and arsenic. You can walk among the lakeshore pools at the **Central Basin** and look at the colorful, thick fudge of the **Thumb Paint Pots.**

Grant Village, named for President Ulysses S. Grant, was completed in 1984 and is the newest of Yellowstone's villages. It has some of the most modern facilities in the park, but it's also the least inspired. On the plus side, this area is a great vantage point for watching sunrises and afternoon squalls move across the lake, and you may see **river otters** and **cutthroat trout** in the old marina's waters. (Come wintertime, the otters like to use holes melted by the underwater thermal features as base camps for ice-fishing escapades.) The **Grant Visitor Center** plays a video that explores the role of fire in the Yellowstone ecosystem.

5 DRIVING THE PARK

Yellowstone has approximately 370 miles of paved roads, and in recent years the park has struggled to catch up with a backlog of maintenance—filling potholes, widening shoulders, and redoing some roads completely. The wear and tear of heavy RVs and trailers undoes the work as quickly as it's done, and since road construction is limited to the warm months of summer, drivers often encounter delays along the park's roads. If you travel in July or August, you'll share these frustrations with a lot of other drivers. But you can see a surprising number of interesting sights along the figure-eight roadways at the

> ## (Tips) Winter Road Conditions
>
> Be cautious if you're planning a winter road trip to Yellowstone. Icy roads and blinding snowstorms take their toll every year. The park itself is largely closed to automobiles in the winter—only the northern entrance is open to wheeled vehicles. The road through Lamar Valley to the northeast gate is kept open to get essential supplies to Cooke City, but from there you can go no farther north into Montana, because the Beartooth Highway is impassable in winter. The rest of the park's primary roads are open during the snowy months to snowcoaches and snowmobiles, along with bison, which find the packed roads convenient and think nothing of lolling along with a line of frustrated snowmobilers waiting for a chance to pass. For up-to-the-minute information on weather and road conditions, call (℡) **307/344-7381.**

heart of the park. You can take in both north and south loops—together known as the **Grand Loop**—in 1 day if a quick blink at each stop is enough for you. Better, though, to take your time, or explore different areas on different trips.

THE UPPER LOOP

At 70 miles, the Upper Loop, which begins at the north entrance, is the shorter of the two loop drives. If you start by going east from **Mammoth Hot Springs** and the park headquarters, orient yourself at the **Albright Visitor Center,** then take in the **Blacktail Plateau** or rustic **Roosevelt Lodge** (a good place for lunch). If you'd prefer, take a side trip up the pretty **Lamar Valley** ★★★ for wildlife viewing at least as far as Slough Creek—checking out the views of **Tower Falls** and **Mount Washburn** (the highest point in the park)—and up **Dunraven Pass** to look out over the Mirror Plateau. Then head west from Canyon Junction to Norris Junction and north to the **Norris Geyser Basin** ★★, with pastel pools and a few burbles and spouts, and its fine museum. You'll continue north past **Roaring Mountain** (a travertine cascade by the road; get out only if you have some extra time) and **Obsidian Cliff** (same advice), and then have dinner in the dining room at the historic **Mammoth Hot Springs Hotel** or the **Park Street Grill** in **Gardiner,** 5 miles north.

If you're doing only the Upper Loop on this trip, you should include the **Grand Canyon of the Yellowstone** ★★★ on your tour—it's a short way south of Canyon Village, where the loop runs west to Norris.

THE LOWER LOOP

The longer **Lower Loop** covers some of the more famous park landmarks in its 96-mile circuit. Beginning at the south entrance, you would join the loop at the **West Thumb** of Yellowstone Lake, an otherworldly shoreline of hot springs and mud pots. If you go east, the loop skirts the west shore of **Yellowstone Lake** to the handsome **Lake Hotel** at the north end, where the Yellowstone River outlet is spanned by **Fishing Bridge.** The route then encompasses the **Grand Canyon of the Yellowstone, Madison Junction,** and the **Firehole Canyon Drive,** the **Lower Geyser Basin** and the **Fountain Paintpots,** the **Midway Geyser Basin,** and the **Upper Geyser Basin** and stalwart **Old Faithful,** where

you can top off the day with a meal at historic **Old Faithful Inn** or the relatively new **289**
Old Faithful Snow Lodge. Then head east over **Craig Pass** to the lake again.

Put the two loops together, and you've done the Grand Loop of approximately 166 miles. At its conclusion, you will have seen most of the major attractions in the park.

OUT OF THE LOOPS: ENTRANCES & OTHER DETOURS

Rapturous descriptions of the **Lamar Valley** ★★★ elsewhere in this guide should encourage you to take a run out of the park's northeast entrance. The valley is wide and beautiful and alive, with elk and bison grazing by the river, and coyotes, wolves, and grizzly bears making guest appearances. Beyond the park gate you'll find Cooke City, a friendly little town, and then a switchback climb north on the Beartooth Highway, with its spectacular views.

Roads to the other entrances also have allure. If you head east along the north shore of Yellowstone Lake, you'll begin climbing into **Sylvan Pass,** the 8,530-foot exit route that will take you through the east gate into the beautiful Wapiti Valley and eventually to the town of Cody (see chapter 14, "Cody & North-Central Wyoming"). The north and east shores of the lake have beaches where you can sun, swim, or begin a paddling journey to the remote southern corners of the lake. The **south entrance road** skirts **Lewis Lake** and follows **Lewis River,** where you'll often see the graceful parabolas of fly-fishing lines at work. You'll also see some of the stark handiwork of the 1988 fires. Similarly, areas along the **west entrance road** are still marked by the burned husks of trees; there are also peaceful views of the **Madison River** along this road.

There are also some trips off the main roads that are worth taking. Try the short **Fire-hole Canyon Drive** (just south of Madison Junction, head west on the one-way loop) for a look at Firehole Falls and a dip in the idyllic spring-warmed swimming hole a bit farther down the road. For a chance at sighting wolves, drive into **Slough Creek** in the Lamar Valley in the early morning or late afternoon. Drive across the Yellowstone River just south of Canyon Village and hike from majestic overlook to majestic overlook along the **South Rim.** Drive to the **Mount Washburn** picnic area off Dunraven Pass (elevation 8,859 ft.), and if you want to see a panorama of the entire caldera, hike 3 miles to the top of the 10,243-foot peak.

6 SUMMER SPORTS & ACTIVITIES

BICYCLING

Considering the vast expanse of real estate the park covers, the challenging terrain, and the miles of paved roads and trails, a cyclist could conclude that the park is a prime area for biking, on or off the roads.

It looks good on paper, but the reality borders on harrowing. The narrow and twisty roads have no bike lanes, so bikers continually fight for elbowroom with wide-bodied RVs and trailers. Off-road opportunities are limited because bikes are allowed on only a small number of trails.

Nevertheless, plenty of bicyclists take the challenge. The following trails are available to bikers, but know that you will share the roads with hikers. The **Mount Washburn Trail,** leaving from the Old Chittenden Road, is a strenuous trail that climbs 1,400 feet. The **Lonestar Geyser Trail,** accessed at Kepler Cascade near Old Faithful, is an easy 1-hour ride on a user-friendly road. Near Mammoth Hot Springs, **Bunsen Peak Road** and **Osprey Falls Trails** present a combination ride/hike: The first 6 miles travel around Bunsen Peak; getting to the top requires a fairly short (but fairly steep) hike. A round-trip hike down to Osprey Falls adds another 3 miles—and a steep climb back up—to the journey.

Bike rentals are available in West Yellowstone at **FreeHeel and Wheel** (© 406/646-7744), and in Jackson at **Hoback Sports** (© 307/733-5335).

BOATING

The best place to enjoy boating in Yellowstone is on **Yellowstone Lake,** which has easy access and panoramic views. The lake is one of the few areas where powerboats are allowed; you can rent rowboats and outboard motorboats at **Bridge Bay Marina** (© 866/439-7375). Motorboats, canoes, and kayaks can be used on Lewis Lake (about 15 miles north of the south entrance).

FISHING

There are two primary types of anglers in Yellowstone. First are the fly casters, purists more interested in the artistry and seduction of fly-fishing than in keeping what they catch. There are stretches of the Yellowstone and Madison rivers where the anglers are packed tippet to tippet and the trout must be punch drunk from catch-and-release.

Then there are the powerboat fishermen who troll the deep waters of **Yellowstone Lake.** Seven varieties of game fish live in the parks: five trout species (cutthroat, rainbow, brown, brook, and lake), grayling, and mountain whitefish. Of the trout, only the cutthroat are native, and they are being pressured in the big lake by the larger lake trout. As a result, you can't keep any pink-meat cutthroat caught in Yellowstone Lake, and you must keep any lake trout. These policies have diminished the number of fishing boats on Yellowstone Lake in recent years, but they're necessary.

The Yellowstone fishing season typically opens on the Saturday of Memorial Day weekend and ends on the first Sunday in November, except for Yellowstone Lake, which has a slightly shorter season, and the lake's tributaries, which are closed until July 15 to avoid conflicts between humans and grizzly bears, both of which are attracted to spawning trout.

The **required Yellowstone fishing permit** is available at any ranger station, visitor center, or Yellowstone General Store in the park. Anyone 17 and older needs a fishing permit, which costs $15 for 3 days, $20 for 7 days, and $35 for the season. Fishers ages 12 to 15 also need a permit, but it's free. Casters under 12 can fish without a permit when supervised by an adult.

In June, one of the best fishing spots is on the **Yellowstone River** downstream from Yellowstone Lake, where the cutthroat trout spawn; anglers head to **Madison River** near the west entrance in July and then again in late fall for rainbow and some brown trout; in late summer, the **Lamar River** and **Soda Butte Creek** in the park's beautiful northeast corner are popular spots to hook cutthroats in September. You'll find more isolation at **Trout Lake,** a small backcountry lake about 10 miles west of the northeast entrance.

You can fish the **Yellowstone River** below the Grand Canyon by hiking down into **Seven Mile Hole,** a great place to cast (thanks to the dearth of vegetation to snag on) for cutthroat trout from July to September, with the best luck around Sulphur Creek.

Other good fishing stretches include the **Gibbon and Firehole rivers,** which merge from the Madison River on the park's west side, and the 3-mile **Lewis River Channel** between the Shoshone and Lewis lakes during the fall spawning run of brown trout.

There is an access for anglers with disabilities at the **Madison River,** 3½ miles west of Madison Junction at the Haynes Overlook. Here you'll find a fishing platform overhanging the river's edge for 70 feet.

HORSEBACK RIDING

People who want to pack their gear on a horse, llama, or mule must either get permits to enter the Yellowstone backcountry or hire an outfitter with a permit (see below). Other visitors who want to get in the saddle but not disappear in the wilderness can put themselves in the hands of the concessionaire, **Xanterra Parks & Resorts** (© 866/439-7375; www.travelyellowstone.com). Stables are located at Canyon Village and Roosevelt Lodge. Choices are 1- and 2-hour guided trail rides (the prices are $37 and $56, respectively) aboard well-broken, tame animals. Wranglers refer to these as "nose-and-tail" tours, and an experienced rider is likely to find them awfully tame.

If you're looking for a longer, overnight horse-packing experience, contact the park and request a list of approved concessionaires that lead backcountry expeditions. Most offer customized, guided trips, with meals, horses, and camping and riding gear provided. Costs run from $250 to $500 per day per person, depending on the length of the trip and number of people. One good outfitter is **Rockin' HK Outfitters** (© 307/333-4505; www.rockinhk.com), offering 3- to 10-day trips for about $450 per person per day. Out of Bozeman, **Greater Yellowstone Flyfishers** (© 406/585-4655; www.gyfly fishers.com) offers fly-fishing pack trips in the park.

---

7 WINTER SPORTS & ACTIVITIES

Yellowstone's average snowfall of more than 10 feet every year—and 30 feet of the white stuff at higher elevations—provides the perfect backdrop for a multitude of winter activities. The north entrance remains open, so you can drive in from Gardiner for a day and drive back out. You can travel throughout the park by snowmobile or snowcoach, and spend the night either at Mammoth or at the handsomely rebuilt Old Faithful Snow Lodge. For additional information on all of the following winter activities and accommodations, as well as snowcoach transportation and equipment rentals, contact **Xanterra Parks & Resorts** (© 866/439-7375; www.travelyellowstone.com). There are also many activities, outfitters, and rental shops in the park's gateway towns.

CROSS-COUNTRY SKIING

The best cross-country trails in Yellowstone are the Howard Eaton Trail to **Lonestar Geyser,** a fairly level 8-mile round-trip through a remote setting, starting at the Old Faithful Snow Lodge, and the **Fern Cascades Trail,** which begins in the Old Faithful housing area on the south side of the road and winds for 3 miles through a rolling wooded landscape. Energetic skiers can tackle the 12-mile **Mallard Lake Trail,** though it may take them all day—it departs north of the Old Faithful Lodge area along the north side of the Upper Geyser Basin, then loops north and east to Mallard Lake and back to Old Faithful.

Equipment rentals (about $20 per day), ski instruction, ski shuttles to various locations, and guided ski tours are all available at the **Old Faithful Snow Lodge** and the **Mammoth Hot Springs Hotel,** the park's two winter lodging options. Discounts are available for multiday rentals of skis or snowshoes. Ski instruction costs around $30 per

Snowmobiling: To Ban or Not to Ban?

During his final days in office, President Bill Clinton approved a ban on snow-mobiles in Yellowstone and Grand Teton national parks. In December 2003 a judge ruled that the ban would become effective in December 2004. It was a win for environmentalists, who argued that snowmobilers brought pollution, noise, and the destruction of natural habitat to the national parks. But hold on: In February 2004, that ban was overturned and another study commissioned, leaving the fate of snowmobiling in Yellowstone up in the air until the National Park Service announced a final winter use plan. New regulations have reduced the snowmobile quota by 25% from 720 per day (65 for Grand Teton and the John D. Rockefeller, Jr. Memorial Pkwy.) to 540 per day. Sylvan Pass—the east entrance—has been permanently closed to over-snow traffic as well.

Snowmobilers have been only allowed access to certain roads, must be accompanied by a licensed guide, and must have a valid driver's license. In addition, snowmobilers must travel in groups of 11 or fewer, including the licensed guide. There are also BAT (best available technology) requirements for most snowmobiles. Snowmobiles and cars are prohibited from 9pm to 7am. Road closings begin on March 7 and typically continue into April when the winter season officially comes to an end.

person for a 1-hour private lesson; a full-day guided excursion costs $75 to $125 per person (lunch may or may not be included). Guided snowshoe trips are also available.

The **Yellowstone Association Institute** ★★★ (✆ **406/848-2400**) offers winter courses throughout the park. Past offerings have included 3-day classes devoted to win-tertime photography, cross-country skiing, and the ecology of wolf reintroduction. The institute's faculty and staff are a knowledgeable and friendly bunch, and a class is one of the best ways to acquaint yourself with the park in any season.

ICE-SKATING

The **Mammoth Hot Springs ice rink** is located behind the Mammoth Hot Springs Recreation Center. On a crisp winter's night, you can rent a pair of skates (free) and glide across the ice while seasonal melodies are broadcast over the PA system. It's cold out there, but there's a warming fire at the rink's edge. There is also an Old Faithful rink; rentals are likewise free. Call ✆ **866/439-7375** for more information.

SNOWCOACH TOURS

It is possible to enjoy the sights and sounds of Yellowstone without raising a finger—except to write a check or sign a credit card voucher—by taking one of the scenic snow-coach tours that originate at the south and west entrances, as well as at Mammoth and Old Faithful. One-way and wildlife-watching trips range from about $30 to $60, while round-trips cost $110 to $140.

If you've never seen a snowcoach, you're in for a treat. Don't be fooled into thinking that this distinctively Yellowstone mode of transportation is merely a fancy name for a bus that provides tours during winter. Imagine instead an Econoline van with tank treads for tires and water skis extending from its front, and you won't be surprised when you see this unusual-looking vehicle. The interiors are toasty warm, with seating for a large group, and they usually allow each passenger two bags. They aren't the fastest, smoothest, or most comfortable form of transportation, but they do allow large groups to travel together, and they're cheaper and warmer than snowmobiles. They're also available for hire by groups at many snowmobile locations. Guides provide interesting and entertaining facts and stories of the areas as you cruise the park trails, and they give you opportunities to photograph scenery and wildlife.

For snowcoach information, contact **Xanterra Parks & Resorts** (© 866/439-7375 or 307/344-7311; www.travelyellowstone.com). Out of West Yellowstone, **Yellowstone Vacations** (© 800/426-7669 or 406/646-9564; www.snowcoachyellowstone.com) and **Yellowstone Alpen Guides** (© 800/858-3502 or 406/646-9591; www.yellowstone guides.com) provide service as well.

SNOWMOBILING

Roads that are jammed with cars during the summer fill up with snowmobiles and bison during the winter. In deference to the shaggier road warriors, moderate speed limits are strictly enforced, but this is still an excellent way to sightsee at your own pace. A driver's license and licensed guide are required for rental, as is a guide. Day tours cost $225 for a single rider or $250 double; custom tours are also available, but considerably more costly. A helmet is included with the snowmobile, and you can rent a clothing package for protection against the bitter cold. **Warming huts** are located at Mammoth, Indian Creek, Canyon, Madison, West Thumb, and Fishing Bridge. They offer snacks, a hot cup of coffee or chocolate, and an excellent opportunity to recover from a chill.

Snowmobile rentals are also available in the **gateway communities** of Gardiner and West Yellowstone, Montana, and south of Grand Teton in Jackson, Wyoming. Most rental shops accept reservations weeks in advance, so reserving at least 2 weeks ahead of time is a good idea. Plan on making reservations for the week between Christmas and New Year's at least 6 months in advance.

8 HIKING

Getting your car snarled in one "wildlife jam" after another in pursuit of a glimpse of one of the park's four-legged denizens is one way to enjoy the outdoors. Another is taking a hike, even a short one, because you'll see a whole new side of the park. There are gentle hikes where you never lose sight of the road; moderate hikes where you might spend an afternoon penetrating the forest to visit a spot of secluded beauty; and overnight trips where you can hike and camp for days without seeing anyone but the people who embarked on the journey with you.

Part of the reason so few people hike and camp in the Yellowstone wilderness is fear of bears. Bear attacks are extremely rare, and usually involve a sow protecting her cubs, but you should carry pepper spray, just in case; when you camp, secure your food and cooking gear in a tree well away from tents. Park rangers can advise you on current bear activity and safe practices. This is true wilderness, but if you equip yourself properly and learn proper techniques, you'll be safer than you are on a city street. If you go into the backcountry, you need a permit (see "Where to Go & How to Reserve a Spot," below), which also ensures that someone knows where you are.

For those who would rather sleep in a bed, there are still excellent day hikes that allow you to escape the crowd and view wildlife in its own habitat, take in the scenery, or climb a peak. Rangers at visitor centers can advise you on a hike to match your interests and abilities, and provide maps of the extensive trail system in the park. Besides a good map, always bring a good supply of water (and, if you can, a purifier or iodine pills) and rain gear.

Here is a small selection of good hikes, long and short. In addition to these individual hikes, the **Continental Divide Trail (CDT)** ★★★ links many of them together as part of a continuous trail from Mexico to Canada, roughly following the spine of the continent. The Yellowstone Backcountry Office maintains a guide to CDT trails. The Howard Eaton Trail system once went all through the park, but was supplanted by the Grand Loop Road. Sections of the old trail are still maintained and will be found in trail guides, though some of them closely parallel park roads. For a more extensive list of trails and details than what follows here, pick up longtime ranger Mark C. Marschall's excellent *Yellowstone Trails* (Yellowstone Association, $9.95) or the maps provided by the park.

HIKES AROUND MAMMOTH

The **Beaver Ponds Loop Trail** starts in Mammoth at Clematis Gulch (btw. Liberty Cap and an old stone Park Service residence) and makes a 5-mile loop to a series of beaver ponds, where your best chances of seeing the big-tailed beasts are early morning or afternoon. There are some good views coming and going, including Mount Everts. More ambitious hikers can link up with the **Sepulcher Mountain Trail,** which features hot springs, gardens of oddly shaped limestone boulders, and scenic views from the ridges of the Mammoth area. Be in shape for this one and bring a good map of the crisscrossing trail system, because you'll cover at least 12 miles, depending on your route.

Nearby is the **Bunsen Peak Trail** ★★, a short but steep trip to the summit of this volcanic remnant, with a 1,300-foot gain in elevation. Make the hike early and you can watch the morning sun strike Electric Peak, which glows with a golden hue. The 2.1-mile trail passes through mosaic burns from the 1988 fires, and when you get to the top you'll have a view from 3,000 feet above the Yellowstone Valley. After topping the peak, you can take an alternative route down Bunsen's east side and come back along the Old Bunsen Peak Road Trail for a 6-mile round-trip. If you're looking for more, hike the **Osprey Falls Trail** ★ and add 3 miles down a series of switchbacks for a great view of a 150-foot waterfall to the trek.

HIKES IN THE TOWER-CANYON AREA

The **Tower Falls** overlook is easy to get to; it's only 300 feet from the Tower Falls parking area. Walk .5 mile more along some steep switchbacks, and you'll be at the less crowded base of the falls for a stunning view. You can also hike 3.5 miles to the falls from Roosevelt Lodge, a good car-free choice if you happen to be staying there. Begin on the **Lost Lake Trail** and take a left when the trail forks .5 mile from the lodge.

Just south of Canyon Village, the **Chittenden Bridge** crosses from the Loop Road to the South Rim Road near the top of the Grand Canyon of the Yellowstone. You can park and hike either the **South Rim** or **North Rim trail,** with spurs that drop steeply (but briefly) down to viewing platforms at the Upper and Lower falls. If you want a more complete and less crowded view of this deep gorge, take the **7-Mile Hole Trail** (which is actually 5.5 miles long) along the north canyon rim. You'll see the Silver Cord Cascade from the rim, and then drop down to the river after a couple of miles in an area where

---

(Finds) **An Old Faithful Secret**

For a spectacular view of Old Faithful from above, take the **Observation Point Trail** ★, a 2-mile jaunt (beginning at the Old Faithful Visitor Center) that will take you by numerous thermal features on the other side of the Firehole River. Follow the Geyser Hill Trail across the river and then climb the switchbacks to the observation point to watch Old Faithful burst in relative solitude.

---

the canyon widens enough for trees. There are some active hot springs along this hike. This is quite a drop (1,400 ft.), and hikers should be prepared for a fairly demanding climb out.

Across the road from Uncle Tom's Trail parking area (the first parking area to the left after crossing the bridge to the South Rim) is the trail head for the **Clear Lake/Ribbon Lake Loop Trail** ★. The hike to Clear Lake is 1.5 miles, a gradual climb across a high plateau, and Ribbon Lake lies less than 2 miles beyond it. Bears are often active in this area early in the year, so check with rangers for current conditions before heading out. Views of the plateau improve with each footstep, until you find yourself surrounded by a panoramic view of the mountains surrounding the canyon area. During early and late spring it's a bit more difficult because snow runoff and rain can make trails wet and muddy, but that shouldn't be an impediment to anyone interested in the spectacular views. Clear Lake itself is intimately small, and gives you the opportunity to see subsurface activity of the thermal areas below the lake. On a circumnavigation of the lake along a trail, you will see and smell venting activity making its way to the surface; in some spots the lake looks like a boiling pot. This trail also connects to the **Howard Eaton Trail,** an arduous, 14-mile trail to Fishing Bridge and Yellowstone Lake.

The **Mount Washburn Trail** ★★★ falls into the "if you can only do one hike, do this one" category. It's a short hike to panoramic views, with wildflowers decorating the way and nonchalant bighorn sheep often browsing nearby. Trail heads are located at the summit at Dunraven Pass (elevation 8,859 ft.), and on Old Chittenden Road, where there's more parking available. Either hike is 6 miles round-trip, with an increase in elevation of 1,400 feet; however, the climbs are fairly gradual and interspersed with long, level stretches. From the summit, the park will lie before you like a map on a table: You'll see the Absaroka Mountains to the east, Yellowstone Lake to the south, and the Gallatin Mountains to the west and north. In addition to sheep, you may see marmots and red fox; bears have also made use of the area in recent years. You'll be climbing a summit that's 10,243 feet, so pace yourself, and bring warm clothing to fend off the storms that often buffet the top. The hike to the summit is an easy 90-minute walk at a steady pace, which can stretch to 2 hours if you take time for breaks. There's a day-use shelter in the base of the ranger lookout, with viewing telescopes and restrooms.

HIKES NEAR OLD FAITHFUL

The popular trail to **Lonestar Geyser** covers a little more than 2 miles of mostly level terrain to the geyser, which rewards visitors with eruptions up to 50 feet tall every 3 hours. The trail follows the Firehole River from the Kepler Cascades parking area, with

Tips ## Wilderness U.: Guided Backpacking with the Yellowstone Association Institute

The Yellowstone Association Institute (YAI) uses the park's backcountry as a 2.2-million-acre classroom for many of its 400 annual classes. In fact, a number of courses are guided backpacking trips into the Yellowstone wilderness.

I went on a YAI expedition with about 10 other customers in August 2004, following the same route the Nez Perce Indians took through Yellowstone in summer 1877 while evading the U.S. Army. Our 4-day adventure—which was preceded by a day in an indoor classroom in Gardiner—traversed 40 miles under the leadership of experienced backcountry guide and park historian Lee Whittlesey, whose wry humor nicely complemented his historical insight.

We learned about the obstacles the Nez Perce faced en route to their ultimate surrender in Montana. Led by Chief Joseph, 600 to 800 people, including a good number of children and seniors, evaded capture from June into October, cutting through a slice of the fledgling national park known as Yellowstone. We also learned about the rugged terrain the Nez Perce crossed, and about differing accounts of their exact path through the park. We learned about wolf tracks, as well as about the "Leave No Trace" etiquette upheld by backcountry enthusiasts. Most important, we learned that the flight of the Nez Perce has been the key event in the tribe's history since 1877. The 5-month ordeal haunts many of its members to this day. The contemporary Nez Perce are a nostalgic tribe, still focused on the events of summer 1877, and thus—for better or for worse—they are quite different from the typically modern people of the United States.

The "Flight of the Nez Perce" backcountry course has become a staple in the YAI catalog, along with guided backpacking classes about wolves, grizzly bears, waterfalls, photography, and the microbes that inhabit the park's thermal features. Taking a course is a great way to educate yourself and to learn the ins and outs of backpacking; plus you meet a bunch of like-minded Yellowstone lovers in the process. Trips typically last 4 days to a week and cost $400 to $700 per person. You need to bring most of your own gear. Call ☎ **406/848-2400** or visit **www.yellowstoneassociation.org/institute** for a course catalog and other information.

a forest canopy to keep it cool in the summer, widening now and then into broad riverbank meadows. The geyser erupts from a brown cone about 12 feet high, and is surrounded by a meadow pocked by steam vents and thermal features. The path begins from a parking lot on the Old Faithful–West Thumb road just south of the Kepler Cascades. It's partially paved to the geyser and open to bicyclists. If you want to try a less busy (and less scenic) route, take the **Howard Eaton Trail** just east of the Old Faithful overpass, 3 miles to the geyser. From the geyser, you can continue on—bicycles can't—over Grants Pass to join the Bechler River Trail to Shoshone Lake.

From the Biscuit Basin parking lot, you can take a fine 3-mile round-trip hike to **Mystic Falls,** which fall 100 feet to the Firehole River. Continue up switchbacks to the top of the falls and beyond, and you'll link up with the **Little Firehole Meadows Trail** to return to Biscuit Basin, with more views on the way. You can make this trip in less than 2 hours, with only a 460-foot elevation gain.

Fairy Falls plummets a more impressive 200 feet, and can be reached by hiking 2.5 miles on the Fairy Falls Trail, which begins from the Old Faithful–Madison road just south of the Midway Geyser Basin parking area. Hikers who don't mind a slightly longer haul (about 8 miles round-trip) will be rewarded with better wildlife-viewing opportunities by starting from the **Imperial Meadows** trail head a mile south of the Firehole River bridge on Fountain Flat Drive. The hike winds through an area populated by elk along Fairy Creek, then past the Imperial Geyser, where it joins the Fairy Creek Trail and travels east to the base of the falls. The total gain in elevation is only 100 feet. If you turn west instead, you'll find an unmarked trail north to the Imperial Geyser.

HIKES NEAR YELLOWSTONE LAKE

At the north end of the lake, the **Pelican Valley Trail** takes a loop north of the lake around an area loaded with elk, bison, sandhill cranes, trout, eagles, grizzlies, and the new kids on the block, wolves. You can take hikes of different lengths, up to a 16-mile loop, but a lot of folks, having had their fill of wildflowers and beasts, go no farther than Pelican Creek Bridge, a 7-mile round-trip. If you continue on, you'll pass through forest and "bear meadows." This is a daytime-only hiking area (9am–7pm), and it's closed in the early summer until July 4 because of bear activity.

The **Elephant Back Loop Trail** ★ is an opportunity to get a bird's-eye view of the island-dotted expanse of Yellowstone Lake, the Absaroka Mountains, and the Pelican Valley—and maybe a moose. It's a great photo opportunity and a fairly easy 3.6-mile loop, beginning a mile south of Fishing Bridge Junction off the road to Lake Village.

You can walk along the north shore of Yellowstone Lake on the **Storm Point Trail** ★, but be aware that it's occasionally closed due to grizzly bear activity. This easy, level 2-miler terminates at a point jutting into the lake where you'll find lovely panoramic views. It begins in the Indian Pond area, 3½ miles east of Fishing Bridge directly across from the Pelican Valley trail head.

HIKES TO REMOTE AREAS & OVERNIGHT BACKCOUNTRY TRIPS

The **Bechler Meadows Trail** enters the southwest corner of the park, an area rich in waterfalls, cascades, and thermal features rarely seen by human eyes. The access is by Idaho 47 from Ashton, Idaho, which will take you to the Bechler Ranger Station in the southwest corner of the park. About 5 miles into the hike, the trail makes several fords of the river as it enters Bechler Canyon, passing Collonade Falls and Iris Falls. There are places on this trail where you can view the Grand Tetons in the distance, and some thermal features bubble and churn on the Bechler River's banks. This is a camping trip—you can cover nearly 30 miles if you hike all the way into the Old Faithful area—best made late in the summer to avoid high water during creek crossings. You'll need a backcountry permit for overnight stays (see "Camping," below).

The **Slough Creek Trail,** which begins in the Lamar Valley of the park's northeast corner, takes hikers through some of the best wildlife habitat in the park. You can see elk, bison, trumpeter swans, the occasional grizzly bear, and the wolves that have quite happily taken up residence among abundant prey. The presence of wolves has made this area more popular, and the trail is also used by horse-packers. The trail starts from the road to Slough Creek campground, following the creek's valley north, then crossing a ridge to a second valley. You can hike a few miles, or take your camping gear and head for the park boundary, 11 miles to the north.

The **Thorofare Trail** follows the eastern shore of Yellowstone Lake and then skirts the Yellowstone River up into some of the most remote and beautiful backcountry in the Rockies. It's a long, steep trail, but you'll be rewarded with views of the Upper Yellowstone Valley, Two Oceans Plateau, and abundant wildlife. Eventually you'll reach a gorgeous alpine valley just outside the park's boundary, with a ranger station known as Hawk's Rest. Fishermen love this area, as do grizzly bears, especially during the cutthroat trout spawning season. This is the most remote roadless area in the Lower 48, a good 30 miles from the trail head at the lake, and even the most capable hikers should consider riding with an outfitter. You can cut 9 miles off the trip by getting a boat shuttle (about $300 round-trip with a maximum capacity of six people) to the mouth of the lake's southeast arm (call the **backcountry shuttle office** at ✆ **307/242-3893**), or you can come in through the Bridger-Teton National Forest to the south (check with the forest's Blackrock Ranger Station in Moran, Wyoming; ✆ **307/543-2386**).

9 CAMPING

WHERE TO GO & HOW TO RESERVE A SPOT

The National Park Service has shifted management of five major campgrounds to Xanterra Parks & Resorts, the park concessionaire, which means, predictably, higher fees, but also allows you to make reservations ahead of arrival. The other seven campgrounds still managed by the park are available only on a first-come, first-served basis. These lower-cost campgrounds ($12–$14 per night) are located at Indian Creek, Lewis Lake, Mammoth, Norris, Pebble Creek, Slough Creek, and Tower Fall. We like Lewis Lake and Indian Creek, which tend to be available when others are full. Check with rangers about campsite availability when you enter the park; some campgrounds fill up as early as 8am.

Xanterra Parks & Resorts operates the large campgrounds at Bridge Bay, Canyon, Grant Village, Madison, and Fishing Bridge, where the fees are $19 per night. The **Fishing Bridge RV Park** is the only campground equipped with water, sewer, and electrical hookups for RVs and trailers, though it accepts hard-sided vehicles only (no tents or tent trailers), and the fees are $35 per night. The **Madison campground** is the first to open in early May, while **Grant Village** is closed until mid-June to avoid bear conflicts during trout-spawning season. These campgrounds are usually busier, and some, like Bridge Bay, are rather barren of trees unless you get a site on the fringes. Most campgrounds close in September, but Madison is open until mid-October, and Mammoth is open year-round. If you plan to travel in July or August, make your reservations 6 months ahead of time by calling ✆ **866/439-7375** or 307/344-7311, or by writing **Xanterra Parks & Resorts,** P.O. Box 165, Yellowstone National Park, WY 82190.

Camping is allowed only in designated areas and visitors are limited to 14 days between June 15 and Labor Day, and to 30 days the rest of the year, except at Fishing Bridge, where there is no limit. Checkout time for all campgrounds is 10am. Quiet hours are strictly enforced between 8pm and 8am.

Black Bear or Grizzly?

Because a black bear can be black, brown, or cinnamon, here are some identifiers. The grizzly is the larger of the two, typically $3^1/_2$ feet at the shoulder with a dish-face profile and a pronounced hump between the shoulders. The black's ears are rounder, just like those you see on stuffed animals. The grizzly's color is typically more yellowish-brown, but the coat is sometimes recognized by its cinnamon color, often highlighted by silver tips. In terms of tracks, the black bear's toes follow an arc around the footpad while the grizzly's toes are arranged in a nearly straight line. The grizzly's claws are also considerably longer.

Caution: Park rangers attempt to keep track of grizzlies to avoid human/ bear incidents. However, it is best to assume that they are always around; make noise when traveling in isolated spots.

There are plenty of opportunities for backcountry camping as well. Some areas in the Yellowstone backcountry include delicate habitat—the southeast arm of Yellowstone Lake is an example—and visitors must camp in designated areas for a limited time only. Check with the **Yellowstone Backcountry office** (© **307/344-2160;** www.nps.gov/yell) for rules, reservations, and advice.

WHAT TO EXPECT

Remember, these are campgrounds, not motels, so the amenities are spare. But some have showers and bathrooms and potable water. Check the chart below to determine the level of comfort at each campground. Showers and laundry facilities are available at Canyon, Fishing Bridge, and Grant Village campgrounds. In addition, campers may use the shower and laundry facilities at Lake Lodge and Old Faithful Lodge.

In the northeast area of the park, the **Tower Fall campground** is near a convenience store, restaurant, and gas station at Tower Lodge, 19 miles north of Canyon Village and 18 miles east of Mammoth. **Slough Creek campground ★** is located in a remote section of the Lamar Valley near the northeast entrance. The good news is there are fewer people, good fishing, and the possibility of wolf sightings; the bad news is that restroom facilities are pit toilets. **Canyon campground** is the busiest in the park. Sites are in a heavily wooded area; the store, restaurants, visitor center, and laundry at Canyon Center are nearby. Because it's in an area of spring bear activity, attempts have been made over the years to close the RV park at **Fishing Bridge.** It's still open, but only hard-sided camping vehicles are allowed here. **Bridge Bay** is located near the shores of Yellowstone Lake, so you get tremendous views, especially at sunrise and sunset. Unfortunately, though surrounded by the forest, much of the area has been clear-cut, so there's not a whole lot of privacy. It's close to boat-launching facilities and the boat-rental operation. **Madison ★** and **Norris campgrounds** are attractive, wooded locations in the heart of the park, close to wildlife activity, hiking trails, and rivers. These camp areas seem less like outdoor motels than the big campgrounds on the park's east side.

Amenities for Each Campground in Yellowstone National Park (Where Flush Toilets Are Not Available, Vault Toilets Are Provided)

Campground	# Sites	Fee	Showers/ Laundry	Flush Toilets	Disposal Stations	Generators Permitted
Bridge Bay*	425	$19	No	Yes	Yes	Yes
Canyon*	250	$19	Yes	Yes	Yes	Yes
Fishing Bridge*	346	$35	Yes	Yes	Yes	Yes
Grant Village*	400	$19	Yes	Yes	Yes	Yes
Indian Creek	75	$12	No	No	No	No
Lewis Lake	85	$12	No	No	No	No
Madison*	277	$19	No	No	Yes	Yes
Mammoth	85	$14	No	No	Yes	No
Norris	100	$14	No	No	Yes	No
Pebble Creek	30	$12	No	No	No	No
Slough Creek	29	$12	No	No	No	No
Tower Fall	32	$12	No	No	No	No

*Reserve through Xanterra Parks & Resorts; ℂ 866/439-7375 or 307/344-7311; TDD 307/344-5395; **www.travelyellowstone.com**.

10 WHERE TO STAY IN THE PARK

For listings of accommodations just outside the park, see section 1, "The Gateway Towns: West Yellowstone, Gardiner & Cooke City," at the beginning of this chapter.

The first thing you should know: no televisions. Private bathrooms have arrived and phones are in place, but televisions are in only two rooms in the entire park (the suites at Mammoth).

Railroad companies built most of the park's hotels and lodges around the start of the 20th century, and they would offer their primped Victorian guests a package tour that delivered them by train and stagecoach to luxurious resorts with rocking chairs on the verandas and gourmet food. A good deal of that old-style ambience has been thankfully retained at Yellowstone. Many of the newer facilities erected by the park concessionaire (in particular, the Old Faithful Snow Lodge and the new lodges at Canyon) are suitably matched to older buildings, at least on the exterior. However, the push for more features may come in the near future, and, during recent upgrades at the Lake Hotel, the wiring was installed for televisions—just in case. Many of the hotels provide beautiful examples of architecture and craftsmanship, but they're not perfect: The plaster walls transmit some sound and the bathrooms tend to be smallish. However, even the most budget-conscious traveler will find a room in the park that fits the pocketbook. Look over the descriptions below carefully, though, because some of the cheaper lodgings are primitive indeed.

Canyon Lodge and Cabins This complex is one of the newer facilities in the park (both Cascade and Dunraven lodges were completed here in the 1990s), but it can't escape the bustle of Canyon Village. However, the lodges are located a mere half-mile

---

Tips   Making Reservations

Yellowstone accommodations are normally open from May to mid-October. Rooms are typically fully booked during the peak season in July and August, so reservations should be made up to a few months in advance. For information or reservations at any of the locations within the park, contact **Xanterra Parks & Resorts** at P.O. Box 165, Yellowstone National Park, WY 82190 (© **866/439-7375** or 307/344-7311; www.travelyellowstone.com).

---

from the Grand Canyon of the Yellowstone and Inspiration Point, one of the most photographed spots in the park. Cascade Lodge offers simple rooms appointed with tasteful log furnishings in the three-story building; the newer Dunraven is similar, although it is more modern (with an elevator); both are located adjacent to a woodland setting. The cabins are single-story duplex and fourplex structures with private bathrooms that are among the largest in the park. They're a bit weathered but generally acceptable, but, given the sheer number of units involved, this isn't the place to "get away from it all."

In Canyon Village, P.O. Box 165, Yellowstone National Park, WY 82190. © **866/439-7375** or 307/344-7311. Fax 307/344-7456. www.travelyellowstone.com. 605 units. $164 double; $70–$149 cabin. AE, DC, DISC, MC, V. Closed Oct to late May. **Amenities:** Restaurant; lounge. *In room:* No phone.

Grant Village   The southernmost of the major overnight accommodations in the park, Grant Village was completed in 1984 and is one of the more contemporary choices in Yellowstone. It's not as architecturally distinctive as the Old Faithful options, consisting of six condo-style units (with motel-style rooms), but it's also less touristy and more isolated. Rooms are tastefully furnished, most outfitted with light wood furniture, track lighting, electric heat, and laminate counters. Nicer rooms affording lake views have mullioned windows, one queen-size or one or two double beds, and full bathrooms.

On the West Thumb of Yellowstone Lake, P.O. Box 165, Yellowstone National Park, WY 82190. © **866/439-7375** or 307/344-7311. Fax 307/344-7456. www.travelyellowstone.com. 300 units. $140 double. AE, DC, DISC, MC, V. Closed late Sept to late May. **Amenities:** Restaurant; lounge.

Lake Lodge Cabins   Value   These cabins surrounding Lake Lodge stand a little way from the lake in a relatively quiet, traffic-free area. The old Western lodge's most attractive feature is a large porch with wicker rockers that invite visitors to sit and gaze out across the waters. The accommodations are in well-preserved, clean, free-standing cabins near a trout stream that threads through a wooded area. (Access is usually restricted when grizzlies emerge from hibernation.) The cabins come in two grades: **Western** cabins provide electric heat, paneled walls, two double beds (and, in some cases, an extra twin), and combination bathrooms, while **Pioneer** cabins are smaller and sparsely furnished, with one or two double beds each and small shower-only bathrooms. Because the dining room here is a tad short on atmosphere, you might want to make the short trek to the Lake Yellowstone Hotel for a more sumptuous meal in a more appetizing setting.

On Yellowstone Lake, P.O. Box 165, Yellowstone National Park, WY 82190. © **866/439-7375** or 307/344-7311. Fax 307/344-7456. www.travelyellowstone.com. 186 cabins. $66 Pioneer cabin; $138–$149 Western cabin. AE, DC, DISC, MC, V. Closed mid-Sept to early June. **Amenities:** Restaurant; lounge. *In room:* No phone.

Lake Yellowstone Hotel and Cabins ★★   The Ionic columns, dormer windows, and deep porticos on this classic yellow building faithfully recall the year it was built: 1891. It's an entirely different world from the rustic Western style of other park lodgings. The facility was restored in the early 1990s, and its better rooms are the most comfortable and roomy in the park, with soul-stirring views of the massive lake. The three- and four-story wings house the hotel rooms, and there's also a motel-style annex and an assortment of cabins. The upper-end rooms here are especially lavish for Yellowstone, with stenciled walls and traditional spreads on one queen-size or two double beds. Smaller rooms in the annex are fitted with two double beds and bring to mind a typical motel chain. The free-standing yellow-clad cabins here are passable, decorated with knotty pine paneling, and furnished with double beds and a writing table.

On the north side of the lake, P.O. Box 165, Yellowstone National Park, WY 82190. ℰ 866/439-7375 or 307/344-7311. Fax 307/344-7456. www.travelyellowstone.com. 300 units, including 1 suite. $143–$216 double; $128 cabin; $565 suite. AE, DC, DISC, MC, V. Closed early Oct to mid-May. **Amenities:** 2 restaurants; lounge. In room: No phone (cabins).

Mammoth Hot Springs Hotel and Cabins ★   Below the steaming terraces of Mammoth Hot Springs, this is one of two Yellowstone hotels open during both summer and winter seasons. (The other is the Old Faithful Snow Lodge.) Established in 1911, the hotel itself is less distinguished than the Lake Yellowstone Hotel or the Old Faithful Inn, but it manages to blend a wide range of rooms into a satisfying whole. The only truly high-end accommodations are the suites. Standard rooms and cabins offer minimal amenities, but make up for it with a fair amount of charm. Some have tubs only, some have showers only, and some share a bathroom down the hall. The cottage-style cabins are clustered in rings adjacent to the hotel, and vary in quality. Make sure you drift into the **Map Room** (named for the massive inlaid map of the United States on one of the walls), a great place to spend an evening reading or listening to a pianist.

At Mammoth Hot Springs, P.O. Box 165, Yellowstone National Park, WY 82190. ℰ 866/439-7375 or 307/344-7311. Fax 307/344-7456. www.travelyellowstone.com. 212 units, including 2 suites. $85–$121 double; $75–$107 cabin; $211 hot tub cabin; $449 suite. AE, DC, DISC, MC, V. Closed Oct to mid-Dec and early Mar to early May. **Amenities:** 2 restaurants; lounge. In room: No phone (cabins).

Old Faithful Inn ★★★   There are three hotels within viewing distance of the geyser, but this is undoubtedly the crown jewel of Yellowstone's man-made wonders. Seven stories tall with dormers peaking from a shingled, steep-sloping roof, it's an architectural wonder that was designed by Robert Reamer to blend into the natural environment, first welcoming guests in 1904.

The cavernous, log-laden lobby is striking, with an ambience that is half elegant palace and half rugged wilderness lodge. You can climb the stairs to its internal balconies, but seismic activity eventually closed the crow's nest, where a chamber orchestra initially performed for the well-dressed guests below. Only 30 miles from the west entrance and 40 miles from the south entrance, this is the first place visitors head when they want a bed for the night, so make reservations well in advance.

Guest rooms are basic, appointed with conservative fabrics and park-theme art, but they don't all have private bathrooms; the wing rooms offer better facilities and more privacy.

At Old Faithful, P.O. Box 165, Yellowstone National Park, WY 82190. ℰ 866/439-7375 or 307/344-7311. Fax 307/344-7456. www.travelyellowstone.com. 327 units, including 6 suites. $119–$206 double with private bathroom; $93 double with shared bathroom; $397–$502 suite. AE, DC, DISC, MC, V. Closed mid-Oct to mid-May. **Amenities:** 2 restaurants; lounge. In room: No phone.

Old Faithful Lodge Cabins (Value) These are the leftovers from the days when crude cabins littered the landscape around the world's most famous geyser. The ones closest to the geyser were hauled away years ago, but you still get a sense of what tourism was like in the park's early days, especially if you rent one of the **budget cabins,** which are only slightly less flimsy than tents and have basic beds and sinks, and nothing more. Showers and restrooms are a short walk away. **Frontier cabins** are the better units, adding a private bathtub to other amenities. If amenities are irrelevant, these rustic, thin-walled cabins are an economical way to put a roof over your head in the park. The lodge is perhaps the busiest spot in the geyser area, featuring several snack shops and a huge cafeteria dishing up varied fast food.

At Old Faithful, P.O. Box 165, Yellowstone National Park, WY 82190. © **866/439-7375** or 307/344-7311. Fax 307/344-7456. www.travelyellowstone.com. 96 cabins, some with shared bathroom. $69–$113 double. AE, DC, DISC, MC, V. Closed mid-Sept to mid-May. **Amenities:** 2 restaurants. *In room:* No phone.

Old Faithful Snow Lodge and Cabins ★★ If your last visit to Yellowstone included a stay at the Old Faithful Snow Lodge, put the memory out of your mind. The old dormitory-style lodge was torn down in 1998, and this new, award-winning structure could aptly be called the New Faithful Snow Lodge. Its contemporary big-beam construction and high ceiling in the lobby echo the Old Faithful Inn, and a copper-lined balcony curves above the common area, where guests can relax in wicker furniture. The folks behind the place paid attention to every last detail: The public areas have a contemporary (but appropriate) style, some of the lodge's wood was recycled from the same mill that provided the lumber for the Old Faithful Inn in 1904, and wrought-iron bears abound on everything from lamps to fireplace grates. The modern rooms are spacious and comfortable, second only to the upper-end accommodations at the Lake Yellowstone Hotel. There's also a small collection of surrounding cabins with motel-style furnishings (many of which were built after the 1988 fires) and—a rarity in the park—in-room coffeemakers.

At Old Faithful, P.O. Box 165, Yellowstone National Park, WY 82190. © **866/439-7375** or 307/344-7311. Fax 307/344-7456. www.travelyellowstone.com. 134 units. $191 double; $94–$140 cabin. AE, DC, DISC, MC, V. Closed Oct to mid-Dec and early Mar to early May. **Amenities:** Restaurant; lounge. *In room:* No phone (cabins).

Roosevelt Lodge Cabins ★ (Kids) This is considered the park's family hideaway, a low-key operation with dinky, primitive cabins; stables; and a lodge restaurant that feels like a big ranch house. The barebones cabins are called Roughriders, and they're furnished with two simple beds, clean linens, a writing table, and a woodstove. A step up, the Frontier cabins have their own bathrooms and showers. The lodge is a rugged-but-charming stone edifice; its large, inviting porch is outfitted with rockers so guests can sit back and watch the world go by. Stagecoach rides, horseback trips, and Western trail cookouts give this place a cowboy flavor, and it's a less hectic scene than the other park villages.

At Tower Junction, P.O. Box 165, Yellowstone National Park, WY 82190. © **866/439-7375** or 307/344-7311. Fax 307/344-7456. www.travelyellowstone.com. 80 cabins, 14 with private bathroom. $64–$107 cabin. AE, DC, DISC, MC, V. Closed early Sept to early June. **Amenities:** Restaurant; lounge. *In room:* No phone.

While they're not world-class establishments, Yellowstone's restaurants are well suited to their location and the appetites of their patrons: The portions definitely won't leave anyone going hungry. Most of the menus include a selection of unadventurous, all-American meat-and-potatoes grub alongside several more creative entrees. Consistency can be a problem, because the volume is high and the kitchen staffs are seasonal.

If you're not up for restaurant dining, but you don't want to cook over your camp stove the entire time, there is counter-style fast-food service at the **Yellowstone General Stores** as well as snack shops and cafeterias at Canyon, Mammoth, Grant Village, Lake Lodge, and Old Faithful. Try the new **Geyser Grill** at the Old Faithful Snow Lodge, or the old lunch-counter scene at the **Fishing Bridge Yellowstone General Store.** The **Glacier Pit Snack Bar** is a nostalgic breakfast counter at the Yellowstone General Store in the Canyon Lodge area, open from mid-May to late September.

Canyon Lodge Dining Room (Kids) STEAKS/SEAFOOD   This is a spacious dining area, a tad sterile perhaps, and when it fills up, it's noisy. The salad bar is long and loaded, but otherwise the dinner fare is largely geared toward the carnivore, with a wide selection of steaks alongside some seafood and pasta selections. The breakfast buffet is a good way to start your day, with all the standard American fixings. The crowds can be large at Canyon Village, but there is a relaxed and unhurried feel to this place that you don't find at some of the park's other busy points. Families, in particular, might appreciate the ability to take their time with their meals.

At Canyon Lodge. ✆ **307/344-7311.** Reservations are not accepted. Breakfast $5–$12; lunch $8–$13; dinner $13–$23. AE, DC, DISC, MC, V. June to mid-Sept daily 7–10am, 11:30am–2:30pm, and 5–10pm.

Grant Village Dining Room ★ AMERICAN   Breakfast and lunch at the Grant Village restaurant are much like those at the other restaurants in the park, although the chef often surprises diners with interesting dinner items that stray from the norm. Lunch might include pan-fried trout covered with toasted pecans and lemon butter, huge burgers, and ham and brie on a pretzel roll. The dinner menu ranges from pistachio-crusted chicken to portobello mushroom cannelloni to prime rib, but the specialty is trout, pan-fried with pecans. Quality and ambience here are comparable to those of the better dining rooms at the major park hotels.

At Grant Village. ✆ **866/439-7375.** Dinner reservations recommended. Breakfast $5–$11; lunch $7–$10; dinner $13–$24. AE, DC, DISC, MC, V. June–Sept daily 6:30–10am, 11:30am–2:30pm, and 5:30–10pm.

Lake Yellowstone Hotel ★★ CONTINENTAL   This represents the finest dining Yellowstone has to offer, with a view of the lake stretching south from a vast dining room that doesn't feel crowded even when it's full. One of the best ways to start your day is with a generous breakfast buffet, but the stuffed French toast is also quite good. Lunch entrees are gourmet sandwiches and burgers. The dinner menu is the most adventurous in the park. Appetizers include chilled cucumber soup and lobster ravioli, while entrees include elk medallions and lobster tail, bison prime rib, and Idaho trout stuffed with mushrooms and tomatoes.

On the north side of the lake. ✆ **307/344-7311.** Dinner reservations required. Breakfast $5–$11; lunch $7–$12; dinner $17–$37. AE, DC, DISC, MC, V. Mid-May to early Oct daily 6:30–10:30am, 11:30am–2:30pm, and 5–10pm.

Mammoth Hotel Dining Room ★ STEAKS/SEAFOOD   At Mammoth, there's a good balance between casual and formal because the dining room is reminiscent of an above-average neighborhood restaurant: comfortable and pleasant without too much of the hotel's Victorian past. The view of the Old Fort Yellowstone buildings and surrounding slopes is also quite enjoyable. The breakfast buffet is essentially identical to what you'll find at other locations here, featuring eggs, French toast, and the like. The lunch menu focuses on an array of sandwiches, including smoked turkey on Parmesan-crusted sourdough, a grilled vegetarian reuben, and smoked salmon club. The dinner menu includes bison top sirloin, Montana whitefish, and tasty pork chops, and the vegetarian entrees are surprisingly good.

At Mammoth Hot Springs. ℭ **307/344-7311.** Reservations recommended in winter. Breakfast $4–$11; lunch $8–$12; dinner $13–$23. AE, DC, DISC, MC, V. May–Sept daily 6:30–10am, 11:30am–2:30pm, and 5–10pm; late Dec to early Mar daily 6:30–10am, 11:30am–2:30pm, and 5:30–8pm. Closed Oct to late Dec and early Mar to early May.

Obsidian Dining Room ★ STEAKS/SEAFOOD   In the snazzy new Snow Lodge, a spacious restaurant provides a comparatively contemporary alternative to the dining room at the Old Faithful Inn. It's a little quieter, a little less expensive, and a little less formal. It still has some flash on the menu—braised bison short-ribs shank and linguine with Tuscan chicken, for instance—and there is a breakfast gem, the veggie breakfast burrito.

At the Old Faithful Snow Lodge. ℭ **307/344-7311.** Reservations not accepted in summer. Breakfast $5–$11; dinner $16–$33. AE, DC, DISC, MC, V. Early May to mid-Oct daily 6:30–10am and 5–10pm; mid-Dec to mid-Mar daily 6:30–10am and 5–9:30pm.

Old Faithful Inn Dining Room ★ STEAKS/SEAFOOD   The food notwithstanding, the true highlight is the gnarled log architecture of this distinguished historic inn. Breakfast is buffet or a la carte, and there's a lot to choose from. There's another buffet at lunchtime (headlined by barbecue beef and chicken), as well as a generous assortment of salads and sandwiches. Dinnertime brings yet another buffet, along with menu entrees like rib-eye steaks, fish, and a vegetarian dish. The fare has gotten more distinguished in recent years, with such creative options as wild game Bolognese and pan-seared elk medallions making regular appearances on the menu.

At the Old Faithful Inn. ℭ **307/344-7311.** Dinner reservations required. Breakfast and lunch $5–$14; dinner $16–$30. AE, DC, DISC, MC, V. Mid-May to mid-Oct daily 6:30–10:30am, 11:30am–2:30pm, and 5–10pm. Closed in winter.

Roosevelt Lodge Dining Room STEAKS/SEAFOOD   This is supposed to be the cowboy alternative to the fancier cuisine served at the bigger Yellowstone hotels, but the unadventurous menu will win over only the most naive city slickers. For breakfast, it's eggs and flapjacks; lunch is burgers and sandwiches. Come suppertime, the menu is dominated by barbecue and steaks. A better idea: Join Roosevelt's Old West Dinner Cookout, and ride by horse or wagon through the Pleasant Valley to a chuckwagon dinner that includes cornbread, steak, watermelon, those famous beans, and apple crisp. It's a daily summer event (reservations required) that costs $66 to $80 for an adult, depending on the route of your horseback ride, or $55 if you go by wagon. Children pay $10 less.

At Tower Junction. ℭ **307/344-7311.** Reservations are not accepted, except for Old West cookouts. Breakfast $5–$9; lunch $7–$10; dinner $9–$24. AE, DC, DISC, MC, V. Summer daily 7–10am, 11:30am–3pm, and 4:30–9pm.

Jackson Hole & Grand Teton National Park

Grand Teton compares to Yellowstone somewhat the way a Generation X snowboarder compares to an old ski patrol graybeard: It's younger, flashier, and closer to the bars. The Tetons are a young mountain range in geologic time, and Grand Teton is a young national park, on the rolls in its present form since 1950; Yellowstone, by comparison, dates from 1872. And whereas the geysers of Yellowstone are a pretty long drive from anywhere, you can come off a climb at Grand Teton and be in a posh Jackson eatery 20 minutes after you hit the valley floor.

That's not a knock on Grand Teton National Park. Jackson, after all, is a spiffy resort town with a little cowboy still in it. And within the park's borders are beautiful lakes and rivers, wildlife galore, and lots of recreational opportunities. In the summer, you can climb, hike, boat, balloon, backpack, raft, bird-watch, and fish. In winter, the park and nearby resorts become a magnet for skiers of every style and skill level. Jackson Hole Mountain Resort is upgrading furiously to keep its status as a premier national skier's destination, and its neighbor on the west side of the mountain, Grand Targhee, has some of the best powder in the Rockies.

1 JACKSON HOLE ★★

57 miles S of Yellowstone National Park; 432 miles NW of Cheyenne; 275 miles NE of Salt Lake City; 177 miles SW of Cody

Of the few communities in the Rockies that have successfully toed the line between promoting themselves as resort towns and retaining some semblance of indigenous character, Jackson is a standout. The million-dollar homes are sprouting all over the valley, but there is still open space, a memory of the cowboy past, and some resistance to letting in too much commercial glitz.

The remaining open spaces allow visitors to imagine what it was like early in the 19th century, when fur trappers first camped here. They were followed by ranchers, who soon became *dude* ranchers. Today, the community holds an interesting mixture of ski bums, blue bloods, nouveau riche, avid outdoor types, and even a few old-time cowboys. The cosmopolitans of this motley crew came not just with a hunger for scenery, but also with a taste for music, art, and good restaurants, too, and the selection here is unrivaled in Wyoming. The big ski hill lures a younger crowd, with the final ingredient for resort status—celebrities—supplied by transplants like Harrison Ford.

ESSENTIALS

GETTING THERE The **Jackson Airport** (© **307/733-7682;** www.jacksonholeairport. com) is located north of town at the southern end of Grand Teton National Park. **American Airlines** (© **800/433-7300)** flies in from Chicago, and regular service is

JACKSON HOLE & GRAND TETON NATIONAL PARK

13 JACKSON HOLE

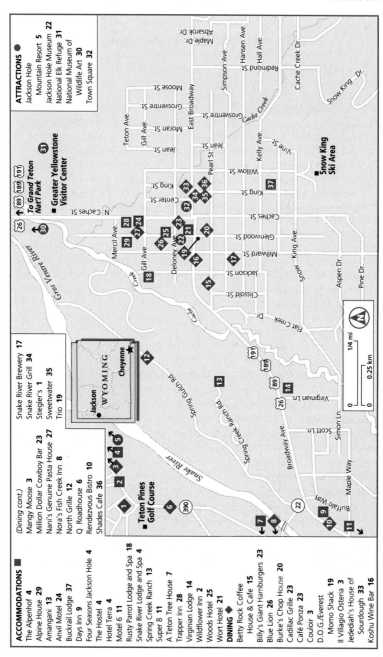

ATTRACTIONS ●

Jackson Hole
  Mountain Resort **5**
Jackson Hole Museum **22**
National Elk Refuge **31**
National Museum of
  Wildlife Art **30**
Town Square **32**

ACCOMMODATIONS ■

The Alpenhof **4**
Alpine House **29**
Amangani **13**
Anvil Motel **24**
Buckrail Lodge **37**
Days Inn **9**
Four Seasons Jackson Hole **4**
The Hostel **4**
Hotel Terra **4**
Motel 6 **11**
Rusty Parrot Lodge and Spa **18**
Snake River Lodge and Spa **4**
Spring Creek Ranch **13**
Super 8 **11**
A Teton Tree House **7**
Trapper Inn **28**
Virginian Lodge **14**
Wildflower Inn **2**
Woods Hotel **25**
Wort Hotel **21**

DINING ◆

Betty Rock Coffee
  House & Cafe **15**
Billy's Giant Hamburgers **23**
Blue Lion **26**
Burke's Chop House **20**
Cadillac Grille **23**
Café Ponza **23**
Couloir **3**
D.O.G./Everest
  Momo Shack **19**
Il Villagio Osteria **3**
Jedediah's House of
  Sourdough **33**
Koshu Wine Bar **16**

(Dining cont.)
Mangy Moose **3**
Million Dollar Cowboy Bar **23**
Nani's Genuine Pasta House **27**
Nora's Fish Creek Inn **8**
North Grille **12**
Q Roadhouse **6**
Rendezvous Bistro **10**
Shades Cafe **36**

Snake River Brewery **17**
Snake River Grill **34**
Stiegler's **1**
Sweetwater **35**
Trio **19**

Jackson or Jackson Hole—What's the Difference?

You'll likely see every kind of merchandise imaginable fashioned with an image of the Tetons and the words "Jackson Hole, Wyoming" scrawled over it. You may notice that on the map, the town just south of Grand Teton National Park is called Jackson. But your plane ticket says Jackson Hole. But wait a minute—the postmark just says Jackson. What gives?

The mystery of the town's name is actually pretty simple. Three mountain men ran a fur-trapping company in these parts in the 1800s: one named David Jackson, another named Jedediah Smith, and a third named William Sublette. Mountain men in those days referred to a valley as a hole. As the story goes, Sublette called the valley Jackson's Hole, because Jackson spent a great deal of time in it. That name was shortened, and when the town materialized, it was also named for David Jackson. So the city itself is Jackson, Wyoming, and it lies in the great valley that runs the length of the Tetons' east side, Jackson Hole.

provided from Denver and Salt Lake City by **Delta** (© 800/221-1212) and **United** (© 800/241-6522). **Northwest** (© 800/225-2525) also connects from Billings, Montana.

If you're getting here on your own wheels, come north from I-80 at Rock Springs on U.S. 189/191, or come east from I-15 at Idaho Falls on U.S. 26 and either come through Snake River Canyon on that highway or veer north over Teton Pass on Wyo. 32. If you are coming south from Yellowstone National Park, you can stay on U.S. 89, which runs north and south through both parks and into town. For up-to-date weather information and local road conditions, contact the Jackson Hole Chamber of Commerce (see below).

VISITOR INFORMATION The **Jackson Hole Chamber of Commerce** has information on just about everything in and around Jackson. Along with the U.S. Forest Service and National Park Service, representatives of the chamber can be found at the informative **Visitors Center,** 532 N. Cache St., about 3 blocks north of Town Square with a view of the National Elk Refuge. For information on lodging, events, and activities, contact the chamber at P.O. Box 550, Jackson, WY 83001 (© 307/733-3316; www.jackson holechamber.com). For lodging information and reservations, call **Jackson Hole Central Reservations** (© 888/838-6606; www.jacksonholewy.com).

GETTING AROUND Once you're on the ground, major car-rental operations serving the airport include **Alamo/National** (© 800/227-7368), **Avis** (© 800/230-4898), and **Hertz** (© 800/654-3131). Also providing rentals in the area are **Dollar** (© 800/800-3665), **Thrifty** (© 800/847-4389), and **Eagle Rent-a-Car,** downtown at 375 N. Cache St. (© 307/739-9999).

Taxi service is available from **Buckboard Cab** (© 307/733-1112) and **Cowboy Cab** (© 307/413-1000). **Alltrans** (© 800/443-6133 or 307/733-3135; www.jacksonhole alltrans.com) offers shuttle service from the airport and national park tours. Many of the hotels and car-rental agencies in the Jackson area offer free shuttle service to and from the airport.

The **Southern Teton Area Rapid Transit (START)** offers bus transport from Teton Village to Jackson daily for $3 (half price for seniors and students; children 8 and under ride free). Service includes about 70 trips a day between downtown and Teton Village in the winter and 15 in the summer; it shuts down around 12:30am year-round. For specific schedule information, contact START at ℂ **307/733-4521** or browse **www.start bus.com**.

SPECIAL EVENTS Held annually in late May, **Old West Days** is a 4-day event dedicated to Jackson's frontier past, with a shootout, cowboy poetry readings, a parade, and a rodeo. The other big annual event is the **Jackson Hole Fall Arts Festival,** a 10-day extravaganza in September with special events every day. Contact the Jackson Hole Chamber of Commerce (see above) for further information on either.

GETTING OUTSIDE
Sporting Goods & Equipment Rentals
Serious climbers with serious wallets will appreciate the gear at **Teton Mountaineering** ★, at 170 N. Cache St. (ℂ **800/850-3595** or 307/733-3595; www.tetonmtn.com), a block from the square, where you can get killer Nordic skis and high-grade fleece jackets. **Adventure Sports,** at Dornan's in the town of Moose (ℂ **307/733-3307**), has a small selection of mountain bike, kayak, and canoe rentals, and advice on where to go with the gear. When snowboards are put away for the summer, the **Boardroom** switches to BMX bikes and skateboards, at 225 W. Broadway (ℂ **307/733-8327;** www.boardroomjackson hole.com). **Hoback Sports,** 520 W. Broadway (ℂ **307/733-5335;** www.hobacksports. com), has a large selection of skis, boards, and summer mountain bikes for rent and sale. **Skinny Skis,** at 65 W. Deloney Ave. off Town Square (ℂ **888/733-7205** or 307/733-6094; www.skinnyskis.com), is a year-round specialty sports shop and has an excellent selection of equipment and clothing. For serviceable factory seconds at steeply discounted prices, head north to the little town of Moose near the entrance to Grand Teton National Park and shop **Moosely Seconds** ★ (ℂ **307/739-1801**).

Biking
You can rent a bike and pick up maps at several of the shops listed above, or take a guided trip in Yellowstone, Grand Teton, or the national forest with **Teton Mountain Bike Tours** (ℂ **800/733-0788;** www.tetonmtbike.com) or Hoback Sports's **Fat Tire Tours,** 100 E. Snow King Ave. (ℂ **307/734-4425**), which places bikes in the Snow King chairlift for an easy ride up the mountain.

Climbing
The sight of the 13,770-foot Grand Teton towering above the valley has been setting hearts pumping for generations. A century ago no one had reached the top; now, thousands have, often carefully roped and cared for by professional guides. Experienced guides and established routes assure a modicum of safety, but climbing accidents and deaths still occur. Overnight climbers must pick up a free permit. The American Alpine Club provides inexpensive dormitory beds for climbers at the **Grand Teton Climbers' Ranch** (ℂ **307/733-7271;** www.americanalpineclub.org). A pair of long-standing operations offer classes and guided climbs of Grand Teton: **Jackson Hole Mountain Guides** in Jackson (ℂ **800/239-7642** or 307/733-4979; www.jhmg.com), and **Exum Mountain Guides** ★ in Moose (ℂ **307/733-2297;** www.exumguides.com). Expect to pay around $700 to $1,000 for a guided 2-day climb of Grand Teton or $150 to $200 for a class. The **Jenny Lake Ranger Station** (ℂ **307/733-3392**), which is open only in summer, is the center for climbing information; climbers are encouraged to stop in and obtain information on routes, conditions, and regulations.

With five Nordic centers and a couple of national parks at your feet, plus the 3.5-million-acre Bridger-Teton National Forest, cross-country skiers have plenty of choices. If you're new to cross-country skiing on any level, you might choose to start on the groomed, level trails at one of the Nordic centers. If, however, you have experience in the steep, deep powder of untracked wilderness, visit or call the National Park Service in **Grand Teton National Park** (📞 **307/739-3300;** www.nps.gov/grte) or the **Bridger-Teton National Forest** in downtown Jackson at 340 N. Cache St. (📞 **307/739-5500;** www.fs.fed.us/r4/btnf), and check in before you go.

The local ski shops are excellent sources of unofficial advice about the area's backcountry. Keep in mind that many of the trails used by cross-country skiers are also used by snowmobiles. For those seeking instruction, lessons are available at the Nordic centers, or you can check the schedule of **Teton Parks and Recreation** (📞 **307/733-5056;** www.tetonwyo.org/parks), which takes visitors on various cross-country ski outings from mid-December to mid-March, weather permitting.

The **Jackson Hole Nordic Center,** 7658 Teewinot St., Teton Village (📞 **307/733-2292;** www.jacksonhole.com), on the flats just east of Teton Village, is a small part of the giant facility that also includes some of the best downhill skiing around (see below). Trail passes ($14) allow access to 11 miles of groomed trails. **Teton Pines Cross Country Skiing Center** (📞 **800/238-2223** or 307/733-1005; www.tetonpines.com) has 7.5 miles of groomed trails that wind over the resort's golf course. At **Grand Targhee** (📞 **800/827-4433** or 307/353-2300; www.grandtarghee.com), you can rent or buy anything you need in the way of equipment and take off on the resort's 9.3 miles of groomed trails.

Dog Sledding

If your idea of mushing is not oatmeal but a pack of yipping dogs, you might want to try your hand at dog sledding, an enjoyable open-air way to tour the high country during the winter. **Jackson Hole Iditarod** (📞 **800/554-7388;** www.jhsleddog.com), associated with Iditarod racer Frank Teasley, offers both half- and full-day trips in five-person sleds (the fifth companion is your guide), and you can take a turn in the driver's stand. The half-day ride costs around $235 per person, gives the dogs an 11-mile workout, and includes a light lunch before you head back to the kennels. For about $300 a head, you can take the full-day excursion out to Granite Hot Springs, a 22-mile trip total. You get a hot lunch, with your choice of trout or steak.

Downhill Skiing

Low temperatures, black-diamond runs, remote location, and an intimidating vertical drop haven't scared skiers away from Jackson Hole—this is what *attracts* them. The two largest ski resorts in the area have been expanding, putting in faster chairs, and eliminating long waits in lift lines. The quality of snow on the mountain can vary, but skiers who seek challenges will not be disappointed. All resorts are open daily.

Jackson Hole Mountain Resort ★★ This resort is booming, with scads of new hotels and timeshares going up at the mountain's foot in recent years, more than doubling the guest capacity in just a few short years. There is special grandeur to this ski resort, from its spectacular mountaintop views to its daring black-diamond runs to its 400 annual inches of powder. Head to the top of **Rendezvous Mountain** and plunge down Tensleep Bowl if you want to get a taste of skiing on the edge. You'll find an inexhaustible supply of steep runs that require skiing expertise: The terrain is rated 10%

beginner, 40% intermediate, and 50% expert. There are lesser runs to the north, including gentler journeys down the sides of **Apres Vous Mountain** that will better suit an intermediate skier. The resort's renowned tram was shut down in 2006; a new $25-million, 100-passenger tram opened in time for the 2008–09 season.

Crowded days have been few in recent years—lucky for skiers, if not the owners. With 2,500 acres of skiable terrain and 4,139 feet of vertical drop, there's plenty of room. Ten lifts, a gondola, and an aerial tram are available from early December to the beginning of April. (The resort turns into a mountain-biking playground come summer.) For an orientation, join the Mountain Hosts, who gather groups at the top of the Rendezvous lift to escort newcomers on a 2-hour tour.

The competition among ski resorts compels growth—not just on the slopes, but also in the resort villages below. A variety of restaurants, lodging, a medical clinic, shops, and entertainment—from sleigh-ride dinners to a skating rink—make it unnecessary to leave the complex during a ski vacation.

If you've never skied in powder up to your kneecaps, make an early-morning trip to the **Hobacks Zone,** just under Cheyenne Bowl. The ski patrol closes it off as soon as the snow gets tracked out.

3395 W. Village Dr. (P.O. Box 290), Teton Village, WY 83025. *C* **888/333-7766** or 307/733-2292; 307/733-2291 for snow conditions; 888/838-6606 for central reservations. www.jacksonhole.com. Full-day lift tickets $55–$91 adults, $40–$66 seniors 63 and over, $32–$54 children 14 and under. Late Nov to early Apr daily 9am–4pm. From Jackson, take Wyo. 22 west to Wyo. 390 and go north to Teton Village, about 5 miles.

Grand Targhee Resort ★ The Grand Targhee resort has struggled at times, changing ownership, wheeling and dealing with federal land managers, and sparring with local conservationists over expansion plans and real-estate development. None of that affects the snow, however, which is terrific. Or the deep, forgiving powder from November through spring (more than 500 in. annually), and a more peaceful, less-crowded village that provides a worthy alternative to Teton Village. Many skiers break up a Jackson ski trip by driving over Teton Pass for a day or two on these slopes.

This may also be a better place for less-aggressive skiers. There is a beginner's powder area and hundreds of acres of wide-open powder slopes for intermediates and other cruisers. You can take a high-speed quad to the adjacent Peaked Mountain and ski in thigh-deep, untracked snow. A problem you might encounter is, oddly enough, fog. Now and then the mountain gets socked in with gray moisture, forcing skiers to ski below the thick blanket. The **Lost Groomer Chute,** a run that takes full advantage of the weather moving west to east, will provide the most insatiable powder hound with enough dust.

Here are a few of the other treats at Targhee: You can ride a sleigh on a starlit evening to a round-table dinner in a snow-buried yurt; your kids can enroll in the Powder Scouts program, which gives kids ages 6 to 12 a full day of instruction, food, and skiing for $128, rental included; and a spa offers everything from massage to an herbal body wrap, along with hot tubs, sauna, exercise room, and heated outdoor pool. Lodging is available at several slopeside hostelries; double rooms start at $139 during regular ski season.

3300 E. Ski Hill Rd., Box SKI, Alta, WY 83422. *C* **800/827-4433** or 307/353-2300. www.grandtarghee.com. Full-day lift tickets $69 adults, $39 seniors 65 and older, $19 children 6–12, free for children 5 and under. Mid-Nov to Apr daily 9am–4pm. From Jackson, take Wyo. 22 over Teton Pass into Idaho, then Idaho 33 north to Driggs, then follow the signs west (back into WY) to Targhee Resort, about 38 miles.

Snow King Resort If you enter Jackson from the north on a winter night, the lit slopes of Snow King are an appealing sight. Snow King offers a variety of recreation, including a tubing hill, ice rink, and snowboard park. Plus, it's conveniently located near the heart of town. It's the oldest ski hill in Wyoming, operating since 1939, and the hotel has attractive, moderately priced rooms. The only problem is the skiing itself: A limited number of fairly steep runs don't offer much variety. The beginner's slope is small and amounts to only 15% of the terrain, the snow is notoriously icy, and there's not enough intermediate snow to satisfy all levels of ability. The two other area resorts are much bigger, with more and longer runs and a greater variety of challenges. "Town Hill," as it's known, has 400 acres of skiable terrain, a triple chair, two double chairs, and two surface tows (one for tubing).

400 E. Snow King, Jackson, WY 83001. ✆ **800/522-5464** or 307/733-5200; 307/734-2020 for snow conditions. www.snowking.com. Lift tickets $42 adults, $32 seniors 60 and older and children 13 and under. Late Nov to late Mar Tues–Sat 10am–7pm; Sun–Mon 10am–4pm. Take Cache St. south to Snow King Ave. Turn left and follow the signs to the resort.

Fishing

Yellowstone and Grand Teton national parks are home to some fabled fishing spots (see the park sections for details), but some of the best angling in the region is found outside the park boundaries.

The **Snake River** emerges from Jackson Lake Dam as a broad, strong river, with decent fishing from its banks in certain spots—like right below the dam—and better fishing if you float the river. Fly-fishermen should ask for advice at local stores on recent insect hatches and good stretches of river, or hire a guide to keep them company. **High Country Flies** ★, 185 N. Center St. (✆ **307/733-7210;** www.highcountryflies.com), has a vast selection of high-quality fishing gear, flies, and fly-tying supplies, along with lessons, guided trips, and free advice if you just want to gab about where to cast. **Jack Dennis Sports** on Town Square, 50 E. Broadway (✆ **307/733-3270;** www.jackdennis fishingtrips.com), is a much bigger store with room to display some big boats, and it also offers lessons and guides. **Westbank Anglers,** 3670 N. Moose-Wilson Rd. (✆ **307/733-6483;** www.westbank.com), is another full-service fly shop. The going rate for guided fishing is about $450 for a full day for two people.

Golf

More than one American president has played a round of golf in Jackson, which despite its short putting season has some world-class links. The semiprivate Robert Trent Jones, Jr.–designed **Jackson Hole Golf and Tennis Club** (✆ **866/915-4482** or 307/733-3111; www.jhgtc.com), north of Jackson off U.S. Hwy. 89, has an 18-hole course that's one of the best in the country—and it underwent a major renovation and saw a new clubhouse open in 2007. Seasonal greens fees range from $65 to $175 for 18 holes, cart included. The **Teton Pines Resort,** 3450 N. Clubhouse Dr. (✆ **800/238-2223** or 307/733-1005; www.tetonpines.com), designed by Arnold Palmer and Ed Seay, is a challenging course; greens fees range from $65 to $160, cart included, depending on the season. Both courses are open to the public.

Hiking

One benefit of having so many mountain ranges converging around Jackson is that you have choices—especially when it comes to hiking. The most popular place to go for a stroll in the vicinity of Jackson is **Grand Teton National Park,** which shows off some glorious aspen colors in the fall. Less traveled are the forests that abut the park, particularly **Bridger-Teton National Forest** just east of Jackson. Bridger-Teton and its east-side counterpart, **Shoshone National Forest,** encompass a huge piece of mountain real estate, including glaciers, 13,000-foot peaks, and some of the best alpine fishing lakes in the world. Among the mountain ranges included in these forests are the **Absarokas,** the **Gros Ventre,** the **Wyoming,** and the **Wind River Range,** or "Winds," as they're called by locals, which stretch about 120 miles from just southeast of Jackson near Pinedale to the South Pass area and the Red Desert. The **Greater Yellowstone Visitor Center,** 532 N. Cache St., in downtown Jackson, provides all of the hiking and access information you'll need for the national forest as well as for the Gros Ventre and Teton wilderness areas. Call the **Forest Service** (© 307/739-5500; www.fs.fed.us/r4/btnf) for additional information.

Horseback Riding

Some hotels, including those in Grand Teton National Park, have stables and operate trail rides for their guests. For details, contact **Jackson Hole Outfitters** (© 307/654-7008; www.jacksonholetrailrides.com), **Spring Creek Ranch Riding Stables** (© 800/443-6139; www.springcreekranch.com), or the **Mill Iron Ranch** (© 307/733-6390; www.millironranch.net). Rides typically cost around $50 for 2 hours or $150 for a day.

Kayaking, Canoeing & Sailing

With the Snake and Hoback rivers and the lakes of Grand Teton National Park, it's no surprise to see all kinds of watercraft towed or tied to the roofs of SUVs in Jackson. Canoeists and kayakers enjoy the upper Snake River, from Jackson Lake Dam down to Moose, and expert kayakers are attracted to the ride through Snake River Canyon and Hoback white water. Beginners should be wary of the upper Snake—snags and spring currents have claimed lives, so a guide is advisable. Canoeists paddle Jenny Lake and, with a small portage or two, String and Leigh lakes. The big lake, **Jackson,** attracts sailboats and sea kayaks, but beware of the sudden afternoon eruptions of gusty wind and thunderstorms.

Several operators in Jackson run schools and guide paddlers of all skill levels. The two major outfits are the **Snake River Kayak and Canoe School,** 260 N. Cache St. (© 800/529-2501 or 307/733-9999; www.snakeriverkayak.com), and **Rendezvous River Sports,** 945 W. Broadway (© 307/733-2471; www.jacksonholekayak.com).

Rafting

The most popular way to experience the Snake River is white-water rafting; these are wet, wild, white-knuckle tours. Several companies offer adrenaline-pumping day trips down the Snake, but don't plan on being just a passenger—this is a participatory sport. Contact **Barker-Ewing** (© 800/448-4202; www.barker-ewing.com), **Sands Wildwater** (© 800/358-8184 or 307/733-4410; www.sandswhitewater.com), **Dave Hansen Whitewater** (© 800/732-6295 or 307/733-6295; www.davehansenwhitewater.com), or **Mad River Boat Trips** (© 800/458-7238; www.mad-river.com). Generally, a full-day trip runs $75 to $100, lunch included, and a half-day trip costs about $40 to $60.

Snowmobiling

Although West Yellowstone is the most popular base for snowmobiling in the Yellowstone area, Jackson has a growing contingent of snowmobile aficionados and outfitters.

The operators who rent snowmobiles (including the necessary clothing and helmets) also have guides to take you on 1-day and multiday tours of Jackson Hole and the surrounding area. **High Country Snowmobile Tours, Wyoming Adventures,** and **Rocky Mountain Snowmobile Tours** share a website and reservation service (© 800/647-2561; www.snowmobiletours.net), offering guided trips in Jackson Hole, Yellowstone, and the surrounding wildlands. **Jackson Hole Snowmobile Tours,** 515 N. Cache St. (☎ **800/633-1733** or 307/733-6850; www.jacksonholesnowmobile.com), offers 1-day trips in Yellowstone and multiday trips along the Continental Divide. A typical guided, full-day outing costs from $250 to $350, with pickup and drop-off service, equipment, fuel, continental breakfast, and lunch included. Also in Jackson, snowmobiles can be rented at **Leisure Sports,** 1075 S. U.S. Hwy. 89 (☎ **307/733-3040;** www.leisuresports adventure.com).

OFFBEAT BUT MEMORABLE WAYS TO SEE THE TETONS

Aerial Touring

For a much quicker climb to the mountaintops, call **Teton Aviation** (☎ **800/472-6382** or 208/354-3100; www.tetonaviation.com), in Driggs, Idaho. You'll actually be looking down at the summits that climbers strain to top, and you'll get a new perspective on the immensity of the Grand Teton (although you won't get too close—the park has some air-space restrictions). Teton has 1-hour flights in planes and gliders ($235–$250 per person) that take you to 11,800 feet on the west side of the Grand.

Ballooning

The folks at the **Wyoming Balloon Company** ★ (☎ **307/739-0900;** www.wyoming balloon.com) like to fire up early, in the still air that cloaks the Teton Valley around 6am. Their "float trips" stay aloft for a little more than an hour, cruising over a 3,000-acre ranch with a full-frontal view of the Tetons. The journey concludes with a champagne toast at the landing site. Prices are $295 adults and $245 for children ages 6 to 12 (no kids 5 and under allowed).

EXPLORING THE AREA

Jackson Hole Aerial Tram and Gondola Rides ★ After the resort's legendary tram shut down in 2006, a new $25-million, 100-passenger tram opened for the 2008–09 ski season. From the top, you can see the Tetons from an elevation above 10,000 feet—or 9,000 for the Bridger Gondola—but don't expect a private tour. During busy summer days, the tram carries 45 passengers, packed in like the skiers that take the lift in the winter. The top of Rendezvous Mountain offers an incredible view; but it can get pretty chilly, even in the middle of summer, so bring a light coat. Atop the Bridger Gondola at 9,095 feet, two restaurants—upscale **Couloir** and the **Headwall Deli**—offer a place to eat before you head back down.

At Jackson Hole Ski Resort, 7658 Teewinot St., Teton Village. ☎ **307/739-2753.** www.jacksonhole.com. Tickets $15–$24 adults and seniors, $10–$18 children 6–14, free for children 5 and under. Early to late Sept and late May to mid-June daily 9am–5pm; mid-June to early Sept daily 9am–6pm. Tram runs approximately every half-hour.

Jackson Hole Museum Dedicated local volunteers maintain this repository of early photographs, artifacts, and other items of historical significance, and they'll carefully guide you through the collections. You can browse the exhibits or go down the street to the Historical Society at Glenwood Street and Mercill Avenue to do some research. At the museum, you'll find collections of trade beads, antique pole furniture, pistols, and Indian artifacts, spread out in 3,000 square feet of floor space. *Note:* The museum is moving to a new location on 225 N. Cache St.; call for current information.

105 N. Glenwood St. (at the corner of Deloney St.). ✆ **307/733-2414.** www.jacksonholehistory.org. Admission $6 families, $3 adults, $2 seniors, $1 students and children. Mon–Sat 9:30am–6pm; Sun 10am–5pm. Closed Oct–May.

National Museum of Wildlife Art ★★   If you don't spot this museum on your way into Jackson from the north, consider that a triumph of design: Its jagged, red-sandstone facade is meant to blend into the steep hillside facing the elk refuge. Within this 50,000-square-foot castle is some of the best wildlife art in the country. There are 12 exhibit galleries that display traveling shows and collections dating from 2000 B.C. to the present, including a gallery devoted to the American bison as well as a showcase for local great Carl Rungius. Younger visitors will be entertained by the many interactive exhibits and a "Kid's Kit" loaner to tote around the museum. The facility also houses a repository of internationally acclaimed wildlife films and there's a good little cafe, too.

2820 Rungius Rd. (3 miles north of town on U.S. Hwy. 89, across from the National Elk Refuge). ✆ **800/313-9553** or 307/733-5771. www.wildlifeart.org. Admission $30 families, $10 adults, $9 students and seniors, $5 children 5–18, free for children 4 and under. Daily 9am–5pm (fall–spring Sun 1–5pm).

WILDLIFE-WATCHING

National Elk Refuge ★   It's not exactly nature's way, but the U.S. Fish and Wildlife Service makes sure that the elk in this area eat well during the winter by feeding them alfalfa pellets. It keeps them out of the haystacks of area ranchers and creates a beautiful tableau on the peaceful flats along the Gros Ventre River: thousands of elk, some with huge antler racks, dotting the snow for miles. Drivers along U.S. Hwy. 89 might also see trumpeter swans, coyotes, moose, bighorn sheep, and, lately, wolves. As autumn begins to chill the air in September, you'll hear the shrill whistles of the bull elk in the mountains; as snow begins to stick on the ground, about 5,000 animals make their way down to the refuge—the world's largest winter concentration of elk. Although the cultivated meadows and pellets help the elk survive the winter, some biologists say this approach results in overpopulation and the spread of diseases such as brucellosis.

Regardless, this is a great opportunity to see these magnificent wapiti up close. Each winter from mid-December to March, the Fish and Wildlife Service offers **horse-drawn sleigh rides** that weave among the refuge elk. Riders early in the winter will find young, energetic bulls playing and banging heads, while late-winter visitors (when the Fish and Wildlife Service begins feeding the animals) wander through a more placid scene. Rides embark from the Greater Yellowstone Visitor Center (532 N. Cache St.) daily between 10am and 4pm on a first-come, first-served basis. Tickets for the 45-minute rides cost $18 for adults and $14 for children 5 to 12 (free for kids 4 and under), and can be purchased at the visitor center.

Located 3 miles north of Jackson on U.S. Hwy. 26/89. ✆ **307/733-9212.** http://nationalelkrefuge.fws. gov. Free admission. Visitor center summer daily 8am–7pm; winter daily 9am–5pm.

SHOPPING

In recent years, big national chains have opened factory-outlet stores in Jackson, and among the ever-changing array of shops (rents are high; so is turnover) you can find everything from American-Indian crafts to cowboy boots to Oriental rugs. But these are what you'll find in most resort towns. The areas where Jackson excels are its art galleries and outdoor-wear shops.

Standouts in the outdoor-clothing category include **Teton Mountaineering,** 170 N. Cache St. (✆ **307/733-3595**), also a great spot for climbing, camping, and winter gear;

JACKSON HOLE & GRAND TETON NATIONAL PARK

13

JACKSON HOLE

(Kids) **Especially for Kids**

Snow King may not have the best skiing in the valley, but it caters to kids and families. In the summer, kids can frolic on the **Snow King's Alpine Miniature Golf Course and Alpine Slide** (© 307/733-5200). A round of 18 holes is $8 for adults, $7 for seniors, $6 for kids 6 to 13, and $3 for kids 5 and under. The **Alpine Slide** is the golf course's untamed neighbor. It's a wild ride down the 2,500-foot ophidian highway running from the top of the blue-and-yellow chairlift to the bottom of Snow King Mountain; it's like a water slide without the water. A trip down the slide is $15 per person.

In the winter, there are ski schools for kids with day-care options at all the ski resorts. Once again, Snow King has a few extras: a tubing hill ($21 for 2 hr. adults, $18 kids 13 and under) and an ice-skating rink, which opens in October and features skating ($6 adults, $4 kids 13 and under; skate rentals $3) and hockey until spring. For more information, call © 307/733-3000.

and **Moosely Seconds** in Moose (© 307/739-1801), where you'll find surprisingly deep discounts on quality outdoor wear.

Collectors, tired of bighorn sheep on the crags and weather-beaten cowboys on their horses, often dismiss Western art. But while Jackson has plenty of that genre in stock, some of its two dozen galleries are more adventurous and sophisticated. **Cayuse Western Americana,** 255 N. Glenwood St. (© 800/405-4096 or 307/739-1940; www.cayusewa. com), focuses on antiques of all kinds, from beadwork to spurs to belt buckles to paintings. The **Center Street Gallery,** 30 N. Center St. (© 307/733-1115; www.centerstreet gallery.com), focuses on contemporary Western art. **Lyndsay McCandless Contemporary,** 130 S. Jackson (© 307/734-0649; www.lmcontemporary.com), showcases abstract wildlife and other edgy work. A mile north of town, at 1975 U.S. Hwy. 89 (toward the park), is the **Wilcox Gallery** (© 307/733-6450; www.wilcoxgallery.com), which showcases more than 20 painters and sculptors from across the nation. The **Wilcox Gallery II** is in town at 165 N. Center St. (© 307/733-3950).

WHERE TO STAY

The thin-walled, dimly lit motels of the past are just memories now—Jackson lodgings these days come with palatial trappings and, in some cases, prices that start at $500 a night. Prices are generally discounted in off season (spring/fall), but not during ski season.

Clustered together near the junction west of downtown where Wyo. 22 leaves U.S. Hwy. 26/89 and heads north to Teton Village is a colony of chain franchises: a surprisingly chic **Motel 6,** 600 S. U.S. Hwy. 89 (© 307/733-1620); **Super 8,** 750 S. U.S. Hwy. 89 (© 307/733-6833); and the more upscale and expensive **Days Inn,** 350 S. U.S. Hwy. 89 (© 307/733-0033), with private hot tubs and fireplaces in suites. High-season prices for the motels range from about $100 to $200.

On the inexpensive end of the scale, the **Anvil Motel,** 215 N. Cache St. (© 800/234-4507 or 307/733-3668; www.anvilmotel.com) offers hostel beds in the well-kept "Bunkhouse" for $25 a night, with ski lockers, a communal kitchen, and a hot tub. Motel rooms run $128 to $148 in summer. I also like the summer-only **Buckrail Lodge,** at the base of Snow King Mountain at 110 E. Karns Ave. (© 307/733-2079; www.buckraillodge.com), a comfortable independent that's been nicely maintained by the two families that have owned it since it opened in the 1960s. Doubles are $85 to $135.

In Jackson

Alpine House ★★ Stylish, environmentally conscious, and melding the best of the B&B and hotel worlds, Alpine House began as a six-room operation in 1996 and expanded nearly fourfold in 2000 when it also opened a spa. Modeled after Scandinavian lodging, the rooms are woodsy and Western but modern and functional, with one king, one queen, or two queens and nice views. Some have lofts with additional beds; all have a shared or private balcony, a fireplace, and a soaking tub. The public areas, indoors and out, are quiet and serene. New in 2009 are five spacious creek-side cottages a block away from the main building. Owners Hans and Nancy Johnstone are former Olympians (she's a biathlete and he competed in the Nordic combined) and great resources for planning outdoor adventures in Jackson Hole.

285 N. Glenwood St. (P.O. Box 1126), Jackson, WY 83001. ℂ **800/753-1421** or 307/739-1570. Fax 307/734-2850. www.alpinehouse.com. 27 units, including 2 suites and 5 cottages. $175–$260 double; $195–$295 suite; $195–$400 cottage. Rates include full breakfast. AE, MC, V. **Amenities:** Lounge; outdoor Jacuzzi; sauna; spa. *In room:* A/C, TV (except original 6 rooms), kitchenette, Wi-Fi (free).

Rusty Parrot Lodge and Spa ★★ The name sounds like an out-of-tune jungle bird, but the Rusty Parrot demonstrates excellent pitch, cultivating a country lodge and spa right in the heart of busy Jackson. Located across from Miller Park, the Parrot is decorated in the nouveau Western style of peeled log, with an interior appointed with elegant furnishings and river-rock fireplaces. One very attractive lure is the Body Sage Spa, where you can get yourself treated to all sorts of scrubs, wraps, massages, and facials. Another is the excellent restaurant, the Wild Sage. The breakfast that comes with your room includes omelets, fresh pastries, fruit, cereals, and freshly ground coffee; food also appears later in the day, but the lodge likes to make that a surprise (sorry). Rooms are gigantic, and several have private balconies.

175 N. Jackson St. (P.O. Box 1657), Jackson, WY 83001. ℂ **800/458-2004** or 307/733-2000. www.rusty parrot.com. 31 units, including 1 suite. $290–$425 double; $625–$750 suite; lower rates spring and fall. Rates include full breakfast. AE, DC, DISC, MC, V. **Amenities:** Restaurant; lounge; outdoor Jacuzzi; spa. *In room:* A/C, TV, Wi-Fi (free).

Trapper Inn ★ Just 2 short blocks from Town Square, the Trapper Inn was reborn as a slick hotel when it opened 36 new rooms in a pair of attractive "mountain contemporary" buildings in 2006. The rooms are stylish and spacious—the newest are all suites that adjoin, with a kitchen in every other unit—and the employees here are some of the most helpful you'll find in Jackson.

285 N. Cache St. (P.O. Box 1712), Jackson, WY 83001. ℂ **888/771-2648** or 307/733-2648 for reservations. www.trapperinn.com. 90 units, including 36 suites. $119–$219 double; $159–$289 suite. Rates include expanded continental breakfast. AE, MC, V. **Amenities:** Indoor Jacuzzi; indoor pool. *In room:* A/C, TV, kitchen, Wi-Fi (free).

Virginian Lodge (Value) It's not brand-new. It's not a resort, it doesn't have a golf course, and the highway is right outside the door. Since its overhaul in 1995, however, the Virginian is one of the better motels in Jackson: The prices remain among the lowest in town; the interior courtyard (with a large grassy play area and central pool) is a world away from the Broadway-facing exterior; and it's a busy, cheerful place to stay. You can get a room with a private Jacuzzi or a kitchenette, and many have "dry" bars and sofa sleepers.

750 W. Broadway, Jackson, WY 83001. ✆ **800/262-4999** or 307/733-2792. Fax 307/733-4063. www. virginianlodge.com. 170 units. $119 double; $159–$220 suite. AE, DC, DISC, MC, V. **Amenities:** Restaurant; lounge; Jacuzzi; outdoor pool; Wi-Fi (free in lobby). *In room:* A/C, TV, kitchenette.

Woods Hotel ★ (Finds)   Originally opening in 1950, the Woods Hotel was collecting cobwebs from 1998 to 2006 until new ownership reinvented the place as a boutique lodging in 2007. The brick exterior (and vintage sign) belies the inn-like rooms, featuring spare Western-chic style: leather headboards, warm earth tones, and a few rugged touches. The standard rooms are small and lack air-conditioning, but the brick structure stays surprisingly cool and the suites and one family room (with bunk beds) give guests more space to stretch out, plus microwaves and minifridges.

120 N. Glenwood St. (P.O. Box 266), Jackson, WY 83001. ✆ **800/963-2200** or 307/733-2200. www.the woodshotel.com. 11 units, including 4 suites. $149 double; $179–$189 suite. AE, MC, V. *In room:* TV, fridge (in some), microwave (in some), no phone, Wi-Fi (free).

Wort Hotel ★★   Located on Broadway just off the Town Square, the Wort stands like a charming old tree. Opened in the early 1940s by the sons of Charles Wort, an early-20th-century homesteader, the Tudor-style two-story building was largely rebuilt after a 1980 fire. Nowadays, it has an old-fashioned style, both in the relaxed **Silver Dollar Bar** (distinctively graced with 2,032 silver dollars) and in the quiet, formal dining room. In the manner of an old cattle-baron hotel, the lobby is graced by a warm, romantic fireplace; another fireplace and a huge, hand-carved mural accent a mezzanine sitting area, providing a second hideaway. The inciting rooms aren't Tudor at all—the Wort labels them "New West." Brass number plates and doorknobs welcome you into comfortable, air-conditioned guest rooms with modern decor, thick carpeting, and armoires. The Silver Dollar Suite features a wet bar inlaid with silver dollars as in the bar below.

50 N. Glenwood St., Jackson, WY 83001. ✆ **800/322-2727** or 307/733-2190. www.worthotel.com. 59 units, including 5 suites. $165–$339 double; $399–$699 suite. AE, DISC, MC, V. Valet parking $10 daily. **Amenities:** Restaurant; lounge; health club; Jacuzzi. *In room:* A/C, TV, CD player, Wi-Fi (free).

Near Jackson

Amangani ★★★   Cut into the side of East Gros Ventre Butte, Amangani's rough rock exterior blends incredibly well so that the lights from its windows and pool appear at night to glow from within the mountain. Understated and rustic, all details are done with high contemporary style. From the high-ceilinged corridors to the idyllic outdoor pool, this place is all about class and privacy, not to mention superlative views. Hotelier Adrian Zecha has resorts like this around the world, from Bali to Bhutan, and while the designs are tailored to the landscape, the approach is the same: personal service, luxury, and all the little touches. To name a few of the latter, there are iPod cradles in every bedroom, cashmere throws on the daybeds, and stunning slate and redwood interiors.

1535 NE Butte Rd., Jackson, WY 83002 (on top of E. Gros Ventre Butte). ✆ **877/734-7333** or 307/734-7333. www.amanresorts.com. 40 units. $565–$1,400 double. AE, DC, DISC, MC, V. **Amenities:** Restaurant; lounge; health club; Jacuzzi; year-round outdoor pool; spa. *In room:* A/C, TV/VCR, hair dryer, Wi-Fi (free).

A Teton Tree House ★ (Finds)   This B&B is an architectural marvel "and a quiet port in the storm" of bustling Jackson Hole, says innkeeper, builder, and longtime Jackson adventurer Denny Becker. Built on a forested hillside above Wilson where flying squirrels glide amidst the sunset canopy, the labyrinthine inn is located 95 steps up from the parking lot and is full of books, staircases, and all sorts of funky nooks and crannies. Most every room has a private deck with a splendid view of the valley; the Downy Woodpecker room has a queen-size bed and an outdoor swing and adjoins with the Clark's Nuthatch room with two queens for larger parties. Denny and his wife Sally eat heart-healthy breakfast (meaning no eggs or meat) with their guests; Denny is known for his breakfast banana splits (with light yogurt), Sally for her baking, and both have plenty of good advice about local attractions.

6175 Heck of a Hill Rd. (P.O. Box 550), Wilson, WY 83014. ☏ **307/733-3233.** www.atetontreehouse-jacksonhole.com. 6 units. $205–$250 double; 3-night minimum. Rates include complimentary full breakfast. DISC, MC, V. Closed mid-May to Mid-Oct. 8 miles west of Jackson. No children 4 and under. *In room:* No phone, Wi-Fi (free).

Spring Creek Ranch ★★ Perched atop East Gros Ventre Butte, 1,000 feet above the Snake River and minutes from both the airport and downtown Jackson, this resort commands a panoramic view of the Grand Tetons and 1,000 acres of land populated by deer, moose, and the horses at its riding facility in the valley below. It seems a little less exclusive now that Amangani has opened next door. But Spring Creek still has much going for it: The rooms, divided among nine buildings with cabinlike exteriors, all have wood-burning fireplaces, Native-American floor- and wallcoverings, and balconies with views of the Tetons. Most rooms have a king- or two queen-size beds, and the studio units boast kitchenettes. In addition to its own rooms, the resort arranges accommodations in the privately owned condominiums and vacation homes that dot the butte—large, lavishly furnished, and featuring completely equipped kitchens. The resort also has an "Adventure Spa," offering a combination of guide service and post-outing treatments, and in-house naturalists who lead guests on "Wildlife Safaris" into the parks.

1800 Spirit Dance Rd. (on top of the E. Gros Ventre Butte; P.O. Box 4780), Jackson, WY 83001. ☏ **800/443-6139** or 307/733-8833. www.springcreekranch.com. 126 units. $340–$500 double; $375–$2,200 condo or home. Lower rates in spring and fall. AE, MC, V. **Amenities:** Restaurant; concierge; Jacuzzi; outdoor pool; room service; spa; tennis court (outdoor). *In room:* A/C, TV/VCR, high-speed Internet (free), kitchenette.

Wildflower Inn ★★ A terrific B&B on 3 lush and secluded acres near Teton Village, the Wildflower Inn is the brainchild of jack-of-all-trades Ken Jern, a log-home builder and climbing guide, and his wife, Sherrie, a former ski instructor who now runs the inn full-time. Besides being founts of local information, the Herns are remarkable hosts who pride themselves on both the big picture and the little details. Rooms, named after local wildflowers, are comfortable and luxurious, with private decks, exposed logs, and a remarkable sense of privacy for an inn. Guests also get access to house bikes, rain gear, and trekking poles—not to mention hammocks. Breakfasts are excellent, including veggie frittatas, sour cream coffeecake, and yeast-raised waffles.

3725 Teton Village Rd. (P.O. Box 11000), Jackson, WY 83002. ☏ **307/733-4710.** Fax 307/739-0914. www.jacksonholewildflower.com. 5 units, including 1 suite. $320–$350 double; $400 suite. MC, V. **Amenities:** Bikes; indoor Jacuzzi. *In room:* TV, hair dryer, no phone, Wi-Fi (free).

In Teton Village

Teton Village is gradually becoming the self-contained resort town now typical of better ski resorts—it has everything you need, from food to powder to a massage, a short limp from the chairlifts. The village is located on the west side of the Snake River, surrounded by ranchlands that have been protected from development. While lodging in the town of Jackson tends to be a little cheaper in the winter than the summer, the ratio is reversed at Teton Village—rooms by the ski hill get more expensive after the snow falls. For a wide range of basic condos and deluxe vacation homes, contact **Jackson Hole Resort Lodging**

(**℡ 800/443-8613** or 307/733-3990; www.jhresortlodging.com). All establishments are open year-round unless otherwise indicated.

Very Expensive

The Alpenhof ★★   No other spot in the village has quite the Swiss-chalet flavor of this long-standing hostelry, which has a prize location only 50 yards from the ski-resort tram. Four stories tall, with a pitched roof and flower boxes on the balconies, it offers a little old-world atmosphere, as well as excellent comforts and service. The rooms feature brightly colored alpine fabrics, handcrafted Bavarian furnishings, and tiled bathrooms with big, soft towels. You can choose from two junior suites with wet bars and five rooms with fireplaces, and many rooms have balconies or decks. Economy rooms offer two doubles or one queen-size bed, while deluxe units are larger. The resident **Alpenrose** restaurant specializes in fondue.

3255 W. Village Dr. (P.O. Box 288), Teton Village, WY 83025. ℡ **800/732-3244** or 307/733-3242. Fax 307/739-1516. www.alpenhoflodge.com. 42 units, including 1 suite. $189–$379 double; $539 suite. Lower rates in spring and fall. AE, DC, DISC, MC, V. Closed Nov. **Amenities:** 2 restaurants; lounge; Jacuzzi; outdoor pool; sauna. *In room:* A/C, TV, hair dryer, Wi-Fi (free).

Four Seasons Resort Jackson Hole ★★★   The most deluxe lodging option in Teton Village, the ultrastylish Four Seasons sets a high bar for ski-in, ski-out luxury. From a year-round pool landscaped to resemble a mountain creek to the cowboy-hatted doorman to the rooms—stately, luxurious, and definitively Western—this is one of the top slopeside properties in the country. The range of rooms starts at the high end and goes up from there, but even the standard kings are large and plush, and most units have a balcony or a fireplace. One especially notable perk: the hotel's "Base Camp," a full-service outdoor-activity concierge who can arrange mountain biking, hiking, fishing, and ballooning excursions, and who will outfit you in style. In winter, the service transforms into a first-rate ski concierge, and s'mores and hot chocolate are served poolside. The eating and drinking facilities are also a cut above, and range from casually hip to extravagant.

7680 Granite Loop (P.O. Box 544), Teton Village, WY 83025. ℡ **307/732-5000.** Fax 307/732-5001. www.fourseasons.com/jacksonhole. 156 units, including 18 suites and 32 condos. $400–$750 double; $700–$4,000 condo or suite. Lower rates spring and fall. AE, DC, DISC, MC, V. Valet parking $24 daily. **Amenities:** 2 restaurants; lounge; concierge; health club; 3 Jacuzzis; year-round outdoor pool; room service; sauna; spa. *In room:* A/C, TV/DVD w/pay movies, hair dryer, kitchen, Wi-Fi ($10/day).

Hotel Terra ★★   The newest—and greenest—property in Teton Village, Hotel Terra combines sustainable design and contemporary Western style, with satisfying results. The LEED-certified hotel incorporates granite stonework and understated decor into inviting and sleek spaces. The rooms, which range from studios to three-bedroom suites with full kitchens, demonstrate superior attention to detail; there are organic cotton sheets and towels, Rain Shower heads, fair trade coffee, and touch-screen telephones. The hotel's facilities are uniformly excellent, including the terrific CHILL Spa and an excellent restaurant, Il Villaggio Osteria (see "Where to Dine," below).

3315 W. Village Dr. (P.O. Box 543), Teton Village, WY 83025. ℡ **800/631-6281** or 307/739-4000. www.hotelterrajacksonhole.com. 132 rooms, including 10 suites. $359–$499 double; $499–$1,700 suite; lower rates spring and fall. AE, DISC, MC, V. Underground valet parking $15/day. **Amenities:** 2 restaurants; lounge; concierge; outdoor Jacuzzi; outdoor year-round pool; spa. *In room:* A/C, TV/DVD, hair dryer, kitchen, MP3 docking station, Wi-Fi (free).

Snake River Lodge and Spa ★★   Under the management of RockResorts, this is one of the slickest spots to hang your hat in Teton Village. Lodgepole beams, wooden floors, and stone fireplaces accent the main reception area. The main lodge provides accommodations where classy overshadows rustic, with exposed wooden-beam ceilings, down comforters, and luxurious furnishings. There are three levels of suites, from over-size versions of the standard rooms to three-bedroom versions with top-of-the-line kitchens, good sound systems, and Jacuzzi tubs. The 17,000-square-foot spa is Wyoming's largest, featuring everything from microdermabrasion to hydrotherapy to free weights. Winter visitors can ski directly to a ski valet and drop their skis off for an overnight tune-up.

7710 Granite Loop Rd. (P.O. Box 348), Teton Village, WY 83025. ℭ **866/975-7625** or 307/732-6000. Fax 307/732-6009. www.snakeriverlodge.rockresorts.com. 130 units. $299–$499 double; $699–$2,000 suite. Lower rates in spring and fall. AE, MC, V. **Amenities:** Restaurant; lounge; children's program; concierge; health club; Jacuzzi; indoor/outdoor pool; room service; spa. *In room:* TV, hair dryer, kitchenette, Wi-Fi (free).

Inexpensive

The Hostel ★ (Value)   If you came to Wyoming to ski, not to lie in the lap of luxury, get yourself a room at the Hostel and hit the slopes. Open since 1967 and fortuitously spared the wrecking ball—and known as Hostel X until 2008—it's a great bargain for those who don't need the trimmings. And it's not just dormitory bunks, either—the comfortable but simple private rooms (about the caliber of a roadside motel) hold up to four people; they have either one king-size bed or four twins. There's also a good place to prep your skis, a library, and a common room with chessboards, a Ping-Pong table, a fireplace, Internet access, and a TV. You can walk to the Mangy Moose (see below) and other fun spots, and nobody will be able to tell you apart from the skiers staying at the Four Seasons.

3315 W. Village Dr. (P.O. Box 543), Teton Village, WY 83025. ℭ **307/733-3415.** www.thehostel.us. 52 rooms, 36 dormitory-style bunks. $79–$89 double; $18–$32 bunk. MC, V. *In room:* No phone, Wi-Fi ($5 one-time fee).

Nearby Guest Ranches

Though there have been ranches in the valley for more than a century, many of Jackson Hole's residents have always made part of their living hosting visitors from Europe and the eastern U.S. who came to hunt, see the sights, and enjoy the outdoors. Somewhere around 1900, the term "dude ranching" came into discourse, and Jackson joined Sheridan and Cody as popular Wyoming destinations for folks who wanted a cowboy experience. You can come out to work hard on horseback, move cattle, eat wranglers' grub, and pay dearly for it; but many of the dude ranches offer a more relaxed vacation, with riding, river floating, fine food, and plenty of boots-up porch time.

Flying A Ranch ★★   Nestled at 8,300 feet between the Gros Ventre and Wind River ranges of Wyoming, the Flying A stuns its visitors with panoramic views. Quaking aspen, stream-fed ponds, and curious antelope are hardly disturbed by this exclusive operation, which hosts only 14 guests at a time. Built in the 1930s, the ranch cabins have been carefully restored, with evocative touches that include wood-burning stoves, handmade pine furniture, and regional artwork. Typical of a dude ranch, everything is included: unlimited horseback riding, fly-fishing (with lessons, if you wish), mountain biking, guided hikes, gourmet meals, and unlimited hot-tub time. The cabins are rustic on the outside but have complete bathrooms and fireplaces, porches, and views. The quiet intimacy of this small operation is underlined by an adult-oriented operation—while children are welcome, there are no specific children's activities. It's a 50-mile drive from the ranch to Jackson for shopping and sightseeing excursions.

771 Flying A Ranch Rd., Pinedale, WY 82941 (50 miles southeast of Jackson on U.S. 191). © **888/833-3348** in winter, or 307/367-2385. www.flyinga.com. 7 cabins. $1,500–$1,950 per person per week. Rates include all meals and ranch activities. No credit cards. Closed mid-Sept to mid-June. **Amenities:** Restaurant; outdoor Jacuzzi. In room: Hair dryer, kitchenette, no phone, Wi-Fi (free).

Heart 6 Ranch ★ (Kids)

Slightly more than an hour's drive north of Jackson, just east of the Moran Junction, is the Heart 6, a fistful of fun for families. The Heart 6 isn't the fanciest of the guest ranches in and around Jackson Hole, but it's certainly not short on entertainment. Fishing, horseback riding, hiking, or just enjoying the fantastic views lead the long list of outdoor activities. A naturalist from the Park Service is also on hand to educate guests on the local wildflowers. The ranch offers Wednesday trips to the rodeo in Jackson, Saturday Yellowstone tours, and extensive children's programs for tykes 3 and over; babysitting service is also available with prior notice.

16985 Buffalo Valley Rd. (35 miles north of Jackson and 5 miles east of Grand Teton National Park on U.S. 26/287), Moran, WY 83013. © **888/543-2477** or 307/543-2477. www.heartsix.com. 15 cabins. $1,995 per adult per 6-night stay June–Aug; $1,095–$1,645 for children 3–12; free for children 2 and under; $75–$250 double Sept–May. Summer rates include all meals. AE, DISC, MC, V. **Amenities:** Restaurant; babysitting; children's programs; outdoor Jacuzzi; outdoor heated pool; Wi-Fi (free). In room: No phone.

Lost Creek Ranch ★★★

The Lost Creek is beloved by guests, most of whom return for another stay after their first visit. Reservations are at a premium with a short season and a maximum capacity of about 50 guests. If you manage to wrangle a reservation, this ultraplush ranch offers a wide range of outdoor activities, crowned by gourmet meals.

After all that activity, you can pamper yourself in the spa (not included in the room rates): Get a massage, a sea-salt body scrub, or a facial, or else take a yoga class or work out. If you want to get away from the kids, there's a lounge with billiards and cards and a skeet-shooting range.

Duplex cabins, representing the height of rustic elegance, can be rented or subdivided; each section is outfitted with queen-size and twin beds and a private bathroom. There's also a two-bedroom cabin with a fireplace that sleeps six.

P.O. Box 95, Old Ranch Rd., Moose, WY 83012. © **307/733-3435.** Fax 307/733-1954. www.lostcreek.com. 10 cabins. $6,450–$15,000 per cabin per week. Rates include all meals, float trips, horseback riding, and many other activities. Call for discounted off-season rates. MC, V. Closed mid-Sept to May. Off U.S. 89, 20 miles north of Jackson. **Amenities:** Children's programs; health club; outdoor Jacuzzi; outdoor heated pool; sauna; spa; tennis courts. In room: Fridge, hair dryer, no phone, Wi-Fi (free).

Red Rock Ranch ★ (Kids)

This working cattle ranch makes room for families amid the peaceful wilderness of the Gros Ventre Mountains east of the park. With excellent catch-and-release fly-fishing on a private stretch of Crystal Creek, horseback riding in the mountains, and activities that include cookout rides for the kids and weekly country dances, this guest ranch northeast of Jackson is a great spot to bring the entire bunch. All ten one- and two-bedroom cabins are comfortable log structures built in the 1950s, each furnished with Western trappings and a woodstove.

The kids will have a blast here. The **Children's Riding Program** (for those 6 and older) takes kids all over the ranch by horseback, but the cookout is the real Western treat. After a horseback ride, the kids cook supper over an open fire with the help of a couple of wranglers. Back at the ranch, meanwhile, parents are served a gourmet dinner with wine pairings.

P.O. Box 38, Kelly, WY 83011. © **307/733-6288.** Fax 307/733-6287. www.theredrockranch.com. 10 cabins. $1,850 per adult per week; $375–$1,375 per child 12 and under per week. Rates include all meals and horseback riding. Minimum 6-day stay (Sun–Sat). No credit cards. Closed mid-Sept to May. 30 miles

Camping

There aren't a lot of campsites for trailers close to this resort town anymore, because property values attract more upscale investments. The standby is the **Snake River Park KOA Campground,** on U.S. 89, 10 miles south of town (✆ **800/562-1878** or 307/733-7078; www.srpkoa.com). Campsites are $39 to $62 a night. If you're looking to set up a tent when the parks are full, **Curtis Canyon Campground** (✆ **307/739-5500**) is a great campground behind the elk refuge in Bridger-Teton National Forest. It's open from early June through mid-September, and a site here costs only $12 a night.

See also section 2, "Grand Teton National Park," for details on camping in Grand Teton National Park.

WHERE TO DINE

Jackson has more dining options than any other city in Wyoming. You'll find the predictable steak/seafood/pasta menus—usually injected with a few de rigueur wild-game dishes, too—but you'll also find more-unusual options. For a morning jump-start, head to **Shades Cafe,** 82 S. King St. (✆ **307/733-2015**), which serves good coffee, sandwiches, and other breakfast and lunch entrees. Another a.m. stalwart, the **Betty Rock Cafe,** 325 W. Pearl Ave. (✆ **307/733-0747**), serves creative breakfasts and plenty of espresso. Serving big, tasty slabs of New York–style pizza, **Café Ponza,** 50 W. Broadway (✆ **307/734-2720;** www.cafeponza.com) is the only place to eat in Jackson proper after the bars close (cash only). **D.O.G.,** Glenwood St. and Broadway (✆ **307/733-4422**) serves coffee, burgers, and superlative breakfast burritos for breakfast and lunch and transforms into **Everest Momo Shack** Thursday through Monday evenings to plate up Nepalese cuisine. And 3,000 feet above Teton Village, **Couloir,** accessible via gondola (✆ **307/739-2675**), offers creative Western fare and incredible views.

Expensive

The Blue Lion ★★ NEW AMERICAN   In the fast-moving, high-rent world of Jackson dining, the Blue Lion stays in the forefront by staying the same. Owned and operated by Ned Brown since 1978, the restaurant is located in a two-story blue clapboard building across from a park that looks like a comfy family home. Inside, in intimate rooms accented with soft lighting, or outside on a picture-perfect patio, diners enjoy slow-paced and elegant meals. The menu features rack of lamb and wild-game specialties, such as grilled elk loin in a peppercorn sauce. Fresh fish is flown in daily for dishes such as the nori-crusted ahi.

160 N. Millward St. ✆ **307/733-3912.** www.bluelionrestaurant.com. Reservations recommended. Main courses $15–$33. AE, DC, DISC, MC, V. Summer daily 5:30–10pm; winter daily 6–10pm.

Burke's Chop House ★ STEAKS/GAME/SEAFOOD   Longtime Jackson chef Michael Burke's ambitious eatery in downtown Jackson features a sleek dining room—punctuated by plenty of dark wood, a sweeping bar, and a few antique car parts and scenic photographs. The understated setting is a perfect backdrop for the unpretentious but excellent fare. The menu includes smoked baby back pork ribs with homemade bourbon barbecue sauce and a nice selection of steaks and chops. The buffalo tenderloin and filets are particularly satisfying.

72 S. Glenwood St. ✆ **307/733-8575.** Reservations recommended. Main courses $20–$40. AE, DC, DISC, MC, V. Daily 6pm–close (usually 9–10pm).

The Cadillac Grille ★ NEW AMERICAN   The nostalgic neon and hip American cuisine give this restaurant a trendy air that attracts see-and-be-seen visitors as well as locals. The chefs work hard on presentation, but they also know how to prepare a wide-ranging variety of dishes, from fire-roasted elk tenderloins to pancetta-crusted Alaskan halibut. A *Wine Spectator* favorite, the wine list is equally long and varied. The Grille's upscale dining room is one of three options at this address; you can also eat at the posh bar, or the '50s-themed confines of **Billy's Giant Hamburgers,** where a great burger runs about $6. For the best of both worlds, order a burger at the bar.

55 N. Cache St. ✆ **307/733-3279.** Reservations recommended. Lunch $5–$18; dinner $12–$35. AE, MC, V. Daily 11:30am–3pm and 5:30–10pm.

Il Villaggio Osteria ★★ ITALIAN   The swankest restaurant in Teton Village, Il Villaggio Osteria features tables as well as a 12-seat wine bar and 8-seat salami bar where imported meats and cheeses are sliced to order. The menu includes gourmet wood-fired pizzas with such toppings as figs, arugula, and hummus, as well as creative dishes with Mediterranean influences: wild mushroom risotto, braised pork with polenta, and house-made wild boar ragout. The tantalizing dessert list includes a delectable tiramisu. The lunch menu focuses on salads, pizzas, panini, and lighter versions of the dinner entrees; from 2:30 to 5:30pm, a limited "café menu" is served.

In the Hotel Terra, 3335 W. Village Dr., Teton Village. ✆ **307/739-4100.** Reservations recommended. Lunch $10–$19; dinner $15–$27. AE, DISC, MC, V. Daily 11am–10pm.

Nani's Genuine Pasta House ★★★ (Finds) ITALIAN   In a warmly appointed dining room with red-and-white checkered tablecloths and a slick wine bar, the food is extraordinary at Nani's. You are handed two menus when you are seated: a "Carta Classico" featuring pasta favorites such as *amatriciana* (tomato, onion, *guanciale*, and freshly ground black pepper) and fresh mussels in wine broth, and a list of specialties from a different featured region of Italy. Depending on when you visit, it might be Sicily, where Head Chef Camille Parker's family has its roots, or Emilia-Romagna, where prosciutto, Parmesan, and balsamic vinegar are culinary staples. Parker ventures to Italy annually for research, and you can literally taste her passion. Your only problem with her restaurant might be finding it—it's tucked away behind a little relic of a motel, but it is definitely worth seeking out.

242 N. Glenwood St. ✆ **307/733-3888.** www.nanis.com. Reservations recommended. Main courses $14–$33. MC, V. Daily 5–10pm. Bar open most nights till 11pm.

Snake River Grill ★★★ NEW AMERICAN   This is a popular drop-in spot for locals, including some of the glitterati who spend time in the valley. The front-room dining area overlooks the busy Town Square, and there's also a more private, romantic room in the back. It's an award-winning restaurant for both its wine list and its menu, which features regular fresh-fish dishes (ahi tuna is a favorite), crispy pork shank, and some game-meat entrees such as venison chops and Idaho trout. The pizzas—cooked in a wood-burning oven—are topped with exotic ingredients such as venison pepperoni or steak tartare.

84 E. Broadway, on the Town Square. ✆ **307/733-0557.** www.snakerivergrill.com. Reservations recommended. Main courses $20–$40. AE, MC, V. Summer daily 5:30–10pm; winter daily 6–10pm. Closed Nov and Apr.

Stiegler's ★ (Finds) AUSTRIAN   Austrian cuisine isn't exactly lurking beyond every street corner, waiting to be summoned with a Julie Andrews yodel, but the discerning

Austrian will certainly appreciate Stiegler's. Since 1983, Stiegler's has been confusing, astonishing, and delighting customers with such favorites as elk *Försterin*, bratwurst, and schnitzel, as well as less recognizable (and not as heavy as Austrian food's reputation might suggest) delicacies. Each plate is served with at least three veggies for a terrific presentation and variety of tastes. The desserts are more familiar: apple strudel and crepes. Peter Stiegler, the Austrian chef, invites you to "find a little *Gemütlichkeit*"—the feeling you get when you're surrounded by good friends, good food, and, of course, good beer. The inviting copper bar has its own menu ($10–$19, with great burgers) and there are intimate tables and booths inside and a poolside patio outside.

Teton Village Rd. at the Aspens. © **307/733-1071.** Reservations recommended. Main courses $16–$37. AE, MC, V. Tues–Sun 5:30–9:30pm. Closed Mon.

Moderate

Koshu Wine Bar ★★ (Finds) ASIAN FUSION   Housed in the back half of the Jackson Hole Wine Company, this small, sleek dining room serves ingenious, addictive, Asian-inspired creations. The Far East is just a starting point, with offerings that meld dozens of influences into dishes such as buttermilk-battered soft-shell crab and pork ribs; the menu changes on a near-daily basis. Thanks to its location in a wine store, patrons can choose from 800 varieties of wine at retail price (plus a nominal corking fee).

200 W. Broadway (in the back of the Jackson Hole Wine Company). © **307/733-5283.** Reservations recommended. Main courses $15–$30. AE, MC, V. Daily 6–10:30pm. Bar open till 2am, depending on crowd.

Mangy Moose (Kids) AMERICAN   Coming off the slopes at the end of a hard day of skiing or snowboarding, you can slide right to the porch of this Teton Village institution. Good luck getting a seat inside, but if you like a lot of noise and laughter, a beer or a glass of wine, and tasty food, you'll be patient—it beats getting into your car and driving into town. The decor matches the pandemonium: It looks like an upscale junk shop, with bicycles, old signs, and, naturally, a moose head or two hanging from the walls and rafters. The food is customary Wyoming fare (steak, seafood, and pasta)—I'm a big fan of the buffalo meatloaf and the fresh Idaho trout. There is often live music in the saloon, which serves both lunch and dinner. An affiliated cafe, the RMO Cafe, serves breakfast, lunch, and pizza in a separate room daily 7am to 5pm.

1 W. Village Dr., Teton Village. © **307/733-4913.** www.mangymoose.net. Reservations recommended for larger parties. Main courses $12–$30 in the dining room, $4–$10 in the bar and cafe. AE, MC, V. Dining room daily 5–10pm. Cafe daily 7am–5pm. Bar daily 11:30am–10pm.

North Grille ★ NEW AMERICAN   The resident eatery at the Jackson Hole Golf and Tennis Club, the North Grille is located at the LEED-certified clubhouse, a slick and stylish new building with incredible views of the Tetons. For sunset watching, I recommend the outdoor patio, but the dining room, clad in dark wood and bookcases, is a cozy setting for the winter months. The menu is neatly organized into categories by price point: $14 nets you a garlic-roasted chicken breast or steamed clams; $20 brings halibut medallions on biscuits with lobster gravy or a spicy pork filet; and $28 allows for rack of lamb or chargrilled king salmon. Lunch brings similar, but lighter fare.

5000 Spring Gulch Rd. © **307/733-7788.** www.jhgtc.com. Reservations recommended. Lunch $8–$12; dinner $14–$28. AE, DISC, MC, V. Daily 11:30am–2:30pm and 5:30–9pm.

Q Roadhouse ★ AMERICAN   This bustling joint on the road to Teton Village offers a casual eatery on one side and a bar favored by locals on the other. There are brick walls, complimentary peanuts (toss your shells on the floor), and a laid-back vibe. The Southern-accented menu ranges from barbecued baby back ribs to veggie enchiladas to blackened catfish. Burgers and sandwiches are also available.

2550 Moose Wilson Rd. ⓒ **307/739-0700.** Reservations recommended. Main courses $10–$27. AE, DISC, MC, V. Daily 5–10pm. Bar open later.

Rendezvous Bistro ★★ AMERICAN/SEAFOOD   The Rendezvous opened in 2001 and quickly garnered a local following. It's easy to see why: The place is contemporary yet casual, the food is affordable but very good, and the service is excellent. Climb into one of the intimate booths and order a dozen oysters on the half shell and slurp away, but save some room for a main course, ranging from steak frites to spicy chipotle trout to grilled chili-rubbed pork chops. It might sound formal, but it's really not—the beauty is that the food is the best upscale value in town, while the atmosphere is very laid-back.

380 S. Broadway. ⓒ **307/739-1100.** www.rendezvousbistro.net. Reservations recommended. Main courses $15–$25. AE, DISC, MC, V. Summer daily 5:30–11pm; fall-spring Mon–Thurs 5:30–10pm, Fri–Sat 5:30–11pm.

Sweetwater Restaurant ★★ AMERICAN   Although this little log restaurant serves American fare, it does so in a decidedly offbeat way. The eclectic menu includes, for example, a Greek salad, a Baja chicken salad, and a cowboy-grilled, roast-beef sandwich. During the summer, there's outside dining. The dinner menu is just as quirky and livened by nightly specials; try the unique chili-lime crab cakes before diving into a giant grilled salmon filet glazed with tequila, lemon, and honey or buffalo pot roast with jack-cheese grits. Vegetarians will want to sample the spinach and feta casserole. The lunch slate is full of creative salads and sandwiches.

85 King St. ⓒ **307/733-3553.** www.sweetwaterrest.com. Reservations recommended. Lunch $8–$11; dinner $16–$25. AE, DISC, MC, V. Summer daily 11:30am–3pm and 5:30–10pm; winter daily 11:30am–2:30pm and 5:30–9:30pm.

Trio ★★ NEW AMERICAN   Opened in 2005 by a trio (thus the name) of owner/chefs who formerly worked at the Snake River Grill, this instant local favorite offers a winning combination of inviting atmosphere and remarkable food. Served in a dimly lit, social room with a fossil-rock bar and semi-open kitchen, the seasonal menu might include appetizers such as sautéed shrimp with Szechuan peppercorns and won-ton crisps, and entrees like elk medallions and a killer Idaho rainbow trout on a bed of blackened corn and avocado. Everything is uniformly mouthwatering, and the portions are perfectly sized and impeccably presented and served. The restaurant is perhaps best known for its killer fries—served with scallions, black pepper, and an addictive blue cheese fondue.

45 S. Glenwood Dr. ⓒ **307/734-8038.** www.bistrotrio.com. Reservations recommended. Main courses $12–$32 dinner. AE, MC, V. Daily 5:30pm–close (usually 9–10pm).

Inexpensive

Jedediah's House of Sourdough (Kids) AMERICAN   You feel like you've walked into the kitchen of some sodbuster's log cabin home when you enter Jedediah's—the structure was built in 1910 and now resides on the National Register of Historic Places. Bring a big appetite for breakfast and a little patience—you might have to wait for a table, and then you might have to wait for food while you stare at the interesting old photos on the wall. But it's worth it, especially for the rich flavor of the sourjacks (sourdough pancakes)

served with blueberries. Lunches include soups, salads, and burgers and sandwiches—on
sourdough, of course. The sourdough starter here is also historic: It dates back to the 1870s.

135 E. Broadway. © **307/733-5671.** Breakfast $5–$12; lunch $7–$11. AE, DC, DISC, MC, V. Daily 7am–2pm.

Nora's Fish Creek Inn ★ (Finds) AMERICAN   If you like to eat among locals, and if you like to eat a lot, Nora's is the place to hang out in Wilson, 6 miles northwest of Jackson—just look for the 15-foot trout on the roof. At once rough and cozy, it's an institution, and if you come here often, you'll start to recognize the regulars, who grumble over their coffee and gossip about doings in the valley. Breakfast is especially good, when there are pancakes and *huevos rancheros* that barely fit on the huge plates. Trout and eggs is another specialty. Prices are inexpensive compared to those at any of the other restaurants in town. Dinner is burgers, barbecue, and smoked trout.

5600 W. Wyo. 22, Wilson. © **307/733-8288.** Reservations accepted for dinner. Breakfast and lunch $5–$10; dinner $10–$15. AE, DISC, MC, V. Mon–Fri 6:30am–2pm; Sat–Sun 6:30am–1:30pm; daily 5–9pm. Call for winter hours.

Snake River Brewery ★ (Value) MICROBREWERY   One of the West's best (and busiest) microbreweries, the industrial-meets-contemporary-looking establishment offers a menu of pasta, applewood-fired pizzas and panini, and salads, plus a few entrees like "Slash and Burn Trout," served with fennel relish. The real standouts are the beers, especially Custer's Last Ale and Zonker Stout, regular winners at the Great American Beer Fest. This place is a local favorite and a great lunch spot, with daily $7 specials like turkey-and-brie wraps and chipotle barbecue sandwiches.

265 S. Millward St. © **307/739-2337.** www.snakeriverbrewing.com. Most dishes $8–$14. AE, DISC, MC, V. Daily 11:30am–11pm. Bar open till midnight.

JACKSON AFTER DARK

Talented musicians from well-known orchestras participate in the **Grand Teton Music Festival** ★ (© **307/733-3050** or 733-1128 for the box office; www.gtmf.org) held in summer in the amphitheater next to the tram lift. Tickets, typically $50 or less, are usually available on short notice, especially for the weeknight chamber music performances, which are often terrific.

Wyoming's only year-round professional theatrical group, the **Off Square Theatre Company,** performs classic and contemporary comedies and dramas at the Center for the Arts, 265 S. Cache St. (© **307/733-3021;** www.offsquare.org). Tickets (typically $15–$25) for all shows should be reserved.

Those less impressed with dramaturgy should head down to the **Silver Dollar Bar,** at 50 N. Glenwood St. in the Wort Hotel (© **307/733-2190**), for a drink with one of the real or wannabe cowpokes at the bar. And, yes, those 2,032 silver dollars are authentic. At the very famous **Million Dollar Cowboy Bar** on the Town Square, at 25 N. Cache St. (© **307/733-2207;** www.milliondollarcowboybar.com), you can dance the two-step to live bands or just mill around and check out the unique details: knobby pine, saddle bar stools, and plenty of taxidermy. For live music and DJs, the young, restless, and intoxicated congregate at **43° North,** 645 S. Cache St. (© **307/733-0043**), near the base of Snow King. If you want some high-octane dancing fun led by some talented local hoofers, head west to Wilson and the **Stagecoach Bar** (© **307/733-4407**) on Wyo. 22 on a Sunday night. It's the only night there's live music in this classic Western joint, and the place is jammed wall-to-wall.

2 GRAND TETON NATIONAL PARK ★★★

12 miles N of Jackson

Since people often think of Grand Teton in conjunction with either Yellowstone National Park or Jackson Hole, they imagine it's been around since the days of exploration, trappers, and ranch homesteads. But it's a fairly new park, about 60 years old, just as the dramatic Tetons are a fairly young mountain range—a mere 10 million years old, give or take a millennium.

It's also a small park, at least by Yellowstone standards, comprising the eastern slope of this brief mountain range and a portion of the Snake River plain below. It lacks the unique geothermal features of its northern neighbor, but few mountains stand in such dramatic relief as the towering Cathedral Group, Les Trois Tetons (or "the Three Breasts," as some lonesome French trappers named them): **Mount Owen, Teewinot,** and **Grand Teton.** The Grand, as the locals call it, rises highest, to 13,770 feet, and it has lured climbers since the Depression era, when young Paul Petzoldt and a friend scrambled their way to the top in cowboy boots, to the astonishment of locals. Now commercial guides take hundreds of people to the summit every year, while adventurers find new and more difficult climbs in the range or new ways of challenging themselves, like snowboarding or paragliding off the summits.

But Grand Teton is not merely an amusement park for risk takers. There are beautiful lakes where you can sail or fish, and hikes that take you to waterfalls and panoramic views of the valley and mountains. There are historic sites such as Menors Ferry, built a century ago to get folks across the Snake River, and some beautiful old lodges where you can experience holidays the way our grandparents did. Alpine wildflowers explode during the late spring, and hikers will often see elk, moose, trumpeter swans, bald eagles, and the occasional bear. There are peaceful nights under the stars when you might hear a chorus of coyotes yapping, or, more recently, the husky howls of wolves.

More than Yellowstone, Grand Teton is a modern park, beset by complex issues that sometimes pit wilderness values against modern conveniences like the commercial airport that operates here, or other uses such as the irrigation water behind Jackson Lake Dam or the cattle that graze the park's meadows.

A BRIEF HISTORY

Your first look at the Tetons, rising like spears from the Snake River plain, will take your breath away. Geologists say these mountains are still growing along a crack in the earth's crust that thrusts the range upward from the west as the valley sinks to the east. The lake-bed sediments of the valley floor are actually "younger" than the pre-Cambrian rock of the peaks. Recent earthquakes in the area indicate the fault is still active. Like much of the Rocky Mountains, this range has been sculpted by glaciers, which gouged out the deep U-shaped valleys between the peaks. When the ice sheet that covered Jackson Hole melted for the last time, 15,000 years ago, it left a depression and a big mound of debris—called a terminal moraine—that formed a natural dam at the end of Jackson Lake.

The receding layers of ice created beautiful glacial lakes such as Phelps, Taggart, Bradley, Jenny, String, and Leigh; polished the sides of Cascade Canyon; and honed the peaks to their present jagged state. The glaciers live on, the most prominent being the five that have survived on Mount Moran.

the tribes that hunted here were the Blackfeet, Crow, Gros Ventre, and Shoshone. Summers were spent here hunting and raising crops; winters meant migration to warmer climes. The trappers and explorers who followed the tribes into the valley were equally distressed by the harsh winters and short growing season, which made Jackson Hole marginal ranchland at best. These early homesteaders quickly realized that their best hope was to market the beauty of the area, which they began doing in earnest as early as a century ago.

The danger of haphazard development soon became apparent. There was a dance hall at Jenny Lake, hot-dog stands and piles of debris along the roads, and vacation homes going up on prime wildlife habitat. In the 1920s, Yellowstone park officials and conservationists met to discuss how the Grand Teton area might be protected, and eventually they enlisted philanthropist John D. Rockefeller, Jr., to acquire lands for a future park. In 1929, a park was established to protect the mountains, while Rockefeller continued buying up ranches at the base of the Tetons, using a dummy corporation to hide his involvement. Wyoming's congressional delegation fought hard against park designation in the valley as Jackson Hole public opinion swayed like a pendulum, so President Franklin D. Roosevelt created the Jackson Hole National Monument in the 1940s. In 1950, the park was expanded to its present form.

JUST THE FACTS
Access/Entry Points

Like the range of mountains it protects, Grand Teton National Park is a strip of real estate centered on a north-south axis. Teton Park Road, the primary thoroughfare, skirts along the lakes that pool at the mountains' base. From the **north,** you can enter the park from Yellowstone National Park, which is connected to Grand Teton by a wilderness corridor called the **John D. Rockefeller, Jr. Memorial Parkway** through which U.S. 89/191/287 runs for 8 miles, where you may see wildlife through the trees, some of which are bare and blackened from the 1988 fires. When you come this way, you will already have paid your entrance to both parks, so there is no entrance station, but you can stop at **Flagg Ranch,** approximately 5 miles north of the park boundary, and get park information. December through March, Yellowstone's south entrance is open only to snowmobiles and snowcoaches.

You can also approach the park from the **east,** via U.S. 26/287. This route comes from Dubois, 55 miles east on the other side of the Absaroka and Wind River Mountains, and crosses **Togwotee Pass,** where you'll get your first—and one of the best—views of the Tetons towering above the valley. Travelers who come this way can continue south on U.S. 26/89/191 to Jackson without paying an entrance fee, though they are within the park boundaries.

Finally, you can enter Grand Teton from Jackson in the **south,** driving about 13 miles north on U.S. 26/89/191 to the Moose turnoff and the park's south entrance. Here you'll find the park headquarters, a visitor center, and a small community that includes dining, rental cabins, and shops.

For details on how to fly into the region, see "Getting There" in section 1, "Jackson Hole."

Visitor Information

There are three visitor centers in Grand Teton National Park. Opened in 2007, the dazzling **Craig Thomas Discovery and Visitor Center** (© **307/739-3399**) is a half-mile

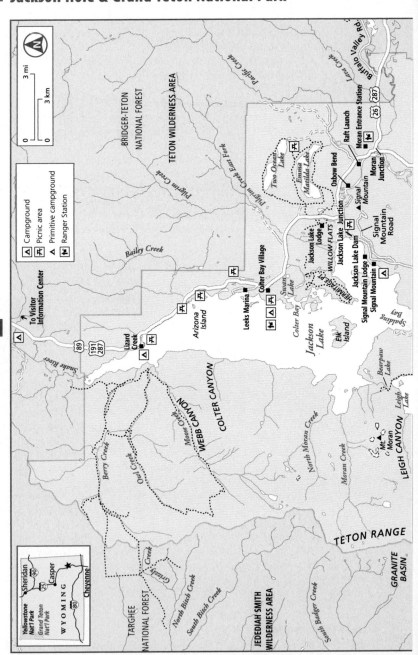

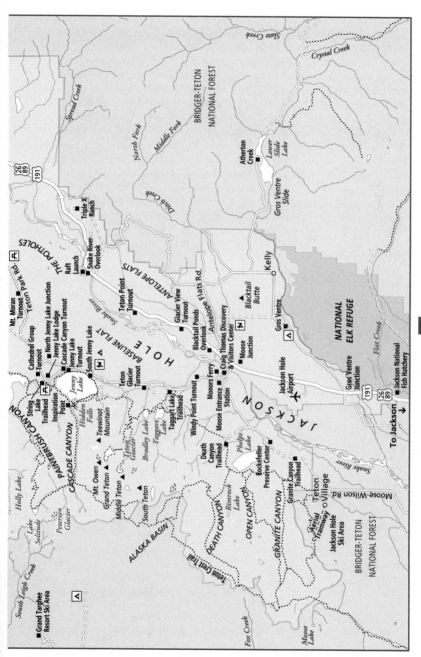

west of Moose Junction at the southern end of the park. Featuring exhibits on alpinism, geology, and wildlife, an art gallery, a "video river" and other multimedia installations, and a theater, it's open daily 8am to 7pm from June to Labor Day, 8am to 5pm after Labor Day through October, and 9am to 5pm the rest of the year. The **Colter Bay Visitor Center** (© **307/739-3594**), the northernmost of the park's visitor centers, is open daily 8am to 7pm from early June to Labor Day, and 8am to 5pm after Labor Day through early October. There is also **Jenny Lake Visitor Center** (© **307/739-3343**), open daily 8am to 7pm from early June to Labor Day, and daily 8am to 5pm after Labor Day through late September. Maps and ranger assistance are available at all three centers, and there are bookstores and exhibits at Moose and Colter Bay. On the Moose-Wilson Road, you'll find the **Laurence S. Rockefeller Preserve Center** (© **307/739-5364**), open Late May through Labor Day from 8am to 6pm and after Labor Day through late September 8am to 6pm. Finally, there is an information station at the **Flagg Ranch** complex (© **307/543-2372**), which is located approximately 5 miles north of the park's northern boundary, open early June through Labor Day daily 9am to 3pm.

To obtain park maps before your arrival, contact **Grand Teton National Park,** P.O. Drawer 170, Moose, WY 83012-0170 (© **307/739-3300,** TDD 739-3400; www.nps.gov/grte).

Fees & Backcountry Permits

There are no park gates on U.S. Hwy. 26/89/191, so you can get a free ride through the park on that route; to get off the highway and explore, you'll pay $25 per automobile for a 7-day pass (admission is good for Yellowstone or Grand Teton). The winter day-use fee is $5. If you expect to visit the parks more than once in a year, buy an annual pass for $50, but I consider the various interagency passes, which are also honored here, to be a better deal (see chapter 3). For information on camping fees at Grand Teton National Park, see "Camping," later in this chapter.

Backcountry permits are required from the Park Service for overnight use of backcountry campsites. The permits are free, but they can be reserved only from January 1 to May 15 (and the reservation itself costs $25); thereafter, all backcountry permits are issued on a first-come, first-served basis up to 24 hours before your first night out. Permits are issued at the Moose and Colter Bay visitor centers and the Jenny Lake ranger station. Reservations may be made by writing the **Permits Office,** Grand Teton National Park, P.O. Drawer 170, Moose, WY 83012, or faxing 307/739-3438. Reservations can also be made online at **www.nps.gov/grte**. Phone reservations are not accepted, but information is available by calling © **307/739-3602.**

Boating permits are required if you bring your own boat (for motorized craft, $40 for an annual permit and $20 for a 7-day permit; for human-powered vessels, $20 for an annual permit and $10 for a 7-day permit). You can get permits at the visitor centers at Moose or Colter Bay; the cost is included in the price of a boat rental. Motorized boats are permitted on Jenny, Jackson, and Phelps lakes; sailboats, windsurfers, and jet skis are allowed on Jackson. Boats paddled by humans are permitted on most park lakes and the Snake River.

State of Wyoming **fishing licenses** are required for fishers 13 years of age and over. An adult nonresident license runs $14 for 1 day, $92 for the season; $3 per day, $15 per season for youngsters 14 to 18; no license is required for kids 13 and under. A $13 Conservation Stamp is also required for all licenses except the 1-day variety. (A Wyoming resident pays $24 for a season permit.) You can buy licenses at sporting-goods stores or

flows into and exits Jackson Lake, different regulations apply to various sections of the river, and several are closed; the prudent angler will become knowledgeable of these laws to avoid a hefty fine.

Regulations

The rules here are similar to those in most national parks. It is illegal to damage or collect natural, archaeological, or historical objects, and even picking wildflowers is prohibited. Pets must be leashed and are not allowed more than 50 feet from roadways; on trails, boats, or boardwalks; or in the backcountry. They are allowed in campgrounds, but must be restrained at all times. Licensed guns are permitted.

Seasons

Spring is an excellent time to visit the park—but remember that spring starts later in Wyoming than in most other parts of the country. In **May** and **June,** mild days and cool nights intersperse with occasional rain and snow. The snow typically doesn't melt in the mountains above the valley until mid-June. Wildflowers are in bloom, and, on a clear day, the snow-covered Tetons stand out boldly against a crisp blue sky. Better yet, trails are virtually devoid of hikers, though at higher elevations snow might still block the paths; check in at one of the ranger stations for trail conditions.

Summer is the most intense season at Grand Teton, with flowers blooming, fish and wildlife feeding, and all sorts of activity crammed into a few months of warm weather, from July to early September.

In **September,** sunny days and cooler nights alternate with rain and occasional snowstorms, and by the middle of the month, fall colors begin to make their way across the landscape.

The first big snow usually arrives by the beginning of **November** (though it's not unheard of in July!). In winter months, temperatures stick in the single digits, with subzero overnight temperatures common.

Avoiding the Crowds

Summer is the busy time here, but crowds thin in the park after Labor Day, and you can enjoy sunny days and brilliant aspen yellows well into October. When there are crowds, you can avoid them by staying away from the centers of activity, which are Colter Bay, Jenny Lake, and Moose. Check out the overlooks, photograph the sites, and take in a few educational exhibits, then abandon the paved areas for unpaved trails.

TIPS FOR TRAVELERS WITH DISABILITIES

Visitor centers at Moose, Colter Bay, Jenny Lake, and Flagg Ranch provide interpretive programs, displays, and visitor information in several formats, including visual, audible, and tactile. Large-print scripts, Braille brochures, and narrative audiotapes are available at Moose and Colter Bay.

Accessible parking spaces are located close to all visitor center entrances; curb cuts are provided, as are accessible restroom facilities.

Campsites at Colter Bay, Jenny Lake, and Gros Ventre campgrounds are on relatively level terrain; Lizard Creek and Signal Mountain are hilly and less accessible. Picnic areas at String Lake and Cottonwood Creek are both accessible, though the toilet at Cottonwood is not.

(Tips) Seeing the Park for Free

Those who are only passing by and never plan to get far from their cars can see the full spectacle of these mountains without paying a park entry fee. If you come from the east, you will pass no tollbooths on your way south on U.S. 26/89/191, but there are frequent pullouts on the west side of the road that give you a panoramic overview of the Snake River and the Tetons. For that matter, you get a more distant, but equally grand, view of the mountains coming over **Togwotee Pass** on U.S. 26/287.

Accessible dining facilities are located at Flagg Ranch, Leeks Marina, Jackson Lake Lodge, and Jenny Lake Lodge.

More information is available by contacting **Grand Teton National Park,** P.O. Drawer 170, Moose, WY 83012 (**$\textcircled{C}$ 307/739-3600;** www.nps.gov/grte).

VIEWING THE PEAKS

Grand Teton National Park is famous for its mountains, and rightly so. The Cathedral Group is composed of **Grand Teton** (elevation 13,770 ft.), **Teewinot** (elevation 12,325 ft.), and **Mount Owen** (elevation 12,928 ft.). Nearby, almost as impressive, are **South Teton** (elevation 12,514 ft.) and **Middle Teton** (elevation 12,804 ft.).

If you come from the north and Yellowstone National Park, you will have paid a park-entry fee and be entitled to explore along **Teton Park Road,** west of the Snake. You'll be looking at mountains as you drive the eastern shore of Jackson Lake, and you'll find plenty of opportunities to pull over and snap your shutter. Four miles south of Colter Bay, you can take an unpaved, 1-mile road heading east from the highway to the **Grand View Overlook.** A large, flat area at the end of the road offers a commanding view of the Grand Tetons, and an excellent picnic spot. This road is great for autos, hikers, and bicycles, but not for large RVs.

You'll also get excellent views of the Cathedral Group on the trails and roads that ring **Jenny Lake** (see "Seeing the Highlights," below).

Signal Mountain, southeast of Jackson Lake, may not rank up there with the other Tetons, but you can drive right up to it to an excellent lookout spot. Navigating the twisting, narrow road pays off at the summit, where you can gaze out over the valley, Cascade Canyon, Jackson Lake, and the Tetons.

Slightly north of Jenny Lake is the underrated, yet astoundingly humbling, **Mount Moran** (elevation 12,605 ft.), the fourth-largest peak in the range; its curiously flattened, sheared-off summit is the result of erosion back in geologically volatile times.

SEEING THE HIGHLIGHTS
Jackson Lake & the North End of the Park

A great many people enter Grand Teton National Park from the north end, emerging from Yellowstone's south entrance with a 7-day park pass that gets them into Grand Teton as well. Yellowstone is connected to Grand Teton by a wilderness corridor called the **John D. Rockefeller, Jr. Memorial Parkway** where the highway runs for 8 miles. Along it, you'll see an interesting area of meadows sometimes dotted with elk; the Snake River as it runs into Jackson Lake; and forests that in some places still show the impact of the 1988 fires.

Some people complain about the sight of blackened tree trunks, but others are heartened to see the mosaic shapes of natural burn and the soft green of new trees sprouting.

Along the parkway, not far from Yellowstone, you'll pass your first lodging option, **Flagg Ranch** (see "Where to Stay in the Park," later in this chapter), with gas, restaurants, and other services. In the winter, this is a busy staging area for the snowcoach and snowmobile crowds, but the new snowmobile quotas led the place to close its rental cabins in the winter in recent years.

JACKSON LAKE The north end of the park is dominated by giant **Jackson Lake,** a huge expanse of water that fills a deep gorge left 10,000 years ago by retreating glaciers. Though it empties east into the Snake River, curving around in the languid **Oxbow Bend**—a favorite wildlife-viewing float for canoeists—the water from Jackson Lake eventually turns south, then west through Snake River Canyon and into Idaho. In 1911, potato farmers downstream were instrumental in getting Congress to fund Jackson Lake Dam, which raised the lake about 40 feet and waterlogged the forest around the shoreline. Stream flow is now regulated at the dam for both farmers and rafters in the canyon, and, for better or worse, we have an irrigation dam in a national park. The dead trees have long since been cleared out, and the dam was rebuilt with an eye for aesthetics in 1989. In general, the lake looks quite natural, except when water level plummets in the fall.

LEEKS MARINA As the road follows the east shore of the lake from the north, the first development travelers encounter is **Leeks Marina,** where boats can launch, gas up, and moor from mid-May to mid-September. A casual restaurant serves light fare and pizza during the summer. But drivers also have the option of stopping at numerous picnic pullouts along the lake.

COLTER BAY Just south of Leeks is **Colter Bay,** a busy outpost of park services where you can get groceries, postcards and stamps, T-shirts, and advice. If this is your first stop in the park, get maps and information at the **Colter Bay Visitor Center.** Here you can view park and wildlife videotapes and attend a park-orientation slide program throughout the day. Ranger-led activities include museum tours, park-orientation talks, natural history hikes, and evening amphitheater programs. Colter Bay has lots of overnight options, from its cabins to its old-fashioned tent camps to its trailer park and campground. There are also a general store and do-it-yourself laundry, two restaurants, a boat launch and boat rentals, and tours. You can take pleasant short hikes in this area, including a walk around the bay or out to **Hermitage Point** (see "Hiking," below).

The **Indian Arts Museum** ★ (© **307/739-3594**) at the Colter Bay Visitor Center is worth a visit, though it is not strictly about the Native-American cultures of this area. The artifacts are mostly from Plains Indian tribes, but there are also some Navajo items from the Southwest. The collection was assembled by David T. Vernon, and includes pipes, shields, dolls, and war clubs sometimes called "skull crackers." Visiting Indian artists work in the museum all summer long and sell their wares on-site. Admission is free.

JACKSON LAKE JUNCTION From Colter Bay, the road veers east and then south again past **Jackson Lake Lodge** (see "Where to Stay in the Park," later in this chapter), a slick, 1950s-style resort with a magnificent view of the Tetons and brushy flats in the foreground where moose often roam. Numerous trails originate here (see "Hiking," below), heading both to **Jackson Lake** and east to **Emma Matilda Lake.** The road then becomes **Jackson Lake Junction,** where you can either continue west along the lakeshore or go east to the park's **Moran Entrance Station.** Here the park's odd entrance configuration comes into play: If you go out through the Moran entrance you are still in the park, and may turn south on U.S. 26/89/191 and drive along the Snake River to Jackson, making most of your journey within the park's borders, though you might not know it.

SIGNAL MOUNTAIN   If you're here to enjoy the park, you'd probably turn west on **Teton Park Road** at Jackson Lake Junction, and arrive after only 5 miles at **Signal Mountain.** Like its counterpart at Colter Bay, this developed recreation area, on Jackson Lake's southeast shore, offers camping sites, accommodations in cabins and multiplex units, two restaurants, and a lounge with one of the few live televisions in the park. This is also the place to fill up on gasoline and provisions from the small convenience store. Boat rentals and scenic cruises of the lake also originate here.

If you turn east instead of west off Teton Park Road at Signal Mountain, you can drive up a narrow, twisting road to the top of the mountain, 700 feet above the valley, where you'll have a fine view of the ring of mountains—Absarokas, Gros Ventres, Tetons, and Yellowstone Plateau—that create Jackson "Hole." Note also the potholes created in the valley's hilly moraines left by retreating glaciers. Below the summit, about 3 miles from the base of the hill, is **Jackson Point Overlook,** a paved path 300 feet long leading to the spot where the Hayden Expedition's photographer, William Henry Jackson, shot his famous wet-plate photographs of Jackson Lake and the Tetons more than a century ago—proof to the world that such spectacular places really existed in the Rockies.

Jenny Lake & the South End of the Park

JENNY LAKE   Continuing south along Teton Park Road, you move into the park's southern half, where the tallest peaks rise abruptly above a string of smaller lakes strung together in the foothills—**Leigh Lake, String Lake,** and **Jenny Lake,** which is the favorite of many park visitors. At North Jenny Lake Junction you can take a turnoff west to **Jenny Lake Lodge** (see "Where to Stay in the Park," later in this chapter)—the road then continues as a one-way scenic loop along the lakeshore before rejoining Teton Park Road about 4 miles later.

Beautiful **Jenny Lake** gets a lot of traffic throughout the summer, both from hikers who circumnavigate the lake on a 6-mile trail and from more sedentary folks who pay for a boat ride across the lake to Hidden Falls and the short, steep climb to **Inspiration Point** (see "Hiking," below). The parking lot at **South Jenny Lake** is often jammed, and there can be a long wait for the boat ride, so you might want to get there early in the day. There are also a tents-only campground, a visitor center, and a general store stocked with a modest supply of prepackaged foods, and even less fresh produce and vegetables. You can take a fairly level and easy hike around the south end of the lake to Hidden Falls or grab a ride with the **Jenny Lake Boating Company** (© **307/734-9227;** www.jennylake boating.com); round-trips cost $10 for adults and $5 for children 5 to 12.

SOUTH OF JENNY LAKE   South of the lake, Teton Park Road crosses open sagebrush plains with never-ending views of the mountains. You'll pass the **Climbers' Ranch** (see "Climbing," later in this chapter)—an inexpensive dorm-lodging alternative for climbers—and some trail heads for enjoyable hikes to **Taggart Lake** and elsewhere. Look closely in the sagebrush for the shy pronghorn, more commonly (and incorrectly) labeled antelope. This handsome animal, with tan cheeks and black accent stripes, can spring up to 60 mph. Badgers also roam the brush here; you might encounter one of the shy but ornery creatures in the morning or at twilight.

The **Teton Glacier Turnout** presents a view of a glacier that grew for several hundred years until, within the past century, it reversed direction, pressured by hotter summer temperatures, and began retreating.

(Tips) Insider Tips

Some of the best spots aren't highlighted on the map. On the west side of the road from Signal Mountain to the Jenny Lake cutoff, a little over a mile north of the Spring Lake–Jenny Lake scenic drive cutoff, is an unmarked, unpaved road that leads to **Spalding Bay.** You'll travel through bumpy moose habitat before curling down a steep hill to a back bay of the lake, where you'll find a small campsite, a boat launch with parking for trucks and boat trailers, and a primitive restroom. Use of the campsite requires a park permit, but we think this site provides an excellent opportunity to find seclusion with excellent views of the lake and mountains. The road is easily negotiable by an automobile or sport-utility vehicle; we would not recommend an RV or towed trailer.

MOOSE The road arrives at the park's south entrance here (well within the park's boundaries) and the **Craig Thomas Discovery and Visitor Center,** as well as park headquarters in the old visitor center across the street. If you are approaching the park from the south rather than the north, this is where you can find maps, advice, and some interpretive displays.

Just behind the visitor center is **Menor's Ferry.** Bill Menor had a country store and operated a ferry across the Snake River at Moose back in the late 1800s. The ferry and store have been reconstructed, and you can buy items similar to the ones Menor used to sell here. Nearby is a historic cabin where a group of locals met in 1923 and planted the seed for the protection of the natural and scenic quality of the area, an idea that eventually led to the creation of the national park.

Also in this area is the **Chapel of the Transfiguration.** In 1925, this chapel was built in Moose so that settlers wouldn't have to make a long buckboard ride into Jackson. It's still in use for Episcopal services spring through fall and is a popular spot for weddings, with a view of the Tetons through a window behind the altar.

DORNAN'S This is a small village area just south of the visitor center on a private holding of land owned by one of the area's earliest homesteading families. There are a few shops and a good grocery store, a post office, rental cabins, a bar with occasional live music, and, surprisingly, a first-rate wine shop.

OTHER PARK HIGHLIGHTS

The highway route through the park on the east side of the Snake has several turnouts for shutterbugs (better have a wide-angle lens!). Among the stops you can make are the **Glacier View Turnout** (where you can view an area that was filled with a 4,000-ft.-thick glacier 150,000 years ago) and the **Blacktail Ponds Overlook** (a beaver-dam subdivision). Gazing out across **Snake River Overlook** at the plateaus that roll from riverbed to valley floor lends vivid insight into the power of the glaciers and ice floes that sculpted this landscape. If you want to go a way off-road and down to the river, you can try the dirt **Schwabacher Road** or the newly repaved **Deadman's Bar Road.**

Only 5 miles north of Jackson on U.S. 26/89/191, you can turn east on the **Gros Ventre River Road** and follow the river east into its steep canyon; a few miles past the little town of Kelly, you'll leave the park and enter the **Bridger-Teton National Forest.** In 1925, a huge slab of mountain broke off the north end of the Gros Ventre Range on the east side of Jackson Hole, a reminder that nature still has an unpredictable and violent side. The slide left a gaping open gash in the side of Sheep Mountain, sloughing off nearly 150 million cubic feet of rock and forming a natural dam across the Gros Ventre River half a mile wide. Two years later, the dam broke, and a cascade of water rushed down the canyon and through the little town of Kelly, taking several lives. The town of **Kelly** is a quaintly unconventional community with a large number of yurts.

Up in the canyon formed by the Gros Ventre River there are a roadside display with photographs of the slide area and a short nature walk from the road down to the residue of the slide and **Lower Slide Lake,** with signs identifying the trees and plants that survived or grew in the slide's aftermath.

RANGER-LED ACTIVITIES

It's got to be the best bargain in the world: National parks offer all sorts of free presentations and guided hikes throughout the summer days, and the rangers are generally personable and knowledgeable. At Grand Teton, these range from a ranger-led 3-mile hike from the Colter Bay Visitor Center to Swan Lake, as well as a relaxed evening chatting with a ranger on the deck of the Jackson Lake Lodge while you watch for moose and birds through a spotting scope. There are numerous events during the summer at Colter Bay, South Jenny Lake, and the Craig Thomas Discovery and Visitor Center at Moose. Check the daily schedules in the park's newspaper, the *Teewinot,* which is available at any visitor center.

From Moose, rangers lead visitors out to the "lek"—the mating ground of the strutting grouse, whose males' displays are dramatic, to say the least, during the springtime mating season. In winter, **guided snowshoe hikes** begin at the visitor center in Moose.

There are guided morning hikes to Phelps Lake at the Laurance S. Rockefeller Preserve and Hidden Falls from Jenny Lake (you take the boat across the lake), among other activities.

Youngsters 8 to 12 can join **Young Naturalist programs** at Colter Bay or Jenny Lake and learn about the natural world for 2 hours while hiking with a ranger. Signups are at the visitor centers (the fee is a mere $1), and the kids will need basic hiking gear.

There are also evening campfire gatherings at most of the campground amphitheaters on a variety of park-related topics.

OTHER ORGANIZED TOURS & ACTIVITIES

The **Grand Teton Lodge Company** (© **800/628-9988** or 307/543-2811; www.gtlc. com) runs half- and full-day bus tours of Grand Teton ($36 adults, $18 children 3–11) and Yellowstone ($66 adults, $41 children 3–11) from late May to early October, weather permitting.

The **Teton Science Schools** ★★, 700 Coyote Canyon Rd., Jackson, WY 83001 (© **307/733-1313;** www.tetonscience.org), have an excellent curriculum for students of all ages, from integrated science programs for junior-high kids to adult seminars covering everything from botany to astronomy. Classes take place at campuses in Jackson and Kelly, and other locations in Jackson Hole. The school's **Wildlife Expeditions** (© **888/945-3567**) offers tours that bring visitors closer to the park's wildlife. These trips range from a half-day to a week, covering everything from bighorn sheep to the wolves of Yellowstone.

HIKING
Day Hikes

Many people cross Jenny Lake, either by boat or on foot around the south end, to hike up into **Cascade Canyon** ★★, a steep but popular journey that takes you first to

Hidden Falls (less than 1 mile of hiking if you take the boat; 5 miles if you walk around) or another .5 mile to **Inspiration Point.** Skip the boat shuttle to avoid the crowds; the easy hike around the south end of the lake is refreshing, uncrowded, and a good prelude to heading up the canyon. Most people go no farther than Inspiration Point, but if you're physically up to it you really should go on. It's a steep climb to the entrance of the canyon, followed by a gentle ascent though a glacially sculpted canyon. At a fork in the trail around 4 miles from Inspiration Point you can follow either the north fork of Cascade Creek to Lake Solitude (3 miles) or the south fork to Hurricane Pass (5 miles). Try the north fork for a more relaxed day hike. Wildflowers carpet the area, ducks nest along Cascade Creek, and moose and bear may be spotted. The round-trip up into the canyon is about 9 miles.

A less taxing alternative to the Cascade Canyon trip is a detour to **Moose Ponds,** which begins on the Inspiration Point trail. The ponds, located 2 miles from the trail head, are alive with birds. The area near the base of Teewinot Mountain is populated with elk, mule deer, black bears, and moose. The trail is flat (at lake level), short, and easy to negotiate in 1 to 1½ hours. The best times to venture forth are in early morning and evening.

Just down the road from South Jenny Lake is the trail head to **Taggart Lake,** a particularly interesting hike that winds through a recovering burn area to a glacial lake. The hike from the parking lot to the lake (a decent fishing spot) is only 1.5 miles along the eastern route, and rarely crowded. After reaching the lake, you can return by the same trail or continue the loop on the **Taggart Lake Trail,** which leads around one end of the pond and loops back to the trail head through a more heavily forested area. This route adds almost a mile to the round-trip, and the elevation gain is 467 feet. At its highest point, the trail overlooks all of Taggart Lake and the stream that flows from it.

Upon reaching Taggart Lake, a second alternative is to continue north .9 miles to **Bradley Lake,** the smaller of the two, and then return to the Taggart Lake trail head. Like others in Grand Teton, this hike is best made during the early morning or early evening hours when it is cooler and there is less traffic.

Yet another hike in this busy area begins at the **Leigh Lake trail head,** next to String Lake at the String Lake Picnic Area. This trail head is between Leigh Lake and Jenny Lake (String Lake is a smaller body of water btw. the two). The Leigh Lake trail is well marked and relatively flat, and goes through a forested area that is always within sight of the lake. Picnickers willing to hike roughly .4 mile from the String Lake Picnic Area to the edge of the lake will find themselves eating in a less-congested area that provides spectacular views of the Tetons. The trail continues along the shore of Leigh Lake, but is rather uninteresting; a better option, if time allows, is to return to the picnic area, cross the String Lake inlet, and explore the western edge of Jenny Lake.

Just footsteps from the entrance to the Signal Mountain Lodge is a sign marking the trail head for the 4-mile **Signal Mountain Summit Trail** ★, which is not generally described in commercial trail books. Though it's well marked, it's not well traveled, since most visitors drive their automobiles in this area. The trail begins steeply, and subsequently opens onto a broad plateau covered with lodgepole pines, grassy areas, and wildflowers. Cross the paved road and you'll arrive at a large, lily-covered pond at the opening of a meadow, home to frogs and waterfowl. The trail then winds along the south and east perimeter of the pond before turning east and heading toward the summit, a climb that will take up to 2 hours. Shortly after passing the pond, you'll come to a fork in the road that converts the trip into a loop trail. Take the northern route and you'll travel the rim of the mountain, meandering to the summit through a forest of sagebrush and pine trees. On the return, the southern trail skirts large alpine ponds where you'll find waterfowl, moose—and, perhaps, black bears.

The day hikes at the north end of the park are less crowded. The easy but lengthy trip to **Two Ocean Lake** begins off the Pacific Creek Road north of Moran Junction and eventually circumnavigates the lake, with much of the mostly level walk through cool conifer forest. Or, located near Colter Bay Visitor Center, the **Hermitage Point trail head** branches out into trips ranging in distance from 1 to 9 miles, mostly in lodgepole pine, with recurring views of the lake and the peaks on the other side. With careful planning, you can start the day with a hike from Colter Bay that leads past **Cygnet Pond** across **Willow Flats** to Jackson Lake Lodge (for lunch). Then, take the same path back to Colter Bay in time for the evening outdoor barbecue—all told, that's 10 miles round-trip.

Among the loops you can take from the Hermitage Point trail head are trails to **Swan Lake** and **Heron Pond** (which share the same point of origin), the kind of country where wildflowers, Canada geese, moose, beaver, and bears all thrive. The two most prominent flowers here are heart-leaf arnicas and Indian paintbrush. Don't be put off by the fact that the first 600 feet of the Swan Lake/Heron Pond trails are steep; after reaching the top of a rise, the terrain levels out and has only moderate elevation gains from that point on. Within minutes, this trail opens to a broad meadow covered with sagebrush and, later in the summer, blooming wildflowers. Here you'll find one of the most spectacular views of Mount Moran, and the peaks reflect on the surfaces of the water.

Finding swans at Swan Lake requires a trip to the south end, where a small island affords isolation and shelter for nests. There are also osprey, kingfishers, and white pelicans in this neck of the woods. The distance from Swan Lake, through a densely forested area, to the Heron Pond intersection is .3 mile; Hermitage Point is 3 miles from this junction, along a gentle path that winds through a wooded area popular with bears. Circumnavigation from the Colter area is doable in 2 hours.

A shorter hike in the Colter area, the **Lakeshore Trail** is a wide, shady thoroughfare that skirts the bay, leading to gravelly beaches that present views across Jackson Lake of the entire Teton Range. The views leap out at you when you arrive at the end of the trail; water gently laps at the shore and, thankfully, you're out of the dense roadside traffic. This 2-mile loop can be completed in about 1 hour of brisk walking.

Longer Hikes

If you decide a day hike isn't enough, you must get an overnight permit and camp in one of the various camping zones reserved through the visitor centers. Much longer trips can be strung together into the mountainous backcountry, crossing the mountains' spine to **Teton Canyon** on the Idaho side, or, at the north end of the park, exploring deep into the **Jedediah Smith Wilderness.**

Within the park, you can go far beyond the day hikes described above—extending a Cascade Canyon hike, for instance, by going north to Lake Solitude, then coming down into **Paintbrush Canyon** (where you can camp, with a permit) and out at String Lake. You can also take the tram to the top of the ski area in Teton Village and follow the **Teton Crest Trail** north into the park, eventually dropping down through **Death Canyon** (another camping area) to **Phelps Lake** (also a camping zone, the closest one to civilization). A trip like this is more than 20 miles and will take several days.

The Park Service has a helpful brochure that delineates the 20 or so backcountry camping zones and lakeshore sites. You'll need to reserve sites, and rangers can brief you

OTHER SPORTS & OUTDOOR ACTIVITIES

For lovers of outdoor recreation, Grand Teton National Park offers one of the most accessible playlands of rock and water in the Lower 48. In addition to hiking, mountaineers and technical climbers can attack the highest hills; paddlers glide across the smooth waters of the lakes or splash along the livelier flow of the Snake River; and boaters will find waters open to motorized vessels and sailboats.

BIKES The roads in Grand Teton were not built with bicyclists in mind, though the flats of the valley seem perfect for pedaling. The problem is safety—there are huge RVs careening about, and some roads have only narrow shoulders. Teton Park Road has been widened somewhat, but traffic is heavy. Debuting in 2009, there is a popular new 8-mile multiuse trail between Jenny Lake and Moose. Road bikers should also try **Antelope Flats Road,** beginning at a trail head 1 mile north of Moose Junction and going east. Sometimes called **Mormon Row,** this paved route crosses the flats below the Gros Ventre Mountains, past old ranch homesteads and the small town of Kelly. It connects to the unpaved **Shadow Mountain Road,** which actually goes outside the park into national forest, climbing through the trees to the summit. Total distance is 7 miles and the elevation gain is 1,370 feet, and you'll be looking at Mount Moran and the Tetons across the valley.

Mountain bikers have a few more options, but keep in mind that bikes are prohibited on the park's backcountry trails and boardwalks. Try **Two-Ocean Lake Road** (reached from the Pacific Creek Rd. just north of Moran Junction) or the **River Road,** a 15-mile dirt path that parallels the Snake River's western bank. Ambitious mountain bikers may want to load their overnight gear and take the **Grassy Lake Road,** once used by Indians, west from Flagg Ranch 50 miles to Ashton, Idaho. Books and maps with biking routes are available at **Adventure Sports** (© 307/733-3307) in Moose, where you can also rent mountain bikes, $32 for a full day and $22 for half a day, as well as road and performance bikes for a few dollars more. Children's bikes are also available.

BOATING Boaters have quite a few opportunities here. Motorboats are permitted on Jenny, Jackson, and Phelps lakes. Rafts, canoes, dories, and kayaks are allowed on the Snake River within the park. No boats are allowed on Pacific Creek or the Gros Ventre River. Bigger boats find room on Jackson Lake, where powerboats pull skiers, sailboats move noiselessly in summer breezes, and fishermen ply the waters in search of wily trout. Those who venture on the big lake need to be aware that the weather can change suddenly, and late-afternoon lightning is not uncommon; sailors should be particularly wary of the swirling winds that accompany thunderstorms. **Scenic cruises** ★ of Jackson Lake are conducted daily by the **Grand Teton Lodge Company** (© 307/543-2811), and breakfast and dinner cruises run twice weekly, both leaving from the **Colter Bay Marina** from May through September. See "Fees & Backcountry Permits," earlier in this chapter, for information on boat permits. Boat and canoe rentals, tackle, and fishing licenses are available at **Colter** and **Signal Mountain.** Shuttles to the west side of Jenny Lake, as well as cruises, are conducted by **Jenny Lake Boating Company** (© 307/733-9227). Additionally, you can rent kayaks and canoes at **Adventure Sports** at Dornan's in the town of Moose (© 307/733-3307), which is in the boundaries of Grand Teton National Park.

CLIMBING Every year there are rescues of climbers who get trapped on Teton rock faces, and many years there are fatalities. Yet the peaks have a strong allure for climbers, even inexperienced ones, perhaps because you can reach the top of even the biggest ones in a single day. But it isn't easy. The terrain is mixed, with snow and ice year-round—knowing how to self-arrest with an ice axe is a must—and the weather can change suddenly. The key is to get good advice, know your limitations, and if you're not already skilled, take some lessons at the local climbing schools (see "Getting Outside," in section 1).

Climbers who go out for a day do not have to register or report to park officials, so they should be sure to tell friends where they're going and when they'll be back. Overnight climbers must pick up a free permit. Climbing rangers who can lead rescue efforts are on duty at the **Jenny Lake Ranger Station** at South Jenny Lake from June until the middle of September. The American Alpine Club provides inexpensive dormitory beds for climbers at the **Grand Teton Climbers' Ranch** (© 307/733-7271; www.american alpineclub.org). A pair of long-standing operations offer classes and guided climbs of Grand Teton: **Jackson Hole Mountain Guides** in Jackson (© **800/239-7642** or 307/733-4979; www.jhmg.com) and **Exum Mountain Guides** ★ in Moose (© **307/733-2297**; www.exumguides.com). Expect to pay around $700 to $1,000 for a guided 2-day climb of Grand Teton or $150 to $200 for a class.

CROSS-COUNTRY SKIING   You can ski flat or steep in Grand Teton; the two things to watch out for are hypothermia and avalanches. As with climbing, know your limitations, and make sure you're properly equipped. Check with local rangers and guides for trails that match your ability. Among your options is the relatively easy **Jenny Lake Trail,** starting at the Taggart Lake Parking Area, about 8 miles of flat and scenic trail that follows Cottonwood Creek. A more difficult ski is the **Taggart Lake–Beaver Creek Loop,** a 3.1-mile route that has some steep and icy pitches coming back. About 4 miles of the **Moose-Wilson Road**—the back way to Teton Village from Moose—is unplowed in the winter and is an easy trip through the woods. You can climb the windy unplowed road to the top of **Signal Mountain**—you might encounter snowmobiles—and have some fun skiing down. There is an easy ski trail from the Colter Bay Ranger Station area to **Heron Pond**—about 2.5 miles, with a great view of the Tetons and Jackson Lake. Get a ski trail map from the visitor centers.

FISHING   The lakes and streams of Grand Teton are popular fishing destinations, loaded with lively cutthroat trout, whitefish, and Mackinaw (lake) trout in Jackson, Jenny, and Phelps lakes. You'll most likely catch fish under 20 inches, fishing deep with trolling gear from a boat during hot summer months. The Snake River runs for about 27 miles in the park, and has cutthroat and whitefish up to about 18 inches. It's a popular drift-boat river for fly-fishing. If you'd like a guide who knows the holes, try **Jack Dennis Sports** (© **307/733-3270**), **Triangle X Float Trips** (© **307/733-5500**), or **Westbank Anglers** (© **307/733-6483**). The going rate is $450 for a full day for two people. **Signal Mountain** (© **307/542-2831**) offers guided half-day trips on motorized craft in **Jackson Lake** for one or two people for $280. As an alternative, stake out a position on the banks below the dam at **Jackson Lake,** where you'll have plenty of company and just may snag something. You'll need a Wyoming state fishing license (see "Fishing" in the Jackson section, earlier in this chapter).

RAFTING & FLOATING TRIPS   The upper end of the Snake River in the park can be deceptive—its smooth surface runs fast during the spring, and there are deadly snags of fallen trees and other debris. Check with rangers before putting your boat in—they'll discourage you if they think your skills may not match the river—and proceed with caution. It's a wonderful river for wildlife, too, with moose, eagles, and other animals coming, like you, to the water's edge. There are many commercial float operators in the park who will allow you to relax more and look around. They run mostly from mid-May to mid-September (depending on weather and river-flow conditions). These companies offer 5- to 10-mile scenic floats, some with early-morning and evening wildlife trips. Try **Solitude River Trips** (© 888/704-2800), **Barker-Ewing Float Trips** (© 800/446-8202), **Grand Teton Lodge Company** (© 307/543-2811), and **Signal Mountain Lodge** (© 307/543-2831).

CAMPING

Since Grand Teton is so much smaller than its counterpart to the north, the mileage between campgrounds is much shorter. As a consequence, selecting a site in one of the five National Park Service campgrounds within the park becomes a matter of preference (rather than geography) and availability. Fees in all campgrounds are $15 per night, and all have modern comfort stations. Campgrounds operate on a first-come, first-served basis, but reservations are available to groups of 10 or more by contacting the **Grand Teton Lodge Co.,** P.O. Box 250, Moran, WY 83013 (© **800/628-9988** or 307/543-2811; www.gtlc.com). You can get recorded information on site availability by calling © **307/739-3603.** Reservations for **trailer sites** at Colter Bay campground may also be made by contacting the **Grand Teton Lodge Co.** Additionally, there is a concessionaire-operated campground located in the Flagg Ranch complex on the John D. Rockefeller, Jr. Memorial Parkway. The area has 97 sites with utility hookups, 74 tent sites, showers, and a launderette. For reservations, contact **Flagg Ranch,** P.O. Box 187, Moran, WY 83013 (© **800/443-2311**).

All the campgrounds but Jenny Lake can accommodate tents, RVs, and trailers, but there are no utility hookups at any of them. **Jenny Lake Campground** ★★, a tents-only area with 51 sites, is situated in a quiet, wooded area near the lake. You have to be here first thing in the morning to get a site.

The largest campground, **Gros Ventre,** is the last to fill, if it fills at all—probably because it's located on the east side of the park, a few miles from Kelly on the Gros Ventre River Road. It has 350 sites, a trailer dump station, a tents-only section, and no showers. If you arrive late in the day and you have no place to stay, go here first.

Signal Mountain Campground ★, with views of the lake and access to the beach, is another popular spot that fills first thing in the morning. It has 81 sites overlooking Jackson Lake and Mount Moran, as well as a pleasant picnic area and boat launch. It has no showers or laundry, but there's a store and service station nearby.

Colter Bay Campground and Trailer Village has 350 sites (some with RV hookups), a general store, showers, and a laundry. The area has access to the lake but is far enough

Amenities for Each Campground in Grand Teton National Park

Campground	# Sites	Fee	Showers	Laundry	Flush Toilets	Disposal
Colter Bay	350	$19	Yes	Yes	Yes	Yes
Colter Bay Trailer Village	112	$48–$54	Yes	Yes	Yes	Yes
Gros Ventre	350	$19	No	No	Yes	Yes
Jenny Lake*	51	$20	No	No	Yes	No
Lizard Creek	60	$18	No	No	Yes	No
Signal Mountain	81	$19	No	No	Yes	Yes

* *tents only*

from the hubbub of the village to offer a modicum of solitude; spaces are usually gone by noon.

Lizard Creek Campground, at the north end of Grand Teton National Park near Jackson Lake, offers an aesthetically pleasing wooded area near the lake with views of the Tetons, bird-watching, and fishing (not to mention the mosquitoes: bring your repellent). It's only 8 miles from facilities at Colter Bay and has 60 sites that usually fill by 2pm.

WHERE TO STAY IN THE PARK

If you plan to visit Grand Teton during a "fringe" season—usually the best, least-crowded time to go, in the fall or spring—you better check first to see if an inn is open. Three different companies run the lodgings in the park, and they all run on different schedules. In early May, you'll find padlocks on the doors everywhere but at Flagg Ranch, which technically isn't in Grand Teton anyway, but in the limbo of the John D. Rockefeller, Jr. Memorial Parkway. Likewise in late fall: By mid-October, there are hardly any beds available in the park, and you'll be bunking in Jackson.

You can get information about or make reservations for Jackson Lake Lodge, Jenny Lake Lodge, and Colter Bay Village through the **Grand Teton Lodge Company,** P.O. Box 250, Moran, WY 83013 (© **800/628-9988** or 307/543-2811; www.gtlc.com). For **Signal Mountain Lodge,** contact P.O. Box 50, Moran, WY 83013 (© **307/543-2831;** www.signalmountainlodge.com). Reservations at **Flagg Ranch** can be made by contacting P.O. Box 187, Moran, WY 83013 (© **800/443-2311;** www.flaggranch.com).

Rooms in Grand Teton National Park properties have telephones but no televisions or air-conditioning. You'll find televisions in the lounge areas at the Jackson Lodge, Signal Mountain Resort, and Flagg Ranch.

Expensive

Jackson Lake Lodge ★★   Much the way that Old Faithful Inn or the Lake Yellowstone Hotel captures historical eras of Yellowstone tourism, Jackson Lake Lodge epitomizes the architectural milieu of the period when Grand Teton became a park. That era was the 1950s, an age of right angles, flat roofs, and big windows. While not as distinctive as Yellowstone's standouts, the lodge is more functional and comfortable than its northern counterparts. The setting is sublime, overlooking Willow Flats with the lake in the distance, and, towering over it without so much as a stick in the way, the Tetons and Mount Moran. You don't even have to go outside to see this impressive view—the lobby has 60-foot-wide windows showcasing the panorama. A few guest rooms are in the three-story main lodge, but most are in cottages scattered about the property, some of which have large balconies and mountain views. Newly remodeled in 2009, rooms are spacious and cheery, and most offer double beds, electric heat, and newly tiled bathrooms. For a premium, the view rooms provide guests with a private picture window facing the Tetons.

P.O. Box 250, Moran, WY 83013. © **800/628-9988** or 307/543-2811. www.gtlc.com. 385 units. $219–$319 double; $550–$750 suite. MC, V. Closed mid-Oct to mid-May. **Amenities:** 2 restaurants; lounge; heated outdoor pool; Wi-Fi (free). *In room:* Hair dryer.

Jenny Lake Lodge ★★★   My favorite property in any national park, this lodge justifiably prides itself on seclusion, award-winning food, and the individual attention that comes with a cabin resort kept intentionally small. Catering to an older, affluent, and exceedingly loyal clientele, the style here is a throwback: a blend of peaceful rusticity and occasional reminders of class and formality. The property is a hybrid of mountain-lake resort and dude ranch, with various extras included in its prices, such as horseback rides, meals, walking sticks, umbrellas, and cool cruiser bicycles. The cabins, each named for a resident flower, are rustic on the outside and luxurious within—decorated with bright braided rugs, dark-wood floors, beamed ceilings, cushy plaid armchairs, and tiled bathrooms. Rooms have one queen-size, one king-size, or two queen-size beds. Some were old dude-ranch cabins from the 1920s, and some were built on the property in the 1990s; the latter have larger bathrooms and more modernity, but less character.

P.O. Box 250, Moran, WY 83013. ☎ **800/628-9988** or 307/543-2811. www.gtlc.com. 37 units. $585 double; $760–$825 suite. Extra person $150 a night. Rates include MAP (modified American plan), horseback riding, and use of bicycles. AE, MC, V. Closed mid-Oct to May. **Amenities:** Restaurant; lounge; bikes; Wi-Fi (free). *In room:* Fridge.

Moderate

Colter Bay Village ★ (**Kids**)   You might call this the people's resort of Grand Teton, with simpler lodgings, lower prices, and a lively, friendlier atmosphere that seems particularly suited to families. Situated on the eastern shore of Jackson Lake, Colter Bay Village is a full-fledged recreation center. Guest accommodations are in rough log cabins perched on a wooded hillside; they are clean and simply furnished with area rugs on tile floors and reproductions of pioneer furnishings—chests, oval mirrors, and extra-long bedsteads with painted headboards. If you want to take a trip back to the early days of American auto travel, when car camping involved unwieldy canvas tents on slabs by the roadside, you can spend an inexpensive night in tent cabins. The shower and bathroom are communal. The village provides an excellent base of operations for visitors because it has the most facilities of any area in the park.

P.O. Box 250, Moran, WY 83013. ☎ **800/628-9988** or 307/543-2811. www.gtlc.com. 166 units. $41–$165 log cabin; $48 tent cabin. MC, V. Closed late Sept to late May. **Amenities:** 2 restaurants; Wi-Fi (free). *In room:* No phone.

Flagg Ranch Resort   At this resort on the Snake River with log-and-luxury ambience, accommodations are duplex and fourplex log cabins that were constructed in the 1990s. The rooms feature patios with rocking chairs, king- and queen-size beds, spacious sitting areas with writing desks and chests of drawers, and bathrooms with tub/shower combinations and separate vanities. There are float trips, horseback rides, and excellent fishing in Polecat Creek or the Snake River. The lodge is a locus of activity, with its double-sided fireplace, fancy dining room, gift shop, espresso bar and pub with large-screen television, convenience store, and gas station. A campground is situated on the grounds amid a stand of pine trees.

P.O. Box 187, Moran, WY 83013. ☎ **800/443-2311** or 307/543-2861. Fax 307/543-2356. www.flaggranch. com. 92 cabins, 171 campsites. $179–$189 cabin double; $50 RV site; $25 tent site. AE, DISC, MC, V. Closed mid-Oct to mid-May. **Amenities:** Restaurant; lounge. *In room:* No phone.

Signal Mountain Lodge ★ (**Finds**)   Signal Mountain has a different feel—and different owners—from the other lodgings in Grand Teton, adding to the sense that any place you choose to stay in this park is going to give you a fairly unique atmosphere. What they all have in common is the Teton view, and this lodge, located right on the banks of Jackson Lake, might have the best. To top it off, it's got lakefront retreats, which you can really inhabit, with stoves and refrigerators and foldout sofa beds for the kids. Other accommodations, mostly rustic log cabins, come in a variety of flavors, from motel-style rooms in four-unit buildings set amid the trees to beachfront family bungalows. These carpeted units feature handmade pine furniture, electric heat, covered porches, and tiled bathrooms; some have fireplaces, and all are nonsmoking. Recreational options include rafting and fishing, and sailboat tours on the lake. A convenience store and gas station are on the property.

P.O. Box 50, Moran, WY 83013. © **307/543-2831.** www.signalmountainlodge.com. 80 units. $131–$300 double. AE, DISC, MC, V. Closed late Oct to early May. Pets accepted ($15/night). **Amenities:** 2 restaurants; lounge; Wi-Fi (free). *In room:* Kitchenette.

Spur Ranch Cabins ★ An outfitter's camp since the 1940s, Spur Ranch is now a collection of year-round cabins built in the 1990s. Located at a family-owned operation in Moose that also includes a market, a wine shop, an outdoors store, guide services, and dining, the dozen cabins here are a good option for families and larger groups. All the units have tub/shower combinations, fitting lodgepole-pine furnishings, and fully equipped kitchens. Two of the cabins are right on the Snake River, but they're often booked a year in advance during peak season.

P.O. Box 39, Moose, WY 83012. © **307/733-2522.** www.dornans.com. 12 units. $175–$250 for up to 6 people. AE, DISC, MC, V. **Amenities:** 2 restaurants; lounge. *In room:* Kitchen.

Inexpensive

Moulton Ranch Cabins (Value) A century-old homestead now offers an off-the-beaten-track alternative to the bustling developments on Jackson and Jenny lakes. The small but comfortable cabins here are a few miles west of Moose Junction, scattered around a verdant, private acre entirely surrounded by the park. The cabins, built in stages from the 1930s to 2004, range from dinky to family-size, and packages are available to those who require numerous cabins. The Granary, Grand, and Bunkhouse are larger, with kitchenettes and space for six to sleep.

Mormon Row, Kelly, WY 83011. © **307/733-3749.** www.moultonranchcabins.com. 5 units. $80–$220 for up to 6 people. MC, V. Closed Oct–Apr. No pets. No smoking. *In room:* Kitchenette, no phone.

WHERE TO DINE

The Bear's Den (Kids) AMERICAN Served at the main lodge at Flagg Ranch, the food at this oasis is better than what's typically found in what most refer to as a "family restaurant," and servings are generous. The dinner menu includes fish, chicken, and beef dishes, as well as home-style entrees such as ranch beef stew and chicken potpie; lunch and dinner are unadventurous but hearty. The ambience is also pleasant during both winter and summer months; wooden chairs and tables with colorful upholstery liven up this newly constructed log building.

At Flagg Ranch, John D. Rockefeller, Jr. Pkwy. © **800/443-2311.** Reservations accepted. Breakfast $5–$12; lunch $8–$13; dinner $12–$26. AE, DISC, MC, V. Summer daily 7–10:30am, 11:30am–1pm, and 5–9:30pm.

Jenny Lake Lodge Dining Room ★★★ CONTINENTAL The finest meals in either park (or, for that matter, in *any* park) are served here, where a talented chef creates culinary delights for guests and, occasionally, a president of the United States. Breakfast, lunch, and dinner are served here, and all are spectacular. (Nonguests should have lunch here if they can.) The five-course dinner is the bell-ringer, though. Guests choose from appetizers that might include elk carpaccio; salads with organic greens, pecans, and dried cherries; and entrees such as pan-roasted squab, herb-rubbed rabbit leg, or a venison strip loin. Desserts are equally creative and tantalizing. Price is no object, at least for guests, because meals are included in the room charge; nonguests should expect a hefty bill. Casual dress is discouraged, with jackets requested for dinner.

At Jenny Lake Lodge. ℂ **307/733-4647.** Reservations required. Prix-fixe breakfast $22; lunch main courses $9–$14; prix-fixe dinner $72, not including alcoholic beverages. AE, MC, V. Summer daily 7:30–9am, noon–1:30pm, and 6–8:45pm.

John Colter Cafe Court DELI/FAST FOOD   Here you'll find the two sit-down restaurants in the village (although there's also a snack shop in the grocery store). Three meals are served daily during the summer months. The **cafe** serves sandwiches, burgers, and pretty good Mexican fare. Breakfasts at the new **Ranch House** are hearty; lunch is a soup-and-salad bar and hot sandwiches; dinner is more of an event but nonetheless family-friendly. Among the dinner entrees are trout, lasagna, pork chops, beef stew, and New York strip steaks. The bar is worth a look, emblazoned with the brands of a number of Jackson Hole–area ranches.

Across from the visitor center and marina in Colter Bay Village. ℂ **307/543-2811.** Reservations not accepted. Breakfast and lunch $6–$13; dinner $6–$22. MC, V. Daily 6:30am–10pm. Closed Oct–Apr.

The Mural Room ★★ BEEF/WILD GAME   Jackson Lake's main dining room is quiet and fairly formal, catering to a more sedate crowd as well as corporate groups; it's also more expensive than other park restaurants. The floor-to-ceiling windows provide stellar views across a meadow that is a moose habitat and to the lake and the Cathedral Group. (The staff applauds sunset every night.) Walls inside are adorned with hand-painted Western murals created by Carl Roters. The food is the perfect complement to the view, and markedly superior to most of what you'll find in Yellowstone. Three meals are served daily in summer. Breakfast items include a "healthy start" breakfast, organic granola, and fruit smoothie. Dinner might be a grand five-course event that includes pan-seared ostrich, butternut bisque and house salad, followed by an entree of blue corn and plantain crusted trout, slow-roasted prime rib, vegetable tart, or peppered elk loin. Dessert includes delicious homemade ice cream and a rich fudge cake. Aside from the dining room at Jenny Lake Lodge and Lake Yellowstone Hotel, this is the most romantic and upscale eatery in either park.

At Jackson Lake Lodge. ℂ **800/628-9988** or 307/543-2811. Reservations not accepted. Breakfast $6–$15; lunch $9–$17; dinner $18–$38. MC, V. Summer daily 7–9:30am, 11:30am–1:30pm, and 5:30–9pm.

Pioneer Grill ⓚⓘⓓⓢ AMERICAN   Bedecked with regional homesteading antiques and photos, this 1950s-style luncheonette, with its curling counter and old-fashioned soda fountain, offers hearty meals and a casual, friendly atmosphere. Breakfasts are basic but ideal for hiking appetites—bagels, eggs, flapjacks, and the like. For lunch, try one of the Grill's ever-popular buffalo burgers, or a plump turkey sandwich. Dinner is similarly laid-back and traditional—you can't miss with the pan-fried rainbow trout. When a tour bus stops at the lodge, the restaurant is often overrun with business, so you might want to head next door to the Mural Room if you're looking for peace or romance. If you're looking for convenience, good service, and a relatively quick meal, though, this is the spot.

At Jackson Lake Lodge. ℂ **800/628-9988** or 307/543-2811. Reservations not accepted. Breakfast $4–$9; lunch $7–$10; dinner $9–$18. MC, V. Summer daily 6am–10pm.

Signal Mountain Lodge ⓥⓐⓛⓤⓔ SANDWICHES/MEXICAN/CONTINENTAL   There are actually two restaurants here, serving delicious food in the friendliest style in the park. The fine dining room and lounge, called **Peaks** and the **Trapper Grill** respectively (there is also a joint called **Deadman's Bar**), supplement Continental fare with Mexican entrees, pizzas, and plump sandwiches. You eat up the scenery, too, with a view of Jackson Lake and Mount Moran.

Bargain hunters flock to the bar for the decadent nachos supreme: a foot-tall mountain of chips, cheese, chicken, beef, beans, and peppers that runs a mere $15. You'll easily fill four people for that price, leaving you plenty of change for the bar's signature blackberry margaritas. Because the bar has one of three televisions in the park and is equipped with cable for sports nuts, the crowd tends to be young and noisy. Full meals are served in the proper dining room, with an emphasis on sustainable cuisine. Entrees include free-range chicken with organic black beans and rice, vegetarian lasagna, and filet mignon served on a potato cake with sautéed spinach, the most expensive entree.

At Signal Mountain Resort. (C) **307/543-2831.** Reservations required for breakfast and dinner. Breakfast $7–$10; lunch $8–$16; dinner $19–$35. AE, DISC, MC, V. Summer daily 7–10am and 11:30am–10pm.

13

3 A SIDE TRIP TO DUBOIS & THE WIND RIVER RANGE

86 miles NE of Jackson

For years, Dubois was a kind of a doppelgänger to Jackson, a blue-collar logging town with some quietly wealthy folks living on nice ranches up the nearby draws. Now the sawmill is closed, and wealthy folks who want to stay ahead of the latest real estate fashion are wandering over Togwotee Pass and buying up the beautiful Upper Wind River Valley. That means Dubois is poised for some serious development, but it hasn't quite happened yet, which dismays some residents and pleases others. Lying as it does along one of the Yellowstone access roads, Dubois is just far enough from the park entrances to be spared the West Yellowstone gateway syndrome, and if locals keep their heads, they'll protect the great trout streams, uncluttered wilderness, and small-town ambience from uncontrolled growth. So far, so good. It's a fun town, often with several bands playing in the bars on weekends. **To get there** from Jackson, go north on U.S. 26/89/191 to Moran Junction, then east over Togwotee Pass on U.S. 26/287.

In the lake-dotted Whiskey Basin, just south of town, one of the largest extant herds of bighorn sheep migrates down in the winter to get away from the deep snows, and so there is a **National Bighorn Sheep Interpretive Center,** 907 W. Ramshorn ((C) **888/209-2795** or 307/455-3429; www.bighorn.org), located just off the highway in the center of town. Just across the park at the **Dubois Museum,** 909 W. Ramshorn ((C) **307/455-2284;** www.duboismuseum.org), is a look at the past of the town, the Sheepeater Indians, and other interesting artifacts with local flavor. The museum is open from 9am to 6pm daily mid-May through mid-September and 10am to 4pm Tuesday to Saturday the rest of the year. Contact the **Dubois Chamber of Commerce,** P.O. Box 632, Dubois, WY 85213 ((C) **888/518-0502;** www.duboiswyoming.org), for additional information on the community.

WHERE TO STAY

Brooks Lake Lodge ★ For many years, this remote and historic mountain lodge, once an overnight stop on the road to Yellowstone, languished; in 1989, it was painstakingly restored and reopened to well-deserved hype. It sits above the shores of Brooks Lake, a prize fishing lake surrounded by soaring pinnacles. This is the entry point to some of the most remote and challenging wilderness in the Rockies, packed with elk, trout, and grizzly bears. Yet the handsome lodge, with its hand-stripped timbers and deep porch overlooking the lake, is as cozy and comforting as anyone could ask. You can lounge or take advantage of the riding stock, guided up steep trails to incredible views. Accommodations are seven guest rooms in the lodge (one room is a suite with a Jacuzzi and a fireplace) and eight cabins along the tree line. The cabins, each decorated with a distinct frontier motif, are comfortable, spacious affairs that have Western pine furniture, woodstoves, and large decks or porches with views of the lake. Snowmobile rentals are available in winter.

458 Brooks Lake Rd., Dubois, WY 82513. ✆ **307/455-2121.** www.brookslake.com. 12 units, 3 family cabins. Summer $300–$375 per person per night; winter $225–$275 per person per night. Rates include all meals and activities. AE, MC, V. Closed Apr–May and Oct–Nov. **Amenities:** Restaurant; exercise room; outdoor Jacuzzi; sauna; spa. *In room:* Hair dryer, no phone, Wi-Fi (free).

WHERE TO DINE

For dinner, the **Rustic Pine Steakhouse,** 123 E. Ramshorn (✆ **307/455-2772**), does a good job with beef, seafood, and pasta. The **Village Cafe,** 515 W. Ramshorn (✆ **307/455-2122**), serves three hearty American meals a day, and also houses a Daylight Donuts franchise.

14

Cody & North-Central Wyoming

Deep, broad valleys, cupped by daunting mountain ranges, provide some of the most livable pockets of the Rocky Mountain West. Not only do the mountains provide some protection from howling storms, but their snowmelt keeps streams running through the summer and their beauty supplies a spectacular backdrop for the communities nestled below.

Such a valley runs down the center of Wyoming, cradled by the Bighorn Mountains in the east and the Absarokas and Yellowstone Plateau in the West. Though the area around the town of Cody gets only about 10 inches of moisture annually, founder William "Buffalo Bill" Cody recognized a century ago that with a few dams and ditches in the right places, the mountains' snowpack could supply water year-round. His legacy continues to shape the basin's economy today: A great summer scene of cowboy fun attracts hordes of visitors, and green fields of sugar beets and grains stretch for miles from the mouth of the Wapiti Valley.

While Cody was staking claims to water rights along the Shoshone River in the early 20th century, the U.S. Bureau of Reclamation was storing that water behind the Buffalo Bill Dam, the world's tallest when it was completed in 1910. The reservoir today irrigates about 100,000 acres in central Wyoming, and the swift winds that skim the lake's surface attract the bravest of windsurfers.

In the post–"Buffalo Bill" era, the charms of north-central Wyoming have taken many a visitor by surprise on their journey to and from Wyoming's famous national parks. And quite a few travelers find reason to linger longer in the nearby valleys, exploring a wealth of American-Indian and Wild West history, geology, mountain scenery, outdoor recreation, and small-town charm. Highlights include fun-loving Cody, the Bighorn Canyon National Recreation Area, the gushing hot springs of Thermopolis, and the forests and rivers of Shoshone National Forest and other public lands.

The combination of stunning scenery and historic cattle operations makes the Cody area a natural center for dude ranches, where visitors can saddle up and swing a lariat. Or you can mount a more stationary seat in the stands at one of the summer rodeos. Cody's rodeo grounds light up every night in the summer, and nearly every town in the basin has its special rodeo weekend. On the Wind River Indian Reservation, the evening outdoor entertainment is often a powwow, featuring drum groups, colorful garb, and traditional dancing, with visitors welcome and food stands offering Indian tacos and other treats.

1 SCENIC DRIVES

The two-lane roads of north-central Wyoming follow the contours of a craggy landscape, tracking the twists and turns of the river and switchbacking over the mountain passes; the roads are narrow but generally not too crowded, except for the constant stream of

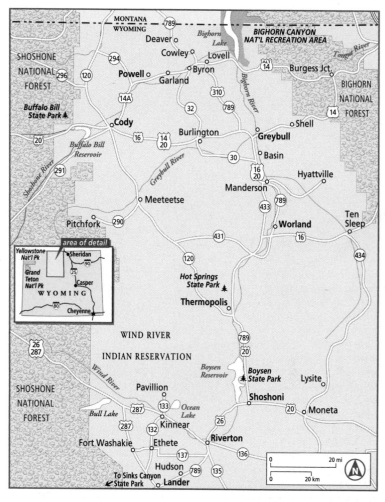

traffic to Yellowstone's east entrance. **U.S. 14/16/20,** the east entrance road (also called the Yellowstone Hwy.), is the major east-west route through this region. The breathtaking views as it snakes through the Wapiti Valley and up over Sylvan Pass into Yellowstone make the traffic and seemingly interminable road repairs worthwhile. West of Cody, almost any road you take will reward you with a canyon or a climb, but many of them narrow into rough dirt byways as they delve deeper into the forest. **Wyo. 291** does that, as it follows the **South Fork of the Shoshone River** upstream toward the white-capped peaks of Yellowstone's Thorofare country. Along the way are prominent volcanic rock formations like Castle Rock, a succession of picturesque ranches, and sometimes a lucky glimpse of bighorn sheep, before the road finally dead-ends on the fringes of the Absaroka Range.

Cody is also an alternative starting point for the **Chief Joseph Scenic Highway,** which links up to the Beartooth Scenic Byway into Montana (see section 1, "A Scenic Drive," in chapter 10).

Note: Most of the sights mentioned in the following driving tours are discussed in greater detail later in this chapter.

DRIVING TOUR 1: BIGHORN MOUNTAIN LOOP

This moderately easy day trip will open your eyes to an extraordinary mountain range, on a route that encompasses the towns of **Powell** and **Lovell,** as well as the scenic **Shell Canyon** area. Begin in Cody by taking U.S. 14A northeast to Lovell and the **Bighorn Canyon National Recreation Area** (see section 3, in chapter 11, for more information on this recreation area). A side trip north along Wyo. 37 provides views of the wild horses of the Pryor Mountain National Wild Horse Range and Bighorn Lake from the Devil Canyon Overlook.

After crossing the Bighorn River, U.S. 14A rises through the foothills and up the steep flanks of the Bighorns, not far from the footpaths of prehistoric travelers who built the **Medicine Wheel,** a 74-foot stone circle with 28 spokes. Like other mysterious wheel designs in the Rockies, it may have served ancient peoples as an astronomical key or a long-distance travel marker. To get here, turn off U.S. 14A at the Medicine Wheel sign and hike 1.5 miles from the parking area to the site. American-Indian spiritual leaders still conduct ceremonies here. Visitors are asked not to remove offerings or disturb American Indians using the site for prayer or fasting. For more information, contact the **Medicine Wheel Ranger District of the Bighorn National Forest** in Lovell (© 307/ 548-6541).

Once you have crested the divide of the Bighorn Mountains, take U.S. 14 southwest at Burgess Junction toward Shell Canyon and the towns of Shell and Greybull. The road drops sharply through steeply cut canyons, and you can stop at the **Shell Falls Interpretive Center** and follow a paved path to a close-up view of the creek, tumbling and twisting amid tall granite slabs. As the road flattens out near the town of Shell, you're surrounded by the deep red sandstones of the **Chugwater Formation,** set off by the rich greens of cultivated fields. This area enfolds some well-packed dinosaur fossil beds. U.S. 14/16/20 takes you back to Cody, toward the embrace of the Absaroka Mountains and Yellowstone. This driving tour can be enjoyed year-round, though winter drivers should proceed cautiously on the steep grades around Burgess Junction.

DRIVING TOUR 2: BIGHORN BASIN LOOP

This all-day trip keeps to the Bighorn River Basin, navigating rolling sagebrush hills, cultivated farmlands, hot-spring terraces, and one-pump (formerly one-horse) Western towns.

Depart from Cody and travel south along Wyo. 120 to the tiny burg of **Meeteetse** on the banks of the Greybull River. From here, continue on Wyo. 120 to **Thermopolis,** self-proclaimed home of the world's largest free-flowing hot springs (New Zealand does not agree). After a relaxing soak and a brief drive east for a glimpse of the bison herd that roams **Hot Springs State Park,** travel northeast on U.S. 16/20 to **Worland,** an important agricultural center. Then, drive east along U.S. 16 to **Ten Sleep,** which lies at the base of another steep-sided canyon cutting down through the Bighorn Mountains. You may want to hike and cast a line in Ten Sleep Creek.

Here, take the Nowood Road north, which joins Wyo. 31, to Manderson and follows the base of the Bighorns. From Manderson, follow U.S. 16/20 north to Basin, take Wyo.

30 west to the junction of Wyo. 120, and continue north to Cody. Along the way, you'll enjoy views of the Bighorn River and the Greybull River Valley. Winter isn't too harsh on this loop, which could include a detour south of Meeteetse on Wyo. 290 to the **Wood River Ski Touring Park.** If it's summer, rangers at Hot Springs State Park have a map and key to Legend Rock petroglyph sites north of Thermopolis, where you can hike around the cliffs.

---

2 CODY ★

52 miles E of the east entrance of Yellowstone; 177 miles NE of Jackson; 214 miles NW of Casper

The legendary scout and entertainer William F. "Buffalo Bill" Cody really knew how to put on a show, and he also knew where to put a town. Cody, founded by its namesake in 1887, is beautifully situated near the juncture of rivers that pour from the rugged Absaroka Range. Every summer, the town of Cody stages a cow-town circus that would do the founder proud, entertaining throngs of visitors on their way to and from Yellowstone 52 miles west. And the drive to the park is sublime: Theodore Roosevelt called the Wapiti Valley "the most scenic 50 miles in the world."

Stop by Cody before the mid-May opening of Yellowstone's east entrance, and it's rather lifeless. For 3 months every summer, though, the town parades its Western charm for masses of travelers. When the sun goes down, the lights come on at the rodeo grounds, and the broncos do a little busting of their own. A world-class museum, a reassembled Old West town, and retail shops all attract the crowds. Though lacking the resort density and sophistication of Jackson, Cody's Western charm feels more authentic.

ESSENTIALS

GETTING THERE Cody's **Yellowstone Regional Airport** (© **307/587-5096;** www. flyyra.com) serves the Bighorn Basin as well as the east and northeast entrances of Yellowstone National Park with year-round commercial flights via **Delta** (© **800/221-1212**) and **United** (© **800/864-8331**) through Salt Lake City and Denver.

If you're driving from **Cheyenne,** travel north on I-25 to Casper, then west on U.S. 20/26 to Shoshoni, where U.S. 20 turns north to Thermopolis. From there, it's another 84 miles to Cody on Wyo. 120. From **Jackson,** take U.S. 191 to the West Thumb Junction in Yellowstone, drive east along the northern boundary of Yellowstone Lake, and continue on U.S. 14/16/20 to Cody. Coming from the southwest, drive north from Rock Springs on U.S. 191 to Farson, Wyo. 28 to Lander, Wyo. 789 to Thermopolis, and Wyo. 120 to Cody.

VISITOR INFORMATION For printed information on this area of Wyoming, contact the **Buffalo Bill's Cody/Yellowstone Country,** 836 Sheridan Ave. (P.O. Box 2454), Cody, WY 82414 (© **307/587-2297;** www.yellowstonecountry.org), or the **Wyoming Business Council Travel and Tourism Division,** 1520 Etchepare Circle, Cheyenne, WY 82007 (© **800/225-5996** or 307/777-7777; www.wyomingtourism.org).

GETTING AROUND If you haven't come by car, you'll probably need to rent one; there's little public transportation. **Budget** (© **800/527-0700**), **Hertz** (© **800/654-3131**), and **Thrifty** (© **800/847-4389**) maintain desks at Yellowstone Regional Airport.

SPECIAL EVENTS The Buffalo Bill Historical Center is a tremendous resource for unique events in Cody. The April festival of **Cowboy Songs and Range Ballads** features

The Mystery of Buffalo Bill's Grave

Buffalo Bill's legend looms large over Cody, but some locals believe that it's more than his spirit looking down from the surrounding peaks. Rumor has it that Buffalo Bill is buried not atop Lookout Mountain in Golden, Colorado, but on Cedar Mountain, just outside of Cody. After the legendary showman's 1917 demise, the mayor of Denver and the *Denver Post* arranged to buy his body as the centerpiece to a tourist attraction. As the story goes, a trio of Cody residents took it upon themselves to see to it that Cody be laid to rest outside the town that bears his name. They swapped Buffalo Bill's body (which sat on ice for 6 months in Denver before the funeral) with that of an anonymous old cowboy who died in Cody without any kin. While there's more than one story floating around regarding the true whereabouts of Cody's grave, longtime Cody residents (and many of Buffalo Bill's descendants) swear that a nameless cowboy is buried on Lookout Mountain in Colorado and that William F. Cody's final resting place is where he wanted it—in Cody, Wyoming.

storytelling, poetry, and some fine yodeling and balladry. In mid-June, the **Plains Indian Powwow** brings alive the Robbie Powwow Garden on the south end of the Buffalo Bill Historical Center parking lot with whirling color. Traditional dance competitions are coupled with craft shows and American-Indian food, and non-Indians are welcomed into round dances. Call the Buffalo Bill Historical Center (© 307/587-4771) for information. Every July 1 to July 4, during the **Cody Stampede,** the streets are filled with parades, fireworks, street dances, barbecues, and entertainment, capped by a top-notch rodeo. Call © 800/207-0744 or 307/587-5155 for tickets (see **www.codystampede rodeo.org** for more information). In mid-August, the Buffalo Bill Historical Center (© 307/587-4771) stages the **Buffalo Bill Celebrity Shootout,** where celebrities and local shooters test their skills in trap, skeet, sporting clays, and five-stand shooting. In late September, Cody hosts the **Western Design Conference (© 888/685-0574)** at the Cody Auditorium and the Buffalo Bill Historical Center, a gathering of artisans to show off their work in Western-style furniture, decor, and clothing.

GETTING OUTSIDE

If you'd rather not be a driver in the park's heavy summer traffic, guided Yellowstone National Park tours are available locally through **Grub Steak Expeditions,** P.O. Box 1013, Cody, WY 82414 (© 800/527-6316 or 307/527-6316; www.grubsteaktours. com). Bob Richard, Grub Steak's proprietor (and one of the most knowledgeable guides you'll find), is a third-generation Cody resident and former Yellowstone ranger. Full-day tours run about $500 for two people and $125 for additional adults, $75 for additional kids 15 and under.

Cody has fewer organized recreation options than Jackson does, but there is no shortage of places to go outdoors. **Buffalo Bill State Park,** located along the canyon and reservoir 6 miles west of Cody, is a hot spot for outdoors buffs, with opportunities for hiking, fishing, and a variety of watersports, particularly windsurfing. The park also has facilities for camping and picnicking.

Biking

If you want to explore the area on two wheels, bike rentals and advice are available from **Absaroka Bikes,** 2201 17th St. (© **307/527-5566**) for $40 a day. Although there isn't a marked network of bike paths in the Cody area, you can ride on the Forest Service trails west of town off U.S. Hwy. 14/16/20 in the Shoshone National Forest. For specific trail information, call the **Forest Service** (© **307/527-6241**; www.fs.fed.us/r2/shoshone).

Cross-Country Skiing

If you favor a groomed course for cross-country skiing, try the **North Fork Nordic Trails** in Shoshone National Forest, near the east entrance to the park off U.S. Hwy. 14/16/20. You can circuit 16 miles of trails adjacent to the Pahaska Tepee Resort.

Downhill Skiing

After slumbering for several years, **Sleeping Giant Ski Area,** U.S. 40 (P.O. Box 400), Cody, WY 82414 (© **307/527-8988;** www.skisg.com) reopened for the 2009–10 winter. With two lifts, 150 skiable acres, and 500 feet of vertical drop, this is a dinky, family-oriented ski area with a mix of beginner, intermediate, and expert runs. Full-day lift tickets run $29 for adults, $24 for seniors and students 13 to 17, $12 for children 6 to 12, and free for kids 5 and under.

Fishing

Yellowstone's legendary fly-fishing waters are a short drive away, though you should try the smaller but excellent angling streams west of Cody: **Clark's Fork of the Yellowstone,** the **North and South Forks of the Shoshone,** and **Sunlight Creek.** To the east, the warmer and slower **Big Horn River** and **Big Horn Lake** nurture catfish, walleye, and ling for boat fishers. For advice on the trout streams near Cody, ask at **Tim Wade's North Fork Anglers,** 1107 Sheridan Ave. (© **307/527-7274;** www.northforkanglers.com), which stocks gear and clothing and also guides day trips for $350 to $400 for two people. If you like to troll or cast from a boat, try **Buffalo Bill Reservoir,** which has produced some big mackinaw, as well as rainbow, brown, and cutthroat trout.

Golf

Greens fees at the 18-hole **Olive Glenn Golf and Country Club,** 802 Meadow Lane (© **307/587-5551;** www.oliveglenngolf.com), are $40 for 9 holes, and $70 for 18, cart included.

Rafting

There aren't lots of Class IV, serious white-water rapids on the rivers around Cody, but the upper stretches of the North Fork of the Shoshone River run pretty fast in the spring. Contact **Wyoming River Trips,** 1701 Sheridan Ave. (© **800/586-6661** or 307/587-6661; www.wyomingrivertrips.com), or **Core Mountain Sports,** 1019 15th St. (© **877/527-7354** or 307/527-7354; www.coremountainsports.com). Prices run from about $25 to $70, depending on the length and difficulty of the trip.

Snowmobiling

The most popular Cody snowmobiling trails originate from nearby **Pahaska Tepee Resort,** located 51 miles from Cody on U.S. Hwy. 14/16/20 (see "Where to Stay," below). Don't take the Pahaska Tepee Trail over 8,541-foot Sylvan Pass if you're afraid of heights; but if you're not, go for it: You'll connect with the Yellowstone National Park trails (guides are required within the park) and the lengthy Continental Divide Snowmobile Trail, and have some breathtaking views, including of Avalanche Peak (10,566 ft.) and Cody Peak (10,267 ft.). The **Sunlight trail system** is located 36 miles north of Cody and winds through the wilds to a stunning view of the Beartooth Mountains. Sledders start from a parking area at the junction of Wyo. 296 and U.S. Hwy. 212 and follow the Beartooth Scenic Byway east for 16 miles to a warming hut. To the east, there are 70 miles of snowmobile routes in the Bighorn Mountains. Snowmobiles can be rented in Cody from **Mountain Valley Engine Service,** 422 W. Yellowstone Ave. (© **307/587-6218;** www.mountainvalleyengine.com).

Windsurfing

The 8-mile-long, 4-mile-wide **Buffalo Bill Reservoir,** which receives wind from three mountain gorges, is one of the top windsurfing destinations in the continental United States. It's best experienced in the warmer months of June to September. There is a boat ramp near the campground on the north side of the reservoir, just off U.S. Hwy. 14/16/20. There are no places to rent a windsurf board in the vicinity.

SEEING THE SIGHTS

If your tastes in wildlife lean to the horned, stop by the visitor center for the **Foundation for North American Wild Sheep,** next to the Buffalo Bill Historical Center at 720 Allen Ave. (© **307/527-6261;** www.fnaws.org), with exhibits on the four different wild sheep that call North America home. Those with a special interest in antique firearms will also want to check out the one-of-a-kind **Cody Dug Up Gun Museum,** upstairs at 1020 12th St. (© **307/587-3344;** www.codydugupgunmuseum.com), showcasing over 500 guns excavated from all over the world, including three from Custer's Last Stand and one that a tree slowly engulfed.

Buffalo Bill Historical Center ★★★   Nicknamed the Smithsonian of the West, this vast museum is top-drawer, casting a scholarly eye on the relics of the West's young history while offering some flash and entertainment for the easily distracted. From its beginnings in a rustic log building, it's grown into a thoroughly impressive modern edifice that now houses five different museums in all.

The **Buffalo Bill Museum** is a monument to one of the earliest manifestations of America's celebrity culture, displaying the wares that turned a frontier scout and buffalo hunter into a renowned showman. Posters trumpet his world-famous Wild West shows featuring "Custer's Last Rally" and "Cossack of the Caucasus," and there are some grainy film clips of the show itself. The **Whitney Gallery of Western Art** showcases work by the adventurous artists who carried their palettes to the frontier to record firsthand the wilderness beauty, the proud Indian cultures, and the lives of trappers and cowboys in the 19th century. Bygone Western artists such as Frederic Remington, Charles Russell, Albert Bierstadt, and Gutzon Borglum share exhibition space with contemporary practitioners. The **Plains Indian Museum** is devoted to the history of Plains tribes, including the Blackfeet, Cheyenne, Crow, Gros Ventre, Shoshone, and Sioux. Interactive exhibits explain the migrations and customs of the tribes and display art and artifacts, including cradleboards, ceremonial dresses and robes, pipes, and beadwork. Situated in an eye-catching rotunda populated by dozens of engaging exhibits, the **Draper Museum of Natural History** focuses on man's investigation of nature over time, with specific attention on the Greater Yellowstone Ecosystem (there's a map composed of 27,000 tiles) and many interactive displays. The **Cody Firearms Museum** displays weaponry dating back to 16th-century Europe in its collection of more than 5,000 pieces.

The center also features rotating special exhibitions, and its research library is an unparalleled resource for all things Western. Additionally, numerous educational programs are held throughout the year. Expect to spend anywhere from 2 hours to 2 days exploring the center, depending on your level of interest.

720 Sheridan Ave. ✆ 307/587-4771. www.bbhc.org. Admission $15 adults, $13 seniors, $13 students 13–17 or with valid college ID, $10 children 5–12, free for children 4 and under; maximum $45 per family. Admission is good for 2 consecutive days. Group tour rates available by request. Nov–Mar Thurs–Sun 10am–5pm; Apr daily 10am–5pm; May to mid-Sept daily 8am–6pm; mid-Sept to Oct daily 8am–5pm.

Buffalo Bill Reservoir The **Buffalo Bill Dam** drops like a slim concrete knife 325 feet into the gorge carved by the Shoshone River west of Cody, and you can walk out atop the dam and look down the steep canyon or back across the deep blue water of the reservoir. Several workers died building it, and when it was completed in 1910, it was the tallest dam in the world. The lake behind it serves anglers, boaters, and windsurfers, while providing irrigation water to farmers downstream. An octagonal visitor center perched next to the dam provides exhibits on the reservoir, wildlife, and area recreation. There is a boat launch along the north lakeshore off U.S. Hwy. 14/16/20 and a clean, spacious campground that lacks shade.

6 miles west of Cody on U.S. Hwy. 14/16/20 at the top of Shoshone Canyon. ✆ 307/527-6076 for visitor center. www.bbdvc.org. Free admission. May and Sept Mon–Sat 8am–6pm, Sun 10am–6pm; June–Aug Mon–Fri 8am–8pm, Sat 8am–6pm, Sun 10am–6pm. Visitor center closed Oct–Apr.

Cody Nite Rodeo ★★ (Kids) If you want to see an authentic Wyoming rodeo, Cody (aka "The Rodeo Capital of the World") offers a sure thing: a nightly tussle between bulls, broncos, and cowboys, as well as roping, cutting, and kids' events such as the "calf scramble"—about 100 young patrons chasing a bewildered young calf. Pay an extra $2, and you get a seat just above the chutes in the Buzzard's Roost. The 6,000-seat stadium sits out on an open terrace above the Shoshone River west of town—not a bad place to be on a cool Wyoming evening beneath the stars. Once a year, some of the nation's top rodeo competitors show up for the Fourth of July Cody Stampede (see "Special Events," above). Before the rodeo, there's a kiddie area with rides, games, and rodeo activities.

Stampede Park (on U.S. Hwy. 14/16/20 west of town toward the Wapiti Valley). ✆ 800/207-0744 or 307/ 587-5155. www.codystampederodeo.com. Admission $18 adults, $8 children 7–12, free for children 6 and under. June–Aug nightly at 8pm; gates open at 7pm.

Cody Trolley Tours ★ An informative, witty look back at Cody's colorful past with a focus on the town's founding father himself, Buffalo Bill, this hour-long tour in a restored trolley takes visitors on a loop that includes historic homes, public art, and the Buffalo Bill Reservoir. The owner/operators, Mike and Margie Johnson, deliver a running commentary augmented by visual aids and recorded snippets that will keep the kids interested. While the couple's narration occasionally comes off as an economic-development pitch for Cody, it also packs a dense serving of fun facts and trivia into the 60-minute drive.

1192 Sheridan Ave. (tours begin and end on the front porch of the Irma Hotel). ✆ 307/527-7043. www. codytrolleytours.com. Admission $22 adults, $20 seniors, $10 children 6–17, free for children 5 and under. Ask about a combination ticket for the Buffalo Bill Historical Center. Tours offered early June to late Sept daily at 11am and 3pm.

Museum of the Old West at Old Trail Town (Kids) Walking the authentically creaky boardwalks here, you'll pass by gray storefronts and clapboard cabins gathered from ghost towns around the region and assembled on the original town site of Cody

City, a short jog from the rodeo grounds. The curators haven't wasted any paint on these relics, which include an 1883 cabin from Kaycee where Butch Cassidy and the Sundance Kid once conspired, a saloon decorated with bullet holes, and what must be the largest collection of worn-out buckboard carriages in the U.S. Also on-site: the relocated graves of a number of Western notables, including John "Liver Eatin'" Johnston, the model for Robert Redford's character in *Jeremiah Johnson*.

1831 Demaris Dr. (©) 307/587-5302. www.museumoftheoldwest.org. Admission $8 adults, $7 seniors, $4 children 6–12, free for children 5 and under. Mid-May to Sept daily 8am–7pm.

Tecumseh's Old West Miniature Village and Museum (Kids) You have to pass through a trading post of Western tourist plunder and handcrafted beadwork to get to this finely detailed miniature diorama of Wyoming and Montana history. Described by proprietor Jerry Fick as his "lifetime work," the room-size landscape depicts everything from fur trappers floating the rivers to Custer's last moments at Little Big Horn. There is also a sizable collection of Indian and pioneer artifacts and taxidermy.

142 W. Yellowstone Ave. (©) **307/587-5362.** www.tecumsehs.com. Free admission. Mid-May to mid-Sept daily 8am–8pm; early May and late Sept 9am–6pm. Call for hours in winter.

WHERE TO STAY

If you want to book lodging before you arrive, a good accommodations resource is **Cody Lodging Company,** 1302 Beck Ave. (©) **800/587-6560;** www.codylodgingcompany. com), which manages numerous properties, from Victorian B&Bs to three-bedroom houses. Rates range from $100 to $500 a night. If you're on a budget, try **Bison Willy's Base Camp,** 1625 Alger St. (©) **307/587-0629;** www.bisonwillys.com), a home converted into a hostel of sorts with dormitory-style bunks going for $20 to $25 a night. There is a communal kitchen, a "beer deck," and a dog kennel.

Buffalo Bill Village Resort: Comfort Inn, Holiday Inn, and Buffalo Bill Village Historic Cabins ★ Consisting of three distinct lodging options at the same convenient location, Buffalo Bill Village has something for everybody. The Holiday and Comfort inns are similar to their chain brethren elsewhere, while the village of historic cabins offers a rustic exterior and a more Western feel, with modern conveniences inside. The former two are priced nearly identically and have similar amenities. The one- and two-bedroom cabins at Buffalo Bill Village are simply equipped—with a bed, phone, and TV—and surrounded by plenty of room for the kids to roam. The cabins themselves first housed the contractors who built the city around 1920, and became the centerpiece of this family-owned resort in the 1950s. The Holiday Inn followed in the '70s, the Comfort Inn in the '90s. Also on-site: an Old West–style boardwalk where you can shop for curios or sign up for tours and river trips, an outdoor heated pool, and several restaurants.

17th St. and Sheridan Ave., Cody, WY 82414. (©) **800/527-5544.** Fax 307/587-2795. www.blairhotels.com. Comfort Inn: 75 units. $89–$169 double. Holiday Inn: 189 units. $89–$169 double. Buffalo Bill Village Historic Cabins: 83 units. $79–$159 double. AE, DC, DISC, MC, V. Historic Cabins closed Oct–Apr. **Amenities:** Restaurant; lounge; exercise room; outdoor pool (summer only). *In room:* A/C, TV, hair dryer, Wi-Fi (free).

The Chamberlin Inn ★★ A boardinghouse opened here in 1903, and the property evolved and devolved over the course of the next century until Ev and Susan Diehl took over the property in 2005 and completely restored it—and then some. Centered on a serene and green courtyard, the new-and-improved Chamberlin Inn is now Cody's best lodging option, just a block from the center of town and featuring charming historic rooms and apartment units. Of special note are the Hemingway Suite—"Papa" stayed **359** here in 1932—with an angling motif and a small Hemingway library; and the lavish Courthouse unit, the original town courthouse reimagined as a luxury apartment.

1032 12th St., Cody, WY 82414. ✆ **888/587-0202** or 307/587-0202. www.chamberlininn.com. 24 units, including 10 suites and apts. $145–$175 double; $235–$650 suite or apt. AE, DISC, MC, V. *In room:* A/C, TV, kitchen, Wi-Fi (free).

The Cody ★★

The Cody immediately became the top modern hotel in the town of its name when it opened in May 2008. Located on the west end of town near the rodeo grounds, the hotel has a colorful, thoroughly Western-chic design in both the common areas and the spacious guest rooms, which have one king-size bed or two queens, warm earth tones, and a Native-American motif. Some have sleeper sofas; those on the west side have balconies with terrific views of Shoshone River Canyon. The facilities are also excellent, including the exercise room and indoor pool, and there are a number of special packages catering to anglers, rodeogoers, and Yellowstone visitors.

232 W. Yellowstone Ave., Cody, WY 82414. ✆ **307/587-5915.** www.thecody.com. 75 units. Summer $209–$249 double; off season $99–$169 double. Pets accepted. Additional person $14. Rates include hot breakfast buffet. AE, DISC, MC, V. **Amenities:** Exercise room; indoor Jacuzzi; small indoor pool. *In room:* A/C, TV/DVD, fridge, hair dryer, MP3 docking stations, Wi-Fi (free).

Cody Cowboy Village ★

This relatively new property is a couples-oriented resort in a family-oriented town. The "village," consisting of a cluster of cabin units near the rodeo grounds, is a world away from the bustling boardwalks of downtown Cody. The log cabins meld contemporary and cowboy in their decor. All have a deck in front; suites feature microwaves and fridges. Most units have one king-size bed, but six have two queens.

203 W. Yellowstone Ave., Cody, WY 82414. ✆ **307/587-7555.** www.codycowboyvillage.com. 50 units, including 10 suites. $79–$159 double; $109–$199 suite. Rates include continental breakfast. AE, MC, V. **Amenities:** Small outdoor Jacuzzi. *In room:* TV, Wi-Fi (free).

The Irma Hotel ★

Buffalo Bill's entrepreneurial gusto ultimately left him penniless, but it also left us this century-old hotel (named for his daughter) in the heart of town. Cody hoped to corral visitors who got off the train on their way to Yellowstone, and one of his lures was an elaborate cherrywood bar, a gift from strait-laced Queen Victoria. You can still hoist a jar on Her Royal Majesty's slab in the Silver Saddle Saloon, or spend the night in a renovated room that might have once housed a president or prince.

Suites are named after local characters from the town's early days: The Irma Suite, on the corner of the building, has a queen-size bed, a writing table, a vanity in the bedroom area, a small sitting area, and an old-fashioned bathroom with a tub/shower combination. While the Irma's aura will surely please history buffs, those acclimated to ultramodern convenience will probably want to look elsewhere. But the hotel's location in the middle of town and the regular schedule of reenacted gunfights out front help compensate.

1192 Sheridan Ave., Cody, WY 82414. ✆ **800/745-4762** or 307/587-4221. Fax 307/587-1775. www.irma hotel.com. 73 units, including 15 restored suites. $105 double; $145 suite; lower rates in winter. AE, DC, DISC, MC, V. **Amenities:** Restaurant; lounge. *In room:* A/C, cable TV, hair dryer, Wi-Fi (free).

The Mayor's Inn ★★

This two-story A-frame, built in 1905 for Mayor Frank Houx, found itself in the path of a wrecking ball in 1997. However, new owners moved it on a truck to its current location, just a few blocks away. It's now one of Cody's best B&Bs, with rooms such as the Yellowstone, featuring a lodgepole-pine bed frame and black-and-white photos of the park's early years, and the Hart Mountain Suite, with romance and floral decor in spades. There's also a carriage house (breakfast not included) with a well-equipped kitchen. The breakfasts here are a hearty treat, featuring sourdough flapjacks and buffalo sausage, and innkeepers Bill and Dale Delph also run a gem of a dinner house here Thursday through Saturday nights in the summer.

1413 Rumsey Ave., Cody, WY 82414. ⓒ **888/217-3001** or 307/587-0887. www.mayorsinn.com. 5 units, including 1 suite. $120–$160 double; $210 suite. Rates include full breakfast. AE, DISC, MC, V. **Amenities:** Restaurant. *In room:* A/C, TV, hair dryer, no phone, Wi-Fi (free).

Guest Ranches & Resorts

Pahaska Tepee Resort ★   Buffalo Bill's hunting lodge, only 2 miles from the east entrance to Yellowstone, was dubbed with his Lakota name, *Pahaska* (longhair), when he opened the lodge to park visitors in 1905. Near the top of the beautiful Wapiti Valley along U.S. Hwy. 14/16/20, Pahaska is a popular stop for people visiting the Yellowstone area. The cabins are scattered on the hill behind the historic (and colorfully decorated) lodge. Accommodations have limited amenities and might best be described as "mini-motels" with two to five rooms, each with a private entrance. Some bathrooms have only showers, some have tubs—it's best to ask in advance. The resort also has a gift shop, restaurant, and trail-ride stables.

183 Yellowstone Hwy., Cody, WY 82414. ⓒ **800/628-7791** or 307/527-7701. Fax 307/527-4019. www.pahaska.com. 47 units. Mid-June to Aug $115–$175 double, $575 condo, $1,095 lodge; off season $70–$140 double, $450–$495 condo, $895–$995 lodge. DISC, MC, V. Closed mid-Oct to Apr. **Amenities:** Restaurant; lounge. *In room:* Kitchen; Wi-Fi (free).

Rimrock Ranch ★   Tucked along Canyon Creek at 6,300 feet above sea level, Rimrock Ranch has an intimate feel not found on larger dude ranches. With a top capacity of three dozen guests, the cabins nestled alongside the creek are fairly modern and definitely a cut above some of the more "rustic" cabins in the area. The weekly package includes backcountry rides, rodeo trips, fishing, cookouts, and river floats. A small outdoor pool perches next to the lodge with a view down the canyon. In summer, horse-packing trips are available; in the winter, there are snowmobile packages.

2728 North Fork Rte., Cody, WY 82414. ⓒ **307/587-3970.** Fax 307/527-5014. www.rimrockranch.com. 8 cabins. Mid-May to mid-Sept $1,650–$1,850 per adult per week; $1,450 per child 6–18 per week; $400 per child 3–5 per week. Rates include all meals. DISC, MC, V (for deposits). Closed mid-Sept to mid-May. Drive 25 miles west of Cody on U.S. 16/20/14 (Yellowstone Hwy.); ranch is on the south side of highway. **Amenities:** Outdoor Jacuzzi; outdoor heated pool; Wi-Fi (free). *In room:* No phone.

7D Ranch ★★   Beautiful Sunlight Creek runs through this venerable ranch, which has a homey, lived-in quality missing in slicker operations. The Dominick family has owned the ranch for 50 years, and they know the nooks and crannies of the Sunlight Basin and the Beartooth Mountains, which guests explore on daylong rides, hikes, and fishing expeditions. Riding and casting lessons, skeet shooting, hiking, trips to Yellowstone, weekly dances, a weekly sweat lodge, and bonfires are all part of the package. And the cabins, cheerfully decorated with heaps of frontier charm, have more personality than the bulk of the 7D's peers. September is adults-only, but the rest of the season the ranch is family-friendly, with numerous children's activities.

Sunlight Basin, P.O. Box 100, Cody, WY 82414. ⓒ **888/587-9885** or 307/587-9885. www.7dranch.com. 11 cabins. May–Sept $1,680–$1,875 per adult per week; $1,050–$1,520 per child 3–12 per week. Rates include all meals, activities, and gratuities. MC, V. Closed mid-Sept to mid-May. Drive north from Cody on Wyo. 120 to Wyo. 296, then head west. Ranch is 50 miles from Cody via Sunlight Rd. **Amenities:** Children's programs; Wi-Fi (free). *In room:* No phone.

WHERE TO DINE

Cody may have more good restaurants than you'd expect in a town of its size. If you need something less than a formal meal, such as a plateful of fuel food or a jolt of caffeine for a busy day, Cody has a good supply of familiar fast-food joints and a few informal, inexpensive places. **Peter's Cafe Bakery,** at 1219 Sheridan Ave. (✆ **307/527-5040;** www. peters-cafe.com), across the street from the Irma, serves breakfast (freshly baked bagels, pastries, and espresso), plus subs and burgers for lunch and dinner. One of the best places day or night to get a steak or a beer and a burger (or Rocky Mountain oysters!) is the thoroughly Western **Proud Cut Saloon,** 1227 Sheridan Ave. (✆ **307/527-6905**), where lots of rodeo riders keep a running tab.

Cassie's Supper Club ★★★ STEAKS/SEAFOOD/WESTERN   Cassie's is the sort of classic roadhouse you might expect and look for in the West: big platters of beef, four bars serving drinks, and ornery roadhouse decor with taxidermy, antelope skulls, and assorted cowboy ephemera. This place has the routine down, having been in business since 1922. Located along the highway west of town in what was once a "house of ill fame," Cassie's is now very respectable and quite good. Besides the requisite steaks—grilled to perfection—there's seafood (including a great walleye dinner), pasta, and chicken, plus a full menu of specialty drinks. In the Buffalo Bar, a 20-foot mural depicts horses, cowboys, and shootouts. The near-mythical dance floor bustles to the twang of live country music every night in summer.

214 Yellowstone Ave. ✆ **307/527-5500.** www.cassies.com. Reservations recommended. Lunch $7–$25; dinner $12–$40. AE, DISC, MC, V. Daily 11am–10pm.

Shiki ★★ SUSHI   An anomalous standout in meat-and-potatoes Cody, Shiki is a superlative sushi bar. With spare Asian decor—consisting primarily of artfully hung cloth and an attractive water feature—and booth, table, and bar seating, the setting matches the top-notch sushi rolls and tempura, teriyaki, and curry. The sushi includes traditional rolls like spicy tuna and eel, as well as a few regional variations—like the Heart Mountain, with crab, cucumber, avocado, and crunchy tempura flakes. Don't be alarmed by the lack of an ocean nearby: Fresh fish is flown in two to three times a week from both coasts.

1420 Sheridan Ave. ✆ **307/527-7116.** Reservations not accepted. Sushi rolls $5–$15; main courses $15–$26. AE, DISC, MC, V. Mon–Fri 11am–2pm and 4–9pm; Sat–Sun 4–8pm. Closed Sun in winter.

Wyoming's Rib & Chop House ★★ STEAKS   One of an upscale regional chain with locations in Billings and Livingston, Montana, and Sheridan, Wyoming, this is the place to head for terrific ribs, chops, and steaks—from chicken-fried steaks to buffalo rib-eyes—but vegetarians will have difficulty finding a meatless main course. Chicken and seafood round out the menu, and desserts like "Pecan Meltaway"—a chocolate crust filled with ice cream, pecans, and more chocolate—provide decadent finales.

1367 Sheridan Ave. ✆ **307/587-4917.** www.ribandchophouse.com. Lunch $6–$9; dinner $10–$33. AE, DISC, MC, V. Daily 11am–10pm.

CODY AFTER DARK

Cody has a lively nightlife, headed by **Cassie's** (see above), with a dance floor laden with real and wannabe cowboys and cowgirls. Downtown, the historic **Silver Dollar Bar,** at 1313 Sheridan Ave. (✆ **307/527-7666**), has tasty burgers, live music, pool tables, and numerous TV screens. Housed in a converted brick garage, **Cooter Brown's,** in the alley behind 1134 13th St. (✆ **307/587-6261**), draws in hordes of hip, young Wyomans with DJs, bands, and regular drink specials. **Dan Miller's Music Revue,** 1549 Sheridan Ave.

(© **307/272-7855;** www.cowboymusicrevue.com), offers a cowboy-style musical variety show Monday through Saturday at 8pm May through September. Tickets are $14.

3 A SIDE TRIP AROUND THE BIGHORN BASIN

Greybull: 40 miles E of Cody; 60 miles W of Sheridan

The prehistoric past of this region is written in the rock, and nowhere in Wyoming is that more true than in **Greybull,** named for a legendary albino bison sacred to American Indians. The town lies amid red-rock formations rich in fossils and archaeological treasures. The **Greybull Museum,** 325 Greybull Ave. (© **307/765-2444**), houses one of the largest fossil ammonites in the world, as well as petrified wood, agates, and American-Indian artifacts. This fine museum is open Monday through Saturday, 10am to 8pm from June to Labor Day, and more restricted hours in the winter, with free admission. Just north of town you'll find a spectacular 15-mile-long, 2,000-foot-high natural fortress named **Sheep Mountain,** a textbook example of a "doubly plunging anticline," geo lingo for a natural arch folded into layered rock.

Greybull is a gateway town to the Bighorn Mountains on scenic U.S. 14 up Shell Canyon. Just 7 miles outside of town heading east is the **Stone Schoolhouse,** listed on the National Register of Historic Places. The one-room schoolhouse was built in 1903 of locally quarried sandstone, and in recent years was converted to a bookstore/gallery, though its hours are unpredictable. Less than a mile farther along the highway, turn south on Red Gulch Road and drive 5 miles to a signed parking area where you can view dinosaur tracks. Driving east from Greybull, U.S. 14 climbs through steep and beautiful **Shell Canyon** (see Driving Tour 1 in section 1, "Scenic Drives").

Fifty miles south of Greybull and east through little Hyattville brings you to the **Medicine Lodge State Archaeological Site** (© **307/469-2234**), where prehistoric peoples decorated the sandstone cliffs along Medicine Lodge Creek with carved petroglyphs and painted pictographs of hunting scenes. You can fish the small stream for brown trout. There is a shady, inexpensive, 26-site campground here, open May through October, with no RV hookups. To reach the site and campground, take Wyo. 789/U.S. 16/20 for 20 miles from Greybull to Manderson, and then drive 22 miles along Wyo. 31 to Hyattville. In Hyattville, drive north and turn right onto Cold Springs Road. Follow the signs 5 miles to the site. There is no day-use fee; campsites are $12.

4 THERMOPOLIS

84 miles S of Cody; 130 miles NW of Casper; 218 miles E of Jackson

Steaming water cascades over pastel-colored terraces and down to the Bighorn River at Hot Springs State Park, one of the undiscovered treasures of Wyoming. Trumpeted as the largest hot springs in the world (it's not quite: New Zealand's Whakarewarewa rightfully claims that honor), the 134°F (57°C) water from the Big Spring supplies two indoor/outdoor pool facilities, two hotels, and a state-run soaking spa. The town of Thermopolis grew up around the hot springs after it was sold to the U.S. government by the tribes of the Wind River Indian Reservation in 1896. Developers dreamed of a health spa to rival Saratoga, but it never quite happened. What did happen is a small, peaceful town with a great place to soak or slide, a nearby canyon of exciting white water, and surrounding hills holding a trove of dinosaur bones and prehistoric petroglyphs.

ESSENTIALS

GETTING THERE The closest airports are the **Riverton Regional Airport,** 55 miles south of Thermopolis, off U.S. 26 W. at 4700 Airport Rd. (✆ **307/856-1307;** www.fly riverton.com), and Cody's **Yellowstone Regional Airport,** 84 miles northeast at Duggleby Dr. (✆ **307/587-5096;** www.flyyra.com). There is a small airport in Thermopolis used by private fliers.

United (✆ **800/864-8331**) and **Frontier** (✆ **800/432-1359**) fly into Riverton. Cody service is provided by **United** and **Delta** (✆ **800/221-1212**).

To reach Thermopolis from Cody, drive 84 miles southeast on Wyo. 120. From Cheyenne, drive north on I-25 to Casper (178 miles), west on U.S. 20/26 to Shoshoni (98 miles), and north on U.S. 20 to Thermopolis. From Rock Springs, take U.S. 191 to Farson, Wyo. 28 to Lander, and Wyo. 789 through Riverton and Shoshoni to Thermopolis.

VISITOR INFORMATION The **Thermopolis Chamber of Commerce,** 220 Park St., Thermopolis, WY 82443 (✆ **877/864-3192;** www.thermopolis.com), sends out packets of information about local attractions.

GETTING AROUND If you've arrived by plane at one of the area airports, you'll need to rent a car to get around. **Hertz** (✆ **800/654-3131**) maintains counters at both the Riverton and the Cody airports.

GETTING OUTSIDE

Hot Springs State Park (see the detailed listing below) offers a variety of outdoor activities, from splashing in mineral water to picnicking on the lawn. South and upstream on the Bighorn River is twisting **Wind River Canyon,** a tricky but bountiful fishing and floating section (you'll need permits from the Wind River Indian Reservation), topped by 19,000-acre **Boysen Reservoir,** about 20 minutes from Thermopolis on U.S. 20. The campgrounds ($17 a site, which includes the requisite $6 day-use fee for nonresidents) on the largely treeless shore of this state park can be a bit buggy and hot in August, but the water attracts boaters to sail, fish, and water-ski. There are three small public beach areas on the reservoir's northeastern and western shores. For more information on the park, contact **Boysen State Park,** Boysen Route, Shoshoni, WY 82649 (✆ **307/876-2796;** wyoparks.state.wy.us), or call Wyoming State Parks and Historic Sites headquarters in Cheyenne at ✆ **307/777-6323.**

Fishing

Whether you like fishing lakes or streams, this area has trophy-size opportunities—Boysen grows record-setting walleye, as well as trout and perch, while the Bighorn River grows some fat brown and cutthroat trout. Check locally to be sure you've got the right fishing license: The canyon requires a tribal permit; the reservoir and other stretches of river require a state license—both available at local sporting-goods stores. If you have your own boat, or hire an outfitter, you can float and fish from the bottom of the canyon at the Wedding of the Waters (where there's a wheelchair-accessible boat ramp) to Thermopolis. During the warmest part of summer, algae can darken the river and hamper fishing, but spring and fall are anglers' dreams.

The **Legion Town and Country Golf Course** is a 9-hole course that overlooks the city from Airport Hill. Call ✆ **307/864-5294** to book a tee time at affordable prices— 9 holes for $16 to $18. The pro shop offers cart rentals, a driving range, and lessons.

Hiking

A boardwalk allows you to explore the bulbous travertine terraces without scalding your soles in the hot-spring water that flows over them. The paths extend to a suspended footbridge across the Bighorn River and a riverside walkway below. For more earnest hikers, there is the approximately 6-mile **Volksmarch Trail,** one of several around the state that are marked with a trademark brown-and-yellow insignia. This one loops through the park and downtown Thermopolis. Just north of town off U.S. 20 you can hike **T Hill** for a bird's-eye view of Thermopolis, the Wind River Canyon, and the Owl Creek Mountains. The 2-mile round-trip up **Roundtop Mountain** is another rewarding hike, culminating in spectacular views of the Hot Springs and Thermopolis, with the trail head beginning near the Monument Hill Cemetery on Airport Road.

White-Water Rafting ★★

The tribes of the **Wind River Indian Reservation** virtually gave away the hot springs, but not the canyon upstream, through which the Wind River tumbles and twists (for reasons no one can explain, the Wind River becomes the Bighorn River as it leaves the canyon). A Shoshone-owned company now takes rafters through rapids named after historic tribal figures like Chief Washakie and Sharp Nose. "Sphincter Rapid" is not an Indian name, but it descriptively tells you that there are some Class III to IV white-water thrills ahead. You can run half the canyon or the entire thing, take a more leisurely fishing trip, or camp overnight with **Wind River Canyon Whitewater,** 210 Hwy. 20 S., Thermopolis (✆ **888/246-9343** or 307/864-9343 in season, 307/486-2253 during off season; www.windrivercanyonraft.com). White-water trips run $30 to $45 for a half-day or $90 for a full day.

HOT SPRINGS STATE PARK ★★

Few state parks in Wyoming are as nice as **Hot Springs** (✆ **307/864-2176;** wyoparks. state.wy.us), with its shady trees, striking flower gardens, and a stretch of the Bighorn River running through it, as well as a roaming buffalo herd and the main event: the magnificent hot springs, with some of its water funneled into swimming pools and slides. It's located at the north side of town off U.S. 20 and admission is free. The park's only shortcoming is that you can't camp overnight, which must please nearby private campgrounds and lodgings. As a Wyoming tourist attraction, the hot springs places a distant third to Yellowstone and Grand Teton national parks, but the sparse crowds allow Thermopolis to retain its small-town style.

At the north end of the park, you can climb a few stairs to look down into the bottomless blue-green depths of the Big Spring—the placid surface belies the fact that the spring pumps out around 15 million gallons a day.

Soaking in the Baths

You can't just plop yourself down in this 134°F (57°C) water, but there are three bathing facilities in the park. To get to them, take the loop road; at the north end are the bathing areas. First, and simplest, is the **State Bath House** ★ (✆ **307/864-3765**), a small spa

Gift of the Smoking Waters Historical Indian Pageant

An annual production, the pageant reenacts the sale of the hot springs and surrounding lands by the Shoshone and Arapaho peoples to the federal government in 1896. The pageant portrays the sale as an act of peace and neighborly brotherhood. In fact, the tribes were starving and desperate. Indians from Wind River play some of the roles in the pageant. The pageant is performed annually during the first weekend in August, along with a powwow. Contact the **Thermopolis Chamber of Commerce** (*(C)* **307/864-3192**) for information.

open to the public free of charge thanks to famed Shoshone Chief Washakie. When the tribes sold the federal government the hot springs in 1896—it would later become state property—Washakie noted that the springs had always been a place of peace and neutrality among tribes, and should therefore always be free to all people. The small, clean indoor and outdoor pools aren't for frolicking or swimming laps—just soaking, wading, and perhaps conversing with some of the old-timers who come here. Soaks are limited to 20 minutes per session. You can rent a towel, locker, and bathing suit for about a dollar each, and it's open Monday through Saturday from 8am to 5:30pm, Sunday from noon to 5:30pm. On either side of this peaceful place are the more raucous commercial pools.

STAR PLUNGE The big lure at the Plunge is its three big slides—the kids' favorite "Little Dipper," the outdoor "Super Star," and the enclosed "Blue Thunder," the latter a 300-foot spin around a 60-foot tower that will thrill you to your claustrophobic, free-falling toes. Indoor and outdoor pools, hot tubs, Jacuzzis, a snack bar, and an arcade make this the favorite of the young set. On a crowded summer afternoon, there are lines at the slides, splashing all around, and a teenage volume level, but you can still find stillness in the "vapor cave." For more information, call *(C)* **307/864-3771.** Admission is $10 for children 5 and over and adults, $5 for children 4 and under, $8 for seniors. It's open daily from 9am to 9pm, except late November to mid-December, when it's closed.

TEPEE POOLS The Pools (*(C)* **307/864-9250;** www.tepeepools.com), sometimes called Hot Springs Water Park or Hellie's Tepee Spa, is a little more peaceful under its big dome than its neighbor to the east, but it has its share of lively teens and a contingent of young families. The slides are not as big here, but you can hear yelps of delight as bodies zip down the twisting indoor open tube. There is a fast-moving open slide outdoors, too, and often a wet basketball game in the roomy outdoor pool. Soaking pools, a steam room, a sauna, and a game room complete the scene. Admission is $10 for ages 6 to 62, $5 for ages 5 and under, and $8 for 63 and over. Open daily from 9am to 9pm.

SEEING THE SIGHTS

Hot Springs County Historical Museum and Cultural Center The original cherrywood bar from the Hole-in-the-Wall Saloon—Butch Cassidy's hangout—is the biggest draw at this local museum, which has some gems among the musty clutter that you learn to expect of rural repositories of historical artifacts. Alongside a trove of Native-American weaponry and art, various modes of transportation are represented, including a caboose and a stagecoach used to tour Yellowstone. Other exhibits trace the local economic threads, primarily coal mining, petroleum extraction, and agriculture. On the lower level are a fully outfitted print shop, general store, and dentist's office. The museum's cultural center features local artwork and crafts on a rotating basis. Expect to spend an hour.

700 Broadway. © **307/864-5183**. www.hschistory.org. Admission $4 adults, $2 seniors 60 and over and children 6–12, free for children 5 and under. Memorial Day to Labor Day Mon–Sat 9am–5pm; rest of year Tues–Sat 9am–4pm.

Legend Rock Petroglyph Site ★ (Finds)   Petroglyphs—prehistoric drawings inscribed in rock—are scattered throughout the foothills of Wyoming's mountains. Legend Rock is one of the richest petroglyph sites in the Rockies, and it is managed—rather informally— by state agents at Hot Springs State Park (© **307/864-2176**). Visitors can pick up a gate key at the State Bath House and then drive up Wyo. 120 to the Hamilton Dome turnoff, then continue 8 miles west, partly on a dirt road, to the site. There you can hike up and down Cottonwood Creek to find pecked representations of turtle-like creatures, birds, hunters, and musicians. To get a good view of some of the panels, you need to scramble up on ledges. Weather has taken its toll on this soft sandstone, and so have souvenir hunters—hands off, please! Be sure to ask for a map to the site when you pick up the key; the route is not well marked. You can drive down by the creek, but you're better off, particularly when it's wet and muddy, parking up by the gate and taking the short hike down.

Near Hamilton Dome, 27 miles northwest of Thermopolis. For information, contact Hot Springs State Park (© **307/864-2176**) or the Thermopolis Chamber of Commerce (© **307/864-3192**). Free admission. Pick up key at park or Chamber of Commerce Mon–Fri 8am–5pm, or at the park only Sat 8am–5pm, Sun noon–5pm.

Outlaw Trail Ride   Butch Cassidy was a well-known character around Thermopolis, although not by any means the only outlaw who favored this rugged country. Visitors who want to relive a Wild West getaway can join the annual Outlaw Trail Ride in August, and journey 100 miles up through the dry, hidden canyons of Hole-in-the-Wall country. Only about 100 people can participate in the weeklong event, and it's popular, so book well in advance. You must BYO horse and sleep on the ground.

Outlaw Trail, Inc., P.O. Box 1046, Thermopolis, WY 82443. © **307/431-2156**. www.rideoutlawtrail.com. $1,200 per rider. The ride occurs annually in early Aug.

Wyoming Dinosaur Center & Dig Sites ★ (Kids)   This dinosaur museum is located right at the site where modern-day paleontologists have unearthed dinosaur bones from the Jurassic period. There are 20 full skeletons on display at the center, as well as eggs, shells, and other remnants from around the world. Except in winter, visitors can take guided tours of dig sites, and then watch workers clean and prepare bones in the laboratory at the center. Visitors can also get dirty with the center's Dig for a Day program ($150 per adult, $80 per child 4–13); reservations are required.

110 Carter Ranch Rd., Thermopolis, WY 82443. © **800/455-3466** or 307/864-2997. www.wyodino.org. Museum: $10 adults, $5.50 children 4–13 and seniors 60 and over, free for children 3 and under. Dig site: $13 adults, $8.75 children 4–13 and seniors 60 and over, free for children 3 and under. Combination museum and dig site tour: $19 adults, $12 children 4–13 and seniors 60 and over, free for children 3 and under. Summer daily 8am–6pm; museum, winter daily 10am–5pm. Closed major holidays. Dig site closed in winter.

WHERE TO STAY

Thermopolis has a number of motels and campgrounds with a little age on them, so if you're arriving in the busy summer season you should have a reservation, or risk landing in a room with the amenities of a closet. Recently, chain affiliates have taken a new interest in lodgings here, so the choices are growing.

Best Western–The Plaza Hotel ★   If you'd rather not have a wildebeest staring at you on your way to breakfast (see Days Inn Hot Springs Convention Center, below), but still want to be in the park (and just an easy walk from the pools), try this alternative, a funky old brick place that once operated as a hostel but now has been nicely fixed up. The 1918 structure is on the National Register of Historic Places and the aura is more urban inn than chain motel. Several of the rooms and suites still have working fireplaces, and new owners have completely renovated the inner courtyard.

116 E. Park St. (P.O. Box 866), in Hot Springs State Park, Thermopolis, WY 82443. ℂ **800/528-1234** or 307/864-2939. www.bestwesternwyoming.com. 36 units. $110–$150 double; $145–$165 suite; reduced rates in winter. Rates include continental breakfast. AE, DC, DISC, MC, V. **Amenities:** Outdoor Jacuzzi; outdoor pool. *In room:* A/C, TV, hair dryer, Wi-Fi (free).

Days Inn Hot Springs Convention Center ★ (Kids)   Formerly the Holiday Inn of the Waters, this is no cookie-cutter Days Inn—it's a hot-springs resort along the Bighorn River within Hot Springs State Park. The huge volume of superheated water that surges from the upturned sandstones is piped into the outdoor Jacuzzi next to the big pool. If lolling under the stars doesn't soften you up, take a turn in the health club and submit to the ministrations of a licensed masseuse. Unique to this property as a Days Inn are its location in the park, several antiques-furnished rooms, and frequent promotions (like the Hot Water Holiday Package: 2 nights, dinner, and champagne for two for $189–$209 from Sept–May). Certainly no other Days Inn has a restaurant like the Safari Room, arrayed with enough big-game trophies from around the world to make Ernest Hemingway blush and vegetarians gag.

115 E. Park St. (P.O. Box 1323), in Hot Springs State Park, Thermopolis, WY 82443. ℂ **800/329-7466** or 307/864-3131. www.thermopolis-hi.com. 80 units. $90–$150 double. Rates include complimentary continental breakfast. AE, DC, DISC, MC, V. **Amenities:** Restaurant; lounge; health club; outdoor Jacuzzi; outdoor pool; sauna. *In room:* A/C, TV, hair dryer, Wi-Fi (free).

Roundtop Mountain Motel (Value)   The Roundtop is the best of the budget bunch in Thermopolis, offering lodging in either a motel room or a log cabin. A redwood deck and patio complement some of the newly renovated units, and kitchenettes are available, which puts the Roundtop ahead of its competition. Though not directly adjacent to the hot springs, the motel is located downtown and within a short drive or walk of the mineral baths.

412 N. 6th St., Thermopolis, WY 82443. ℂ **800/584-9126** or 307/864-3126. Fax 307/864-3905. www. roundtopmotel.com. 12 units, including 7 cabins. Summer $75–$79 double; winter $45–$55 double or cabin. DISC, MC, V. *In room:* A/C, TV, kitchenette, Wi-Fi (free).

Super 8 Thermopolis (Kids)   The tile-roofed Southwest style of architecture distinguishes this new motel from other Super 8's and from the many older, somewhat drab lodgings in Thermopolis. Inside, the decor is not particularly distinguished, but there is a big indoor pool, a pleasant lobby and eating area for the full breakfast, and a honeymoon suite with a marble Jacuzzi. And it's a good bet for kids, offering eight family rooms, each with a bunk bed, two queen-size beds, a VCR, and a Nintendo for only $15 extra.

Lane 5 S., Hwy. 20, Thermopolis, WY 82443. ℂ **800/800-8000** or 307/864-5515. Fax 307/864-5447. 52 units, including 1 suite. Summer $89–$129 double, $189–$229 suite; winter $65–$99 double, $189–$229 suite. Rates include full breakfast. AE, DISC, MC, V. **Amenities:** Indoor Jacuzzi; indoor heated pool. *In room:* A/C, TV/VCR (in some), hair dryer, Wi-Fi (free).

Camping

The **Fountain of Youth RV Park** (ℂ **307/864-3265;** www.fountainofyouthrvpark.com) has tent and RV sites available year-round and is located 1½ miles north of town by the river on U.S. 20. The campground features a large hot mineral spring pool, barbecue grills, showers, laundry room, dump station, and camp store. RV sites cost $33 to $35 for two people (tent sites are $30 for two). When things are busy in the summer, you may find yourself overhearing the unmuffled conversation of the Harley riders parked in the next slot. Open April through October, the **Eagle RV Park** (© **888/865-5707** or 307/864-5262; www.eaglervpark.com) offers RV sites for $31, tent sites for $20, and log cabins for $40 to $70—and peace and quiet. It's located at 204 S. U.S. 20, just south of Thermopolis.

WHERE TO DINE

Pumpernick's (Finds) AMERICAN   The three rooms where meals are served at Pumpernick's clearly weren't designed as a restaurant, but the bric-a-brac-bedecked quarters add a friendly intimacy to good food. In the summer, you can escape the elbows by eating outside in the roomy adjacent arbor. Pumpernick's serves three-egg omelets to breakfast noshers, then crepes and plump specialty sandwiches for lunch. Dinner features generous portions of T-bone steaks and seafood, including rainbow trout and steamed shrimp. The place bakes its own breads, which it uses for hoagies, soup bowls, and dinner loaves. Try the Hertle Turtle for a melt-in-your-mouth chocolate treat.

512 Broadway. © **307/864-5151.** www.pumpernicksfamilyrestaurant.com. Breakfast $2–$8; lunch $3–$7; dinner $12–$22. AE, DISC, MC, V. Summer Mon–Sat 7am–9pm; winter Mon–Sat 7am–8pm.

---

5 WIND RIVER VALLEY

Riverton: 164 miles E of Jackson; 140 miles N of Rock Springs; 140 miles S of Cody

The deep curve of the Wind River Valley is shaped by the snowcapped Wind River Range to the West and the Absaroka and Owl Creek ranges on the east, forming a cottonwood-lined bottom that many consider one of the most beautiful areas in Wyoming. A sizable portion of the valley belongs to the Eastern Shoshone and Northern Arapaho tribes of the **Wind River Indian Reservation,** where there is considerable poverty but also productive ranches and spectacular wilderness reaching up to the Continental Divide. The largest towns are Riverton and Lander, but there are smaller communities like Dubois, Shoshoni, Fort Washakie, and the historic gold-mining town of Atlantic City.

RIVERTON

Notched in a big bend of the Wind River is **Riverton,** a settlement that was carved out when the federal government opened the northern portion of the reservation to non-Indian people a century ago. Riverton has established itself as a retail commercial center for west-central Wyoming. Contact the **Riverton Area Chamber of Commerce,** 213 W. Main St., Riverton, WY 82501 (© **307/856-4801;** www.rivertonchamber.org), for information, including useful suggestions for day trips in the area and a list of events. That calendar includes a summer **Riverton Rendezvous and Balloon Rally,** held during the second and third week in July, when colorful balloons from all over the Rockies rise against the majestic backdrop of the Wind River Range, and the town puts on arts and crafts fairs, a demolition derby, a family dinner with live entertainment, and even a treasure hunt. Also in July, there is the nostalgic **1838 Rendezvous** staged at the junction of the Wind River and the Little Wind River, with black-powder shooting, Indian dancing, tomahawk throws, and bead trading. A **cowboy poetry gathering** is held here in September, and there is the

February **Wild West Winter Carnival** with drag races, ice sculpting, and fishing derbies on the frozen surface of Boysen Reservoir.

GETTING THERE The **Riverton Regional Airport,** 4700 Airport Rd. (✆ 307/856-1307; www.flyriverton.com), is served by **United** (✆ 800/864-8331) and **Frontier** (✆ 800/432-1359). By car, from Thermopolis, take U.S. 20 south through scenic Wind River Canyon to Shoshoni, then U.S. 26 south to Riverton.

WHERE TO STAY If you plan to stay overnight in Riverton, your best bet is the **Holiday Inn** (✆ 800/465-4329 or 307/856-8100). Located at 900 E. Sunset Dr., it has 122 rooms that rent for $99 to $149 double. Or you could head 24 miles farther west on Wyo. 789 to **Lander** (see below).

LANDER

If you head 24 miles farther west of Riverton on Wyo. 789, you hit **Lander,** tucked snugly into the foothills of the Wind River Range where the three fingers of the Popo Agie River draw together. When railroads were the nation's primary mode of travel, Lander was "where the rails end and the trails begin": the takeoff point for backcountry trips to hunt, fish, or explore the lake-dotted wilderness that climbs to the Continental Divide. The trains are gone, but this is still where you put on your hiking or riding boots. For more information, contact the **Lander Area Chamber of Commerce,** 160 N. 1st St., Lander, WY 82520 (✆ 800/433-0662 or 307/332-3892; www.landerchamber.org).

Just west of town on Wyo. 131 is **Sinks Canyon State Park** (✆ 307/332-3077 or 332-6333; wyoparks.state.wy.us), where the Middle Fork of the Popo Agie disappears into a limestone cave and reappears farther down the canyon at a pool with an overlook where you can feed kibble to giant trout (no hooks allowed!). Day use is $6. The park has a nature trail, a visitor center with naturalist displays, a campground ($17 a night, includes day-use fee), and tumbling waterfalls for those willing to hike some switchbacks. For a different kind of experience, drive south 37 miles on U.S. 287 to the **South Pass City Historical Site** (✆ 307/332-3684; wyoparks.state.wy.us), which re-creates a gold-mining town from the 1860s and where Esther Hobart Morris became the nation's first female justice of the peace. There is a $4 day-use fee.

Lander has a justly famous **Fourth of July parade and Pioneer Days Rodeo** (✆ 800/433-0662), and later in July it hosts the **International Climber's Festival** (✆ 307/349-1561; www.climbersfestival.org). Slide shows by climbing greats, clinics, an equipment show, and climbers testing their mettle on the walls of Sinks Canyon and Wild Iris draw hundreds of serious climbers to the event. Some of the climbers are resident here, partly thanks to the **National Outdoor Leadership School** ★, which has been teaching out-door types responsible ways of enjoying the wilds since 1965, and now has branches all over the world. For course offerings from India to the Rocky Mountains, write the school's Lander headquarters at 284 Lincoln St., Lander, WY 82520 (✆ 800/710-6657 or 307/332-5300; www.nols.edu).

If you want an exotic element to your trail adventure, try the **Lander Llama Company,** 2024 Mortimore Lane, Lander, WY 82520 (✆ 307/332-5624; www.landerllama.com). Their naturalist-led Red Desert trip is as enlightening as it is enjoyable, incorporat-ing ancient American-Indian history and fossil viewing with stunning Wyoming scenery. Three-day trips start at $675 per adult and $630 per child 12 and under. If you'd prefer to horse around, check out **Allen's Diamond Four Ranch,** P.O. Box 243, Lander, WY 82520 (✆ 307/332-2995 or 330-8625; www.diamond4ranch.com), for guided horse-back tours in the Popo Agie Wilderness and Wind River Range. The ranch's overnight accommodations are barebones—woodstoves, propane lights, bring your own bedding—but the emphasis is on riding, fishing, and seeing the high country. Trips are about $300 per person per day on the trail. There are special programs for kids.

Winter transforms this country into a snowmobiler's playground, with 250 miles of the **Continental Divide Trail** from Lander to Yellowstone. Call the **Wind River Visitors Council** (✆ **800/645-6233;** www.wind-river.org) or the Lander Area Chamber of Commerce (see above) for information on this and other trails.

Where to Stay & Eat

As far as lodging and grub go, there are quite a few options in Lander, from pizzerias and roadside motels to supper clubs and historic B&Bs. The **Pronghorn Rodeway Inn,** 150 E. Main St. (✆ **800/424-6423** or 307/332-3940; www.pronghornlodge.com), is a reliable choice, with frontier-style trappings and a riverfront setting. Standard doubles run $79 to $129. The Lander Llama Company (see above) rents the **Bunk House,** a stylishly rustic cabin (with a kitchenette) on the Popo Agie River, for $115 a night or $575 a week in high season ($60 a night in winter), with a five-guest limit. If you *really* want to get away from it all, head to **Louis Lake Lodge,** about 30 miles down the highway and 9 miles down a dirt road from Lander at 1811 Louis Lake Rd. (✆ **307/330-7571;** www.louislake.com), where there is no electricity and most cellphones don't work. Cabins are a reasonable $80 to $200 a night, and lodge rooms go for $100 to $140 nightly; there are discounts for longer stays. For dining, try the **Gannett Grill,** 126 Main St. (✆ **307/332-7009;** www.landerbar.com), with a more-interesting-than-it-sounds menu of thick burgers, sandwiches, pizzas, and salads. Under the same ownership next door is **Cowfish,** 128 Main St. (✆ **307/332-7009;** www.landerbar.com), which specializes in beef and seafood, and has an organic garden and a microbrewery on-site.

WIND RIVER INDIAN RESERVATION

The starting point for a tour of the Wind River Indian Reservation is Fort Washakie, located 14 miles north of Lander on U.S. 287, or 146 miles from Jackson (U.S. 26/89/191 to Moran Junction, then U.S. 287 over Togwotee Pass to Dubois and then on to the reservation).

More than 2 million acres of the **Wind River Indian Reservation** surround the town of Riverton, encompassing an area that stretches 70 miles east to west and 55 miles north to south. Wyoming's sole reservation is home to more than 2,500 Eastern Shoshone and 5,000 Northern Arapaho tribal members, governed by a council made up of representatives from both tribes.

The Shoshone were given a huge reservation to buffer westward travelers from more hostile tribes to the north such as the Sioux and Blackfeet. A reservation that once included parts of Wyoming, Utah, and Colorado was reduced greatly when non-Indians discovered gold, grazing land, and water on tribal lands. Today, the Wind River Indian Reservation is a still-sizable 2.2 million acres, including oil and gas fields, several small communities, and some of the most pristine wilderness—and best fishing—in the United States.

The Northern Arapaho came to Wind River in the late 1870s for what they thought was a temporary placement before moving to their own reservation farther east. However, government promises were forgotten or ignored, and the Arapaho settled in to stay. The two tribes have unrelated languages and a history of warfare, but their relationship has gradually improved.

There is poverty and high unemployment on the reservation, but there is pride, too, quite evident at the powwows. Outsiders are welcome at these dances, which are held May through September at various sites (the Wind River Visitors Council can provide a schedule; © **800/645-6233;** www.wind-river.org), where you'll see a more open, friendly side of the Arapaho and Shoshone, as long as you are respectful. Sun dances are more spiritual affairs, and while visitors are not banned, these moving ceremonies are not for tourists, and no photographs or videos are allowed.

Services for visitors are not well developed on the reservation, but you can learn more about the Shoshone tribe at the **Shoshone Tribal Cultural Center** (© **307/332-9106**) in Fort Washakie, and about the Arapaho tribe at the **St. Stephen's Mission** (© **307/856-7806**). At St. Michael's Mission, in Ethete (5 miles east of Fort Washakie), there is a **museum** (© **307/332-2660**) of Arapaho cultural artifacts.

Sacajawea, the famed Shoshone scout for the Lewis and Clark expedition, is supposedly buried on a reservation that bears her name, west of Fort Washakie. There is some debate about whether she is buried there, but it's a beautiful cemetery on a hill and worth a visit (ask for directions in Fort Washakie). You might also stop by nearby **Roberts Mission**—John Roberts was an Episcopal minister who lived most of his life on the reservation and had a tremendous influence on the tribes, founding a school and recording useful historical and anthropological information about the tribes. Chief Washakie, the venerated Shoshone chief, is buried in a cemetery along the Little Wind River on the north side of Fort Washakie. He lived to be more than 100 years old and was buried with full honors by the U.S. Army—the only Indian chief to be so honored.

In late June, American Indians from around the country converge at Fort Washakie for **Shoshone Treaty Day,** a celebration of American-Indian tradition and culture. The **Eastern Shoshone Powwow and Indian Days** follow on the next weekend, with one of the West's largest powwows and all–American Indian rodeos, including thrilling bareback relay horse races.

There are hundreds of lakes in the reservation's high country, and in the summer they come alive with trout—browns, cutthroats, brook, and golden. You can purchase a reservation fishing permit at local sporting-goods stores and find your way with maps to Bull and Moccasin lakes by car, or pick up USGS topographical maps and head for the high country on foot. Check with the fly-tying experts at **Rocky Mountain Dubbing Company,** 115 Poppy St. (© **800/866-4094** or 307/332-2989; www.rmdstore.com), off U.S. 287 just south of Lander, for permits, maps, equipment, and advice.

Sheridan & Eastern Wyoming

As you enter Wyoming from the east, the plains begin to roll like ocean swells, rising and falling until they break against the Rockies. As the elevation rises, the grass grows shorter. Rains taper from dependable downpours to sporadic cloudbursts. The wind races across the surface, combing down the grass and sculpting the snow.

Bison once roamed these prairies in enormous herds, and people were few. But the modern era brought rapid change. In the 18th century, Indian bands mounted horses that had escaped from Spanish conquistadors and enjoyed a brief era of prosperity on the plains, hunting buffalo with great skill. Then the white people arrived: trappers searching for beaver pelts, and pioneers who wanted to either settle here or just pass through on their way to Utah, California, or Oregon. But it was the Texas trail drives, moving north, not west, that most shaped the history and culture of eastern Wyoming.

The landscape hasn't changed much since then. There are still widely scattered settlements; a few small, irrigated fields; and lots of grass and cattle. The billboards announce WELCOME TO THE COWBOY STATE, but these days it's more often the coal and oil and gas beneath the prairies that subsidize the human population in

these wide-open spaces. But the cowboy life is still vibrant and friendly to visitors: You can see rodeos or join a cattle drive, or just buy a hat and pair of boots and pretend. You can explore the mostly unchanged landscapes where cattle barons and their hired guns battled homesteaders in the Johnson County War, where outlaw Butch Cassidy and the Hole-in-the-Wall gang did their "work," and Indian chiefs Crazy Horse and Red Cloud clashed with the cavalry.

Adventurers come to climb **Devils Tower**, a natural skyscraper of volcanic rock that suddenly rises more than 1,000 feet from the flatlands of eastern Wyoming. Visitors also come to hike and fish in the Bighorn Mountains, a handsome range somewhat overshadowed by the peaks of the Continental Divide farther west.

You can explore this region by interstate—I-25 runs north-south, while I-90 dips down from Montana and then east to Gillette and Devils Tower—or take small highways like U.S. 18 and Wyo. 59 to reach smaller towns and more remote country. But since Sheridan is often the target of travelers to the area, this chapter begins there, exploring south to Buffalo and then east to Gillette and Devils Tower before backtracking to Casper, Wyoming's second-largest city.

1 SHERIDAN

144 miles N of Casper; 130 miles S of Billings; 156 miles E of Cody

Sheridan looks right at home where the Rockies meet the plains, its deep roots evident in its well-preserved historic downtown. The Bighorn Mountains cast afternoon shadows

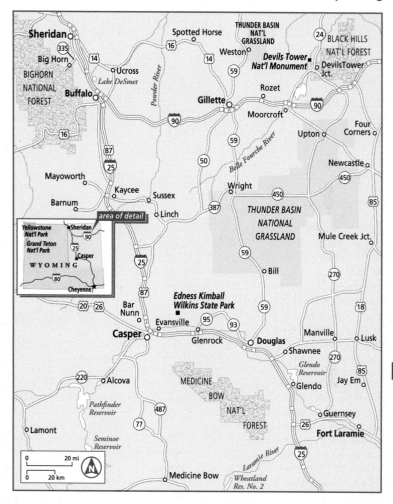

in this direction, across the ranches in the foothills where dude ranching was defined and perfected. One of the largest of Wyoming's small towns, with about 16,000 residents, Sheridan, named after Civil War general Philip Sheridan, retains its small-town charm with century-old buildings along Main Street and the mansions of cattle barons.

The source of prosperity in more recent times lies in the massive coal deposits to the north and east. After decades of production, the big strip mines are in a slow decline, and tourism is on the rise, with an influx of adventurous mountain bikers, rock climbers, paragliders, snowmobilers, and cross-country skiers who are lured by the Bighorns. Ranching these days is less about beef and more about providing saddle time for vacation dudes and retreats for wealthy corporate kings. Or queens—Queen Elizabeth of England, who has distant relations here, stopped by in the 1980s, and like any sensible horse-woman would, she dropped by **King's Saddlery,** known worldwide for hand-tooled tack and ropes.

ESSENTIALS

GETTING THERE The **Sheridan County Airport** (© 307/674-4222; www.sheridan countyairport.com), just southwest of town on Airport Road (take exit 25 off I-90), has daily service from Denver on **Great Lakes Airlines** (© 800/554-5111; www.greatlakes av.com).

If you drive from Billings, take I-90 south 130 miles to Sheridan. From Sheridan you can continue south on I-90 then I-25, sliding along the eastern side of the Bighorn Mountains, 147 miles to Casper, or drive the full 325 miles to Cheyenne. From Yellow-stone and Cody, follow U.S. 14 across the basin and over the Bighorns, and drop into Ranchester, where you'll take I-25 15 miles south to Sheridan.

VISITOR INFORMATION **Sheridan Travel and Tourism,** P.O. Box 7155, Sheridan, WY 82801 (© 888/596-6787 or 307/673-7120; www.sheridanwyoming.org), is located at the State Information Center, off I-90 at exit 23. Across 5th Street is the **Wyoming Game and Fish Visitors Center** (© 307/672-7418), with information on wildlife habitats, fishing, hunting regulations, and the best places to spot wildlife.

GETTING AROUND You can rent a car from **Avis** (© 800/230-4898) or **Budget** (© 800/527-0700) at Sheridan's airport. In summer, there is a trolley that runs from the visitor center to downtown and other destinations; fare is $1. Or call **Sheridan Taxi Service** (© 307/674-6814).

SPECIAL EVENTS Held every Labor Day Weekend, **Don King Days** attracts about 1,500 people to the Big Horn Equestrian Center. Named for late, great local saddlemaker Don King, the event is a rodeo with few fences—spectators get a great view of the action. Call **Sheridan Travel and Tourism** (see above) for additional information.

GETTING OUTSIDE

The **Bighorn National Forest** offers some of the best outdoor recreation in the country, with hundreds of miles of marked trails for hiking, mountain biking, cross-country ski-ing, snowshoeing, and snowmobiling; plus campgrounds, fishing streams, and fantastic wildlife-viewing opportunities. For maps and advice, contact the forest headquarters and Tongue Ranger District office, 2013 Eastside 2nd St. (© 307/674-2600; www.fs.fed.us/r2/bighorn).

In town, there is an excellent trail network dubbed **community walkways.** Pick up a map at the visitor center at I-90, exit 23.

For advice on local hot spots for hiking, mountain biking, fishing, camping, and the like, plus topographical maps, check with **Big Horn Mountain Sports** ★, 334 N. Main St. (© 307/672-6866; www.bighornmountainsports.com). This extremely well-stocked sporting-goods store sells equipment and supplies, and also rents practically anything you might need for fly-fishing, backpacking, camping, snowshoeing, downhill and cross-country skiing, and snowboarding. Next door is **Back Country Bicycles,** a full-service mountain-bike facility (© 307/672-2453), with sales, repairs, and rentals. Big Horn Mountain Sports also coordinates fly-fishing classes and guided trips.

Ron Spahn of **Spahn's Big Horn Mountain Bed and Breakfast** (© 307/674-8150) offers daylong tours of the area, with a focus on the off-the-beaten-path sites that are representative of the "real West," looking at Indian history and modern social problems, mining and environmental issues, outlaw hide-outs, wildlife, and the wild horses of the Pryor Mountains. Ron drives customers in a four-wheel-drive vehicle and offers a field lunch and an engaging, educated perspective. His tours run $95 per person with a $325 minimum.

The scenic drive, the **Bighorn Mountain Loop** (discussed in section 1 of chapter 14), can easily be undertaken with Sheridan as the starting or ending point, or as both.

Equestrian Events

Polo? In Wyoming? Well, they ride horses, don't they? Introduced by early English cattle barons, the tradition continues with matches every summer Sunday at the **Big Horn Equestrian Center** south of Sheridan near the town of Big Horn at 351 Bird Farm Rd. (© **307/674-6969;** www.thebighornpoloclub.com) and Thursdays and Saturdays at the **Flying H Polo Club** (© **307/674-9447;** www.flyinghpolo.com). Admission is free (unless a benefit match is scheduled).

Fly-Fishing

The Tongue River is the Bighorns' blue-ribbon stream. There are browns, rainbows, and brook trout up to 20 inches. Inquire at the **Wyoming Game and Fish Visitors Center,** 700 Valley View Dr. (© **307/672-7418**), for local catch limits and licenses. For equipment needs, advice, and guided trips, contact the **Fly Shop of the Big Horns,** 227 N. Main St. (© **800/253-5866;** www.troutangler.com).

Golf

Dubbing itself the Golf Capital of Wyoming, Sheridan offers several excellent courses with views of the Bighorn Mountains, including one of the state's best, the **Powder Horn ★★**, 6 miles south of Sheridan in Big Horn (© **307/672-5323;** www.thepowder horn.com). The semi-private course includes 27 beautiful holes that mix Scottish-style golf with plenty of wide-open fairways and target golf. Greens fees for 18 holes run $64 to $84 plus $15 per seat for a cart. There are also the 18-hole **Sheridan Country Club,** west of Sheridan at 1992 W. 5th St. (© **307/674-8135;** www.sheridancountryclub. com), with greens fees of $30, plus $16 per seat for carts; and the 18-hole **Kendrick Golf Club** on Big Goose Road (© **307/674-8148**), charging $28 for 18 holes, plus $12 per seat for carts. In Buffalo, the **Buffalo Golf Club,** 550 W. Hart (© **307/684-5266;** www. buffalowygolf.com), is a hilly 18-hole public course with greens fees of $28 for 18 holes, $24 for a cart.

Hang Gliding

Sand Turn in the Bighorn Mountains west of Sheridan is a hang-gliding mecca in the summer. There are fly-ins in late May and over Labor Day weekend; spectators are welcome. Call **Sheridan Travel and Tourism** (© **888/596-6787**) for additional information.

Winter Sports

In the winter, snowmobiling, cross-country skiing, and snowshoeing are all popular activities in the Sheridan area. The 218-mile **Bighorn Mountains Trail System** is a perpetually top-rated snowmobiling area, with the nearest trail head just 15 miles southwest of Sheridan. Call **Sheridan Travel and Tourism** (© **888/596-6787**) for additional information.

SEEING THE SIGHTS

Ask at the State Information Center at I-90, exit 23, for the excellent *Historic Downtown Walking Tour* leaflet, which has summaries on 31 notable structures and a handy foldout map. Another good guide to pick up is the *Art on Display* brochure, detailing temporary and permanent installations of public art around town.

Bradford Brinton Memorial Ranch ★ From a distance, surrounded by cottonwoods and dwarfed by the hills and horizon, the Brinton ranch house doesn't look much different from most other two-story, white wood-frame homes. But the house, dating from the late 1800s, is not the real reason to visit. Yes, this 20-room residence offers a fine example of how a "gentleman rancher" lived in the early 1900s—the tables are set with china and the shelves filled with gold- and leather-bound volumes—but on the walls hangs a first-class art collection. Here you'll see *Fight on the Little Bighorn* by Frederic Remington, and *When Ropes Go Wrong* by Charles Russell. Will James, John Audubon, and a host of other notable artists show up in one of the best but least known Western art collections in the Rockies.

239 Brinton Rd., Big Horn (10 miles south of Sheridan on U.S. 87). ✆ 307/672-3173. www.bradford brintonmemorial.com. $4 adults, $3 children 13–18 and seniors 62 and over, free for children 12 and under. Memorial Day to Labor Day Mon–Sat 10am–4pm, Sun noon–4pm; limited hours fall–spring depending on exhibition; call or check website for details.

King's Saddlery and Museum ★ Founded by the late saddlemaking legend Don King, this Main Street emporium is a cowboy's candy store, with an extensive collection of Western tack, and any size, length, and lay of ropes. Wander the shop to see the tools of the modern cowboy, and watch the King brothers hand-tool leather. Then step back in time to their museum, housing one of the largest collections in the world of Indian artifacts and cowboy trappings—including high-back saddles, chaps, Spanish bits, silver spurs, and quirts.

184 N. Main St. ✆ 800/443-8919 or 307/672-2702. www.kingropes.com. Free admission; donations accepted. Mon–Sat 8am–5pm.

Sheridan County Museum Located in a former barbecue restaurant near I-25, the Sheridan County Museum offers an interesting glimpse into Sheridan's rich history. The stories of mining and logging are told through intricate dioramas, and works by local artist Bernard Thomas and local photographer Elsa Spear Byron are spotlighted, alongside historic ranching artifacts and other displays.

850 Sibley Circle. ✆ 307/675-1150. www.sheridancountyhistory.org. $4 adults, $3 seniors, $2 students, free for children 11 and under. May and Sept to mid-Dec daily 1–5pm; June–Aug daily 10am–6pm. Closed mid-Dec to Apr.

Sheridan Inn The majestic Sheridan Inn was hailed as the finest hotel between Chicago and San Francisco when it opened in 1893, and visitors today can step back to that time as they explore the restored first floor. Modeled after Scottish hunting lodges, the hotel has dormer windows for each of the 62 rooms and three impressive river-rock fireplaces. The back bar was imported from England, and the building boasted the town's first electric lights, running water, and telephone. The Sheridan Inn has hosted a variety of visiting celebrities and dignitaries, including Buffalo Bill Cody, Calamity Jane, Theodore Roosevelt, Will Rogers, and Ernest Hemingway. Although it hasn't operated as a hotel since 1965, the Sheridan houses a restaurant, **1893 Grille & Spirits** (✆ 307/673-2777)—and the handsome and historic bar still serves drinks. A complete restoration of 22 rooms will allow overnight stays, perhaps by late 2010 (rates are expected to be $150 and up nightly).

856 N. Broadway. ✆ 307/674-2178 or 673-1747. www.sheridaninn.com. $3 self-guided tour of the 1st floor and museum. Call for appointment.

Trail End State Historic Site   The Kendrick Mansion, the only example of Flemish Revival architecture in Wyoming, sits on 3¾ acres of manicured grounds. John Kendrick, orphaned in Texas, arrived in Wyoming in 1879 at age 22 on a cattle drive. By 1912 he'd built a 200,000-acre cattle ranch and amassed a net worth of $1 million. The next year, he completed construction on a home so large it took a ton of coal each day to warm its 20 rooms. He later became Wyoming's governor, then U.S. senator. Visitors today can marvel at materials not common in pioneer Wyoming: silk, mahogany, Italian marble, Georgia pine beams, and a maple floor in the ballroom. Also on the grounds is a carriage house, which serves as a community theater.

400 Clarendon Ave. ℭ 307/674-4589. www.trailend.org. $2 adults 18 and over. June–Aug daily 9am–6pm; Mar–May and Sept to mid-Dec daily 1–4pm. Closed mid-Dec to Feb.

The Ucross Foundation   Retreats for writers, artists, and musicians are not all that common in the West, but Ucross has gained an international reputation by providing a quiet, beautiful setting for seclusion and creativity. This ranchland, 27 miles east of Sheridan, was once the headquarters of the Pratt and Ferris Cattle Company, established in 1879. Now over half of the 22,000-acre ranch is protected with a conservation easement with the Nature Conservancy. You don't need an artist's residency to stop in and visit **Big Red,** a magnificently restored structure that once served as the main ranch house but today is a showcase of antique furniture; and the **Big Red Gallery,** which every year mounts four exhibits. If you're in the area on the Fourth of July, this is the place to be; more than 4,000 people show up for the fireworks.

30 Big Red Lane, Clearmont. ℭ 307/737-2291. www.ucrossfoundation.org. Free admission. Mon–Fri 8:30am–4pm. From Sheridan, drive 27 miles east on U.S. 14 to junction with U.S. 16.

WHERE TO STAY

The Sheridan area has a great range of lodging establishments, running the gamut from modern hotels to Victorian B&Bs to authentic dude ranches. The two best chain properties are the **Best Western Sheridan Center,** 612 N. Main St. (ℭ 877/743-7432 or 307/674-7421), with double rates of $119 to $149 in the summer, $79 to $99 in the winter; and the **Holiday Inn,** 1809 Sugarland Dr. (ℭ 307/672-8931), with rates of $108 to $126 double and $159 to $229 suite. The **Wingate Inn,** 1950 E. 5th St. (ℭ 307/675-1101), is another solid option, with double rates of $129 summer, $99 winter.

Mill Inn   From 1921 to 1972, the Sheridan Flouring Mills served as, yes, a flour mill, but a maverick businessman soon turned the place into a motel with office suites. It's since been upgraded; the very nice rooms have a mild Western motif (historical photos, cowboy-speckled bedspreads), with the trademark concrete grain elevator still in place. The only downside is traffic noise, as the inn is close to both the interstate and the main drag through town.

2161 Coffeen Ave. (at I-90, exit 25), Sheridan, WY 82801. ℭ 307/672-6401. www.sheridanmillinn.com. 44 units. Summer $110–$175 double; fall–spring $75–$85 double. Rates include continental breakfast. AE, DISC, MC, V. In room: A/C, TV, hair dryer, Wi-Fi (free).

Sheridan Cottages ★   Located 2 miles from downtown, these colorful metal-sided cottages meld quaintness and modernity in their exterior and feature comfortable and stylish "New West" interiors. Great for couples or families, all of the cabins have maple hardwood floors and kitchens with granite counters; some feature a den area. There is a shared laundry room and nicely landscaped yard area out front. The location, between a commercial district and a residential neighborhood, is unremarkable but quiet and convenient to the interstate.

1185 Sugarview Dr., Sheridan, WY 82801. ℂ **307/751-0793.** www.sheridancottages.com. 5 units. $135–$150 double, with a 3-night minimum stay. Discounts available for longer stays. DISC, MC, V. *In room:* TV, kitchens, Wi-Fi (free).

Spahn's Big Horn Mountain Bed and Breakfast ★★ Spahn's Big Horn Mountain B&B prides itself on being the oldest B&B in Wyoming, and it's certainly one of the best. Picture this: a four-story log cabin; a common room with a crackling fire, shelves of books, and a piano; and outside, a deck with a 100-mile view of prairie stretching to the east. The rooms glow with varnished peeled logs, and have such country comforts as patchwork quilts and claw-foot tubs. Ron Spahn (he's run the place for more than 20 years with his wife, Bobbie) leads evening wildlife safaris in search of moose, elk, and deer on Monday and Thursday; he also takes customers on daylong tours of the area (see "Getting Outside," above). The cabins here burned in a 2007 fire that left a lasting mark on the mountainside.

P.O. Box 579, Big Horn, WY 82833. ℂ **307/674-8150.** www.bighorn-wyoming.com. 3 units. $100–$175 double. Rates include full breakfast. MC, V for reservation deposit only; payment by cash or check. 15 miles southwest of Sheridan via U.S. 87 and Wyo. 335. *In room:* No phone.

Guest Ranches

Eatons' Ranch ★★ (Kids) This is the country's oldest guest ranch, and one of the best. Founded by Howard Eaton (the namesake of the Howard Eaton Trail in Yellowstone), the ranch got its start in North Dakota in 1882 before relocating in 1904 to remote and rugged Wolf Creek Canyon, about 20 miles west of Sheridan and a picture-perfect spot for a guest ranch. The third through fifth generations of Eatons now run the ranch, which has repeat guests year after year thanks to a first-rate horseback-riding operation, hearty meals, and terrific rustic cabins that range from truly historic to modern, with big river-rock fireplaces, elk trophies, and a rich dose of Western ambience. Other diversions include fishing in a stocked pond, pack trips (for an additional charge), movie nights, barbecue dinners and dances on Sunday nights, and Wednesday afternoon softball games (guests versus staff).

270 Eatons Ranch Rd., Wolf, WY 82844. ℂ **800/210-1049** or 307/655-9285. www.eatonsranch.com. Reservations required at least 2 months in advance. 51 cabins. Late May or early June to mid-Aug $210–$235 per adult per day; $145–$180 per child 17 and under. 3-day minimum stay required. Rates include all meals and ranch activities. DISC, MC, V. Closed mid-Aug to late May. About 18 miles northwest of Sheridan via Wyo. 331. **Amenities:** Dining room; children's programs; outdoor Jacuzzi; outdoor heated pool; Wi-Fi (free). *In room:* Hair dryer, no phone.

HF Bar Ranch ★ (Kids) With reasonable rates and plenty of activities for children, the HF Bar Ranch really caters to families—nannies are encouraged to come along at half-price. This hospitable ranch is a real working ranch and a hoedown of old-fashioned fun, with weekly hayrides and dances. Ice and wood are delivered daily to each of the cabin's front porches, and hearty family-style meals are served in the main lodge. Guests can take daily trail rides or arrange a pack trip to the remote and rustic "mountain camp" 15 miles into the Bighorns. For an additional fee, the sports enthusiast of the group can fish the miles of stream banks, shoot on one of the six sporting-clay courses, or hunt pheasant and chukar on a private bird reserve.

1301 Rock Creek Rd., Saddlestring, WY 82840. ℂ **307/684-2487.** www.hfbar.com. Reservations required at least 6 months in advance. 30 cabins. $260 per person per day; free for children 4 and under. Rates include all meals and most ranch activities. No credit cards. Take I-90 35 miles south of Sheridan to exit

47. Drive west on Shell Creek Rd. and Rock Creek Rd. for 12 miles to ranch. **Amenities:** Dining room; babysitting; children's program; outdoor heated pool; Wi-Fi (free). *In room:* No phone.

Paradise Guest Ranch ★   Aptly named, this guest ranch 45 miles south of Sheridan adds modern conveniences to the ambience and activities you expect on a ranch. The log cabins not only have decks with views of the surrounding valley, mountains, or streams, but also come equipped with their own washers and dryers. As with most resort ranches in the West, several trail rides depart daily for guests of all levels of ability. And if you're riding all day, you can get a chuck-wagon dinner. There are ample after-dark activities for the entire family, with evening entertainment in the ranch's saloon and recreation center.

Box 790, Buffalo, WY 82834. ℂ **307/684-7876.** www.paradiseranch.com. 18 cabins. $1,400–$2,000 per adult per week; $550–$1,850 per child 12 and under per week. Rates include all meals and ranch activities. No credit cards. Closed Nov to mid-May. From Buffalo, drive 13 miles west on U.S. 16, then turn right at Hunter Creek Rd. to the road leading to the ranch. **Amenities:** Dining room; lounge; Wi-Fi (free). *In room:* Kitchenette, no phone.

Camping

The **Sheridan/Bighorn Mountain KOA Campground,** 63 Decker Rd. (ℂ **800/562-7621** for reservations, or 307/674-8766), a half-mile north of Sheridan at the Port of Entry exit, offers quiet and shady tent and RV sites, plus all the usual commercial campground amenities, including an outdoor swimming pool and miniature golf. The campground is open year-round, with rates from $20 to $40. Another option is **Peter D's RV Park,** 1105 Joe St. (ℂ **307/673-0597** or 674-4613; www.wyomingrvpark.com), with rates of $25 to $30 for a site. For those who prefer roughing it, the **Bighorn National Forest** has several primitive campgrounds in the area, with sites costing $12 to $14 per night. Contact the **Bighorn National Forest office** in Bighorn (ℂ **307/674-2600**) for further information.

WHERE TO DINE

Oliva's Kitchen ★ (Finds MEXICAN/ITALIAN   Beginning as a dinky takeout counter down the street, Oliva's is a new restaurant on Main Street and has quickly emerged as a local favorite. Serving Mexican standards like burritos, *chile verde,* and enchiladas, the eatery also plates up some more-than-respectable pasta dishes (I favor the spicy shrimp), burgers, and steaks. The breakfast burritos are also hard to beat. The basic restaurant has tables and a counter and great service.

437 N. Main St. ℂ **307/673-0986.** Main courses breakfast $3–$6, lunch and dinner $8–$23. AE, DISC, MC, V. Mon–Thurs 6am–9pm; Fri–Sat 6am–10pm. Closed Sun.

Oliver's ★★ CONTEMPORARY AMERICAN   Oliver's brings some big-city flair to the cowboy environs of Sheridan. Opened in 2002 by Matt Wallop, the son of former U.S. Senator Malcolm Wallop, the monthly-changing menu has some Western touches among its wide range of influences. You might get pheasant ravioli; a filet of locally raised beef tenderloin, with applewood-smoked bacon, caramelized onions, and Gorgonzola; or maybe macaroni and cheese made with Gouda, white cheddar, and Parmesan. Like the menu, the space itself is contemporary, with a San Francisco–inspired design that melds elegant and industrial with a hint of the West. There is also a nice inventory of wines and such tantalizing desserts as espresso crème brûlée.

55 N. Main St. ℂ **307/672-2838.** Reservations recommended. Main courses $12–$39. AE, DISC, MC, V. Mon–Thurs 5:30–10pm; Fri–Sat 5:30–11pm; Sun 10am–2:30pm. Bar open later.

Sanford's Grub & Pub CAJUN   The maze of rooms at Sanford's, located in a 1907 historic building, is decorated like the dorm room of a junkman's son: Televisions, beer signs, and license plates are crammed to the rafters. You might even say the same about the dinner menu, which leans toward Cajun dishes, with really good jambalaya and Cajun-flavored burgers and steaks—try the New York strip Cajun style. But the restaurant also has a whole lot of other things, including some items, such as fried okra, that you wouldn't expect to see above the Mason-Dixon line. Sanford's is a good spot for beer drinkers, with a seemingly unlimited selection of bottled beers, plus the restaurant's own on draft.

1 E. Alger St. (at N. Main St.). © **307/674-1722.** Burgers and sandwiches $5–$10; main courses $10–$20. AE, DC, DISC, MC, V. Daily 11am–10pm (9pm in winter).

SHERIDAN AFTER DARK

The doors of the legendary **Mint Bar,** 151 N. Main St. (© **307/674-9696**), first swung open in 1907. The place operated as a speak-easy until Prohibition ended, then evolved into the prototypical Western bar; "Meet me at the Mint" became a catchphrase in these parts. It's still decorated just as it was in the 1940s, with all sorts of taxidermy and historical photos. There's an 8-foot Texas rattlesnake skin (said to have formerly sheathed an 80-pounder) above the bar and plenty of local color seated in front of it.

WYO Theater   Built in 1912, the WYO is a model for other old theaters in the West. It was a broken-down movie palace facing the wrecking ball in the early 1980s when locals stepped in and saved it, restoring the proscenium and reviving live entertainment in Sheridan. Classical music, local choral groups, touring dance companies, and popular performers like B. J. Thomas and the Bellamy Brothers fill the house. It sits at 42 N. Main St. (© **307/672-9084;** www.wyotheater.com) and tickets are usually between $9 and $30.

2 BUFFALO ★

35 miles S of Sheridan; 182 miles E of Cody

Though Sheridan remains the busy hub of this Wyoming region, it is surrounded by interesting little towns like Dayton, Story, and Ranchester, plus one big enough to deserve its own slot: Buffalo. A short drive south of Sheridan on I-90, this old ranching town is near the site of the infamous Johnson County War (a battle among settlers over the use of rangeland), and not far from the Hole-in-the-Wall country favored by Butch, Sundance, and other outlaws.

Though this was a favorite area of Indian bison hunters, it was not named for a shaggy beast: The original settlers drew names from a hat, and the winner had written his New York hometown.

The historic downtown area is compact enough to explore on foot. Follow the **Clear Creek Centennial Trail** on a wheelchair-accessible path from downtown to a pleasant grassy area where it joins a 3-mile unsurfaced road to the base of the Bighorn Mountains. Maps are available from the **Buffalo Chamber of Commerce,** 55 N. Main St., Buffalo, WY 82834 (© **800/227-5122** or 307/684-5544; www.buffalowyo.com). You'll see the old **Occidental Hotel** at 10 N. Main (see "Where to Stay," below). At the excellent **Jim Gatchell Memorial Museum,** 100 Fort St. (© **307/684-9331;** www.jimgatchell.com), you'll find American-Indian artifacts like arrowheads and medicine rattles, as well as

cavalry items and the bridle Tom Horn braided while awaiting execution. The museum
is open May through early October and closed the rest of the year ($5 adults, $3 children
ages 6–17, free for kids 5 and under).

Buffalo lies on the route of the Bozeman Trail, a 19th-century shortcut to the gold
country of Montana that cut right through the hunting grounds of several resentful
tribes. The U.S. Army built forts to protect travelers, and engaged in skirmishes with the
resident Sioux, Cheyenne, and Arapaho. The largest fort was **Fort Phil Kearny,** exit 44
off I-90 (© 307/684-7629; www.philkearny.vcn.com), where soldiers endured repeated
raids by hostile Indians. Though the original fort is gone, the site today is a national
historic site with a visitor center and tours of two major battlefields nearby: the 1866
Fetterman Massacre, in which Crazy Horse and his band overwhelmed a small army
contingent; and the Wagon Box Fight, which went the other way. The visitor center is
open daily 8am to 6pm from mid-May to September; and Wednesday through Sunday
noon to 4pm the rest of the year; admission is $4.

Robert LeRoy Parker (Butch Cassidy) and his partner, Harry Longabaugh (Sundance
Kid), assembled their infamous group of bandits known as the Wild Bunch to rob trains
and banks and steal herds of horses and cattle. One of their favorite places to hide was
the **Hole-in-the-Wall,** a red-rock canyon area above the Middle Fork of the Powder
River. The Hole-in-the-Wall is located about 45 miles south of Buffalo near the town of
Kaycee. Take I-25 south from Kaycee to the Triple T Road exit, continue south 14 miles
to County Road 111, go west 18 miles to County Road 105, then north 8 miles to the
U.S. Bureau of Land Management directional sign for Hole-in-the-Wall. It's a 3-mile
hike into the actual site. The Hole itself is no more than a notch in a butte, disappointing
to folks used to Disney-like re-creations of outlaw hide-outs. But for the intrepid on
horse or in four-wheel-drive vehicles, you can explore the spacious **Outlaw Cave.** There
are tipi rings in the surrounding area and large pictographs and stenciled handprints
under a rock overhang.

Note: Most of this area is private land. Be sure to check with the U.S. Bureau of Land
Management office in Buffalo (© **307/684-1100**) before exploring on your own.

Just a few miles northwest of Buffalo along I-90 is **Lake DeSmet,** an excellent fishing
and boating destination, with opportunities for picnicking and camping.

WHERE TO STAY

The Occidental Hotel ★★   The Occidental started as a tent in 1878 and evolved
into a hotel that was demolished and rebuilt in 1900. It was lost in a poker game in 1919
to the Smith family, ranchers who ran it as a hotel for more than 50 years. It closed in
1980, and the dust and cobwebs took over for 20 years. But new owners John and Dawn
Wexo breathed new life into the place and the grand hotel reopened in 2002 as one of
the most intact historic lodgings in the West. The rooms—often fashioned out of two or
three of the old rooms—are decorated with original furnishings and reproduction wall-
paper, as well as vintage radios that pick up old radio programs from an in-hotel trans-
mitter. We like the masculine Teddy Roosevelt Suite, with an original sink and tub, and
the dinky Hole-in-the-Wall room, with brick walls and tasteful decor. We also adore the
historic saloon downstairs, its woodwork pocked with bullet holes from Buffalo's Wild
West past, and great bluegrass jams on Thursday nights.

10 N. Main St., Buffalo, WY 82834. © **307/684-0451.** www.occidentalwyoming.com. 14 units (2 with
shared bathroom). Summer $75–$165 double, $185–$210 suite; winter $50–$125 double, $135–$165
suite. AE, DISC, MC, V. Pets accepted (fenced yard outside). **Amenities:** 2 restaurants; lounge. *In room:* A/C,
TV, no phone, Wi-Fi (free).

3 GILLETTE

103 miles E of Sheridan; 243 miles E of Billings

Gillette is now "Energy Capital of the Nation" and boasts the local convention and visitors bureau, but just a century ago it was a huge sea of open range. Where there were once herds of cattle, you can now see several massive surface coal mines such as the RAG Coal West–Eagle Butte Mine. The mine, which opened in 1978, shipped its 250-millionth ton of coal on April 15, 1998, and continues to produce more than 40 million tons a year. The huge coal mines, along with recently discovered coal-bed methane gas, have made Gillette a booming community of about 25,000 residents, which means that this is a pleasant enough place to live, with a variety of modern facilities, including a first-class swimming pool and water park. There is still plenty of undeveloped plains habitat, too, particularly in the 1.8-million-acre **Thunder Basin National Grassland.** Anyone who likes geological wonders, and anyone who enjoyed *Close Encounters of the Third Kind,* will want to visit the nearby **Devils Tower National Monument.**

ESSENTIALS

GETTING THERE Great Lakes Airlines/Frontier (© 800/554-5111; www.greatlakes av.com), **Delta/SkyWest** (© 800/221-1212), and **United/Mesa** (© 800/864-8331) fly into the **Gillette-Campbell County Airport** (© 307/686-1042; www.iflygillette.com), off U.S. 14/16.

By road, Gillette is 103 miles east of Sheridan via I-90 and 61 miles southwest of Devils Tower National Monument.

VISITOR INFORMATION Contact the **Campbell County Chamber of Commerce,** 314 S. Gillette Ave., Gillette, WY 82716 (© 307/682-3673 or 686-0040; www.gillette chamber.com).

GETTING AROUND You can rent cars from **Avis** (© 800/230-4898) or **Hertz** (© 800/654-3131) at the airport or in town; or get a taxi from **City Cab** (© 307/685-1000).

GETTING OUTSIDE

Golf addicts can get their fix at either the **Gillette Golf Club,** 1800 Country Club Rd. (© 307/682-4774), or the **Bell Nob Golf Course,** 1316 Overdale (© 307/686-7069). The former is a 9-hole course; Bell Nob has 18.

Bird-watchers will enjoy the waterfowl of **McManamen Park,** near the corner of Gurley Street and Warlow Drive. **Hunters** are drawn here to bag elk, mule deer, pronghorn, and upland birds. Numerous hunting guides operate in the Gillette area; contact the Campbell County Chamber of Commerce (see above) for assistance in finding one.

SEEING THE SIGHTS

If you are impressed by big holes and big machinery, you've come to the right place. The RAG Coal West–Eagle Butte Mine has an impressive overlook near mile marker 100 on U.S. 14/16, about 1 mile north of Gillette's airport. The mine company and the Gillette Convention and Visitors Bureau jointly sponsor **free summer tours** to the mine site, where you can see the massive equipment used to extract the coal. Reservations should be made by calling © 307/686-0040.

The **Campbell County Rockpile Museum** ★, 900 W. 2nd St. (© **307/682-5723**), is the place to learn something about the history of this area. Displays include artifacts of the area's past such as saddles, rifles, arrowheads, and the like, but I prefer the big stuff—antique vehicles, including several Ford Model Ts, and a wagon collection that includes a horse-drawn hearse and an old sheep wagon. Kids like the vintage tractors they can climb on, as well as the other hands-on displays, including one that helps children identify the area's animals. There's also a "Grandma's Attic" section, where kids can dress up in historical (and funny-looking) fashions from days gone by. Adjacent to the museum building is a historic schoolhouse and a homesteader's cabin from the early 1900s. Both of these buildings were relocated to the museum grounds from other parts of the county. Finally, for those who like firecrackers—we mean really, really big firecrackers—don't miss the 10-minute big-screen video on coal mining that shows what dynamite can really do. Admission to the museum is free. It's open year-round Monday through Saturday from 9am to 5pm.

The **CAM-PLEX** (© **307/682-0552;** www.cam-plex.com), a massive event pavilion, has been the host in recent years of the National High School Rodeo Finals, as well as an array of other exciting events. Call or visit the website to find out what's scheduled.

WHERE TO STAY & DINE

Lodging rates in Gillette are highest in summer, and sometimes as much as a third less at other times; the rates below are peak rates. The largest lodging property in town is the **Best Western Tower West Lodge,** 109 N. U.S. 14/16, Gillette, WY 82716 (© **800/762-7375** or 307/686-2210), which charges $89 to $179 double or $189 to $229 for a suite. The **Clarion Western Plaza,** 2009 S. Douglas Hwy., Gillette, WY 82718 (© **307/686-3000**), charges $149 to $169 double; and the **Holiday Inn Express,** 1908 Cliff Davis Dr., Gillette, WY 82718 (© **307/686-9576**), charges $159 to $239 double.

The restaurant I like in Gillette is the **Prime Rib Restaurant & Steakhouse,** 1205 S. Douglas Hwy. (© **307/682-2944**), an upscale steak and seafood place where you can get tender, slow-roasted prime rib, charbroiled filets, sautéed halibut, and shrimp scampi, among other items, as well as a wine list that's garnered acclaim from *Wine Spectator*. Lunch prices are in the $6-to-$12 range, and most dinner entrees cost $15 to $45. The restaurant is open Monday through Friday from 11am to 10pm, Saturday from 4 to 10:30pm, and Sunday from 4 to 9:30pm.

4 DEVILS TOWER NATIONAL MONUMENT ★

62 miles NE of Gillette; 230 miles SE of Billings; 110 miles W of Rapid City, South Dakota

Once upon a time, so the Kiowa legend goes, seven sisters were playing with their brother when he suddenly turned into a bear. Fleeing, the girls scrambled onto a small rock and prayed. The rock started to grow, pushing them into the sky. While the bear clawed at the rock's sides, trying to get at the girls, the rock thrust them so high that they became the points of the Big Dipper. Rising 1,267 feet above the Belle Fourche River below, the formation became named Mato Tipila, or "Bear Lodge." The site is sacred to the Lakota and other tribes native to the northern plains.

Col. Richard Irving Dodge, who commanded a military escort to a U.S. Geological Survey party that visited the Black Hills in 1875, is credited with giving the formation its current name. In his book *The Black Hills,* written the year after his journey, Dodge described Devils Tower as "one of the most remarkable peaks in this or any other country."

As a battle to preserve the monument from commercial encroachment was being waged in 1893, two local ranchers decided it was time someone made the first recorded climb to its summit.

William Rogers and Willard Ripley planned for months before making their first attempt on the southeast face on July 4, 1893. As the date approached, the pair began distributing handbills offering such amenities as ample food and drink, daily and nightly dancing, and plenty of grain for horses. The flyers also touted the feat as the "rarest sight of a lifetime."

Rogers and Ripley used a wooden stake ladder for the first 350 feet of the climb. As more than 1,000 spectators watched, the pair made the harrowing climb in about an hour, raised Old Glory, then sold pieces of it as mementos of the occasion. Thereafter, the tower became a popular place for Independence Day family gatherings. At the annual affair in 1895, Mrs. Rogers used her husband's ladder to become the first woman to reach the summit.

In 1906, Congress declared it the nation's first national monument. The tower was further popularized in the 1977 movie *Close Encounters of the Third Kind.*

While the 50-million-year-old tower itself is composed of hard igneous rock, much of the remaining exposed rock within the 1,347-acre monument is composed of soft sediments from the warm, shallow seas of the Mesozoic era. These colorful bands of rock encircling the igneous core include layers of sandstone, shale, mudstone, siltstone, gypsum, and limestone.

Any visitor will understand immediately the allure of this striated column of volcanic rock. It's especially evocative in the evening—as darkness shrouds the surrounding hills, Devils Tower stands above the horizon, glowing amber.

ESSENTIALS

GETTING THERE From Gillette, take I-90 east to Moorcroft (exit 154) and follow signs to Devils Tower; from Jackson, take U.S. 26/287 to Riverton, then U.S. 26 to Casper, then I-90 through Gillette to Moorcroft; from Sheridan, take I-90 to Gillette, then see above.

VISITOR INFORMATION Contact **Devils Tower National Monument,** P.O. Box 10, Devils Tower, WY 82714-0010 (© **307/467-5283;** www.nps.gov/deto). The **Devils Tower Natural History Association,** P.O. Box 37, Devils Tower, WY 87214-0037 (© **307/467-5283**), operates a bookstore at the monument's visitor center and offers a variety of publications.

VISITOR CENTER Open from early April to late November only, the visitor center is located 3 miles from the monument's entrance, with exhibits about the tower's history and geology.

FEES & REGULATIONS The entrance fee is $10 per vehicle (motorcycles included) or $5 per person on foot or bike. Disturbing any wildlife or gathering items such as rocks or flowers is prohibited. Especially do not feed, chase, or disturb prairie dogs; they bite and may carry diseases. Abandoned prairie-dog holes are often homes to black widow spiders and rattlesnakes.

SEEING THE MONUMENT

It's easy to experience much of what Devils Tower has to offer in less than a day. Rangers recommend that you allow 2 to 4 hours to walk a trail, stop at the visitor center, and view the prairie dogs.

At Day's End

Visitors to Devils Tower should take the time to stay a night, if only to watch the drama that unfolds at dusk. Head to Joyner Ridge via Joyner Ridge Rd., about 2.5 miles up the main road from the park entrance, with a picnic dinner on a nice night and just gaze at the tower and watch the moon rise. It also offers a tremendous vantage point to photograph the tower. There are also occasional guided full moon hikes here in the summer; contact the park for details.

Surrounded by ponderosa pines and bathed in blue sky, the towering rock obelisk is visible for miles, and it's easy to imagine the reaction of the first lonely American-Indian scouts and French fur trappers who stumbled upon this stunning geologic anomaly a few centuries ago. The paved 1.3-mile round-trip **Tower Trail,** rated easy, goes all the way around the formation, offering close-up views of the tower on fairly level ground. Wayside exhibits tell the Devils Tower story. It connects to the 1.5-mile **Joyner Ridge Trail,** which has some wide-open grassland that makes for a sublime view of the tower.

Home to the feisty black-tailed **prairie dog,** the grounds of Devils Tower National Monument are perfect for picnicking and viewing wildlife. You can watch the sociable prairie dogs in their colony, or "town," just inside the park's east entrance station. The critters excavate elaborate networks of underground passageways, then guard their burrows with warning "barks" when predators such as hawks, eagles, bullsnakes, coyote, red fox, and mink come too close. Walk the leisurely .6-mile round-trip **Valley View Trail** to see a prairie-dog town, or savor a picnic lunch among the wildflowers at the monument's picnic area on the banks of the sleepy Belle Fourche River.

CLIMBING THE TOWER

Climbers have been wedging their fingers in the tower's cracks for more than a century, at a rate in recent years of about 5,000 climbers annually. (About one-third actually make it to the summit.) Climbers must register with a ranger before starting and upon their return; otherwise, there are no permits or requirements for climbing the tower. Be prepared for sudden storms; carry rain gear and a flashlight. Rockfall is common, so helmets are advised. Ask a ranger for additional safety and climbing information; the visitor center has a list of the guides permitted to lead climbs up the tower. We recommend Frank Sanders's **Above All Climbing Guides and Instruction** (© 888/314-5267; www.devilstowerclimbing.com), which specializes in working with novice climbers and has rates starting at $300 per day. Above All has a climbing gym on the monument boundary where its introductory packages begin and always has at least one guide for every two customers. *Note:* A voluntary climbing ban is observed each June out of respect for American-Indian religious ceremonies that are held on Devils Tower at that time.

WHERE TO STAY

Immediately outside of the monument's boundaries, climbing guru Frank Sanders runs the **Devils Tower Lodge,** P.O. Box 66, Devils Tower, WY 82714 (© **888/314-5267** or 307/467-5267; www.devilstowerlodge.com), an eclectic four-room bed-and-breakfast in

SHERIDAN & EASTERN WYOMING

15

DEVILS TOWER NATIONAL MONUMENT

Impressions

A dark mist lay over the Black Hills, and the land was like iron. At the top of the ridge I caught sight of Devils Tower upthrust against the gray sky as if in the birth of time the core of the earth had broken through its crust and the motion of the world was begun. There are things in nature that engender an awful quiet in the heart of man; Devils Tower is one of them.

—N. Scott Momaday, Pulitzer Prize–winning author of *House Made of Dawn*

the former superintendent's residence. The rooms all have private bathrooms; the facilities are geared toward climbers and the communal mood makes guests feel as if they're staying in a home instead of an inn. Rooms are $150 to $225 a night, full breakfast included. MasterCard and Visa are accepted. In Hulett, try the **Hulett Motel,** 202 Main St., Hulett, WY 82720 (© **307/467-5220;** www.hulettmotel.com). Double rates are $65 to $85 year-round; MasterCard and Visa are accepted. Rooms are clean and well maintained, and there's also a row of trim and tidy cabins on the Belle Fourche River.

CAMPING   Located a mile from the monument's headquarters, **Belle Fourche Campground** is open April through October and rarely fills up except for Sturgis (South Dakota) Motorcycle Rally time in August. Its 30 sites accommodate RVs (up to 35 ft. long) and tents on a first-come, first-served basis. Each campsite has a cooking grill, table, and nearby drinking water. There are no showers, RV hookups, or dump stations. Sites cost $12 per night, and there are three group sites, which cost $2 per person per night, with a six-person minimum. The adjacent Valley View Trail skirts a giant prairie-dog town, and the campground's amphitheater offers excellent ranger programs.

Those looking for a commercial campground with RV hookups and hot showers will find the **Devils Tower KOA,** P.O. Box 100, Devils Tower, WY 82714 (© **800/562-5785** or 307/467-5395; www.devilstowerkoa.com), just outside the monument entrance. Open from May through September, it offers 56 RV sites, 100 tent sites, 11 camping cabins (which share two bathhouses and other campground facilities), and a camping lodge. Rates for two adults are $25 to $80 in hookup sites, $20 to $60 for tents, $75 to $300 for the camping lodge, and $45 to $80 for cabins. Amenities include a heated outdoor pool, self-service laundry, free Wi-Fi, game room, cafe, two gift shops (featuring homemade fudge), horseback rides, hayrides, propane sales, and a nightly showing of *Close Encounters of the Third Kind* Memorial Day to Labor Day.

5 CASPER

153 miles S of Sheridan; 178 miles NW of Cheyenne; 300 miles S of Billings; 240 miles NW of Denver

Casper is a pleasant little city between the Great Plains and Rocky Mountains that owes much of its success to the oil and gas industry. Its first oil refinery was built in 1895, and though, like most boom towns Casper has had its share of ups and downs, the petroleum industry continues to help the economy keep rolling along. But what keeps many residents here, and what makes the community of interest to many visitors, is not what's under the ground but what is on the ground.

Casper has a small but fun ski area, and there is a lot of wildlife in the vicinity, including more than 75% of the world's pronghorn. Also look for mule and white-tailed deer, fox, and a variety of birds. The North Platte River, which meanders through the city, is a premier year-round trout fishery.

This is also an ideal spot to see the real history of the West. Casper stands at the crossroads of westward expansion, and in the ruts of the Oregon, Mormon, California, and Pony Express trails. Fur traders stopped here in 1812 on their way back East, building a hovel from rocks and buffalo hides, perhaps the first building constructed by non-Indians in Wyoming. Later, pioneers and Mormons crossed the North Platte River here. Then came the oil miners, and Casper boomed.

Today, Casper is the second-largest city in the state, with about 50,000 residents. It is also the former hometown of U.S. Vice President Dick Cheney.

ESSENTIALS

GETTING THERE Casper's **Natrona County International Airport,** 8500 Airport Pkwy. (*©* **307/472-6688;** www.iflycasper.com), 12 miles northwest of Casper on U.S. 20/26, has daily flights from **Allegiant** (*©* **702/505-8888**), **Delta** (*©* **800/221-1212**), **Northwest** (*©* **800/225-2525**), and **United** (*©* **800/864-8331**).

To reach Casper from **Sheridan,** drive 153 miles south on I-25. From **Cheyenne,** take I-25 north for 178 miles. From **Jackson,** take U.S. 191 to the Moran Junction, then drive 255 miles east on U.S. 26/287.

VISITOR INFORMATION Visit the **Casper Area Convention and Visitors Bureau,** 992 N. Poplar St., Casper, WY 82601 (*©* **800/852-1889** or 307/234-5362; www.casper wyoming.info).

GETTING AROUND Rent a car with **Avis** (*©* **800/230-4898**), **Budget** (*©* **800/527-0700**), or **Hertz** (*©* **800/654-3131**) at the airport. Need a cab? Call **RC Cab** (*©* **307/235-5203**).

SPECIAL EVENTS Casper draws its largest crowds during the 5-day **Central Wyoming Fair and Rodeo** (*©* **307/235-5775;** www.centralwyomingfair.com), which takes place each summer in early to mid-July. Call for details. On the third weekend of July each year, the **Beartrap Summer Festival** (*©* **307/266-5252;** www.beartrapsummer festival.com) takes place on top of Casper Mountain, with blues and bluegrass musicians plus the Wyoming Symphony Orchestra.

GETTING OUTSIDE

To escape the heat of the summer or ski a few runs in the winter, head up **Casper Mountain,** being sure to stop at the pullouts to take in the view of the plains stretching north toward the Bighorn Mountains. The mountain rises 8,000 feet above sea level, and there are campgrounds, hiking trails (try Garden Creek Falls), ski tracks, groomed snowmobile tracks, and mountain-biking trails. Another popular destination for outdoor recreation is **Muddy Mountain.** Much of the public land here is under the jurisdiction of the **Bureau of Land Management,** 2987 Prospector Dr. (*©* **307/261-7600**). The office has maps and other information available. At **Mountain Sports,** 543 S. Center St. (*©* **800/426-1136** or 307/266-1136), you'll find winter and summer outdoor equipment and plus rentals. The **Ugly Bug Fly Shop,** 240 S. Center St. (*©* **307/234-6905;** www.crazyrainbow.net), is a great angler's resource, with advice, gear, and guides ($350–$380 per day per boat).

There are some great hiking opportunities on Casper Mountain, including the **Lee McCune Braille Trail,** which enables visually impaired visitors to enjoy the beauty of Beartrap Meadow, with interpretive Braille markers describing the area's ecology. The Casper Area Convention and Visitors Bureau (see above) can provide you with maps detailing this and other hiking trails.

Edness Kimball Wilkins State Park (© 307/577-5150; wyoparks.state.wy.us) is a pleasant day-use park just 6 miles east of Casper off I-25, where you'll find huge old cottonwoods over the North Platte River. The park has hard-surfaced walking paths, a canoe- and raft-launch ramp, a swimming area, picnic tables, and a playground. There is also an accessible fishing pier, and excellent bird-watching opportunities for species including cormorants, yellow-billed cuckoos, golden and bald eagles, and numerous ducks. The park is open daily from 7am to 10pm; admission costs $6 per vehicle.

Skiing

A cheerful little ski area is a big plus in an area of sometimes howling winters, and Casper has a fine one in the **Hogadon Ski Area** ★ (© 307/235-8499; www.hogadon.net), situated atop Casper Mountain (drive south on Wyo. 258 from I-25 to Casper Mountain Rd.). It has a 600-foot vertical rise to a top elevation of 8,000 feet. Two double chairs and a Poma lift cover its 60 acres of groomed trails, and there are also on-site equipment rentals, a snack bar, and a ski and snowboarding school. Nearby, a county-owned cross-country ski area (© 307/237-8098) is groomed for skating and track skiing. The ski area generally opens around the first of December and closes sometime in April. Lift tickets are $40 for adults, $35 for students 13 to 18, and $25 for children 5 to 12. During ski season, Hogadon is open Wednesday through Sunday, plus holidays (except Christmas Day), from 9am to 4pm.

SEEING THE SIGHTS

Casper Planetarium This planetarium offers a multimedia jaunt into space, with changing programs ranging from a basic exploration of the night sky to trips through the solar system. There are also other astronomy-related programs, such as one on the possibility of life beyond earth, plus special kids' shows. The planetarium also offers telescope-user workshops, instruction on how to build your own rocket, and lectures. There are hands-on science displays and exhibits of meteorites and tektites, plus a gift shop.

904 N. Poplar Ave. © 307/577-0310. $2.50 per person per program. June–Aug showings daily at 4, 7, and 8pm; Sept–May Sat 7 or 8pm. Call for additional holiday programs.

Fort Caspar Museum and Historic Site Come to Fort Caspar for a look at what the "good old days" in these parts were really like. The first occupation of this site was in 1847 when Brigham Young and the Mormon Pioneer party constructed a ferry to cross the North Platte River. The post also served as a relay station for the Pony Express, and the transcontinental telegraph crossed the river here. The U.S. Army occupied the site in 1862, naming the post Platte Bridge Station. While attempting to reach an army supply train on July 26, 1865, members of the Sioux and Cheyenne tribes attacked Lt. Caspar W. Collins and troops from the fort. Collins and 26 other soldiers were killed during battles that day, and the fort was later renamed Fort Caspar to honor the lieutenant.

Today the site includes the reconstructed fort buildings furnished as they would have appeared in 1865—the mess hall, telegraph hall, officers' quarters, store, blacksmith shop, stables, commissary, and the like. Newly expanded in 2007, the museum features

Moments **Time Travel**

Historic Trails West, P.O. Box 428, Mills, WY 82644 (© **307/266-4868;** www.
historictrailswest.com), organizes trips that take you back in time as you rattle in
a wagon, or sway in the saddle, along the Oregon, California, Pony Express, and
Mormon trails. Trips range in length from 3 hours ($45 adults, $35 children 10
and under) to all day ($95 adults, $75 children 10 and under), which includes
lunch. Prices are slightly higher for those who opt to ride horses instead of sitting
in the wagons. There are also overnight and multiday wagon-train trips, with
5-day trips priced at $995 adults, $795 children 10 and under. Trips are scheduled
May through October.

exhibits on the social and natural history of central Wyoming. During the summer there
are living-history programs and lectures. Allow 1 or 2 hours.

4001 Fort Caspar Rd. © **307/235-8462.** www.fortcasparwyoming.com. $3 adults, $2 for students 13–18,
free for children 12 and under. June–Aug daily 8am–7pm; May and Sept Tues–Sat 8am–5pm. The
museum is open year-round, but the fort buildings are open May–Sept only.

National Historic Trails Interpretive Center ★★ This excellent facility opened
in Casper in 2002, using state-of-the-art exhibits to give modern travelers an idea of what
life on the "road" was like to the emigrants who passed through here in the mid-1800s
on the Oregon, Mormon, California, and Pony Express trails. A number of engaging
multimedia exhibits cover the pioneer story from the packing of the wagons to the fer-
rying of the rivers—the latter is demonstrated by a faux wagon that visitors ride across
the Platte River, simulated with motors and a movie. Be sure to take in the informative
18-minute film that tells the trails' history with real-life accounts of pioneers' journeys
before the railroad rendered the trails obsolete. The final "exhibit" is the trails themselves,
leaving from this spot and marked by BLM markers, for those that want to see a landscape that's changed little in the past 200 years. Allow 2 hours.

1501 N. Poplar St. © **307/261-7700.** www.blm.gov/wy/st/en/NHTIC.html. $6 adults, $5 seniors 60 and
over, $4 students 16 and over with valid student ID, free for children 15 and under. Late Apr to mid-Oct
daily 8am–7pm; mid-Oct to late Apr Tues–Sat 9am–4:30pm.

Nicolaysen Art Museum and Discovery Center This attractive facility presents
changing exhibitions of works by national and regional artists, with an emphasis on art
by Western artists or with a Rocky Mountain West theme. There are one large and six
small galleries, and three exhibitions take place simultaneously, for a total of a dozen
different shows each year. Works range from traditional Western to contemporary. The
Discovery Center is a hands-on self-guided studio with about a dozen stations, some
often related to the current exhibits, where participants of all ages can create their own
art. Allow 1 or 2 hours.

400 E. Collins Dr. © **307/235-5247.** www.thenic.org. $5 adults, $3 children 5–17, free for children 4 and
under. Tues–Sat 10am–5pm; Sun noon–4pm.

Tate Geological Museum You like rocks? If so, this is the place to come. You can
see a vast collection of Wyoming jade, a variety of minerals, and meteorites here. The Tate
also has a section on dinosaur excavations from the Natrona County area, including a

T. rex skull and the leg and skull of a brontosaurus. There's also an interactive computerized weather station, plus "please touch" exhibits of fossils and minerals.

125 College Dr. © **307/268-2447.** www.caspercollege.edu/tate. Free admission. Mon–Fri 9am–5pm; Sat 10am–4pm.

WHERE TO STAY

In addition to the lodging properties discussed below, reliable chains in Casper include the **Days Inn,** 301 E. E St., Casper, WY 82601 (© **800/329-7666** or 307/234-1159), with double rates of $89 to $99; and the attractive **Ramada Plaza–Riverside,** 300 W. F St., Casper, WY 82601 (© **800/272-6232** or 307/235-2531), with double rates of $89 to $119.

C'mon Inn ★ This impressive new hotel on the south side of town is my pick for a night in Casper. Modeled after the grand national park lodges, the C'mon Inn looks like no other chain property in town, and has a slick Western interior that nicely matches the wood exterior. The rooms have lots of exposed wood, river rock, and Western art, and are available in a number of different options, from basic doubles to grand suites. There is also a pair of kitchenettes. The best thing about the hotel is the central Jacuzzi Courtyard, with a pool, baby pool, five hot tubs, and faux waterfall.

301 E. Lathrop Rd., Evansville, WY 82636. © **866/782-2690** or 307/472-6300. www.cmoninn.com. 125 units, including 3 suites. $119–$149 double; $189–$249 suite. AE, DISC, MC, V. **Amenities:** Exercise room; 5 indoor Jacuzzis; indoor heated pool. *In room:* A/C, TV, kitchenette (some units), Wi-Fi (free).

Hotel Higgins ★ Built by area oil tycoon John Higgins in 1916, the Hotel Higgins is a small historic hotel—listed on the National Register of Historic Places—that is plain on the outside but beautiful within, and a wonderful place to soak up the post-Victorian ambience of the early-20th-century American West. It has mahogany and oak woodwork with distinctive decorative touches that include alabaster chandeliers, beveled glass doors, and terrazzo tile floors. Standard rooms are somewhat small by today's standards (as is the case in most historic hotels), decorated with antiques, including some original pieces from the hotel. The brass, iron, or massive wooden beds have attractive quilted bedspreads, and dressers are oak or walnut.

416 W. Birch St. (P.O. Box 577), Glenrock, WY 82637. © **800/458-0144** or 307/436-9212. www.higgins hotel.com. 9 units. $70–$80 double; $85–$95 suite. AE, DC, DISC, MC, V. From Casper, take I-25 south for 20 miles to the 1st Glenrock exit. **Amenities:** Restaurant; lounge. *In room:* TV, no phone, Wi-Fi (free).

WHERE TO DINE

In addition to the restaurants discussed below, you can get a good burger or traditional American breakfast at a reasonable price at **Johnny J's,** 1705 E. 2nd St. (© **307/234-4204**), a '50s-style diner open for three meals daily.

Bosco's Italian Restaurant ★ ITALIAN Other than cowboy cooking—translate that as beef, beef, and more beef—the only cuisine that seems to shine throughout Wyoming is Italian. This friendly little restaurant, owned and operated by Susan Bosco since 1974, is a standout. It serves excellent food, and stays open as long as the customers keep coming (usually about 10pm). The scampi is excellent, or you can create your own fettuccini dish from ingredients such as fresh vegetables, smoked salmon, and shrimp. The menu also includes veal, homemade ravioli, and gluten-free dishes for those with wheat allergies.

847 E. A St. © **307/265-9658.** Reservations recommended. Lunch $5–$10; dinner $10–$20. AE, DC, DISC, MC, V. Tues–Fri 11am–2pm and 5pm–close; Sat 5pm–close.

> ### (Fun Facts) Douglas: "The Jackalope Capital of the World"
>
> Douglas, about 50 miles east of Casper via I-25 S., is the self-proclaimed "jack-alope capital of the world," because, as the tall tale goes, pioneers first spotted the legendary critter near town in 1829. For the uninitiated, the mythical jacka-lope is a jack rabbit with a full rack of antlers growing between its ears, measur-ing about 4 feet at the shoulder. The city honors the beast with an 8-foot statue at the aptly named Jackalope Square (3rd and Center sts.) and an annual festival in May or June. Jackalope hunting licenses are even available from the **Douglas Area Chamber of Commerce,** but the season is limited to only 2 hours each year. For more information, contact the chamber at 121 Brownfield Rd., Douglas, WY 82633 (℮ **877/937-4996** or 307/358-2950; www.jackalope.org).

The Paisley Shawl ★ CONTINENTAL   This is the area's best fine-dining establish-ment. Located inside the historic Hotel Higgins, 20 miles east of Casper, the Paisley Shawl is the dining complement to a very good guest inn/restaurant combination. Specialties include filet mignon, roast duckling, jumbo shrimp done in a variety of preparations, and an apple-marinated pork tenderloin. Set inside the hotel's former ballroom—next to a fun little bar—the restaurant is expansive, with seating for 60.

In the Hotel Higgins, Glenrock. ℮ **800/458-0144** or 307/436-9212. www.higginshotel.com. Reservations recommended on weekends. Lunch $7–$10; dinner $20–$26. AE, DC, DISC, MC, V. Tues–Sat 11am–2pm and 6–9pm. From Casper, take I-25 south for 20 miles to the 1st Glenrock exit.

Wonder Bar AMERICAN   A Casper stalwart where drinkers once rode their horse to the bar, the Wonder Bar has reinvented itself as a slick, smoke-free microbrewery in recent years. Served under an amazing tin ceiling and inside walls clad with Western bric-a-brac, the menu includes half-pound burgers with all sorts of toppings as well as salads, sandwiches, pasta, seafood, and meatloaf. Skip the W.B.B.F.B.—a 5-pound burger that costs $22—in favor of some tasty fish tacos. The brewery makes five beers, including a stout and a wheat.

256 S. Center St. ℮ **307/234-4110.** www.thewonderbar.net. Reservations accepted. Main courses $6–$14. AE, DC, DISC, MC, V. Mon–Sat 11am–10pm. Bar open later (usually until midnight on weekdays and 2am on weekends).

15

6 FORT LARAMIE NATIONAL HISTORIC SITE

125 miles SE of Casper

On a hot day in 1834, mountain man William Sublette stopped his pack train laden with goods for the Green River rendezvous. Looking at the confluence of the Laramie and Platte rivers, then to the east, across the dusty plains, and then to the west, toward the mountains, he decided that this was a good place for a trading post. Over the next 15 years, the fort served as a hub of the buffalo trade, then as a way station for weary travel-ers who needed a break on their way to the Pacific.

In 1849—the year of the California gold rush—the U.S. Army bought the fort to "defend" the rising tide of immigrants from the "savages." The Indian Wars hadn't really started yet, not until 1854, when a lame Mormon-owned cow wandered off and was eaten by a starving Miniconjou. A young lieutenant marched into the tribe's camp and demanded that the cow-eater be turned over for swift justice; soon his troops opened fire on the village, and the wars had begun. Many battles later, the Indian tribes gathered here to negotiate the Treaty of 1868, which gave the Sioux and their allies the Powder River country and the Black Hills for "as long as the grass shall grow and the buffalo shall roam."

Soon thereafter, gold was discovered in the Black Hills, and the promise was broken. The army corralled the Indians onto reservations, the railroad replaced the wagon trails, and the beaver and the buffalo were exterminated; the fort closed down in 1890. It wasn't until 1938 that Franklin Roosevelt designated Fort Laramie a national historic site. In its time, travelers from Jim Bridger to Mark Twain stopped at the fort; today tourists ramble through many of the site's 22 original structures.

For an in-depth look at life at the fort, stop by the **visitor center** and watch the 18-minute video about the fort and its role in the settlement of the West. You'll see historical photos there, and a gift shop sells a wide selection of Western-themed books and gift items. Pick up a paper copy of the self-guided tour of the fort's historic buildings, or for $3 rent the audio tour, which not only tells the history of the fort but also brings it alive with the voices and sounds of the past.

Some of the more notable (and restored) buildings you'll see are the **cavalry barracks,** where dozens of soldiers slept, crowded into a single room; **Old Bedlam,** the post's headquarters, which later served as housing for officers, bachelors, and married couples; the **guardhouse,** a stone structure that housed the fort's prisoners; and the **bakery.** Living-history programs are conducted every summer, from June to mid-August, when rangers dress in period costumes, give talks, and answer visitors' questions.

Before leaving the fort, consider driving to the **Old Bedlam Ruts** (ask for a map from the visitor center), 2 miles northwest of the fort. The bumpy gravel road allows you to view the rutted trail marks left by the wagon trains of early Western settlers. Look for Laramie Peak and the grave of Mary Homsley, one of the many who died along the trail.

The grounds and buildings are open daily from sunrise to sunset. From mid-May to mid-September, the visitor center is open daily from 8am to 7pm, and daily from 8am to 4:30pm the rest of the year. Admission costs $3 for adults, free for those 16 and under. To get to the fort from Casper, take I-25 east past Douglas to U.S. 26 (exit 92), and head east to Wyo. 160, which you take southwest 3 miles to Fort Laramie. For more information, contact **Fort Laramie National Historic Site,** National Park Service, 965 Gray Rocks Rd., Fort Laramie, WY 82212 (✆ **307/837-2221;** www.nps.gov/fola).

Southern Wyoming

Southern Wyoming has long been less a destination than a land passed through. All of the famous transcontinental trails—the Bozeman, the California, the Emigrant, the Mormon, the Overland, and the Pony Express—lead somewhere else. Even today, if you stand on a hill just outside the state capital of Cheyenne, where two major interstates intersect, you'll see a cluster of mega–gas stations crowded with RVs, autos, and big-rig trucks, fueling up before speeding east or west.

In the middle of the 19th century, nearly a half-million people passed through Wyoming on the Oregon Trail. They paused at Independence Rock only long enough to rest and to carve their names in the stone (it's still there—west of Casper on Wyo. 220). This cross-state journey, which can now be done in less than a day, took a month in the 1840s. Along this route travelers left wagon tracks, cast-iron stoves, worn-out boots, crippled livestock, and their dead. It was no easy passage: On average, they dug 10 graves for every mile of trail.

By 1868, the railroad had forged across the plains, following the more southerly route of the Overland Stages. The arrival of the railroad brought shantytowns of gambling tents, saloons, and brothels, known as "Hell on Wheels." Left behind as the rails moved on, the makeshift towns collapsed, and a cycle of booms and busts began. New discoveries of coal, oil, gold, or uranium would spur a revival, followed by another bust.

Today that legacy colors the character of towns along I-80, which follows the same path used by the first transcontinental railroad. A new generation of miners dig coal and trona (a mineral used in cleaning agents) and keep the oil and natural gas flowing. Mineral money builds sparkling new schools and government buildings, but there is still a rough-and-ready quality to the downtown districts.

But unlike the old days, the communities now have a better grip on the landscape. **Cheyenne** is the state capital, home to thousands of government workers. The holdovers from the ranching families that once dominated the area come out in force every year for **Frontier Days,** a rodeo extravaganza known the world over. West over the pass in **Laramie,** the University of Wyoming is the state's cultural and intellectual nexus. From Laramie west, I-80 climbs around Elk Mountain and races across the high desert—an expansive (some might say bleak) view from behind the windshield, and a sometimes-harrowing drive during winter blizzards.

Cross-country travelers often miss the unexpected beauty in this land because they steadfastly stick to the interstate instead of the two-lane roads that lead to chalk buttes and rust-colored mesas. Take an offramp and head north among the stirring buttes of the Red Desert, read the ancient archaeological record at Fossil Butte, hike the mountain cirque of the Snowy Range, or dip in the clear waters of Flaming Gorge. On summer afternoons, the dry air turns humid, the sky blackens, and lightning dances on the red rims. When the sun breaks again, the cliffs burn copper.

I-80 runs the length of southern Wyoming along the same path followed by the first transcontinental railroad: straight, fast, convenient, but not often scenic. To the curious eye, though, there are interesting sights along the way.

Geology buffs will be interested in the road cuts made by the interstate—eons of geologic history are revealed. Historians will appreciate the remnants left more than a century ago: Take exit 272, 41 miles west of Laramie, and visit **Little Arlington,** where you'll find what's left of an old stage station and a log cabin, back in the trees. Here along the interstate you'll also see one of Wyoming's latest contributions to the nation's energy pool: a wind farm of spinning propellers lining the ridges like an infantry on stilts.

But to break the monotony of the long drive across southern Wyoming, you need to take a loop off the interstate. There's plenty of great scenery out there, including the landscapes you'll see on the following trips. Many of the sights mentioned here are discussed in further detail later in this chapter.

DRIVING TOUR 1: THE SNOWY RANGE SCENIC BYWAY: LARAMIE TO SARATOGA

The **Snowy Range Road** (Wyo. 130), designated the nation's second scenic byway, twists up and over the Medicine Bow Mountains south of I-80 and west of Laramie, through corridors of pines and between snow banks (even in midsummer), and tops Snowy Range Pass at 10,847 feet. During the winter, heavy snows block the pass, but you can reach a ski area (both Alpine and Nordic) on the Laramie side, 6 miles past Centennial.

To reach the Snowy Range Scenic Byway from Laramie, take exit 311 off I-80 and head west along Snowy Range Road. Once past the little town of Centennial, the road switchbacks uphill at a steep grade. As you top the pass, you'll see sharp granite peaks to the north, often skirted by snow, bordering a group of snowmelt-fed lakes. This is the top of the range, with elevations more than 12,000 feet above sea level. On a summer day you'll have plenty of company at the turnouts—people stopping to look, to fish, to hike a nature trail, to picnic. Half a day of vigorous hiking (if you're adjusted to the altitude) will get you atop Medicine Bow Peak, the highest summit in the range. The road then descends the east side of the range, following French Creek to the **Upper North Platte River** (known as the Miracle Mile), which is popular with anglers. When you come to a T in the road, turn right on Wyo. 130 and drive 8 miles north to **Saratoga,** a friendly little town where many boats are launched to fish the excellent waters of the Platte. Continue north from here to rejoin I-80 at Walcott.

FINISH THE LOOP: A DIFFERENT WAY BACK TO LARAMIE You can return on I-80 to Laramie, or take a more adventurous route by going north from Walcott on U.S. 30/287 toward Medicine Bow. This road follows the rail line and, as such, bypasses the mountains—in the winter, it's often a better route than the interstate. The landscape is sagebrush plains and hills, where antelope roam. Every 20 miles or so, you'll hit a crumbling town. One community with a little life still left in it is **Medicine Bow,** location of the Virginian Hotel (another model for Owen Wister's *The Virginian*) and of a watering hole with character, the Diplodocus Bar. Take a look at the bar itself—a solid slab of Wyoming jade, 40 feet long. Some of the great historic dinosaur discoveries were made in this area, at nearby Como Bluff. Continue east to finish the loop in Laramie.

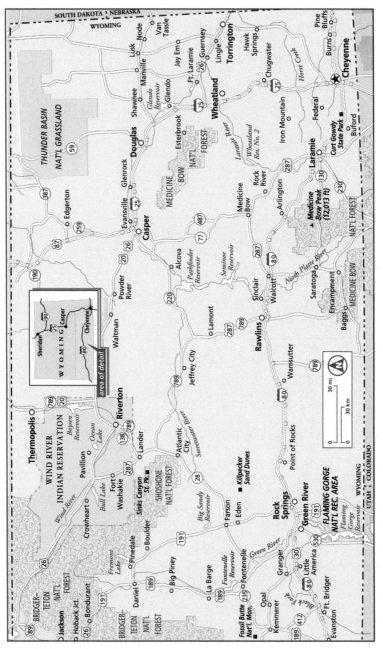

This scenic drive goes from Laramie to the town of Baggs along Wyo. 230 and a recently completed stretch of Wyo. 70. **Wyo. 230** (also known as "the Rivers Rd.") winds its way southwest from Laramie along the Laramie River to the town of **Mountain Home,** where the road dips south into Colorado. Here it makes a loop along Colo. 127/125 for 18 miles and reenters the state of Wyoming on the other side of the Medicine Bow Mountains. The route then continues northwest along Wyo. 230 to the old logging town of Encampment. This last portion offers beautiful river scenery with aspen and lodgepole pines, and opportunities for trout fishing. From Encampment, take Wyo. 70 west to Baggs across 58 miles of Carbon County land in the Sierra Madre Mountain Range. Because of the altitude, views can stretch for miles around this virtually uninhabited belt of southern Wyoming. But the altitude also causes road closures in the winter. Wyo. 70 climbs to 9,955 feet to Battle Pass, named for a nearby conflict that took place in 1841. Here it crosses the Continental Divide before descending to the small towns of **Savery, Dixon,** and **Baggs,** a trio of hamlets with a combined population of fewer than 500. Early settlers came to the area in search of gold and silver. The history of Baggs also includes a different kind of business: Outlaw Butch Cassidy pulled off several robberies here, and quick-triggered livestock detective Tom Horn frequented the area during the late 1800s.

At Baggs, turn north off Wyo. 70 onto Wyo. 789, then drive north for 51 miles through high-plains ranching country. At Creston Junction, you'll rejoin I-80. From here, you can either drive west to Rock Springs and the Utah border or return east to Laramie. You won't have traveled as far as you think, but you'll have seen a lot more along this route than you would have staring at the back of an 18-wheeler along the interstate.

---

2 CHEYENNE

93 miles N of Denver; 180 miles S of Casper

Cheyenne is located in the southeast corner of the state. Legend has it that when Gen. Grenville M. Dodge's surveying crew trudged across the prairie, picking a route for the transcontinental railroad, night came, they were tired, they stopped and said, "Good as any," and thus was born the present site of Cheyenne.

By horse or by highway, you can't miss Cheyenne, not only the largest city in Wyoming (population: 56,000) but also its capital. Visitors enjoy the many historical and political sights, from the **Capitol Building** to the **Historic Governors' Mansion.** But Cheyenne's biggest event, hands down, is that wild and woolly weeklong cowboy extravaganza, **Cheyenne Frontier Days.**

ESSENTIALS

GETTING THERE **Great Lakes Aviation** (© 800/554-5111; www.greatlakesav.com) flies daily into the **Cheyenne Regional Airport** (© 307/634-7071; www.cheyenneairport.com) on East 8th Avenue, but most people choose to fly directly in and out of **Denver International Airport** (© 800/247-2336; www.flydenver.com), 101 miles south of Cheyenne in Colorado on I-25, and rent a car to drive into Wyoming from there.

By bus, you can get here with **Greyhound** (© 800/554-5111; www.greyhound.com). The **bus depot** (© 307/635-1327) is at 5401 Walker Rd.

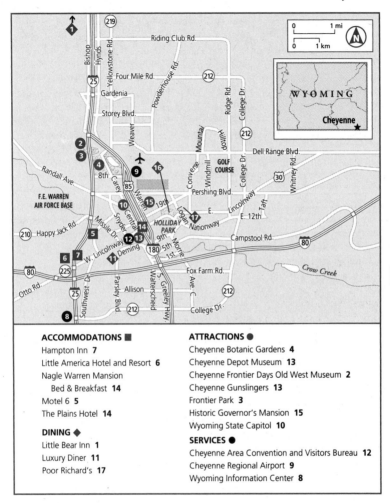

ACCOMMODATIONS ■
Hampton Inn **7**
Little America Hotel and Resort **6**
Nagle Warren Mansion
  Bed & Breakfast **14**
Motel 6 **5**
The Plains Hotel **14**

DINING ◆
Little Bear Inn **1**
Luxury Diner **11**
Poor Richard's **17**

ATTRACTIONS ●
Cheyenne Botanic Gardens **4**
Cheyenne Depot Museum **13**
Cheyenne Frontier Days Old West Museum **2**
Cheyenne Gunslingers **13**
Frontier Park **3**
Historic Governor's Mansion **15**
Wyoming State Capitol **10**

SERVICES ●
Cheyenne Area Convention and Visitors Bureau **12**
Cheyenne Regional Airport **9**
Wyoming Information Center **8**

SOUTHERN WYOMING

16

CHEYENNE

To get to Cheyenne from **Casper,** take I-25 south for 180 miles. From **Rock Springs** in the southwest part of the state, take I-80 east for 258 miles.

VISITOR INFORMATION The **Cheyenne Area Convention and Visitors Bureau** in the lovingly restored Cheyenne Depot, 1 Depot Square, 121 W. 15th St., Ste. 200 (© **800/ 426-5009** outside Wyoming, or 307/778-3133; www.cheyenne.org), has a variety of brochures and local maps, including the "Cheyenne Historic Downtown Walking Tour" and the "Downtown Cheyenne Map." Just outside of town, you can also get information at the **Wyoming Information Center,** operated by the Wyoming Division of Tourism, located just off I-25 at College Drive.

GETTING AROUND   Avis (© 800/230-4898) and Hertz (© 800/654-3131) have airport counters. For a taxi, call **Capital City Cab** (© 307/632-8294). Expect to pay about $10 for a ride from the airport to downtown.

CHEYENNE FRONTIER DAYS ★★

In the world of rodeo, there are three must-see classics: the Pendleton Round-up, the Calgary Stampede, and the "Daddy of 'em All," Cheyenne Frontier Days. Since the inaugural event in 1897, it has grown into one of the largest rodeos in the world. The Frontier Days committee and thousands of volunteers organize this 10-day-long Western spectacle of parades, a rodeo, dances, and concerts each summer, the last full week of July. It's safe to say that this is the most vivid demonstration of Western hospitality you'll encounter in the modern world.

Though the rodeo lasts for a full 10 days, picking and choosing activities carefully can save you a lot of time and money. Rodeo ticket prices range anywhere from around $12 to $40 per person, and nightly shows featuring popular country music acts cost $20 to $60.

VISITOR INFORMATION   Contact the **Cheyenne Frontier Days Ticket Office** for brochures, ticket forms, and information on all shows and activities during upcoming Frontier Days celebrations at Cheyenne Frontier Days, P.O. Box 2477, Cheyenne, WY 82003 (© 800/227-6336 or 307/778-7222; www.cfdrodeo.com).

GETTING AROUND DURING THE RODEO CELEBRATION   Parking is provided at Frontier Park for $10 per vehicle, but shuttle parking is also available and makes much more sense. The shuttle picks up visitors at several locations and delivers them to the rodeo grounds; round-trip fare is $6 per carload. The city also runs a special bus service to Frontier Park from downtown Cheyenne that stops at nearby campgrounds and hotels. Contact the **Cheyenne Area Convention and Visitors Bureau** (© 307/778-3133) for bus stop locations and scheduled pickups.

The Grand Parade   With the exception of Buffalo Bill's walk through the streets of Cheyenne in 1898 and a docile march led by Theodore Roosevelt in 1910, Cheyenne's Frontier Days Grand Parade in its early days was similar to a stagecoach holdup. Guns blazed as cowboys rode through the streets with little regard to form or style. In 1925, things took a turn toward civility when the "Evolution of Transportation" theme was introduced. Today, many horse-drawn vehicles make their way through the streets of Cheyenne as part of the Old-Time Carriage section of the parade. In addition to the carriages and antique cars, marching bands, local clubs, and various Plains Indians groups march. Viewing sites are as near as the closest curb, but you'll want to claim a position 45 minutes before the start.

The parade starts at Capitol Ave. and 24th St., runs down Capitol Ave. to 17th Ave., and continues up Carey Ave. to the finish at Carey Ave. and 24th St. Free admission. During Frontier Days, Sat, Tues, and Thurs, starting at 9:30am.

The Rodeo   An anthropologist might see rodeo as a fading ritual to a passing way of life, but don't tell that to the fans who pack the stands at Frontier Days. It's actually one of the most popular spectator sports in the nation, as American as apple pie and baseball. Cheyenne's annual rodeo draws people from across the nation, and the best of the best cowboys.

Spectators from around the world pack into the stands to watch such events as steer wrestling, barrel racing, team roping, and the classic event—and Wyoming's state symbol—saddle bronc riding. It's enormous fun, but part of the attraction is that these men

and women put themselves in harm's way, working enormous animals with a wild streak.
In a world where risk is often an illusion created by entertainers, this is the real thing. Champion bull-rider Lane Frost died in the ring at Frontier Days in 1989.

Daily ticket prices start at $12 for bleachers at the far end of the arena; $16 for seats closer to the roping gates; and $24 for the center of the action—the bucking chutes. Bull riding tickets cost more, from $29 to $39. Each night after the rodeo, country stars take the stage. Concert tickets run $20 to $60.

Frontier Park, exit 12 off I-80. ✆ **800/227-6336** or 307/778-7222. Tickets $12–$24. During Frontier Days, daily at 12:45pm.

The Pancake Breakfast   Since their inception in 1952, these free breakfasts have become increasingly popular. Legend holds that a cement mixer churns up enough pancake batter to cook 100,000 flapjacks for 30,000 people. The breakfasts are held downtown at the Cheyenne Depot Plaza on the corner of Lincolnway and Capitol and served by the local Kiwanis Club, including, sometimes, an unassuming governor.

Depot Plaza, Lincolnway and Capitol. Free admission. During Frontier Days, Mon, Wed, and Fri 7–9am.

SHOPPING

The can't-miss retailers in Cheyenne are **Sierra Trading Post,** 5025 Campstool Rd. (✆ **307/775-8090**), for outdoor gear and close-outs of all kinds; the **Wrangler,** 1518 Capitol Ave. (✆ **307/634-3048**), for cowboy boots and Western duds; and **Wyoming Home,** 210 W. Lincolnway (✆ **307/638-2222**), for Western furnishings and decor.

SEEING THE SIGHTS

Stop in at the **Nelson Museum of the West,** 1714 Carey Ave. (✆ **307/635-7670;** www.nelsonmuseum.com), to see a collection of cowboy trappings, American-Indian artifacts, taxidermy trophies, and Western memorabilia. The **Cheyenne Botanic Gardens,** 710 S. Lions Park Dr. (✆ **307/637-6458;** www.botanic.org), is a showcase of lush flower beds.

Cheyenne Depot Museum ★   This good museum details Cheyenne's beginnings as a dusty railroad town and tells the story of how rails shaped this part of the West. Exhibits include fascinating historical photographs, models, and the original cargo scales used when the depot was active (late 1800s–1980s). The Union Pacific Depot was restored to its original condition and is worth visiting even if you're not a railroad buff—but if you are, start here and then pick up the brochure "Tracking Trains in Cheyenne" from the information center in the depot lobby: It's a great resource for trainiacs, covering historic rail landmarks and the best places to gawk at the real thing. There are occasional excursions on a historic steam train; call for the current schedule.

121 W. 15th St., in the Union Pacific Depot. ✆ **307/632-3905.** www.cheyennedepotmuseum.org. $5 adults, free for children 11 and under. Mon–Fri 9am–6pm; Sat 9am–5pm; Sun 11am–5pm.

Cheyenne Frontier Days Old West Museum   Frontier Days has been around long enough that folks have become interested in its history, so sponsors established this museum to warehouse memorabilia from the rodeo and other historical artifacts. The Old West Museum, located next door to the rodeo arena, is a convenient place to take a break from the action. There are carriages, temporary exhibits, photos, a video-screening room, and a treasure-trove of rodeo gear.

4610 N. Carey Ave., Frontier Park. ✆ **307/778-7290.** www.oldwestmuseum.org. $7 adults, free for children 12 and under. Mon–Fri 9am–5pm; Sat–Sun 10am–5pm; longer hours during Frontier Days and peak summer season.

Cheyenne Gunslingers (Kids) June through July, this nonprofit Cheyenne group puts on an Old West shootout downtown in "Gunslinger Square." You'll recognize it by the stage set of an Old West saloon, jail, and gallows. The volunteer actors love to ham it up. Their shows include jailbreaks, near-hangings, and shootouts—starring corrupt judges, wily villains, and white-hatted good guys. It's not necessarily the most accurate portrayal of the Old West (and it's not intended to be), but it is great entertainment for the family.

Gunslinger Sq., Lincolnway and Carey. ✆ **800/426-0059** or 307/778-3133. Free admission. June–July daily at 6pm; Sat at noon.

Cheyenne Street Railway Trolley No longer used as a mode of mass transit, the local trolley offers visitors a ride around Cheyenne's main tourist sites, including the Governors' Mansion, the Wyoming State Capitol, and the historic homes of the area's late-19th-century cattle barons.

Purchase tickets at the Cheyenne Area Convention and Visitors Bureau in the Cheyenne Depot, 121 W. 15th St. ✆ **800/426-5009** or 307/778-3133. Tour $10 adults, $5 children 4–12, free for kids 3 and under. May to mid-Sept 2-hr. tours Mon–Fri 10 and 11:30am, and 1, 2:30, and 4pm; Sat 10am and 1:30pm; Sun 1:30pm.

Historic Governors' Mansion If you're interested in the political history of the state, you should continue 6 blocks from the capitol to the Historic Governors' Mansion. Built in 1904, it housed Wyoming's first families until 1976; today, many of the rooms have been restored to their 1905 appearances. Over the years, the decorative styles mixed, and you'll find everything from Chippendale to Colonial Revival to Art Nouveau. There's even a steer-horn chair in the entrance hall.

300 E. 21st St. ✆ **307/777-7878.** Free admission. Summer Mon–Sat 9am–5pm, Sun 1–5pm; winter Wed–Sat 9am–5pm.

Wyoming State Capitol In the summer, when the streets of Cheyenne are shaded by large old oaks, it's easy to come upon the capitol building a bit by surprise. It's not a large capitol, as such things go, but it's a traditional one, with a gold-leaf dome and carved stone. The main structure was built in 1888; the wings were added in 1917, but otherwise, the stately building has undergone little change over the years. Inside you can admire the beautiful woodwork, stained glass, and sparkling marble floors, and view historical photos and exhibits on the state's wildlife. Outside, you can stop by three statues: a monument to the first female justice of the peace, Esther Hobart Morris; a bronze bison; and the *Spirit of Wyoming*—the wild bucking horse emblazoned on every license plate in the state.

Capitol Ave. at 24th St. ✆ **307/777-7220.** Free admission. Self-guided tours Mon–Fri 8:30am–4:30pm, except holidays. Guided tours available by appointment.

WHERE TO STAY

Thanks to its crossroads location, there's a plethora of accommodations in Cheyenne, from basic motels to ornate B&Bs. The chain properties include **Hampton Inn,** adjacent to the junction of I-25 and I-80 at 1781 Fleischi Pkwy. (✆ **307/632-2747**), offering double rates of $119 to $159 ($199 and up during Frontier Days); and **Motel 6,** 1735 Westland Rd. (✆ **800/466-8356** or 307/635-6806), with double rates of $44 to $62 ($110–$120 during Frontier Days).

A reservation caution: Hotels fill up quickly during Frontier Days, and rack (published) rates are much higher.

Little America Hotel and Resort ★   Renovated and expanded into a full-fledged convention center in 2007, this is one of the largest hotels in Wyoming and a noteworthy oasis. The main building and low-rise brick lodges are surrounded by an executive golf course, duck pond, and mature evergreens. The main building harbors a tasteful lounge warmed by a fireplace and Navajo rugs; shops offer boutique clothing, jewelry, and Western souvenirs; there's a stuffed penguin, the hotel's unofficial mascot, in the hall. Accommodations, in four low-rise brick lodges, provide 31-inch TVs, balconies, and bathrooms with tub/shower combos and marble counters. Rooms come in three categories: standards, minisuites with king-size beds, and executive suites. Meals are available in the coffee shop, open from 5am to 1am with very modest prices. The Olympic-size pool is open summer only, but a fitness center and jogging path can be used year-round.

2800 W. Lincolnway (I-80 at I-25), Cheyenne, WY 82009. © **800/445-6945** or 307/775-8400. Fax 307/775-8425. www.cheyenne.littleamerica.com. 188 units. $109–$259 double; during Frontier Days $149–$299 double. AE, DC, DISC, MC, V. **Amenities:** 2 restaurants; lounge; exercise room; outdoor heated pool. *In room:* A/C, TV, fridge, hair dryer, Wi-Fi (free).

Nagle Warren Mansion Bed & Breakfast ★★   This gem of an inn is the centerpiece of an increasingly nice stretch on 17th Avenue. Originally built in 1888 by famed architect Erasmus Nagle (it was the first house in the state with indoor plumbing), the mansion was converted into an elegant bed-and-breakfast in 1997. Grand and spacious, the three-story structure oozes luxury, from the furnishings (almost exclusively regional antiques) to the stately spire that anchors the building's southeast corner. The rooms, named after the mansion's former residents, feature lavish, late-19th-century style, tempered by a few modern perks—CD players, televisions, and modem-ready phones. Half of the rooms are located in the main building, and half are in the adjoining carriage house (the latter have fireplaces), but they all have their own unique allure.

222 E. 17th St., Cheyenne, WY 82001. © **800/811-2610** or 307/637-3333. www.naglewarrenmansion.com. 12 units. $142–$172 double; during Frontier Days $294–$324 double. Rates include full breakfast. AE, DC, MC, V. Pets accepted. **Amenities:** Lounge; exercise room. *In room:* A/C, TV/VCR, hair dryer, Wi-Fi (free).

The Plains Hotel ★   Built in 1911, the stalwart Plains Hotel went through a long period of decline before enjoying a complete overhaul that was finished in 2003, giving its rooms, lobby, and restaurant a much-needed face-lift in the process. Under a stained-glass ceiling, the lobby is a multipillared space with its original tile floor and a retouched mural on the walls ringing the ceiling. Rooms run the gamut from standard (with a king-size bed or one or two queen-size) to larger parlor suites (a king-size or two queen-size) to true two-room suites, one of which is done up in high cowboy style thanks to the help of *American Cowboy* magazine. The rooms on the whole are comfortable and attractive, with a subtle Western motif, with bathrooms that vary in terms of amenities and quality—some are a bit old, some have showers only, and others feature the vanities in the rooms. The elevators are also quite dinky: As the story goes, they built them that way so people couldn't take their horses up to their rooms.

1600 Central Ave., Cheyenne, WY 82001. © **866/275-2467** or 307/638-3311. Fax 307/635-2022. www.theplainshotel.com. 131 units, including 17 suites. $89–$139 double, $219 suite; during Frontier Days $169–$239 double, $339 suite. AE, DC, DISC, MC, V. **Amenities:** Restaurant; lounge; exercise room. *In room:* TV, hair dryer, Wi-Fi (free).

Camping

The biggest campground is the **Restway Travel Park,** 4212 Whitney Rd., 2 miles east of Cheyenne (© **800/443-2751** or 307/634-3811). Catering to RV and tent campers alike,

Restway boasts a heated seasonal swimming pool, miniature golf, and a store stocked with basic supplies; nightly rates run from about $18 for a basic tent site to about $35 for a site with full hookups during Frontier Days. For something a bit different, head to **Terry Bison Ranch,** located 6 miles south of Cheyenne via I-25, exit 2 (© **307/634-4171;** www.terrybisonranch.com), a working buffalo ranch with tent ($18 per night) and RV sites ($19–$32 per night), as well as a bunkhouse, guest cabins, gift shop, and restaurant. The ranch also offers cabins, lodge rooms, and a variety of tours.

WHERE TO DINE

Little Bear Inn STEAKS/SEAFOOD   A Cheyenne-area stalwart since 1958, the Little Bear's story actually begins in the 1870s. The original Little Bear was a way station (read: saloon and casino—the proprietor figured that people wouldn't come all that way just for the food) for travelers, traders, and outlaws right up until it closed in the 1950s when the county sheriff came down on gambling. In less than a decade, the new one opened about 20 miles closer to town than the original, and has been a Cheyenne institution ever since, serving up quality steaks and seafood in a fun roadhouse atmosphere, featuring plenty of taxidermy (including a not-so-little grizzly bear). For the adventurous, the menu includes frog legs and Rocky Mountain oysters (deep-fried bull testicles), as well as a creative array of steaks that includes buffalo, filet mignon, and a New York strip.

700 Little Bear Rd. (near I-25, exit 16). © **307/634-3684.** www.littlebearinn.com. Main courses $15–$29. AE, DISC, MC, V. Sun and Tues–Thurs 5–9pm; Fri–Sat 5–10pm. Closed Mon.

Luxury Diner Finds AMERICAN   A favorite blue-collar breakfast counter, the Luxury Diner is a real down-home greasy spoon. We say that affectionately, of course; the food is good, the coffee always hot, and the waitresses sassy. Breakfast is served all day. The pie: apple. The special: meatloaf. It's the real thing—no Buddy Holly posters, no 45s dangling from the ceiling for that retro look. In fact, the small dining area ran as a trolley from 1896 to 1912 before becoming a diner in 1926. Pictures of trains cover the walls, Christmas lights blink around the trim, and the menu says, "Friendliest place in town." It's right.

1401-A W. Lincolnway. © **307/638-8971.** Breakfast and lunch main courses $3–$11. AE, DC, DISC, MC, V. Daily 6am–4pm.

Poor Richard's ★★ STEAKS/AMERICAN   The locals' choice for a nice dinner, Poor Richard's has been serving excellent steaks, seafood, chicken, and pasta dishes since opening its doors in 1977. I recommend the blackened prime rib, but all steaks are USDA Choice Beef, aged for 4 weeks and cut fresh daily. Lunches are lighter, but include several pasta and seafood dishes beyond the sandwiches and burgers that dominate other Cheyenne eateries. The staff is efficient and sharp, working several rooms that feature stained glass, wood-backed booths, and an ambience midway between romantic and casual. This winning combination—plus the subtle Benjamin Franklin motif—attracts everyone from politicians to ranch hands.

2231 E. Lincolnway. © **307/635-5114.** www.poorrichardscheyenne.com. Reservations accepted for parties of 6 or more only. Lunch $8–$13; dinner $13–$27. AE, DISC, MC, V. Mon–Sat 11am–2:30pm; Mon–Thurs 5–9pm; Fri–Sat 5–10pm.

CHEYENNE AFTER DARK

The **Atlas Theatre,** 211 W. Lincolnway (© **307/635-0199**), is Cheyenne's prime performing arts venue. The hippest watering hole in town is **Shadows Brewing Company,** 115 W. 15th St., in the Union Pacific Depot (© **307/634-7625**), a sports bar/microbrewery that serves good barbecue and other pub fare. Free **concerts** are staged in front of the depot on summer Friday evenings. **Bit-O-Wyo Ranch** puts on a barn dinner show on summer weekends about 20 miles west of Cheyenne at 470 Happy Jack Rd. (© **307/638-6924;** www.bitowyoranch.com); the price is $40 per person ages 6 and over.

3 LARAMIE ★

49 miles NW of Cheyenne; 360 miles SE of Yellowstone/Grand Teton; 207 miles E of Rock Springs; 124 miles N of Denver

Though the political capital is 49 miles to the east, Laramie is the cultural and intellectual capital of Wyoming. It's home to the state's only university, public or private. Unlike Jackson, which has a prefabricated feel designed to appeal to visitors, Laramie has an earnest charm that seems to have developed by accident, and it has been this way for nearly a century. Located just east of the beautiful Medicine Bow Mountains, at an altitude of more than 7,000 feet, Laramie is sometimes buffeted by chill winds. But it has university-town amenities like bookstores and coffee shops, and a few Western features to boot, including outlying ranchlands and some rowdy downtown bars.

ESSENTIALS

GETTING THERE   The **Laramie Regional Airport** (© 307/742-4164; www.laramie airport.com), west of town along Wyo. 130, services daily flights on **Great Lakes Aviation** (© 800/554-5111) from Denver.

Or go **Greyhound** (© 800/231-2222), which stops in Laramie at a bus depot/convenience store at 1300 S. 3rd St. (© 307/742-5188). The bus stops at several Wyoming cities along I-80, including Rock Springs and Cheyenne.

Laramie is an easy 49-mile drive from Cheyenne on I-80; driving from Salt Lake, it's just more than 300 miles once you hit Evanston. The fastest route from the Yellowstone–Grand Teton area is via U.S. 287 S. for 259 miles to Rawlins and I-80 east for 101 miles to Laramie.

VISITOR INFORMATION   Contact the **Albany County Tourism Board,** 210 Custer St., Laramie, WY 82070 (© 800/445-5303; www.laramie-tourism.org), or the **Laramie Area Chamber of Commerce** (© 307/745-7339; www.laramie.org).

GETTING AROUND   Hertz (© 800/654-3131) and **Enterprise** (© 800/261-7331) maintain outlets in Laramie.

SPECIAL EVENTS   **Jubilee Days** (© 307/760-9920; www.laramiejubileedays.com) is a Western party that runs early to mid-July with rodeos, parades, and fireworks.

GETTING OUTSIDE

Curt Gowdy State Park (© 307/632-7946; http://wyoparks.state.wy.us) named for the television sportscaster who hailed from Wyoming, is quite pleasant, if not spectacularly beautiful. Located 23 miles southeast of Laramie, the 1,645-acre park is a great spot for a picnic ($6 day-use fee). Or stay the night in one of the five campsites for $17 per night. There are two lakes here, but no swimming is allowed (they provide part of Cheyenne's water supply). Boating is permitted, but no rentals are available at the park. Call for further information. To get to the park, take I-80 east until you see the exit for Wyo. 210, the scenic back road to Cheyenne.

About 10 miles southeast of Laramie, on the edge of the Medicine Bow National Forest, are **Pole Mountain** and the **Vedauwoo Recreation Area** (© **307/745-2300**). Vedauwoo and the Happy Jack trail head near the Summit exit of I-80 have some excellent summer and winter recreational opportunities. The name Vedauwoo (pronounced *Vee*-duh-voo) is Arapaho for "earth-born." The rock formations—soft-edged blocks shaped like stools, turtles, and mushrooms—were considered the sacred creations of animal and human spirits, and young Indian men sought visions there. Today rock climbers pursue their quests for challenging climbs here, and find tough technical pitches. Other folks see a great place to mountain bike, hike, and scan the vistas. There is a campground with sites for $10 per night. To get there, take I-80 east toward Cheyenne, past the second-biggest Abe Lincoln head in these parts (10 miles outside town) to exit 329, to the Vedauwoo turnoff.

SEEING THE SIGHTS

The **Laramie Plains Museum,** 603 Ivinson Ave. (© **307/742-4448;** www.laramie museum.org), is housed in a gorgeous three-story Queen Anne Victorian home built by Laramie settler Edward Ivinson, with furnishings from the 1890s. Admission is $10 adults, $7 seniors, and $5 students (free for kids 5 and under). The **Wyoming Children's Museum and Nature Center,** 968 N. 9th St. (© **307/745-6332**), has enough things to keep kids busy, including a frontier general store where children can handle items and do face painting. Admission is $3 children 4 to 12 ($1 for those 3 and under) and $2 adults.

University of Wyoming   The only 4-year college in the state, the University of Wyoming was established in 1887 with the funding of Old Main, its first building. At that time, there were five professors, two tutors, and 42 students on the 20-acre campus, which included Prexy's Pasture, where the school's first president kept his cows. Today, the University of Wyoming has more than 2,000 faculty and staff members and an enrollment of about 13,000. The university has boomed along with oil and gas prices and the coal-bed methane market, with the legislature loosening the purse strings in recent sessions.

A campus tour is worth the effort, if for no other reason than to check out the campus architecture, which ranges from the solid sandstone castles of a century ago to the spaceship designs of today (stop at the **Visitors Services Center,** 1408 Ivinson Ave., for a map). To catch a glimpse of student life in Laramie, swing by Prexy's Pasture.

With no pro sports teams in Wyoming, the college's athletic programs take on special importance. Fans drive from all over the state to root for the **Cowboys** as they compete against Mountain West Conference foes. For event information and tickets, contact the ticket office (© **800/922-9461** or 307/766-4850; www.wyomingathletics.com).

The university plays an important role with its museum spaces, and most of the exhibits are free. Located in the Knight Geology Building, in the northwest corner of Prexy's Pasture, the **Geological Museum** (© **307/766-2646;** www.uwyo.edu/geomuseum) has plenty of dinosaur fossils as well as some from mammoth, camels, and other extinct Wyoming denizens, not to mention a life-size T. rex statue out front. It's open Tuesday through Friday from 1 to 4pm, Saturday from 10am to 2pm, and Sunday from noon to 4pm. Also worth visiting is the **Rocky Mountain Herbarium** (© **307/766-2236;** www.rmh.uwyo.edu), open Monday through Friday from 8am to 5pm (7:30am–4:30pm when school is out of session). The **Insect Gallery** (© **307/766-2298;** in the Ag Building, just north of Prexy's Pasture) is primarily a research facility and a bit esoteric to the average visitor; call for current hours. The **Centennial Complex** (on the east side of campus, east of 15th St.) houses the **UW Art Museum** (© **307/766-6622;** www.uwyo.edu/ArtMuseum), with works by Audubon, Charles Russell, Thomas Moran, and even

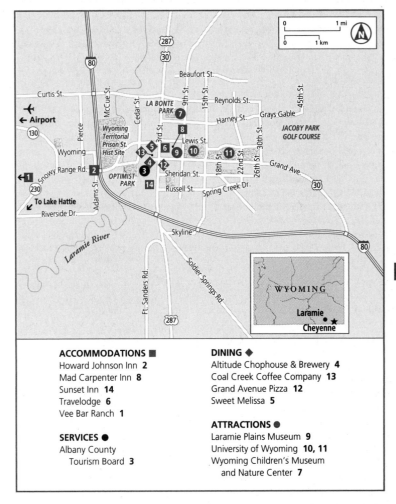

ACCOMMODATIONS ■
Howard Johnson Inn **2**
Mad Carpenter Inn **8**
Sunset Inn **14**
Travelodge **6**
Vee Bar Ranch **1**

SERVICES ●
Albany County
   Tourism Board **3**

DINING ◆
Altitude Chophouse & Brewery **4**
Coal Creek Coffee Company **13**
Grand Avenue Pizza **12**
Sweet Melissa **5**

ATTRACTIONS ●
Laramie Plains Museum **9**
University of Wyoming **10, 11**
Wyoming Children's Museum
   and Nature Center **7**

Gauguin. It's open Monday through Saturday from 10am to 5pm (until 9pm Mon when school is in session). Also in this building is the **American Heritage Center** (🕾 **307/766-4114;** http://ahc.uwyo.edu), a top-notch research facility with extensive collections of Western-history materials and some unexpected archives, such as some of Jack Benny's papers, open Monday 10am to 9pm and Tuesday through Friday from 8am to 5pm.

Bordered by N. 9th and N. 15th sts. on the west and east and E. Lewis and E. Ivinson Ave. on the north and south. 🕾 **307/766-1121.** www.uwyo.edu.

Wyoming Territorial Prison State Historic Site ⓀⒾⒹ Formerly a penitentiary where Butch Cassidy served time, the Territorial Prison transmogrified into an experimental livestock station before becoming the historical park it is today. Almost everything having to do with frontier life before the start of the 20th century can be found here, from a funky frontier town, to stagecoach rides, to a ranching exhibit with a homesteader's cabin and farm animals.

975 Snowy Range Rd. (just east of I-80, exit 311). ℰ **307/745-6161.** http://wyoparks.state.wy.us. Admission $5, $2.50 for children 12–17, free for children 11 and under. May–Oct daily 9am–6pm; call for winter hours.

SHOPPING

Since Laramie is a university town, it has its fair share of bookstores. Our favorites are the peaceful **2nd Story Books** and **Personally Recommended Books,** both at 105 E. Ivinson Ave. (ℰ **307/745-4423**). To see what's hot on campus, visit the **University Bookstore,** 1 block north of Ivinson Avenue and 13th Street (ℰ **800/370-2676**).

If you're looking for the gear you need for an adventure in the Medicine Bow, try **Cross-Country Connection,** 222 S. 2nd St. (ℰ **307/721-2851**), for skiing and climbing equipment (you can rent skis here, too). For Western clothing and souvenirs, hit **Martindale's,** downtown at 217 E. Grand Ave. (ℰ **307/721-4100**).

Downtown Laramie is also home to all kinds of artists and craftspeople. **Earth, Wind, and Fire** (ℰ **307/745-0226**), 216 S. 2nd St., is a pottery lover's dream come true. **Hart's Jewelry & Gifts,** 111 E. Grand Ave. (ℰ **307/742-9386**), is another excellent gallery and gift store. The prime antiques store is **Antique Fever,** 211 S. 2nd St. (ℰ **307/721-8398**).

WHERE TO STAY

Among the chain properties in town are **Travelodge,** 165 N. 3rd St. (ℰ **800/942-6671** or 307/742-6671), with rooms for $70 to $100 double; and **Howard Johnson Inn,** 1555 Snowy Range Rd. (ℰ **307/742-8371**), with double rates of $65. Outside of the chains, the **Sunset Inn,** 1104 S. 3rd St. (ℰ **800/308-3744** or 307/742-3741; www.sunsetinn-laramie.com), is a small motel with an outdoor pool and indoor hot tub. Doubles cost $65 to $75.

Mad Carpenter Inn ★ Before Lawrence Thomas bought this huge Victorian near from the University of Wyoming Campus, it was just a "shabby old house." But Thomas, a one-time basketball star at UW, renovated the place and crafted the woodwork that earned him the nickname "the Mad Carpenter" from his daughter. The end result is a first-rate B&B with equal parts elegance and whimsy in its three guest rooms, two of them with queens in the main house. The third room is actually its own structure, the Dollhouse, with an ornate staircase leading to a sleeping loft and the adjacent balcony. In the main house, there is also one of the best game rooms I've ever seen in an inn, complete with slick hardwood floors, a piano, dartboards, and pool, Ping-Pong, and foosball tables.

353 N. 8th St., Laramie, WY 82072. ℰ **307/742-0870.** www.madcarpenter.com. 3 units. $85–$115 double. Rates include continental breakfast. AE, MC, V. **Amenities:** Game room. *In room:* TV, no phone, Wi-Fi (free).

Vee Bar Guest Ranch ★★ A jewel of a guest ranch, the Vee Bar is definitely pricey, but perfect for those looking to delve into the ranching lifestyle as they get away from it all. The property itself, 800 acres in all, features lush fields, cottonwood and willow groves, and a stretch of the crystalline Little Laramie River. Alongside the historic main lodge, the accommodations here are comfortable cabins and a trio of "Riverside Suite" duplexes that manage to balance the rustic with the convenient. Two of the free-standing cabins are more than a century old, restored and furnished with antiques of local origin; the third is modern (1990), but blends into the old-fashioned atmosphere with ease.

Activities such as horseback riding, fishing, river tubing, and overnight camp-outs are **407** included, as are all meals. For breakfast, expect flapjacks, eggs, and bacon; for dinner, steaks and seafood. Guests can unwind in the historic John Wayne Saloon.

2091 Wyo. 130, Laramie, WY 82070. © **800/483-3227** or 307/745-7036. Fax 307/745-7433. www.veebar. com. 9 cabins. $3,350–$3,750 per 7-night stay for 2 adults; $1,445–$1,645 per week each additional person. 3-night packages also available. Rates include all meals and activities. Fall–spring (and summertime Sat), single-night stays are available for $120–$150 for a double. AE, DISC, MC, V. Located 21 miles west of Laramie via Snowy Range Rd. (Wyo. 130). **Amenities:** Restaurant; lounge; children's programs; exercise room; outdoor Jacuzzi; Wi-Fi (free). *In room:* Fridge, no phone.

Camping

The **Laramie KOA**, off I-80 at 1271 W. Baker St. (© **307/742-6553**), is open April through October, depending on the snows. There are 100 pull-through sites here, as well as a rec room, small store, and unobstructed mountain views. Full hookups cost $28 to $32; there are also tent sites and cabins. There are also campgrounds at Curt Gowdy State Park and Vedauwoo Recreation Area (see "Getting Outside," above).

WHERE TO DINE

Thinkers and talkers fuel up on good java at the **Coal Creek Coffee Company,** 108–110 E. Grand Ave. (© **307/745-7737**); there is sometimes live music in the evenings. You can get pasta or pizza at **Grand Avenue Pizza,** 301 E. Grand Ave. (© **307/721-2909**), which hides in an old corner space downtown.

Altitude Chophouse & Brewery ★ AMERICAN/MICROBREWERY This downtown eatery, effortlessly melding woodsy and swank, features tree stumps for bar stools and blue banners hanging from the rafters to dampen the sound of friendly chatter. The smoke-free atmosphere is a rich complement to the excellent fare, which includes pub standards (burgers, pizzas, and cheese sticks) as well as excellent steaks and seafood. We like the cedar plank salmon and the orange-braised pork loin, but the steaks are also held in high regard. The prices are right, and the beers aren't bad at all, either.

320 S. 2nd St. © **307/721-4031.** www.altitudechophouse.com. Reservations accepted. Main courses $8–$20. AE, DC, MC, V. Mon–Sat 11am–10pm. Bar open later.

Sweet Melissa (Finds) VEGETARIAN A meatless menu in Wyoming might sound like something of an oxymoron, but this funky cafe by the rail yard will satisfy most any patron, carnivorous or not. The three-bean chili is terrific, and makes me long for another trip to Laramie, but the menu also includes salads, eggplant subs and hummus sandwiches, sweet potato–black bean burrito, lentil loaf, mushroom fajitas, and several pasta dishes. Attached is the **Front Street Bar,** which opened in December 2009.

213 S. 1st St. © **307/742-9607.** Reservations accepted for large parties only. Main courses $6–$10. DISC, MC, V. Mon–Sat 11am–9pm. Bar open later.

4 A SIDE TRIP FOR THE OUTDOOR ENTHUSIAST: THE SNOWY RANGE & CARBON COUNTY

Snowy Range: 32 miles W of Laramie

You can very quickly leave behind the dry plains around Laramie and find yourself up among lakes, forest, and substantial peaks in the north end of the Medicine Bow

SOUTHERN WYOMING

16

THE SNOWY RANGE & CARBON COUNTY

Mountains, known as the **Snowy Range.** Just take Wyo. 130 west, through the foothill town of Centennial, past the **Snowy Range Ski Area** (© **307/745-5750;** www.snowy rangeski.com; full-day lift tickets are $39 for adults, $24 for children 12 and under), and up into the mountains, where peaks rise well over 10,000 feet. Though **Medicine Bow Peak** is 12,013 feet tall, it's a relatively easy day-climb, starting at the parking lot by Lake Marie and covering about 5 miles. You can loop around the west side of the hollow in which the peak stands and return on the east side among the lakes. Trails are well marked and you'll meet people as you hike. Just keep an eye out for thunderheads, as you'll be above timberline, exposed to lightning. For **detailed trail maps,** contact the **Medicine Bow National Forest,** 2468 Jackson St. in Laramie (© **307/745-2300;** www.fs.fed.us/r2/mbr).

If you drive on over the Snowies—it takes only about an hour—you'll drop down into the valley of the **North Platte River,** with its old mining and timber towns such as Encampment and Saratoga. **Saratoga** is the roost of several fishing outfits that guide on the North Platte, one of the finest trout fisheries in the state. If you spend the night, you'll probably enjoy the creaky, old-fashioned style of the historic **Hotel Wolf,** 101 E. Bridge St. (© **307/326-5525;** www.wolfhotel.com), with double rates of $67 to $110, or the **Saratoga Resort and Spa,** 601 E. Pic Pike Rd. (© **800/594-0178;** www.saratogainn.com), with its own hot-spring-fed pool, golf course, and double rates of $100 to $175 in summer and $85 to $160 in winter. At the foot of the mountains in Centennial, try the **Old Corral Hotel** (© **866/653-2677** or 307/745-5918; www.oldcorral.com), $89 to $109 for a double with Western decor ($79–$89 double in winter), or the rustic **Brooklyn Lodge** (© **307/742-6916;** www.brooklynlodge.com), a log-laden B&B with rockers and wagon-wheel tables; double rates are $175. Another area attraction of note is **Woods Landing** in the dinky town of Jelm (© **307/745-9638;** www.woodslanding.com), a historic Western dance hall built on 24 boxcar springs—when the dance floor is full, the place literally bounces. A restaurant, a complex of rustic rental cabins ($55–$100 double), and a riverside guesthouse ($175–$190 a night) are on-site. North of the Snowies off of I-80, the **Historic Elk Mountain Hotel,** 102 E. Main St., Elk Mountain (© **307/348-7774;** www.elkmountainhotel.com), is a first-rate restored hotel with double rates of $130 to $170 and a restaurant on-site.

CAMPING

Medicine Bow National Forest (© **307/745-2300;** www.fs.fed.us/r2/mbr) maintains a number of semiprimitive campgrounds June through September, scattered throughout the range west of Laramie. Fees at most campgrounds range from $10 to $12 per night, although a few are free or $5 per night.

FISHING

The Upper North Platte River cuts right through Saratoga, and those in the know consider it one of the state's top trout-fishing spots. **Stoney Creek Outfitters,** 216 E. Walnut, Saratoga (© **307/326-8750;** www.fishstoneycreek.com), charges $450 for a full-day, two-person float-fishing expedition.

5 ROCK SPRINGS

258 miles W of Cheyenne; 178 miles S of Jackson

Rock Springs began as a stage station on the Overland Trail, named after a natural spring that dried up after extensive mining in the area. In 1894, Jack London wrote of Rock Springs: "It seems to be the Wild and Woolly West with a vengeance." It's still true: Rock

Springs shows the rougher side of Wyoming, powered by a coal-burning power plant, freight trains roaring through, and all-night truckers stopping for coffee, adding to a blue-collar sensibility.

For more than a century, boom followed bust followed boom, and in the late 1970s, oil, gas, and coal caused the area population to skyrocket. So did the crime rate, and corruption raised its ugly head, but things have improved dramatically since.

The city is not far from some fine outdoor attractions: **Fossil Butte National Monument** (see section 7) and **Flaming Gorge National Recreation Area** (see section 6).

ESSENTIALS

GETTING THERE **Great Lakes Aviation** (℡ 800/554-5111) and **United Express** (℡ 800/241-6522) fly into **Rock Springs–Sweetwater County Airport** (℡ 307/352-6880; www.rockspringsairport.com), 15 miles east of town on I-80, and the **Greyhound** bus rumbles in at 1695 Sunset Dr. (℡ 307/362-2931; www.greyhound.com).

Rock Springs sits at the intersection of U.S. 191 and I-80. From Cheyenne, drive I-80 west for 258 miles. From Jackson, take U.S. 191 south for 178 miles.

VISITOR INFORMATION The **Rock Springs Chamber of Commerce,** 1897 Dewar Dr. (℡ 800/463-8637 or 307/362-3771; www.rockspringswyoming.net), and **Sweetwater County Travel and Tourism,** 404 N St., Ste. 404 (℡ 307/382-2538; www.tour wyoming.com), put a positive spin on Rock Springs and its immediate area.

GETTING AROUND **Avis** (℡ 800/230-4898), **Enterprise** (℡ 800/261-7331), and **Hertz** (℡ 800/654-3131) maintain counters at the airport. For a **taxi,** contact **City Cab** (℡ 307/382-1100).

SEEING THE SIGHTS

While strolling around town, pop into the **Community Fine Arts Center,** at the Sweetwater County Library, 400 C St. (℡ 307/362-6212; www.cfac4art.com), which contains a few original paintings by Grandma Moses and Norman Rockwell. The **Rock Springs Historical Museum,** 201 B St. (℡ 307/362-3138), is a fine piece of Romanesque architecture housing exhibits covering the city's rough-and-tumble past. The **Western Wyoming Community College Natural History Museum,** 2500 College Dr. (℡ 307/382-1600), has several dinosaur displays and a few fish and plant fossils. All three museums are free.

WHERE TO STAY

The two hotels listed below have swimming pools, free continental breakfast every morning, and well-maintained modern rooms. **Wingate Inn,** 525 Gateway Blvd. (℡ 307/382-5181), offers rooms for $129 to $149 double. The **EconoLodge,** at I-80 exit 104 (℡ 800/548-6621 or 307/382-4217), has rates of $79 to $99 double.

WHERE TO DINE

Bitter Creek Brewing MICROBREWERY LIFE IS TOO SHORT TO DRINK CHEAP BEER, reads the sign behind the oak bar. If you agree, then Bitter Creek is the place for you. In four fermenting vats adjacent to the bar, they concoct their own special microbrews, including the popular Mustang Pale Ale and the cleverly named Coal Porter, a darker beer with a slight chocolate aftertaste. The ever-changing menu includes gourmet salads, pizzas, and pasta dishes.

604 Broadway. ℡ 307/362-4782. www.bittercreekbrewing.com. Lunch $5–$15; dinner $10–$26. AE, DISC, MC, V. Mon–Sat 11am–10pm.

6 FLAMING GORGE NATIONAL RECREATION AREA ★

24 miles W of Rock Springs

By May 1869, the Union Pacific had laid its tracks across Wyoming and pinned them to the eastbound rails with a golden spike. The town of Green River, 15 miles west of Rock Springs, was only a year old. And that May, 10 frontiersmen and ex-soldiers climbed off the train, led by a veteran who'd lost his arm in the Civil War. They jumped into stout wooden boats and set off down the Green River. As they slid through red canyons with the cliffs peaking high above, almost singed yellow along the rims, they named the place Flaming Gorge.

The expedition continued down the Green, which merged into the Colorado River, and then continued on into the Grand Canyon, weaving through boulders, portaging sandbars, and being sucked through rapids. Three men decided to hike out rather than risk the rapids. They were later found bristling with arrows. The remaining seven survived. The leader went on to map and record the "Great American Desert" and later helped organize and direct the U.S. Geological Survey. The one-armed Civil War veteran, a famous river runner, was of course John Wesley Powell.

Today a 455-foot dam, 15 miles into Utah, backs the river onto itself for 91 miles, nearly to the town of Green River. Each summer, jet-boaters, water-skiers, and anglers skim the surface of the reservoir, while paddlers drop in below the dam for scenic and adventurous floats in the wake of Powell's boats.

ESSENTIALS

GETTING THERE   Take I-80 west from Rock Springs for 15 miles to the town of **Green River** at the junction of Wyo. 530. (See "A Driving Tour," below, for information on driving through the area.)

VISITOR INFORMATION   For information before you arrive, contact the **District Ranger** (© 435/784-3445; www.fs.fed.us/r4/ashley). Once you're in the area, stop at the U.S. Forest Service's **visitor center** in Green River at 1450 Uinta Dr. (© 307/875-2871) to pick up maps and brochures.

ADMISSION & REGULATIONS   If you're boating, admission to the 190,000-acre Flaming Gorge National Recreation Area is $5 per vehicle per day or $15 for a 7-day pass. The Forest Service's regulations here are mostly common sense, aimed at preserving water quality and protecting the forest and historic sites. In addition, Wyoming and Utah fishing and boating regulations apply in those states' sections of the recreation area. Leashed dogs are permitted on trails.

A DRIVING TOUR

As you drive south from Green River on Wyo. 530, the cactus and sagebrush-filled **Devils Playground** badlands and the rock formations of **Haystack Buttes** will be to your right. Wyo. 530 runs the length of the recreation area's west side and provides access to the Flaming Gorge Reservoir at the **Buckboard Crossing Area,** 20 miles south, where a full-service marina operates during the summer.

From Wyo. 530, pick up Utah 44 just across the state line in Manila, Utah. Utah 44 runs south then east for 27 miles to pick up U.S. 191. Along this route you'll catch

Impressions

The river enters the range by a flaring, brilliant red gorge, that may be seen from the north a score of miles away . . . We name it Flaming Gorge.
—Explorer Major John Wesley Powell, May 26, 1869

glimpses of Utah's Uinta Mountains to the west and may see bighorn sheep in nearby **Sheep Creek Canyon,** which has been designated a special geological area by the Forest Service because of its dramatically twisted and upturned rocks. A mostly paved 11-mile loop road cuts off from Utah 44, offering a half-hour tour of this beautiful, narrow canyon, with its lavish display of rocks that have eroded into intricate patterns, a process that began with the uplifting of the Uinta Mountains millions of years ago. This loop may be closed in winter.

Eventually, you'll come to the **Red Canyon Overlook** on the southern edge of the gorge, where a rainbow of colors adorns 1,000-foot-tall cliffs. The **Red Canyon Visitor Center** (open daily 8am–6pm in summer) is nearby, as is **Flaming Gorge Dam.**

To head back to Wyoming, take U.S. 191 away from the eastern edge of the gorge. From the junction of Utah 44 and U.S. 191, it's 16 miles to the border. Once you're at the state line, it's 30 miles to the turnoff for **Firehole Canyon,** an access to the gorge that offers views of the magnificent spires known as **Chimney Rocks.** Keep going north on U.S. 191 and you'll hit I-80 again.

GETTING OUTSIDE

For more information about the Utah portion of Flaming Gorge National Recreation Area, including additional outdoor recreational activities and outfitters, lodging options, and other nearby sites of interest, see *Frommer's Utah.*

BOATING   Three marinas on **Lake Flaming Gorge** provide boat rentals, fuel, launching ramps, and boating and fishing supplies. **Cedar Springs Marina** (© **435/889-3795;** www.cedarspringsmarina.com) is 2 miles west of Flaming Gorge Dam; **Lucerne Valley Marina** (© **435/784-3483;** www.flaminggorge.com) is on the west side of the lake, 7 miles east of Manila; and **Buckboard Marina** (© **307/875-6927**) is also on the west side of the lake, off Wyo. 530, 22 miles north of Manila.

CAMPING   The U.S. Forest Service maintains about 20 RV and tent campgrounds in the area (about $10–$30 a night), and there are also many primitive riverside sites. Contact the **Forest Service visitor center** in Green River (© **307/875-2871**) for more information.

FISHING   You might want to bring along a muscular friend if you plan to fish Lake Flaming Gorge, which is famous as the place to catch record-breaking trout, such as the 51-pound, 8-ounce lake (Mackinaw) trout caught in 1988; the 26-pound, 2-ounce rainbow caught in 1979; or the 33-pound, 10-ounce brown caught in 1977. You'll also see other cold-water species such as smallmouth bass and kokanee salmon. Fishing is popular year-round, although ice-fishermen are warned to make sure the ice is strong enough to hold them. For fishing information and excursions, call **Conquest Expeditions** (© **435/784-3370** or 801/244-9948; www.conquestexpeditions.com).

7 KILLPECKER SAND DUNES & FOSSIL BUTTE NATIONAL MONUMENT

Killpecker Sand Dunes: 40 miles N of Rock Springs; 140 miles SE of Jackson

KILLPECKER SAND DUNES

North of Rock Springs and east of Eden (I'm not kidding…it's a small town) swell the **Killpecker Sand Dunes**—the largest active dunes in North America. Here hikers can scale and descend the heaving hills of white sand, where the noon heat shimmers and the midnight cold cuts. Rock climbers trek to **Boar's Tusk,** a standing volcanic plug, ethnography buffs seek the **White Mountain Petroglyphs,** and photographers with high-powered telephoto lenses should be on the lookout for wild horses.

Bird-watchers will especially enjoy the **Seedskadee Wildlife Refuge,** where they may see geese, sandhill cranes, and great blue herons along the miles of marshes along the Green River.

GETTING THERE   To get to the dunes, drive Wyo. 191 north from Rock Springs 36 miles to Eden. Turning east, you'll bump along at least 20 miles of gravel road. Bring a compass, plenty of emergency water, and a map. It's best to contact the Bureau of Land Management (✆ **307/352-0256**) before blazing the trail on your own. *Note:* When it rains, the bentonite on these rough roads turns to glue, and smart drivers stop trying.

FOSSIL BUTTE NATIONAL MONUMENT

Standing at the base of Fossil Butte, gazing up 1,000 feet at the rust- and ocher-stained cliffs, with the crackling desert wind rattling sage and tumbleweeds, you'd never guess that aeons ago you'd have been looking up from the bottom of a subtropical ocean. Some 50 million years ago, during the Eocene Epoch, millions of fish wriggled across what's now the sky. With the ebb and flow of millennia, they sifted into the mud and fossilized.

Today, visitors join paleontologists during the summer to dig for the ancient remains of fish, insects, turtles, birds, and even bats. You can also hike (be watchful for rattlesnakes) on two short trails—the 1.5-mile Fossil Lake Trail and the 2.5-mile Quarry Trail. This is also a prime wildlife-viewing area, where you're likely to see pronghorn, mule deer, white-tailed prairie dogs, and ground squirrels, and you might be lucky enough to spot moose, elk, and beaver as well. A variety of birds are also seen here, including Canada geese, great blue herons, Clark's nutcrackers, yellow-headed blackbirds, great horned owls, and red-tailed hawks.

The excellent **Fossil Butte Visitor Center ★** (✆ **307/877-4455**) exhibits more than 75 fossils, including a 13-foot-long crocodile and the oldest known bat, plus it offers video programs. It's open daily from 8am to 7pm June through August, but only until 4:30pm the rest of the year, and closed during winter holidays and bad snow.

GETTING THERE   From Green River, head west on I-80 to U.S. 30 (exit 66), which you follow north about 40 miles. Past Kemmerer, follow the signs to the visitor center (about 3½ miles). Admission to both the monument and visitor center is free. Advance information is available by writing to Superintendent, Fossil Butte National Monument, P.O. Box 592, Kemmerer, WY 83101 (✆ **307/877-4455;** www.nps.gov/fobu).

ALSO WORTH A LOOK   No need to rush through Kemmerer, an old mining town with a pleasant central square and some fine old buildings, set along the Hams Fork

River. Here you'll find the very first **JCPenney store** (© 307/877-3164) and the original home of the chain's founder, James Cash Penney. The store, despite being small and historic, is a regular JCPenney, open year-round. The house is open Memorial Day to Labor Day, Monday to Saturday 9am to 6pm, with free admission. The flagship store is on the town's central square, at 722 JC Penney Dr.; the home is 1 block north. Another good local attraction: **Pine Creek Ski Resort** (© 307/279-3201; www.pinecreekski resort.com) is about 50 miles northwest of Kemmerer, though calling it a "resort" is a bit of hyperbole. Full-day lift tickets are $35 for adults, $30 for children 17 and under.

17

Fast Facts

1 FAST FACTS: MONTANA & WYOMING

AREA CODES The statewide area code for Montana is **406.** Wyoming's area code is **307.** Intrastate long-distance calls also require these prefixes.

AUTOMOBILE ORGANIZATIONS Motor clubs will supply maps, suggested routes, guidebooks, accident and bail-bond insurance, and emergency road service. The **American Automobile Association (AAA)** is the major auto club in the United States. If you belong to a motor club in your home country, inquire about AAA reciprocity before you leave. You may be able to join AAA even if you're not a member of a reciprocal club; to inquire, call AAA (© **800/222-4357;** www.aaa.com). AAA has a nationwide emergency road service telephone number (© 800/AAA-HELP [4357]).

BUSINESS HOURS Banks are usually open Monday through Friday from 9am to 5pm, often until 6pm on Friday; some have hours on Saturday. Small stores are usually open Monday through Saturday, with some also open on Sunday. Most department stores, discount stores, and supermarkets are open daily until 9pm. Some supermarkets are open 24 hours a day.

DRINKING LAWS The legal age for purchase and consumption of alcoholic beverages in both states is 21; proof of age is required and often requested at bars, nightclubs, and restaurants, so it's always a good idea to bring ID when you go out. All liquor stores in Montana are state-controlled with minimum hours of 10am to 6pm, although individual stores may be

open longer. Most are closed on Sunday. Liquor may also be bought at bars with package licenses during their operating hours. Beer and wine are available at convenience stores and supermarkets from 8:30am to 2am.

Do not carry open containers of alcohol in your car or any public area that isn't zoned for alcohol consumption. Interestingly, however, Wyoming is the last state in the country without an open-container law; many cities do ban it. The police can typically fine you on the spot. And nothing will ruin your trip faster than getting a citation for DUI ("driving under the influence"), so don't even think about driving while intoxicated.

ELECTRICITY Like Canada, the United States uses 110–120 volts AC (60 cycles), compared to 220–240 volts AC (50 cycles) in most of Europe, Australia, and New Zealand. Downward converters that change 220–240 volts to 110–120 volts are difficult to find in the United States, so bring one with you.

EMBASSIES & CONSULATES All embassies are located in the nation's capital, Washington, D.C. Some consulates are located in major U.S. cities, and most nations have a mission to the United Nations in New York City. If your country isn't listed below, call for directory information in Washington, D.C. (© **202/555-1212**) or check **www.embassy.org/embassies**.

The embassy of **Australia** is at 1601 Massachusetts Ave. NW, Washington, DC

20036 (℡ **202/797-3000;** www.usa.embassy.gov.au).

The embassy of **Canada** is at 501 Pennsylvania Ave. NW, Washington, DC 20001 (℡ **202/682-1740;** www.canadianembassy.org). Canadian consulates are in Buffalo (New York), Detroit, Los Angeles, New York, and Seattle.

The embassy of **Ireland** is at 2234 Massachusetts Ave. NW, Washington, DC 20008 (℡ **202/462-3939;** www.irelandemb.org). Irish consulates are in Boston, Chicago, New York, San Francisco, and other cities (see website for complete listing).

The embassy of **New Zealand** is at 37 Observatory Circle NW, Washington, DC 20008 (℡ **202/328-4800;** www.nzembassy.com). New Zealand consulates are in Los Angeles, Salt Lake City, San Francisco, and Seattle.

The embassy of the **United Kingdom** is at 3100 Massachusetts Ave. NW, Washington, DC 20008 (℡ **202/588-7800;** www.britainusa.com). British consulates are in Atlanta, Boston, Chicago, Cleveland, Houston, Los Angeles, New York, San Francisco, and Seattle.

EMERGENCIES Call ℡ **911.**

GASOLINE (PETROL) A gallon of unleaded gasoline cost between $2.50 and $3 at press time. Taxes are already included in the printed price. One U.S. gallon equals 3.8 liters or .85 imperial gallons.

HOLIDAYS Banks, government offices, post offices, and many stores, restaurants, and museums are closed on the following legal national holidays: January 1 (New Year's Day), the third Monday in January (Martin Luther King, Jr. Day), the third Monday in February (Presidents' Day), the last Monday in May (Memorial Day), July 4 (Independence Day), the first Monday in September (Labor Day), the second Monday in October (Columbus Day), November 11 (Veterans Day/Armistice Day), the fourth Thursday in November

(Thanksgiving), and December 25 (Christmas). The Tuesday after the first Monday in November is Election Day, a federal government holiday in presidential-election years (held every 4 years, and next in 2012).

For more information on holidays see "Montana & Wyoming Calendar of Events" in chapter 3.

INTERNET ACCESS In Montana and Wyoming's major cities and resorts, Wi-Fi is commonplace. It's harder to find in some of the less populated areas, but generally not difficult to access the Internet in any conurbation.

LEGAL AID If you are "pulled over" for a minor infraction (such as speeding), never attempt to pay the fine directly to a police officer; this could be construed as attempted bribery, a serious crime. Pay fines by mail, or directly into the hands of the clerk of the court. If accused of a more serious offense, say and do nothing before consulting a lawyer. Here the burden is on the state to prove a person's guilt beyond a reasonable doubt, and everyone has the right to remain silent, whether he or she is suspected of a crime or actually arrested. Once arrested, a person can make one telephone call to a party of his or her choice. International visitors should call their embassy or consulate.

MAIL At press time, domestic postage rates were 28¢ for a postcard and 44¢ for a letter. For international mail, a first-class letter of up to 1 ounce costs 98¢ (75¢ to Canada and 79¢ to Mexico); a first-class postcard costs the same as a letter. For more information go to **www.usps.com**.

If you aren't sure what your address will be in the United States, mail can be sent to you, in your name, c/o General Delivery at the main post office of the city or region where you expect to be. (Call ℡ **800/275-8777** for information on the nearest post office.) The addressee must pick up mail in person and must produce proof of identity (driver's license, passport, and the like). Most post offices will hold your mail for up to 1 month, and generally are open Monday to Friday from 8am to 6pm (some Sat 9am–3pm).

Always include zip codes when mailing items in the U.S. If you don't know your zip code, visit www.usps.com/zip4.

NEWSPAPERS & MAGAZINES Montana's major daily newspapers are the *Missoulian* (www.missoulian.com), the *Great Falls Tribune* (www.greatfallstribune.com), and the *Billings Gazette* (www.billings gazette.com). In Wyoming, the *Casper Star-Tribune* (www.trib.com) is the only statewide paper, while the *Wyoming Tribune-Eagle* (www.wyomingnews.com) is Cheyenne's daily. Magazines of note include *Big Sky Journal* (www.bigsky journal.com) and *Montana Magazine* (www.montanamagazine.com).

PASSPORTS See www.frommers.com/ planning for information on how to obtain a passport. See "Embassies & Consulates," above, for whom to contact if you lose yours while traveling in the U.S. For other information, please contact the following agencies:

For Residents of Australia Contact the **Australian Passport Information Service** at © 131-232, or visit the government website at www.passports.gov.au.

For Residents of Canada Contact the central **Passport Office,** Department of Foreign Affairs and International Trade, Ottawa, ON K1A 0G3 (© **800/567-6868;** www.ppt.gc.ca).

For Residents of Ireland Contact the **Passport Office,** Setanta Centre, Molesworth Street, Dublin 2 (© **01/671-1633;** www.irlgov.ie/iveagh).

For Residents of New Zealand Contact the **Passports Office** at © **0800/225-050** in New Zealand or 04/474-8100, or log on to www.passports.govt.nz.

For Residents of the United Kingdom Visit your nearest passport office, major post office, or travel agency or contact the **United Kingdom Passport Service** at © **0870/521-0410** or search its website at www.ukpa.gov.uk.

POLICE Call © **911** for emergency police help.

SMOKING In 2005, Montana enacted a law banning smoking in public buildings and restaurants; bars had until 2009 to comply. In Wyoming, most restaurants have separate smoking and nonsmoking areas, and most hotels in both states have nonsmoking rooms.

TAXES The United States has no value-added tax (VAT) or other indirect tax at the national level. Every state, county, and city may levy its own local tax on all purchases, including hotel and restaurant checks and airline tickets. These taxes will not appear on price tags. Montana has no state sales tax, but there is a lodging tax of 7%, and certain resort communities can also charge an additional tax for goods and services. Wyoming's state sales tax is 4%, and local communities can add up to 1% more. Communities can impose a lodging tax of up to 4%.

TIME Montana and Wyoming are both in the **Mountain Standard Time Zone.** The continental United States is divided into **four time zones:** Eastern Standard Time (EST), Central Standard Time (CST), Mountain Standard Time (MST), and Pacific Standard Time (PST). Alaska and Hawaii have their own zones. For example, when it's 9am in Los Angeles (PST), it's 7am in Honolulu (HST), 10am in Denver (MST), 11am in Chicago (CST), noon in New York City (EST), 5pm in London (GMT), and 2am the next day in Sydney.

Daylight saving time is in effect from 1am on the second Sunday in March to 1am on the first Sunday in November, except in Arizona, Hawaii, the U.S. Virgin Islands, and Puerto Rico. Daylight saving time moves the clock 1 hour ahead of standard time.

TIPPING In hotels, tip **bellhops** at least $1 per bag ($2–$3 if you have a lot of luggage) and tip the **chamber staff** $1 to $2 per day (more if you've left a disaster area for him or her to clean up). Tip the **doorman** or **concierge** only if he or she has provided you with some specific service (for example, calling a cab for you or obtaining difficult-to-get theater tickets). Tip the **valet-parking attendant** $1 every time you get your car.

In restaurants, bars, and nightclubs, tip **service staff** and **bartenders** 15% to 20% of the check, tip **checkroom attendants** $1 per garment, and tip **valet-parking attendants** $1 per vehicle.

As for other service personnel, tip **cabdrivers** 15% of the fare; tip **skycaps** at airports at least $1 per bag ($2–$3 if you have a lot of luggage); and tip **hairdressers** and **barbers** 15% to 20%.

TOILETS You won't find public toilets or "restrooms" on the streets in most U.S. cities but they can be found in hotel lobbies, bars, restaurants, museums, department stores, railway and bus stations, and service stations. Large hotels and fast-food restaurants are often the best bet for clean facilities. Restaurants and bars in resorts or heavily visited areas may reserve their restrooms for patrons.

VISAS For information about U.S. visas go to **http://travel.state.gov** and click on "Visas." Or go to one of the following websites:

Australian citizens can obtain up-to-date visa information from the **U.S. Embassy Canberra,** Moonah Place, Yarralumla, ACT 2600 (✆ **02/6214-5600**) or by checking the U.S. Diplomatic Mission's website at **http://usembassy-australia. state.gov/consular**.

British subjects can obtain up-to-date visa information by calling the **U.S. Embassy Visa Information Line** (✆ **0891/200-290**) or by visiting the "Visas to the U.S." section of the American

Embassy London's website at **www.us** **417** **embassy.org.uk**.

Irish citizens can obtain up-to-date visa information through the **Embassy of the USA Dublin,** 42 Elgin Rd., Dublin 4, Ireland (✆ **353/1-668-8777;** or by checking the "Visas to the U.S." section of the website at **http://dublin.usembassy.gov**.

Citizens of **New Zealand** can obtain up-to-date visa information by contacting the **U.S. Embassy New Zealand,** 29 Fitzherbert Terrace, Thorndon, Wellington (✆ **644/472-2068**), or get the information directly from the website at **http:// wellington.usembassy.gov**.

VISITOR INFORMATION Travel **Montana,** P.O. Box 200533, 301 S. Park St., Helena, MT 59620 (✆ **800/847-4868** or 406/841-2870; TDD 406/841-2702; www.visitmt.com), provides information about Big Sky country and specific locales in Montana. It puts out two well-designed vacation planning kits—one for summer and one for winter—that include maps and the *Montana Vacation Planner.* The planner includes contacts with agencies that can provide information and travel services, such as airlines and rental-car agencies; it also has listings, by town, of places to stay and eat, with charts specifying price ranges and such amenities as hot tubs and access for travelers with disabilities. Travel Montana will also send you separate guides to some of Montana's more popular sports activities: snowmobiling, fishing, and skiing; as well as site-specific guides for each of six travel regions: Glacier Country in the northwest, Gold West Country in the southwest, Russell Country in north-central Montana, Yellowstone Country in south-central Montana, Missouri River Country in the northeast, and Custer Country in the southeast.

For additional information about attractions, facilities, and services at specific Montana destinations—national parks, cities, or towns—contact the **Montana Chamber of Commerce,** P.O. Box 1730, Helena, MT 59624 (© **406/442-2405** or 443-7888; www.montanachamber.com), for the address and phone number of the nearest chamber office.

The **Wyoming Business Council Travel & Tourism Division,** 1520 Etchepare Circle, Cheyenne, WY 82007 (© **800/225-5996** or 307/777-7777; www.wyomingtourism.org), distributes summer and winter editions of the *Travelers Journal,* an informative guide with information about sights and towns in the state's five travel areas—Devils Tower/Buffalo Bill Country in the north and east, Oregon Trail/Rendezvous Country in central Wyoming, Medicine Bow/Flaming Gorge Country along the southern border, Jackson Hole/Jim Bridger Country in the west, and Grand Teton and Yellowstone—as well as special features on everything from geology to adventure travel. They also furnish maps, cultural and park guides, and other information.

2 AIRLINE, HOTEL & CAR-RENTAL WEBSITES

MAJOR AIRLINES

Aer Lingus
www.aerlingus.com

Aeroméxico
www.aeromexico.com

Air Canada
www.aircanada.ca

Air France
www.airfrance.com

AirTran Airways
www.airtran.com

Alaska Airlines/Horizon Air
www.alaskaair.com

Allegiant Air
www.allegiantair.com

American Airlines
www.aa.com

British Airways
www.british-airways.com

Cape Air
www.flycapeair.com

Continental Airlines
www.continental.com

Delta Air Lines
www.delta.com

Finnair
www.finnair.com

Iberia Airlines
www.iberia.com

Icelandair
www.icelandair.com

JetBlue Airways
www.jetblue.com

Lufthansa
www.lufthansa.com

Midwest Airlines
www.midwestairlines.com

Northwest Airlines
www.nwa.com

Southwest Airlines
www.southwest.com

Spirit Airlines
www.spiritair.com

Swiss Air
www.swiss.com

United Airlines
www.united.com

US Airways
www.usairways.com

Virgin America
www.virginamerica.com

Virgin Atlantic Airways
www.virgin-atlantic.com

Best Western International
www.bestwestern.com

Clarion Hotels
www.choicehotels.com

Comfort Inns
www.comfortinn.com

Courtyard by Marriott
www.marriott.com/courtyard

Crowne Plaza Hotels
www.crowneplaza.com

Days Inn
www.daysinn.com

Doubletree Hotels
www.doubletree.com

Econo Lodges
www.econolodge.com

Embassy Suites
www.embassysuites.com

Fairfield Inn by Marriott
www.fairfieldinn.com

Four Seasons
www.fourseasons.com

Hampton Inn
www.hamptoninn.com

Hilton Hotels
www.hilton.com

Holiday Inn
www.holidayinn.com

Howard Johnson
www.hojo.com

Hyatt
www.hyatt.com

InterContinental Hotels & Resorts
www.ichotelsgroup.com

La Quinta Inns and Suites
www.lq.com

Marriott
www.marriott.com

Motel 6
www.motel6.com

Omni Hotels
www.omnihotels.com

Quality
www.qualityinn.choicehotels.com

Radisson Hotels & Resorts
www.radisson.com

Ramada Worldwide
www.ramada.com

Red Roof Inns
www.redroof.com

Renaissance
www.renaissancehotels.com

Residence Inn by Marriott
www.marriott.com/residenceinn

Rodeway Inns
www.rodewayinn.com

Sheraton Hotels & Resorts
www.starwoodhotels.com/sheraton

Super 8 Motels
www.super8.com

Travelodge
www.travelodge.com

W Hotels
www.starwoodhotels.com/whotels

Westin Hotels & Resorts
www.starwoodhotels.com/westin

Wyndham Hotels & Resorts
www.wyndham.com

CAR-RENTAL AGENCIES

Alamo
www.alamo.com

Avis
www.avis.com

Budget
www.budget.com

Dollar
www.dollar.com

FAST FACTS · 17 · AIRLINE, HOTEL & CAR-RENTAL WEBSITES

Enterprise
www.enterprise.com

Hertz
www.hertz.com

National
www.nationalcar.com

Rent-A-Wreck
www.rentawreck.com

Thrifty
www.thrifty.com

INDEX